SAKYA
OR
BUDDHIST ORIGINS

SAKYA
OR
BUDDHIST ORIGINS

BY

MRS RHYS DAVIDS

"All the worth in my figure of the Way is based on this: that man is not, but is becoming. The Wayfaring is nothing if it be not an advance. Man's life is nothing worth if he stay where he is."—*Gotama the Man*.

GYAN

Published by

GYAN

Gyan Publishing House
5, Ansari Road
Daryaganj, New Delhi-110002
Phone: 011-47034999, 9811692060
E-mail: books@gyanbooks.com

Distribution Network
gyanbooks.com
India, USA, Canada, UK, Australia, France

ISBN : 978-81-212-1165-9 (PB)
First Published, 1931

2nd Impression 2021

Printed at: Gyan Press, Delhi.

Sakya or Buddhist Origins
Author: Mrs Rhys Davids

SAKYA
OR BUDDHIST ORIGINS

By

MRS RHYS DAVIDS

D.Litt., M.A., President of the Pali Text Society, Lecturer on Pali and Buddhism at the School of Oriental Languages, London, author of *The Milinda Questions*, etc., etc.

"All the worth in my figure of the Way is based on this: that man is not, but is becoming. The Wayfaring is nothing if it be not an advance. Man's life is nothing worth if he stay where he is."—*Gotama the Man.*

LONDON

KEGAN PAUL, TRENCH, TRUBNER & CO., LTD.

BROADWAY HOUSE: 68–74 CARTER LANE, E.C.

1931

CONTENTS

INTRODUCTORY

This book is intended to be a help to those who would approach the study of a great religion with a very long history in the intensive way known as at first hand. As such it is not a supplement, but a complement to my other manual, *Gotama the Man*. In that work I sought to help the otherwise busy man and woman who have too little leisure or inclination to take up the history of that religion seriously, the study of its records, the study of their language. It is to those who have the inclination and are carving out the leisure to consider that history more closely and, it may be, to further what is known of it that I turn here and now. And to such I would at the outset say this :

You have the will to take up the study of what is called Buddhism, and more especially, just now at least, the study of the Buddhism to be got from what is known as Pali literature. You, in taking up this book, are asking to be told something about the beginnings of the one and the other : what was Buddhism at first ? how did it come to be what it now is ? is it very like what at first it was ?

To your first question I would say : Put away, for your origins, the word "Buddhism" and think of your subject as "Sakya". This will at once place you for perspective at a truer point. You are taken away from a quite modern term—convenient, it is true, for inclusive import—and are deposited in the history of the first three or more centuries of the life of this religion. Emphasis for you shifts at once. You are now concerned to learn less about "Buddha" and "Buddhism", more about him whom India has ever known as Sakya-muni, and about his men who, as their records admit, were spoken of as the Sakya-sons, or men of the Sakyas. It is only when Sakya was lingering on in India as a moribund cult, as a decadent quasi-philosophy, that Indian writers mentioned it as "what the Bauddhas say".

In the next place, you will have been directed, for the carrying out your purpose, for the finding replies to your questions, to devote possibly your first inquiries to a study of the collection of books—all, as books and not as manuscripts only, made accessible to you in this last half-century by the labours of a handful of scholars and by the gifts of a handful of donors [1]—the collection entitled the Pali Canon of the Three Piṭakas. Of these three, the first two, containing

[1] The work of the Pali Text Society, founded in 1881 by Rhys Davids.

respectively a mass of monastic rules and comments thereon (with a few scraps of narrative), and an immense number of recorded sayings in verse and prose (with a book of commentary and one of folklore) are earlier than the third. This is internally admitted and is demonstrable. You will further be referred to two or three extra-Canonical books and to a number of commentaries on the Canonical books. For these last a much later fixed wording, and writing down in such, is claimed, although as spoken comment they may be as old as much in the canon itself.

Hence for a reply to your first question you will mainly concentrate on the first two Piṭakas, the while you keep a watchful eye on the Commentaries. If herein you are first directed to the scraps of narrative in the second Piṭaka and to a few more adduced in the first Piṭaka (mainly to vindicate the main sanctions of a community of the Rule and the making of some particular rule), you will probably not, at this time of day, be first struck, as I was half a century ago, by this: that the appearance of a devoted Helper of Man, with an inspired mandate, becomes no longer for you a phenomenon that is unique. Your day is different; it has learnt more. For you comes possibly a different first impression; one that belongs more to your second and third question. You may, as a child of your day, get the impression that what you read in the records is other than what a World-Helper will have said to the world—that is, to the men and women about him there and then. If not, what will he really have said there and then, and how will he have said it there and then?

If this comes over you, you are *at the right standpoint* to take up the historical study, the one and only right study, of "Buddhism". And if this be not your impression, it is what I seek to give you in this book. What he, called "Buddha", is made to say; what it is likely he will have willed to say; what it is unlikely he will have willed to say; what it is impossible he can ever have said and yet is made to say: here is sound outlook; here is the attitude of the man or woman bent on a quest of high worth. Your quest is one of high worth. It concerns so much more, in your own growth, than the eliciting truth from a dead past. It is a quest in what is true in your own nature, your own life, when you seek, as now you are seeking, wherein lay, in the long-ago delivered message of this Man to the Man in everyone about him, what he will really have said, what he tried to say, what a want of new words hindered him from saying, which was of new meaning, new light; what these old records you are now sifting may in course of time have made him out as not saying, as saying differently.

You ask : How am I to distinguish ? How can I possibly know ?

My son, you have not entered upon a light matter of just gleaning the contents of a mass of old books, and then saying you know from them what were the origins of Buddhism. That would be as if you were to reconstruct a Roman basilica from the materials prepared for a late Gothic church ; or, from the elaborate Glastonbury Abbey of the twelfth century, a model of the little "vetusta ecclesia" wherein St. Joseph and his Keltic converts foregathered fraternally. Yours it is to follow our archæologists and to dig for the original Troy beneath more than one superimposed city. For that which was Sakya is not that which you find displayed in category and formula, in sermon and reiterated refrain in the Piṭakas. I would go so far as to say in utmost seriousness, that could you now put into the hands of, say, Sāriputta any portion of Vinaya or Sutta, he would tell you it was hard for him to recognize in it anything that he taught as the right-hand man of Gotama ! Yet you have no reason therefore to despair of getting at something of original purport beneath these many palimpsests. Nay, your position as serious student becomes so much more interesting. Yours it is, not to follow in a newly made "by-pass road", but to aid in the road-making. You are coming to this study just when the labours of a generation and more of pioneers have cut a clearing for the Road of the True through the jungle of our ignorance about Sakya and its birth. The Road has now to be made.

To leave figure, this is the position : Pali literature has just won a claim to be considered as, so far, containing, among much that is later, the most archaic records we yet have available for reconstructing Buddhist origins. The quest is now gone further east, to seek whether in Chinese and other literature we may possibly find translations made by men who bore eastward earlier versions of Sakya than the version which we have derived from Ceylon, recast into the form of literary Prakrit called Pali by the missionary monk centres of Ceylon. I have given reasons at the end of this book to show that this hope is not ill founded. Nor is this the only quest of the future into other sources of Sakya. Not as yet has even a beginning been made to sift the contents of the oldest known Sinhalese literature written in Sinhalese, yet quoting doctrine of "the Men of Old" as often in Sanskrit as in Pali : doctrine, that is to say, which was first taught in India more likely in Prakrit than in either of these tongues.

But meanwhile you and others who have as yet not turned eastward or southward have all your work cut out for you to winnow, in the Pali Piṭakas, the older grain from all the later chaff. For even scholars as yet take the emphases and values in the Piṭakas pretty much as they are given by the monastic editors, rating as fundamental, as of most worth, just what is so rated by the relatively late statements emanating from the altered ideals of the monk.

" The monk ! "—here it is that I would have you see what comes between you and the real gospel of Sakya. That gospel brought to Everyman a new word of a " More " in his nature, in his life and destiny. The monks who became its vehicle worthily kept the ideal of the More of which a man is capable to the front. You will recognize this in *their* theory of the saint or " arahan ". But you will also recognize that their saint is not ideal Everyman, but ideal monk. This shows you that, in the monastic compositions called Piṭakas, you are not considering scriptures for all men and all women. You have in them the interests put forward of certain men and women who have selected a certain kind of life detached from earthly life taken as a whole, and who have become a world within a world, with aims and ideals suited to that inner world. This is not to withhold appreciation of a man's coming out of a groove of average living, in the will to live up to more than average values. But when a man so willing enters into a group who have chosen the same way as he out of that groove, he does but get down into another inner groove. To that extent he has become a groove-man in the Less ; he is no more an out-of-the-groove man in the wider world of the Whole. Out of his, her life such an one has cut all human relations—father, mother, husband, wife, child—save those of friend and of teacher and pupil. He has chosen to become in a selected range an expert. But the expert is properly such in some proficiency of body or mind or both. As *very man*, using mind and body, but not being either, he needs life as a whole in which to develop. His outlook on life is narrowed and oblique. And historically considered, the Piṭakas show you the birth and growth of Sakya in the swaddling clothes of a monastic nursing, such as was coming into vogue at the time. You get the gospel brought by the Man to Man twisted and re-valued and otherwise emphasized to suit a monastic set of ideals.

Another octopus which gripped the young Sakya, mightily diverting it from its birth-words, was the vogue known as Sānkhya, still new and spreading when Sakya was born, of considering the mind as distinguishable from the very man. You will not go rightly to work on Sakya till you realize all that this meant for India of that day. You are so much in a similar vogue yourself, that at first it will not strike you. There were other time-spirit influences at work, but these two were the strongest.

With these influences, into which this book inquires, you will need especially to heed carefully the worthiest religious ideals of India at the time when Sakya came (as later did Jesus elsewhere) " not to destroy " those ideals " but to fulfil " them, bringing into them a New Word, where they fell short, or were falling into misuse. And do not mix these ideals with those of the later growth of monk-values.

Further, see that you keep ever in view the peculiar difficulties attending the faithful transmission of any formulated teaching down many centuries in a bookless world. You have here and now great difficulty in adequately realizing this. Do not be misled by any supposed constancy in other bookless channels in Indian literary traditions. Study the *openings for change*, together with the *growing* motives for making changes.

So working and so watching, you may help to make ready against the day, when disclosures from the Further East and from Southern Asia will test the values of the monastic Piṭakas to rank as giving us genuine Sakya ; you may find that genuine Sakya more in what the Piṭakas *betray* and have *suffered to survive*, than in what they affirm as chief and fundamental ; you will come to realize, that, short of the best thing in life : the welcoming in of a New gospel—and we are not yet ready for that—you are taking part in what is perhaps the next best thing : the discovery, the reconstruction, the rehabilitation of that which, at its birth, was a new and a true word from very man to very man, true always and everywhere.

Such has it been to me, who as wren on eagles' backs have flown, I think, a little higher than my pioneer bearers. To no pioneer is it given perhaps to see in perspective to where he is breaking through. And in what he has so far said over his work, I see conclusions more or less premature, conclusions based on too slight an historical and intensive weighing of materials which, after all, it is only now becoming possible to make. Let us like Elijah pray that we may perish if we are no better than our fathers ! If in these pages I have not gone much into these conclusions, it is because I would not take up your time with worrying over bones in the food I have been helped by feeding on. It has seemed less impertinent to put before you such positive contribution as I believe you will here find. If here or there in it I may be proved to have been forestalled without admitting it, this was done in ignorance. The field of " books about Buddhism " is strewn with pioneer and immature conclusions. And the profound confidence of certain recent writers, who shall be nameless, of such books that they have won to final truth has often made me gasp. Only they who have tried to study historically have known, that they were groping, that they were not out of the jungle. The future will see groping also (and rightly) in this book, and in those which I have published since, let me say, 1923.[1] But let me be judged by these later works, and not by the yet more immature gropings of my earlier work. It has taken a long time and no little pioneer work to get only so far. The thing most worth while is not easy to win.

In the following chapters I have incorporated much from certain articles in the *Journal of the Royal Asiatic Society*, the *Indian Historical Quarterly*, and the *Calcutta Review*, published during the last three years. For permission to do this, I would here to Council and Editors respectively tender my thanks.

[1] Especially *Gotama the Man, Kindred Sayings on Buddhism*, and *The Milanda Questions.*

CORRIGENDA

Page 11, *l.* 7 : *read* Mahāyānist.

„ 22, *l.* 1 : *insert* colon *at end.*

„ 22, *l.* 8 fr. end : *insert comma after* anticipated.

„ 28, *l.* 7 „ „ : *read bhū* ; so on p. 30.

„ 29, [1] : *read* Rāmānuja.

„ 41, *l.* 20 : „ Nigaṇṭha ; so on p. 49.

„ 55, [1] : *for* sakya *read* satya.

„ 60, *l. last but one* : *read* Hīnayāna.

„ 79, last *l.* : *read* than.

„ 87, *l.* 4 : *read sankappa.*

„ 94, *l.* 9 *from end* : *read bhāvanīya.*

„ 158, *l.* 6 „ „ : „ *vijñānamayaḥ.*

„ 187 ff., *headlines* : *read* Sānkhya.

„ 196, *l.* 7 *from end* : *add*, or, not *for* me the self.

„ 223, *l.* 6 *from end* : *read agghayati.*

„ 227, *l.* 15 *for* in the *read* in a.

„ 238, [1] : *read pūraṇī.*

„ 250, [1] : „ *Brāhmaṇa.*

„ 297, *ll.* 13, 12 *from end* : *after* child *read* pupil, and rearrange following 4 words.

PART I

I

THE BIRTH OF A NEW RELIGION

When we come to study a religion, it is the birth of it that most interests us. The legends about just that show where the interest in it has lain. When we consider that birth, as we say, historically, there arises for us the further interest, namely, in the religion coming to birth where and when it does. And if it be a religion with a very long history, it becomes a very complicated task to get at the truth, not only as to this, but also as to the original nature of the religion itself as a mandate, and as to the man or men who first gave utterance to that mandate.

Our interest in the religion itself is really due to its having been, at its birth, as mandate for the Many, a New Word. It does not follow that its sole value lay in its being, to that extent, new. Its real value lies in its message, a message of vital interest to every man and woman, having come to be virtually accepted by succeeding ages of civilization as something true and of value for all the world at all times, and as such to have been wrought up into the essentials of that civilization. "Wrought up into" with limitations. These will be due, in part, to the way in which the views held by the long series of transmitters of the teaching have been changing. "Hereby hangs a tale," and a long one: the tale of that religion's history. But at its birth, and there and then the religion will have been new, for till then man, the Many, had not been ready for such a message.

In the Christian religion, with a beginning less remote from us, and with records written nearer in time to its birth than those of the religion with which we are here concerned, we can better see its message as something waited for, listened to, and taken up, in a way that is beyond all bounds of the usual and the probable, and spread among the Many with a truly wonderful vitality. It opened up a "more" in the life of each man. This was, that to ward, not only his fellow-Jew, but his fellow-man, fraternally, as his "neighbour", was a part of the worthy life here, and was *the test of his worthiness* when judged hereafter in another world. This is not usually pointed to as the message of Christianity, but rather as its result. I would contend that it is the teaching of the very message, and that the warding of man by man, chiefly in the body, to a less extent in the mind, has ever been all down its history the very worthy "long trail" of a religion which has many less worthy traces left by its course. This, and not faith in a sacrifice, it is that is taught as a message in the Gospels. That Jesus mandated man in the Many as the children of a loving Father I am not for a moment disputing. But it is equally true that when he showed man as brought to the tribunal of the worlds, he did not show him as asked: Did you believe in my sacrifice? but, Have you done this and that for your brothers?[1]

In the Sakya religion, which came to be called Buddhism, with a beginning more remote from us, and with records written very much more remotely in time from that beginning than those of Christendom, we may, it is true, there also see its message as something waited for and eagerly taken up and spread, but we find even more difficulty in discerning what the message to Everyman really was. From the records both early and late it might well be concluded that it taught, as to man's nature, that diagnosis of Ill known as "the four truths", or a trinity of attributes known as "the three marks", and as to man's life, that the best life on earth was that of casting off worldly ties and living mainly in seclusion. And these are still the notions held about it by many, not only in lands called in religion Buddhist, but even among such as are drawn to that cult from other lands and other religions.

But it happens that, here also, we can apply a parallel test, to bring out the very marrow of the message as touching the very man, to that which Christian teaching offers. For in the Buddhist records we also find the man brought in the hereafter, that is, on his leaving the earth, to the judgment-bar, to be passed as worthy, or not passed. And the question put to him is not: Did you believe in the truth of the truths, of the marks? Or, Did you believe that to leave the world was the best life? but, Did you see our messengers on earth, bidding you again and again to lead the worthy life? Here surely if anywhere the very touchstone of the message would be recorded. Here we see the newness of the new word as touching the very man in his testimony to his faith: not merely that a man should lead a worthy life: such a message would not then have been a New Word, even to the Many. The New Word was, in its bearing on conduct, the supreme importance of the worthy life, not so much to the short life of body and mind on earth but to the whole life of the very man

[1] Matthew's Gospel, xxv.

as wayfarer in the worlds. It was more important than belief in either the efficacy of rites or the select seclusion of an artificial mode of life. And the New Word was more than that.

The message of the later of these two religions was not needing that of the older. It was known then by the Many that the worthy life was of deepest importance hereafter. Nor did the older message convey the New Word of the later religion. The earth was not ready for it. It is true that its Messenger was very alive to help his fellows. Yet even that is not made out clearly in the records, when the way he took to do so is told. He is troubled at sight of the "messengers": old age, disease, death, but his trouble is so expressed that it might well be understood he was thinking of his own escape. There is no clear word in the story, "gest" (*apadāna*), or legend of the older scriptures, that in brooding over the ills of the world, and a way out, it is not his own fate only which is troubling him; that it was the Many he was concerned about. There are those even to-day who see in his trouble self-interest only, even when the record runs: "Alas! the world is fallen on trouble . . . Where on earth will a way out be shown?"[1] We cannot reasonably doubt that he did mean "way out for the world". He would not have lived in men's memory as "he-of-compassion-for-all-beings" had his earth-life not made it very clear that he did mean this. Nevertheless, the warding of all men by each man was then very far from being in men's minds and values, and hence, in men's wording. And thus we have to *read into* the story of his troubled thought the meaning "care for all men", and not for himself only.

Now the New Word with which this great "son of the Sakyas" opened up a "more" in the nature, and also in the life, of man was, I repeat, the importance of the moral life, or conduct, not in this world only but in the worlds, or in life as a whole. This was a new valuation, a new emphasis. Good conduct was then relatively speaking an amenity in earth life, and weighed lightly in trans-mundane values when compared with the accomplishment and efficacy of the Ritual. And the men who were charged with the Ritual were they who held the field in the regard and attention of the Many. But the New Word saw "the way out" as different.

It saw it as only in the man himself. No external methods as such can help. The man must find the way. In himself must each seek salvation. But let the reader not understand this in the way we now understand it. The "man" in our day is no longer the "man" of the day when Sakya began, any more than he was the

[1] *Digha-Nikāva*, ii, 30 f.

"man" of the day when Sakya was becoming what we call Buddhism. In the earlier day the "man" meant he who had "within", latent yet astir, the very Divine, the Highest, the Most. This Self it was, and no external deity, on whom man was thrown back, to whom man was referred, to follow whom was the way out. It is of the first importance that this be realized; the ignoring of it, the substitution for it of the later Buddhist limited view of the man, the self, and *of our own limited view of the man, the self*, is ever vitiating modern treatment of Buddhist teaching.

Man, as and by the Self, must find the "way": here we have the "sailing orders" in Sakya. This is, for me, vital in the teaching of the Man of the Sakyas, whose disciples were called after him Sakya-sons and his teaching "Sakya" for centuries. Men had long been herded along prescribed ways, with rite and sacrifice, with fixed gest and chanted mantra, if so be they might thereby elude mishap, both here and also in the next step awaiting the end of life on earth. It was a new thing for the Many to be told that in each man and woman was a vital spring whence could be evolved an ever greater fitness to meet and mould the To Be. It had been hinted at in Vedic teaching, but no more.[1] How did Sakya word that "spring"?

What have we surviving of Sakya teaching? Hereon, if my book prove unsatisfactory in brevity, the reader knows that I have not set out to deal with what we may call the external history of Buddhism. It would take me far beyond its more intensive scope. But I would at least have my reader make bowing acquaintance with the sources from which I have deemed it most worth while (and why) to draw. And I would also remind him of how very much, in the perspective of the history of our times, those sources are themselves to us a "New Word", one of the wonderful phases of the "More" that have so opened up our earth-horizon during a little over a century. Readers who have sampled books of the seventeenth and eighteenth centuries, dealing with Southern Asia, will know how few and fragmentary were the glimpses of "Buddha" and "Buddhism" shown to Europeans. Interesting examples are to be found in Mr. E. J. Thomas's *The Buddha in Legend and in History*,[2] to which may be added the curious references to both the Buddha and also to "Promb" (Brahman), supreme impersonal "Deity"

[1] Cf. *Śatapatha-Brahmaṇa*, vi, 2, 2, 27 (*SBE*, xli, p. 181): "Hence they say, Man is born into the world made (by him)."

[2] Page xiv.

(Tipedah = Devatā), in Alexander Hamilton's travels in Siam and Cambodia, now being edited by Sir William Foster. But the beginning of the nineteenth century reveals the dawning of new interest, of livelier inquiry. This is very natural when we remember that we won Ceylon from the Dutch at the end of the eighteenth century, retaining possession at the Treaty of Amiens, 1802. To the excellent historical references of the Oxford Dictionary we owe the ability to see how, at that time, the subjects "Buddha, Buddhism, Buddhist" were coming under discussion in the periodical *Asiatic Research* and in books. And the newness is intensified by the varied spellings, such as Bhoodha, Boudhou, Bhooddhist, Boudhist, Bhuddist, Bhudist, Buddhite, Buddhic, with the Sanskrit form, Bauddhas.

Such inquiries had been carried on practically, if not entirely, without access to anything that we should now call Canonical writings. The interesting tale of how these first poured into the hands of European libraries, first through Tibetan versions by the labours of Csoma de Körös, a Hungarian, then in Sanskrit Mahayānist compositions through the generous agency of Brian H. Hodgson from Nepal, and lastly in a completed, closed Pali (text) Canon through the labours of Upham, Turnour, and Robert C. Childers from Ceylon is already told elsewhere. It is needless and not in the scope of this inquiry to repeat the story, absorbing in interest though it be. I leave it repeating only, in inverse order, the reasons why it has been just touched upon :—

The general reader may incline to the conclusion that everything about Buddhism has been said, and said often enough. I would remind him that the problem of Christian origins has been, for us of Europe, "always with us," and that there was a mountain of books about Christianity in existence before a serious effort to solve the problem of its origins in the historical study of its records was begun. Speaking approximately, it took thirteen centuries before such an effort began less than one century ago. Modern conditions make it less likely that the corresponding effort over the problem of Buddhist origins will be delayed so long. But because there is already a mountain of books—a very little mountain comparatively—about Buddhism, it does not follow that that effort has got very far, much less that it has got as far as it will get. Only an ignorant person would say—as was recently said to me by a London firm of book-purveyors—that all the books that were needed on Buddhism had been written. On the contrary : the effort to disentangle the real sources from the later values, values which became orthodox and authoritative, is relatively new and untried. This little work will not get very far, and is at best a call to the world to take note of what remains to be done. But to think it has been done is that little knowledge which is indeed, in the cause of truth, a dangerous thing.

And if I call upon readers to make a "bowing acquaintance" with Pali literature only as my field of excavations, it is not to maintain that there are no other fields presently available or to be available for digging. It is, in the first place, that I would deal with that about which I have first-hand knowledge ; in the second place, because, when we compare Pali books and one other source, Buddhist Sanskrit books, we cannot be in doubt that, among the former, we have writings which are, as compared with all that I have seen of the latter, records of what had already long existed as *uttered sayings,* while in the latter we have *written compositions*, works far less archaic, works of a later date. Into this I have gone elsewhere, and may go a little into it here. But the style is not the only historical guide. Sayings in the Pali books are cited as authoritative by Buddhist Sanskrit works, and if the world of scholars is not yet in a position to come to finished conclusions in this matter of relative antiquity, the present position is well worded by Mr. E. J. Thomas when he writes, that what has become recently available in other Buddhist literatures emphasizes "the relative importance and antiquity of the Pali against the late and degenerate forms that have survived in Nepal and Tibet. It is no longer possible to pit the (Sanskrit) Lalita-Vistara against the Pali as a source of history, and to base theories on documents that can be proved to be accretions and inventions of later centuries".

As to the contents of the Pali scriptures, I have here tried the reader's patience to a minimum, by giving a statement of them only in an Appendix, and that just for convenience of reference. He will find a thematic list of them both in Rhys Davids's *Manual of Buddhism* (S.P.C.K.) and in Mr. Thomas's book, *The Buddha in Legend and History*, pp. 257 ff.

Those Pali scriptures have one special feature distinguishing them from all other "bibles" known to us, and which should never be lost to view. They are the compilations of men whom we should now call monks. Now it may be, that the Christian scriptures were in time preserved and propagated by clerics who, to all purposes, were as much separated from the external world as were the monks of the Sangha. But we cannot say that it was an Order of such clerics who first committed to writing the memorized sayings out of which the first three or even the fourth of the gospels were compiled. They are sayings addressed to—as we now say—

Everyman, and bearing no sign that they were the utterances of clerics. The Pali books differ from them of course in many ways, but mainly in just this :—It is claimed that they are compiled by Buddhist clerics, that is, by monks, and they are, in their present form, *almost wholly addressed to monks*. This is not realized by those who are not conversant with these books. And because of this want of acquaintance with this distinctive feature, it is not realized that the books are concerned, not so much with the world of Everyman as with a world within that world : a world of men (and of some women) who had renounced life in the world as parents, sons, brothers, citizens, workers, who *as such* had renounced the attempt to live worthy lives, and who, having made a violent purging of all that from their lives, were adapting themselves to other interests, other occupations, other ideals.

It does not follow, from this altered and narrowed range, that the Pali books do not contain much that is of high religious and moral value, not only for the monk, but also for Everyman. But it does follow that, as teaching for Everyman's needs and aspirations, they make a narrowed appeal, they word a mandate less fitted for the world than if they were addressed, in every case or in most cases, to the man in the world's life. And it does follow from this that in their present written composition they are *no true expression* of a real world-gospel, a message that is to Everyman, to the very Man in all men.

How then, it may be asked, is it that, in these Pali books, we are asked to see the oldest surviving mandate of what was and is indubitably a world-religion? To this the answer is : Well, it is the best documentary survival that we yet have ; but being such a mandate as they are, we must not accept its wording of this *in just the form it has come to take*. We must use our reconstructive imagination. This is to use neither constructive (creative) imagination or fancy, as we shall surely be accused of using. We have to make of these Pali scriptures an intelligible whole. Such a whole many now try to make by interpreting much in an over-modern way, reading ideas of our own time, such for instance as solidarity and altruism and fraternity, into these old-time scriptures. And hence comes much of the appeal Buddhism makes here and there to men and women of lapsed creed, or of no creed.

This is not the way to take if we really care for truth. The way I would ask the reader to take is the historical way. This means, broadly speaking, that we should consider these scriptures in the light of the fact that man is ever changing, ever becoming other, ever shifting his values even where he is not changing his skies, more where he has changed his skies.

In the lifetime of the coming-to-be of the Pali scriptures there was time, and opportunity, for many changes. Even if we place the formulating of the oldest Sayings, long precedent to any series corresponding to a " book ", as early as 500 B.C., more than three centuries, more likely four, or even five, centuries elapsed before the Pali Canon can safely be said to have been finally closed. And it is agreed that it was about as long a time as that, namely, about 80 B.C., before, in the new vogue of writing, and not only memorizing records, they were committed, at least in one country, to the form of written documents. Our only evidence, as yet, when and where this was done is a statement in Ceylon literature[1] that it took place to meet a possible emergency in that island. It is more likely that the canonical records were written there in imitation of an earlier commitment to writing in India, made about the time of the " Fourth Council " under king Kaniṣka, but our scanty evidence inclines scholars to place the date of that after the date alleged in the Ceylon epics.

After this long interval, with all that it actually brought of changes internal and external, it is not wilful scepticism to say that when we accept " Buddhism " as we find it held in worth in the Pali scriptures, we are *not near to its origins.* It is because it is generally supposed that those scriptures put the really original teaching in the chief place, that we are not very near to a true idea of it. There is but little left in them of the way in which the Founder of Sakya and his first men taught. We are not worthy reconstructors if we do not face this difficulty.

We are often reminded of the remarkable power of memorizing past and even present in India. This is only natural in a country where good writing materials were late in being found, so that the reign and power of the spoken word was, so to speak, artificially prolonged. But we may help out the Pali scriptures, as true mandate, with this subterfuge too much. It is questionable whether we should look, among Sakyan repeaters, for such highly developed memorizing as was ancient and traditional among not all, but certain of the Brahmans. And even among these there is no absolute certainty that their mantras never varied. We have for that matter evidence that revision of these from time to time was an ancient institution. Never to vary is only possible for automata. A repeating cleric is, relatively, an automaton. But the more he is worth as a *teacher*, the more will he tend to vary from the automatic.

[1] *Dīpavaṃsa*, xx, 20, 21. *Mahāvaṃsa*, xxxiii, 100, 101.

To word his own convictions he will change a memorized record here in emphasis, there in order of wording, there again even in wording. And his following will come to imitate him herein. Hence, long before there were scribes to scratch in with their styles the mistakes we now meet with in manuscripts, it is not only possible, it is very probable, that Sakyan repeatings underwent change in versions carried on at different places, at different times. It is well to rate the Pali scriptures for what they are ; it is better not to rate them for what they are not and cannot be.

And that which they are not, that which, from the circumstances of their coming into being, they cannot be, is a truthful adequate presentation of Sakya, the gospel taught by Gotama the Sakyan and his first fellow-workers. Where, then, and how are we to find, if find we may, that very gospel ? I do not think we need despair, as a few are inclined to do. The task of the modern archæologist in this ancient site and that has seemed at first no less formidable, and yet by patient dogged digging he has come upon sites and their spoil more truly showing the city of his quest than the remains nearer the surface. We too must dig. We too may find more meagre remains underneath, as he does. It would ill accord, did we not, with what is disclosed in other historical religions ; and Sakya is among existing religions very old, while the oldest documents for our digging are relatively new.

But we must ever dig as the most sagacious archæologist digs, and as the wiser scientific researcher observes : and that is by the light of a hypothesis. "Tell me what to look for !"—was it not Faraday who used to say this ? I am aware that a hypothesis is faith in process of being tested, not faith held as proven, or as above proof. But, till shown unworkable, a hypothesis is a guide held most worthy by the man of science. By the investigator in our field I find it is not used enough, perhaps because our observed particular instances are so few. To work consistently with this opinion I would ask the reader to bear with me while I set out my own hypothesis. No less than the worker in natural science, research in world-religions should be questing in these for a natural, or cosmic law, or uniformity. So wonderful a phenomenon is the birth and growth and later life of a world-religion, succeeding under apparently the most untoward circumstances where most similar attempts would fail, nay, have failed, that either each has been, in its own field of success, held to be unique, a law unto itself, or the partisan chronicles of them have been discredited. But a wider view recognizes on the one hand that we are dealing with things which, if wonderful, are not unique, and on the other, with things which, whatever we may discredit in their origins, are, in their development and present status, very world-facts.

And I would repeat here, as very pertinent to the subject, that few contributions of scholastic Buddhism are so worthy of our note as the discernment, not only of a fivefold cosmic order (*niyama*), but as fifth therein of a gospel-order, or order of the Better, the May-be, the Should, or Ought to be (*dhammaniyama*). The view was more possible to Buddhist sectaries than to those of other religions, in that for Buddhism the Saviour is himself not a unique phenomenon, but one in an august succession. The wording I gave eighteen years ago to this great conception [1] was traversed for me later by an account sent me of the wording of it accepted in the Burmese Buddhism of to-day. But this explanation makes the scholastic explanation of the exegesist Buddhaghosa himself quite pointless, and for myself I hold it erroneous and of no worth, not even worth adducing here.

Now here is the hypothesis with which I try to work. I restate [2] it here and somewhat fully. Let us consider (1) the gospel or New Word itself; (2) the response when and where and how made to such of gospels as have grown and persisted; (3) the messenger or man of the mandate.

(1) Wherever and whenever "gospels" were uttered and spread, we note in them certain great common features. In the first place, they are each and all addressed to the "man", not to anything external about him, to what is of the nature of an adjunct or a factor, or an instrument, but—by implication, if not explicitly—to what we might call the "man-in-man", the very self of him. Next, they are concerned with man's life, and its great significance for the man himself, now and hereafter. Lastly, they speak, in terms of high worth and faith and hope, of man's nature, namely, of what he may become, of that which, in virtue of his nature, however he lives now, he has it in him to become. What is that? It is variously worded: to become Deity, to become perfect, to put an end to ill, to become entirely happy.

I think—perhaps it is part of the hypothesis—that one word might claim to include all these, when we come, as come we may, to give it due worth: the word "well". Man, say the great religions, imperfect, minor, infant, as, in his earth-stages, he more or less always is, has it in his nature to become *utterly well*. Poor hackneyed

[1] *Buddhism* (Home University Library), p. 119.

[2] Cf. *Kindred Sayings on Buddhism*, Calcutta, 1930.

little monosyllable that it is, not suffered in my language to figure as the great noun it is in many European languages,[1] few may be ready to see the depth, the breadth, the height in the range, the scope of it. Yet its negative equivalent, the "end of ill" (*dukkhass' antaṃ*) has stirred the earnest Buddhist imagination for ages. And again, it is a bigger ultimate conception than that of happiness, pleasure, bliss. To be well, utterly well, is not only a state to be enjoyed or contemplated as a consequence of actions or good fortune: it is a state of supreme attainment after much becoming. It may be not so much a state, as itself a hyperbecoming in a glory of bringing to pass, of making to become. Happiness, or its equivalents, may be accompaniments, but they are that also in much that is not well. They are like the perfume, the colour of the flower. The "Well" belongs to the very growth of the plant. This is because the "well"—if the reader will overlook the unfamiliar use, and bethink him of "le bien", "das Wohl", "il bene", and so on—like the Platonic "good", is a term of the very man, or soul, or spirit, and not of his instruments, body and mind. These two grow from infancy to adulthood, no less than does spirit. Soon body enters on decay, and to some extent mind also, that is, in so far, as it is the body's servant, and has its scope limited in outlook by the body's lifespan. But growth of the very man is not so limited, not so rounded off, not so ephemeral, nor need there be decay. Its beginning we do not know, nor its end. But the index of its growth is not the more or less of happiness, but the Better, the more well. The Well belongs less to the little present world of things enjoyed, more to the world of one who would become fit to enjoy. The world of the Well is the world of Dharma—of which more presently—in the true fundamental meaning of that word.

(2) It is not easy for us, to whose world no recent gospel-mandate of any proven power to grow, to sway men, and to persist has come, and who have very fragmentary records of the days when such a mandate was just come, to be wise about the response which met the bringer of such and the message as such. Even were there no such fragments, some explanation of the phenomenon of his and of its success would be needed. As it is we seem to see this: the message made a singular appeal, a strong appeal, the appeal of a supply to a demand; the response to something waited for. They who were waiting were not in every case the very worthy, the very wise. But they were in a way feeling the need of someone to give

[1] *Le bien, il bene, das Wohl*, etc. Aristotle once uses τὸ εὖ, probably as forced a word as is my "the well". I sin in great company.

expression and guidance, of a kind yet unworded for the Many, about the "man" and the life of him. In the man who thus expresses and guides they find one who appeals to the very man in them, not to anything external about each, not to any actual worthiness in each, but to that in each where there is very need of him. Something there will have been in the message to this and that man about his changing for the better that flashes like an electric throb from man to man; something concerning the very nature of the man in his long wayfaring toward That who is also of his very nature, his nature in very perfection as he is only perfection's germ. I believe that in no other way can we account for the extraordinary growing and expanding power shown at the inception of each great gospel-movement. It is true that the written testimonies are the work of votaries. But I repeat that, independently of the way in which these made record, the patent fact remains, that there was both astonishing growth and expansion. And this will have been because the movement met some felt need, felt more especially there where the response to that need was first brought, but beginning to be felt elsewhere too. Something in the message, something put in a new light will have appealed to the growing, the becoming man. For of no religion can it be said that it was the work of message and messenger alone.

Man in this includes woman. Woman, in the very self of her is "man". (Sex runs deep in mind as well as body, deep in character, for character, though it is the imprint on mind and body of the man, is an outcome in, and hence affected by, body and mind. But sex is not of the very man.) And woman has ever been the friend of religion, although the converse is less true, if, by religion we mean the framework of religions, churches. She is admittedly so, and the cause has usually been sought in her intellectual inferiority. Perhaps it were truer to say, it is because she values the "man" above the mind, the minder above the minding. She rates as supreme the things that belong to the very man, the self, the spirit, that is, the things that make for the Better, for growth in the very man. She, too, will at such a given epoch be seeking after and responding to the New of the kind with which we are concerned. But it will be a seeking and a responding in her own way. And that will not be quite men's way.

That she will seek and will respond is for her a more natural thing than for him; it is nearer to her woman's life to be doing so. As mother, she is ever contemplating and caring for the "new" and the "more". Her child is a new creature, not identical with anyone else, not wholly like anyone else. In him she is witnessing growth, becoming; she is caring for a "more" in him, that is, for a better. It is the mother potential and actual who will better respond to the message of a new which is a more; and so it was in India. She responded in a more intimate, a deeper way than most men: she welcomed the new in the way not of men, but of the "man". This may be seen from such records as survive, both in the Upanishads and in the Piṭakas. There is also evidence of similar response, in women of the Jains which, though it is chiefly in Pali Commentaries, has yet the appearance of being very old tradition, when, that is, it is found in Nikāyan Commentary. Such a tradition is in the Majjhima Commentary as to the founding of the Jain community at Vesālī by a little group of women.[1]

(3) Something in the messenger too will have made special appeal; something that made him one with his message, so that it came to be said of him: his message is he, he is his message. I am not going here into the deep matter of his being specially mandated, i.e. "inspired". Let the fragrance of mankind's tribute to that be here sufficient:

> ". . . Benedictus qui venit in nomine Domini!"
> "Yen' eva maggena gato Vipassī . . . ten' añjasena agamāsi Gotamo."[2]

Let it be enough for purposes of my hypothesis to affirm that he owed the heed which from the first some paid him, the worth in which some held him—the number of such growing quickly—to this: he as just very man, and not otherwise, spoke to the very man in each man, bringing a message about that very man, about his "good", or "well", now and to come, about his growth toward it, about each man's own work as willing and choosing in that growth, that changing for the better. No doubt he will have been personally attractive; even Sokrates was clearly that, and who will say truly, that Sokrates taught no gospel, made lasting in scripture? But there will have been more in the man of the message than what we usually understand by attractiveness, unless indeed under the word we mean the total drawing power of him. Something that I believe all bringers of a new gospel, or even of a lasting reform in a religion, will have had in common, despite differences in time, in place, in race, language, birth, and breeding. Many words to this or that man they may not have said, but the will and the word and ways of

[1] *Papañca-Sūdanī*, p. 268 (P.T.S. ed.).

[2] "The very way by which Vipassī went . . .
By that same road (now) hath gone Gotama." (*Theragāthā*, ver. 488–90.)

them will have gone straight past externals to the very man, as if a living flame, a live wire had been communicating. In their one aim, and in the way of putting that aim into action, I see in such helpers of men, not totally detached individuals, but a type, the vehicles of a cosmic law, a great Fraternity such as Te Deums have been at pains to word.

Let it not be supposed that I see, in such Helpers, any one who is more than man. I only plead that in order to be and become what he was, we must heed and measure him for the very man he will have been, and not credit him with saying that which cannot have come from him. This, as we shall see, is a vital factor in my hypothesis; one that should do much to guide our digging.

Briefly summed up (1), (2), and (3) amount to this: In a world-religion we have a special relation of two terms and the bond between them: the mandated, the mandater, and the mandate. Man does not respond to an appeal which is not to his inmost self. (Man here includes woman.) When he does respond, he has, perhaps unawares, been seeking it. The worder is one to whom the "man" in men pays instant heed. In the whole relation: man the taught, the teaching on man, the man teaching, it is the very man, not just body, not just mind, not just the dual complex, that is in question.

And I would maintain that it is of great importance to have these interrelated factors as a working hypothesis when we are sifting old scriptures. For instance, in the last factor, the man teaching: here the growing tradition has been to see in him more than the man, and then to credit him with any- and every-thing he is recorded to have said. The very human man, as speaking to "the man", is lost to view. Then in the linking factor, the teaching-on-man: this is also twisted and covered over by tendencies in teaching which are of secondary importance, or which are later, or which are both. Let me not be taken as supposing that twisting and covering are the work either of wilful impiety, or of carelessness. Nor that changes were made without adequate motive. Non-automatic (i.e. human) repetition of sayings through many generations, in many regions had resulted in diversity of versions. When authoritative revision took place, one of such versions had to be made "authentic". Very naturally the version most consonant with the (changed) views of the day of revision would be selected. Lastly, the first term of the relation, man the taught, is not always rightly considered. He is too much treated of as just multitude, mass, men. There is in the Sakya Sayings a fine simile about this. They to whom the teacher comes are likened to lotuses growing beneath, on, or above the water's surface ; even so are the many not all alike. And there will be some with eyes but little dust-dimmed : "there are they who will understand." These are of the many or of them who are also concerned about the many ; these it is who have "set going the wheel" of a new movement. With this setting going it is usual to credit the messenger alone. But a great movement, such as is a world-religion, is no one-man matter. Between helper and multitude there is a mighty bond, welded by that Who calls in the one to the other. And that is the manhood in man, rightly understood : the "man-in-man" who is also the More-than-man.

I have herewith explained the hypothesis or theory, which is, I venture to think, that which should guide our reconstructing the almost lost features of the original message in a world-religion. Reconstructors will not fail to have it cast at them, that they, in sifting old scriptures, are selecting and rejecting according to caprice and predilection. And they may deserve the casting, if they make it not clear that they are working according to nothing of the sort, but by a theory really worthy of their high emprise. When, guided by such a theory, they say, "This saying is true" ; "That saying cannot be true", it is because they believe that, in the original message, in the messenger, in the conditions of the uttering by him of it, they have the working of a universal law or uniformity, in the mandating of man in a "more" concerning his nature, his life, his destiny. And this, not in a capricious way, but as gradually revealing more as man becomes ready for more. Thus guiding ourselves, we shall not look, for true origins, to any mere protest against, or revulsion from some older, other established mandate. We shall not look in the messenger for a man who set himself in direct opposition to, or subversion of the established doctrines, but rather for one who led the New, yet was not too far ahead of his day in leading. We shall seek for one who will not have "come to destroy . . . but to fulfil". And I believe we shall find our origins in a new and positive addition to the ideals of the Many, ideas which the man among the Many will come, through the message, to hold in a worth never before held. Thereby the man will grow. And in the conditions of the impetus to that fresh growth, we shall look for something which we may illustrate in the physical world by the electrified oxygen and nitrogen elements of the air when thundery conditions are favouring growth. We shall also look for a man or men giving voice or other expression to the new in a way, not necessarily eloquent, but a way that "draws a man with cords as of love".[1]

[1] "I drew them with cords of a man, with bands of love."—Hosea, xi.

II

THE WORLD AWAITING SAKYA.

I will begin with the first factor in the triad of the hypothesis the man to be mandated, and try to reconstruct the world, the particular section of mankind, to which the original message came. This has several times been attempted, but not altogether as I find it might be. Writers have been guided, it may be, overmuch by the Pali records. And reacting in their reading to the sense of something later and much other than certain Brahman records [1]—the earlier Upanishads—they have come to, I think, a mistaken conclusion. They have not said : These Pali records are mainly pictures of conditions much later than the day of Sakya beginnings, and we are more likely to find a truer picture in those earlier Upanishads of those beginnings. No, they have said, these Pali records represent more or less the day of Sakya beginnings ; therefore those earlier Upanishads are very pre-Buddhistic. I think that this is scarcely a true perspective. I think that we should see in the Piṭakas much of the usage, seen in Renaissance paintings, of depicting older happenings in the raiment and the customs of the painter's own day. I think it may be a truer way to take Brahman works *assumed* to be pre-Buddhistic, and with them to compare certain ideas, which we find emerging in the Pali records, but which do not fit well with the most of what we there find. I mean such ideas as "the Way", the "self", the "man" as very real, "*prajñā*," the life beyond, the very man as "becoming". So proceeding we may find, that whereas in Sakya there are affinities with those Brahman works, it is rather the cult which we call "Buddhism" and not "Sakya" which is akin to the Pali works known as Piṭakas.

For if Sakya was indeed a New Word, only anticipated in the emphasis it laid on how a man lived as more of religious importance than ritual, by the Jain movement, we need not therefore look to find it put forward in a time of religious chaos, where no established cult was left standing. Some evidence of this we might see surviving in the Pali and other books. But the contrary is true. We have to picture a world where certain ideals or concepts about man were generally held, where certain institutions were well and strongly

[1] Cf. for instance Oldenberg, *Lehre der Upanishaden*, etc., p. 282 f.

established. I am referring especially to man's nature as being the immanently divine, and to the social acceptance of Brahman and Kshatriya (or noble). And the problem for us is the relation of the Founder and his men to those ideals and concepts, and their attitude to those institutions. In what way were they concerned "not to destroy but to fulfil" those religious ideas and ideals? In what way were they, as both of Brahmans and Kshatriyas themselves, concerned to bring a More into the concepts and life of their fellows?

There was in the first place the Brahman world. This was then much more important than when the Buddhist Sangha or "church" became influential. It stood very high in men's esteem. The Brahman stood for the learning of the time, for the holiness of the time, and for the lore in the unseen, as teacher, as mantra-bearer, as celebrant, as mediator. Herein he was unlike other men; he was a man of privilege and monopoly. He could utter words that others might and could not; he could work, he could claim, he could give what others could not; he could assign values in the things of high religious import as others could not.

And there is another aspect of him to which writers scarcely do justice, an aspect which may be equally applied to the noble or Kshatriya. Both he and the Brahman were rated at that time as higher, finer specimens of manhood in the social standard of the day. Not just because they were rated in the mass as belonging to a certain "colour" (*vaṇṇa*), i.e. social class or caste. The caste-system, in any proper or exact use of the term, did not exist—to quote Rhys Davids—in the age in question.[1] It was a day more like our own of yesterday, without *sharply* defined class barriers, with an uncertain demarcation of four classes of society, but with a fairly clear idea of what we describe as *noblesse oblige*. I mean that more was expected from the manhood of one who was Kshatriya or Brahman than from one who was not. The class was, not so much an external matter, as a guarantee, that a member of the first two classes would be likely to conform to a worthier standard of what we call "breeding" than one who did not. Kshatriya and Brahman were, whatever else they were, the "gentleman" of the day, expected to obey what in the Pali books—to speak only of them—was termed his own dhamma: that is, what or how he should behave. I am not overlooking that, in the context where this is emphasized, a "dhamma" is also assigned to each of the other classes, trader and serf; but equally I would not have it overlooked that the assignment here is rather (like the "dhamma" itself) of what should be or might be, than of *what really had weight* in current standards.

[1] *Dialogues of the Buddha*, i, Introd. to Sta. iii, esp. p. 101.

This was, not so much men in the lump, as the man, the individual. In worth it is the man that India has looked to, and not so much the men. We may see this emergent in the context just quoted and others,[1] thus : " This verse was well sung, Vāseṭṭha, . . . I too say :—

The Khattiya is the best among this folk
Who put their trust in lineage ;
But one in wisdom and in virtue clothed
Is best of all 'mong devas and 'mong men."

It is here the man who is the held in worth ; not nobles, not the worthy men, but the individual, the very man. It is only when Gotama is criticizing the current cases of laxity in maintaining the Brahman " dhamma " that he speaks again and again of " Brahmans " in the plural.

I am not wishing to emphasize these special contexts, as in themselves very evidential. They are at best but reflections of a very positive feature in the conditions of Sakyan origins, to which sufficient justice is not done. A comity such as the Indo-Aryan, which in its religious ideals rated so high the worth of the man, the person, cannot be too much heeded by us, who are in the throes of trying to get away from the man and to " think racially ". Nor could such a theory as the Arahan, the ideal man-in-worth, of monastic Sakya have evolved save under conditions in which the highest worth in the " man " was, or had been current.

If I stress the influence and prestige of the Brahman institution at this time, it is not to maintain that the members of it were as a whole in a condition of high moral or spiritual health. It is very possible that, in the West of Northern India, where as I read Brahman prestige was higher than in the Eastern valley of the Ganges, there was, at the time in question, less of decadence and of a lowered standard than there appears to have been in the latter region. Nor even, for the state of Brahmanism here, can we safely follow what we read in the Pali books. But it is fairly safe to infer, that where new movements in religious reform first showed themselves, to wit, in that eastern region, it is there that the state of Brahmanism was less commending itself to the serious will of earnest men. And hence we can give the more credence to such strictures on the average moral conduct among Brahmans, as often leaving much to be desired, of which the Tevijja Suttanta speaks (Dīgha Nikāya, xiii), as well as on the " muttering " (*japanā*) of mantras for fees alluded to in the Sagāthā Vagga (Saŋyutta Nikāya).

[1] Cf. op. cit., iii, p. 94.

It does not follow that a low moral and spiritual standard prevailed among all. Many were doubtless slack and unworthy, but probably the majority, even in the East, were worthy according to their light. And there will have been, as in any ecclesiastical community now, at once both stricter and more lax conduct in clerical and in secular work. There was, for instance, a certain feeling against cultivation of the soil by Brahmans, nevertheless many Brahmans are shown tilling their farms and estates,[1] without apparent opprobrium. Much more was permitted than was thought worthy. In such professions there are always and everywhere these shades of opinion and grades of worth.

A more adequate description of the Brahmanism of this time and of the probable degree in which it was and yet was not a great force, barring in any way the inception of new movements, is to be found in the late Hermann Oldenberg's *Buddha* (especially the last, the 6th, edition)[2] and *The Upanishads and the Beginnings of Buddhism.* Specially worthy is the emphasis in the former work on the error it is to see in Brahmanism and Sakya two forces in mutual opposition. We have on the one hand to avoid seeing, in the former, anything resembling the judicial hierarchy of the Catholic Church a few centuries back, enforcing its will by secular authority, and we have on the other hand to see in the first Sakyan teachers a high appreciation of what was truly worthy in the Brahman. The ideally good man was and remained in the Sayings of Sakya "a Brahman",[3] the word holding its own even when the term Arahan, or as we might say "saint", had come into its loftier signification. There were Brahmans who disdained the upstart New; there were Brahmans who appreciated it and its exponents. But there was everywhere civic and ecclesiastical tolerance.

To one phase, however, which, I incline to believe, was apparent among the more enlightened Brahmans of the day, I do not find attention given, and that is the extent to which some Brahman teachers *were themselves responding to the call of the New*, and introducing ideas new to the orthodox teaching of the day into the instruction they gave professionally, ideas which were professionally repeated and handed on (in the absence of writing) in their schools. It has not come to my notice that, in the Vedântic estimates of to-day concerning the Upanishad literature, this or that book is held in greater reverence than others. It is generally accepted that all

1 E.g. *Saṃyutta-Nikāya*, i, 171.

2 Only the first edition is translated into English.

3 Especially *Dhammapada* and *Sutta Nipāta, passim.*

are held in high worth ; nevertheless it is reasonable to assume that, as in the case of a man, an added reverence may attach, in any one of the books, to its greater age. That the Upanishads are of different age is no new problem, but an established conclusion for many years past. The varying nature of their contents, varying in outlook, in emphasis, in ideals, leaves no doubt on the matter. But there is room for further internal comparison of one part of the same Upanishad with other parts. As a result we may find that each of the older Upanishads is a little history in itself. And a lack of adequate internal analysis in such studies as I find has made my own problems harder.

For of any one Upanishad, however venerable be now its time-status, there was a day when its utterances, or at least some of its utterances, were new ideas. I say, some at least, since this also is patent in the contents, especially of those reckoned oldest : an apparent interfusion of new with older matter. Nowhere perhaps is the editorial hand more sensibly felt, nowhere is the work of "gloss" so evident as in the greater Upanishads [1] which are deemed older if not oldest. Now it is only reasonable to imagine (reconstructively imagine) that, when these utterances had not before been put forward, the utterer on the one hand was a teacher in touch and in sympathy with the new ideas of the spirit of his age, and on the other that, as a "new man", he would not be looked upon with full uncritical approval by his fellow-teachers, in so far as, in the greater segregation of district branches in an ancient community, they would be aware of what he was teaching. He will doubtless have had a convinced and loyal band of pupils, youths, it may be, also ready for and feeling after the new. And he will have had his repeaters, as now we have publishers, Brahmans of professionally trained memory, whereby, as pupils went and pupils came, the utterances were maintained, and survived the careers of both pupils and finally of the teacher himself.

Meanwhile the utterances will have become known more or less widely, and in so far as they worded those new truths which come, as has been contended, to man when he is ready for them and feeling out after them, they will have found acceptance among other teachers, and been incorporated into the body of Upanishadic lore. They will not necessarily have been kept as a separate item ; they may have come to form accretions in an older framework, in which we see upheld the older absorbed interest in ritual, mantra, celebrant.

[1] By these I mean Chhāndogya and Bṛhadāraṇyaka, coupled with Kauṣītaki, Aitareya, Taittirīya, and one or two others.

Nor will this be the end. Other accretions will have come testifying to a newer, even more absorbing interest which had crept up and over Indian thought: the finding in the study of man not so much, or not only the engrossing contemplation of the "man" as opposed to body, but the contemplation of the man in the ways and modes of mind. In parts of the Upanishads reckoned oldest, we meet with the mind (*manas*) referred to as an important unitary, undiscussed factor, parallel with speech and breath, etc. In other parts of these Upanishads the interest in the mind has undergone a notable development, as readers will have recognized. And this analytical "new word", when it had not only been approved and its sayings incorporated in the older framework, became at a yet later date, and in still younger Upanishads, cited by name as a commendable and even necessary training in the Brahman lore, namely, as Sānkhya.

I have mentioned the historical fact of change in Upanishad utterance and emphases as having been at one time both new and unapproved, and only becoming accepted gradually, not only because due attention has scarcely been given to it, not only because it may help us in determining the really original in Sakya, but also because I would show that the history of the Pali Piṭaka evolution, as I conceive it, is not unique, but reflects an analogous history in the evolution of the Upanishads.

But what then may have been that new word in the greater Upanishads, which I see as overlying the oldest matter of rite and mantra cult, the less old cult of the man as Deity, and as, in its turn, overlaid by the mind-analyses of early Sānkhya leavening? I consider it is to be found in the discourses of the teacher who has the (probably) assumed name of Yājñavalkya in the Bṛhadāraṇyaka Upanishad. Here it is not so much the ultimate oneness of the man with the Highest or Brahman that is introduced. This was, when "Yājñavalkya" taught, an accepted belief, a very vital doctrine. It is in the insistence on the consummation of the man's life and nature as being, not a matter of great wisdom or insight to be attained *here*, but the outcome of stages-in-becoming figured as a Way (*marga* or *yāna*) through worlds of rebirth till full maturity or realization is won.

This will have been, I venture to think, a new word at some time in India's religious history. Not in the use of the figure—*yāna* is, if I mistake not, a Vedic figure—but in its earnest and solemn emphasis, and its application to the conception of man's betterment and ultimate consummation as Man, this being none other than

Deity, and to this climax being realizable, not proximately to earth-life or lives, but after another world-stage or stages :—

> Scarce visible and old there lies a Way
> That touches me, e'en me, was found by me.
> Thereon the wise whose is the Brahma-lore
> Fare onward to the world of light, and thence
> O'erpassing that are utterly released.
>
> *Bṛhad. Upan.*, iv, 4, 8.

The kinship in these lines with the central figure in the Sakyan message is fairly obvious, and into both we need much searching of thought to see, as writers mostly do not see, all that is implied in it. To that we shall recur. That the one utterance suggested the other I do not believe, in whichever order they are taken. That the same source inspired both utterers is very conceivable, but who is able to go into that? But that the two represent the religious aspiration of the same place and time in the voice of two (or more) gifted men—here is a quite plausible hypothesis. The more so, in that this new word comes to be obscured in each corpus of sayings, Brahman and Sakyan, by the same later preoccupation, to wit, the inquiry into mind as the "man's" way of self-expression, and as possibly the ultimate expression of the "man" himself!

I said "all that is implied in" the figure of the Way. In its use by this Brahman-of-the-new-word is an implication, a significance as great as in its use by Gotama-of-the-new-word, and one just as much passed over. It is not the figure as such that is important; it is the thing meant by the Way. And that is man's nature as not static, as not "being", but as a becoming, a "werden", a coming to be, a progress in the "More". That man, as being, was ultimately the supreme Ātman, was the prevalent creed among the thoughtfully pious Brahmans, when that new word of the Upanishad was uttered. It was a pre-Sakyan view, and it was that which among them held the field.

But here, implied in this Brahman's "Way" (*marga*), and patent in the pre-occupation of the older Upanishads with the word *bhu*, to become, is a new note, even one that implicates the very idea of Deity Itself.[1] Namely in this: that the very exercise of divine creative power is now deliberately worded as "desire-to-become": "It desired being One to become More." Now since the man was Deity in microcosm, desiring-to-become was also essentially the man's natural self-expression. Becoming was no longer a mere matter of body,

[1] I have found 300 passages in these Upanishads using the word as finite verb. It does not appear to me to have received adequate attention.

of mind, of external phenomena ; it was of the very man. In it we see a passing on beyond the static concept of man as being. The Divine Itself is a becoming, a growth in the More in the very man, till he, fully attaining, and become Most, can exercise that creative becoming, which can no more be rightly described as growth, but may more fitly be described as Play.[1]

I am not saying that this mighty new word was incorporated into the religious ideal of India as it merited to be. It was a mandate to the very man or self. And had the warning of another man of the new thought, Kauṣītaki of the Upanishad so named, been rightly heeded, the true conception might have been upheld. He it was who warned his students not to consider the ways of man's mind without considering the man, the minder.[2] But the growing influence of the new analysis of mind, wherein mind was rated as ways in which man acted, and, so to speak, had always acted, was adverse to the consideration of how he might *come to act*, i.e. think, feel, etc. So the new idea died out, even as it was worsened in Sakya, and to-day the Indian's conception of the Divine is, once more and still, not "becoming" but "being" (*sat*). He has a cramped idea of becoming ; and his defective grasp of will is a contributory cause. Had he worded this, in his crude psychology, as the most fundamental self-expression, he had not lost sight of becoming. Hardly may we blame him, however, for has not our own psychology been equally blind, and with less excuse, both as to the "man" and the will to become ?

It is the more strange, that the idea of becoming, as essentially the nature of man, the microcosm, should not have retained its hold on the mind of India, when the new teaching, put forward perhaps at this very time in all the three Upanishads (Bṛhad., Chhāndo., Kauṣ.), concerning the man in dreamless sleep is considered. He was then held to have the opportunity of, as it were going home, becoming Himself, with all that was alien discarded. It is not easy for us, with our materialistic ideas about sleep, so utterly unworthy of our great heritage, to ascribe fit worth to this theory. We have left ourselves orphans herein. Moreover, our mediaeval tradition of attaching supramundane values to height and distance is hindersome. For the Brahman teacher of this day, to go home to the Highest Who he really was amounted to an intensified sense of *inwardness*, expressed as a going into the heart. The Most High was at the same time the Most Within. But there was transition, that is,

[1] Cf. Ramānuja (*fl.* A.D. 1100); "highest Brahman . . . who in play produces, sustains and reabsorbs the universe. . . ."

[2] *Kauṣ. Up.*, iii, 8.

there was a becoming That (in deep sleep) in a more entire sense. THAT is waiting for him who is of Itself, for him for whom it was shown to be natural to revert to his fountain-head, natural to become, to re-become That. Nevertheless, so lost was the precious insight into the need and fact of becoming, of which we just get these glimpses, that the wording best known to us, by which the belief in identity of nature was confessed, is that which survives in the Kauṣītaki Upanishad: "That thou art"; not "That thou becomest". That the word for becoming *was there* (*bhu, bhava*) is perhaps no mean guarantee that the idea found utterance: "It did not develop (*sambhava-*) . . ." we do get that much. But anyway the vision of the man, realizing his divine nature as an unfolding-in-becoming wilted away, either through the cause suggested above, or otherwise. Yet the vision, albeit quite beyond adequate conception, of Deity as "desiring to become", and as "becoming", persisted, and became scripture. And this is the more singular, since it is actually as That Who is, not as That Who has become, that the idea of the self has been upheld ever since.

I have ventured to maintain that the new ideas concerning the very man (that is, the "soul") which heralded the rise of Sakya may be found in the paramount religion, in Brahman culture, itself. But they were not confined to that. It is generally admitted that the movement known now as Jainism led the movement of the Sakyans by about a generation, and had then their headquarters at Vesālī. It is true of both movements that absolute novelty of teaching was, or rather came, later to be denied. Both claimed to only revivals; both came in time to claim what would now be called a Messianic succession. But we need not be at pains to discover in either case a prior origin to the origin we seek. It sprang from the felt need of having an ancient tree of tradition to set up against the relatively true antiquity of Brahman prestige. I see something analogous in the early editing of Jewish followers of Jesus, tracing for him a descent (through Joseph) from all that would give weight to Hebrew genealogy, although from the Christian point of view it was irrelevant. It was an attempt to give weight *of race* to a man who was in no need of it.

The Jains were probably calling themselves Nātaputras, a name which is parallel with Sakyaputtas or -puttiyas, of the Pali books, for the followers of Gotama the Sakyan. Their leader Vardhamāna was of the Nāta family. The name under which they appear in the Pali books, Nigaṇṭhas, the undraped, with probably an included reference to their dissent, or nonconformity with any recognized cult, may well have been given them by others almost in derision. We may see an analogy in the word Quaker which now evokes nothing of the sort. I do not know when the more honorific term Jainas—men of the Conqueror—Jina, was introduced, but, in the Pali books, whereas "jina" is a poetical term applied to the Sakya leader, the Nātaputras are there invariably called Nigaṇṭhas. Their teaching concerning the "man" was, in this important respect, that which was adopted by the Sakyan teachers: the value of man's will working on the deeds of the past as bringing about happiness or sorrow in the after-life. It was not, as such, a new word; the new thing about it was that, in accepting it, they stressed the possibility and importance of altering by deliberate deeds the consequences of deeds. A man's past was, in its present and future effects, not a dead matter, but could be affected in these by such willed action. This they called karma. They did not take it in its literal meaning as action as a whole. The word meant also business or procedure of a certain kind, as when the Brahman applied it to sacrificial business, and the Sakyan monk, later, to matters of lodging and clothing.

It is curious that, in the important Upāli Sutta of the Majjhima, where Gotama is shown in discussion with a Jain, the latter uses the word *daṇḍa*, chastisement, for karma (as thought, word, and deed), and is corrected by the former, who uses karma. The conversation may have been worded in the first instance to repeaters by the Jain, Upāli himself, who became a disciple of Gotama after the conversation, and it is conceivable that he was careful to give his new teacher the credit of the right word. But it remains a curious thing.

To repeat, the Jains used the word karma in speaking of the procedure by which the consequences of a man's deeds might be annulled, so that his future would not be worried by them. This procedure was a variety of austerities, mainly (but not only) fasting, so familiar to India under the elastic word *tapas*, or heat. The heat was not necessarily connected with those forms of austerity consisting in self-exposure to heat from fire or sun; it was symbolically meant in the sense of a wearing or consuming away ill deeds in the past; and more: it meant effort of energy, will, concentration, conceived as "fiery", as ardent fervour. Sakya came to adopt a finer word for this glowing will: *tejas*, which also means heat. But it was never associated with austerities or "penance"; it symbolized a greater thing, the ardour of growth, the keener life, the more sensitive will. In *tejas* also was purifying; but it was a positive, and therefore a nobler idea. In the man who was "awake" (*buddha*) the glow of the better burnt out the glow of the worse.[1] And the flame of it drew to the man help from the unseen, as when we read that Sakka's throne waxed hot with the moral glow of a good deed, and he would hasten to earth to help.[2] The aspirant to the Better cries:

> O when shall I have power to draw the blade
> Of insight, potent ardour of the seers . . . (*paññāmayam ugga-tejaŋ satthaṃ isīnaŋ*).[3]

For the Brahman of the time we are considering, *tejas* necessary to win insight, or otherwise achieve, was merged in the need of practising *tapas*, which probably consisted in fasting and concentrated musing. So closely was achievement conditioned by *tapas*, that old Upanishads describe the All-Father Prajāpati as practising *tapas* before exercising creation.[4] And much more was the pupil bidden to practise it if he would win insight.[5] It was not the ignoble way of the fakir, to impose on the wonder and generosity and wish-to-win-merit of his fellows. It was a serious valuation, in the need of the individual "soul" to place his welfare on a sounder basis in his world-wayfaring. Karma, as of the Jainas, karma as willed procedure with a religious aim, will certainly have greatly interested the founders of Sakya, and herein the Suttas give us doubtless true glimpses, albeit coloured by sectarian feeling.

The other leading idea which Jain and Buddhist books have in common is *ahiŋsā* "not-harming", wherein the "man" (soul) is seen as in every form of life, and hence as giving value to all life. It is a mandate for the greater welfare of the "man", and is thus a teaching of the "More" in man. But I do not hold it was in the original Jain teaching, else we should have probably found it raised in the Pali books when Jain and Sakyan met in talk. We do not find it; perhaps agreement about it made discussion unnecessary. And the term only finds its way into a cut-and-dried Buddhist category of quite indefinite inception in the Pali scriptures. Warding of life is in the Suttas; warding of life unseen in water is there too, though very seldom mentioned,[6] and the strainer (*paris-savana*) appears in the Vinaya Rules, as having at some time become

[1] *Dhammapada*, ver. 387; cf. the Commentary here. *Patisambhidā*, i, 103.

[2] *Jātaka*, iii, 53, etc.

[3] *Theragāthā*, ver. 1095.

[4] *Taittirīya Up.*, 2, 6; *Bṛhad. Up.*, 1, 2, 5.

[5] *Taittirīya*, 3, 1.

[6] E.g. *Majjhima*, i, 78.

part of the monk's equipment,[1] not as safeguarding his own health, but as the very inadequate warding of not-to-be-swallowed life. But this will have come in, whenever it did come, not through Jain influence, but as a form of that moral scrupulosity which is so prominent in the values of the upgrowing monasticism.

I come to another set of conditions into which Sakya was born, by which the Jain movement, for some reason unknown, was *relatively* uninfluenced, but which strongly affected the Brahmanism of the day, and yet more strongly the youthful Sakya—influenced it so strongly that distinguished Indologists such as Professor Jacobi have "derived" Buddhist "philosophy" from it,[2] and which certainly went far in giving birth in Sakya to the worsening of the concept of the "man" as real, when thought of apart from the mind. I have alluded to this movement above as having gradually come into Brahman teaching, first as a new and absorbing interest, seen in the great Upanishads often termed pre-Buddhistic, later as a definite, named system of values.

Kapila, the founder of a teaching—not yet a system—known later as Sānkhya, was teaching perhaps about a generation previous to the time I am considering, but nothing definite is known of him. He was a non-Brahmanic secular "sage", and not, I think it is safe to conclude, one who had a religious mandate, else the after-men, in whose hands his teaching grew into the system known as Sankhya, would have quasi-deified him in some way, so great was his influence. I do not think it amiss to call him the founder of Indian psychology. Till his day the "man" or self was both thought and thinker, word and speaker, feeling and feeler. He was never, it is true, will and willer, as distinctly worded from thought and thinker—a dangerous defect. Now Kapila, it seems, brought in the "new word" of distinguishing the "man", not only from his body, but also from his mind. It is more than improbable that he *merged* the "man" in mind. He will have wished the rather to exalt the divinity, the uniqueness of the "man" by more utterly disentangling him from all modes of earthly self-expression, the immaterial as well as the material. And as an effort to compute in a new way this important aspect of a distinguishable self-expressing, the better therewith to distinguish the high worth of the self, his teaching became taken up and discussed as Sānkhya, that is, for the

[1] E.g. *Vinaya*, Mhv. vi, 15, 9; cf. *Jātaka*, No. 31, introduction.

[2] "Der Ursprung des Buddhismus aus dem Sānkhya-Yoga," *Nachr. d. Gesellschaft der Wissenschaften*, Göttingen, 1896.

word includes them all, computing, naming, numbering. It has been defined, as the last only, but this is to narrow the meaning overmuch, as Pali readers will know.[1]

That Kapila's teaching was at this time much agitating Brahman pundits is very plainly seen in the Upanishads to which reference has been made. New discussions on ways of mind and their relative values abound. There is no idea in them of identifying the "man" with mind. Always the self (*ātman*) has the last word. But there is a note of agitation sounded as to the tendency of the new vogue, to which I have referred. It is not usual to regard this as a warning, but if we are watching for the new features as not only come, but as *coming* into the Upanishads, we may discern it as so meant. We may be the more sure, because the man who warns was not likely to have seen danger, had he not ,with many teachers and pupils, felt the strong influence of the new study. Kapila's contribution, if I justly give it, to Indian culture was very notable, for there can no great advance be made in an intelligent estimate of the "man", unless we have come to distinguish him, as *sui generis*, from his instruments. This is not to take the way of modern psychology, which tries to build him up out of his instruments. Brahmans of the new ideas took a more intelligent view. Jains may have held the new teaching at a greater distance. But Sakya was profoundly influenced by it, as we shall see. It is very possible that among the early disciples were students of Sānkhya, and the Founder himself may well have known and approved of this ancient attempt at mental analysis as clarifying, for the better understanding, that inner world of the self-expressing "man", which was so necessary to the right valuing of him.

The original aim of Sānkhya, I repeat, was more likely to have been the giving greater distinction to the concept of the "man" than the less. The more his ways of self-expression were disentangled from himself, the more supramundane would the self-expresser tend to become. Thus the man's awareness of himself as "I" was analysed as being a function, not of the very man, but of his mind, called "I-making" (*ahaŋkāra*). It was not fit to see in such an attitude an activity of the self, who was held as being a passive quasi-onlooker. (We find the term strayed over into Sakyan sayings.)

[1] Cf. *Dhammasangaṇi*, § 1307, where it is equated with "name". Cf. also the use of *paṭi-sankhāna*, as defined, e.g. in *Anguttara*, i, 52, and the idiom *sankhaŋ gacchati* and *sankhāta*.

Cf. also Oldenberg, *Lehre der Upan.*, 208, Dahlmann, etc. Oldenberg concentrates too much on the "numbering" only.

But the new conversance with all available words expressing the mental ways of the minder, the new appreciation of them considered apart from the minder, coupled with the current ideal of the Highest as the man himself, led to a rewording of the conception of Deity in terms of mind. Man's highest self-expression came to be held to be "mind" at its most exalted, its most effectual power, withal at its most sensitive intensity. Thus, if the reader will look at one of those earlier Upanishads, the Aitareyya, he will read of Deity conceived wholly in terms of mind: mind in sense, in purpose, in understanding, in wisdom. Especially are the last two emphasized in the word for which we have no good parallel, *prajñā*: more-wisdom, more-knowledge, coming-to-know. Man, in it, is wording the more which he seeks in quest of the Most. That eloquent summary *is the accretion*, maybe, to an older work. The utterer was groping, as we too grope, when we say God is love, light, love, goodness, power, will. That such ideals have value is obvious. The danger in them lay in the attribute tending to obscure the fact believed in, man, the *purusha*, as immanent Deity. And this is precisely what we find in even the early history of Sakya. Sakya found *prajñā* as a term for Deity in man. It retained, gradually came to use it (*paññā*) as we should, as just a way of mind. But with a difference, a difference in which the older glory of the term peeps out, as we shall see.

We have now to consider other conditions under which Sakya took birth. One of these, an older way in the man, but not to be called cult, was the very opposite to the newer vogue of mind-analysis, the way of the man in Yoga—that is, devotion, or strenuous study of a special kind. This, I cannot say why, had come at this time to be called Dhyāna (Pali: *jhāna*)—a word which means brooding, or musing. It is often, but wrongly, rendered "meditation". This means active thinking, and that is the reverse of Jhāna. Meditation requires, if it be worthy, the whole synergy of the thinking man. Jhāna is a deliberate putting off (*pahāna*) of applied thinking (*vitakka*) and of sustained, or discursive thought (*vichāra*). The resulting final mental residuum is bare "mindfulness" (*sati*), with emotional neutrality (*upekkhā*). But this is inadequate for describing the habitual attitude of ourselves toward concentration, and hence the error in the word "meditation", in which the modern Buddhist follows us, ignorant of what the ancient Buddhist tradition was much concerned to teach.

When Sakya took birth, Jhāna was the individual, deliberate

effort to put off, or recede from one world in order to gain access to another. This was not necessarily by way of trance, let alone deep sleep; it was, so to speak, letting moon and starlight replace sunlight; it was to give room to those dual faculties we all perhaps have in a more or less entirely stunted state, which at that time appear to have been called by such names as sight and hearing of devas,[1] but which we should now call clairvoyance and clairaudience. Into Jhāna, as it was cultivated in original Sakya, and as it worsened within that same cult, I shall go presently. Here it is the profoundly significant change of Yoga into Jhāna before that time which I would emphasize as one of the conditions we are considering.

The original object of Yoga was in a deliberately induced recession from earthly awareness[2] to confront That Who was the Most-in-the-Man, the greatest Self, of whom the man was the little self. This was held to lead to a growth of the "More" in the man. The sacramental process is perhaps best described in the Mahābhārata, though I cannot vouch for the redaction that we have being as old as the time in question. "How can a man find deliverance without a lord (to guide him)? . . . let the yogin bearing Me within sit solely devoted to Me. . . . Let him behold the Self (Ātman) in the yogin's self. . . (let him say) This Ātman here is my true Kinsman; I can no other than be with Him; won even to evenness and unity with Him, then only become I He Who I really am."[3] We see here that in Yoga the Yogin, the "man", is in full view from first to last, and there is no doubt about What is sought. It is the man, and not his mind only, that is before us, the man breaking his bars and bonds, waxing in strength and fearlessness (I quote the epic), winning to absorption in, to vision of, the Man in him, Who is one with himself.

But round about the beginning of the sixth century B.C. there will have come a change over the Indian time-spirit from that which we see more or truly reflected in these lines, and which is to be found in the greater Upanishads. It is a wistful yearning for knowledge of the Beyond, a will to know of the worlds in man's wayfaring. "Son of the Gotamas, is there an ending in the world in which you put me? Or is there any Way?" And "This thing whereon they doubt, O Warder (Death), what there is in the great passing on: tell us that".[4] And many a word of this sort. Much had thus come that stretched out as a long long Way between the seeker of earth and the consummate realization of himself, in wonderful

[1] *Dibba-cakkhu, dibba-sota-dhātu.*

[2] "Thinks as little as a bit of wood" (*Mhbh.*).

[3] Mokṣadharma, Adh. 309.

[4] *Kauṣ. Up.*

moments here and now, at the sacrament of self-introversion in Yoga. And the knowledge that lay between: this for some might be acquired in an *adjustment* of the Yoga attitude. This world was still to be eliminated in the musing, but it was a world of space, not the spaceless, that was to be substituted. It was not an ecstatic, a mystic communion, much less a union that was to be attained in and as the musing; it was a state of attention, more akin to that of the boy Samuel in the Hebrew scriptures: "Speak, lord, for thy servant heareth!" It was *an attitude for coming to know*. The world of North India had thus been getting ready for the new mandate and the mandater, if our hypothesis be right.

And more: there had been coming into the words "deva, devaputta, devatā" (god, god's son, deity) a changed, a modified meaning, which was for India not so great a step as it would be for other, at least for Western, peoples. Men were coming to think of those beings, less as powerful, if interested aliens, and more as fellowmen who had been men and might again be men. To arise from death on earth and live in their worlds was called not "union with" (as it has been defectively rendered) but "in the companionship of" (*sahāyatā*; Pali *sahavyatā*).[1] This has not yet been as clearly recognized as it should be, and the words *deva*, etc., in later Vedic and Pali works are still rendered too indiscriminately by "gods". Since our vocabulary is too poor to give us a fit word, *deva*, *devatā* are best left untranslated. We cannot speak of "god" in just the friendly way in which we find the oldest Pali books alluding to *devas*, etc., the seeing and conversing with them, the learning from them, the teaching them. It is true that even here a *deva* was nominally not *manussa*, or man-of-earth. But he was anything but an alien; even as governing the next world, his earthly antecedents might be known[2]; and when it was a deva who had not long left earth, he might by the clairvoyant be discerned as a visitor, recognized by name, and in speech be conversed with.[3] We come in these days of Sakya origins far more out of the region of the wraith, the phantom, than we ourselves were in mediaeval Europe, nay, than we still are. We still seem to be now and then in a ghost world in the Pali books, but actually we are scarcely ever so, the fact being that translators, used to such notions, translate by the word ghost when the term is not fit.

There is nothing to which we can point in records as showing the actual breaking down of the Yoga purpose in Dhyāna to the

[1] E.g. *Dīgha*, i, Tevijja Suttanta. [2] Cf. *Jātaka*, No. 31, Kulāvaka.
[3] *Dīgha*, ii, 204; iii, 15; *Saṃyutta*, i, 55.

early Jhāna purpose in Sakya. As I have said already, it is very rare to find transition in progress in early documents. They give us only what they look upon as accomplished, whether it be to our seeming progress or regress. And if they refer to other views, they cannot be trusted to give them truly. The Pali books never, I believe, apply the (unmodified) word Yoga to Jhāna practice, but we can see in the earliest of them that Jhāna was much practised, and also that no explanation of it as of something introduced by Sakya is ever called for. It was there and it was understood.

I have spoken of early records as giving us the "become", the accepted, the established, the valued. They are not, as now are books, to a great extent, the views of some one man or woman put forward as new, or in a new way, to win over the approval and acceptance of readers. They are, in so far as they are Indian, very different; they are written memoranda substituted for oral memoranda of utterances, which have already existed, first as spoken, then as potential re-utterances in a succession of speakers. And the bodies of such potential utterances as composing all the "literature", all the scripture, all the books that then existed, constitute one of the circumstances attending the birth of Sakya which it is of great moment to have before us. There is nothing new in what is here said. But this to us unknown, unexperienced, bookless world tends, in the view usually presented of our subject, to fall too much into the background.[1] As usual, it is our reconstructive imagination that is hardly yet awakened. In some circumstances in which we are placed, deliberately it may be, or involuntarily, we too are in a relatively bookless world. But even then it will not be such wholly; it will not be such long. Nor while it lasts can we come out of our bookish tradition and upbringing.

We need here to imagine ourselves in a very different world. We have to place ourselves in a world of speakers, and not in one of silent marks on paper, which to-morrow will tell us just what they do to-day. It is the world of the tongue and the gesture, the cadence and the emphasis. And it is not a very wise world as to what is true. It is more the world of the will to move, to impress, to persuade. It is more akin to the world of the actor, the pleader, the preacher, the apologist; it is less akin to the world of scientific exposition, or of history as distinct from its mother, the "-story".

[1] Thus an artist has lately composed, for the Paris Theosophical Society, a picture apparently of "the Buddha" speaking and being "reported" by attendant writers!

In such an old world of the Word, men will accept and applaud both word and speaker the more readily, if by word he give what is already acclaimed as very worthy. The new is not so easy to make acceptable. It is not recognized ; it is alien ; it is the unwonted. We of to-day do not greatly seek acceptance of the new by the spoken word. Uttered it may well be to select audiences, but we lose no time in endorsing it with developments in print. Print is our staple means of bringing out the new idea. In a time and place where no books were, the welcome of a new mandate depended much more than now on not only the speaker himself, but *on them to whom he spoke*. Putting the speaker, till the next chapter, on one side, it is when, in a world which is absolutely or relatively bookless, there comes over that world a wave of interest in "the new" concerning the "man", that a new religion arises.

We are not here and now in such an age. We have no experience of the social or human atmosphere of it. But we read of it, of a spirit of curiosity about the New, when the new meant not just the unknown in general, but what the English reader would call God and the soul. All will recognize the allusion to St. Paul's noting the Athenian preoccupation with this at such a time.[1] This curiosity was not entirely a new appearance among Greeks, but it had then apparently become an obsession. Nor was the Israelite a stranger always to such curiosity ; but it was only when the new mandate was at hand that this "new" was being much looked for. And there is enough left perhaps in such clues as we have to betray a similar curiosity in North India before the birth of Sakya. For we have eloquent witness to it in the action of the Messenger himself, taking the very unwonted step for an Indian nobleman of setting out on a quest, as it is worded of him speaking on his death-bed :

> Thirty less one of age, Subhadda, I
> Went forth a seeker after something Good,
>
> . . . .
>
> A pilgrim in the onward-way and Right.[2]

And a similar unrest of inquiry is on record in the Commentarial tradition of another nobleman of North India at the same time ; the rajah Kappina. For us of European traditions the riding forth of the noble on a quest is familiar, but we do not find the Indian noble so doing in a similar tradition. We have the Jātaka quest of king Kusa after his lady, but it is as a very exceptional procedure.

[1] Acts xvii, 21 : "for all Athenians and strangers . . . spent their time in nothing else, but either to tell, or to hear some new thing (*kainoteron*)."

[2] *Dīgha*, ii, 151.

The Christian knight went on a worthy quest: the aid of those who needed him. Kappina's interest was said to be in the new in knowledge. The purpose of the Sakyan prince was the combined purpose of the new in knowledge in order to bring help to men. That which is perhaps the first Sutta ever put together, the first in the first Nikāya, testifies to much current inquiry about the nature here and hereafter of the "man" or "soul". And anxious inquiry by this and that bereaved Everyman as to the fate of the recently departed is also testified to in the Suttanta of the Founder's decease and elsewhere.[1] To satisfy this felt need of more of the knowledge of which we are here treating, new light on life as a whole, on "God and the soul", man even now would, if he willed to learn, learn not only by the written word; he would listen as did Elijah, nay, he would now so learn in more ways than he was learning only yesterday. But in that day to listen was the only way. We, when once we will to hear, to learn, can satisfy our curiosity in many ways; we need not be at such pains to seek. When once more comes the day of a new mandate in that line of knowledge, curiosity may not be so imperious as to take the form it took at Athens. But in that day the one way by which man could learn "some new thing" in things most worth while to know made him need a stronger wave of desire to hear, a curiosity which had to assert itself in a marked degree.

I tried in the previous chapter to show, that a hypothesis, which can account for the phenomena attending and preparing the birth of a new world-religion, must include an abnormal condition of this kind in the particular "world" in which the birth is healthy. I may not find credence with the modern reader. He lives it is true in a day of eagerness to enlarge knowledge. But it is not knowledge having the objective of which this book speaks. It has not as object that whom the Indian calls the man, and we call soul or spirit. Its object is man as mind in body, and as what is called "character" as an outcome of that. Its object is the "visible" world and men's life in that; it is not the worlds of the man's life as a whole. We are therefore not the men living on earth during or just before the birth of a world-religion. Hence men are sceptical in regarding such abnormal conditions either as true at any time save once or twice in the past, or indeed as having ever been actual events. Imagination jibs.

Or again, it may be said, do you then place credence in the assertion of the little minority blended of east and west, who are to-day

[1] Especially in the Janavasabha Suttanta in the same collection: *Dīgha.*

claiming that a new mandate on the "man" and his life as a whole is already at hand? Frankly, I would say "No!" We have yet to hear any matured expression from the man elect on any central theme. So far no *new word* has been heard by the great public. Men have been bidden to set and hold themselves free—so I have heard. This is a good preparation, but it is nothing more. It is but a negative ideal. No, we are not ready. Hence the new mandate for us is not at hand. It is well to be eager for the new as to matter and as to mind. But the new, I repeat, for which we are not ready, is new light not on these, but on the very "man". And just this, that the reader may say: "What then is the very man, if not these?" does but show that the nobler curiosity has not arisen in us.

The word "free" brings me to one more feature in the reconstruction of the pre-Sakyan conditions. The charge to be and keep free in that recent utterance comes fitly from a son of India. Freedom or its equivalents, liberty, emancipation, release, deliverance, has for ages been a religious ideal of India. In no other land has the religious quest been so largely bound up with the notion of the riddance from bond or tie. We see this in such names for religieux as Achélaka, Nigantha, Ājīvaka, and in such equivalents for "salvation" as *mukti*, *mokṣa*, *vimutti*. This is not, however, an earliest Aryan trait. It does not appear in the Vedas. The word (*vimutti*, etc.) abounds in the Piṭakas, but they are no fit index to ideas abroad when Sakya was born. Concordances, dictionaries reveal the idea *emerging* in Indian records. The age of Aryan invasion was probably too recent, an age when solidarity and not liberty was the prime consideration. When the Aryan became firmly established in India the tendency in him to independence, which so markedly developed the concept of the "man" or self as unitary, evolved into the idea of personal freedom, or the surmounting of ties as essential to any higher religious life. This done he described himself as the *śramaṇa* (Pali *samana*)), the man at peace.

The word in its first intention means the tryer, toiler; in its second intention it means one who has tried, toiled, and has reaped the result. We need not go far for parallels, even if we cannot equate the very word. To "worth" is to be judging, rating, but the noun "worth" is the decision, the estimate. The word *samaṇa* is frequently met with in the Pali books, and there it indicates high worth. Thus as a class, *samaṇas* together with brahmans, in the compound *samaṇa-brāhmaṇā*, compose what we might term the religious world. It is thus that Greek chroniclers of the third century B.C. wrote, when they described the North Indian world of "philosophers" as consisting of sophists (presumably Brahmans) and *sarmanai*, or *samanaîoi*,[1] placing them in inverse order from that used by the Sakyans. Further, there are references here and there in the Piṭakas to the duties, the advantages, the privileges of a *samaṇa* and of his status or *sāmañña*. Further, the leader is himself spoken of, or addressed in the third person by non-Sakyans as the "*samaṇa* Gotama". But more often than not, an individual *samaṇa* is referred to as an "almsman" or *bhikkhu* (*bhikshu*; *bhikkhā* = broken meats), and for some reason the latter word has come to oust the former. *Sāmaṇera* (*-eraka*) was and remained the term for novice.

We may take it that the *samaṇa*, as one who had broken with world-ties and "gone forth", as the Pali books word it, "from housedom into the houseless," was a social feature preceding the birth of Sakya. It was not a new feature, but it was very possibly still a young feature. The *samaṇa* was already not merely tolerated, but was respected, by the many, with of course exceptions. But his prestige was spreading. There would seem to be a testimony to this in the Sāmaññaphala-Suttanta, second of the Dīgha, and one of the only two apparently existing as an oral compilation at the First Council. King Ajātasattu, asking "if it paid", as we should say, to be a *samaṇa*, is reminded that were even a slave of his household to leave the world as *samaṇa*, he would be treated as a very noble or brahman by the king himself. The first reference to the word *samaṇa* is in the Bṛhadâraṇyaka Upanishad (4, 3, 22), where in deep sleep the man who is awake to his divine identity casts off all the ideas he and his environment have formed as to earthly relations. "Then is ascetic not ascetic, śramaṇa not śramaṇa." There is but "the man". In none of the Upanishads may a second allusion be found, save only an imitation of the given passage in the later Brahma-Upanishad.

This is of importance in the picture we are trying to form of pre-Sakyan conditions. With the recent growth of the *idea* "release" from world-ties, *words* for it, both nouns and verbs, were being coined, and the *human embodiment* of the worded idea was becoming a feature in the picture. But we need in our picture to use, in artist language, lower values for this feature than is usually the case. Were we to be guided by the Pali books alone, and by a superficial reading of them at that, we should use high values for the world of the monk. I shall try to show presently what I mean, in the case of those books. But we can hardly doubt that, had the

[1] See McCrindle, quoting Megasthenes, *Ancient India*, 98, 101 f.

time and place been largely characterized by "recluses", we should inevitably have seen these bulking less meagrely than is the case in the books held to precede, if only by a little, the birth of Sakya. The brahman would regard as customary the retirement of his elderly men, and women too, it might be, to the āśrama retreat, when, the years of vigour ended, their duties in and towards the world had been observed. But for him that retirement as a worthy course in the young, as *śramaṇa*, was a new thing, and the novelty of it, as a subject of surprised comment, has survived in many passages in the Suttas of Sakya.[1] Not all *śramaṇas* were of the Sakyas. The movement, we saw, had begun to invade, together with the ascetic proper (*tapasvin*), the brahman world. And had the invasion progressed there as it did with the Sakyans, as it evidently did not with Brahmans, references to the *śramaṇa* would not be absent.

If now it be asked, why did the movement in "release" through "recluseship" begin, and begin just when it did, the answer has been, not to account for it causally, but to point to a wave of pessimism spreading then or earlier over India. But this is no explanation and can satisfy no one long. It is true enough that life and the world as "ill" was an idea which we find somehow grown up, but this was, I suspect, the recluse's main apology or framed reason for his procedure, rather than the true cause of it, and we must go further back to explain the *śramaṇa*.

I have referred to the Aryan characteristic of independence. To launch out in the tremendous adventure of a community-trek to new lands argues a strong common development of "will" in independent self-expression. And will, in the most general terms, is self-expression exerting itself. In the Indo-Aryan, will took its special development, once solidarity became less vital, of not social or political, but personal, individual independence. It found, in time, its supreme expression in the theory of oneness with Deity conceived as Highest Self or Man. But it did not find expression in a corresponding, a complementary theory of oneness with his fellows. On the contrary, the Highest was conceived as not to be found among "men". To realize That better, the ties with these had to be broken. The "Man" had to be self-expressed in the man alone. Higher worth in the man was a matter of the individual alone. Be it remembered that "self" was then never used in the plural.

We do not know when it was that the gospel of immanent Deity, of the Highest as being potential in the very nature of each man and woman, in the nature of the "man-in-man", was uttered in India.

[1] See e.g. the Raṭṭhapāla Sutta, Majjhima, No. 82.

It was long after the earliest Vedas were compiled. It had become accepted when Kapila arose and taught what came later to be called Sānkhya. But it must have been at its inception a new outbreathing of a wonderfully inspiring kind. It may come trippingly over the lips of pundit and pupil nowadays, but when considered in a quiet hour it is even more tremendous for us than perhaps at its birth, so have we grown, or so ought we to have grown in the concept of Deity. And it must have, in any case, been a word of tremendous weight then. Then it will have come about, that here and there a man, willing to realize the new word that the man was, had in him, as man, the More, nay, the Most, felt it needful to "come apart", in a way he had not felt so needful before, and ponder this thing about the "man" away from "men". It was too wonderful a thing to be well made clear amid the values of the world, the aims, the unquiet, the warring, the playing, the work, the troubles, the futilities of worldly life. It was a matter needing quiet; it was a matter calling for realization by each man for himself.

I am not saying that it was needful to give the whole of life to compass this aim. But there was a real truth in the question being one that, as new, needed seclusion and concentration for a time, and times. It was a "God-intoxicated" idea, and to such Divine madness men have ever been prone. Why wonder, then, that to some it seemed as nothing to sacrifice all to brood upon it. Such a life—it is perpetuated in a curious old phrase of the Pali records: "with mind become that of the wild (*miga-bhūtena cetasā*)"—might conceivably not have first taken root in a cold country. It needed a climate where a man could maintain himself without taking life, since this was incompatible with fostering the ideal of man in the Most, or at his Best. He would need to be where he could maintain himself on wild roots and fruits, and not perish for lack of shelter or clothing. But I incline to believe that it was in the reaction to the impact of this world-mandate, uttered it may be by the semi-mythical, but once real man Yājñavalkya (not the Upanishad teacher or teachers named after him), "THOU (the man) art THAT," that the pioneer recluses, the first *śramaṇas*, led the way to life in the alone in India. They "went forth" far more thoroughly than did the alms-fed almsman or *bhikshu* of later days. There was in their day no question of receiving support from the "laity". They were the forest-recluses, not the almsmen who haunted the doorstep in the village. They lived on roots and fruits.

Now of these men the formula begins sometimes in a way which suggests a genuine old saying about not a dogma, but "the man":

"He tormenting neither the self, nor another, lives as to the seen uncoveting, finished, become cool, experiencing happiness, *with the self become God* (*Brahma-bhūto*)."[1] It is true that, when the Commentaries were put into fixed form, the last phrase is explained with all the historical significance gone, as "the self become best". It is true, no less, that this, read in its highest possible meaning, is not an explaining away. The immanent Deity to be realized *was* the Best, the Highest, the Most into whom the man could ultimately blossom. But it had ceased to mean this (as we now say) transcendental idea for Buddhaghosa and his little Ceylon world. For me it is a precious fragment of that ancient world of religious ideas lingering on in the Piṭakas.[2]

I do not think we need to be much exercized over the extent to which the concept of Deity as immanent in man's nature was, in the West Indian religious world relatively to that of the East of India, an esoteric teaching. The dual distinction was doubtless drawn by teachers on this and that point; we find Gotama using the terms once in *repudiating* such teaching for himself.[3] But nowhere does there appear any hard and fast line between teaching as so divided; nothing remotely near, in the matter under consideration, to the Greek mysteries. All deep religious truth is esoteric to the average worldly man and woman everywhere and at any time; all religion may need to take on, for such, a relatively esoteric shape. In the Suttas erudition is claimed for and by certain brahmans, but nothing—and here I follow Oldenberg—that can fairly be rendered by mysteries. If the high religious conception of Man, as identical with the World-Self in his nature, is not questioned in a nonconformist way, in Sutta interviews with brahmans, I infer that it was, at the birth of Sakya, the view held very generally by thoughtfully religious persons, not gainsaid in any marked way. The controversial positions in the appendix of the very first Suttanta of the Dīgha Nikāya and elsewhere, are for me all of later emergence. And when at that earlier date a teacher like Vardhamāna or Gotama began a mission with a new word of needed reform, there was no need to support the current central conception of immanent Deity in an assertive way. We may compare the case of Luther or of Wesley, each with a new word, but neither deeming it needful to maintain the concept of the Fatherhood of God.

[1] *Majjhima*, Sta. No. 51 and others; *Aṅguttara*, ii, 250. The term is repeatedly applied also to Gotama.

[2] Oldenberg drew attention to it in the last edition of *Buddha* in a footnote only.

[3] *Dīgha*, ii, 100: "I have taught making no inner, no outer . . ."

But when, as we see in the Piṭakas, the *samaṇa* had become less of a recluse, and nearly always an almsman or *bhikshu*, the fresh wonder and glory of the inspiring indwelling Holy Thing had died away. He was no longer valuing the world-life as too unquiet and difficult for self-realization; he was estimating it as, in itself and hopelessly, "ill" (*dukkha*). This is a different attitude, a later attitude, which is not clearly understood as such. And very gradually there had grown up a great respect in the majority for men who, not waiting for their later years, as with brahmans, but at any age, cast aside all that the world valued, and so the *samaṇa* had no longer to undergo privations, cut off from the neighbourhood of his lay patrons.

It is hard to trace this growth; early books, I repeat, are not inquiries into movements, but "sayings" about things moved. Nevertheless whereas, in the Suttas and Vinaya, the support of the laity in the maintenance of the *samaṇa* has become an institution, and the only uncertainty as to getting support lay in the varying popularity of this or that company of them, we can see that, especially among brahman householders, there was not seldom adverse comment on these men of the bowl, who looked to be supported for standing aloof from the productive work of their fellows, and with whom social status counted for nothing. This will be illustrated in a later chapter.

I come back to where the Indo-Aryan stood, with solidarity become less imperative, with the lone-recluse movement launched, when the new Sānkhyan values touched him, not long before the birth of Sakya. He had been living his life as man-having-body, in, or aloof from the world, without being consciously curious how he was related to that body or to that world by way of what we call mind. But now he began to heed the minding itself, and ideas or mental expressions in themselves. Among these were his relations to both body and external world, as coming, in a way, between him and the supreme "man" Who and Whose he was. And then it will have been, that those relations, that is, *the ideas of them*, emerged as so many ties, bonds, fetters.[1] Then stood up his Aryan independence, his will to freedom, saying "Break!". Had the new interest in mind, in ideas, not weakened his grasp of his very nature as "man", he would not have, as man, fallen under the bondage of the idea. It is the child in man to see ideas as the very man. Had he seen himself as very man, maker, worther, user of his ideas, but not as very man subservient to them, he would not have seen anything in world or body as tie or bond over himself.

[1] *Gantha, yoga, sanga, saṃyojana.*

Hence it may appear that, between the birth and growth of Sānkhya-mind-values and the *spread* of the Indian monk-world, there is a causal connection which is not yet acknowledged as, I believe, it deserves to be. Sānkhya, not only in its much later systematized form, but also in its pre-systematic influence, has been considered perhaps too much as an already broken down attitude, and not sufficiently as the solvent that was in process of effecting the breaking down. As a solvent or leaven, it was at this time already having a potent effect on outlook and values in what was then at once religion and philosophy. The contemplation of mind as such was for the first time pre-occupying the thoughtful, and was felt as of new and immense interest. The discussions on its phases in the greater Upanishads are alone explicable in this light. It is the dawning of the consciousness of man as self-expressed in, and as mind.

It is not sufficiently realized what a strange, new development was here going on, however much we may find crudeness in the results. We forget how we have ourselves gone through a somewhat analogous period—similar yet different—in the development of a so-called psychological or mentalized outlook on the "man" or soul, out of and away from the older philosophico-religious outlook.

Here too, then, the reconstructive imagination needs quickening. Here most of all, namely, that with the new stimulus to introspective alertness, the *idea* about the man—his nature, his life—was beginning to bulk more importantly than the man who framed it ; the "idea" overshadowed the "framer of the idea" ; the man, framer, valuer, user, was beginning to lose the self first, in such an idea as the tied one, bonds, fetters, and next over against this, in the idea "release", the freed one, the escaped, the gone forth. This is well shown in the favourite definition of "Buddhism" in German writers as a religion of release or "Erlösung". The Upanishadic cult of the self or man had broken down into a cult of an idea about the man. Man as valuing his essential nature had been cloaked by man as valuing his instrument the mind, and himself in it.

Such is, to the best of my belief and word-craft, a rough sketch of the conditions in which the message of the men of Sakya came to be uttered. In so far as it adds to what is accepted the critic may or may not approve. However that be, the general reader will possibly see it as more alive, if I tell it afresh as from the lips of a teacher of that day, giving us what is for him a still living memory, if severed by many a rebirth. How gladly would he not listen did he hold that such a telling brought with it, to one told, the sense of the possible and the true! Shall we listen?

I was a Brahman teacher who lived at Rājagaha. I had not many pupils, for Brahmans were not held there in the worth they had further west, but they were devoted to my teaching, for I was like them in this, that I was not only teaching the things that were old. They liked to hear me talk of the mind. This was very new, for till my day the man had been spoken of as in the body, but not as in a way in the mind. Man's ways in mind had been introduced some fifty years or so earlier by the man known as Kapila of Mathurā, and it was becoming a vogue in our more east-lying region, albeit the older teachers held aloof from it. They foresaw danger in it, and they were right; it led men away from the self or very man to see mind as man, as came to pass in Sakya. One of our teachers, Kaushītaki, who was much interested in this new way himself, uttered the danger in words known to you in writing, beginning: "Not speech should one desire to understand; one should desire to know the speaker," and ending "Not mind should one desire to understand; one should know the thinker." He saw to what it might lead. I was greatly taken by it none the less, and what has been written of my wordings is full of it. The newer world has never taken these teachings for what they really were, namely, a new word by inquirers into the new. They have been taken to be the teaching all Brahmans were agreed upon. They were not, and I was not much commended in my interest in them. I was that later, when the vogue of mind-analysis became usual and no more an innovation; then my utterances were held quite orthodox.

At the same time the man was ever for me the man, and in no way was he mind. Mind was a way of him, and for us mind was unfolding as a world of ways, a system; in no way was it, for us, the man. No one then thought so; it would have been a very madness in the teacher to have taught that. Yet it came later to be virtually what Sakya taught; it is virtually what is taught to-day among *you*.

Now in converse with other men, the new things would take utterance, and not only among Brahmans. Among the many attent to the new were men who were "men of the Jina"; the world called them, partly in derision, Nirgranthas, Nigaṇṭhas: the Untied. They were disciples of the teacher who had lately died, Vardhamāna. They were much teaching willed courses of action, as able, in retrospective effect, to bring about happy consequences for the doer in after-lives. Result of action was of course not a new teaching. The new thing was, not to acquiesce in the result, but to alter it in effort through acts which they called karma. Not karma or action as a whole, but a special course of action. We, you will know, used karma in such a special way in connection with ritual, as if you were to say procedure or business. I was very interested in their belief, and in the *tapas* procedure by which they tried to escape from this tie, upon their future, of the past, the old. I myself had tried by fasting and brooding to win to more light on the very nature of man, but without success. I only grew weaker. I was seeking the more in me, but was doing it in the wrong way. I was not listening for the help that might come. *Tapas* was so far new, that these men set a high and special worth upon it, for the end I am telling you. But it did not appear to me worthy of being imitated. I thought it was a very carnal view to think to cure what the *man* had done by ill-treating his present *flesh*. It was as if one should visit one's wrath on an instrument because of the misdeeds of the user. But there was a sincerity about the men which I respected, and I asked them one day : Why do you not attend the ritual with us ? They replied : You are taking the wrong way to cure evil. You try to cure what you have done with one thing by what you now do with other things. The offerings have not offended : why burn them ?

I was deeply impressed by his reply ; I had no answer to make. They did not make of me a convert, but I began to see in our ritual something that was irrational, and I was never a sound Brahman after that. I was not much with the Nirgranthas ; they were more at Vesālī than at Rājagaha, and their austerities gave me a distaste for their opinions. But I did highly appreciate their will in the new ways, I mean the way in which they planned their lives on a new method which was not that of the majority, nor of the things accepted.

I come to other men of new thought. I am thinking of the Sakyas : they were then called so by most, or else Muṇḍakas, shavelings, namely, as to their faces, not their heads. They were a very worthy set of men, who had considered and tried *tapas*, and had rated it as not wise. They were more concerned to teach the importance of the moral life in its effect on a man's life hereafter, in another world. It was not a new teaching in itself, among the minority, but in the high worth in which they held it, it was new. I wondered why they were holding themselves aloof for just such an emphasis, for it did not seem to justify them to keep away from the ritual for that. And they were not disparaging us ; they honoured the Brahman ; they were in no way attacking us.

Remember, that whereas you of here and now may consider the sacrifice as cruel, this was not so with us there and then. The beast slain was believed to be reborn much more happily for the choice of it as the sacrificial victim.

One day I was listening to the teaching of one of the Sakyas. It was a man in the dress adopted by all *śramaṇas*, or *bhikshus*, as they were called. There were coming to be a good many of them about; and they all wore the same kind of yellowish raiment, no distinctive feature being made for any following or "order". They all lived by alms. It had not always been so; it was among the new movements. I was not looking upon it with approval, for I held that if a man wished to leave the world—it was called going forth—the only fit time was when he had fulfilled the duties of house-father, teacher, and other work in the world, but not till then. We did not look for a man to shrink from these duties while in the prime of life.

I was much fascinated by this man. He was in the prime of life, and he had a very lovely expression. He was speaking about *artha*, the "good", that which is well for man. And he was speaking of the very man as one in the "way", the way of the worlds. He was speaking of the way as the right thought, word, and deed, of the man in the worlds in very worth. It was a world-utterance, a word for Everyman. And I was thinking: Here is a very simple utterance; all can understand it; he speaks not of any ritual; he is speaking of man's daily life. We are not uttering it so earnestly in the mantras. We have it, but we are less urgent in it. We do not make real its importance as he does; we do not bring out the true man-worth. Very worthy is the way he shows the man as self-mandating. We do not do that as we should. We tell the man too much what to do. It is he who must bid himself what he must do. We make too little of this.

When he had ended I spoke to him. We all spoke Prakrit then as man to man, not the early Sanskrit of the mantras. He was very pleasant when spoken to. I found he was Brahman. He no more wore any marks about him to show he was one. He said he belonged to the Sakyas; that their leader was one Gotama of the Sakyas of Kosala. They were speaking to men about the "way of the worlds", meaning thereby the whole of life. They were looking upon life as the one Way, in which every stage was very important in a man's becoming ever worthier.

There was the deepest earnestness in his teaching; he was saying what he himself utterly believed, and for this I was greatly taken by him. I wanted to see him again, but I never did. I heard he had passed on not long after, and that he was the chief of the Sakyas after the leader.

I tried to meet the leader ; I did one day, and I was impressed by a similar earnestness in him. Every word was from the heart. It was not his choice in wording that charmed me ; he was not eloquent, but it was as if he was speaking to each man, not to men. I was very drawn to him, and felt as if his own high worth lent a higher worth to every man. When he had finished, it was as if the world was made the holier. I was deeply moved ; I could not go. Then he saw me and he said : I am *puruṣa* ; I am the *puruṣa* in you ; we have in each of us the very *puruṣa*. The *puruṣa* bids us attain the more : the *puruṣa* heeds the way in the worlds ; the *puruṣa* looks to the Most in the more. I said : You are the very worthy man in your teaching ; I am honouring you ; I would learn more of you. He said : Come ! I will tell you. I went with him. I felt a deep regard for him and would have joined his Order. But he said : You have pupils who would miss your teaching. I would have you stay with them and help them. You will take up what I have been saying in your teaching. I wish you not to leave them.

There was something else come to pass in my day : not anything in itself new, but an old thing regarded and used under a new aspect. It had been Yoga ; it was now called Dhyāna. It was a way by which the man with us sought to become the more than the average man. The more, gained in Yoga, was the intercourse of the man with the self, the very man "within" regarded as the Highest. And this gain revived later on. But just then the men who were in the new ideas were using absorption or musing to induce access to, converse with, men of other worlds. And inasmuch as this involved a special sort of seeing and hearing, it was an effort to be something more, in sense, than the average man. I had it a little ; I could hear in the inner kind of way ; I could not see. And the words that I heard were very wise, and were concerning the new things, in the more that was in man. The practice was become very prevalent, and men's eyes were being opened to the reality of the worlds. And it was man as being of the worlds that we taught. Thus it was that man was now turning from the Man within to men in the unseen.

Such were some of the ways in that day in which many among us were seeking after that New which should mean the More for and in each man, in and with men. It was this that I was seeking, and giving word to in my teaching. It was that man should become what he was not before. This faith and aim is not usually attributed to the men of the mantras. And in truth it was only the few among us who so believed and taught. But your people see in the Upanishads what was approved by all at any given time, and do not take into account that things there written may, when new, have been new utterances of the few, and not approved when uttered. And when some of us said that the ātman (man) and the Ātman (Deity) were the very same, we did not mean that the man was Very Brahman now; we meant "same in nature". To be That, he had to become, and that becoming was for each the way through the worlds, of which you show that we spoke. That was true for us then; it is true for me now.

III

THE MESSAGE OF THE SAKYAN

We now come to the foreground in the picture: the mandate and the messenger. I shall deal mainly with the mandate; with the messenger I have dealt in the book, *Gotama the Man*, to which this is a complement. Here again I shall try to fit the message worthily, that is truly, into the picture of the men who were mandated, linking up these men with the will and work of the messenger, so that the fact and truth of their interdependence may stand out.

The man, who, in the days when in India books were not, made a public utterance, had to make it impressive in a special way. Much depended on its being impressive as utterance. And this it only became in India when he "mantra'ed" it, turned it into a "rune", delivered it as an intoned or semi-chanted utterance. It then ceased to be a "talk". It was not necessarily metric speech or Gāthā, but it was other than conversational prose. In the Pali books, as in the Upanishads, we have samples of both: now it is the talk; now it is the mantra either in prose or in verse: the public general utterance, calculated to appeal in matter and in form to the many. The talk-word may it is true also be more or less in stilted form, but that is due to the "accident" of its fate as orally transmitted. There are other ways in words, which have become "Scriptures", for achieving weighty impressiveness; in the Hebrew books we have: "Thus saith the LORD"; in the Rules of the Pali Vinaya we have each rule made to begin with: "I (the Bhagavā) allow you, monks. . . ." And the Indian mantras have their own words of exordium. But the way of the speaker will have been, in voice at least, a mighty factor in the impressiveness of his message.

In the first two utterances ascribed to the Founder of Sakya, called in the tradition "the Setting in Motion the Wheel of Dhamma" and "the Not-Man-features", we have two mantras worded in the authoritative way described. This is that; this is not that. It is true that in the middle of the second utterance we have the categorical ousted for a moment by the catechetical: "What think you as to that?" But this way, which may well have been a favourite method with the Founder, so often does it occur, may be said to have become inherent in the new wording of the Sakya Mantras. Now it is possible that these two utterances were originally delivered as mantras, and not as talks—that is, so far as any part of them was an utterance by him. It is true, that they are said to have been addressed to a mere handful of listeners, the so-called "Five-set recluses". But these were men waiting for a decision as to how in word to approach the Many for the good of the Many. And the talks may have taken, from the first, the mantra form which best went down with the Many. On the other hand, under the special circumstances, all the "Five" being friends and fellow-students, who had doubtless discussed a best new mandate together, it is very possible that the utterances were first in the form of "talks", but were subsequently, perhaps long subsequently, altered to mantra-form when not only their growing worth required it, but also when changes in ideals and emphases called for a good deal of editing.

What do I conclude, from these impressions, as to those two first utterances of the Sakyan mandate? I conclude this: In a gospel, or world-religion-message, I look for a word on the "man" (soul), a word which tells of a something more which *is he*, which *may be his*, which *he may become*. This "more" is not coming to him as manna from heaven; it is a more that he must will to win. It calls for more-will in him to win a "more-well", a something better. Now such a message is hinted at in these utterances, but no more. It is impossible to call them well worded. And I judge that, as the mandate of a great world-religion, they are very wrecks, and that in them we have but a fragment, in each case, of what was really spoken when they were first uttered. For it was a great soul that is said to have uttered them, and such an one would not have spoken like that. He may very well not have been an eloquent speaker. He had new matter, but he had not new words. Yet even without them, he would have spoken more worthily.

Why then should such an unworthy patchwork, with the small but precious remnants in them, yet held still in unquestioning reverence, be all that is left of the first public teaching of such a man?

It may be due to several reasons. There is the fact that it was not committed to writing for quite a long time. There is the probability, that it was not committed to fixed oral version for many years, during which men had come to regard the mandate with different ideals and emphasis. There is the fact that the speaker was new to public speaking. There is the fact that the mandate was one that needed new words, words to clothe ideas, or at least emphases which were suitable for and needed by the Many, but which had not come for them into present highest values. All these will have tended to mar the first wording of the utterance. We must look closely, allowing for much, if we would see anything in it of the nature of a New Word. But it is there. This is how it *now* begins.

"Monks! these two extremes by one who has gone forth are not to be followed. Which two? Both this that is the cleaving addiction to pleasures of sense in sense-desires, low, pagan, of the many-folk, unworthy, not belonging to *Artha*, and this that is the addiction to what is fatiguing to the self, painful, unworthy, not belonging to Artha. Now, monks, both these two extremes not having taken up, a midway course has by the man so wayfaring been well understood, making vision, making knowledge, leading on to peace, to wisdom, to enlightenment, to nirvana. But what, monks, is that midway course? Just this worthy way. That is to say, right view, right purpose, right speech, right action, right livelihood, right endeavour, right *smṛti*, right concentration. Now this very midway course, well understood by the man so gone, making vision, making knowledge, leads on to peace, to wisdom, to enlightenment, to nirvana. But now, monks, this is the 'ill' (*noun*) worthy truth[1]: birth is ill (*adjective*), old age is ill, disease is ill, dying is ill, union with the not-dear is ill, separation from the dear is ill, the wish that one gets not, that too is ill, in brief, the five grasping *khandhas* are ill. But now, monks, this is the 'arising of ill' worthy truth: this craving which is again-becoming-ish, accompanied by what is sensual and (wish-for-)the-happy, enjoying now here, now here. That is to say, craving for pleasure (of sense), craving for becoming, craving for many becomings.[2] But now, monks, this is the 'ending of ill' worthy truth; that which is of that same craving the utter fading out and ending, the giving up, the letting go, the release from, the not being cloven-to. But now, monks, this is the 'course going to the ending of ill' worthy truth: just this worthy eightfold way. That is to say . . . right view . . . (*as above*)."

I have given the mantra in curious English, but in as close keeping with the original as it was possible. How it goes on I give in an Appendix. I consider that the portion given is *in substance* probably older than the rest; I consider also that the treatment of "ill" bears the marks of later editing under a changed emphasis about "ill", and is not, in that emphasis, in keeping with the mantra about the choice of ways. There we have a way enjoined making for "well". Ill is incidental. It was first pointed out thirty-four

[1] Or fact, *sacca*, i.e. *sakya*. 'Painful' and 'ill' are both *dukkha*.

[2] I disagree with the Commentaries which see here "not becoming" in *vi-bhava*.

years ago by Kern, that in the formulation of the four truths we have the four cardinal articles of Indian medical science, applied to the spiritual healing of mankind, exactly as in the Yoga doctrine.[1] This connection with medical diagnosis he sees virtually admitted in two passages of the Lalita Vistara, the well-known Buddhist-Sanskrit poem on the Founder. The fourfold "truths," *not* in the Sūtra, but in the "talk about it": the Yoga-bhāśya of a mediaeval date,[2] are life itself (*saŋsāra*), cause of it, health, treatment. Kern only points to the striking coincidence, drawing no inference, there at least, as to coincidence in date of compilation

Nor do I. The interval is too long. And the healer's way of procedure is after all a formulated procedure of everyman's way of seeking to win to a better state from a worse. For me the conviction that the four Ill-mantras are a late monastic gloss, rewording it may be an older reference to the quest of health (*artha*) in the original mantra, lies in the changed emphasis. Had there been that later emphasis on ill when the Founder spoke his mantra, he would have begun, as do the truths, with ill. It is not Indian way to formulate with the chief item, as climax, at the end; it is put first. Moreover, when it is a case of ailment barring our way, the thing first and foremost in our mind is the ailment; the "not well" has to be met and overcome. Health is our ultimate object, but we are bending over its absence. But in a gospel of a world-religion it is just the ultimate health that is to the fore. Ill in it is incidental.

To revert to our message of health: first, I would point out that in it I find two main implications. If we leave them out the message is relatively meaningless. The first is that it is *a call to man's will.* Were it not so, it were useless to have spoken to men of a way, a course, or progress. The way is the course chosen by the man in willing. Way is not just wayfaring. It is *chosen* way, plan, method. Yet it is more, as we can gather from the books. Man's life as a whole, involving more worlds, more lifespans than one, is inseparable from Indian religious ideals, and was being stressed at the time, as the Upanishad showed us. The words *yāna*, *magga* meant this. And the word *saŋsaraṇa* (wayfaring or proceeding onward) was coming to mean it also. So we have here a way within a way: the long, long "upward way"[3] and the right wayfaring in it. I come to the other implication presently.

"Way" then was (*a*) how to walk, (*b*) in the way of the worlds;

[1] *Indian Buddhism*, 1896, p. 46 f.
[2] Cf. J. H. Woods, *Yogasūtras of Patañjali*, p. 135.
[3] Edwin Arnold's phrase (*Light of Asia*).

(*a*) without (*b*) is just advice as to culture and conduct ; it is not the call of a world-religion. Now the " how " meant a choosing. And the choosing meant will. It is not alone on the way chosen that emphasis is laid ; it is also on the choosing. This has been too much overlooked. We tend to take a teaching too much as a thing prescribed. A teaching is something willed by teacher to willer, who must accept and make it his own will before it can be of any use. This is the more easily overlooked, because the words are so inadequate for what the message meant. We have here to estimate both the man who willed and the man he was willing. It was a great word he was willing to utter, but the language at his command, judging by this fragment, was not great. It was a great will he was putting forth, but not so the way in which he expressed it. I find the *figure* of the " way " very fine and true. It came, as the full text will remind the reader, to be developed in ways of good thought, word, and conduct, to the number of eight, or ten, usually eight. Another rival development not inserted here, is into the worldway considered as four stages of progress. This brings out better the way, or progress in the way as of the worlds. But in both, the main implication, as I see it in the Utterance, is lost sight of : that of the man, as he wayfares, *choosing* or *not choosing* a way " belonging to Artha ". Only by putting aside those details, eight or other, only by contemplating the one fact of the way shall we get at the real mandate, the vital mandate for the wayfarer ; the faring aright to his goal. And that, not so much because he is sent, herded, but because he says " I will ". Any teacher can give good advice. It needs the world-helper to point to what the man has within him and link that up with the whither of him.

But the figure of the Way, as we have it here, was not expressed in such a way as to cut out the possibility of mistake. We see nothing about choosing or will. There was, it is true, no really fit word like will for a man there and then to use. But there were good makeshifts, words for " stirring up effort " (*viriyaŋ ārabhati*), a phrase much used in the Suttas, words for desire (*chanda*), intent or purpose (*sankappa*). Any of these, had they figured, as *I* do not see them figuring in the original mantra, would have helped, if not so well as our words *will* and *choosing*, to clear up the real purport of the utterance.

But, it will be said, are not effort and purpose worded in the very statement of the Way : " This very worthy eightfold Way, to wit, right view . . . purpose . . . effort. . . . " ? This is true, in the First Utterance as it has come down to us. The " eightfold " list is stated at once, and again in the reappearance of the Way as a fourth "truth". And I do not expect to carry readers with me in writing my conviction, that the elaboration into eight limbs" is later, and is part of the elaboration of the truths and following refrains. I willingly concede, that it was found both necessary and fit to expand the message of the Way as implying a need for the Wayfarer to use purpose and make effort, so much so that certain terms about the wayfarer became closely associated with exposition of it. But, once we concentrate on these ideas about the man in the Way, we obscure the great figure itself, and what it ultimately stands for: the man's nature and life in course of becoming, a course calling for will in choice. So much obscured is it, that I have never yet seen a book on Buddhism which is not more occupied about these "right" ideas attaching to the Way, than about the Way itself as Way, as figure, as symbol. Way was, even more than Wheel, the very symbol of Sakya, as have been to Christians the Cross, the Lamb.[1] But it is the symbol and what it symbolizes that is ever being lost to view over attention to those eight details.

Had those eight—I may also say, had the ten, had the four limbs which we also meet with—been held from the first as of equal importance with the symbol itself, we should be likely to find them stressed in the very few surviving sayings where the Founder teaches some man with the use of the figure. But in those, alas! so few extant passages, the eight are not mentioned at all.

Again, he was hampered it may be by want of such a word as we have in "choice". This brings me to the second main implication. This is that the utterance is a call to the "man" as his own inward monitor. In willing to choose the "right" or "fit" life in word, thought, and deed, by what standard herein shall he direct himself? The developed factors, four, eight, or tenfold, of the Way give no guidance. But there was that within him which said: "This is the better, that is the worse way." We do not find this clearly worded in earlier Indian literature. What the man should do, or not do is there, but it is given to him in codes of procedure. He is not himself left to be the chooser, or made aware that he is chooser. Look at the word for choice and chooser: it was used, not in our general way, but in a very limited way, namely, as meaning a privileged choice, a boon (*vara*), or the special case of a maiden choosing her husband. Even here, when she did choose, her action is worded as "taking this man", not as choosing.[2]

[1] The Wheel too is symbol of the Way, figure within figure, but it was wrongly applied, as revolution without progress.

[2] E.g. *Jātaka*, No. 31; cf. my *Stories of the Buddha*, pp. 6, 42, 182.

This narrow use is the less strange in view of India's failure to develop the same word, *vara* (our *val*), as "will". The two, will, choice, are almost of necessity present or absent together. With the one there will be the other. Man is needy when he lacks these words, for the lack indicates that he is not yet aware of the need to use will, nay, of the will he has to use. If he had been aware, if he had valued that of which he was aware, he would have found the word.

These implications I have as yet found passed over by those who have written on Buddhism and its beginnings. The textual value in the books has prevailed too much. They are taken as wording what was said, not of telling the little that had been remembered, in a wording much altered from what it had been. There is after all not a single original teaching in any religion which has remained unaltered. And in saying "altered", I take the word in its dual European sense of changed and worsened.[1] But in this utterance, if we see in it a call to everyman to will to choose for himself the way which That Who is somehow within bids, wills him to take, why then surely for that time, for that place, yea, for always and everywhere, it is a message of highest truth and meaning.

The men who are first won over to aid in such a call are no ordinary men. But, and in part as such, they will each wish to carry on that message in his own way. And that way will not always be coincident with that of the messenger. They will be giving varying emphasis to it. It is perhaps noteworthy here[2] that, of the first "Sakyans", one only has remained singled out in the records as having been commended by his leader as turning the wheel, i.e. carrying on the word, as he himself did. (The saying has been oddly misrepresented as carrying on in succession to himself, but this he, as one predeceasing his Master, could not do.) They will be slightly altering the wording each in his own way. They will be full of goodwill, but they will not be seeing just as the messenger does. When we consider this we need no longer wonder that a first utterance, a manifesto, as this has ever by Buddhists been held to be, should have become altered, altered in both meanings.

An utterance so regarded will never be worded by earnest men in a way they deem other than very worthy, and intelligible, if—and much depends on this—if the utterance is the expression of what they in their day are holding as vital, as central teaching. But it may well be, that what they are so holding is no longer the vital,

[1] *Altéré*. [2] See Chapter VII for the episode in detail.

central teaching in the original utterance of an earlier day. They have come to hold something else. The utterance may still be preserved as a treasured relic, a venerated mantra. We ourselves have such in the Hebrew Ten Commandments, the Magna Charta. But neither are these for us the vital, central teaching they originally were, even though, so far as we know, they have not as scripts been edited. They are virtually fossils. They are not the live wires they were. We deem we have now something that is more in line with our present religious or political standards. So also the men in whose hands were the Sakyan records had come to place another teaching as more vital, more central than the will and the choosing of the Better, figured in the Way. This was the teaching about Dukkha: the ills of life and of the worlds.

Now there will very probably have been, in the original utterance, a simple direct talk on Ill, not put in the forefront as a fourfold mantra, as we see it in the records, but appended to the positive Way-statement, to show how right wayfaring was (in itself) a gradual decreasing of the manifold modes of "ill". For after all it was the ills of life: old age, disease, death, which apparently moved the Founder to take the drastic step (for one in his position) to leave his home to study a remedy. But he had got past the former brooding over ill, the cry: "Alas! the world has fallen on ill!" He had found in man's nature a radiating effort, an onward striving, which he could not word, but which he figured by Wayfaring, whereby in the long run ill could be overpast, and the utterly-well of Artha reached. And this it was which he put first and foremost, Artha and the Way thereto; not Ill. As the years rolled on and his teaching became ever more and more borne by the vehicle of a monastic machine, it became necessary to put in the strongest *mandamus* for the justification of that system. This was the hopeless Ill of the world and of life. And since it had been going too far to insert this *mandamus* at the head of the mantra, we get it stuck on at the end: a non-organic whole, as Deussen truly called it. The Indian, or at any rate the Sakyan, method in wording is not, I repeat, that of leading up to climax. The chief matter is placed first. There can be little hesitation in calling the chief idea in the appendage, that is, the four truths, Dukkha and not the Way. But analogously, in the Utterance as a whole, with its probably original opening left in place, the chief idea is the Way, the Way belonging to, leading to Artha. Had the Founder intended to have taken, as Buddhists now do (at least those of the Hīnayana persuasion) his stand on Dukkha, he would have begun with it.

But why, some may say, make this rally round the Way as being in truth the chief idea in the will and word of the Utterer?

I fall back on my hypothesis of the Message in a world-religion, and its Messenger. We are herein dealing with a man who mandates a new word to the "man" about his nature and his destiny, which is what I would call a "More" therein, an enlargement of outlook, a telling of power to evolve more from life than he has done, always taking life in the whole, never in one world-span of it only, a call to use more will to become more well. Now to see in a theory of "ill" the great reality in life, to see it as the main value, dictating to a man what shall be his relations to the world of his fellowmen, to the worlds of all beings: this is to see something that is not of the original gospel, not of the original inspiration of the Messenger, but a gospel of the Less. If my hypothesis is to stand, we must see, in the real essence of the first utterance, not a gospel about the supreme importance of ill; we must see on the contrary a new word about "well", and the "more" in man's nature, making for that "well".

I shall, I know, be told: But the truths are after all a theory how to become well. I admit they are saved as to their face by admitting the Way to that as the fourth and last mantra of "truth". But my point is this: that in this fourfold formula the Way is no longer the chief subject, and Ill very surely is. The formula is obviously not "about" the Way; it is obviously a formula "about" Ill. What men hold very important in life, that will they put into words; that will they make the chief subject of their words. And accordingly, for the men who, on to this uttered "talk", grafted, or rather stuck the mantra about Ill, Ill *had become* for them, as it was not for the Utterer of the Talk, the chief subject to be mandated.[1]

Hence it is that the true subject of the Utterance has got covered over, and we have to dig for it. We must put that into it which will have been there, if the message ever had the "More-value" of a world-gospel. It is a woeful thing that this has to be done. I would we had not to put in, or leave out, a single word. As it stands, it is manifestly corrupt, leading those who take it at its face-value into error. One of these errors is this: Whereas a world-religion is essentially a message to everyman—else is it no world-religion—the editors, who were contemplating Ill as the chief matter, have made the utterance to be concerned only with the "man who has gone forth" (the recluse, because of the Ill of the world); and hence we find one writer seeing the utterance as dealing with laxity, or strictness in the life *only* of the recluse,[2] and another seeing in it

[1] See also Chapter XXI. [2] De la Vallée Poussin, *Nirvāṇa*.

a "popular-poetical" conception of a world-forsaking recluse's escape from Ill.[1]

Is it really true vision which sees in the Utterance such pitiful abortions as these? Is it indeed only a message for monks? Was it no message of help to the laity also, to the Many the Compassionate One of world-fame came forth to help? Were we, in a world religion, dealing with externals of body and mind, time and place, I should not venture to reword the Message as I see it. But we are dealing with a word from Very Man to Very Man, reverberating across time and space to the same in ourselves. And in this sense I can hear a missioner speaking that message to the heart of men somewhat like this :—

I am telling you of the better way in which a man should walk in life. Most men choose to walk either in the way of self-indulgence and worldliness or in the way of being the slaves of rules. I am willing you to take a different way. It lies between the two. It is like the former because it calls upon you to walk according to your will. It is like the latter because it calls upon you to have some principle according to which you will to walk. You have yourselves the knowledge that when two ways lie before you, one is what you would call better than the other. That is, the one is the way which, if followed, will lead to your doing and so becoming, better than if you follow the other. It is not always quite clear but a man usually knows. Now if this better way be followed as long as you live on earth, the result will be better for you when you leave the earth. And this is true for all the rest of your life. You will by such choosing come in the future to the very goal of life. You will then know what it is to be utterly well, even though now you have no clear idea how or what that will be. Now you are often not well. You are often unwell in body and in mind; you are unwell in your very self. As very man, as the spirit you are, you are not well; you are very imperfect, you are truly as a babe. You suffer in many ways. You want not to suffer. Use that want to become better. Use your will to choose the way to become better. Let it be your firm belief that you can become better. Do not turn away from the will to the better. Word the better to yourself. Hold the better to be indeed better. See yourself in a long, long way of life, long enough for you to grow to what you do not dream of. You see but a very little of the way. As you keep on choosing the better, you will be seeing ever more and more of it. You will be wayfaring in the way to the utterly well.

[1] Heiler, *Die Buddhistische Versenkung*.

I am not saying that the above is a correct reinstatement of lost words and phrases. Who could pretend to make that? I only claim that, clothed in simple English fit for a gospel for Everyman, it reproduces something of the essential meaning of the fragmentary utterance out of which grew a mighty world-religion. It presents the utterance in the one and only way in which, given those first "talked" fragments, it can possibly have been a gospel message from Very Man to Very Man, and not from a sectarian among men to a section among men, a monk to monks.

Does the question here again arise: Why was it that, during so long a life of mission work as the Founder's, and with a Community and an influence becoming extended, no better wording of the first mandate was drawn up with at least his sanction? It is not easy for us to get at the truth here. We need first to recollect that Sakya is the only world-religion in which we get even the patched-up wreck of a first mandate at all. Religions do not begin with the making of records, nor in the decades of strictly missionary work does the need of charter-statements show itself. More especially in a bookless world. It is true, that in the companion volume to this and in this also, it is put forward that fixed wordings were begun in the Founder's old age. But the reader is there also vividly reminded, that by that time Gotama was in the midst of a relatively new and growing monk-vogue, vigorously wording its own monastic views of life. In his old age it was too much for him to control, and after his passing, these would hold sway unchecked. But affectionate reverence for him would be likewise then growing apace, and it would be then, that memories of how he began to teach, as well as fresher memories of how he ended his career would call for revival, for restatement, and in the latter case for compilation of wording.

It may again be asked, would a mandate of such high significance have been originally uttered as a "talk"?

Here most fortunately, as many of us know, we have in the record the circumstances under which the talk took place. We have there, as it were, a man returning home from a journey with a treasure he has won. He had left the friends with whom he had been experimenting in *tapas*, the better to think things out. He came back to them (or perhaps he had to seek them out in Benares whither they had gone in his absence), with things thought out, to lay before them his message for mission work. It is only reasonable to suppose that, before leaving them, he had talked much with them, and they with him of a line of teaching best calculated to help the many. For there was no question here of founding a School for philosophic study, or a return to *tapas*. We have also most fortunately the record (as we have in the Christian gospels) that once the group became enough in numbers, it was missionizing, and not academic debate, that they set about. This tends to be forgotten over very much development, in a much later, established Buddhism, in what we now call philosophy. Now the friends will have known the trend of Gotama's mind, and the alternatives in the new ideas of the day over which he had been hesitating. Hence it is not impossible that, when he came back with a solution and a decision, he did not express himself in the explicit way about the springs of action, in the man mandating himself in the Way, that he would have used before strangers, before pupils, before a public audience. They will have understood, when he told them as " talk ", with much left implicit, what he felt strongly moved to try, in such words as he could find, to tell his fellow-men.

My belief then as to the original form of the first two utterances is, that, deducting the added glosses, they are mantras, following on talks between the teacher-band, and were so worded by them or by the Leader, to serve as outlines, as schemata, to be expanded in the mission to the Many.

There is this one more thing to be said about the Utterer, judged by that Utterance. It is reasonable to hold that he did not reel off in well-worded sentences what his will was trying to say. When we are charging our will with a new word, we are making articulate, in matter and word, something to which we are not accustomed. We have no preconceived precedent in the values. We are *valuing in the making*. We are giving value to the yet unvalued. Gotama was bringing new values into India and making them articulate. We shall not understand Sakyan origins if we fail to see this. It was a question of putting something into new words where words most needed were not. *Now* we may reel off a clear restatement of what in my judgment he was trying to say, and sorely should we be, as heirs of the ages, to blame, if we could not do so. But we shall not regard his message truly if we continue blind to his difficulties. A New Word, we hear him saying, is never worthily worded.

He might have left worthier fragments, had he been an accomplished speaker. He was that in legend only. He cannot be said to have shown the orator's gift. Nowhere in the Suttas is there an eloquent speech of which we can say, These were truly his very words. Wherever they rise to eloquence, the sentences have been refashioned in those prose refrains which are a special feature of the Suttas, and which herein betray, probably as an aid to memorizing, the later hand of the editor. It is not the way of one who is giving a new teaching. Such does not flow out in easy periods, in the way of a purposely drawn-up wording. That may be the way of the preacher, of a pundit. It is not the way of a man afire with a new word he is willed to utter, stammering it may be over the unworded ideas he is inspired withal.

If we are content to see in the Sakyamuni the pundit, then does the following quotation worthily picture him : "Artificial as this arrangement (in Sutta method) sounds when analyzed, it is a natural procedure for one who wished to impress on his hearers a series of philosophic propositions without the aid of writing, and I can imagine that these rhythmical formulae, uttered in that grave and pleasant voice which the Buddha is said to have possessed, seemed to the leisurely yet eager groups who sat round him under some wayside banyan or in the monastery park, to be not tedious iteration but a gradual revelation of truth growing clearer with each repetition."[1]

It is because I see in him the latter kind of teacher and not the pundit, that before me, as I read those words, there rose a different vision of one who saw, who heard . . . and said, "Woe is me ! for I am undone ; I am a man of unclean lips . . . Then flew the seraph . . . and laid upon my mouth a live coal from the altar . . . I heard the voice saying, Whom shall I send ? Who will go for us ? Then said I, Here am I ; send me. And It said, Go and tell . . ."[2]

I do not for a moment reject the belief that here was a man who could and did during many years of ministry with gentle voice impart good counsel. But when it comes down to reiterating refrains, there I find that the passionate ardour surmounting the stumbling utterance of the Hebrew prophet fits better. It fits better with the lines ascribed to him in the Sutta :—

> I lay no wood, brahman, for fires on altars ;
> Only within burneth the fire I kindle.
> Ever my fire burns ; ever tense and ardent
> Worthily I work out the life that's holy.[3]

"Afire," *tejasā* : so he was, when from solitude he came back to his friends and spoke what had been willed he should try to utter ; radiant he looked with the new word of the new will.[4] And it is with this in mind that I have sought to re-kindle the dead embers of the few words of that utterance which have survived.

[1] C. Eliot, *Hinduism and Buddhism*, i, 286. [2] Isaiah, ch. vi.

[3] *Saṃyutta-Nikāya*, i, 169 :

> *Ajjhattam eva jalayāmi jotiŋ*
> *Niccaggini . . .*

[4] *Vinaya*, I, i, 6, 7.

IV

DHARMA (DHAMMA) IN SAKYA

I have said, that in the First Utterance of the Sakyan mandate, I find two implications, implications so vital that without them the message is relatively worthless. As recorded, it can in no way fail to have interest historically considered. It is undoubtedly an ancient record; as ushering in a new religious movement with a formal pronouncement, it is unique; and as the ostensible mandate, in its added mantra, of the monk, it is a good apologia for his motive of a diagnosis of world-woe. But as a call to the Many, shedding new light on man's nature and man's way in the worlds, it is, I repeat, without those two implications lifeless, irrational. These are (1) that man must himself will the Better, the Best, and choose to follow after it; (2) that he is aided herein by an inward monition, which is at once himself and more than himself. I propose to seek further for the original Sakya by way of these two vitally important values. And I will begin with the latter.

There is a word which we do not find in that utterance, but which none the less became of the first importance in the whole history of Buddhism. I have worded it in the restatement thus: "It is not always quite clear, but a man usually knows." Now this awareness as to which of two or more courses is the better or best is, for the history of man, as we all know, a very real and vital phenomenon. It has been diversely named; I need only refer to the "daimôn" of Sokrates, to the "I find a law" of St. Paul, to the "conscience" of our own day. In India the word was *dharma* (Pali: *dhamma*). In its truest sense it expresses this inward monitor. It has a long history, and has been used with various shades of meaning. But as singular and substantive, ever with a "solemn, holy meaning". These may be studied, admirably set forth, in the monograph from which I quote, *Pali Dhamma*, by Magdalen and Wilhelm Geiger.[1] Especially to be noted, in connection with our First Utterance, is the nearness, "in pre-Buddhist times"—I would add, contemporaneously with the birth of Sakya—of the word *dharma* to *Brahman* (the Supreme, Divine), and, again, the equivalence in Vedic thought of *dharma* with *ṛta*, that impersonal concept of the

[1] *Abhandlungen d. Bay. Ak. d. Wiss.*, München, 1921.

Fit, the Right, to which, like the Greek "Necessity", the very gods were subject. This meaning is never absent, whatever be the aspect taken of *dharma*, whatever is the emphasis used with it at different stages of Buddhist history. We even find it reverberating in a Commentary in a unique wording: *dhammo karaṇakātabbo ti*, "*dhamma* is the ought to be done of a doing."

The, to us, singular absence in the First Utterance of any reference to a supra-mundane mandate has often been commented on. And many a modern has swallowed, has accepted the monkish values, because he appreciates, in the message, that which seems to be a wonderful anticipation of the rationalism of his day.

This is because he reads without seeing in the Utterance what it will have meant to the average worthy man or woman of *its* day. He has taken, and rightly taken, the utterance, in spite of its having been elaborated into a "monk-mantra", as the very world-"sermon" the Buddhist world has ever taken it to have been, as the message of a man whose vast compassion included, not men on earth only, but "all devas", "all beings"; as the mandate which unseen inmates of the worlds came thronging to hear. In so doing, he has unwittingly substituted for "one who has gone forth", the reading "man". And he has been right in so doing. But, for him, "man" will have meant no more than it does in other religious mandates. It will have meant the external person, complex of body and mind, who "has", or "has not, a soul". This was not the meaning for the thoughtful, the religious Indian of the seventh and sixth centuries B.C. When for him a call came, in which he appeared as, by implication, both the bidden and the Bidder, it would not therefore have appeared to him as what is now called Rationalistic or Atheistic. And why? Because, for him, the "man" *included in his nature* the "More than man".

I am not, of course, referring to the word in the Utterance "tathâgata". This title, "he who has thus-come, or -gone," constantly applied in the Suttas to the Founder, but now and then to any good man, may or may not have been in the original utterance. I incline to think it was not; but if it was, it cannot possibly have referred to the speaker. He was not yet acclaimed as one to whom any honorific titles were due, and to have assumed such a title at the outset would be but part of the pious after-editing, which makes him assume a pompousness which would have ill become him then—especially before a few friends—and indeed at any time. But even if "tathāgata", may not have been in the original word-outline, it may well have been used by the first Sakyas in the teaching of the Way to mean the Wayfarer, the man who thus fares in the way to the Better. It will have been a much later value in the term which practically reserved it for a "Buddha", or for "Buddhas".[1] Similar has been the fate of *su-gata*, 'well-farer'.

For that matter, whereas such a word as Wayfarer was supremely wanted when the little original outline was taken over as The Teaching by the founders, there can scarcely be said to have been such a word. We may look long in the Piṭakas, even in the Jātakas, yet never find such a word. I have only run such a word to earth in two Commentaries, that on the Dhammapada and that on the Dhammasangaṇi, and in the treatise (5th cent. A.D.) *Visuddhi-Magga*. We there at length find[2] *maggika* (way-er), *paṭipanna*, or *-annaka* (fared, fared-er) and *gamaka* (goer). And therewith the very pertinent remark in the second: "Given a faring-course (*paṭipadā*) there must be a (way-)farer." I cannot help thinking we may have here another difficulty with which the New Word had to contend, another word needed, yet not to hand. The Utterance is referring to a middle way which the man who takes it, i.e. has willed, has chosen to take, will have "understood", namely as the Better Way. But the words "*tathāgatena abhisam-buddhā*", "understood by one-so-gone", have been distorted, with the waning importance of the Way, and the growing Buddha-cult, to mean "understood by the Buddha".

Now in the Sakyan message the man was thus "becoming in the Way",[3] the man thus going was he who walked according to *dhamma*, *dhammena*; according, that is, to that hidden Divinity, Who, in virtue of his manhood, he was. There is nothing more solemnly deliberate in acts ascribed to Gotama, than his confessing worship of *dhamma*, as That under Whom he vowed to live. Very dehumanized has he become in the stilted prose and verse of the little Sutta "Gāravan" (honouring),[4] very far is it from the very man in the attitude he is made to assume about himself, yet it is most unlikely there is no basis of truth in the confession. Buddhology would not have invented it. And it appears as a step taken before he began his mission work. Why do Buddhists so ignore it?

To say: "This is to put the Brahmanic Theism, or Ātmanism into Buddhism, which was its religious opposite," is to talk at cross purposes. We are not dealing with what has come, late in time,

[1] The student of the Piṭakas will find it useful to consult the article "Tathāgata", by R., now Lord, Chalmers, *JRAS*. 1898, 391 ff.

[2] On Dhp. v. 24, and *Atthasālinī*, p. 164; *Vis. Magga*, 513.

[3] On this idiom, see Chapter VI.

[4] *Saṃyutta*, i, 139.

to be called Buddhism ; we are dealing with that New Word which soon came to be called the *dhamma* of the Sakyans. And when it was spoken, the whole religious world of North India was then seeing in every man, not a "man who somehow has a soul", but man who *is* THAT ; a self (ĀTMAN) who is the world-self (ĀTMAN). We cannot too carefully keep this in view : that to take the man as most of us here and now see him, and see that man in the time and place of the beginnings of Sakya is to be incapable of understanding its gospel. I shall return to this in another chapter.

Again, *dhamma* is often translated, especially by men of Buddhist countries, by "law". If by this is meant that inward monition which St. Paul called the "law" (*nomos*), wherewith he fought against his lower nature, the rendering is not amiss. But there is a tendency to read into it the newer idea of natural uniformity (popularly called laws of science). This, if brought in to explain Sakyan concepts, is out of place. There was then no such scientific culture as to enable a teacher to say that the Better for man has been shown to be the conforming to a law of this kind. It is to read the new, the later, into the old. Even the wiser few did not so think, or at least so speak ; much less would there have been in such teaching any possible appeal for the Many. On the other hand, there would be an appeal, not only for the wise few, but also for the thoughtful Many, in a teaching addressing a call to the man-as-such, because the man-as-such was more than he is for us ; he was More-than-man *in the very fact of being man*.

I am not saying this would be a true saying for India earlier or again later. We are concerned with the valley of the Ganges at a certain epoch. And with much uncertainty as to precise dates, we can see this much, that at this epoch the older cult of great gods had waned ; the newer cult of great gods (with a difference), especially the Vishnu and Śiva cults, had not yet shown a theistic renaissance. "The gods" sat lightly in man's firmament.[1] Their real, their earlier weight had been transferred to the Impersonal and the Within.

There has been too much tendency to see in the birth-time of Sakya a period of decadence in belief in the Divine, a waning in faith in unseen world-governance. I hold this to be a mistake. There was, there had been Götterdämmerung, twilight of gods ; there was no waning of faith in a Divine Principle. Externalized faith had been made to "enter in". The Upanishads of the epoch are full of it. Deity was come to be held as an impersonal (neuter) "Brahman" ; as a somewhat analogous to the breath (*ātman* and

[1] So sat they in Plato's, in Aristotle's firmament.

prāṇa)[1] in one's self. The inner world of the man had assumed a rich import of highest significance; a word had taken birth for it: *adhyātman*, not used before, but to be so much used in the Pali records as *ajjhattaŋ* and *ajjhattika*: self-referring; within the man dwelt the very Principle of world-governance Itself. "Know you, O Kapya, that Inner Controller (who makes to go[2]), who from within controls this world and the other world and all things . . . *this*[3] is self, inner controller, immortal."

It was into this new world of "God made immanent" that Gotama's message came: into a world of the man made so rich, so much More, that in the glory of the idea the dazzled self-communer would easily forget the very babe he was in growth toward that More-in-him-in-idea; forget the need of transforming that More into the living of life; forget the need of insight into that More in each fellowman; forget the long way of becoming that stretched before both the one and the other through the worlds. Let no man say: Into such a world of new insight into the Divine what need was there for a new gospel? The new insight, had India understood it, was the very vantage-point on which the new gospel might have become a marvellous world-word in man's advance.[4] On the other hand, let no man say: Here was a religious mandate shorn of the Divine; a wonderful anticipation! when at that time the very word "man" breathed the Divine nature; when the very word for what the man should do (*dhamma*) had become tantamount to Divine guidance, and to speak of holy living was to speak of the God-conduct (*Brahma-chariya*).

To resume: In any scheme or summary put forward, at that day, of a religious kind capable of appealing to the majority, the very word "man" as its subject, his nature and life as its object, would call up associated ideas of immanent deity and of divine monition or *dhamma* to an extent to which we here and now are very much less responsive. To that extent we are very orphans.

If it be said: But there is no mention in the Utterance of the word "man", I would remind the reader again that we are dealing with an ancient husk, with a plastered superstructure. We have seen reason to find two plastered items in the very places where the word "man" is called for: the place for the wayfarer on the Way, and the place filled in by "recluse", which in a world-gospel (let alone the context) is unfit. The recluse (unless the mere monastic explanation on which one writer, as I said, has fallen back, is adopted), *had*

[1] *Taitt. Up.*, 2, 3, etc.
[2] *Antara-yāmin. Bṛhad. Up.*, iii, 7, 2.
[3] *Eṣa ta.*
[4] See below, Chapter VI.

already chosen the one of the two extremes deprecated ; and the place filled in by "tathāgata", which, as understood, was on that occasion impossible. Here we need some such phrase as "the man usually knows".[1] And why? Because in him as man That is working by *dhamma* (*dhammena*, in Pali idiom), That Who, as was then taught, he is : "*Tat tvam asi.*" The word "man" in these two places would appeal somewhat in this stronger, Indian way both to the Many on whose behalf the utterance was thought out, and also to the chosen few, who had been looking to hear it in the will to work with the speaker among the Many.

The actual word for "man" which the speaker will have used was in all probability the Prakrit forms *purisa*, *pulisha*, both corruptions of the earlier *purusa* (Vedic). It was the last named which, in the greater Upanishads is, in passages innumerable, used to identify immanent deity with the man : "he saw this very man (*puruṣa*) as veriest Brahman."[2] "In the beginning this world was *ātman* alone in the form of the man (*puruṣa*)[3] . . . that bright immortal man incorporated in the body, he is the same as that Self, that Brahman, that All,"[4] and so on. It is to weaken the specific nature of the Indian conception to translate *puruṣa* here as is constantly done by "person", when *in any other connection* the translator would have rendered it by "man". That it is not the present vogue with us is no real excuse. Before this century is over we may see, even here, the "man" come into his own, who now is disinherited, and we may then be seeing a kinship with this early fetch of Indian thought, and no more value the wording that helped to keep him aloof.

There is another word for "man" in Pali, which in the Pali Piṭakas has an interesting if unwritten history, and that is *puggălă* (Sanskrit *pudgala*), or "male". In the Sayings or Suttas, it has practically ousted the word *purisa* as signifying the human individual or self or soul. *Purisa* was still used in the records, but merely in the sense of the man as a useful machine, such as a messenger, a policeman, or again as meaning male in a context as complementary to female. But there is one very notable exception (not to mention others of less significance), and this is that when, at passing from earth, the human being is, at the tribunal of his deva-fellowmen, brought to book for his earthly career, the judge addresses him, not as *puggala*, but as *purisa* ! It is possible that we have here in the Sutta (of which more later on) a true early Sakyan record. There was the further word *manussa*, but this is never used in an individual personal

[1] See p. 62.
[2] *Aitareyya Up.*, iii, 13.
[3] *Bṛhad. Up.*, i, 4, 1.
[4] *Ib.*, ii, 5, 1 ff.

way, only as "men", "human beings", in opposition to beings not termed human, and we can here disregard it.

It remains for me a strong presumption, that as monastic Sakya came to set itself against the ultimate reality of the man as entity, the words *manussa* and *pulisha*, *purisa*, with very positive, real associations, with superman implication, were dropped, and the less lofty word *puggala*, the centre of later ecclesiastical dispute, was substituted. We see the Sakya admitting the having adapted Brahmanic terms to a new meaning: *tevijja*, *brāhmaṇa*, etc. It is not unreasonable therefore to conclude that they had effected a complementary rewording where ejection seemed desirable.

But we are now in an older day than this of Sakya monks editing with changed values. We are trying to reconstruct a day when a new idea here, a new idea there, was struggling to become articulate in a world pre-empted by set ways of articulate thought. To be understood at all, the new idea would have to be expounded with all the swathing draperies of the words of the day of its birth. And hence it is that I am insisting so strongly that, even when we have got rid of the more obvious "plasterings" in the original matter (if aught indeed be left) of the first Utterance, we have yet to read the meanings current at its birthday, and which have dropped out, into the essential words, instead of insetting words bearing either the later Sakyan values, or our own modern values. And thus I would suggest, that not only would the speaker have used the word *purisa* (or *pulisha*), but that for his hearers the word would have, in such a talk or schema, the meaning I have tried to show. In such a connection "man" meant very much what a similar utterance here and now would mean by "soul"—but *more than soul*.

I have spoken of many meanings of the word *dhamma* or *dharma*. I have suggested in which of these it will have been implied in the first utterance, nay, must have been implied, if the words, as we have them, were to have any driving power at all. It will not have always been left unsaid in the first Sakyan teaching. In fact, it became of such central importance as to stand for the teaching itself. "What is that 'dhamma'"—it might be more literally rendered "What kind of *dhamma* is that (*ko nāma so dhammo*)—which your disciples when trained therein, finding comfort, confess as their choice and the beginning of the Godlife (*ādi-Brahmacariyaŋ*)?"[1] Unfortunately it was not suffered to be left in this meaning of "basic principle of holy living", a term by which we might very truly define conscience. It came to mean the principle made articulate, the inner guide

[1] *Digha*, iii, 39.

brought outside, in formulated teachings, in sayings, rules, sermons, discourses, and what not. So that, in reply to such a question as that quoted, the usual reply is, that the Dhamma is in nine parts, enumerated somewhat like the above. We even find the Founder himself made to describe Dhamma as a thing of these nine parts which the monk learns ! (*Majjhima*, Sutta 22). No such scholastic schedule mars the reply to the question quoted above, and that, as far as it goes, points to a possibly more genuine Saying.

Externalized though *dhamma* came to be in what we might call its church meaning, it ever remained that which *implied* a teaching of the " things that ought to be done ". And so meaning, the word, for which we have nothing equally rich in import to render it by, is better translated by "law" or "norm" than by "doctrine". Doctrine is true only of the much later Buddhism, the Buddhism of the monasteries, of the schoolmen. But even law and norm are not clean equivalents ; law, if not perhaps for St. Paul, is for us either too statutory, or too scientific ; norm is too much the "good average". Neither term has in it that secret of the Way, the " coming-to-be ", the stage by stage further than we were before, which calls through early Sakya. *Dhamma* was in it that which *ought to be* as above and beyond that which *is*. It transforms the nature of the early records sometimes, if we read this meaning into *dhamma*. Take the passage in the unique (Vinaya) account of the beginnings of the movement, where the word occurs, I think, for the first time. The Founder is, like Jesus, sending his early disciples out two by two from the first settlement at Rājagaha for the day's missionizing. He is no longer leaving *dhamma* implicit in what they have to say. " Fare in a round that may be for the good of the many . . . teach *dhamma* beneficent in the beginning, in the middle, in the end . . ." This description recurs often in a famous formula in praise of the triad, Buddha, Dhamma, Sangha, and we may some of us have vaguely imagined it referred to periods in formulated doctrines, much as we refer to periods in a man's, a poet's, a composer's work. But it cannot here have meant a system of doctrine, when for the first missioners there was not yet any set form of words. When we take *dhamma* as the working of the Antarayāmin, the inner controller, we get a thing true for all time and for every man at every stage in his life, we get that which is present to guide for his good the man *as child, as adult, as aged.* We have the very spring of the holy life. Yet no Buddhist, no writer on Buddhism, so far as I have seen, has noticed this. They do not even translate the passage as if they had. The usual rendering is inapt. It is not " *dhamma* which is beneficent " or " good " or "lovely"—*kalyāṇa* may be rendered by any one of these—but it is "*dhamma* (doctrine) which is glorious", which is not the meaning at all!

Still less suitable is "doctrine", or "the Dhamma" suitable in the case of the very first five converts, who were, we read, after the Utterance of the Message, instructed and admonished in *dhamma*. The right way to read this is surely to see in it a very ancient link between the Way as the message to be taught to the many and *dhamma* or the inner guide in choice of Way, by which alone, urging him, a man would know how to choose aright.

V

MAN'S WILL IN SAKYA

I come to the second vital implication in the First Utterance : Man must himself will the better, the best, and choose to follow after it.

This is not there given utterance, any more than is *dhamma*. None the less, to make that brief Utterance worth while, to give it any weight at all as a World-Word in the New and the True, both of these things must be taken as implied. But they must not be taken as they are taken in most that has been written on this subject. *They should not be left latent.* We see what a lamed word those writings have been made in consequence of acquiescence in this latency. Namely, no two writers are at one on what is the central conception of Buddhism. Writers have been too content to take the explicit at its face-value ; they have too little brought the inlying burden of the message to the surface. And so we get emphasis laid mainly on the over-neat explicitness of the appendage called the Four Truths, and on the over-elaborate explicitness of the modes in the Way. These jump to the eye. And just because of that, we had done well to have been less content, and to have suspected work of aftermen in those categories, of the men who had themselves, before us, lost sight of the real heart of the Utterance, that great, but halting, poorly worded feeling-out-after a mandate in the New for all men, and had reduced it to a mere message for " the man who had gone forth ", the recluse, the *samaṇa*, the monk. Rightly to understand the Utterance we should wholly shift our emphasis ; we should ignore the neat categories, eightfold and fourfold ; we should listen to the undertones in the opening sentences.

So listening, it may then be that we shall hear, we, the very soul that we are will hear the call that came : " you *will* the better in this way, in that way ; the way you feel you *ought to go* : you 'thus-gone' will go towards the highest weal, the end of all ill. Choose that way. *You* must will. *You* must choose."

Long after these days it is to be seen in the rock edicts of a layman addressing laymen, how for Asoka this will, this choice in conduct, was worded as the gift of *dhamma* from man to man : " should tell him, that 'this is good', 'that ought to be done' ; this will bring benefit now, happiness hereafter." It is the very refrain of the edicts.

Why was this left so largely implicit? Why was it not better worded?

Some reasons for this I have already suggested: the fact that the Utterer was telling to friends a schema or outline only (he is recorded as engaged immediately after on the subject of *dhamma*, miscalled "the Dhamma"). He was not a gifted speaker. He was still in travail with the new, the unusual, the greatness of what he willed to do. All this leaves yet untouched these other two reasons, why the two matters before us have been left implicit. Firstly, there may have been that in the Utterance which *became implicit* when, in editorial hands, first as spoken, then as written, first in one tongue, then in another, the Record of it took its present shape. Secondly, there may have been that in the Utterance which *had to be left implicit* for want of a fit word.

About the former reason I shall have more to say in a later chapter. About the latter reason I have already said much elsewhere. But whereas I hold it to be both true and important, it is not yet accepted as such by fellow-writers. Hence I must once more deal with it.

We are slow as yet, so far at least as some of us have put words about this matter on paper, to bring out the striking difference between the wording of the will in the Christian scriptures and those of other religions. In the first, words for the will are there ready for use, in Hebrew, Aramaic, Greek. And those words, or that word, is often used, often in ways where no other word of approximate meaning would have expressed the agent as forcefully as does "will". It takes two and a half quarto columns in the Biblical Concordance to exhaust the references to will, and its derivatives. In contrast to this, the references to Will in Dr. Winternitz's Index to the fifty volumes of the Sacred Books of the East occupy eight lines, Volition one and a half, and Saṅkalpa, Sankappa, five lines. And of these, it should be noted, *only one reference* is to Buddhist books. The other references are to Taoist, Pahlavi, and Vedântist texts. The articles, I may add, on Desire and the peculiarly Buddhist word (I doubt if it came into early Sakyan teaching) *Taṇhā* (thirst, craving) are almost equally meagre. Again, other indexes to recent works on Indian philosophy, Indian religion, are even more meagre, or wholly silent. Deussen, historian, philosopher and translator, was in strong sympathy with Indian concepts. His works contain excellent indexes of, as he says, noteworthy ideas. In not one of these indexes is there a single reference to the mention of will in any original. There is a little article on "freedom of the will" in one of the works (omitted from the index), but it might as fitly have been called "freedom without will". In the histories of Messrs. Das Gupta, O. Strauss, Radhakrishna we find the same silence, the same blank.

Now the Indian mind is very introspective, and very fond of definitions. The Indian, the Hindu liked from of old to ponder over and talk about the powers, the needs, the limitations of man. He began early to study man and his body, and then man as distinguishable from his mind. He believed in learning, in knowledge. He honoured the teacher, the man who talked about the man, exceedingly. He studied the way of impression and idea. He grew early to be deeply concerned with the taming and training of the "self", with right choice at the parting of the ways, with the innate upward trend of effort towards the better. The more curious then is his failure to develop his own strong Aryan root for "will", *var* (the bifurcate, it would seem, of the Western Aryan *val*), or to find an equally strong equivalent to express that in man which is so vital throughout all religion, all life. To discern that in man, by and in which man, having an inward monitor, turns to a Better, words it as such : I ought to walk in this way! and tries to walk in it, seem to call for more than "dharma", seem to call for both "will", and also for "willer".

Yet when we try to express the man so acting in Indian idiom, we have no words. *Vara* is there, but it is restricted to (*a*) the *result* of an act of will, (*b*) to the *negative aspect* of will, namely, to repression to what a man should not do, should will not to do. As (*a*), in "better", or excellent", it expresses the chosen, the selected. When, I repeat, in the *svayaṃ-varaṃ*, or personal choice of bridegroom by a maiden, she wills this man and not those, she says, not "I will", or "I choose", but "I take him". *Kāma* was there, and *kratu* : both strong, excellent words for will. But *kāma* was suffered to become depreciated currency, as sex-, or sensuous-desire only ; and *kratu* was suffered to die out. *Vasī* was there, but used for the having willed, not for the putting forth will. *Saṃkalpa*, a compound at best, when a strong simple term was the only fit one, was used for aim or purpose. But never was it felt, never was it worded, that in it we have a radical factor in man's nature. Students are warned by a, teacher, as I have said, that they should not, in the processes of *thinking* and the like, lose sight of the *thinker* and the like, but there is no inclusion of man as aimer, or purposer (*samkalpetar* is a no-word).

Then there is *cetanā*. Now it is overstressing the will-coefficient to see in *cetanā*, as do Burmese Pali-ists, the equivalent of volition. It is called action in one Sutta, but then all mind-work was action (*mano-kamma*). *Cetanā* does literally mean thinking. It is the verbal noun of *cetas*. The word in the Vedic appears to have a volitional implication: thinking in relation to action, intention. And in the Nikāyas it occurs in contexts where it seems reasonable to translate it by will. Thus it occurs (1) as if in apposition to *patthana* (wishing) and *paṇidhi* (intent, aim)[1]; again (2) in a mid-position between these two and *vitakka, saññā, diṭṭhi*,[2] words of purely cognitive meaning; again (3) as *ceteti*, as if in apposition to *pakappeti*[3] (intends to do, plans); again (4) Gotama, in a Sutta describing his early austerities, is made to say: he bethought him of restraining *citta* by *cetas* (*cetasā cittaŋ abhiniggaṇheyyaŋ*).[4]

But when we look about us for passages to test the apparent will-force in the meaning, as actually explicit, in either *cetas* or *cetanā*, we find no support. On the last instance (4) the Commentary gives us none; it paraphrases with: "that I might make evil thought energy-crushed by good thought," thus curiously inverting matters, and placing the more volitional energy (*viriya*) in the *citta* rather than in the *cetas*. Again, when terms of energy are defined, *cetanā* is never brought in to help; nor is *cetanā* ever defined by any such. It is not used to define *chanda*, where in *later* books we do come across one really good equivalent of will, *kattu-kamyatā* desire to do.[5] And I am fain, after seven years, to record here my regret that I suffered Burmese Buddhist influence to cause the change in my revised translation of Dhammasangaṇi, from "thinking" to "volition".

It would indeed be truer to say that Sakyan, like other Indian teaching, in so far as it recognized what we call will in man at all, took it up into mind or cognition, than that it anywhere thought of mind as distinctly volitional. It must never be forgotten that it adopted the very significant view of mind as action, no less than deed and speech as action. But it limited this position to its teaching in what we may call world-worth, or rather inter-world-worth. Man's worth as a wayfarer through the worlds is determined by his actions, including therein his thoughts, his purposes. But when it is a question of his nature and his life on earth, and of the training and growth of him there, we hear very much less of mind-action. There and then it is only the *manas*, the *citta*, the *viññāṇa*, that is made to represent the inner self-expressing world of man, and when

[1] *Saṃyutta*, ii, 99. [2] *Ibid.*, 154. [3] *Ibid.*, 65.
[4] *Majjhima*, i, 242. [5] *Vibhanga*, 208.

these are defined they are invariably defined as the man contemplating, the man receiving impressions, never as the man radiating, the man efferent, the man reaching out after, the man becoming, willing. We are no better, after all, in our term "consciousness".

Is it not now seen to be a very possible thing that a man who had a mandate in the New, the unwonted, for the India of an early day, a mandate calling on man to arise and use by and for himself, not a new set of ideas about life, not a way in which to contemplate life, but a way in which he might will, might desire to walk in living, a way in which he had himself to decide as to the better, and not have it decided for him, a way which he had himself to "make become"—that such a man would have not a little difficulty in finding fit words?

Take such a man and place him in the time and world of Jesus. Jesus could stretch forth his hand and say "I WILL! be thou clean!" That other man's tongue would not suffer him to say this. He could only have said: "Be thou clean!" (*suddho*, or *arogī hohi*). The "I will" would have been left *implicit*, shown, not by word, but by the act of beneficent psychic power. He might, it is true, have put into words his "wish", his "desire", that the healing should come about. But the synergy in the "I will", the *savena*, the Aramaic equivalent of the late Greek *thelō*, would be lacking. We can see how the Jesus-word would be weakened by such a substitute. And the very message in the legend acclaiming his advent to earth is in terms which no Vedic or Prakrit message could have used: "and on earth peace among men of good will, or, in another version, good will towards men". Here the Greek equivalent of the original is weak, and Greek is almost in this matter as weak as Indian idiom; it is the Latin recensions which give the adequate word: *bonae voluntatis, benevolentis*. But neither here could Indian devas have sung a fit equivalent. When, as we shall see later, an Indian teacher taught a gospel of man willing good will to fellow-man, he had no fit word; he had to say (I quote the older wording) "make become a mind accompanied by amity".[1] Had Jesus so taught, he had the fit word. "The poor ye have with you always, and *when you will* (*ōtan thelete*[2]) you can do them good . . ." In the case of the Indian teacher, the will to be exerted by the benevolent willer had to be left as implicit. And no attempt is made to use any substitute of more dynamic, more kinetic force then "mind" (*citta*). There

[1] See below, Chapter XI. [2] Mark xiv, 7.

is no use even of a Prakrit equivalent for that *kinesis*,[1] which was all Plato had to work withal.

I hold that this was a real difficulty which that teacher and Gotama himself were up against. For that matter, for all that we have, in the word "will", a treasure, a vantage-point India had not, and for all the earthquake of Schopenhauer's hurling it into European philosophy, we do not yet appraise rightly what we have in it. Nor do we see in will but the way of *the man who wills*. It is almost forced to speak of the "willer" in English, as I have ventured to do, but when turning it into French there was literally nothing for it but *celui qui veut*. And is any European tongue as to this better off than the French? How do we not, as the French would say, *gaspiller*, trifle with, fritter away, our noble heritage, unworthy that we are! How will not the future wonder at us! India was not ready for such words. The world was not ready for such words. But we are scarcely yet ready for will and for willer. If we were, we should hold the one word in proper worth and "make-to-become" the other. But like the Indian, we merge will in the inevitably more static conception of mind. Unlike the Indian, and yet like the later Sakyan, like the Buddhist of South Asia, we merge also the willer in the mind. We aim at greater efficiency of body and mind, and we judge that therewith all has been said. At the most we profess, besides, an interest in what we are pleased to call "character", which is but the outcome to be looked for in our mental and bodily activity. We forget that character is but the "impress" that the willer will show in that activity. Him and that activity as fundamentally will: this we leave implicit. We do not see that the radical need, the test, the hall-mark and the end of growing efficiency is the willer growing in will.

Hence we have failed to see this feature of great moment in Buddhism: that whereas, in the teaching set on foot by Gotama and his men, we get a very gospel of will, and becoming in and through will—the evoking of will, the training and taming of will, self-salvation by will, good will—we get this without any explicit grasp of the fact, the nature, the importance of will, and without any distinctive word for it. Jesus, having the fit word, worked in a world which had come to feel and therefore to word itself in this. It was the easier for him to develop that awareness, and this he did, making his mandate appear as a very harmony between will in man and will of the Highest—that "kingdom of God" which is "within you". But for that older Indian world it was not so easy.

[1] I am much indebted to Miss M. H. Wood's fine study, *Plato's Psychology in its bearing on the development of Will* (1907).

I have often spoken of this curious and most interesting anomaly in Buddhism, in Sakya, early and late. It was the first vivid general impression I experienced from a study of psychological data in the Piṭakas,[1] a study suggested to me by Rhys Davids now nearly forty years ago. I found scriptures teaching religion very emphatically as a matter of training the will, when there was in them no word we could quite honestly translate as "will" (let alone willer). I referred, I remember, to Matthew Arnold's remark about the people of Soli uttering solecisms, and knowing no such term for them. There seemed to me a curious dumbness in wording the very key-note, around which those scriptures played so closely. There were terms in which will was implicit, but when these were defined, one of two things was evident. Either (*a*) the thing defined was to be stopped, put away, got rid of; or (*b*) it was the mode of it, not will itself, which was made explicit.

(*a*) Thus man's will to become was, in the four truths, given the bad name of *taṇhā*, and called, not the very basis and spring of man's advance—as it surely is—but the cause of ill and of that alone. Desire, too, *chanda*, was treated very stepmotherly, the getting rid of it was called the aim of the holy life, and only here and there was it admitted as possibly of an ideal kind (*dhamma-chanda*). *Kāma*, too, the very nature of man according to one Upanishad,[2] was utterly deprecated; *āsā*, longing, no less so; and the fine *kratu* was never used. *Sankappa* was only tolerated in an occasional half-hearted way, felt perhaps to be a weak word.

On the other hand, when (*b*) the mode and intensity of what *we* are able to call "man exerting will" was to be defined, the definition is generously carried out as to mode, as to intensity; but that the man exerting will in such ways is the one main point to keep in view is left out. Thus: "What is then the faculty of effort or energy or endeavour (*viriya*, *vāyāma*)? The inception (*ārambho*) of *viriya* (or *vāyāma*) which there then is, the striving and the onward effort, the exertion and endeavour, the zeal and ardour, the vigour and fortitude, the state of unfaltering effort, the state of sustained desire, the state of unflinching endurance and solid grip of the burden . . . this is the *viriya* that there then is."[3] This is quite a notable collection of terms to describe the ways in which the man puts forth will,

[1] *Bud. Psychology*, 1923; "Will in Early Buddhism," *JRAS*. Jan. 1898; "Will in Early Buddhist Scriptures, *I.H.R.*; "Man as Willer," *Bulletin, Sch. of Oriental Studies*, 1926; "Kindred Sayings on Buddhism," *Calcutta Review*, 1927–8, re-issued by the Calcutta University Press, 1930; *Gotama the Man*, 1928, etc.

[2] *Bṛhad. Up.*, iv, 4, 5.

[3] *Dhammasangaṇi*, §§ 13, 22, 26.

but the willer and will are out of the picture *save as implicit*. And what man values, what he comtemplates as object, he does not as a rule leave implicit. In conversation maybe he does, but not when he is teaching what he holds most worth while, in the way he holds most worth while. Now in the First Utterance the thing held most worth while has come down to us as implicit. And one of the reasons I am suggesting is that a gospel in the New, meaning what is there implied, had then and there no fit words.

Let me once more note other (implicit) will-points in the teaching. With the one exception of the perfected man, the arahan, it conceives the " man " in nature, in life, as no finished being, good or bad, but as capable of changing, nay, as inevitably in a process of changing. In ways of mind especially, the man is infinitely capable of being worked, of being made to become better or worse.[1] Man may ripen from life to life, or worsen; it is in his power (will) to do, to become either. Mind is conceived as action (the carrying out of will, *manokammaŋ*), no less than are speech and deeds action (*vacī, kāya*).[2] In moral weight, nay, in power over matter, his mind-action takes precedence over the deed that follows the mind's activity.[3] Desire[4] may dominate him for good or ill. The willed entry on the Way is a process of " desire, zeal, weighing, earnestness "[5]—all dynamic concepts. When in the Way he is fighting evil thoughts, he is putting forth " desire, effort, endeavour ".[6] There is " nothing like stirred up energy for making good to become, and for the waning of evil ".[7] Any psychic power he may develop is work of will, lit. effort (*padhāna*) with effecting (*iddhi*).[8] The training in will under the four heads called the Four Great Struggles or Assays (*samma-ppadhānāni*), namely, for the not arising of any bad states (*dhammā*), for the getting rid of risen bad states, for the arising of good states, and for their persistence, growth, further becoming—is reckoned-in among the last injunctions of the Founder.[9] To a young noble asking how long it would take to graduate in his teaching, Gotama is made to say that, as with the art of riding, it depended on five conditions, which are worded as so many factors in endeavour.[10] The 19th and 20th Suttas of the *Majjhima* are interesting discourses on thinking as " willing ", the former of the two being of great interest as depicting the maturing of the Way-gospel in the preceding meditations of Gotama—a Sutta which, unless it be pure invention, must be based on memories of

[1] *Anguttara*, i, 5. [2] *Ibid.*, iii, 4, 15, etc. [3] *Majjhima*, , 373 f.
[4] *Chanda*. [5] *Majjhima*, i, 480. [6] *Ibid.*, i, 119; ii, 11.
[7] *Ibid.*, i, 480. [8] See below, Ch. XII. [9] *Dīgha*, ii, 120.
[10] *Majjhima*, No. 65.

what he will himself have told. And there is a graphic formula, occurring more than once and specially associated with him, which runs: "Verily may skin, nerves, bones, flesh and blood dry up and wither, or ever I stay my energy (*viriya*), so long as I have not attained whatsoever by human endurance, energy and effort (*thāma*, *viriya*, *parakkama*) is attainable."[1] Lastly a word, attributed to Sāriputta, shows us yet another aspect of will worded in a way which conceivably might have served for "will": the word *vasī*. The man is commended whose mind is under his own will (*vasippatta*).[2]

Finally, three chief points in the teaching can only be understood of will and a willer: (1) man is the heir of deeds he has done and willed to do; (2) man as wayfarer of the worlds goes as he wishes, according to those deeds; (3) man is in a becoming (*bhava*), and "makes to become" what he was not before: a process of will.

It is conceivable that, with such a teaching reverberating through the scriptures as it does, the Sakyans, in spite of the monastic damning of the very spring in man's nature whence his "effort" came, might have grasped the fact of that spring, and found a name for it—as we do when we grasp facts in which we are really interested—had they not, in theory—they did not do so in practice—eliminated the willer in eliminating the very man. They anticipated our own psychological limitations in this, without, however, for all that, getting beyond the first steps in psychological analysis. The call upon man's will to save himself, coupled with the faith in the capacity of that self to be trained, might, with a sound conviction as to the self, have taken them far.

And yet perhaps hardly so. There was always dominating Indian thought (and Greek thought too) the old-world conception of man the spectator, man the recipient. For this conception of himself those lands had found names in plenty. Man was the beholder, the appraiser, the contemplator. He was "speaker, seer, hearer, smeller, taster, feeler", and he touched. In all of these phases forthputting of will was essential, but in the messages received in them he overlooked what he gave out to get them. He also did, acted, worked (using one word where we have three). But he could do so little to make or mar his world, that he found that little not so much worth wording as what he took in as spectator. Mainly he let, or had to let his world come to him, and like Adam he named what he saw so come. He did now and then go to find his new world, when perhaps hunger drave. That, by sea or by land, was a tremendous business; all his world had to come along. And

[1] *Ibid.*, i, 480 (cf. *Jātaka*, i, 71). [2] *Ibid.*, No. 32; cf. *Saṃyutta*, v. 71.

it may be that for some sections of him thus wandering, overcoming many and great difficulties, he found, in the adventure for the "making-to-become" a new world, the pregnant word "will", *uelle*, *uolo*, *wollen*, *well*, *weal*, *wealth*. For other sections this result did not follow. Little could man do, as worker, as willer, in proportion to the wealth of the messages that sense, especially sight, brought to him as recipient, as beholder. Hence he went on speaking of himself in names of receiving and beholding. He *stood amongst* things: "understanding," "intelligent." He *accepted*: perceiving, conceiving, apprehending. He *watched*: contemplating, meditating. *He measured*: minding, weighing, comparing, reasoning. He *moved*, but not much. He *chose*, but the world of things choosable was very little.

The Greek set out betimes to learn more of this world and life that were so interesting. Death was to him not interesting; it was as the blind spot in his vision. The seen man, the seen world, the nature of these was his study, the form of man his will's delight. His self-expression was individualistic. He founded modern science; he opened the way to our realizing to-day, through science, that in us which is the spiritual analogue of world-movement: radiant will. But he saw man as intelligent rather than as willing. He did not, in his very little world, *will together*. There was a noble exception to this, one brief day, when Persian conquest threatened, but it passed unrepeated, not followed up.

The Sakya started with a far wider, far longer conception of life than the narrower vision of the Greek. Death was no blind spot for him. The noble figure of the Way was a way of all the worlds: the Pārāyana, the Going-beyond, with his fellowmen dwelling in and awaiting him in each and any of them. But there was rising about him a vogue, on the one hand, of a way of life, on the other hand, of a mode of analytic thought, which half paralyzed before long the means of developing the pregnant strength of the fine will-data in his gospel. The latter influence paralyzed the grasp of the Way as will, by banishing the reality of the Wayfarer. The former influence paralyzed man's concerted efforts to will his welfare, by removing him from the world, that great laboratory of experiment in goodwill to men.

And so, for all its earnest teaching on Way and Act, on energy and becoming, Buddhism found no words worthy to name that which is the very spring and fount to make that teaching fruitful: the will of the willer seeking welfare, seeking the goal of the supremely well. Isolated from exercising that will among his fellows in all human relations, the Buddhist scripture-compiler fell back again and again on negative words—on *nibbāna*, *nirodha*, *virāga*, *nibbidā*, *alobha*, and the like—and on ambiguous words and worsened words.

Whereas in Sakya we find a movement bringing to man's use a new attitude on life *as itself a religion*, a new earnestness as to conduct and the future as involved in conduct, on the possible potency in what we now call, or should call, will, we find that this teaching, when formulated, could not see just so much ahead of the old world as either to grasp a unifying principle of will, or of man as willer, and therein find a word for the same.

I may be reminded by readers without first-hand knowledge of the Pali records that they not infrequently meet in translations with the word will, with volition, with will-power and the like. I may again be rallied by translators themselves, that I am captious merely, and that there are here and there passages where the use of will is fully justified.

To both readers and translators I would say : then has once more the *tradduttore* proved himself or herself *traditore*. In will, they have used a word transcending in force and depth anything in the Vedic or Pali original. But it was convenient to do so, and so they (I too once) have read the West into the East, the newer into the older. Nor is there agreement among translators of the same material, when some see fit to use " will ", neither with each other, nor always each with himself. Thus Deussen, when in one passage he translates *manas*, suggests *Wille* as an alternative to *Verstand* ! And I borrow the following table from my article " Man as Willer ",[1] which shows anything but agreement in the rendering of the word *saṃkalpa* (purpose, intent) :—

	Saṃkalpa	Max Müller	Deussen	Tatya, Cowell, & Röer	Hume
1.	Ait. Up. 5, 2	conceiving	Vorstellung	determination	conception
2.	Kau. Up. 3, 2	conception	Erkenntniss	resolve	„
3.	Kena Up. 30	imagination	vorstellen	ascertained	„
4.	Chhā Up. vii, 4, 1	will	Entschluss	will	„
5.	„ viii, 2, 1	will	Wunsch	wishes	„
6.	Bṛh. Up. i, 5, 3	repre-sentation	Entscheidung	determination	imagination
7.	„ ii, 4, 11	percepts	Strebungen	„	intentions
8.	Śvet. Up. 5, 8	thoughts	Vorstellung	„	conception
9.	Katha Up. i, 10 (*santaś-*)	pacified	beruhigten Gemüths	appeased in thought	intent appeased

[1] *Bulletin of the School of Oriental Studies*, London, 1926.

Clearly here the word *saṃkalpa* gives out no definite unambiguous meaning. It is a weak makeshift of a culture which, in respect of something in man's inner world, had not grasped the work of values with true insight, had not lit upon the fit word for that something. We are in no better plight ourselves in other values. We have only to look at our makeshift terms in a matter which the relatively new interest in history evidentially considered has brought into our foremost values—the terms for the happening of something which shows a convergence-point in causes; such terms as the borrowed "conjuncture",[1] the borrowed and distorted "psychological moment", i.e. factor, or momentum; resultant. We have not yet here the right, the fit word.

Yet *sankappa* was the best word which Sakya found to hand, with which to treat of will much as now we treat of it in our manuals. These, when dealing with the radical factor in man of "reaching out after", do not (since Alexander Bain wrote) use will. They speak of conation, of other newer alien terms, *hormè* and the like. In such contexts the Sakyan term is effort—"*viriya*," "*vāyāma*," usually. But when the context requires a term for what my teacher would have called "intellection with a co-efficient of conation and feeling", for what another teacher called "synergy", a term for the thoughtful man facing the need of action, then there is a use of *sankappa*. At least so it would seem to have been in the Upanishads, all old ones, quoted. But as a fact very little use, very little distinctive use of *sankappa* is made in the Pali records. The word is nearly always used as a variant of other general terms for "thought"—*vitakka*, *saññā*.[2] The only distinctive use I find is of volitional import: "his *sankappa's*"[3] are fulfilled; something he has wanted is satisfied. And the devoted aged disciple Pingiya is in the Pārāyana made to say: "Ever I follow him with a going by *sankappa*. So is my mind bound up with him."[4]

It is not till the day of "abhidhamma" development that *sankappa* acquires a distinctive definition as fixing, or (*we* might say) focussing of the mind, lifting it on to"; and even here it is given first the emphatically cognitive equivalents of *takka*, *vitakka*. We know too that "right *sankappa*" is the second *anga* or factor in the scholastic division of the Way (of the good mind, word and deed) into eight such. Also that there it precedes the factor of "effort", in which the attempt to give the more fundamental aspect

[1] German (also borrowed) *Konjunktur*.
[2] E.g. *Dīgha*, iii; *Saŋyutta*, ii, etc.
[3] *Majjhima*, i, 192, 200; iii, 276 f.
[4] Sutta-Nipāta, ver. 1144.

of will had to be expressed. We know finally that, stripped of that effort at cataloguing, the Way, as set forth in the surviving fraction of the ancient schema, as a new aspect of life, makes no reference either to *sankappa*, or to *viriya* (or *vāyāma*).

But then there was only one will-term which was actually needed in the schema. This was "choosing". The only word recorded is "not to be followed (*a-sevitabba*)". For the "will", the "choice", which resulted in a man following this or that turn in the way of life, I feel little doubt but that the fit word was not there. "Effort" was not adequate, for choosing is not distinctively effort as such. *Sankappa* was inadequate; perhaps it was no "mantra"-word, but a little too "learned". Will, choosing were left implicit.

That both the makeshift terms found much later very honourable inclusion in the Way made "eightfold" shows the tradition surviving of just that call on the individual will, as at once effort and purposive thinking, which was really implicit in the Sakyan mandate, and which was for the first teachers the point to make very explicit in Way-mission-work, so far as the words at their command suffered them to do so.

One of our eminent psychologists wrote, that in psychology words are things.[1] In a way this is true; in a way it is not true. They are the only visible results of our observation of man's inner immaterial world, and a jealous care in the seen use or misuse of them may seem mere captiousness to those who may not have undergone training in the ways of that world. On the other hand, so far are even psychological terms, for me, "things", as we usually reckon things, that I should gladly have hailed the *thing* I call "will" in any Pali *word*, could it have been shown as meaning what I hold is in man so vitally important. For me will is man's reaching out after, with or without awareness of, a better than he is or has. The learned have called it "conation", a worthy but weak Latin alien, without a verb to it—it of all things to have no verb! We need to make will our fundamental, as it is our crowning term for inner immaterial things. In religion it is the base; of salvation it is the supreme guarantee, and heaven is will made perfect.

Now in one Saying imputed to the aged veteran Ānanda, there is a notable approach to *chanda* as equating will. And yet it is exactly wherein *chanda* falls short of will thus adequately conceived, that we see how it actually amounts to no more than our "wish".

A Brahman[2] asks Ānanda what is the object of the God-life lived in his Gotama-Order? "It is for the getting rid of *chanda*."

[1] James Ward, *Principles of Psychology*. [2] *Saŋyutta*, v. 272.

"That would surely be an unendingly impossible." "Well, had you not *chanda* when you sought me to-day and when you found me was not that (specific) *chanda* (wish) abated?" "It was." "Even so, in the monk who, as become arahan, has lived the life, done what was to do, laid down the burden, outworn the fetters of rebirth, is released by perfect insight, that *chanda* which he had, to win where he has won, is it not abated? If so, then is there possibility, then is there an end."

Here we have *chanda* meaning in the Brahman just a wish, a want, a desire of a worthy kind, terminable when satisfied. But in the man aiming at the Best as the Sakyan *had come* to conceive it—too limited a best for any world-religion—it meant the persistent will-to-the-Better, not satisfied till the man consummate was achieved. Nor, as will, ending then! And had it been consistently so used in the Piṭakas, I should have ranked *chanda* as, for the Buddhist at least, a worthy word for will.

This episode shows, in a very crucial way, the utterly unworthy conception of will which passed for such in the Sangha, when this possibly very posthumous Sutta was compiled as it stands. For look! will is only used to name something which it is the object of the God-life to get rid of! And this miserable negative aspiration is put into the mouth of the companion of the world-helper, who came to reveal a More in the life and power of the man to bring about: even the choosing by the man himself of the way, wherein wayfaring he would become the Most. But *could* the Most be That, the achieving of which involved the getting rid of that *whereby he had attained* to the More, to the yet More? Would not the Most prove to be a very perfecting of the will which had been the willer's *way of becoming fully That*? Could it be rightly conceived as the Ending of that will?

Verily is the Sakyan world shown herein to have been not ready to word will and willer! Nor, in spite of the way in which Jesus opened up these words, shall *we* be shown ready, unless and until we see the man as the willer who, in willing, is becoming, is coming to be.

VI

THE WAY AND BECOMING

I have now tried to show in some detail that which appears to me as two main implications, implicit, unworded in the First Utterance; two meanings which are necessary if we are to see in it the genuine worthy "message" of a world-religion. The one is, that it is through his will, to which the call makes appeal, that the man must choose the way for himself, of himself. The other is, that the man, the self, who wills, who chooses is not just the man as here and now understood, or as he came to be understood in "Buddhism", but the man as understood in that day, in that land: the man as at once human and divine; the man as human self and as immanently God-self; the man as Dhamma-bidden. I now wish to develop further all that I see implied in this figure of the Way. It is a figure not peculiar to Sakya alone. Its prominence in Taoism—"the Way of heaven"—may possibly have opened a "way" of least resistance for the propagation of Sakya among Chinese hearers. We are familiar with the "Way" in teachings ascribed to Jesus. And I have shown that, in the day of Sakyan origins, it had found or was finding place in newer Brahman teaching. But in no religion does it occupy the centre, as a figure for the centre, as it did in what I hold was the original Sakya.

What was that centre of which the Way was to serve as figure?

I believe it was a deeper meaning which was revealed to the Teacher and his men as they taught. At first we have the Way symbolizing man's life in the worlds towards the uttermost goal as a becoming better, more, further, as he willed, as he heeded the inner bidding. But there was more in it than this. It was, that *the man*, the very man, not body and mind only, the man-in-man, as wayfarer in the Way of the More, is by his very nature *becoming more.* He was not static "being" only; he was "becoming", evolving into That who in germ he as man ever was.

I do not for a moment anticipate that to make readers here see eye to eye with me is an easy task. With most I may fail. But that does not make it less worth while to try. No writer on Buddhism known to me puts becoming, *werden*, *devenir*, to the front, either in treatment, or in allusion, save now and then to "growth" in a general way. And if I suggest, that the Sakya-muni himself came to realize, as he taught, meeting all sorts of inquiries, how great, how pregnant a figure there had come to him, before he began, in that symbol of travel-adventure, I shall be met by the Buddhist with the bar of orthodox creed: "He became first supremely enlightened; he knew everything; for him there was no more 'becoming'." But this does not bar me. If he could see with me in becoming, a fitter attribute of Deity than in being, he might transcend the heavy mortmain of both Buddhism and of Indian thought.

I would say this, before trying to see this expanding significance in the Way of Gotama. Sakya, in its later Pali dress and its Ceylon change of sky, underwent loss of features which in India lingered on. In the Milinda Questions, for example, we find the question of man's past and present activities treated in connection with both duration and becoming, as we nowhere find is the case in the Piṭakas.[1] That is, we have conversations taking place in the Panjab in Prakrit, in which the factor of "becoming" is dealt with as it is not in similar contexts in the Ceylonized Piṭakas in Pali. Again, we find Indian philosophy referring to the Saugatas (followers of the "Well-farer") and Bauddhas, as insisting on the reality of becoming (as virtually against the fact of previous "being").[2] This probably indicated a surviving emphasis, which in Ceylon has been lost to view.

This, then, I would say at the outset: We must not lose sight of the necessity, in our research, of holding before us (*a*) a vanishing Sakya in India, and (*b*) a growing, much modified, very monastic "Buddhism" in Ceylon (both of these during the same period). There is thus the likelihood that in (*a*) we may have the main theme of the original Sakya yet visible, and more so than in (*b*).

This one thing more I would also say, harping on it, it may be, for there can be no understanding of Sakya if it be lost to view: Let the Western reader shed his traditional view of the very man, soul, spirit, self, and don that of India. In that, the man is never the "mere" man, adopted in redemption, in mercy, in grace by Deity Who he himself is not. In that the man is "He", in his very nature; he has but to will to make It become within him. As he becomes "more", there is waking in him the Highest, who he is in germ.

But for India of Sakya's day, this awakening was a coming to

[1] Cf. my *Milinda Questions*, 1930, p. 80 f.

[2] *Sarva-darśana-saṃgraha*, ed. Cowell and Gough, p. 224; *Sāṅkhya-Kārikā*, Commentary on Sūtra, ix.

know, a realizing *in idea*. And hence for the Many it had no grip on the life. For the Sakyamuni it was no mental concept of being such and such ; it was an unfolding of the very man, a coming to be. But for the Indian, becoming was of the perishable ; only Being was divine. And so over this point, Sakya which sought to fulfil, was thwarted, and eventually declined on a lesser ideal. Now "becoming" (*bhava*, *bhavya*), as noun or as verb, is not in the First Utterance, the Way-mantra. Does this rule out that for which I am here contending? I think not ; but the reader must dig with me.

He will, if he do so, notice that in a group of Suttas, to wit Section 5 of the Collection on Origin (Nidāna) of the Saŋyutta-Nikāya, the identical words are used in which the Way, in the First Utterance, is led up to : "The man-so-gone, not having gone after either of these extremes, has understood"—here the verb is "teaches you *dhamma* (thus). . . ."

There then follows a formula which, on the face of it, gives no rational solution. Had the solution been stated as "The man-so-gone is becoming", or as we should now say, is in process of becoming, the reply would be rational. I give here the least unknown of these Suttas (No. 48) : that called Lokâyatika, the Natural Philosopher, for the ancient world-lore of the day, existing doubtless from pre-historic time, and "becoming" doubtless in its own way, was termed Lokâyata.

A Brahman lokâyatika puts to Gotama the queries, whether he thinks that (*a*) everything is, (*b*) that nothing is, (*c*) that everything is a unity, (*d*) that everything is a plurality. The reply is so far significant, that it advocates a "middle (way)". It then breaks down into mere formula. The formula is the conditioned arising of "ill" (*dukkha*).[1]

The fairly clear inference is, that the man neither is (*sat*), nor is not, but is becoming (*bhava*, *bhavya*). But since this word stood also for rebirth, which the monk had vetoed, the formula of applied causation is substituted, showing *bhava* as a mere factor in ill. The man, *Gotama* will have answered, is "he who becomes".

In the other Suttas of the bunch, the "two extremes" propounded by inquirers are, "Is the doer and the experiencer of the deed's results the same, or different?" Again, in Section 1 are similar Suttas, with the problems of the section cited first, somewhat differently worded, but of identical import. Always, *yet only here*, we have the words of the First Utterance introducing the solution,

[1] Known as Paṭicca-samuppāda, or causal genesis.

with the exception I have given, and further, the term Middle does service for Mid-Way, or Course. And here again we have the one rational reply absent: Man is not being, nor not being; he is becoming. Man, the doer, in becoming, becomes the experiencer. And everywhere the formula describing the serial causes of Ill is the reply.

Eight years ago I suggested, in this connection, that the live word of the Sakya-muni had here fallen out.[1] I went no further than to suggest: the reply might have been in terms of his general statement of causation: Given this, that comes to be, etc. I knew then as much and as little of Hegel as I do now. I knew that for him "the new and higher concept of Werden (devenir, becoming) reconciled the opposites of being and not-being". And had Hegel been more human with his pen, had he not been submerged in the stupid flood of "words, words, words" imposed by his time and country on a thinker's expression, he might have made the world of plain men wiser, and I might have been met here by helpful suggestions. However that be, since the translation I cite from appeared, no word of comment from Buddhist or non-Buddhist has reached me, and I must here and now be my own commentator.

Thus: It seems to me of the very highest significance that we have here (1) a hiatus (misfilled by a formula of later origin; monastic; not fit for a world religion), where the rational reply would be: Man neither is, nor is not; he is becoming. Again, the man who did and the man who experiences the consequences is not an unchangingly identical person, but is the doer who has become and is becoming when experiencing the consequences. And (2) that this hiatus has been led up to by the wording which is only to be found, elsewhere, in the first Mantra of holy repute: the Mantra of the Way. The man to whom such a conjuncture tells nothing must be somewhat deaf. I was deaf, but now I hear.

As to the alleged reply, apparently so formal and here so unintelligent, it will seem to the reader, who has not gone carefully into the whole problem of editing in the Piṭakas (editing both oral and then written), an arbitrary thing to see here a deliberate insertion of a formula, even if it gives no solution to the nature either of man, or of things in general, but only states a process in the happening of Ill. If he will read this book to the end, he may in part at least absolve me. Let him here consider, *why that formula* was inserted. Inserted, I add, very possibly not at some important revision, but previously here and there by teachers, and only selected and

[1] *The Book of the Kindred Sayings*, 1922, Introduction, p. viii.

confirmed by revisers in council, from possibly various repeated versions.

That formula, called the Paṭicca-samuppāda, and beginning "Conditioned by ignorance (arise) activities", or sometimes "Conditioned by name-and-form (arises) mind" . . . is (*a*) concerned with a certain coming-to-be), (*b*) contains the word "becoming" (*bhava*). This is redundant, coming between the "substrate of birth" or "grasping, attachment (*upādāna*)" and birth; and has puzzled writers. Now *bhava*, by itself, meant for the monk rebirth; not an opportunity for becoming better, but rather an occasion for further ill. But as used in a sanctioned formula, *bhava* was correct and in place.

Before the critic puts this judgment aside, let him dispassionately consider the Suttas I have quoted, and ask himself if a wise and enlightened man of old India, or of anywhere would conceivably have replied to such deep-going questions in terms of a set wording, in which the queries were not candidly and directly met, and yet where the reaction on the inquirer would be of the enthusiastic nature recorded (though even this is in terms of formula). Let him imagine the very-live man Gotama answering in live terms: that the Way he taught was that of Everyman, not body, not mind—the very man-in-man—being he who, as having in him the germ of the Highest, Best, Most, was no mere "being" eternally the same, yet, as real, was in no way a not-being, but was a Becoming more, and yet more, as he wayfared toward perfecting, in himself, the Self, the very Most. Then verily, especially in India of that day, yea, everywhere it becomes conceivable, that the live Message would evoke the live, the grateful response.

More hereon when we deal with the subject of Cause. But this negative evidence is not all our digging brings up. There emerges the development of the discredited *bhava* into its causative form: *bhāva-*. *Bhava*, becoming, is as strong, as important a word in Indian word-treasure as it is in that of the Teuton: *Werden*. Its English weakening, in the ambiguous "becoming", hampers the translator at every turn. Unworthy we to have dropped our own strong *weorthan*, *wairthan*! *Bhava* is of the ancient Aryan tongue. *Bhāvanā*, the causative "making to become", is of a much later growth. No Vedic book appears to use it; the epic Mahābhārata (a work of many dates) appears to use it but once. If we accept the Piṭakas as evidence of any worth whatever for words of Gotama's date, the word was there for the using, and that in such venerable poems as the Sutta Nipāta. We find it in the Four Nikāyas, or books of Sayings, doing service for meanings where the word "will" is wanted. It is for instance contrasted with phrases for purely thought-procedure: "What is to be put away by vision" with "what is to be put away by *making-to-become*"[1]; "what is to be *made to become*"[2] with "what is to be well known"; "what is to be *brought to pass*"[3] with computation;" the Way as "made to become",[4] as other than "understanding, realizing, etc." In each case *bhāvanā* is the contrasting "dynamic" complement. It is not an unwarranted step to suggest that the early influence of Sakya, and of Jain too—the Jain books have *bhāvanā*—promoted the use of this word in Indian culture, a use in which it is just possible—I go no further—that early Yoga teaching pioneered. For Yoga needed the word for its characteristic rite or attitude, just as Sakya needed it for Jhāna—and used it.[5]

But the strong distinctive meaning of the word *bhāvanā*, albeit worthily treated in the classic Sanskrit Dictionary, and clearly defined in the newer Pali Dictionary, is *not as a rule rightly rendered* by Sanskrit or Pali translators. Their favourite renderings are "meditation", "reflection", "pondering"; for these the texts have plenty of fit terms in the proper place. "Cultivation" is sometimes given a turn, and this is much better, for cultivation without an implicit resultant "coming to be" is as nought. Now in the Buddhist Commentarial tradition there was no question that *bhāvanā* meant this, rather than meditation. Buddhaghosa thus defines it: "*Bhāveti* means beget, causes to arise, causes to grow; that is what it means here (in Jhāna). Elsewhere the meaning is modified by prefixes."[6] Yet so little, for all this clear description, do the scriptures themselves bring to the front the vital connection between *magga*: the figure of man the wayfarer—and *bhava*, *bhavanīya*:—the man as growing, as becoming, as bound to become—that it was no more evident to me, or even suspected by me than it is yet for either Buddhist, or writer on Buddhism.

Then, nearly a generation ago, I had to find a good translation for the phrase: *Yasmiŋ samaye rūpûpapattiyā maggaŋ bhāveti*: "at the time when he makes to become a way of access to (the world of) the Seen"[7] . . . and it was then that the seed—not more—of the term's full significance was sown. A decade perhaps passed—and then Sāriputta came to help foster the seedling. He is called

[1] *Bhāvanāya*. [2] *Bhāvitabba*. [3] *Bhāvanā*.
[4] *Bhāvito*. [5] See below, Chap. IX on "Musing."
[6] *Expositor* (on *Dhammasangaṇi*, p. 217, on § 160.
[7] I.e. Brahmaworld, *Dhammasangaṇi*, *ib*.

in one Sutta the parent, the mother (*janetti*); for me he took over the office there assigned to Moggallāna: he was the *jātassa uppādetar*: rearer of what is born.[1] It was in a possibly very old Sutta: the Greater Miscellany, where two leading disciples are (according to the Commentary) coaching each other in playing the pupil and teacher. "Is there any difference between *viññāṇa* (mind, or cognizing) and *paññā* (the divine mind in the 'man')?" "Yes, this:" is Sāriputta's reply, "*paññā* is to be made to become; *viññāṇa* is to be thoroughly known: that is all the difference." And I saw another saying of Buddhaghosa's on *paññā*: *paññā* having striven wins manifestation of the Way."[2] I was then compiling a Buddhist psychology, and the placing of *paññā* in the ragged garden of the four *skandhas* (i.e. mind) was an old difficulty. That *paññā* stood in the old Upanishads for immanent Deity: that I knew and I said so.[3] That *paññā* had this force also for Sāriputta's world (though no longer for that of Buddhaghosa) I did not then allow for. That *paññā* was the "man", willing the new, the not yet become, the good, the better, the Best, the man making himself come to be what he was not before; well, I was not so grown up as to see that. None the less those two notable personages had shown me a truer thing than our own psychology books do: that to come to know is an active process of making to become. There can be no true study in the way of the spirit where this is not kept well in front.

For want possibly of a better opportunity I halt yet a moment longer over the word *paññā*, taken in a context of solemn emphasis in which it very often occurs. The context is "known, or considered, or seen) as it really has come to be, by right *paññā—yathābhūtaŋ sammappaññāya*, with now this or that verb of the meaning given above. I have traced this phrase in upwards of 224 contexts in the Four Nikāyas, in ascending frequency from the First to the Fourth. It is not a phrase easily to be rendered in such few Western tongues as I know. The German *der Wahrheit gemäss* of Neumann is tidier than my rendering, and for *yathābhūtaŋ* it is to be conceded that possibly *bhūtaŋ*: "become" had come to mean just "fact". On the other hand, we have to note this: there were other words to hand: *saccato*, *ṭhetato*, etc., which might have served the speaker's purpose, but in these there was not, nor is in the German idiom, any hint of "becoming". Next, the word *yathābhūtaŋ* never

[1] *Majjhima-Nikāya*, iii, 248.

[2] *Visuddhi-Magga*, chap. xiv, p. 437 (or, risen up: *ussuk-* or *ussak-*).

[3] "Paññā and the Khandha Doctrine," Congress of History of Religion, Oxford, 1910.

appears to occur in early Vedic literature. I have seen one reference only to a line in the Mahābhārata,[1] a work of various dates. And the Vedic Concordance gives me one reference only, to the Atharva-Veda, a work long posterior to both early Sakya and also to the Nikāyas, where never more than Three Vedas are mentioned. But the passage in the Atharva-Veda shows the word as meaning not "really", or "truly", but "as become": "As that which is become and as that which is to become, do thou fear not." (*yathā-bhūtam ca yathā-bhavyam ca.*) Lastly, whereas the Jains may also have developed the use of the word in asseverating, as the Sakyans certainly did, I have not found them using it in contexts where the Sakyan usage leads us to expect it, e.g. . . . he knows! he sees! But here I speak with reserve, having access to but very few of the Jain Angas.

As to Pali contexts I speak naturally with a little more confidence, and although the views, put forward some eighteen years ago in my little *Buddhism*, I have in many respects outgrown and put aside, I would still endorse what I there wrote on this term *yathābhūtaŋ*. Utterly rejecting the virtual support there given to the scholastic denial of the self as fundamental in Sakya, I would repeat with more confidence what I there put forward tentatively[2]: that *yatha-bhūtaŋ*, for early Sakya, did not mean in a merely idiomatic way "according to truth" or "to fact", but that it was closely bound up with the teaching of becoming as more true than being. Listen!

"See you, Sāriputta, that this has become (*bhūtam-idan-ti passasi*)? See you, Sāriputta, that this has become? Yes, sir, one sees it by right *prajña* as become (*yathā bhūtaŋ*)."

The association is repeated in another context.[3]

Here we have something tangible to rest upon. This is, that in *yathābhūtaŋ* we have a word laid hold of and developed by Sakya, at some not very late period, as expressing something they were out to stress very strongly, in a way which had not been done before. And further, that the *bhūta* in this word had probably not become as meaningless to them as is, say, the "doing" in the word "fact" to us. So far may the word have been from a mere expletive of "truly", that as late as the Atharva-Veda we see the force in the "*-bhūta* . . . *-bhavya*" as very significant.

Now let us apply this significance to the word *paññā*. As to

[1] See Böhtl. and Roth, *s.v.* (?).

[2] P. 224 ff. Cf. above with Katha Up. 2. 14.

[3] *Saṃyutta*, ii, 48, and *Majjhima*, i, 260 The contexts are too much worsened by monastic editing to be worth quoting at greater length.

paññā, I am not saying that even in Sakya's earliest days, it may not have had a varying meaning, much as has for instance the French *esprit*. And I certainly think that the word underwent a worsening down the centuries, and was, long after Buddhaghosa's time, practically ejected from religious manuals, like the standard Abhidhammattha-sangaha, *vipassanā*, i.e. insight, having replaced it. But when Sakya began, *paññā* was capable of bearing the high import to which I have tried to do justice.

We cannot equate it by our own psychical terms, because we have never frankly recognized, in our man-nature, that fundamental divinity which the Indian did recognize. Thus it is wide of the mark to render *paññā* by intellectual terms when we are on religious ground. We can do that when we are on secular, or worldly ground. We can then see in our mind, that is, in our "mindings", our ways of meeting outward circumstances, foreseeing, handling, reflecting upon them. And we know very well, that like the body, the mind is a very limited instrument, train we it never so well, and that we are limited by it from effecting all that we would, even while by it we effect what we can.

Now as the mind (that is *citta-mano-viññāṇa*) is to the man when he confronts his worldly business, so was *paññā* to the man when viewed as being one with the Highest. It was the Divine Way of him at work. And the early Sakyan—so far as we can trust the many repetitions to be giving us a true record—called this the *paññā* of his highest values: the "right wisdom", *sammā paññā*. It was the working of the Very Self in man. But he was persuading men to listen to a new conception of that Self, namely, that It was not being so much as becoming. In proportion as a man realized the need of "making-to-become" in him this holiest manhood, "so far was become" (*yathā-bhūtam*) in him by divine growth a More, ultimately to become Most, Perfect, Highest.

There need be no implication here that to have become That, was to revert to a Being, a ceasing from Becoming. Rather should That be conceived as perfection attained as and in becoming.

India, neither then nor since, has been able to grasp this. Still is Deity, for her, *sat*, *cit*, *ānanda*: being, thought, bliss. And the high value of becoming, in Sakya, sank away. We have indeed nothing beyond a few remains in word and phrase, and in the jibe of later Indian writers, to betray her early effort to transform that barrier to Becoming which was Being. India, between philosopher and monk, threw away the given opportunity, which I hold that

Gotama tried to expand. And the Sakyan monks transferred the "making-to-become", the while it banished the becoming (*bhava*) as evil, to the mind, instead of the self.

We are to-day getting ready to see, indeed we are backward if we do not see, more in the meaning of *bhāvanā* than did any Indian cult of the past, whether it was Buddhist or another. The Sakyan saw a little more in it than did any other. He will have forgotten, or dropped out in his records—for reasons I shall show—many sayings of the founders, in which they will have shown the close bond between the Way and Becoming, between man the wayfarer and man as grower, as progressive, as coming to be, as "making to arise" (*uppādeti*). These things will happen—do we not see it has happened elsewhere?—when the followers have not been big enough to rise to the level of the Messenger of their gospel and of his true helpers? But the tradition of the early teaching flickered on in the life of the Order, and here and there we come, shifting the metaphor, to an outcrop of it. Very slight they are, yet they need to be accounted for.

To the allusions given above I will quote a reply ascribed to Visākhā, charming lady and distinguished, wealthy lay-disciple, well known to the Founder. The reply bears traces of scholastic editing; but her use of *bhāvanā* is where those traces are not. It is in the Vinaya,[1] and the translation (Rhys Davids's contributions) is not very apt, albeit there are thoughtful footnotes. Visākhā is pleading the benefit she will herself reap, if she is permitted to extend her generosity to the Order. She speaks of the joy, content and peace she will feel (so much has been put into a Piṭaka formula); she goes on: "and that will be to me a becoming (or causing to become) in moral sense, in moral strength, in wisdom." (The last three phrases are in ecclesiastical terms.) Now "becoming" has been translated "an exercise"; but Visākhā is clearly speaking of effect, of fruit, of the *result* of exercise. No one of the laity made better response to the teaching than she, and it is for me possible, that she was reacting to the stress Gotama will have laid on the very man, the self (not mind or body) as he who becomes. She says: "There will be *in* (or 'of') *me* a becoming."

Once more: very noteworthy is in the Pali books the choice, and the persisting choice of the verb *bhāveti*, when a word is needed to express, as express we alas! cannot, such an effort of will as Maudsley called synergy, and I have once or twice ventured to call "more-will". (I do not like such hybrids as plus-will, hyper-will.)

[1] *Mahāvagga*, viii, 15.

In other words, when the man who is seeking to exercise will in a new, or an unwanted, or an abnormal way, the word *bhāveti*, "he makes to become," is used.

In the exercise of "musing" (Jhāna) it was access, in this earthlife the Sakyan strove to "make-become", to the next or other worlds. *Bhāveti* invariably goes with "musing". And in the development of "psychic sense" called Iddhipāda, he was "making to become", strenuous and ardent, those other-sense reactions of which he happened to have found himself capable: the "deva-sight", or the "deva-hearing", or levitation, or thought-reading, or the like. Once more we find, in the Sutta-Nipāta, the man who, while "bearing his human burden" is out for fruition, "making-to-become that joy-bringing occasion" (ver. 256); and further, that the willed state in another, called "the Mood of Amity" (with which I have to deal in a separate chapter) is worded as the "making mind to become" (*cittaṃ bhāvayaŋ*, ver. 507).

In such expressions the use of the strong causative verb, by those lucky enough to have it to hand, is in no way forced. But we also meet with the verb in conjunction with the idea of road or way, used, not so much as "means" only, but as a parable of life wayfared toward its goal. Here the less forced verb would have been "proceeding" (*paṭipanna*), as we find it in records of tours in mission-work,[1] also used here and there as a figure.[2] Actually however we find here too, and emphatically the word "make-to-become" used, when the Way or the First Utterance is the subject. Thus in the solemn mantra of the four truths, appended to the First Utterance, the Founder is made to say: "The first truth 'ill', as a matter to be understood, I have understood; the second truth, as 'origin (of ill)', as a matter to be got rid of, I have got rid of; the third truth 'stopping (of ill)', as a matter to be realized, I have realized; the fourth truth, 'Way' *as a matter to make-to-become*, I have made to become." The forced use here of *bhāveti* may be seen in the translation (*SBE.*), where "realize", the exact rendering of the Pali *sacchikaroti*, is replaced by "see face to face", and is made to serve for *bhāveti*.

This forced use should not thus be slid past. It should be well weighed and given its full weight and significance. I contend, it is true, that the mantra of the truths was not in the original talk to the few friends. Indeed it is for me an indefinitely later gloss, in which

[1] E.g. *Dīgha*, i, 1.

[2] E.g. the Sangha formula, *Saṃyutta*, i, 220, etc., and cf. Comy. on *Dhammasangaṇi*, § 160.

the venerable traditional verbal yoking of this noun and this verb are mixed with obviously scholastic phrases as "the three modifications and the twelve constituent parts".

The yoking of Way with Becoming we see again in the old Pārâyana of the Sutta-Nipāta:

> Making the way incomparable to become.
> (*bhāvayaṃ maggam uttamaṃ* (ver. 1130)).

How are we to account for this curious presentation of wayfaring as a road made to become, and not as a road proceeded along, travelled along (which is all that Buddhists unversed in their texts see in it), or not as "becoming in the Way" or in "Wayfaring"? We do not meet with it in travel-stories, nor in references to religious touring. I suggest this:—

For the founders of Sakya, the mandate they brought to men was a call to each man to develop, to make become the Man-soul, the Divine Man who he really was. It was a call to the "more-will" in him to become more, by heeding *dhamma*, the divine sense of right, of the ought-to-be, within him. The becoming more was to lie in the better life he led; living better he became better; he was progressing thereby in a Way-of-the-worlds.

Now there was no good word for this will, this "mea sponte" of his choice. But there was the word *bhava, bhāveti*: becoming, making to become. And there was the figure, the parable of wayfaring towards a goal. Incidentally be it said, there was also no word for Wayfarer. Yet did concentration on the great figure wring out the needed words: "the man thus-gone", "the man well-gone" (*tathāgata, sugata*): words cramped by coming to be used for the Way-shower only. And I believe, that it was because the mandate of Becoming (the word was there) and the figure of a Way (the word was there) were closely linked together in that early teaching, with the idea of the Wayfarer as *choosing* (the word was not there), that Sakya has come down the ages to us in just this idiom: "making the Way to become."

So much then at least—and I am not pretending to have exhausted the traces—remains in the Pali books of a teaching on becoming which dates for me from very early days. And I hold that it belongs to the full and the true conception of what the Way of the first utterance implied and involved. For I would say it once more, so has it been overlooked:—Way means progress, unfolding, coming to be, the very "man"-in-the-More. This is the old Sakyan emphasis, more than any *external* goal of fulfilment, any consummation *externally* conceived. For Dhamma is not anywhere, as Nirvana is not anywhere. The Divine is "within" the man. But the fully becoming That is a long, long process. "Way" means this also: the fully becoming That, for that is the End of the way. To be in a wayfaring to which no way's end is held up is alien to world-religions; they may have conceived it in their formulated doctrines diversely, but it is there. To see in the Way a figure of the "man in-the-More" is to include in it a reference to the "man-in-the-Most". "In the Highest" is for us a more usual phraseology, but it is only that; it is more usual; it is not more apt.

Now here the First Utterance is not an implying only; it has explicit terms. And if I see, in the four terms for the Goal in the text, later ideas, a gloss, it is not because there has been insertion of the expressed where originally there was only the unexpressed. I think the four: "approach to calm, more-knowledge, thorough (or continuous or collective) enlightenment, going out (nirvana)" [1]—to translate them quite literally—are a later insertion for at least two reasons. If the reader will turn to the First Utterance, he will see that, in the clear wording of the two extremes, the "midway course", to agree with this wording, requires the use of the word *artha*. The midway can only here be shown as best, because it does belong, as they do not, to *artha*; it does lead to That. Now the best *artha*, the *summum bonum*, the Utterly Well was at some early time in Sakya's history expressed as "*paramartha*": highest or furthest *artha*. Thus in two venerable hymns of the Sutta-Nipāta we find it:—

> He who has stirred up effort for the winning of *paramattha* (verse 68),

and:

> Knowing the world, having vision of the *paramattha* (verse 219).

And again in the Nuns' Anthology (ver. 210):—

> Even the rune she spoke
> Fraught with its burden of sublimest good (*paramattha-saññitā*).

But somehow, used in this way, the compound would seem to have been current in poetical diction only, for we do not meet with it in the prose sayings. And it is just possible that for this reason it was not, where it seems eminently in place, uttered in the Talk of the mandate. Or—and this is for me the more plausible— it *was* current in the Prakrit (pre-Pali) prose, and *was* uttered in the mandate, but when the

[1] *Upasama, abhiññā, sambodhi, nibbāna.* See above, p. 55.

Sayings were finally revised in present form, *or* when they were written down in Ceylon, then a change had come into the meaning of the compound *paramattha*, such that it could no longer stand for the Goal of the Way, of man's life-consummation. Namely in that it had come to be used for "ultimate meaning". For this is the way in which it is used in the great debate-series on man's ultimate reality, in the book said to have been compiled expressly for the Patna Congress in king Asoka's reign: the Kathā-vatthu. (And in this sense, its use in the one Sutta of the Majjhima Nikāya, No. 22, is coupled with what appears from the Commentary to be certainly a gloss.) Anyway, if *paramartha* was not used, it is at least "*artha-saṃhita*", belonging to *artha*, that is wanted in the context.

Instead of such a clear, straightforward, consistent wording, we find these four compound terms, which do not, as they stand, *express the Way's End at all.* They are terms of the More, not of the Most or Highest or Best. They express a more than ordinary knowledge (*abhiññā*), the process of winning calm (*upasama*; *samatha* is calm); the advance or improvement in enlightenment (*sambodhi*: the Commentaries parse *sam* as is given above, in alternatives), and away-from-going, or out-going (*nib-bāna*). Now I would not dispute that these terms, placed to stand for the Goal to which the Way would lead, did mean, had come to mean, much for scholastic Sakya. For that matter each of them means much in the Pali books. But the much means, I repeat, *only the More*. Not one of them can be said to be free from ambiguity; the last of them least of all. It is still to-day very ambiguous among Buddhists themselves. Not one of them is an unambiguous term for *paramartha*: supreme Good or Goal. And this can only mean one thing: that in monastic values, the Way was no longer the worlds-journey from more to more, ending in the Most.

Somehow, in the teaching world of Sakya, the Way as a becoming (*bhava*) in each man's life had ceased to draw, to have value. The Way had been supplanted, for the layman, by a code of five moral ways, or habits, negatively worded, called *sīla*,[1] for the monk, by one of four statements about the woes of life, called true things (*saccāni*).

This is a historical event of deep interest. Will the reader bear with me if I go into it?

That man's life is a wayfaring—a *Magga*—is one of the great figures in human speech, because it is so close to world-truth. Even were there no greater way of the worlds, wherein Man-soul, the *purusha*, is in a sense more literally a wayfarer, the figure would

[1] The term in use to-day in "Southern" Buddhism: *pañ-sil*, is very late.

still be most apt. For, to repeat, way implies choice, brings growing fitness in wayfarer, way brings the new, the further view, way heads for a goal. For the young especially there is nothing which so brings at its close, in the return to the familiar, a sense of "having become"—and not in body or mind only but in the self, the very "man"—as does a lengthened bout of wayfaring. In the resumption of work and of play, even after disuse, there will be a little stronger, wiser grasp of things, which is not in skill of body or mind, but is felt as better vantage-point in view. It is growth in the very "man".

To the superficial reader the figure of the Way may seem to stress but little or not at all the individual Wayman; it seems to call up the many, the travelling host. And it would not be a figure of world-truth if it were not of all. But it is curious how empty of comment on its significance for the individual is the literature of and on Buddhism. I am not saying that a man's growth towards saintship as a "way", or that man's conquest over birth and death, as stages in a *Magga*, are not prominent teachings. But I do say that the doctrine of man as wayfarer in a way, taught as a figure full of meaning and attractiveness for the Everyman to whom, as intended, it will have been addressed, is lost sight of. And why? Because the Buddhist exponents, as monks, did not welcome all that wayfaring means; and again, because their cramped use of the great figure has put European exponents off the scent. I would justify both these assertions.

I have said that the figure *magga* for man's life as a whole to a consummation of life was, when Sakya began, not peculiar to Sakya; it was also a Brahman figure. The first group of Sayings in the venerable Dīgha Nikāya ends with the Tevijja, or Three-Veda Suttanta. In it two young Brahmans are shown disputing whether any of the Ways (*maggāni, sic*) taught by this and that Brahman teacher is right, that is, "the straight way, the thither-faring road leading to companionship with Brahmā (not Brahman, but a personalized conception of deity; in Sakyan teaching the ruler of this Brahma-world ranked as "higher" than the next world). The luminous reply ascribed to Gotama shows how, in his message, the Way was *so much more* than any course of prescribed teaching, which might be associated with his name. The Way, for him, was man's very life. And it was thus, and thus alone, that the Way would be a faring to the Highest, in that the wayfarer, conceiving the Highest as what he thought Best, would by persistently choosing to live at his best, be ever becoming more and more like that Best, more fit for the divine *sahavyatā*, or companionship (see above, p. 37). Worthy in truth is a word like this to stand beside that of Hosea, prophet: "Then shall we know if we follow on to know"; beside that also of John the Elder: "Dearests, now are we sons of God, and it doth not yet appear what we shall be, but we know that we shall be like . . ."

But the Way has come down to us so congealed in its rather unfortunate "eightfold" uniform of prescribed states of thought, word, and deed, that we have not seen its true significance. It is when we cut these shackles off, noting where and how Way and Wayfaring survive in the records, when it is unhampered by them, that something of its original strength and significance stand out. Notice, for instance, the context in the Pārâyana (Sutta-Nipāta, a portion old enough to be quoted in the Nikāyas), from which a line has been cited: here is no detail of Eight, no harping on "ill"; here it is the forward wayfaring and the Goal:—

> He who would practise as the Teacher taught,
> 'T is he may go from hence to the Beyond;
> Yea, hence to the Beyond 't is he may go,
> Making the Way-Incomparable to become;
> The Way this is for going to Beyond,
> And therefore is it Yonder-faring called.

Nor in our sampling be it overlooked what is the name by which some early Sakyan poet called his Founder: Satthavāha, "caravan-leader":

> Arise, thou, leader of the caravan, and tour the world![1]

a name which came, in two anthologies, to be applied also to former "Buddhas". And it should not be overlooked that in the amazing treasury of folklore in the Pali Canon, the Jātaka, the place of honour as the first two is given to two caravan tales, in which of course the Bodhisat, or future Buddha, is the caravan-leader. On the fascination which adventure by travel and knowledge by travel may have had for Gotama, both before and after he set out himself a-quest, I have written in the companion volume. Here I would not stress this feature of the Way. For the very pith of the figure was, that each wayfarer should himself be a *satthavāha* (a word meaning literally *sa-attha-vāha*, "cum-goods-bearer", the Good within him), choosing the Way. I bring it in here to show the lingering, dying tradition of the Way as once a great symbol of man's life, and not merely the ethical rune, which is *not truly ethical at that*, as which it is usually valued.

Such picturesque developments in Way-allegory may or may not

[1] *Dīgha*, ii, 39; *Majjhima*, i, 169; *Samyutta*, i, 137.

have been in the Founder's thought when the figure occurred to him or when he first put it into words. It is not a matter about which we need to come to any conclusion. When new will in the shape of a new idea stirs within us, we may not at first see all the scope and richness of it; we come to see that by degrees. We may at first have but a worded outline by which to express it. Now the First Utterance, I repeat, will have been just that, a schema, not a "sermon", as it is usually inaptly called, but a worded outline on which to build, out of which to draw, all that it rightly could be said to imply, for the purpose of bringing help and guidance to this man and that, who together constituted the Many for whom the word of new will was intended. We should not see, in the fact of its utterance, the genuine historical event we do, had it been more than a schema—had it been a floridly worded discourse, such as we see in Buddhist Sanskrit effusions.

And when, launched in his new career as missioner, Gotama spoke to this man and that woman of life as a "way", full of adventure, unknown, unpredictable, appealing to the young, and having a wonderful "beyond", it is then, and probably only then, that he would himself come to see what a rich and strong appeal lay in it. I see in it for him no mere "overture" to the music of his long career, but a Leitmotif, a leading theme ever recurring, brought to bear now thus, now thus. The very last man whose question he sought in dying weakness to answer, was told of the Way.[1] And what would we not give to have his very words and not the pædagogic version in the book! I can see nothing unreasonable in the surmise that the swift success (if swift it truly was) of his teaching among the many, the merchant and the land-tiller, the craftsman and the beast-tamer, the woman and child, the hunter and bandit, the cowherd and the flower-sweeper, was in part due to the fascinating and stimulating picture of man as wayfarer from the known to the unknown, of how welfare lay in getting further, of how getting further depended upon right wayfaring here and now. The figure as I have said, was not his monopoly; but his emphasis was new. And this was a bringing of life as travel, in Bacon's immortal words, "home to men's business and bosoms." Could the men who were the vehicle of the teaching have remained laymen, could we have had in Ganges valley a little world of John Bunyans, teaching the notion of the "pilgrim's progress" as the "way through the jungle", not so much with a load of sin to be discarded, as with an ever growing force of *artha*—the good, the needed, the better—to be carried along,

[1] *Dīgha*, ii, 151,

we should not now be seeing the Buddhist Dhamma so lamentably misrepresented as a gospel of "Ill", of world as good for nothing, of "not-man", of "becoming to be stopped" as in its records it came to be, as in its monasticism it has continued to be.

Laymen and monks, Buddhists have ever been keen and pious pilgrims. The sadder it is, and the stranger, to see how in the past they failed to value rightly the figure and the truth of the Greater Pilgrimage. The lure of the roadway, and of the seaway, and now of the airway calls to man, even though, when his ostensible purpose is that of pilgrim, he may have missed the true call of his religion. And I fail to find any grasp, in either Buddhist scriptures or Buddhists, of the Way as a parable of life for the man as a whole: the Way in and through the way: *magga* in *saṃsāra*, of the worlds.

Some will say I am forcing parable or figure of life on to what was a mere term of means or method only. If such a charge be seriously maintained it does but show how much monastic teachers and editors have so displaced the once central feature, so that we have to look hard for the hidden treasure. I will disclose three such out-of-the-way applications, and leave the reader to judge whether or not we have in them "means", "method," or a picture of the right life-as-a-whole itself.

In the canonical anthology called Verses of the Elders there is one poem, and one only, about the Way. It is claimed for one Migajāla, "Deer-snarer," and very eloquent it is. Here and there it shows real insight, yet not where it is most needed. In both respects it is well worth a brief consideration.

In the first place, full though it is of epithets for what the Way is judged to bring to the life and help of man, there is no word of reference beyond the one word "eightfold" (*aṭṭhangiko*) to the analysis so-called or to any of the parts. Emphasis on action (*kamma*) is the only approach to one of these, *kammanta*, and even that is in depreciation and not, as in the eight parts, an appreciation (of right conduct). I cannot conceive a (Hīnayāna) Buddhist of to-day composing a psalm to the Way with such an omission. We have at this time of day no idea how much later this (?) Prakrit poem was turned into Pali. But according to the Commentary Migajāla was a son of the lady Visākhā, contemporary of the Founder. As such he ranks among the older verse-composers. And had there been in his day the eightfold division, on which I find Buddhists of to-day much busier than they are on the real teaching of the Way *quâ* Way, it would surely have found mention in his verses.

In the next place he implies that the Way is not *saṃsāra*; he sees in it "chosen advance", and not "whirling round". This is in the epithet *sabba-vaṭṭa-vināsano*. I have rendered this "all rolling on is razed away". It should have been "rolling *round*" ("rolling *on*" would be *pavattana*, *anuvattana*). To roll *on* is that of the wayfarer in the way, which he rightly goes on to call *niyyāniko* : "it leadeth on and out" (the word means both). This is the true movement of the "wheel of dhamma". It is the wheel in the air that merely whirls *round*, and it was a very worthless perversion of the figure when Buddhaghosa, of himself, or with his tradition, calls life in the worlds a wheel of becoming (*bhavacakka*), as if it were a wheel of Ixion. How with such a simile was not the worth in the Way become changed for the worse ! For Migajāla the Wheel of Dhamma in its progress crushes out the miserable figure of the wayless whirling wheel. Yet are we in the poem almost at once dragged back into the nightmare of rebirth as a thing to be dreaded. Whom are we to see at work here ? Migajāla or his editors ?

For in the monkish doctrine of Ill, *saṃsāra*, which in Gotama's day had come to be used for the flowing *on* of life from world to world, came, after his day, to be conceived as a round, an eddy, *āvaṭṭa*, *dukkhavaṭṭa*, with no maintenance of *parakkama*, going forward, but rather of *niyyānika*, faring out of, away from. Negatively then Migajāla has got the idea of progress. The Buddhist idea came to be to get out of *saṃsāra* into *magga*. The sounder idea would be thus: *in saṃsāra*, in the life-faring, choose the *magga*, the right faring. But then the world-despairing idea of the monk was to bring life in worlds to an end. Life in worlds as the true, the only way of self-fulfilment was not accepted.

The poem also speaks of act and cause in the Way, and rightly. The Way was conduct ; it was man in his conduct becoming the cause of his progress, only Migajāla didn't see this.

> Action as such it knoweth, and the fruit as fruit,
> True world-view of all things as risen causally.

But he adds, ending on a noble note :

> *Mahākhemangamo santo pariyosānabhaddako.*
> Yea, to the mighty Haven doth it wend,
> Holy (the faring), well (for thee) the End.

Where then does he miss wording with true insight ? Herein :— There is nothing to show the very essence of the Way, there is nothing to keep the hearer off from the idea, that here is a road along which mankind, like sheep, were being shepherded by "Buddha, Dhamma, Sangha" to salvation, there is nothing to show the hearer, that the Way means a man's so living as to be and to do his best, *as himself the "caravan-leader"*. Yet it is this, just this, and the End well kept in view that make of the First Utterance, not a mere good-compelling mantra, not a mere code of good thought, word and deed, but a very gospel, an inspired Call to the "man" from That Who is both Source and End.

Nor is there anything in the verses to show an awareness, that wayfaring in the Way meant in the wayfarer a continual progress, becoming, growth. Words, I have shown, were not lacking here. Besides *bhāveti*, "making to become," "developing," there was *vaḍḍhi* or *vuddhi*, growth, a word which peeps out just here and there like an unsubmerged rock in an engulfing sea. Thus we come across praise of "Ariyan growth" in a good woman,[1] and the nun, mother of Vaddha, in her verses, plays on his name in inciting him to growth towards the Utterly well, or, as she negatively puts it, the making an end of ill, connecting her admonition with the Way (*magga*) and with the Goal (*param'attha*).[2] Survivals these just here and there, but very precious in dealing with records, in which the main theme has become Ill rather than Way to the Utterly Well, in which Becoming is the very thing that must be stopped. *Bhava-nirodho nibbānaṃ*: the stopping of becoming is Nirvana, and the effecting this is named among the chief aims of the holy life![3]

Quite a thrill it gives when, in the midst of these records with their Leitmotif of world-woe, we come on the passage where the bald wording in the First Utterance is changed to one of loftiest meaning; in a speech accredited to the Governor of the next world:[4] that the Way and the Goal flow one into the other, as flow Ganges and Jumna.

But perhaps for us the most interesting survivals, out of probably a very great number, are the two that remain showing the Utterer of the Way-figure himself applying it in his teaching. (I cannot recall meeting with any others.) The one is in the Saṃyutta Collection, the other in that called Majjhima. In the former he is represented as heartening up his cousin Tissa, bilious or certainly sick at heart, in a Way-parable telling him of difficulties met and surmounted in the way of the new and unwonted, till at length the view of way's end breaks upon vision. And then the healing

[1] *Saṃyutta*, iv, 250.
[2] *Theragāthā*, ver. 207–12.
[3] *Saṃyutta*, ii, 117.
[4] *Dīgha*, ii, 223.

is driven in with words like so many electric shocks, words so unlike in phrasing to the wonted Piṭakan flow, that we wonder if we have not here something very near what was actually said.[1]

It may be said, that in one respect the alleged implication in the essence of the Way-utterance is absent. Tissa, namely, *is told* which way now here, now there he is to take. It is true that the monitor in that is, in the Saying, interpreted as being not the "inward" *dhamma*, but "Tathāgata, Arahan, Fully Enlightened One". This does but show how externalized as the set Doctrine of a Person, and no more the inward divine urge of *dhamma*, the orthodox teaching had become. And after all, for all the guide's advice, Tissa had himself to choose to accept or reject it.

This, the wording of the man's own will is better shown in the other application of the Way-message. "Why," a brahman asks him, "with the End as real, and the Way to it as real, and with you to show it, do not all your men, as you yourself admit, win to the end?" (There is perhaps some corrupt wording crept in here; but on the other hand it had become, when the Suttas were compiled, correct to speak of a saint or "arahan" as one who had definitely won all there was in life to win, hence in a way, he had won Nirvana.)

"What think you, brahman?" is the stated answer, "Suppose a man asked you the way to Rājagaha, and you gave him detailed guidance, and he none the less went west where you had said east . . . what then?"

"What fault were there in me, Gotama? I only had shown the way."

"So I too only show the way . . ."[2]

Here in all but explicit words the choice is referred to the wayfarer. We have the "man" standing at a dividing of the ways, and willing to choose the best way, the way that is right or fit (*sammā*, *samyak*). But it is left to him to know, to "understand" which is best. "Yours," runs a verse, "is the arduous thing to be done; tathāgatas are (but) they who declare." (*Dhammapada*, ver. 276.)

I confess that for me these simple object-lessons in the far-reaching implications lying in the word of the Way, pointing to what it meant, not so obviously to "men" as to each "man", pointing also to the

[1] *Saṃyutta*, iii, 109.

[2] *Majjhima*, Sutta 107. Lord Chalmers' trans., "where is my responsibility?" is not inapt, but it is very free. The Pali has only: *Ettha kv' āham karomi*? "Here now what do I?" or "Here where do I come in?" according as we see in *kv'*, *ku* or *kva*.

manner in which we may, I think, believe that the great Teacher did use it as man to man, are worth more than all the wearisome reiterations of the Way as being Ariyan and Eightfold.

We may consider later with other scriptural sophistications this curious elaboration of man's way in conduct into eight dispositions, neither more nor less. To me it is more likely that the original wording in the Utterance was the much older, the Aryan, not "Ariyan" threefold division of right thought, word and deed. It is a division we often meet with in such portions of the Nikāyas as may have been earlier compiled. Moreover it occurs in a very striking way in the Jātaka book, a way which shows the Founder waiving aside a growing ecclesiastical complexity in the monks' teaching of novices. Now this I do not see monkish editors putting in as emendation of older versions. It is, we might say, a story told against themselves, and we are fortunate it has survived. It is true that the Jātaka Book, which is a great "Apocrypha" included in the Sutta Piṭaka, came —it is supposed—very late into written form for it is, practically all of it, Commentarial talk, for which the teaching monk was given a free hand. But it does not follow that the "episodes of the present", that is, which gave rise it was said, in the Founder's own day, to the old folklore story being told, do not contain very old survivals.

The episode—it is that of the Bar of Gold Jātaka—is that a lay convert, entering the Order, was so overwhelmed at the complexity in the various Moral Codes (forms of Sīla) taught by his tutor that he decided to return to the "Low Thing", as life in the laity was called. Brought before the Teacher, the "Bhagavā", the latter is made to say this: "Come, what use is for you a mass of moral rules? Will you be able to keep just three precepts?" "I shall be able, sir." "Well then, do you henceforth ward the Three Gates: the Gate of the Act, the Gate of the Word, the Gate of the Thought; do no evil action in act, word, or thought. Go . . . just ward these three."

This taken alone will not be held as very "evidential" in a theory as to a wording of the Way, in the First Utterance, older than the Eightfold schedule. On the other hand it is suggestive, and as yet it has not been brought to notice. It uses, as Bunyan showed us, a metaphor of the City, rather than of the Way, and I do not quote it for the figure. I quote it as showing the existence of a tradition, that the Sakyan Founder preferred the simpler Three Ways of conduct to a longer list, in which is an arbitrary, inadequate, inexhaustive distribution of those Three Ways. Such a list is the Eightfold. And as to the story giving us but a suggestion towards reconstruction : well, we are digging for a buried city, and as with the archæologist, our inductions may have to rise out of a cumulative pile of suggestions.

Into the difficult criticism of editorial emendation I shall be going further in a later chapter. I have been charged here and there with upholding "ecclesiastical distortions" for which no sufficient motive is brought forward. Now it were not wise did I say : "That is prejudice and blindness on the critic-reader's part." I prefer to think that I have not made myself sufficiently clear, have not marshalled my reasons well. I hope before the curtain falls to convince him, that to speak of choosing one version among many as "authentic", because it best accords with the view of the chooser (the view that is of a later day), as distortion, is to miscall acts where the *motive* was very worthy. I hope also to show that from the editorial chooser's point of view there *was* such a motive, worthy and cogent.

So far let it suffice that I have tried to show in the First Utterance, as we have it, certain fragments which are all I judge to be original, and why I judge them to be so. And I have, I hope, made it clear that even had we the Utterance in its actually original wording, we should at best have "a talk disclosing a schema or outline" and not at all a "sermon", or even an impressive "heart to heart" talk to a given individual. We see the Sakya-Muni as a man who started his man-helping mission as no orator, with no confidence in his own powers of convincing hearers on what we should call philosophic lines, but with a great gift of going straight to the heart of some one man's need. Now as a far-reaching truth conveyed in a popular figure—the "man's" ultimate welfare in a long existence of coming to be, in accordance with his own inwardly guided decision in conduct pictured as the traveller's ways in wayfaring—he had thought out the brief sketch we have discussed. He had thought it out as a guide-code, not only for himself, but also for men he at once sought out, who would understand and be wanting to help with him.

In this little outline I have come to see two implications at least—Dhamma, Will—*without which* the Utterance (as we have it) falls out from such momentous words as may be rightly called messages of world-gospels or religions, and is reduced to an apologia for the monk's renunciation of life in the world, together with a rule for his own conduct in so far as this is deemed to be (*a*) right for his own mind-culture, (*b*) right in giving no offence to other men. But those two implications—dhamma, will—lift the outline at once to a different plane. They entitle it to be looked upon as a call to the man, not to the recluse only. When read into the outline as belonging to its essential meaning, they reveal it as saying to the man, then regarded by the religious world as *God-Man immanent in earth-man*: Choose in your long life-way how to act in thought, word and deed, guided by *dhamma*, the urge which is in and of you (*ajjh'atta*). So will you in your wayfaring become. So will you in becoming reap the fruit, even to the uttermost Good (*artha*).

If we dare thus to reconstruct, if we dare, in the teeth of endless Buddhist reiteration down centuries of ecclesiastical routine, in the teeth of Western acquiescence in that reiteration, to lighten the caravan and drop from it the monk-diagnosis of the Four Truths about Ill, then shall we at least better understand, it may be, how in the ancient book of the Sutta-Nipāta, the man is linked, not so much with Ill, as with the Way to "Well": "way-liver," "way-victor," "way-teacher," "way-corrupter."[1] In the Majjhima it is the Founder only who is thus linked: "Way-shower," "Way-upraiser."[2] That each man, each woman was wayfarer, waymaker, waychooser, way worth-er: of any of this we find nothing remaining save in the Sutta-Nipāta. And it is only too consistent with the gradual dropping of the "man" from the caravan that went on, the Man-soul who is its leader, that in the Jātaka, in the Indian figure of life's chariot-driving,[3] whereas the usual feature of mind as charioteer is retained, the king no longer stands directing beside him.

And therewith the Way's End is virtually dropped also. Nirvana, it is true, that apex of ambiguity, is there. But I repeat, the word was a closing of the view, not a vista. It was as a shouting by the exiled wayfarer Not-land! when the innumerable laughter of the sea, and its home-suggestion broke on his view. We know that was not his cry. And it is significant that, in that other often used scheme of the Way, oddly divided as "four" ways and four "fruits", the culmination of it is no more called Nirvana, but "worthiness" which we try despairingly to render by "arahantship". I have no wish to do anything so myopic as to undervalue a conception of the Goal of the Way expressed as man consummate—for that is what *arahatta* comes to in meaning. But by the Buddhist it was, not by me, that the term became depreciated. For he used the word to express human consummation attainable on earth, and that can only be managed by holding a woefully cramped idea of what consummation

[1] Verses 84–9 continued. Of course we do not now accept the pioneer Fausböll when he sees here four sections of Samaṇas!

[2] iii, 6, 8, 15.

[3] No. 544.

is, and more, of what in finer, more than earthly states of life it may come to be. "Eye hath not seen, ear hath not heard, nor hath the heart of man conceived . . ." Faintly the Sutta Nipāta anticipates that :

> Nowhere is measure for one gone to oblivion,
> That whereby we speak of him, that for him is not . . . (ver. 1075).

But herein again this book, albeit mainly a manual of the recluse, has so far the wider vision of the poet that it is now and again less cramped in idea than are the Suttas.

In the Fourfold Way Nirvana, it is true, is let go, but still it is the backward view that we find, the thinking of the sea as "not-land". The view of the Way as in stages of progress would seem to be the reverse of this. And this view was indeed a great opportunity for Sakya to have expressed its ideal in what we might call a Coué-istic fashion, namely by dwelling on the Better than had come to be, and was yet still more coming to be. But no ! the opportunity was lost ; life in the Four stages is measured, in *name*, not by the so much of effort accomplished or to be grappled with, but by the amount of Becoming got rid of :—"Once-(more) going-(back to earth)" ; "Not-coming-(back)".[1] I hasten to contrast with these, the intermediate stages, the name for the First Stage : Streamwinning.[2] Here at least we have, albeit in oddly mixed metaphor, a strong positive word of Becoming. It is akin to similes, favoured in the Pali books of mountain streams reaching the river, of Gangā's tributaries blending with her, of Gangā's finding the sea. It may well have been, in early Sakya, a figure used parallel with the Way, for man's life as heading, as drawing irresistibly onward to the Ocean of its natural tendency. In its place in the Fourfold Way it is as a round peg in a square hole. It obviously does not belong there, and in the Suttas it is repeatedly treated as belonging to a separate scheme of salvation from the monks' scheme of desire stopped, of becoming quenched, and of Nirvana. It has its own triumph song, the song of happy rebirth.[3] It is part of a gospel not of the monk for the monk. It is the gospel for the Many, for Every man. It *is* Sakya.

I do not overlook that, when we get past the names in this Fourfold Way, we find the great idea of progress in holiness given utterance, such as the gradual reducing of the sensual nature to a minimum, etc.[4] Again, but only in the later Abhidhamma, we find a very noble utterance associated with the first stage, the disposition

[1] *Sakad-āgāmin* ; *an-āgāmin*.
[2] *Sot'āpatti*.
[3] *Saṃyutta*, ii, 67.
[4] *Dīgha*, i, 156.

named in the compound: "I-shall-come-to-know-the-unknown."[1] But only there. Men's names for things are a mirror of their values in things. And it is in the *names* of the Fourfold Way that we see the values. What values, what an outlook it is! Outlook of the timid, the burnt child, the shipwrecked on the sands of time, the man who has given up. It has been a great disutility to the real message of the Way. It has drained from that a fit wording of the Way's Goal (for to its credit this later way *is* a world-way with a goal). And the real Way, thus blooded, has shrivelled up to being practically a Way of this earthlife only. So much so, that I have heard Europeans asking whether Buddhism taught survival at all. And I have read young Ceylon saying in print that the Buddha taught, it was only this life that mattered and that the "other life" could take care of itself.

How have the founders of great religions been crucified anew times without number!

How do not the votaries of great religions cast aside treasures of great worth committed to them!

When the Christian knight set out on a journey he took of the cup of remembrance, the bread of compassionate sacrifice, took them with prayer. Symbols of "more-will" in becoming in his wayfaring were these:

> Wein und Brod des letzten Mahles
> Wandelt' einst der Herr des Grales
> Durch des Mitleids Liebesmacht
> In das Blut das Er vergoss,
> In den Leib den dar Er bracht . . .[2]

When two friends of mine and of Ceylon left the island, the kindly farewell ceremony given them by monks was the confession thrice of refuge in the Buddhist trinity, the five *sīlas*, the little Sutta about what is the highest luck.[3] Not a word about the Way, of which the journey was a fit symbol, not a word of wellwishing in the Making it to Become, not a word of "the love-might of compassion" to all men, which the very Man-in-the-Founder breathed forth, as did that other Founder, to the world!

[1] *Dhammasaṅgaṇi*, §§ 277, 296, 362.
[2] The poem of Parsifal.
[3] "Memories of Ceylon," by W. Geiger, *JPTS.*, 1924–27.

VII

THE FIRST SONS OF THE SAKYA

Let me now return to the first of the three terms in the hypothesis of a new religion considered as a world-happening or -phenomenon. This is "they to whom the message comes". I considered this in a former chapter in a very general sense, as the particular "world", the world round about 600 B.C. in the middle Ganges valley, and I considered it, not in its ethnological or political aspects—others have done that—but mainly with respect to certain prevailing religious attitudes, and in particular with respect to certain changes in attitude which had come in and were coming in. I now wish to reconsider this subject in a more intimate and specific way, namely, in the persons of the first group of men to whom the new message is recorded to have come.

So slight and fragmentary is the ancient chronicle about them, that few subjects offer more difficulties to the reconstructive imagination. The men are named, to be almost immediately dismissed again, and with two exceptions without recall. Their appearance in legend and in bas-relief is of what I would call of the most hide-bound nature; they might be called fossilized figures. As such we see them in the Borobudur bas-reliefs; as such we see them (with one exception) in the unique Piṭaka record of them: the Mahā-vagga of the Vinaya Piṭaka; as such we see them in the Nidāna-kathā, or Introduction to the Jātaka. Yet is "fossilized" never applicable to ideas; the legend had in it elements of change. Thus in the Vinaya the first "five" appear, as hearers for the first time; in the Nidāna-kathā and Commentaries, one of them appears twenty-nine years before as Brahman augur at Gotama's birth. The legend I put aside; the Vinaya Commentary is not within reach, and I shall keep to the record in the canonical text. The narrative is always in very slight outline; much would seem either to have been forgotten or suppressed, as not relevant to the formal registering of some Vinaya statute, and why it came to be. We get the impression that we are reading about persons and places which, for the compilers, are just names, bound up it is clear with an ancient and venerated tradition, but not belonging to any actual memories either in their possession or even in their own preceding generations. The places named do not seem to be places known.

About the families and circumstances of the group of friends, to whom the Founder spoke his schema for a teaching-message, nothing is told. About a certain recluse, Upāka, by whom he was accosted and asked as to the reason of his ardent, radiant mien, just before he found those friends, we do learn a little from text and from Commentary. And it is not impossible that this man was actually the very first to hear the message. The words actually put into Gotama's mouth in his reply are so bombastically improbable as to suggest, that there had come here a hiatus in the oral record, which was filled in when, with the growth of the "Buddha"-cult, nothing was too magniloquent to say of him, or be made said by him. It strikes us now as not less repulsive than the self-vaunting of the Homeric hero before he lays to with the sword.

But it is a very natural feature in the story that the Man-with-the-Message should be seeking first, not some one to whom he could speak as missioner, but a man or men whom he considered able and worthy to come in with him and help him.

He was not blind to the heavy work that lay before him. No other scripture so lets us peep behind the scene in this respect as does the Pali. He is shown us, during the weeks of absence from the group of fellow-inquirers, as depressed with a sense of "It's not workable", and with the sense of failure in the attempt as likely to hurt—himself. I do not stand out for this sentence: "This would be wearisome to me; this would be hurtful to me" as being a true saying.[1] But it is worth noticing for two reasons. It is the attitude of an Indian recluse even to-day, namely, that his own *artha* is his primary concern; failure will, in hurting him, only in a secondary degree also affect others, who are in a way being lifted under the ægis of his lofty merit. Again, and on the other hand, when he was an experienced teacher, this self-pity is no more given as the mind that was in Gotama. In the Lakkhaṇa Saṃyutta, where Moggallāna is smiling at the clairvoyant vision of some wicked folk finding retribution in purgatory, Gotama's comment is: "Disciples live the life of vision, yea, of insight, since a disciple will know, or will see, or will testify to a thing like this. I also had seen that thing . . . I might have revealed it; and others would not have believed me. Had they not believed me, it would have been *to their hurt and their sorrow*."[2] That we have here, assuming the record in both cases is true, an unnoticed glimpse of the Messenger himself growing in the "More", becoming "more" as he himself wayfared, will be to readers acceptable and possible,

[1] *Vinaya*, Mahāv, i, 2. [2] *Saṃyutta*, ii, 255.

or the contrary, according to their view of Gotama the Man. Once accepted, their view of him as a man attaining at a bound to consummate manhood, or more, beneath the Bo-tree, falls.

That Gotama was induced to surmount diffidence and take up the work of winning his fellows to see a "more" in life and live it, through the persuasion of a wise adviser from the Unseen, may again be writ down as myth, or be accepted. It will very largely depend on the reader's belief in the range of life's possibilities—depend much more on this than he is usually willing to admit. Either the account is sheer legendary invention, inserted by monk-editors, or it is more or less true. No one but Gotama himself can in the first instance have related the experience, for by all accounts he was alone at the time so far as anyone of earth was present. Hence for a Buddhist it is a matter difficult to get round. And only ignorance of, or indifference to these ancient records in their scriptures can justify the saying referred to in the last chapter concerning their "Buddha" and his indifference to other worlds (p. 114).

There is another feature in this very impressive narrative, one of the most moving in any scripture, and that is: the Messenger hesitates to place before men a matter he has thought out, seeing how habit-bound most men are; but this matter is quite different from that which he did eventually bring out. I would invite the reader to note this carefully, for not only is it much passed over, but that his message did take a different form readers who are not given to passing over will not always admit. The text in essentials runs thus: "I have penetrated this *dhamma*, deep, hard to discern, hard to understand . . . but this is an age (lit. race) devoted to the habitual;[1] for it, hard is it to understand how 'this is conditioned by that'; that 'all happens by way of cause'; hard too to understand 'the calming of all material interests, the renouncing of the substrate (of rebirth), the destruction of natural cravings, (the attainment of) passionlessness, ending, going out.'"[2]

We have here a dual theme: a teaching of causality on the one hand, and on the other the monastic ideal of the day. With the exception of the allusion to the worldly life, and to "going out" (*nirvana*), it has *nothing in common with the wording* of the First Utterance till we come to the four truths. Nor, if we still exclude those, has it aught in common with the Utterance *in idea*. The

[1] *Ālaya* is not usually so translated, but I do not see why not. The word means point of rest or attachment, and is used both in connection with sense and *with opinion*.

[2] *Vin.*, loc. cit.

Way is not there, neither in word nor in idea. In that dual theme the More for man *is* there, both in the notion of popularizing the idea of universal causation, which seems to have been occupying the new thought of the day, and in the monastic ideal. But had he continued in that first intention, it is hardly conceivable that he would not have given it expression somewhat at least in the terms of the citation. Causation *is* in the four truths, but they are not *on it*; they *assume it as a foregone datum.*

No, a new religion does not take birth by a message which holds up to the man a formulated idea, cut and dried. In this way or that it will go straight to the very man, and to man's *will.* Man in some way has been seeking a new mandate for will; the new message takes him by the hand, saying: "This is the way; walk in it." In that fit of depression the message will not yet have taken shape in the Way-figure. But he thought, we read—it may well be he saw, as well as thought—of lotus-flowers in water, and he thought of them as growing, growing in varying degrees of becoming, some more strongly than others. He was thinking both of the "more" of which the man was capable, and, as the man in the Many, variously capable. "There would be some who would understand."[1] And with this quickened vision of fellow-men at different stages of growth, but of all as growing, he resolved to teach. When he went forth ready to teach, the vision of the flowers had passed, but he saw the better for it. The 'man' also grew, but not just here and now only. The growing of him, the human flower, stretched out as if to distances immeasurable, and the End of him was not yet. And so somehow "the man becoming through the worlds" presented itself as a Way; for in wayfaring the fact of growth was assumed, but the how of it, the more of it was no mere matter of a plant's earth-bound fate. Will, choice was now called into play, and afar there was the coming to be in a way, in a degree of which the earth-bound "foot-drinker", as India called the plant,[2] would never be capable.

That we have here, very dimly presented in the text, evidence of a change coming over the Messenger, as he pondered over his Message to come, will be accepted, or rejected, by the reader more or less in accordance with the how much, or how little he accepts of the text of the First Utterance, and I leave it at that. Let us resume the Messenger's quest of efficient fellow-workers.

I use the last word with emphasis. It was imperative for him

[1] *Vin.* loc., cit. [2] *Pāda-pa.*

to find such. The "Come with me, and I will make you fishers of men" was a reasonable wish, not only in the Founder of the World-Brother Mandate, but also in every Utterer of a new world-word. But the tendency, in books about the subject, is to be led by the emphasis *in the text*. And the result is to see, in the quest, a monk, seeking and finding men who are also already monks, and who, moreover, appear as merely acquiescent listeners and converts, with no will akin to his own, to work with him in teaching the Many.

But the text is at least equally clear that his wish was to find men who would be fellow-teachers, rather than docile adherents. His first thought is said to have been to tell the two of his former teachers who are mentioned by name (there may have been others), under whom he had studied what had come to be called Jhāna. And this appears to be, not because he wished to win them over from their own speciality, but because of their high intelligence. "Āḷāra is wise, clever, sagacious; he has long seen things clearly. What if I were to teach him *dhamma* first; he will quickly come to know 'this dhamma'." (The reader may note the older and later use of the word *dhamma* in close contiguity: to this I have referred above.)

It may have been characteristic of the still young man's optimism, to think he could so easily win over to a new word two men noted and sought after by students in their own line. Yet he knew them as we do not, and it must be remembered that each of them is said to have invited him into teaching-partnership. It is not impossible that it was in his mind to ask each of them to reconsider his own refusal of their separate offers, and blend his new word with their older, more established teaching. Such a blend Sakya *held to be wise and practicable*, as we may see later on. Had either teacher proved to be, as they were not, still on earth when Gotama sought for them, and had such a partnership been carried out, it is then not impossible, that we might have now a Buddhism of which, in its foundations, it could justly be said—as has lately been said—that it is "through and through nothing but Yoga". Even then, however, so wild a word would have needed modifying, when the new element in the "blend" had been so strong and distinctive. But, for this man, the way lay not to be the teacher in the accepted, the accredited, the established, or to be as such himself accepted, accredited, established. He was not to be merged in anyone else. He was to be Founder.

This does not mean he was to be sole teacher, lonely oracle, captain of sheep and dolls, seer in a kingdom of the blind. His next thought is described as being of certain men with whom he had strenuously practised *tapas*, and who had been "of great help to him (*bahûpakārā*)".[1] Of what nature will that help have been? It was not in the nature of bodily service. When he is made to say he so overdid matters in training, that he nearly died, he is made to acknowledge receiving aid at the time, but it was from "devas".[2] And we are left to conclude that the "help" was of the kind *we* call, inclusively, mental: help in thinking and discussing lines of teaching, and help of the more intimate kind in valuing ideals and ends, and the fostering of growth in these. What is there unreasonable in taking "upakāra" to mean help of this kind? The word was later used to figure (it could do no more) the conception of the "transeunce" of cause into effect; thus it is not tied to meanings physical. Now helpers of this kind will have been well judged as worthy to help in bringing the gospel of the Way to the Many. Worthy *just because* they were not pale reflections of their leader, but capable of complementing his own untried teaching, by lending other, that is, their own individual values to it.

I confess that I take the text very lightly by the hand in its other words on them. "Helped me much" is very significant, and is too much passed over. But I do not see them as of a certainty "five" only, or as men only, or as already monks. The curious way of alluding to them always as the *pañca-vaggiyā bhikkhū*, or "five-set-ter" almsmen is parallelled by the curious way of alluding to any and every schismatic or mutinous clique in the Vinaya rule-making episodes as "*chabbaggiyā*" or "six-setters". There may have been a very old tradition in the first hearers being five. I refer to the legend of the eight Brahman augurs called in by Gotama's father to prognosticate, all of whom are said to have died before he began to teach but one, who was young and survived to become, as Aññā Kondañña, the first of the five. Of the *sons* of the other seven, four are said to have become recluses with Aññā, in order to await Siddhattha Gotama's advent, three refused. As if, in the legend, the majority are for the triumphant Word and Worder, the minority against. It is true that we have five names in the story to amplify the group-word (*pañca-vaggiya*), but then they are not the Peter, James, John of this gospel. They are all so many Nathaniels, or even less.

No women are named as present. But we should not expect to find an ancient record mindful of them, if they had been. It has taken the other sex a world of centuries to recognize in the woman the real support, yea, the wire-puller of a religion, and they have

[1] *Vin.*, loc. cit. [2] *Majjhima*, i, 245 (Mahā-Saccaka-S.).

scarcely come to it yet. We have to dig out how early she will have been ready hearer and also helper in this, as in other religions.

Nor do I judge the first men to have been monks at or before the utterance of the Message. Equally can we place on one side the legend unworthy and fantastic of Gotama becoming a monk immediately after leaving his home. For this reason : we do not find men, once committed to samaṇaship or monkish Orders, seeking to train themselves under secular teachers, or teachers of other religious bodies. I see the first Sakyans as laymen studying *tapas* probably under the Jains, studying *nyāya* under Sañjaya, and probably studying Sānkhya (since, let alone tendency, one of its aphorisms came to be rooted in their fixed wordings) under some successor of Kapila. Further, the first men were out to become missioners. The starting of organized mission work appears very early in the incidental history of the Vinaya books. This is not conclusive evidence, since it is the entry into a monk order with which the compilers were interested, and not with helping the world. Yet it should be given due weight. Now, in India at least, a man did not become a monk primarily to be a missioner. It was to leave the world, not to go and help it.

Just when and why the first Sakyas, or early Sakyas, became monks we do not know. But it is noteworthy that the legends differ slightly in versions about the monk-status of the "Five". I hold they will have been Paribbājakas, "wandering" students, like those of mediæval Europe, a not less interesting institution, and a very live and recurrent feature in the records. They were not recluses proper, not celibates, but seekers after this and that form of accredited teaching, after the new also, the not yet accepted, wherever they had heard it might be found and freely discussed. And there seem to have been "parks (*ārāma, āśrama*)" specially reserved for their lodgment and debates. As Paribbājakas they would have absorbed, no less than Gotama (himself a Paribbājaka, "seeking the Good, the Guiding, the Ideal")[1] the current and debated theories of their day in the districts they visited. They will have been familiar with the state of brahman orthodoxy and perhaps also with the new ideas seething here and there in that. Two at least of them are called Brahmans in a Commentary. (Most of the inner group in fact were Brahmans.) They will have been presumably young, or youthfully mature. They will have had their individual training and antecedents, tendencies and theories. And with Gotama *they will have had the will* to centre on and begin a life of mission work.

[1] *Dīgha*, ii, 151.

Such I believe, because I must believe, to have been these men who, in throwing in their lot with the Sakyan, before his own kinsmen rallied to his cause, became, with loyal conviction, at least at the start, not so much pupils as comrades and fellow-teachers. It is no ordinary man who on such an occasion calls, who speaks not as other men speak, who tells Everywoman "all things that ever she did".[1] But again it is no ordinary men to whom he first goes for help, and who as willing helpers respond. And these men will each, as teachers, have taught in his own way, and as teachers of the Way, will have brought in their own cultural ideas to amplify their new line of doctrine.

What then is it that the records actually tell us of them?

Just their 'conversion'. After this they all, with one brief exception fade out of that picture. Verses ascribed to two of them, revealing nothing of biographical interest, are in two Anthologies of the Canon. Two Suttas mention one of them: Assaji, one: Aññā Kondañña; and that is all. What sort of help they actually gave, whether they preached, whether they invited and answered questions, whether they healed, whether they gave lessons in Jhāna, or whether finally they did nothing beyond collecting alms (they are shown doing this at first) and acting as repeating reporters: of any of this we hear nothing. To the silence about all this there is, I have said, one brief exception; but that exception is for me full of significance.

Here are the positive data in the Vinaya record, in the Mahāvagga, sections 1, 5, 6, 23, 24:—

(1) Gotama, at the end of a quest of some years after religious truth and religious welfare, believes he has worked out a sound gospel of salvation for the many on a basis of modifying faith and action in the light of the working of causality and in world-renunciation.

(2) This gospel he rejects, as having in it no power to draw men from the grip of the habitual (in sense and in idea).

(3) Urged by the messenger of another world, he decides anyway to teach.

(4) To find co-workers, he returns from lone thinking to a few friends, and declares in a talk, round a certain word-schema, a new gospel, different in emphasis, wording, and appeal from the causation-cum-renunciation gospel which he had put aside.

(5) The friends accept his mandate. They are instructed by

[1] Gospel of John, iv: "Come, see a man who told me all things that ever I did! Is not this the Christ?"

their new Leader, and successively "ordained", and a system of alms-quest is begun.

(6) One of the friends is named Assaji, the others named being Aññā of the Kondaññas, Vappa, Mahānāma, and Bhaddiya.

(7) After this another (?) friend appears, Sāriputta, a brahman, a student disgruntled with his own teacher Sañjaya, who is a noted sophist and dialectician. Sāriputta, too, like Gotama, is seeking not just culture, but a gospel, salvation, immortality (*amata*). He meets Assaji, who is looking unusually radiant, as if his quest were found. He asks him, what has he learnt? Assaji tells him that his teacher, the young Sakyan, has taught him a religion of explaining things causally. Sāriputta accepts this gospel, and brings over to it a brahman friend, Moggallāna. The two and their friends desert Sañjaya and join the new group of the Sakyan.

(8) Assaji hereupon fades out of the picture, as a teacher, for good and all. The other two do not; they become eminent fellow-teachers with Gotama. (Neither of them appears, later on, as given to teaching a doctrine of theory and practice regulated by causal explanation.)

Such is the account in the Vinaya; there is no other record in the Suttas; and the later record, the Nidāna-kathā, is even more meagre.

I cannot see a critical, unbiassed reader, reading this chronicle for the first time, failing to come to the conclusion, that somehow in the course of its long existence, oral and then scriptural, a twist here, a twist there has got into the telling of these fragmentary episodes. I am, it is true, not unmindful that readers who may claim not without right to be such, may *not* do as I think they fain must do. If such a reader does not so conclude, he is for me either too sceptical, rejecting the old chronicle as altogether fictitious, or he is too apologetical, in which case he is yielding to bias. I do not agree that the chronicle is to be treated as just ballad, or else as untouchable. I am for the midway of looking upon it as a set of truthful fragments wrongly pieced together. And I suggest the following resetting.

Gotama leaves his home to seek, in new thought, new teaching, a way of salvation, wherein the decay and death of the body should no longer form the woeful drag on man's happiness that it was. He sought out teachers. We find him associated, for an indefinite time during his quest, with at least five other men, men like himself of the Paribbājakā, or wandering student world, themselves in search of culture. There was the new world of the Nigaṇṭhas, or Jains, with one of its principal seats at the busy, thriving town of Vesālī. There, in the Mahāvana, went on the well-meaning but foolish worsening of the body in ways of *tapas*. The students try it together. Gotama gives it up to beat out some better way alone. There has been much and long interchange of views between the six. They have learnt much of the new Zeit-Geist while together : the new views astir about orderly process in nature (*prakṛiti*), about orderly process in man's world way (*karma*)—this from the Nigaṇṭhas—about system in musing or Jhāna, from Ālāra or Uddaka, about the academic lay or secular training of thought [1] in naming, numbering, analysis (Sāṅkhya), which had come much into vogue since Kapila taught at, was it Taxilā ?, Mathurā ? and much besides. One of the friends in particular, Assaji, was deeply interested in the first, in what we should now call natural causation, and that in a way it is not easy for us, late heirs of the ages, to understand. When Gotama left them, the friends travelled east to Benares, another centre of new thought.

Gotama, meanwhile, also deeply interested in his friends' talks on causation, tries to weld it into a gospel for the ending of ill. Could not man, in the very process of coming-to-be, as himself the working cause, so choose, so work, as to bring about this effect, avert that effect ? To some extent man as *ātman*, abode and "image" of World-Ātman, was able to say "Let this be so ! Let that not be so!" He could "will", he could choose . . . Now he had no fit words here ; none for "will" save approximations, and a very cramped word for "choose". But when one set out to get a thing done, one said course or method (*paṭipadā*) ; to reach a goal one followed a way (*magga*, *añjana*, *addhāna*) : here were words a-plenty. And the man in the way (*paṭipanno*) was, as such, a working cause making for the way's end, the effect. The multitude would not respond to a new message preached in *terms* of cause and effect (*paticca-samuppāda*), but the way, the road, the wayfaring, the adventure :—here was an idea that would grip them. They were at all and every stage of this great way, at every stage of progress therein . . . of growth therein—yes, like those lotuses in the pond—he would show life and its ills and the way on and out *as a Way*, and each man as a caravan-leader, one with the goods (*satthavāha*). So he follows the friends to the wood near Benares and proposes the message of the Way.

Now two others of the student-world at Vesālī (or elsewhere),

[1] Non-brahman.

Sāriputta (more fully Upatissa, son of the lady Sārī) and Moggallāna (viz. Koliya) had also come to Benares. The former meets Assaji (whom he apparently knows) and asks : "Why ! What have you found to look so blissful ? What new thing have you learnt ?" Assaji, in reply, has nothing to say about the teaching of the Way, nor about any other of the first Utterances ascribed to Gotama ; he answers in terms of causal law : that the saving truth is to see, that since all arises causally, all, as effect, *ends* accordingly ; and that Gotama can tell what is the cause of any given thing. Nor is this reply given in terms which would appeal to a man who is seeking what he sees in the one word *amata*.

I judge that the fragments of what were once two remembered episodes, have here long after, been evidently fitted in wrongly to the much patched up chronicle. Assaji is an enthusiast chiefly in the subject of natural causation ; he has made it his own, and has made the more practical teaching of the Way, to which he has given his allegiance, a matter of secondary interest. Gotama, friend and leader, is at first glad to win over any of his worthier student-comrades to form a missioner-group. And he is great-minded enough to be glad to have his own teaching enriched and supplemented even by men who are more interested in, and as such are more likely to stress in teaching, this and that factor in the new thought than his special gospel for the Many—the Way—which the band nominally represents.

Here I finish the reset mosaic with just this : Assaji's answer shows clearly that at Benares he had met, or had found again (not only Gotama, but) the (unnamed) teacher of natural causation under whom he had acquired his interest in the subject. That this teacher came to be identified with Gotama the Sakyan is only one of the results of what I shall consider again later—the merging of all the teaching virtue of the Order, the Sangha, in the "Buddha".

The conclusion I draw as probably true from this resetting is, that the prominence given to the subject of causation in some sections of the Piṭakas—a prominence which is very unequally distributed—is due directly to Assaji, and indirectly to his unknown teacher, rather than to Gotama himself. Gotama apparently welcomed the wording of the subject in the sayings taught and recorded. It may even have been he who framed it properly in its abstract form : *Idaṃ sati, idaṃ hoti*, etc. "Given this, that comes to be," and so on. It is possible that the unknown teacher was drawn into the Order only to be submerged, as was Assaji himself, in the "Buddha" and his "Dhamma". For we never find Assaji, any more than the two eminent disciples he introduced to the new mandate, speaking, or speaking habitually on just that topic in which he worded a teaching which to him appeared of primary importance, namely, causation.

There may, it is true, be other reasons why we do not meet with Assaji discoursing on Paṭicca-samuppāda. Even in the surviving fragments where he reappears, Assaji would seem to have been a mighty poor speaker. When in the Cūḷa-Saccaka Sutta of the Majjhima he is asked by the Jain what sort of doctrine his leader teaches, he is made to say, not any of the leading tenets, *not* the Way, *not* Causation, but a rudimentary monkish formula, to the not unreasonable contempt of Saccaka. He probably *did not make* that reply, yet it may fairly be inferred that, worthy disciple though he was, whatever he did say was neither lucid nor impressive. Nor when he is a-dying and Gotama visits him, does he speak as a teacher, even a very sick one, would have spoken, let alone a teacher on cause and effect (*Saŋy*. iii, 124 f.).

Again, the way in which the encroaching outlook and interests of the monk-world took over the teaching of causation, and twisted it to serve that outlook and those interests, was *probably not the way* in which either Assaji or Gotama himself taught it. Assaji's interest may have been more what we should call scientific interest in causal law as true, rather than as a practical organon. Gotama, as I have suggested, may have wrought it up into the teaching of the Way. But in so doing he *must* have put into it just the opposite emphasis to that of the monastic teaching. He must, namely, in the Way-figure, have dwelt on *uppāda*, *samudaya*, that is, on coming to be, and on making to come to be, not on *nirodha* : the " stopping " the effect by " stopping " the cause.

Now as Gotama grew old in body, and became more revered and less obeyed—as is the rule when even well loved teachers and guardians grow old—the workers in the Order who drew up the Sayings in fixed formulas would not be chiefly interested in causal law *as a cosmic induction*. Such a notion was not absolutely new. It lies implicit in the Vedic term *ṛta*. But the laity did not share in such Vedic lore. There was, it is true, a movement afoot toward such a sharing, but only among the few. We shall consider this in the next chapter. A statement of causal law had found utterance in early Sakya : " Given this, that comes to be, etc." framed very possibly, I have suggested, by Gotama himself. But it is rarely introduced in Sayings on cause and effect, and practically the only use made of causation is the identification of life, past, present, future, with "Ill"—the wail of the world-lorn, the recluse, the monk.

With the other first men of the Sakya, and with the first women too I have dealt in *Gotama the Man*. It is alas! very rare in these much faded memories that we are given more than their names and some external incident. With hardly an exception they are not depicted, in the slight sketches, as men of character or of wisdom. Yasa, first convert of "the Many", shows an uprush of "more-will" in breaking out of the groove, but we do not meet with him again, nor with his parents or wife, thrust for a moment into interesting departures of will. The same is true of the next converts, and is true alas! of that very interesting man Kassapa of Uruvelā, who with his brothers and adherents saw in fire—very possibly derived from Persian travels—a symbol as efficacious of man's inner radiating energy towards the Better and ultimate Best as Gotama saw the symbol of the Way might be. We see another vivid will in Kaccāna, dubbed Mahā, famed in exposition, who founded a school at Avanti, whence has survived a solitary compilation probably of a date not later than the Third Piṭaka: the "Book of Guidance".[1] But he is little more than a name. Cunda, Revata, brothers of Sāriputta, also rank among the ten to twelve names clustering about the Leader in Vinaya, but beyond a talk to one and verses by the other they are but names. Kappina, another such, should surely, to judge by an allusion in two Suttas and the Commentaries, have been of all a most live figure, yet is he too merged in the one dominant Teacher. Puṇṇa, ardent missioner, leaves the Leader to help men; Kassapa, the Leader's double, leaves him to hug seclusion. They come clearly to the front, these two, for a moment now and again, but swiftly fade out. It is not always the worthier fellow-workers who, on this little stage, come as living actors to the front in these brief episodes. Vangīsa, the ever ready improvisatore, and Vakkali, the doting disciple, for instance, are men of whose characters we know more than we do of wise, earnest and sagacious teachers like Sāriputta and Moggallāna. Of Moggallāna and of Panthaka Junior I shall have more to say in a later chapter. I would fain know more of two others who elude us, both among the men who had been in close touch with the Leader:—the teacher who had "heard *dhamma* and *vinaya* from the mouth of the founder," and knowing refused to conform to the wording of it as fixed by the first Conference: we should surely know his name, but he has been ostracized in the records with the name of Purāṇa, the Man of Old; and the

[1] *Netti-pakarana*. ed. E Hardy. *PTS*.

venerable recluse, Gavampati, a very Moses in psychic power, the friend of Yasa in his youth:

> Who by his might reared up the Sarabhū,
> Who standeth self-reliant and unmoved,
> Him mighty seer the unseen worlds acclaim . . .[1]

Gavampati has been lost, in his last acts, by the Piṭaka tradition and we have to seek him in Chinese translations of possibly Mahāsanghika originals.

Of those who were Sakyans not by adoption only but by birth, we meet with the Leader's half-brother and his son here and there, silent listeners in Suttas, and in the only talk made historic by the Asokan Edicts: that of deliberate lying, the latter, Rāhula, is by implication made to appear not, in this respect, impeccable. But neither of these men, younger than Gotama, and associated with his work from an early date, appears with him in his last years. At his passing they are not seen. Had they perhaps turned back to the "low thing", the lay life? Many may very well have done this.

Then there were the kinsmen and fellow-Sakyans who, when the Kumāra of their clan had established his position as a teacher patronized by the king of Magadha, left their northern home in Kosala, and came in to swell his Order: first, Mahānāma, then six more: Bhaddiya, Anuruddha, Ānanda, Bhagu, Kimbila, and Devadatta. Of these, two are certainly very live wires in the records: Devadatta, the schismatic, attractive, psychic, ambitious, who all but succeeded in wrecking the continuity in "Theravāda" Buddhism, and Ānanda, loyal, gentle and courteous, the loving, but often, and wrongly, described as "beloved" disciple, deferring overmuch to the majority. These two certainly prevent the much dehumanized records from being as lifeless as they would otherwise have been. Anuruddha was gifted psychically as was Devadatta and Moggallāna and Gotama himself, yet we find him resorting to peace and quiet in seclusion with Kimbila and another, instead of using his gifts to good purpose. Bhaddiya we only meet with elsewhere in the Anthology; Bhagu is but a name. Their great adventure makes a pretty Jātaka tale in the Vinaya; renunciation, by the telling of their motive in leaving home, it does not deserve to be called.

I have suggested, that the one rift in the all-shrouding veil of oblivion, hiding from us the nature of the work and influence of each of those first co-helpers, happens—if only for a moment—in

[1] *Theragāthā*, ver. 37. See below, Chapter XIX.

Assaji's case in a glimpse of what, in the (probably) new thought of the day was his special preoccupation. But we do not get any such rift in the case of the other factors in the body of doctrine which has come down through Sakya as Hīnayāna Buddhism, factors sufficiently prominent to be confused now by this, now by that writer with Gotama's own central teaching. Who, for instance, was it who brought in, probably very early, the way of the "computing" (Sankhā, Sānkhya) theory, so much coming into vogue, even as we saw, in Brahman teaching (unacknowledged as yet *as* Sānkhya), with its discipline of mental clarity in name, number, categories, mental analysis, and its guarding the nature of the very man by the "not I, not Mine, not the Man of me" formula? Which of the pupils of Āḷāra, among Gotama's fellow-students—was it Gotama himself?—made the practice of rapt musing important?

Such are some of the so far unsolved problems of the coming to be of the heterogeneous aggregate called Hīnayāna Buddhism, which has been transmitted, welded together, edited with additions and subtractions by long "apostolic successions" of Sanghas of monks. And I venture to think that, in saying many things about what "Buddha" and "Buddhism" teaches, when what we really have in mind is the complex of the written word, we have lost sight, we have never had sight, of the man Gotama *as working with* those other actual, if less inspired, personalities, the men who with him set going the "Wheel of Dhamma". In the first concept, the first word, of its triple slogan: Buddha, Dhamma, Sangha, Buddhism has tended to merge the other two; Dhamma and Sangha have virtually become Buddha; all the teaching was practically word of Buddha; all the teachers were virtually Buddha: what he "said", or "said he would have said".[1] And when this or that in the body of doctrine is said to be derived from Brahmanism or from Sānkhya or from Yoga, either Gotama is said to have annexed it, or, in a quite impersonal because unknown way, the body of doctrine or Buddhist "philosophy" is said to have imported it.

The result of this confused point of view is, that something different is ever being brought up as the "Central Concept of Buddhism". Either it is *Erlösung*—emancipation—or it is *anatta*—denial of the very man, *puruṣa*, *puggala* (usually referred to as self, soul, or "I")—or it is "*dhamma*", or it is "*dhammā*" (plural), or it is causation, or a form of mysticism, of Brahmanism, or of Sānkhya, or it is *karma*, or *ahiṃsā*, or atheism, or just ethics. Each theorist is quite or fairly confident that he has got hold of the truth,

[1] E.g. *M.*, i, 304; iii, 29; *S.*, iv, 379.

and that it is what "the Buddha" taught! That the Sangha, when it started as a handful of men, might claim credit, were the truth known, for much of the teaching which Buddhists and exponents of Buddhism rank as equal to the indisputable message of the leader of those few men—the message of the Way—is very possibly a fact, but it is a submerged fact. I am not assuming for a moment that Gotama during his long mission taught one theme only, or that his fellow-teachers never taught it. To this I will return.

The one slender clue of Assaji, and the queer misfit of his reply to Sāriputta remain to suggest to us how the composite "Dhamma" came into being. And we may apply that clue thus: It is not fit to see in that teaching the work solely of one man, no matter if he did teach many years and learn much the while, and then to say this or that is its "central idea", ignoring in part, the alleged, solemn statement of what that central idea really was. Again, it is not fit to see in "Buddhism" or "Buddhist philosophy" a homogeneous whole borrowed from this or that "system" presumed to be older. It is more fit to see, in its complex of teaching, *first*, an inspired message for the welfare of the many, appealing simply and directly to the very nature of every man and woman in the "wayfaring" of life here and through the worlds; *secondly*, contributions from the current much-stirring new thought and will, i.e. culture of the country and time, brought in, collectively or individually, by the little band of ardent men who, with their comrade Gotama—*satthavāha* and *maggakkhāyin*—started their teaching as the Sakyaputtas; *lastly*, the influence of the monk-world of guardians and transmitters on the recorded sayings. Had Gotama alone, or Gotama together with his first colleagues planned a doctrine or "system", we should have a homogeneous teaching, instead of one which every critic gauges differently. Again, had Gotama and his friends been real utter "monk-men", born anchorites, to whom the inner world of the monk is the only world that counts, we should have found a simpler, more homogeneous teaching. But there was not only that type of monk; there was the man concerned to teach new knowledge as such, and there was the brother-man seeking world-betterment. These were not monks by nature, but men of the world, "mondial" men. But they could only be respected as teachers if they taught as *religieux*.

And so they decided, at some early date in their mission to become samaṇas, almsmen, monks. This would not mean the winning an altogether unanimous welcome from their world of laymen. We come across complaints voiced here and there in the Suttas, quite apart from the frequent allusion to lay criticisms adduced in the Vinaya as leading to some new, or changed rule. These former strictures are all I believe, imputed to brahmans. Brahmans would not unnaturally resent the way in which the samaṇa detached himself too previously from carrying on the duties of work in the world and at home. We see the brahman farmer telling Gotama that who works has the right to dine ; we see Rohinī's brahman father blaming her for giving alms to

> . . . the lazy crew ;
> They make their living off what others give.
> Cadging are they, and greedy of tit-bits. (*Therīgāthā*, ver. 273.)

Other brahmans pour scorn on the " shavelings ", who, so to speak, simulate the brahman retired recluse, while associating with companions of any or no class.[1] It was a mixed reception for the samaṇa, whether he came out to turn his back on the world, or to help it. Herein the men of Sakya were as was Gotama himself. Theirs was, *must* have been the incorrigible, ineradicable will to help the Many ; and more—to help them in a new way. It was not will to help the bodies of them nor their minds as such ; it was to help the very man in men, the spirit, soul, very man. It was a great task, and no easy one, the nature of which is still much overlooked. It was a " More " they were to bring to man, a new More in man's worth. This was to bring out and stir up the individual will, in each man, to the Better ; that he himself (*sayaṃ*) must choose the way to his *artha*, which had hitherto been a matter prescribed for him, and that the winning of it hereafter depended not on observances, ritual and rule, but on how he carried out his choice in his life—a matter which had not been stressed. Will-missioners : no word is more fit to describe Gotama and his first men.

Will-missioners they appear to me. Similarly the first men of Jesus will appear, with their Master himself, to one coming fresh to a reading of the Gospels, to have been Healing-missioners, far more than Word-missioners. The " gift of healing ", however it be *explained* by those who accept it as fact, must have been abnormally on the increase, to have made it possible for Jesus to meet with several such men in one small corner of a small land. I conceive a similar *abnormal growth in will-power*, or synergy, in that small area, where Gotama and his men were reared and where they worked. It was men with such a " gift of will ", who will have drawn Gotama and who were drawn to him. That we know so very little of them

[1] *Sutta-Nipāta*, *Saṃyutta*, i, *Theragāthā*, *Majjhima*.

is our misfortune. We would give much for just one Saying in the Suttas on what, in world-help, the causal law meant for Assaji, by Assaji. We feel the mutual love and esteem in the senior disciple's, Kondañña's, greeting after long absence, in old age, of the beloved Leader—the disciple described by verse-maker Vangīsa as *daḷhaviriyo*: strong in energy.[1] But we have enough for all that to feel sure, that for all their differences in outlook, in ideas old and new, the very strong will, working mainly as will to help, must have linked them closely with their Leader, and that it was men, as he said, like himself, whom he sent to and fro as missioners to "tell man of the "lovely dhamma", in them, of the "God-life."[2]

[1] *Saṃyutta*, i, 193; *Theragāthā*, ver. 1238 f.
[2] *Vin.*, loc. cit., p. 21.

VIII

THE MANDATE ON CAUSE

I have tried thus far to show, that in the first adherents of the Man of Sakya, we should see, not mere listeners, satellites, disciples, but men very fit to be fellow-workers, men who as such would not merely echo his teaching, but enrich it by what they themselves brought into it. I have already indicated one and others of these enriching factors, and I would now deal with each of these in some detail.

But let this strong presumption that we have here in Sakya the work of not one man alone, but of men of individual capacity and manifold tendency, not mislead us as to the equally strong presumption that they were one and all bent on a common quest. Their object was the man and his welfare, the one and the other was to be worded in terms of a new value, but a value which a man would understand and appreciate as it was meant he should. In other words it was a "More" which they were bringing to Everyman about himself. Not about things external; not about the external universe; just about himself. However much their own predispositions might cause them to teach with varying emphasis; however much this might and did lead to a manifoldness in the teaching they handed down; they were all, so far as the scanty record shows, at one in that common quest: the bringing as mission-teachers a gift to man.

Of what I have called enriching factors, none has left a deeper mark on the Founder's mandate of man's progress in the "More", pictured as a Way, than that which we saw working at the very outset: the teaching of that "More" by way of cause and effect. So deep is the mark that in books on Buddhism, whether old, mediæval, or modern, the religion is more often said to have "causation" as its base, or essence, or credo, than the saving importance of the Way of the good life.

I said "old" books, thinking of the Piṭakas themselves. There we read, that he who sees *paṭicca-samuppāda* (happening as causal) sees *dhamma*; he who sees *dhamma* sees *paṭicca-samuppāda*,[1] words said to have been said by the Founder, and, in the passage, ascribed to him by Sāriputta. Again, Gotama is recorded as saying to Udāyin,

[1] *Majjhima*, i, 190.

a paribbājaka or wandering student: "Let be the end (limit) of the past; let be the end of the future; I will show you *dhamma*: where this is, that becomes; from the uprising of this that arises; where this is not, that does not become; from the stopping of this, that stops."[1] In other words, I venture to interpret, *dhamma* is in that becoming which you can now be causing by your will. Again, to the abstract statement just cited, followed by the statement of the Paṭicca-samuppāda formula (that is, by the usual application of the general wording to the cause and stopping of "ill") is given the special title of ariyo Nyāyo,[2] or Ariyan Teaching. This is enough to show at least the titular importance of the subject in the records earlier and later, apart from the Suttanta devoted to it in the Dīgha, and the Collection devoted to it in the Saṃyutta.

With mediæval schoolmen, such as Buddhaghosa, who deals at length with Paṭicca-samuppāda in his *Visuddhi-magga*,[3] and those who wrote in Sanskrit, such as Vasubandhu, this book is not concerned. Our business is with the beginnings of this deep mark set upon a gospel, which in its first authoritative utterance, has not a word to teach about cause and effect *quâ* gospel. The figure in that much submerged gospel of the Way is, it is true, capable of being interpreted in terms of a working cause to bring about a desired effect. But this is not its first, its overt meaning. A world-message would not take a line so crooked. The appended "four truths", it is true, are an application of cause diagnosed and the stopping of it indicated. But even were they part of the original utterance, which I hold they were not, they are not a statement of "the essence and spirit of Buddhism" *as a gospel of cause*. They *assume* a belief in causality, as a man would do who put a bucket of water into our hands to pour on our blazing turban. (A Sakyan figure suggests the simile.) It was, as I have said, Assaji, and not Gotama, who spoke, of the new teaching he is made to ascribe to the man of Sakya, in terms of a gospel of causation. And it is with the words imputed to him that we are concerned.

Let us go more critically into these. Sāriputta, having accosted Assaji as we saw, asks: "What is the doctrine (*kiṃvādī*) of your teacher, the Samaṇa Sakyaputta? . . . Tell me little or much, (but) tell me just the *artha* (the well, the good, in it); it is *artha* that I need. What need to make much wording?"

The reader should note here that I take the older, the Indian,

[1] Ibid., ii, 32. [2] *Ñāyo. Saṃyutta*, v., 388.

[3] Now published as *The Path of Purity*, by P. Maung Tin, B.Litt.Oxon., *PTS*.

not the "Buddhist" meaning of *artha*, used by Oldenberg and Rhys Davids, and rendered "spirit", as = "meaning". They would seem to be justified by the following question with the word *vyañjanaṃ*, which I have rendered "wording".[1] In later records the two Pali words of the text: *attha, vyañjana*, are frequently used in this sense of spirit or meaning and letter or form. But I can find no instance of the pair of words either in Vedic or in early Pali literature, and I am constrained to judge that we have here a genuine Vedic and Sakyan term *Artha*, edited and embroidered in later idiom and antithesis. It was just *artha* as "Good" or spiritual health, "salvation," that Sāriputta is declared to have been seeking, albeit in this Vinaya record it is called *amata*, and in the later Dhammapada Commentary "*dhamma* of release (*mokkha*)". And as we saw, "belonging to *artha*"[2] was the term used in the record of the First Utterance, where "spirit" or "meaning" is clearly not meant.

Assaji thereupon "uttered this expression of *dhamma* (*dhamma-pariyāyaṃ*) :—The things which have come to be from a cause, of these the tathāgata has spoken the cause; and the stopping which is of them: such-a-speaker is the great *samaṇa*." (*This is in two lines of verse.*)

"Then in Sāriputta, hearing this expression of *dhamma*, arose the dustless spotless *dhamma*-sight, namely: whatsoever is arising-thing, all that is ending-thing."

"This verily is *dhamma*, if so be ye have thereunto reached, which is the Estate Unsorrowing, Unseen, and by many myriad ages the Long-ago-gone Past."

I have given these lines as literally as possible.

The last paragraph has been by the translators given to Sāriputta. More accurately, for me, it is a pious editor's comment, in quite poetic idiom if not in any recognized metre, on the foregoing, by him revered, "expression of *dhamma*". That "expression" (*pariyāya*) had evidently come to mean for him and his fellow-votaries something very "central" and essential.

Now the two previous paragraphs make together a very bad fit. Thus: the *verse* claims to say what the "great recluse" taught. The following *prose* sentence does not, and makes a different statement. The *verse* says: This man (is able to) assign its arising and its ending to everything that is caused. The *prose* sentence says, that when Sāriputta hears, he sees by a flash of insight that whatever arises comes to an end. Or, more truly interpreted, as I hold,

[1] Page 134. [2] *Atthasaṃhita*.

whatever is a causing is also a stopping. Namely, the willing agent can both produce and also stop. Now this is not what the *verse* said. The *prose* makes a statement we call a law, or uniformity. This is usually identified as the law of impermanence (*anicca*). More justly it means: anything a man can produce he can also stop. For this and this only was the interest felt in those days in such a matter. But the *verse* says only: Here is a man who can tell the specific cause and ending of any given thing. Further, the word "cause" (*hetu*) is only in the verse. Further, the verse makes a claim, "out of the blue", of omniscience for a brand-new teacher. Further, the verse, found in inscriptions on ruins at Benares and elsewhere occurs nowhere else in the Piṭakas. Further, the prose rejoinder of Sāriputta is a stereotyped phrase occurring elsewhere in the Piṭakas.

How is it that a Church so insistent on formulas, in verse and prose, as the Sangha should have neglected to reiterate a verse, which has come to seem to writers, even to such an one as Oldenberg, and in the latest edition too of his *Buddha*, "the Buddhist confession of faith briefly comprised"? Nor, for that matter, without supporting evidence, if we are to believe Brian Hodgson's statement that the verse can, or could in his day, be repeated by almost every man, woman and child of the Bauddha faith at Katmandu (Nepal).[1]

My answer is, that this verse, so charged with weight of office, is a later compilation than Vinaya and Suttas, and was interpolated in the former work, when Sakya, call it Way-cult or Cause-cult, had become Buddha-cult. The botchwork of the episode is then in some degree explained.

Yet not wholly. As I said in the last chapter, I do not see in Sāriputta a champion of any teaching of salvation based on willed action *as causal*. Gifted and impressive speaker he appears to have been, valued by his teacher Sañjaya the sophist much as Gotama was valued by his teachers, Āḷāra and Uddaka.[2] But he appears as "fed up with" Sañjaya's sceptical sophisms. Much, it is true, is fathered upon Sāriputta (as upon his Leader) with which he had nothing to do, for instance, the book called Paṭisambhidā-magga, schoolmen's work of a much later date, and the last two Suttantas of the Dīgha, numbered categories, evident supplement and appendix to the earlier contents, compiled probably subsequent to his predecease, and not by any of the original Sakyans. But if we combine text and commentary in which are thumbnail sketches

[1] Spence Hardy, *A Manual of Buddhism*, 196.
[2] *Vinaya*, Mahāv., i, 24, 2.

of Sāriputta, we seem to get what, in spite of opposing cries, I should call, as a known Western writer was called, a God-intoxicated man. By that I mean the Indian sense, the sense of realizing the "More" in each man Who can grow into, become the "Most", and the Sakyan sense of *dhamma* as the Inner Controller, the Antara-Yāmin, urging the man's will in that growth. In his quest for Amata, or Mokkha [1]—he may not, as to that, be rightly worded in either word—he was seeking the best way to further that Becoming. He is repeatedly said to have been commended by the Founder—whose dearest friend, if any one was, he was (the calling of Ānanda "the beloved disciple" is nonsense)—as the man who alone taught Gotama's message as he himself taught it. The Anthology praises him as speaker and teacher, yet so unassuming would he seem to have been that he impressed some as slow in mind :

> Not dull is he, though he seem dull of wit,

says a verse [2] ascribed to him. And if a novice hinted that his robe was disarranged, he would thank him as his teacher.[3] I see him as a thoroughly good and lovely man—the best type of the Sakyan *sappurisa*—teaching salvation by Right Wayfaring, by the God-conduct, by *dhamma*, rather than one to whom the power that lay in uniformity of happening as causal would appeal. We do find him, once only [4] I think, alluding to "contact" as *cause* of ill, and it is always possible, that we have here a mere fraction surviving of what was, when first spoken, a purview of the subject. But nothing further has survived, save this and his reference quoted earlier in this chapter.

All this, however, is a little by the way, and serves but to show how hard it is to get at the true residuum in these ancient records, wherein they who have handed them down have forgotten so much, are so indifferent as to historic truth (the episode is only incidentally included as one instance among many of the original method of ordination !), and where the chroniclers are not careful to be consistent, or at least did not always know, as we now can know, what was contained in other versions beside their own. Thus as to consistency, the chronicler in the Dhammapada Commentary makes Assaji say only the first part of the metrical reply to Sāriputta, and makes Sāriputta himself add the second part ! Truly the tampering

[1] In *Vinaya*, i, loc. cit., and *Dhammapada Comy.*, i, 90, respectively.
[2] *Theragāthā*, ver. 1015 : *ajaḷo jalasamāno.*
[3] *Kindred Sayings*, i, 88, n.
[4] Ibid., ii, 28 f.

hand of the editor, encountering, poor man! many lacunæ, has been busy.

I come to the very kernel of this matter of causation as taught already in early Sakya, before it bulked even bigger than the teaching of the Way. My inquiry is twofold: who introduced it? what did it mean as gospel when introduced?

Who introduced it? Why not, it will be said, hold to the record with which this section of the Vinaya begins, where the Man is shown (I, i, 2) as meditating in full formula on the production of what brings sorrow or ill, and on the ending of it? Or where, in the "Great Legend" of the Dīgha Nikāya he is actually asking himself what brings and what ends ill? and answers again in formulated terms identical with those of the Vinaya, save that here, again inconsistent, the two ultimate links in the causal chain are omitted?

I go with the legend so far as to believe that he was much occupied with formulating a cause-gospel, when he had absented himself from the men who wished to teach, as well as he. And this is not because the legendary account is in itself at all convincing; I do not find it so. But even without writing, the chroniclers were here and there able to word episodes which strike the hearer as true. I could quote several did I not fear to clog the argument. It is not even because the Man's self-communing is worded in formulæ or quasi-mantra: there was more or less of a reason for that. But once he has questioned himself on the origin of ill, he is not made out *as seeking the reply*. The reply is given him; it is placed as a finished argument into his mouth. But later he *is* depicted as wanting to talk to men about the fact of causal uniformity being something by which, as by a lever (the figure is mine) the man could uplift himself from his lower nature, yet he fears that habit, custom, the wonted, will prove hostile to this new gospel [1]—and so when he does begin, it is with a more popular "way". Here I find something more deserving the name of evidence, that he had thought much and wistfully on the idea of causal uniformity as a spiritual lever or spring, with which he could enlist man's will in his own betterment.

But, as I have said already, so far from having such words as lever, or spring, wherewith I of our mechanical day can glibly picture incentive, he may quite possibly have felt he had no words to make such a gospel practicable. Now among his men, one or more did find it possible, did succeed where he anticipated too great a difficulty, did find, as he did not, convincing words, and so brought in to the new Sakyan Word this factor which proved so greatly influential in its

[1] *Dīgha*, ii, 37; *Saṃyutta*, i, 171, f. *Supra*, p. 117.

development. But can we make any plausible guess who it was, seeing that Buddhist tradition has let the memory of those cause-missioners die by fathering their work on the Man who was Way-and-Will missioner?

I am venturing here to repeat my own guess.[1] Assaji, we can see, was certainly much preoccupied with the teaching of cause, whether or no we accept as true the record of his referring it as gospel to Gotama. But I have said that I cannot see in Assaji an original messenger, or effective speaker of a new mandate, and why I cannot. Rather am I inclined to see in his answer to Sāriputta a reference, not to the Sakyan Gotama, but to another man, who had the gifts and power he himself was less endowed withal, and who had actually formulated a way of teaching for the Many based on causation. And just when he made that answer—and we cannot say with respect to those other first occurrences when it was, so mixed, so incidental is the inclusion of them in the Vinaya—he had come straightway from meeting that teacher, and possibly hearing him enunciate *his* First Utterance as a message worthy to launch on his world. Assaji was evidently a fervent disciple, a deeply convinced man, even if he felt tongue-shy at attempting the difficulty—Gotama had felt it as difficult—of putting the case for a gospel based on causation, so as to do it justice, to a man he knew to be as gifted as was Sāriputta. "I am new . . . lately come to this teaching; I am not able to set it out fully, but I will state it in outline." We may look upon him as abettor of an original teacher, but not as able to make the teaching what it actually became: a rival factor to the message of the Way.

It is not in anyone of the so-called Five-men that I see such an *original* teacher, nor in any of those named among the earliest converts. But—and I give it here as no more than a surmise—I incline to see him in one of the twelve Theras (seniors), who are several times named especially in the Vinaya, as being about the Founder. These were Sāriputta, Moggallāna, Kassapa, Kaccāna, Koṭṭhita, Kappina, Cunda, Anuruddha, Revata, Upāli, Ānanda, Rāhula. This list is not always the same; in the group of the moonlight talk in the Gosingavana,[2] Nos. 4–8 are omitted; in the group of Udāna, i, 5, commended by the Bhagavā as true "brahmans," i.e. sincerely religious men—Nos. 10–12 are omitted, and Devadatta, the formidable schismatic, is included, which is a testimony to the age of the Sutta. A further comparison of such lists shows a certain number of "constants" among the twelve;

[1] *JRAS.*, 1927. [2] *Majjhima*, No. 32.

of these the man I have in mind is all but such; I refer to Kappina.

Kappina was then undoubtedly one of the leading, shall I say, apostles in the inception of Sakya; and Kappina is signalled out, in the Anguttara chapter of men and women commended for this or that gift or office, as the best of those who exhorted the monks.[1] Yet there is not a single Sutta surviving in which he is the speaker! The commending of him in this way is explained in two Commentaries:—that on this passage, and that on the verses attributed to him (*Theragāthā*, verses 547–56), thus: Become not only a convert to Sakya, but a Senior with a thousand pupils, he became slack in teaching, musing on his happy state. The Founder inquired into this and bade him: "Brahman! (holy man) do not so; from to-day teach *dhamma* to them who have come in." He did so, causing the thousand to attain saintship. So far then we see Kappina as eminent among first apostles, credited in tradition with a mighty persuasiveness in teaching, but as teaching what, and with what emphasis, not a word remains to guide us.

Does he then figure in the Suttas only in this wordless way? No, in two widely detached Suttas, both of the Saṃyutta Nikāya,[2] both entitled "Kappina", we see him pointed out to disciples by Gotama, as approaching or as seated, and spoken of in terms of respect. The former Sutta runs thus: "Do you see that monk coming to us, pale, thin, with prominent nose? (I do not feel satisfied about the word pale, "odātakaṃ". Kappina was a noble, nor would an Indian brother-noble comment on that. The Commentary also, if I recollect rightly, is silent here. It is probably a corrupt reading, possibly some form of *ovādatar*, preacher.) That monk is highly gifted, of wondrous power. No easy matter was it to win what he once had not won . . ." the rest tails off in the usual formula for the religious career: "even that uttermost goal of the God-life which he has attained, wherein he abides, having come even here to know it thoroughly for himself and to realize it."

In the other Sutta, his rapt absorbed stillness is pointed out.

There is yet another little Sutta following the former of these, in which Gotama points out two unnamed disciples of Kappina in the same terms as their teacher. And we are left wondering whether one of them was Assaji? I judge we have here very old fragmentary sayings relating to an early date in the Order, when Kappina had

[1] By scanty materials, or oversight, I have wrongly said "nuns" (*bhikkhuniyo*) in *Psalms of the Brethren*.

[2] Vol. ii, 284, v., 315.

very likely not yet cast in his lot with the Sakyans, and that we have the two teachers meeting, it is just possible, for the first time: the ex-raja from the border-country, its capital named Kukkuṭa, with the kumāra from the uplands of Kosala. That Kappina is referred to as if he were a monk, already in the Order, may well be just the way of the monastic editor making his fragments of oral sayings more plausible. That the names of the two distinguished students, about whom there follows a little poem, are forgotten is evidence that we have here very old stuff.

Then there is the traditional story of Kappina in the Commentaries of Buddhaghosa's Pali recast (from the Sinhalese, which was from the Māgadhī) and of Dhammapāla.[1] They are in agreement that Kappina as raja, i.e. squire, petty chieftain, of a remote estate somewhere in the north-west, was athirst for coming to know new ideas, and stationed men at the gates of his town to ask incoming traders, if they could tell of any teaching (*sāsana*) of such. At length traders arrived from Sāvatthī, who told him of "the Buddha" there. At that he put all his home business aside and set out with his cavalcade towards Sāvatthī. The Buddha meanwhile aware, when at dawn he surveyed the "world", of his coming, went forth to meet him.

We have very possibly here a legend, not unlike that of Siddhattha Gotama himself, and which, had there been only not

room enough at Rome but for one man,

room for two such men, had the Sakyan Sangha not fathered the other man's teaching on one and the same teacher, had Buddhism kept alive the memory of the man who turned the mandate largely from one of the Way to one of the Cause, would now bulk as largely in the popular lore of Buddhism as does that of the accredited founder.

So far then we now see Kappina recognized both by tradition, and also by the Sakyan leader *as in a way akin to himself.* Yet not akin as brother-teacher in just the same way as he declared Sāriputta to be. I think this merits attention. Kappina was clearly a teacher to be reckoned with, yet not of him was it said:

> The Wheel I set a-going, Dhamma-wheel,
> Above which, Sela, there is none, 't is that
> Doth Sāriputta after my example turn,
> Who hath become like him-who-thus-hath-gone,[2]

[1] On *Anguttara* (Etad-agga-vagga) and *Theragāthā*, resp.
[2] *Sutta-Nipāta*, ver. 557; *Theragāthā*, ver. 827.

even though there was plenty of opportunity to have done so, in such Suttas as those cited above.

I come now to the verses, *Theragāthā*, 547–66, ascribed to Kappina. That Kappina compiled them as they stand, who shall dare to say? Far more likely is it, that gnomic aphorisms, such as these, were very possibly prose sayings repeated by his many pupils and, as utterances of a leading "apostle", were metrically recast by those clerical monks who, as the years went on, were gradually amassing a Smriti, or worded tradition fit to set beside the more venerable thesaurus of the brahmans. I do not see all the poems in the Anthology as of this nature. There were, as I have pointed out, genuine poets among the compilers. But these verses are different, and should be contrasted with, say, those of Migajāla, cited in an earlier chapter. They are in a way a misfit with the sentiments, monastic, anchoritic, æsthetic, prevailing in the book as a whole. The reader will thank me for giving him to hand the opportunity of judging for himself. I give them not metrically, as in my translation, but in literal prose:

"He who sees a matter (or end, object, *attham*), not yet come, beforehand, as beneficial or as harmful, in him neither ill-seekers nor well-seekers scrutinizing see a defect.

"He by whom meditation in breathing has been perfected, well made-to-become, practised duly as by the Buddha taught, he lights up this world as the moon freed from cloud.

"Lo now! the mind of me white, boundless, well made-to-become, penetrated and grasped, illumines all directions.

"The holy man is truly alive, though his wealth be destroyed; with the not getting of holiness (*paññā*), though rich he is not alive.

"Holiness is arbiter of the heard (*suti*, learning); holiness is increaser of repute and fame; with holiness as friend a man even here finds happy things in things of ill.

"This is not a thing of to-day, nor abnormal nor anomalous: 'where ye are born ye die': what is here that is anomaly? For to one born the sequel is perpetual dying from life; here this one and that, when born, die: verily such are all breathers.

"Verily not for the welfare (*atthāya*) of the dead is it that (there be) weeping of other men; not honouring (them is it), nor of world-(value), nor praised by recluses and brahmans. Weeping wastes eye and body; comeliness, strength and intelligence is wasted. To one joyous, (joyous) become the world-quarters; well-seekers become they, if he be not lucky. Hence should one desire the wise and the cultured, (if) in family dwelling. Verily by their abundant holiness (men) accomplish what should be done, as by a boat the full river [is crossed]. Great-Kappina uttered these verses."

Of these verses I wrote recently: "They are neither Hindu, nor Buddhist, nor Jain, nor monastic; they are frankly pagan. But if we look at them as the verses of a man absorbed in the study of the external world and of this earth-life only, they become a very voice speaking from a nearly forgotten past. There is nothing in them, save one verse, that Thales might not have written! Take the first lines: how could a Causationist better commend the practical benefit of the prevision and prediction of specific causes? Note, too, the gloomy pagan outlook." Here I should have added: "and the pagan ground of joyousness and well-being." Well, to-day I propose to modify to some extent this conclusion. Two years is not too short a time in which to become a little wiser. I will first make one or two incidental remarks.

(1) On the cultivation of breathing in *sati* (here "meditation") I shall have a word to say later.

(2) I do not associate the words "the mind of me (is) white" with the words in the commendation quoted above: "that *odātaka* man." The latter is probably a misreading; the former refers to mental "purity" or lucidity. In this meaning the word is usually *pariyodāta*, thoroughly white, and it would have probably been used here, had the metre permitted.

(3) In passing, the insistence on the man, whose is the mind, *me cittaṃ*, should be noticed. The man is not merged in the mind.

(4) If I have substituted "holiness" for the more usual "wisdom", in the important word *paññā*, it is not that I judge the Sakyan thought lightly of wisdom as we understand it. It is because he saw in *paññā* more than what we see in wisdom to-day. Occasionally this more of meaning confronts us in other Scriptures, e.g. in Psalms, in Proverbs, in Epistles of the Bible, and into it I have gone in an earlier chapter.[1] It is the Divine nature in man, the More that may become the Most, which is truly the old Sakyan *paññā*. The very phrase *paññā-sahita*, "holiness-comraded," reminds us of the Mahabhārata term to which I referred: "This Self is my true kinsman; I can no other than be with Him."

(5) Save for the opening lines, I do not see that these verses, imputed to Kappina, strengthen my surmise, that in him we have the man chiefly responsible for Sakya becoming, in repute, a religion based on causation. The opening lines are, none the less, distinctive as a pragmatic rune in causality. But we are too much in the dark

[1] See p. 95.

as to the historical relation, if there be really any, between verses and putative author to build anything definite about the latter as a teacher of any special subject. All that we can say is, that there was a tradition existing, for the Theragāthā editors, linking Kappina the "Great" with a verse which gives practical value to prediction, or the foreseeing effect from cause.

(6) The one other line in the Anthology mentioning a Kappina is of interest, even though it has nothing to do with causation. Kassapa the apostle is *credited* with a number of poems, He may very likely have been the author of none of them. I may appear to be infected with what, in another connection, Garbe called "barren dubietitis",[1] but I have here anyway the leading of Dr. Winternitz, the eminent author of the *History of Indian Literature*. Kassapa *may* have been addicted to compiling verse; we know that Vangīsa, whose many poems follow his, was so addicted; but we know also that Kassapa was first and last, as Vangīsa was not, the ascetic, and as such, and also as coming to the front in his old age, he is more likely to have had verses written about him than to have compiled them about either himself, or about his earlier fellow-disciples. There will, I imagine, have been quite a number of verses, the repeating of which was kept up as the generations went by, but the authors of which had become forgotten. If there is one thing of which, in most men, we can *not* say "liveth for evermore", it is the name. Now Kassapa, as at the front in a great crisis, Moggallāna as the great wonder-worker and Vangīsa, as a famous improviser: was it not likely that in the case of these orphaned verses, the editors, feeling that "the child must have a name", would include now and then a poem under the collections bearing severally these famous names, much as Persian editors have done in the case of Omar Khayyam?

Perhaps one of these is that ascribed to Kassapa, in which he is beholding Brahma-devas doing homage to great Sāriputta. Detached, and at the end, we read:

> Then, seeing Sāriputta thus adored
> By hosts divine, saint most adorable,
> A smile stole o'er the face of Kappina.

Now there is a precedent to this smile somewhat earlier, in the case of Sunīta, the rubbish-sweeper, who in the verses ascribed to him, tells of a similar astounding honour done to himself, and

[1] *Beiträge zur indischen Kulturgeschichte*, 110: Das ist nicht mehr historische Kritik, sondern unfruchtbare Zweifelsucht.

of the Master smiling at the sight and commenting on the beauty of holiness. There are, moreover, a few other smiles—never tears—recorded of the Founder in Sutta and Jātaka, chiefly over memories of former lives. (And of only, I believe, one other son of Sakya. This is Moggallāna.) Now, I conceive the Founder and his first men as a joyous company, among whom smiles as of those embarked on a happy quest, on a happy basis, in their theory of man's nature and destiny, would be frequent. But that a smile and its apparent cause should get into the records is perhaps significant, as of a tradition linking in some way the smilers. I say not, that Kappina actually did smile on that occasion; much less that Kassapa, or whoever compiled the odd little appendix, composed an imaginary smiling for æsthetic reasons. I have a different guess about it, but it is not pertinent to the present inquiry.

This I here leave, only too aware how very far it stands from constituting anything evidential for seeing in Kappina, rather than in Gotama, let alone Assaji or any one else, the real founder of a Sakyan gospel of causation. As the Founder used to say: *Alaṃ! Tiṭṭhatu Kappino*: "Enough! Let that stand (aside)!" Let us sum up briefly why I think it was less likely to have been Gotama than another.

(1) A Saying followed by an Act, both ascribed to him, both being recorded as of the first importance. (2) The testimony of the man who had been in unbroken companionship with him, first as disciple, then for 25 years his personal attendant and what we should call his chamberlain, Ānanda.

(1) It were a hard thing to try to move people rooted in and content with tradition (or the habitual) by a teaching of causation [1]: this is the Saying. The Act was the wording a scheme of teaching salvation as the choosing of the right Way where most took the right or the left. It was not a compassing of salvation (eventually) by the certainty, that what and how a man caused *this* would bring about *that*. The scheme has also, it is true, come to include a stopping "that" by not causing, or by stopping, "this". But (*a*) this has been called "truths", not cause and effect; (*b*) world-gospels are not likely to have been negative in form.

(2) After Gotama's death, Ānanda, while at the "mother-church" of Rājagaha, went, we read, to look at the repairs in fortifications going on. The supervising military engineer, Moggallāna of the Cowherds, a brahman, welcomes him back to Rājagaha after his long absence, and then asks whether they reckon

[1] *Dīgha* ii, 37; *Vinaya*, Mahāv., i, 5, 2, etc.

to have among them any one "almsman" who is in every respect the equal of the great Gotama? And Ānanda said: "There is none such, brahman. For he, brahman, was the maker-to-arise of a Way not arisen, he was the maker-to-perceive of a Way unperceived, he was the declarer of a Way undeclared, he was the Way-knower, the Way-witter, the Way-master. And followers in the Way are now the disciples who in this later day have fallen in." [1]

Now this is a solemn, heartfelt confession of faith both in the beloved Leader and in what his teaching had meant to Ānanda. And about it these thoughts arise in me: (1) Granting that Ānanda did so speak, he of all men was best qualified, aged life-witness as he then was, to say what his deceased leader's teaching distinctively had been, what in a word truly represented it. And of causation he says nothing. (2) If the Sutta is a later compilation, and the answer, to give it high authority, was put into Ānanda's mouth, it would be in words sanctioned by the Sangha of the day. This means that for the Sakyan Community Gotama was Way-mandater, not Cause-mandater. I cannot otherwise explain the direct and splendid emphasis in the reply. Causation does not even come in as accessory mandate, let alone co-mandate. In it Gotama is the Man of the Way. And in the Sutta just preceding the reader can see, as I pointed out earlier, one of the few surviving examples of how, in his teaching, he verily was so.

Herein I do not for one moment mean that the full significance in a message to man to carve out his own salvation of cause and effect was either underrated by Gotama and his men, or did not expand into a *virtually* twin gospel with that of the Way. I should be blind not to see the testimony to this in the Piṭakas. Indeed, my first lispings on Sakya were about just these two things: "the Will in Buddhism"—and that is the Way-doctrine without the figure-head, the Wayfarer—and on Causation as a new word *in religion*, to wit, in Sakya.[2] I do not think, that Gotama started his mission with it, nor does it come into the recorded charge he gave his first commissioners. But I think that some man or men among those about him, either at first or later, missionized more as a teacher, or teachers, on Causation than on Wayfaring. It may have been Kappina; it may have been another; it may have been Kappina with others. We have seen that, of the twelve sometimes named as grouped about Gotama, not one is recorded as teaching prominently on the subject of causation. And Kappina alone, while he is recorded

[1] *Majjhima*, iii, 8; Sutta 108.

[2] Congress of Orientalists, Copenhagen, 1908.

as best in teaching in the Order, is never recorded as teaching on any particular subject. Eliminating these, save Sāriputta, all that we have of the other quite first men is Assaji's answer to the former, and Sāriputta's recorded reaction to it.

But albeit the evidence I have so far found is alas ! either quite or mainly of a negative character, I will yet briefly sum it up to help the reader's goodwill. Of the twelve Theras associated as such with Gotama in the records, we have, in the case of each and all, records of utterances by them, or at least of conversations with them, *save in the case of Kappina.* Kappina was a raja according to tradition, keen for new ideas, who like the Founder, left his home to learn the new from a teacher. He was twice pointed out by the Founder, and declared to be one who had achieved something very difficult. He was one of the list of men and women of the Order commended for specific excellence, namely, in the teaching of men who were, nominally at least, themselves teachers. To him are attributed verses of a very distinctive kind, the first of which has a bearing on causation. In verses accredited to another man he is likened to the Founder by a little trait rare in the records.

In leaving the trail of our *x*-teacher, I have a word for those who will say : This is all very well, as far as it goes, and that is saying little. But (1) what can there have been to make his contemporaries (or immediate followers) silent in associating causation with the main teaching of any Thera, if indeed it was more his teaching than that of the Leader and Founder ? (2) The records explicitly associate cause and effect with the ill of the world and the remedying of it in the preliminary meditations of the Founder, and with no one else. Is not this sufficient ?

That my answer to the last question is in the negative I have tried to show. That, in answer to the first question, a reason might be found for a movement or cult letting a man's, an eminent man's, name die, while his distinctive teaching is fostered, I shall presently bring forward in the case of another important phase of Sakya missionizing. The reason is, in the case of both teachers, the same. I suggest it may have been that the two men in question were strongly drawn to the Founder, and the Founder himself strongly appreciative of their doctrines ; some of his most loyal co-workers no less so, but beyond this, there was a potent determinant of such men's after-reputation which should be ever kept in view. Into that I shall go later.[1]

Here let it suffice that in Sakya we have a world-mandate which

[1] Chapter XI.

I am persuaded was started for Everyman, *not for the man as monk, nor by men as monks.* And in saying this I speak counter to its traditions, its legends, its belated *written records.* Now the men of original messages might be drawn to the Founder, but not at all to the growing trend in the new community towards the adoption of the status of the *samaṇa*, likely though this was to invest a religious teacher with that weight and prestige which our Scottish congregations used to see in the minister, when they called him a "man of God". They may have seen and deplored, in the *samaṇa*, the tendency to look upon himself as in a world within a world, as well as the effect which what we now call industrial parasitism had upon his disinterestedness. As dependent on the laity he taught, he ceased to be over against them a free man. And as of an inner clique, he ceased to be with them fellow-man. Their anti-monasticism would tell, both in his dealings with his colleagues, and in their estimate of him during and after his life with them. His teaching, it may be, had come to stay. But he, as not having endeared himself to the monk as monk, would as a personage wane with the years. Can we not see such disappearances in a nearer creed—the first teacher for instance of Madonna-worship? What man was here the lever? Or what woman, perhaps of those in "Thrace, Scythia, Arabia" of whom Epiphanius wrote as making offerings to Mary as to a goddess?

I come now to the second part of my inquiry: What did causation as a gospel mean for the teacher, or teachers, by whom it was first taught as such?

Causation as a gospel, that is, as a new word of help to Everyman on the way and the mystery of life, will not have been fraught with the emphasis and the significance which it might now have for the Everyman of to-day. It will not have interested that Everyman of a past day as a statement of cosmic truth. It will not have been a revelation, transcending everyday knowledge of cause and effect, of uniformity in "Nature's" way. It will not have been to him as a Stoical tonic, in an age when certain personal conceptions of deities were in the melting-pot,[1] reassuring him, as in the "Necessity" of the Greek, that "law" in the universe was a stable chronic fact "behind" the personal god. Even had it been all this, there would have been no new word here for the man of India, whose wise men had spoken before the day we are considering of cosmic Order (*ṛta*), of which gods were but the mouthpiece (*vrata*).

[1] This is the case made out for it in my relatively immature study *Buddhism*) of eighteen years ago.

But, it may be said, only the few, the wiser men would know and appreciate that older teaching; it would yet be a new word for Everyman.

This may well have been the case. But whether the Cause-gospel was in effect a popularization of the Vedic *ṛta* on the one hand, and whether on the other, it was accepted as such by an Everyman ready to receive it, we must check by such evidence as we have in our documents. This is far from being the easy matter it would seem. Not because there is any lack of Sutta-references to causation, but because (*a*) almost every reference has been worded in terms of two formulas, (*b*) of these the greatly preponderant formula is not a proper exposition of causation as a "means of grace" to develop the "More" in man, but only of a mutilated aspect of it, which alone appealed to the monk-teacher and the monk-recorder. I will go further into this presently. I have yet to say what, for me, causation as a gospel did mean in the will of its first teachers.

Now, this was indicated at the beginning of this chapter. I have tried in these pages to suggest that the growing need of that day, albeit dimly felt as such, a need which took effect in (*a*) a new note in Brahman teaching, (*b*) the "Nigganṭha" or Jain movement, (*c*) the Sakyan movement, was for a man to take over into his own hands the shaping and control of his life. And by life I mean his life as a whole, with an indefinite past and an indefinite, but very real future not of earth only.

In this connection two points stood out with a clearness which, if not new, was now enhanced, and was therefore newly worded. These were, firstly, that for each man "life", as we say—and *only we* use this word, not they—was, as to the whole of it, a faring on (*yāna*, *añjana*, *magga*, *saṃsaraṇa*, *pavatti* [1]) and in faring a changing, a becoming. In fact the nearest equivalent to our "life", when not worded as births and dyings, was just "becoming" (*bhava*), too often translated by the inadequate word "existence". Secondly, it was in the man's power to determine the nature of this constant "becoming". And this he could do, so he was coming to believe, less and less by external applications of will: rite, oblation, invocation and the like, and more by chosen conduct in thought, word, and deed. This, the importance, not so much of "ethics" properly understood, as of individual conduct, is the burden preponderant in the Sakyan books. And in this conduct of life, so fraught with the future outlook, it is not the pleasing of an externally conceived Providence which is the guide, nor the standing in the good graces

[1] *Santāna* and *santati* are later terms.

of earthly guides (albeit this is by no means a negligible motive [1]); it is the conduct which is by, or according to "dhamma". Nor was the man in whom "dhamma" made appeal just body worked by mind; the man was self; not "himself"—that is our idiom, and ours only—the man was self, the self, the One self ("selves" was a much later, a Sānkhyan term). And when once this self—God-self and man-self in one—was conceived as moral, as "good" (and not only powerful and creator), it became fit (*samyak*, *sammā*),[2] —the Greek would have said it became "according to nature" —for the individual man also to become moral, good.

But there was much in the way obstructing his so becoming. Now what spring or leverage could the teacher, who as a man elect desired man's weal, call to mind to stimulate this desirable becoming? To stimulate in him the natural, the inevitable becoming-other, as the years passed, so that it should be a "fit" becoming? Well, to this end there was the invoking what we now call will, but which the Indian could only word as "stirred-up effort", or plan, or desire.[3] And one great teacher pictured this as the progress, the effort, the adventure of the Journey (*magga*). Another great teacher (together with the former) ventured on the more abstract way of appealing to his hearer's ability to *cause*, to produce, bring to pass, create, effectuate, or, where he willed, to stop, end, destroy, desist from. So might we depict a teacher of to-day seated in a motor-car, showing a child how, by manipulating this or that "gadget", he could produce progress, or regress and the like, and using this to enjoin the bringing to pass such a better habit, the stopping of such a bad habit. The body, the mind: here was his car, his *ratha*, his chariot; listen!

Thy chariot is the "Silent Runner" named,
With Wheels of Righteous Effort fitted well.
Conscience the Leaning-board; the Drapery
Is Heedfulness; Dhamma the Driver is,
I tell you; Right View he who runs before.
And be it woman, be it man for whom
Such chariot doth wait, by that same car
Into Nibbāna's presence shall they come.

(*Saṃyutta*, i, 5, 6.)

This is said to have been the Founder's response to the earnest appeal: Declare to me what insight is the cause of saintship? [4] And so

[1] Cf. the frequent comment "commended by the wise".
[2] See Chap. III: the First Utterance.
[3] *Āraddhaviriya, saṃkappa, chanda.*
[4] *Commentary*, i, 87.

close is Cause and Way blended in his reply—he opens with the words :

> " Straight " is the name that Way is called, and " Free
> From fear " the Quarter whither thou art bound,

—that we can imagine how much both aspects of the man, " wayfarer " and " creative worker ", meant for him. Both aspects meant the man making-to-become, not change as change, but a change from the less to the more, the More that was in him, the More which, developed from life to life, would one day blossom into the Most Who was in him. This was the " Fit " (*sammā*) wayfaring, this was the fit work of cause, the fit, because it was according to nature the Greek and we might say, because it was *ajjhatta*, according to Self, the Sakyan would have said.

This is the way, I now think the only way, in which the first Sakyans, Gotama, Kappina, and others, saw in " all things as arisen through cause " a mandate such as we call religious. For them, as for that old world in general, the proper study of mankind was man, and not external Nature. I was feeling after this in the chapter, (The) Dhamma as Cause, in a book written 18 years ago, but the mortmain of Western tradition, the heavy hand of the past in the present Western outlook was very strong and withheld vision. For that great movement in religion, as a matter of the individual Man, in India of the seventh century B.C., effect as dependent on antecedent condition was a fact taken to heart as of immediate and intimate importance *for the man*.

That the fact was true of the external material world nowhere appears as of interest. It was with regard to the nature of *the man*, and the life of *the man* (I purposely do not say just " man "), that the growing interest in the fact of uniformity in succession was showing itself. Cosmic uniformity in succession was already latent in the old Ṛta, and the notion and the word survived in the idiom of the day, appearing in Pali later as *utu*, or seasonal phenomenon.[1] But nowhere in Pali books is *utu* ever associated with talk on cause and effect, in or out of formulæ. Where at length we find *utu* re-expanded in Buddhism to cosmic breadth, is in a synthesis appearing only in Buddhaghosa. He, in naming the fivefold world order of his day, calls the *physical* (not the cosmic, or universal) order *utu-niyama* (= *ṛta-niyama*).

And why the fact of causation was being just then realized as tremendously true for the inner world, the immaterial world of the

[1] Or, in Burma, just seasonal " heat ".

man, was a factor, a co-efficient in the conviction which was then stirring that the man was not solely or rightly to be conceived as being (*sat*), but that he was becoming (*bhū*). There is perhaps no older group of words in Vedic thought than that around *bhū*, but it was not to the man's essential nature that they were applied. The concept was now being turned inwards and deepened. Not in the plant only was the "season" of coming to be and of waning. Not in immaterial things only did visible cause precede visible effect. That was, as I have admitted, very pristine experience, and the wording of such visible certainties, in our so-called "accumulative jingles", is of the hoariest: "The cat began to kill the rat; the rat began to gnaw the rope; the rope began . . ." but I forget what the rope did; I know that certainty lay in the old woman getting home that night, even as in the monastic formula, the landing in *dukkha* in all its shapes was the culminating effect of a causal series, and the only effect on which, in the Piṭakas, any emphasis on the fact of causation is laid.

Here we have the real interest of that early day felt in the new talk about cause. It was the truth of causality for the inner world of man. We have come to see causality in everything within and without. We do not dream of trying to prove it in any one series, just to show it is actual and effective. But then the idea of causation within as well as without was new, and it had to be shown in an authoritative way *as happening within*. This we have to bear in mind when considering the crudely fitted formula called the Paṭicca-samuppāda. Greater far is the new fetch of mind in the abstract, not the applied formula: Given *a*, *b* comes to be, etc. But this was in advance of the "time-spirit". It was not grasped; it is usually omitted before the concrete application to *dukkha*. Here and there the two occur together; very rarely the abstract statement occurs alone—I am coming presently to the most interesting example [1]—but the concrete application is frequent and has, moreover, a lengthy Collection to itself.

This is no evidence for the applied formula being of the truly early Sakya sayings. There is evidence indeed that it was a much later compilation. It is not included in the list of Sayings adduced as final charge to his men by the dying Founder. Nor for that matter are the "truths" included, which assume causation in the man. It is an intensely monkish view of that causation *as a sinister functioning needing stoppage*, and belongs to the growing monastic vogue.

[1] Page 154.

Later, too, is the definition of cause put forward when Buddhists began to frame the rudiments of a scholastic philosophy, perhaps only in Ceylon. It has affinity with our own mediæval conception of causation. We have now reduced causality to the ætiolated idea of uniformity in succession, and we may perhaps not stop at that. But it used to mean uniform "transeunce" of a somewhat-in-the-cause "going-over" into the effect. And this was also the function of cause in the Buddhist East. This we see in the term *upakāra*, helping, literally, "contributory- (*upa-*) factor", as the salient feature of cause.

"Condition has *upakāra* as its mark, for that thing which is *upakārako* (helper) in the persistence, or the coming to pass of a given thing, in its condition." [1]

Here, unfortunately, being himself not of a philosophical temperament, Buddhaghosa leaves us. But in that he has just this one feature in cause *quâ* its causality to give us, we see how wide of the mark we should be were we to read our idea of mere successional uniformity into the Sakyan tradition. "Cause," was the idea, "is that which contributes to the coming to pass of *x*." Unfortunately, I repeat, for it is just here that a greater man would have explained what his tradition meant, by limiting the function of cause to the *upa* in the *kāra*, by limiting it to the contributory office only. Had the cause produced the effect, of becoming or of perduring in becoming, he would have found that the right word was *kāra*, *kāraka*, without the prefix. As it evidently was not in order to see the cause as maker, producer, he might have told us what that was. But readers of Buddhaghosa will know, worthy man though he was, what a perpetual disappointer he also is.

To find the producer, the *kāraka*, we must come to the man in his very nature. Ever potential becomer, he needs, to bring the new, the unwonted, the Better to birth, a *plus*, a more, a super-effort as midwife. Ever willing the becoming, it is now and again the more-will that he needs. And thus, in this gospel of causation, is the man self-creator, self-causer.

You would I should help you choose the best Way, to the companionship hereafter with That whom you hold the Best, Gotama is recorded to have replied. Think not to effect it by just "going to church" (rites of invocation), nor by such bonds as will not leave you free for right effort, nor by just doing nothing, as one asleep. But see that in this life you are making to become, in the man, that which you hold most worthy in your idea of Him you call

[1] *Tikapaṭṭhāna and Commentary*, i, pp. ix, 11, etc.

the Best. Faring in this Way you will be fit for companionship when you pass hence.[1]

Let there be no misunderstanding; there is no use here of causal terms. We have to read them into the teaching from first to last. For there is, I hold, no way rightly to interpret the teaching here given as religious advice of the first importance to the questioners unless we show the Way, unless we show the Causing, one and the other, as a *right choosing* in man's mobile nature, as a right more-effort in man's *engendering* the becoming of what he was capable as man. But it is as if some blight had fallen upon these Pali records, that with such pregnant, far-reaching symbols and hallmarks of a great gospel as the Way and Cause, we scarcely ever find them being brought home in very word to the listener.

Take the conversation with the "Wanderer" Udāyin, to which I have referred. How near we are there to seeing what causation, rightly stated in terms of "law", could mean as a religious mandate, yet how the veil drops at once leaving us with nothing but formula. And so obviously corrupt is the version as recorded of the opening remarks that we are constrained to allow for forgotten matter. Anyway, Gotama interposes his characteristic "*titthatu*": Let be the beginning, let be the end; I will teach you "dhamma": where this is, that comes to pass; where this arises, that arises . . . where this is not, that comes not to pass; where this is stopped, that is stopped.[2]

And that is all! The record may be right in making Udāyin break away in his turn, and complain he "had no use" for such talk, and turn the conversation. But is it conceivable that Gotama will have to be content to leave it with a formula, notable and world-true though it was? We must at least see in the brief "I will teach you dhamma" that which Buddhist and exponent have quite lost sight of, namely, that here is no "doctrine", no "the Dhamma", but the inner urge or will to the Right of which I have spoken. Where this is heeded, the man causes or makes *that* to become, or again the man stops *that*. Only surely in this way can we be satisfied that we have here, if all too briefly, what a cause-gospel

[1] *Dīgha*, No. xiii.

[2] In Pali *idaṃ* . . . *idaṃ* . . . this, this; not this, that. It is the usual Pali idiom for a pair, just as in *añño* . . . *añño*, "the one, the other," (as in Latin); *ca* . . . *ca* . . . "both (x) and (y)". But in the repeated *idaṃ*, x and y are certainly meant. Yet I have in mind a French scholar who tried to make a specific Buddhist feature out of the two *idaṃ*'s taken as identical in meaning.

can reasonably be supposed to have meant in the mouth of such a teacher. No original mandater would have referred to his own mandate as "a Dhamma", or as "the Dhamma", or even as just "doctrine". Let a Christian ask himself if he can hear the Christ beginning: I will teach you (the) doctrine: Love your enemies . . . It was "But *I say unto you*: Love . . ." and again: "A new commandment *give I unto you*: that ye love . . ." The Pali permits, as we know, but do not always remember, of no preceding "article", and this is often a translator's difficulty. It has contributed not a little in making *us* see, in the word, what the Buddhist *came to see in it* in the different medium of his own tongues—came to see, when in his world that dhamma which had once meant "inner monition" (working as cause) was now externalized as verbal teaching. The inner principle of the teaching, of the Faith was the inner principle in the man, the principle, I repeat, which we now call conscience, that which stirred in the man, at a crisis great or small, to act "according to *dhamma*": *dhammena* (rightly), not *a-dhammena*; *charati dhammaŋ*, "to walk by *dhamma*."

Great is our loss that in the Sutta the narrative gives only Udāyin's interruption, and changed subject. To have seen Gotama proceeding to apply his own general statement of causation to the man's difficulty, in rightly appreciating the aims and worth of a religious teacher, might have thrown much light on to this very subject of causation as a vehicle in religious teaching. One thing is worth noticing as we leave the episode. This is Udāyin's confession of inability to follow what the Teacher meant in the terms with which he was opening his remarks: "I am wholly at a loss," are his words, "to follow your utterance about 'this' and 'that'." To us, suckled in a tradition of causality in "Nature", which we express in virtually the same terms as Gotama, there is no such difficulty in following him here. And we cannot fall back on uncultured intelligence in the listener, for the "Wanderers" were, as we might say, the intelligentsia of that day, men of the student or inquiring world, a-foot to learn the new, and discuss it in the *sālās* (open halls) specially provided in parks. And if the cause-thesis was met at the outset by lack of both understanding and of interest in a man of this class, it was surely a wise premonition which made the Sakyan Founder shrink from teaching it as a religious principle before he made his début.

Indeed, I am led to ask, though it be only in asking to wonder, whether, especially since the context here is unique, it was not by way of experiment in putting forth cause as a religious "text" that Gotama spoke as he here did (or is said to have done). For, in the light of what I have said just above, the association of causation with "dhamma" or inner sense of right is not to be lightly passed over, as it hitherto has been. Let it be noted that (*a*) the occasion was deliberately brought about for the holding of a public debate in such an aforesaid park, (*b*) the thesis opened by the Wanderer (like that on a similar occasion three Suttas previous) was, not so much the teacher's actual message, as the way in which he taught it and responded to its effect upon the man taught. Thus it was not an occasion which called for help to be given to one of the Many needing it; it was rather an opportunity as between a teacher, acknowledged as such—the text here leaves no doubt as to that—and an audience of alert intelligent inquirers. And the experiment is made: "Can I stimulate in a man the heeding *dhamma* within him, by showing him that it is the man, the self, working in the self as "that which being present, this comes to pass"; or as "that which, being absent as such (as cause), this is stopped? What will be its effect on him? He is much occupied with the effect of teachers upon himself; but it is with their behaviour. Incidentally I will note the effect upon him of what is taught. Would he respond to the *dhamma* as cause, as Assaji and I have wondered?"

Unique in the juxtaposition mentioned, this Sutta is not the only one in which we read of (*a*) instruction given by Gotama in terms of cause and effect, (*b*) a statement of the fact of causation as a postulate in both natural and religious "philosophy" (as *we* should say). Here is a case of the former.

Next to the First Utterance, Buddhist tradition has ascribed chief importance to the utterances known as the Sakka-pañha, or Questioning of Sakka, governor of the next world.[1] The visit of the unseen deva, accompanied by Pañcasikha, the musician, has been depicted in sculpture, and the Sutta which is No. 21 of the Dīgha Collection, is referred to in the Saṃyutta Collection, and in later Pali works. No formula of cause is cited—neither the adequate statement as in the foregoing Sutta, nor the mutilated application of causation more usually cited—we are spared that—nevertheless the effect on the listeners, namely, on Sakka and his attendant devas present in great numbers, is recorded in the identical formula with which Sāriputta is said to have responded to the (later) verse put into the mouth of Assaji. And the whole dialogue turns on how a man can make of his inner world an efficient causal process, producing this or that effect either of making to become, or of stopping.

[1] *Dīgha*, ii, 283.

So far as I know, the significance of this has been overlooked. I have myself overlooked it till now, who ought to have seen it first, when translating it.[1] Namely, that this Sutta is an example, an object-lesson, of how a man, once he admits the datum of causal happening as ever present, can (*a*) see the fact of its working in his own nature, and (*b*) apply it as an engine in his own power to become better and to remove obstacles to the same. The reader will remember the general statement spoken to Udāyin. If he will refer to the Suttanta of the Sakka Questioning, he will see the application of this statement in a number of cases of (*a*) and (*b*). "Envy, sir, and selfregard: what is the . . . cause thereof? how do they come to be? What being present, are they also present? What being absent, are they also absent?" "Things as dear and not dear to us, ruler of devas: this is the cause of envy and selfregard . . . this is how they come to be. In the presence of what is dear or not dear, envy and self-regard come about, and in the absence of these, they do not come about." And so on.

It may be said: well, there is here a statement of uniformity of happening as applicable to the processes of the mind. But there is nothing leading me to see a teaching of *using this uniformity* as an "engine" in his religious growth.

I may say here, that the very application of cause and effect, familiar externally, might have been so far a new and impressive feature for an intelligent listener of that day. For it is not till centuries later, in the work called Milinda Questions, that we find the idea of *process in mind* newly worded as a thing to be taught.[2] But let that pass. Let us read further. "Attachment as engendered by desire, as engendered by fixing of mind, as engendered by obsession: now how does a man practice a way suitable for leading to the stopping of this idea, this thing called obsession?" And the reply? Well, we here get the answer of an original inspired man reclothed in the monastic, scholastic verbiage of the later editor, dressing up the fragments of a very ancient oral saying (for be it noted that the speaker appears to have been alone, and exercizing "psychic" hearing and sight, and will therefore have probably himself have related the conversation afterwards, instead of memorizing repeaters doing this). But the gist of it is, that obsession, thought, desire, attachment are to be as so many causes, abandoned in so far as they bring about effects which are seen to make for the reverse of what is well.

This is what we should call the Utilitarian standpoint. And

[1] Viz. for *Dialogues of the Buddha*.

[2] Cf. my *The Milinda Questions*, 1930, pp. 52 ff.

this, if taken as more than endorsement of the mandates of *dhamma* or conscience—this, if it is made to take the place of the divine prompting of *dhamma*—will not, in my opinion, have been Gotama's teaching. It will have belonged to the same agency as that to which we owe the dressing up of the answer. More of this later. The Sutta is none the less an interesting instance of the application of the causal proposition, not only as a statement of what happens, but —and here is its significance—of what a man may *make to happen.* Anyone falling into the sea will rise again, but the swimmer and diver, ware of this absolutely reliable fact, *will use it* to enjoy himself, to save life, to recover property.

"How does a man practise" to put the causal law into effect? It is in those words that we need to see a correction of first importance to much that is said about Buddhist fundamentals. For Buddhists, as we of to-day in our own way, became very mechanical in their outlook in this matter of causation. We hear much, even *ad nauseam*, about this mental thing being conditioned by that mental thing, but too little about that which alone gives meaning and force to the conditioning: the fact, namely, that, as religious teaching, it is upon the conditioning, as the actual or possible work of the man, that we are really concerned withal.

But the monastic view became very busy ejecting the man from the causal process. This may be seen in the conception of cause as food or nutriment (*āhāra*). In body as in mind, "all beings are persisters-by-food," ran the formula.[1] Food was accordingly seen as fourfold: material food, contact, purpose and *vinnāṇa*, literally cognition. (Actually *viññāṇa* meant more, namely, the principle persisting from life to life. This we must concede, with the alternative of landing early Buddhism in an illogical distinction. *Viññāṇa* stood for the mind*er* as much as for the mind. It is true that the "minder" *came to be* dropped out of the term. But we are dealing with an earlier day when this had not come about. For the religious thought of that day the man was, *in his nature, viññāṇa* [*vijñāṇa-nāmayaḥ puruṣaḥ*].[2] And this is not saying that the man was merely *viññāṇa* plus body; *viññāṇa* was an essential attribute of his nature, a nature one with the Divine: *vijñāṇamânandam Brahman.*[3] It was as *viññāṇa* that the man "as speaker and knower, himself, not another," was held to "fare on" through births and dyings[4]; it was *viññāṇa* that watchers in the unseen [e.g. Māra]

[1] *Anguttara*, v., 50, 55; *Khuddakapāṭha*, iv.

[2] *Bṛhad. Up.*, ii, 1, 16.

[3] Ibid., iii, 9, 28.

[4] *Majjhima*, No. 38.

looked for, when man was freed from this body [1]; it was as stations [*ṭhitiyo*] for *viññāṇa* that the worlds in rebirth were considered).[2]

We might say then, that of the last two "foods" or bases or causes, the third was psychical, viz. the will (as *we* should say), and the fourth was the willer or minder. And we can see how it was over survival at death that man-as-*viññāṇa* came to the front, and also how confused became this concept of "food", between the older and the later aspect of *viññāṇa*. The question "Who feeds on the *viññāṇa*-food" [3] was indeed "no fit question". It should have been "What effect does the knower, considered as nutriment, fuel, or food, *bring forth*?"

Another curious instance of the unfit, this time in the reply, is the Sutta imputing to Sāriputta, and then by way of endorsement, to Gotama, the idea that effect is caused by "touch", or contact.[4] (The actual effect is "ill", but it was then become the type-word, as being the one effect in which the monastic teaching was professionally interested.) The Sutta does not give the whole causal catena, in which contact is but one link. And the omission may not be without significance as indicating a later trend of ideas, in which the term *sparśa* (contact) apparently came to be extended to mean the whole field of sensation. This was not yet the case where the formula of the Catena "Paṭicca-samuppāda" was accepted, since the field of sensation is represented by the preceding item *saḷāyatana*" (the sixfold sphere).

In either case the misfit is the same: the man who senses, who experiences contact is left out, with the result that the teaching as a religious mandate is hamstrung.

Very different is the emphasis in other Suttas in this group, where the question is about the causer and the effect-experiencer. I have already dealt with this group in connection with the Way, and the central meaning it came to have for the teacher. Here I come back to it in connection with its importance both for the monastic exponents of a mutilated theory of causation—namely, as a force to be stopped—and for us who seek what will have been the fuller, the positive richness of the idea of causation in the conception of the man and his destiny.

"Is he," it is asked,[5] "who does the deed the same as he who experiences the result? Is the experiencer a different person?

[1] *Saṃyutta*, i, 122; iii, 106.
[2] *Dīgha*, No. 15.
[3] *Saṃyutta*, ii, 13.
[4] *Saṃyutta*, ii, 28 f.
[5] Ibid., 75 f. Cf. *Kathāvatthu*, § 212 f.

Is he both? Is he neither?" In other words, is the very man apart from what his body and mind at any time are doing and suffering? Here we are involved in the man, and no amount of editing could drop him out. (The newly established orthodoxy of the Patna Sangha in Asoka's day sought to evade the question, but could only do so by throwing the burden of proof on the champion of the man as real. Let him show that the man was equally real when he was *not* doing or experiencing results!) The teacher is recorded as giving a negative answer to all four alternatives, and further as not admitting for a moment, that the results of the man's deeds are a hedonistic illusion: "Nay, *I*[1] am not one who knows not pleasure and pain. I know, I see pleasure and pain." And had we the reply in the words actually given, we should see that he knew, he saw the man in a new, a fuller meaning than did his questioners. For him deed, result, the man, the experience were very real. And the man-as-real was the man-as-becoming. As becoming he was the same yet not the same; other yet not other; not both at the same time; not neither, for it was his, in becoming, to be using therein body and mind, and his, in that using, to be ware of both pleasure and pain.

And let us not here forget, amid our own wealth of such terms, that the teacher had no word for "using", "use," and none for "tool" or "instrument"!

Surely in some way will he have thrown light on the tangle in the questioner's mind as to occasion the outburst of devotion which in each case follows! Actually the recorded answers are mere formulæ, in part misfitting formulæ. We have first a rejecting of alternatives borrowed from the wording of the First Utterance, with an indication of a "middle Way". Then comes an insertion of the application of the Causal Formula to the genesis of Ill. Had the record given the general statement I have cited: "Given this, that comes to be, etc.," the result would still have been profoundly disappointing, but at least it would not have presented an appearance so logically anomalous as the explaining man's *progress* as causing his own destiny (experienced as a mixture of good and bad, better and worse, pleasure and pain, the more or the less well) merely through antecedent conditions leading to ill. But the less ill-fitting statement is not even given in the case of the answer, where the question is of the more abstract, very general kind: "Everything is; everything is not: which is the fit view?"[2] Here the man is merged in the larger concept of "all". The aspect of him as suffering pain or

[1] *Khv'âham*. [2] See supra, p. 92; *Saṃyutta*, ii, 17; iii, 135.

as anything else, save as just coming under "Everything", is out of count. Here the view in the general statement, where the static "is" and "is not" are blended under the kinetic "is becoming", would have been a fit, if terse reply to the terse question.

Yet even here, where the live word of the live man has been lost, the dead formula inserted is not the broader mantra of the causal fact, but the narrower detailed mantra of the Conditions of Ill. And the only apology I can make to myself for the editors, is that the Abracadabra of the longer mantra had come to *stand for* the great pregnant term Becoming, in which it had tried to word one phase. For let the reader, who sees a captious cavilling only in thus criticizing these old records, try to imagine any man exercizing the vivid instant effect upon the listener, as here shines through the dead formulas, by the words in which he is said to have spoken, words so wooden and inept. Let him try to imagine the listener responding to them convinced and enthusiastic. It is surely not impertinent here to seek an apology, when apology is so obviously needed.

I conceive that, for the monk, the difficulty in the Sayings, in so far as they were truly perpetuated, lay in the speaker's, the original speaker's use of the term which *we* can use without fear of blame: the term *bhava*.

For consider:—It would have been impossible for a teacher to have set out a theory of the man's nature and of the man's life, as that which neither is nor is not, but which is a process of becoming, a growing, a growing which he can cause to come about, without his using the words *bhava*, *bhavati*, *bhāveti*. And in Gotama's day, I believe that he both could and did so use them, without fear and without reproach, as an essential feature in his great gospel of hope for man. This hope was, that in the long, long Way of becoming, the man would at last burgeon and blossom into the maturity of That Who he in the germ really was. But with the rise of the Samaṇa vogue, the world, and life in the world, in any world, became a thing to be dreaded and avoided. For every case of such life, especially in the plane of sense-desire (*kāma*), meant a bodily becoming. Bodily life with its three "fires" of disease, old age, and dying: *this* is what *bhava* actually stood for in monastic eyes. Branded as canker (*āsava*), as latent morbid tendency (*anusaya*), as wrong view (*diṭṭhi*), as flood (of ill, *ogha*), as yoke (of ill, *yoga*), the stopping of it ranked as Nirvana. Becoming came to be looked upon, not as the very guarantee of man's attaining perfection, but as the outlook of despair, rescue wherefrom lay alone in "*nirodha, nirodha*", "stopping, stopping." No more was the Way the symbol of Becoming; the wheel was substituted, the *bhava-chakka*, bound to which the man was pictured in Buddhist literature as turning eternally round and round, till he had forsworn desire to become again. It is not easy to picture a greater tragedy in religious teaching than this which befell the hope-radiating gospel of the Way. But it seems to me a not unlikely explanation of the otherwise inexplicable botching patchwork of editing which we find in the Suttas on Causation.

The only way in which monastic Buddhism could atone for thus dropping the strong, vigorous and, I believe, original teaching of *bhava* from their records, and for blasting the word in this way, was to emphasize the newer causative form of the word in *bhāvanā*, *bhāveti*. I have gone into this in an earlier chapter. As a mode of study in the growth of worthy dispositions, *bhāvanā* appears chiefly in Abhidhamma. But there remains nothing of this in the composition of that relatively worthless formula, the Paṭicca-samuppāda. Banished from it is both the man and his innate will and power to be, for and in himself, a cause; there remains only the negative implication that the causes of Ill being unfolded can be dealt with, can be stopped. The pure gold of the teaching has been thrown away; the worse, the weaker has been let stand.

NOTE.—As I conclude my chapter there comes to me an article in a Ceylon Annual by a European Buddhist, in which the vanished significance (as I have here given it) of causal teaching in Buddhism is claimed to be latent in the Paṭicca-samuppāda. But the very words in which my good friend Earl Brewster sets forth that significance *can not be supported by the Pali records*, nor does he try *there* to find that significance which he has found elsewhere. "It means," he writes, "that man is himself a force which is self-directing; that he is part of all force; to use an expression which by repetition has lost its meaning: he is divine . . . all that he is to become he must create . . ."

"Force," "self-directing": here are great words; here are *modern* words; here are *not* Pali terms of a scholastic monasticism. That "a man is divine": here is a great word, but it belongs not to Pali Buddhism; it belongs to the religious standpoint of India, which was the nursery of original Sakya, but which Sakya, *as* what we call Buddhism, rejected.

IX

MUSING (DHYĀNA, JHĀNA) IN SAKYA

I now pass to consider a feature in Sakya which was there from the first. It is true that no older Indian literature supports us in this. It is true also, that this feature, which is known as Jhāna, came to be referred to in a fixed form of words, not less inadequate and misleading than the formula we considered in the last chapter. It is true also that Jhāna plays no part in the first mandatory utterances attributed to the Founder. We have only indirect evidence to bring to bear on the matter. But that indirect evidence fails to make me feel, when Jhāna is brought in, the sense of an added, a not original exercise, the jar at something superimposed that I get for instance in references to the Brahmavihāra formula. That formula was in one case superimposed on sīla-exordiums. The Jhāna formula is one, on the contrary, on which higher or abnormal states are said to supervene. The term "*pādakajhāna*"[1] is perhaps later than the Piṭaka strata of thought and wording, but it is suggestive of a tradition of Jhāna as being essentially the "base" of further development in the "more" to which the man could rise. And as basic in the Sakyan movement it will have been an instrument at hand for the Co-founders, as known to and practised by anyone at that day who aspired to realize in himself the More of which, as very man, he was capable.

Nowhere do we find the question, often occurring, about matters or words which may have been at the time unfamiliar, "Musing, musing—what is this that is called musing?"[2] This is worth noting, but is not in any way conclusive, for neither do we find the question put about the Four Moods.

Stronger evidence is it perhaps that the state of Jhāna is closely associated with Gotama. It is the only thing come down to us of a religious character about his boyhood, as a state he himself is recorded to have told of himself, as he sat in the shade while his father, the laird in chief, opened the ploughing season.[3] It is associated with his adult love of solitude.[4] And he is called in early verses "the muser in the wood".[5]

[1] Cf. *Compendium of Philosophy*, p. 62; also *Visuddhi-Magga*, 397, cf. 371, etc.

[2] E.g. on Nirvana, *Saṃyutta*, iv, 251, 261, and on several other terms.

[3] *Nidānakathā*, Jātaka, i, 58.

[4] *Vinaya*, Mhv., x, 4, 7.

[5] See *infra*, p. 178.

If then Jhāna was a practice known to the religious world in the earliest days of Sakya, how did it stand in the sanctions of the "Established Church" of the Brahman cult? To the best of my knowledge we have hardly anything in the way of reference to guide us. *Dhyāna* in the Upaniṣads is a *specialized* musing only when it had become the vogue in Brahmanism to recognize and adopt Yoga ideals and outlook.[1] These saw in *dhyāna* an inner concentration, miscalled I think meditation, preceded by *dhāraṇā*, a first negative exercise of binding thought to preclude distraction, and to be followed by *dhyāna*-at-a-higher-power known as *samādhi*. In such a state the yogī could best come face to face with that Most in himself, his divine nature, and so be advanced in the becoming-the-more when emerging to the duties of life. But the fact that Brahman literature is otherwise so silent about this practice of inner self-centred concentration inclines us to think that *dhyāna* may have been, in the orthodox cult, somewhat akin to the position taken up in the Christian Church towards mysticism. It was there from the first; it was not a matter enjoined as essential; it was a legitimate side-track; and mystics, as men and women, who found what they most needed in the way of silence, did little to make the practice in which they could spiritually thrive articulate. But the date when Brahman teachers could be orthodox, while at the same time expressing a sense of value in Yoga is not yet ascertained. They being for the most part conservative in being orthodox, *dhyāna*, as meaning introspective self-communion, is likely to have had its votaries long before that date, but not, I am inclined to hold, the use it had in Sakya.

In the Buddhist formula known as that of the Four Jhānas, later expanded to Five, we are it is true concerned with the serial exercise, which after a fashion combines those of *dhāraṇā* and *dhyāna* with developments which were classed, including Jhāna, as *samādhi*, another name being *adhipaññā*, or super-wisdom.[2] But whereas on the one hand the more to be gained in this Buddhist exercise was (*a*) a series of conscious states of a very vacuous content or nature, and purging of anything we should call intellectual, (*b*) a series of abnormal psychic developments, there is never claimed for it an introversion of the man into that Highest Man within, whereby he could draw support and a coming-to-be of the More of which he was as yet capable. Such is the difference between (α) the true Yoga and (β) Jhāna as it was developed according to formula at some time in the growth of Sakya.

But the object of this book is to get, in time, at the back of the formula-stage, and to find, if the finding is possible, how it was part

[1] *Śvet.* i, 14; *Maitri*, 6, 18. [2] *Anguttara*, i, 236.

of the newly quickened will of the first men of the Sakyas to use and to enjoin the use of this systematic musing. How was it part? Why was it part? If the aim of the Yoga "mystic" was eliminated, what aim reckoned yet worthier, to be compassed by musing, was there to take its place?

We have been told by learned writers that there is no mysticism in Buddhism.[1] And by Buddhism they include, as I do not, the Sakyan beginnings. In so saying they say truly to some extent. But this is because they, with fellow-writers in the *Encyclopædia of Religion and Ethics*, have certain preconceptions about what we have come to call mysticism. And perhaps it is also because a critical, i.e., a historical knowledge of the Buddhist texts is as yet, and was yet to a greater degree when they wrote, very immature.

The word mysticism is a newcomer among us. Johnson's dictionary knew it not. But Johnson defined "mystical" as "sacredly obscure", as having a hidden meaning, and again as just "obscure". Jhāna too is an obscure subject; Dr. Heiler's study in it, of a decade ago,[2] shows it clearly as, at least for him, a "sacredly obscure subject". For him its obscurity lies more in the history of its appearance, growth, and decadence in Buddhism, than in its object. He makes wise and suggestive comments about its history, but about the object of Jhāna he reckons to have found in the texts adequate explanation. He sees in Buddhist, Jaina, and Vedantist Dhyāna a triple expansion, the roots of which run down to obscure pre-Yoga beginnings. But the object of Buddhist Jhāna he claims to have been a gradual but sure way to attainment, cathartic and strenuous, of that Nirvana here and now which is different only in degree from, and is the antechamber of the final goal, Parinirvana. In other words, he sees in Buddhism "not philosophy nor metaphysic nor ethic, but a mystical religion of deliverance", *the* way to which was the way of rapt musing or absorption known as Dhyāna or Jhāna. With a worthy jealousy for the genius of the Founder—the genius of warding and leading individually the individual—he repudiates the idea that Gotama himself taught this "way" in the stereotyped, fourfold Jhāna formula (much less in the four- and five-fold formula of the abstractions called Arūpa-jhāna). With a less worthy rejection of Gotama's significant "manifesto" of the Way, the Magga of life, a wayfaring according to a man's inner guidance through the worlds to the goal as his very gospel—this he calls "an incomplete and inexact popular-poetical conception of the path of salvation"—he makes the Founder

[1] *Encyclopædia of Rel. and Eth.*, art.: Dhyāna.

[2] *Die Buddhistische Versenkung*, 1918.

turn away from the need and the call of a world he had set out to help, turn away from the warding of Everyman, and hold out his way of salvation to the world-lorn, world-forsaking recluse (a strange picture of a world-saviour !).

For me early Buddhism may be rated as "mystical" or not. The word of course means now not merely obscure. But the ascription may produce more obscurity than it clears. Mysticism in its broadest, its most real, because its (for us) most practical meaning is *converse, usually solitary, with the unseen.* Converse is access. It is comm-union ; it is not necessarily union. When the earth comes to accept this humbler, more practicable aspect of mysticism, instead of using terms of an as yet inconceivable union with the Highest, we may then come to hold in wider worth a mysticism that is not attainable only by a saintly aspirant now in this continent, now in that century, but one that is a way for the help of the many, *ye keci sikkhākāmā* ; whosoever are willing to learn.[1]

If we take converse, communion, with the unseen as our meaning of "mystic", we can, as I shall show, claim that there is mysticism, and much of it in early Buddhism. But so-called mysticism is of both the old world and the new, both of primitive culture anywhere, and of riper culture in East and West. And the tendency at present is for the new and the riper to read later traditions and concepts into the old and the more primitive. I propose here as elsewhere, to drop the words "mysticism" and "mystic" as more hindersome than helpful, and try to show whether the Pali books do not betray, when closely scanned, an evolution in the specific form of Indian Samādhi called Buddhist "musing" (Jhāna).

I find myself in disagreement with much that has lately been written on Buddhist Jhāna. Whatever Dhyāna may now mean in Japan or elsewhere in the East, in the Pali books it does *not* mean "meditation".[2] Or at least it does not mean the modern, Western meditation of "threshing a matter out" in concentrated thought. Such meditation requires, if it be worthy, the whole synergy of the thinking man. Early Buddhist Jhāna is a deliberate, explicit putting off (*pahāna*) of applied and sustained thought. What is stated to be left is *sati* coupled with emotional indifference (*upekkhā*). Now *sati* was just lucid, introspective awareness, the very state needed by the listener who is purged of preconceptions, has made his mind a *tabula rasa* and *is waiting to learn.*

This final state in what is known as Fourth Jhāna is not enough kept in view by writers on Dhyāna. Is it because alert receptiveness

[1] *Mahāparinibbāna Suttanta.* [2] *E.R.E.*, art. : Dhyāna.

is so little valued by the man to-day who is about to will what to say, to write, to do? Bach was receptively alert, judged by the "J. J." (*Juvet Jesus*) in his MSS., as headline to his compositions. And it was a great word to America and to us, given by Ramsay Macdonald the other day in a great cause: ". . . so that our two lands may be standing side by side straining our ears and listening to the Divine call, competitive in nothing except which is to be the first to obey." He also showed the need of being receptively alert for that which is not of this world, but which this world sorely needs. Nevertheless that any response not of this earth was looked for does not usually appear, either in the Jhāna formulas, or in any development to which they in most of their contexts are said to lead. Yet there are three striking exceptions to this, which should open our eyes. I shall quote them presently.

I agree that Buddhist Jhāna and Yoga Dhyāna may have a common root in India's remote past. But when it comes to calling the former the latter, I would say they have naught in common save the fact of the solitary muser and the unseen. The values placed in the muser and imputed to the musing are in each cult very different. So different that between the formularized Jhāna and the Yoga aphorisms some historic link is needed, a link which may not show the one as derived from the other, but which may show them as at one time less widely divergent.

Once more, the object in Buddhist Jhāna is not to me so clear as it seems to be to some. Dr. Heiler, like other German writers, sees in the object both of Buddhism and of Jhāna the fairly general Indian religious ideal of deliverance or release (*Erlösung, mokśa, vimutti*). This is not a Vedic doctrine, and it is not very clear whether its first appearance in Indian literature is pre-Buddhistic. It became a familiar word in the Buddhist tradition, as we shall see later, but I repeat, that for me it is not in the Sakyan mandate, and it is with that mandate that we are concerned. Nor is deliverance by any means given as the constant object of Jhāna. What we do find in the Piṭakas is a double set of formulas, expressing, not release, but a practice without a definite object, and inserted in different contexts. Taken in themselves, they suggest a ladder placed against a wall, but not reaching to the top.

Dr. Heiler admits that, in Buddhism, Jhāna is but a preliminary, a preparing, not an end in itself. But he calls the culminating step in the fourfold formula the immediate threshold (*Vorstufe*) of full deliverance, i.e. of "visible nirvana" (*paramadiṭṭhadhamma-nibbāna*), which for him is "in essence one and the same saving-good and deliverance-ideal as the otherside nirvana" (p. 37). But this is by no means the position clearly and unvaryingly assigned to Fourth Jhāna in the canonical books. I can find only one case of a monk making Jhāna basic (*pādaka*) to his winning arahanship, and he was an exceptionally competent jhāyin: Kankhā-Revata.[1] But this is by no means the position clearly and unvaryingly assigned to Fourth Jhāna in the canonical books. In the highly authoritative Brahmajāla Suttanta[2] the four Jhānas are classed in the same category as the enjoyment of bodily health (which was also a form of Nirvana, as the Māgandiya Sutta testifies [3]), and are stated to be outclassed by many other higher and better things felt and known by the "tathāgata". It is true that these "things" may refer to Nirvana-experience, the error being to see in Jhāna the *patti* or attainment itself. But it is very improbable that had Fourth Jhāna been held as the very "threshold" of the highest, it would have been so *classed* as it is there. It is true that we find a baser kind of Jhāna contrasted with that of the formulas, when a man brooding over one of the "hindrances" to right Jhāna "muses and bemuses, unmuses and de-bemuses".[4] But it is not this but the Jhāna of the formulas which is here classified. The Dhammapada declares that it is the combination of Jhāna and wisdom (*paññā*) that makes a man "near to Nirvana" [5] But the less poetical, academic procedure in Abhidhamma sees in Fourth Jhāna, not only a stage in "transmundane" (*lokuttara*) study, but a stage no less, a stage in access to the conditions called Rūpa, or Rūpaloka, the world, or conditions of Brahmādevas. Now these were not for Buddhists coincident with Nirvana; they are even referred to on one occasion as "hīna", inferior.[6] *Yasmiṃ samaye rūpûpapattiyā maggaṃ bhāveti*: "at what time . . . he makes a way to become for access to (or rebirth in) the Rūpa-world)": such is the unvarying formula in Jhāna when undertaken with this object. In supramundane Jhāna, where we might have expected to find no less a clearly stated object, and that object Nirvana, or anyway arahanship, none is given. We are only told that this Jhāna is a "going away from", or "going out" (*niyyānika*), and not-making-for-upheaping" (*apacayagāmin*), and we are left with these negatives. And so little is Jhāna here considered the one and only threshold, that nineteen other forms of "making-to-become" are added,

1 *Anguttara*, i, 23; the attainment is told only in the Commentary.
2 *Dīgha-Nikāya*, i, 36 f.; cf. *Majjhima-Nikāya*, ii, 228.
3 *Majjhima-Nikāya*, no. 75.
4 Ibid., no. 108. Lord Chalmers's transl. Ānanda is the speaker.
5 Verse 372.
6 *Majjhima*, no. 97.

beginning with the "Way," as equally important with Jhāna. I may add in passing, that the Jhāna placed between these two, Rūpa and Lokuttara, namely, Arūpa-Jhāna is, like Rūpa-Jhāna, said to have the definite object of "access" to the hypothetical incorporeal (?) world.

Let it not however be supposed that this relatively tidy treatment of Jhāna appears throughout the Abhidhamma Piṭaka. If we pass from the first book just cited, the Dhammasangaṇi, to the second, the Vibhanga, we seem to light on curious confusions. The Jhāna formulas remain unchanged. Here also the aspirant is said to eliminate all desires of sense and of things evil, then all active work of intellect, then all commotion of emotion, remaining in a state of utterly cleansed indifference and awareness. But we read in what immediately follows, e.g. in the chapter on the Four Infinitudes, that "at that time" the contents of the aspirant's thought (*citta*) include many factors of intellect and emotion, even after attainment of Fourth Jhāna, prior to which all modes of such (viz. *vitakka, vicāra, sukha, dukkha*) have been eliminated. Now it is not easy to understand how a man in Fourth Jhāna, with this purging completed, can be developing the "emancipating thought" of pity or of a fellow-feeling of joy, or be understanding the cause of Ill. Emergence from Jhāna, technically called *vuṭṭhāna* may have first been necessary and be here implied, but there is, though often the case elsewhere, no recorded indication of it. I do not forget that the word "jhāna" came to be applied to musing or brooding, when the officially prescribed procedure *was not being carried out*. Such are the cases of Subhūti and of Nandā, who according to the Commentary were prone to be rapt in willing amity to others while about their daily avocations. But in the Vibhanga, the formula is in every case trotted out.

Then there are those abstractions said to be serially attained in the Arūpajhāna: "from the transcending all perceptions of things visible, from the waning of all perceived resentment (through sense), from inattention to perceptions of diversity, he attains to and abides in the sphere of what may be called infinite space . . . infinite mind . . . nothingness . . . neither perception nor non-perception." I think we may more justly call these vacuities of mind rather than intellectual "fetches" of mind. I do not mean that the aspirant was trying to reduce himself to idiocy. I mean that he, being obsessed with the pre-occupation of mind on things material, and convinced that the only life worth having was one of release from both these and "the particular in things immaterial", was striving to make his consciousness not a *plenum*, but a void. The striving meant of course that he was using his will, but this there were no fit words to express. And it was a willing not to think, since thinking inevitably involved the particular. Meanwhile he sought to let his mind float in a wholly empty medium, only delimitated by some most general name, when thereafter he came to try to make it articulate. It is not then in Arūpa-jhāna that I would see anything anomalous in the elimination of thought prescribed in the Rūpa-jhāna which apparently always preceded it.

Any way, it may be said, the *object* of Jhāna (*Rūpûpapatti*, *Arūpûpapatti*) is here clear enough. That is true. The Commentary concedes, from the Suttas, that there are higher things to be got by *samādhi*, or *jhāna*, but that, for this access, the fourfold Jhāna is the only way.[1] And I am not yet aware of any teaching in the Suttas urging a man to practise Jhāna for rebirth's sake. Rebirth was " becoming " and that, it had come to be thought, led rather to Ill than to the end of Ill.

Is there then more consistency of treatment in the subject of Jhāna in the first two Piṭakas? What do we learn in them about the purpose, end, or object of Jhāna?

The Vinaya almost entirely ignores Jhāna. This is not a little remarkable, seeing how much it was commended in the Suttas, how much it was said to enter into the life of the earnest monk. Yet there appear to be only four distinct references in this bulky work to the Jhānas as a formulated system, and the same number of references to monks as Jhāyins, needing as such the quiet of the cave (*leṇa*) or other separate lodging.[2] It may of course be replied that the Vinaya rules deal mainly with the bad monk who would not be Jhāyin. The reply does not satisfy. The more worthy protesting monk, who brings about the making of new rules, is a prominent feature. If we had a corresponding encyclopædia of Christian discipline, we should never read far without reference to prayer or prayers, a factor to which some writers refer as the equivalent to Jhāna. For me there is no doubt that had the Sangha, during the centuries when the Vinaya was growing by accretions, held Jhāna in its original worth, it would have produced a disciplinary chronicle glowing with Jhāna atmosphere throughout. It is true that, in the over-elaborated set-off, given at the beginning of the Pāṭimokkha-Commentary in the Vinaya, the Founder declares himself to have been a muser, but it is a mere passing allusion in stereotyped sequence, and there is no recurrence in the work even of this, in connection with any other saint. So low could the Sangha at one time and place fall in piety, both in general and with reference to Jhāna, that during a

[1] Commentary on *Dhammasaṅgaṇi*. [2] *Cullavagga*, iv, 4.

scarcity at the important town of Vesālī, the monks decided by a majority not to lend a hand and work with their distressed lay fellow-men, but to advertize each other as holy Jhāna-experts, so as the better to wheedle alms. Public rebuke, ascribed as usual to the Founder himself, albeit probably after his day, was duly given and an older rule enforced, but the occurrence is suggestive.[1]

In the Sutta-Piṭaka on the other hand there is never a long silence about Jhāna. In the four principal Nikāyas alone I have noted some 240 references at least, the *average* distribution being as follows :—

Dīgha-Nikāya : once in 39 pages
Majjhima-Nikāya : „ 26 „
Saṃyutta-Nikāya : „ 19 „
Anguttara-Nikāya : „ 20 „

The formulas never vary, but the context does considerably, giving thereby more or less of living actuality to the congealed ritual of the fixed wording. Certain results are said to be obtained consequent upon attainment of Jhāna, albeit uttermost consummation is nowhere, I believe, given as one. In the fifth Nikāya, excluding the Jātaka, as consisting mainly of much later commentary, and three other later works, I have the following rough approximate quantities :—

In the Dhammapada, 12 references.
„ Sutta-Nipāta, 19 references.
„ Khuddaka-Pāṭha, no reference.
„ Udāna, 1 reference.
„ Iti-vuttaka, 4 references.
„ Peta-vatthu, 1 reference.
„ Vimāna-vatthu, 1 reference.
„ Theragāthā, 5 references.
„ Therīgāthā, 3 references.
„ Niddesa (Mahā), 5 references.
„ Apadāna, 30 references. }
„ Buddhavaṃsa, 2 references } not included in estimate.[2]
„ Cariyā-Piṭaka, no reference }
„ Paṭisambhidāmagga, 33 references.

This is a very rough estimate,[3] but is sufficiently informative to show an average frequency of reference which is about the same taken together, as that in the other four Nikāyas. And the average frequency is sufficient to show Jhāna as a very prominent feature in

[1] *Vinaya*, Pācittiya, viii.
[2] Poems in later diction, probably written when compiled.
[3] Based *mainly* on Index references to *Jhāna* and *jhāyin*, and therefore erring on the side of omission.

the doctrinal part of the Canon. The frequency would loom even greater had I included all references to the contexts where "samādhi" occurs. This is sometimes equated with Jhāna, but it is the genus of which Jhāna is a species, and hence the inclusion would not be justifiable. For instance in the *Udāna*, when Sāriputta is said to be rapt in a certain samādhi, the Commentary claims that this was the fourth Brahmavihāra of indifference or equanimity. And the calling these states a kind of Jhāna, as in the case of Subhūti of the Theragāthā, is a commentarial, not a Piṭaka usage.

Taking then *Jhāna* and *jhāyin* only, I ask my readers to consider what conclusion can we infer from their frequent occurrence? For it may be a different conclusion from that which might safely be drawn (1) were the Sutta-Piṭaka the whole of the Canon, and (2) were it the work of a group of men compiling and completing the group of sayings at the same time and in the same place. We know that Jhāna and jhāyin anticipated the beginnings of Buddhism, just as we know also that even in the Buddhism of to-day we find their resultants, to mention only the Zen school of Japan and the Diyan centres of Tibet.[1] We are then, in this matter of Jhāna, up against what would seem to be a chronic need of the Buddhist religious mind, and not only of that, but of the Indian religious mind when Buddhism arose. This is by no means to agree with the opinion of a writer that "Buddhism is through and through nothing but Yoga"[2]. Buddhist Jhāna may represent what current Yoga became in Buddhism. But Jhāna is not the whole of Buddhism, save by a gross misrepresentation. What men value much, they word often. But we find the first Piṭaka almost silent on Jhāna, and the third Piṭaka dropping the subject more and more after the first two books, portions of which treat of it. We come back to the proportion in reference to it in the second Piṭaka, and to the question: what did this frequency of wording mean in terms of value? What did the recorders and editors of the sayings in prose and verse hold there was of welfare and of interest in Jhāna, to warrant the preserving of these references, amounting to a mention in about one out of every twenty of our pages here, or perhaps rather more in the middle collection of their scriptures?

Our answer is made the less easy by there being no simple reply to the second point above. We are coming to admit that the Sutta Piṭaka, as well as the other two, was not the work of one inner group

[1] See "Dhyāna and Samādhi im Mongolischen Lamaismus", A. M. Pozdnejev, *Zeitsch. f. Buddhismus*, 1926, 3–4.

[2] H. Beckh, *Buddhismus*, ii, 11; quoted and criticized by Dr. Heiler.

at the same time and place. And when this is conceded, other complications arise. Was it always one and the same good that was valued and sought in Jhāna? It is true there was a fixed wording in some detail to serve—I borrow the Vinaya simile [1] on a more general case—as a string (*sutta*) to bind the bunch of flowers together. But as to that, we have no sound evidence to feel sure, that the formulas now in the books were either the original fixed wordings, or whatever even those, if there were any, truly expressed what Jhāna really meant for Gotama and his first fellow-workers, men, and women. If Buddhism is indeed a sort of imported Yoga, that is of the very spirit of Indian Yoga, we are forced to postulate some earlier formulas showing less sharp severance between the two—which would show us at least the more gradual, the more usual method of pouring an old wine into new bottles.

Some likeness there is between Jhāna formulas and the Brahmanized Yoga (nothing earlier being, I find, available), but it is in detail only. The antithesis to Sānkhya is in both literatures, albeit almost hidden in Buddhism. The Mahābhārata sets it out more than once and clearly; in the Piṭakas we trace it in such outline as "There are these two strengths: reasoned calculation and making-to-become (*paṭisaṅkhānabalaṃ bhāvanā-balaṃ*) [2]" where the latter is explained by the fourfold Jhāna-formula. And there is, in both Yoga and Buddhist procedure, elimination of sense-impressions and mindwork on them. But in the latter, that which in Yoga is the heart, the very object, the very justification, is lacking. "How" asks the Yoga inquirer, can a man find deliverance without a God (*īśvara*)? . . . "Let the Yogin bearing Me within, sit solely devoted to Me." [3] The Buddhist formula not only sees no perfection of concentration resulting from devotion to God, not only sees no "beholding of the Self in the Yogin's self" [4] in Jhāna, but even bars out all reference to the jhāyin as such. Gotama, it is true, is shown investing it with his characteristic personal emphasis in his own case:—*So kho ahaṃ . . . jhānaṃ upasampajja vihāsiṃ.* "*I* indeed abode in the attainment, etc." [5], or in the case of others,[6] but no person finds mention in the bare formula, save as understood in the verb and the pronoun *so* (he). Even where the Jhāna is connected with a definite personal object—access to Rūpa or Arūpa—the aspirant is wholly merged in the verb (*bhāveti*).

This may seem a modern Western captiousness, but no, the

[1] *Vin.*, iii, 9.
[2] *Anguttara-Nikāya*, i, pp. 52, 94.
[3] Mokṣadharma, Adh., 302.
[4] Ibid.
[5] *Vin.*, iii, 4; *Majjhima*, i, 21, etc.
[6] Ibid., p. 40, etc.

Commentator himself takes note of it. "Why," he says, "should the foregoing analysis of mind presuppose things only, and this teaching presuppose a person (*puggala*)? Because we have here a way (or course, *paṭipadā*), which he makes-to-become. . . . And a way has to be accomplished, and this must be accomplished by somebody."[1] O wise little Buddhaghosa, why were you not elsewhere, as here, a "man who sees"? Let no man call you here pernickety. You are here giving away the whole of that "anatta" dogma which you for the most part so doughtily defend! You were not afraid to write that a way required a wayfarer, a *paṭipadā* needed a *paṭipannaka*. But had you lived six centuries earlier, when even the Master's use of the word *puggala* had to be in a sense explained away, as in the Kathāvatthu, you might not have trotted out "the man" so airily. You were writing in Ceylon, far away from renascent Brahmanism, and you did not fear to have to eat your words when you thus brought in the *ātman* and the *puruṣa*.

Both in Sakyan Jhāna and in Yoga the process of concentration sets out with the individual, the man, the solitary aspirant. But as soon as we touch on attainment, the values alter. In Buddhist Jhāna the man vanishes; we are left with his mind only, purged, emptied to a state of "purity, indifference and mindfulness". And we hear nothing of any object partly or wholly won beyond the mental state itself. I have in mind here the fourfold Rūpajhāna, but even where, as is often the case, the jhāyin is made to pass on to Arūpajhāna, the serial attainment reached cannot, even from the Buddhist point of view, be called truly a religious or spiritual Better. A certain vantage-point in musing in a vast vacuous vagueness is the utmost that can be claimed, unless this Jhāna was ever seriously held to promote a man's prospects of rebirth in a world believed to be *arūpa*, or incorporeal. But in Yoga the *Yogin*, the *man*, is in full view from first to last, and there is *no doubt* about what is sought. It is the man and not his mind only that is before us, the man breaking his bars and bonds, waxing in strength and fearlessness, winning to absorption in, to vision of, the Ātman in him, who also is that Ātman.

And with the man thus prominent, the Yoga literature leaves us with no shadow of doubt as to the good, the "well", the *artha*, which comes to him through attainment. It is the vision or conception, as "within his heart", of Man transcendent, akin to the man himself, but above and beyond the best, the finest he has ever realized. This is declared to bring him release, that is from

[1] *Dhammasaṅgaṇi* commentary, p. 163. He is referring to the analysis of *citta's* preceding the Jhāna chapters.

prakṛti, i.e. in brief, from body and mind. Nearer perhaps to Western religion is the expression of the good in the associated description of Sānkhya-attainment, albeit it fits even better with Yoga-attainment: "This (Ātman) here is my true Kinsman; I can no other than be with Him; won to evenness and unity with Him, then only become I really he who I am" (Mokṣa: Adh. 309).

What is there in the way of a worded welfare-in-purpose to set over against this when we contemplate Sakyan Jhāna? It may be said that, when such ideas are held to be error and delusion, it is also "release" to attain to and rest in a state where they are not. To this we might reply, in the first place: It is true that Sakyan saints are shown, in their own works, as actually deriving an amount of peace and even rapture from a negative form of "release" coupled with a purely backward view, such as can scarcely be found in any other cult.[1] But man's nature is such that this attitude cannot very long be maintained in fervour and purity; it will degenerate as such into a complacency which we word sometimes as "that blessed word Mesopotamia"! In the second place, whereas it is true that the "Ātmanism" in the last quotation is closely allied to the (possibly older) Brahman-Ātmanism which is attacked in the Buddhist Suttas, it is not correct to hold, that there was nothing of "divine immanence" in the mandate given by the founder of Buddhism. For the message of the Way words the wayfarer, by implication, as "self-resorting" (*attasaraṇa*), naturally choosing the way he thinks right, that is, willing the better. And I have tried to show that, at the birth of Sakya, "self" had the divine implication for *all* cults. But for long I could find in Buddhist Jhāna, as such, no clear connection made out, as is made out, however all too briefly, in the Way-mandate:—a connection between practice and object, as we find in Yoga.

I used to puzzle over this and wonder whether, in what was so evidently a fourfold series in *preparation only*, the benefit (discounting rebirth-prospects) was held to lie in the preparation itself? Coming into Buddhism by way of Abhidhamma, I missed at first the varied contexts of the Sutta-Piṭaka. I was inclined to see, in the detached mental lucidity of Fourth Jhāna, a possible starting-point for concentrated work on concepts, such as the otherwise aimless insertion of Jhāna formula in parts of the Vibhanga seemed to suggest.[2] For I found also a shrunken and specialized meaning of the thinking—*vitakka*, *vicāra*—which is suppressed after First Jhāna, and not the

[1] See *passim* in *Psalms of the Early Buddhists*.

[2] Chapters on Paccayâkāra, Iddhipādā, Magga, Appamañña.

more inclusive, unspecialized meaning of these two words as used in older Suttas. The object was not trance: save in an occasional appendix added to the Arūpajhānas, that was quite clear. Then was it perhaps keener, sublimated work of intellection? Modern training in the building up of inductions and the applying of deductions told me, that no good beginning to such work could come in a process which made nugatory mental application and discursive thinking. Was it that, by concentrating without these, fresh insight might come as in a flash, a thrill of new knowledge, new worded thought, not got by conscious reasoning? There is talk now about this that we call intuition, not using the word quite as Bergson does, and it is well that there should be. But is intuition really a beholding from within? The great musician or artist would not always grant that. Why should any other muser be so confident about it? Aristotle was not. *Thurathen*, "from without," is his conclusion as to our constructive thinking.[1] And is our "inspiration" a mere fancy? Or did the mental exercise in Jhāna, whatever other advantage is offered, serve as a respite and withdrawal, otiose yet strenuous, from the pre-occupations of daily life, much as books now afford us? It is not easy for us here and now to fill out the mental day of the studious meditative man in a bookless world, nay, a manuscriptless world, who had turned away from the life of his fellow-men, nor saw any good in the study of the world of nature.

Then I came to learn a little of the Zen (Jhāna) sect of Buddhism in Japan, mainly through Daisetz Suzuki's essay (*Journal of the Pali Text Society*, 1906-7).[2] In that interesting article there are quoted some sayings of Zen adherents that are quaint and even foolish, but this essential point was clear: in a world where imported Buddhism had found, not a bookless world, but a world of books, the jhāyin flouted books, and professed to find the good sought in musing in the seeker himself. If he would, through his musing, divest himself of everything he considered morally lowering and intellectually hindering, and seek to win to the best self he could conceive, enlightenment would come from within. Jhāna is pictured here as a sort of cure or tonic, purging, restful, stimulating. And the writer considers that "this special discipline came to be emphasized . . . as a saving power, when the Buddhist faith began to wither under the baneful influence of scholasticism".

[1] *Peri Neotétos*.

[2] I apologize to Mr. Suzuki for ascribing his interesting article to another distinguished scholar, in *Ind. Hist. Quarterly*, where this subject was alluded to.

It is always interesting to see an idea, or course of action, or attitude, when transplanted to new soil, flourishing there with a new and fresh energy. In Zen, Jhāna regains that central well-spring of "the man", his nature, his objective, which was in Yoga, but which became blurred and lost in Sakya. And yet it is not exactly a replica of Yoga. It is more positive, more self-concentrated, less religious, less super-personal than Yoga. It is still Sakyan, in that it seeks the divine in man rather than to develop man into, or raise man to the divine. It bids man look within, not beyond himself.

In Indian Buddhism we see both emphases in ātman—man-self and divine self—blurred and lost. What do we find in Jhāna replacing them? The emphasis, I would say, is on, not man, but *mind*. It is from first to last the mental process in which we are kept informed: first the deadening of sensations by way of the self-hypnosis of the "kasiṇa", or artifice of concentration on a special object of sense; then the deadening of active work of mind, and so on, in a curious and psychologically interesting procedure. Those who approach Buddhism through the "legend" or story of its founder, and its early church and rule (Vinaya), do not always realize the absorbing interest that is betrayed in its scriptures in mental phenomena, in the mind. But this interest colours very markedly its Sutta literature, and points, I venture to think, to a very notable feature in the spirit of the time, when Gotama was teaching. To this feature I shall come in the next chapter. I have said it already and I say it again—there seems to be herein, if in nothing else, something akin between that time-spirit and our own; the interest in, not the very man—*we* call him, self, soul, spirit—but in his complex of body and mind, the interest in mind-procedure, and with this the blurred, lost vision of "the man".

But when Gotama's mission began, the man was not yet blotted out; the blotting out was nascent only. But blotted out he was, and that, it may be, at an early date. It is Ānanda himself, who, as an exponent of authority, is shown teaching Jhāna as pure and simple mind-practice (*cittaparisuddhiyaṅga*), to be perfected and kept up, as one of four such factors, conducing to an end of highest worth, definitely worded.[1]

But so markedly, in the self-willing process of Jhāna, has the blotting out of the self taken place, and the mental process itself become solely of interest, that we come—if we are thoughtful—to a halt, and ask ourselves: If Buddhism was indeed a daughter of Yoga, how did she come so much to value Yoga-samādhi and to

[1] *Anguttara*, ii, 195.

word it in a way so different, that it is as if we were to reckon mechanical power with no machinist, or to value the music of an instrument leaving out the player? Can a period of transition be shown? Can we show it from the Pali books, late in date as, in their present form, they are? Can we draw out of them (1) that Gotama was an ardent *jhāyin*, and with him many of his early fellow-workers, (2) that for Gotama, and for these, Jhāna was valued, not for just what the Yogin (of any age) valued it, still less as mere mind-practice, but for something else—for an "access" felt to be, in their work and their "wayfaring" through the worlds, as a help and an enlightening?

(1) That Gotama was an habitual muser has hardly perhaps till now received the attention it merits. And yet, apart from the frequency of mention in the discourses fathered on him, we find him called muser more than once:—

> *Muniṃ vanasmiṃ jhāyantaṃ ehi passāma Gotamaṃ*
> (Come, see we Gotama the seer, the muser in the wood).[1]
> *Jhāyiṃ virajam āsīnaṃ*[2] . . .
> to the muser, the pure, the seated (am I come).

The tempter rallies him:—

> *Sokāvatiṇṇo nu vanasmiṃ jhāyasi*[3]
> Art thou sunk in grief that in the wood thou musest?

The muser's posture is said to be peculiarly his,[4] and Ānanda's memory of him declared him as "having both practised and engaged in Jhāna, and advocated it".[5] Of his fellow-workers we note musing associated with Sāriputta,[6] Anuruddha, Kankhā-Revata,[7] and Moggallāna,[8] Nandā the nun,[9] and Uttarā Nandamātā the laywoman.[10]

Now this man and these persons and others were at the wellspring of the movement, and to them the work of spreading and making acceptable among the many a gospel of a self-directed living, such as would bring "well", welfare, to man here and in the worlds to come, was the all-absorbing thing. Can we believe that they would have often gone aside to cultivate a stereotyped way of musing

[1] *Sutta-Nipāta*, 165. [2] Ibid., 1105. [3] *Saṃyutta*, i, 123.
[4] *Tathāgata-seyya*; *Anguttara*, ii, 245. [5] *Majjhima*, iii, 108.
[6] *Apadāna*, Sāriputta's poem refers five times to Jhāna. Cf. *Buddhavaṃsa*, i; *Sāriputto samādhijhānakovido*; *Udāna*, iv, 4.
[7] *Anguttara*, i, 24. [8] *Saṃyutta*, ii, 213; iv, 262 f.
[9] *Anguttara*, i, 25.
[10] Ibid., 26; also iv, 63, where she is shown (in a curiously edited record) to be clairaudient.

which was nothing more than a sort of glorified practice in mental, mind-worsening scale-playing? Would they not be far more occupied with the question of man's salvation, witness Sāriputta's inquiry about it (*amata*),[1] than about a practice expounded as an elimination of mental phases? So near are we to-day to analysis of these phases, so far are we from the conditions attending the birth of a world-gospel, that we need a more quickened imagination than such as our psychology is usually content to graze upon. What we actually find Gotama first bidding men seek was *not the mind, but the self*: "Were it not better that you sought the *attan*, the *ātman*?"[2]

(2) Did he then bid men seek, in musing, the world-ātman—Brahman—an Īśvara? He did not. Much had come to this man that lay between the Highest and the new pre-occupation with man's mind as such, and, as I think we might add, the rising pre-occupation with man's life in this world. He had, at some time in his life, come to acquire clairaudience and clairvoyance. It was owing to this psychic development that he was able to be willed and induced to become a teacher, for he must have *himself* told of his lonely hesitation, and of the entreaty of a man of another world, whom the books came to call Brahmā Sahampati.[3] And he admitted more than once that something he knew was due to information from a *deva*, a *devatā*, a man of another world.[4] (It is true that he is also made to say, "I knew it of myself"; but whereas the worshipping recorders of a teacher, ranked later on as omniscient, would not have invented the informing *deva*, the case is different as to the clause vindicating that omniscience.) Again, there are frequent talks recorded between him and *devas*, notably the governor of the next world, entitled Sakka, as we have seen, and others called *devaputtas* (so called, says the Commentary, because their names were known). Among these were sometimes men whom the clairvoyant Gotama recognized as still resembling, in their new bodies, men he had known on earth, notably his wealthy friend Anāthapiṇḍika, his first patron, king Bimbisāra, and a Licchavi officer, Ajita. His gifts as a psychic medium were well-known, for we read that he was consulted in many places where he taught as to what had befallen this person and that whom death had removed.[5] And that he should have been thus consulted points as much to a widespread need for light as to interest in his person and powers.

[1] *Vinaya*, i, 39. [2] Ibid., 23.
[3] Ibid., 5. [4] *Dīgha*, ii, 10. Cf. 39 f.; 241; iii, 14.
[5] *Dīgha*, ii, 200 ff., cf. 91 f.; 206; iii, 15; *Saṃyutta*, i, 46, 55; v, 358 f.; cf. *Therag.*, 1263 f.

Now is it unreasonable to hold that Gotama used Jhāna as the best way of obtaining, or at least of facilitating, access to, and converse with, worthy men who had been reborn in other worlds? If the word "reborn" be too Eastern, let us say, "had survived the death of their earth-body." Do the books help us further?

We read that, on leaving home to find help for men subject, without light and leading, to old age and death, he resorted to one after another noted teacher of Jhāna; it may be, in order to develop himself psychically, so as to bring light and hope to men in that way.

Further we may note a recurrent appreciation of the practice of Jhāna shown by *devas* in the chapters on them in the Saṃyutta. "The monk should be a *jhāyin*," says one, Kassapa. "The man awake (*buddho*) who has understood Jhāna," says another, Pañcālacanda. Another, Candimāsa, commends Jhāna; two others do no less.[1]

Further, the Jhānas (the Four) are in many places made to serve as a preparation to certain "higher knowledges" (*abhiññā*) which are all, with the exception of the last, forms of psychic or "supernormal" development. These *abhiññās* are given in two series. The series we usually find has only three of the six: memory of former lives, clairvoyance and awareness of "cankers" as destroyed, called together "*te-vijjā*". The other, which gives the six *abhiññās*, and adds two others, gives, as No. 4, clairaudience and as No. 6, clairvoyance. By a misconception of the word *dibba*, these have been rendered in translations "heavenly" or "celestial" ear and eye. But *dibba* is for Buddhism just "belonging to *devas*", that is, men happily reborn. A man gifted with Nos. 4 and 6 can both see such persons when they are near him, and can hear what they tell him, tell for instance, of the fate of X, Y, and Z, who have passed over and have undergone the verdict of Yama, or tell concerning other matters in which he may seek guidance. Thus a man in Fourth Jhāna was held to be in the most favourable conditions to profit by such seeing and hearing, if they were either inborn gifts, or had been acquired.

But I have not yet found any writer commenting on why clairvoyance and clairaudience take such an important place in venerable Suttas, not as ultimate objects of Jhāna but as abnormal states to which Jhāna often appears as a preparation. If Jhāna was a condition of deva-converse, then those two states fall, as also essential conditions for that converse, into their natural places. If early Sakya, on the

[1] *Saṃyutta*, i, pp. 46–52.

other hand, did not in some at least of its apostles cultivate deva-converse, I fail to account for these two *abhiññās* of hearing and sight. Disuse in the Sangha gives them the appearance of atrophy, but was there not a time when they were " live wires " ? Writers, however, call them just " mystic ", or " hallucinations " and pass them by. Or they do not even stay to call them that.

Modern writers have their own way—a way of to-day which may ere long be that of yesterday—of dealing with this very prominent feature in Sakya. They either push it into a corner as ancient supernaturalism, or they speak of it as so much hallucination which is true subjectively only. Both views hinder the earth from getting at much in Buddhism that is historically and objectively true.

Take these three passages: two are canonical, one is in a Commentary:

(1) *Anguttara-Nikāya*, ii, 184: " How does a monk become one who has reached the devas (*devapatto*) ? " The answer is the Jhāna formulas.[1]

(2) *Vimānavatthu Commentary*, 4: The eminent Sakyan co-founder Moggallāna comes in solitude to the resolve to aid his leader's teaching by getting access to the next world, and questioning this and that inmate as to what had been the kind of reward to which he or she had been reborn for good deeds done on earth. He obtains his leader's sanction, *enters fourth Jhāna*, and then as an expert clairvoyant and clairaudient finds himself in the (interpenetrating) next world, and the little poems of the *Vimānavatthu* are the metric memoranda of his experiences.

(3) *Majjhima Nikāya*, ii, 37. This is ascribed to Gotama when—a very precious context—he is commending the use of Jhāna: he is asked, during a conversation, " when is a purely happy world made present ? " He replies: " As long as a man in Fourth Jhāna has attained to converse with those *devas* who are living in a purely happy world, is present (*santiṭṭhati*) with them, talks with them." Do not these show that, at least at one period in the history of Buddhism, Jhāna was not a mere discipline of sense or of mind, any more than it was a straight short-cut to Nirvana, but was something that lay between the two ? That it was *then* not merely a training of the earth-body-and-mind, with the Inner-goer, the *antarayāmin*, left out, nor an effort to precipitate a mysterious, inconceivable state of " going out ", but a seeking to enlarge and enrich earth-welfare, so bedimmed with sorrow and evil, by converse of man to man with those who, not yet by a long

[1] *Anguttara Nikāya*, ii, 184.

way knowing the highest things, *knew more* than the man of the earth?

How does it not enrich and enlarge our little knowledge of Gotama the man, if we picture him, the Muser, musing in this way! Too cramped and prejudiced is our view of him, for either it is of a monk among monks, preaching a forced growth or "making-to-become" (*bhāvanā*) in this life, which shall do away with all becoming (*bhava*) hereafter, or it is of a teacher of just earthly ethics, or it is of a superman who knew everything. Why do we not take the truer view of him, which we may also find in the books, if we look a little more closely and historically: the view of the noble man who (*sânukampī anuddayā*)[1] "moved by compassion and by kindness" for men, sought to help them and himself by "making present" to himself more worlds than one, and by converse with their inmates learning how this might best be done? Of him it was said:

> And rolling back the (murky) veil,
> And pain gone by and weariness,
> He sees both this world and the next.[2]

By him we are told, it was said, repeatedly, that the man-who could-see, standing between, saw "the two houses" clairvoyantly with separate doors and men faring from the one to the other.[3]

He is recorded as not overrating the value of psychic gifts in religious ends, but as clearly affirming their reality. "Yes, Mahāli, such deva-sounds (or words or speech) *are*; they are not things of nought. If he (Sunakkhatta) is clairaudient only, not clairvoyant, it is only because he has not concentrated on both, as may be done. But in the matter of joining the religious life, there are higher considerations than these."[4] (I have condensed in translating.) His experiences while exercizing these gifts figure in a great number of records, over which modern writers quickly slide. He is listener; he is interlocutor; often he is recorded as relating the experience; often we are left to infer it. One series of such he decided not to tell, for men would not have believed him, and that would have hurt them.[5]

I see this helper of men as neither the atheist concerning the world-ātman, nor the denier of man the "ātman" as some make him out, nor as one who spoke of himself as a little god on earth, nor as just an ascetic, monastic mystic. I see him as a man with

1 *Saṃyutta Nikāya*, i, 206.
2 *Dīgha*, iii, 178.
3 *Majjhima*, i, 279; ii, 21; iii, 178.
4 *Dīgha*, i, 152.
5 *Saṃyutta*, ii, 255; cf. *sup.*, p. 116.

an inspired mandate to the "man". There was in his day a worthier conception of the Highest; there was a dawning sense that religion was mainly a matter of *living*, and there was a very general belief that living was no mere matter of a brief three score years and ten, but a matter of *worlds*, wherein men needed guidance. And like a good guide, his immediate aim was not to dwell only on the ultimate goal, but like England's most famous general, to try to judge what lay on the other side of the hill, round the bend of the way [1]; the next step, and the next after that. That was enough for the worthiest; more than enough for most.

And in his habit of "musing in the wood" he will have found that quiet and concentration which he judged necessary, and for which he is often made to show his preference. He found too the "*jhāna-sukha*" [2]—that fine delicate sense of added well-being known to those who claim to have been in converse with the very worthy of the other side. Some of his disciples knew of it; we note it in the verses of both women and men; we can hardly wonder that they call themselves "lovers of musing" (*jhānaratā*). And the tradition at least of it yet lingers in Burma.[3]

That the traditional memory of him was closely associated with the Jhāna habit is betrayed by the curious insertion of the Jhāna formulas into the account of the moment of his passing.[4] The Buddhist would say that the back and forth narrative of the process (knowable by none save a thought-reader) indicates the deliberateness with which the great man put off mental and bodily life. The critic of my theory will say that at any rate the absence of any allusion to deva-visitants during that Jhāna disproves its soundness. To both I would say that whatever induced the insertion here of the formulas, silence as to presences at the end, when at the beginning at the first "sermon" there is not silence, may only mean that, when the man passed, Jhāna *for the men about him* no longer meant musing for access to the unseen. Only Ānanda and Anuruddha were left, the latter, though a jhāyin, a very timid aged recluse, the former recorded as willing to "make true inferences" when his cousin Gotama told of his psychic experiences.[5] The newer cult of the positive, the earthly, the things seen, as alone important was prevailing; psychic gifts were held as possible only for the very few; the man of the two houses was suffered to depart with no one listening, let alone seeing, whether in Jhāna or not.

[1] Gleig's *Life of Wellington*.
[2] *Dīgha*, iii, 78.
[3] *Compendium of Philosophy*, p. 57.
[4] *Dīgha*, ii, 157.
[5] *Saṃyutta*, i, 55, "as far as it is to be got by inference, you have got it."

Here then was what I conceive may have been for the co-founders of the Sakya movement, later called Buddhism, the more especial advantage which they sought in musing. In their days there would seem to have been the contrasted cultures of Sānkhya (*paṭisankhā*) and Yoga (the *bhāvanā* of *samādhi* or *jhāna*). Never do they appear to *call* the latter "Yoga". But for them too it meant not a merely negative eliminating of things seen, for them it was a coming to see or at least to hear the unseen and therein not only to taste joy, but also to come to have the veil shrouding the long way rolled back for a little (*vivaṭṭachadda*).

Faith in the old Great Devas was in the melting-pot, but devas, devatās, the men who had passed on, had come with a new significance to man's help; they were seen as intermediaries along the whole upward way to Amata, aiding their fellow earth-wayfarer with such knowledge as he was yet able to bear. Modern books, as is natural, estimate them and their wording variously. But *on the whole* devas appear as worthy and kindly warders of the man they have left behind, who (discounting a Sabbaññu) must, as behind the veil, have known more than those they warded. They held Gotama in high worth, but not the monk as monk; they believed in "the man" as real; they believed in the good life; they believed in man as willing to seek the Better. We may with most writers on Buddhism minimize all that this converse meant for the founders of the movement; we may with immature pen write it down as rubbish; or as not "of the essence" of the matter. But we shall only do so by shutting our eyes to very much in the records that we do not wish to see.

But Buddhism blotted out the "man" from its creed, and that already, it may be, little by little during the Founder's day. Not heeding his warnings, "not body, not mind", men came to see in man just body and mind. Then they came to see in Jhāna an interesting procedure in bodily and mental training. And then the kindly deva-warders are less and less heard of. Rūpajhāna and Arūpajhāna became associated with after-death prospects only, and to-day not even with that. As worded in the Abhidhamma they would seem to be now dead words in a stereotyped routine.

All the more significant is the wording used for Jhāna in the first book of Abhidhamma, which I have quoted above. It would certainly not have been so worded at a time when the object of Jhāna had ceased to be that of communication with other worlds, and when it had become merely an exercise in inducing vacuous unthinking reverie, or the being, as we say, just lost to the world. Never, when that had come to pass, would an account of it have been introduced with the words : " at what time he makes to become a way for access to the Rūpa-world . . ." Nor can I think that " access " means here rebirth, for we are dealing here with monk-values, and rebirth in any world whatever would not, in those, be an end to which a way was to be made to become.

Here at all events we have a reef of the submerged Sakya still visible above the waters of oblivion. But I have in mind another passage where, to make the record intelligible, we need to fish up and replace the submerged reef. In the little Sutta called Kolita,[1] the disciple of that name, better known as Moggallāna, is telling of how his leader had rebuked him for the way in which he misused Jhāna. I am not capable of rightly reconstructing the twisted defective record, but as it stands it would seem that Moggallāna was mistaking the preparation itself, or a stage in it, as itself the object of the exercise, this being called " the Ariyan silence ". It is conceivable that the formula at the time was very new, whether it was the one we have, or *an earlier one*. The rebuke was that he should not be careless, but should " establish, lift up and plant his mind " in the object. The record sticks to it, that this was silence. And this has apparently satisfied the editors, and for the rest the Sutta is probably not known to more than a handful of Buddhists. But can we seriously suppose that an abnormally gifted man like Moggallāna would be bidden by an abnormally willed man like Gotama to establish, lift up and plant his mind in the effort to keep silence ? The only way to make the story of such a pair intelligible is to see *in the silence*, which is elsewhere held as characteristic of the Sakyans, that vivid attention which in another literature is shown as preceded by the prayer : " Speak, Lord, for thy servant heareth ", and as followed by that " access " for which the prayer was uttered.

[1] *Kindred Sayings*, ii, 184.

X

SAKYA, SĀNKHYA AND THE SELF

I have tried to show how the "man", all-important in Indian Yoga, became in Sakyan Jhāna, dimmed, even blotted out, so much so that the Commentator has to remind his hearers that there was a man at work in the exercise of it. This strange reminder might seem less odd to us, if we used our verbs with the subject implicit in them, as was possible in Pali—we know it in our own classics—e.g. *bhāveti* : "(he) makes become." That it was thought needful to use the reminder is significant. It may have become needful; it would not have been needful in the day of Sakyan origins. When students of Buddhism will in their study not suffer the Piṭakas to be their unquestioned guides to "early Buddhism"; when they will be more cautious before consenting to see in the dozen or so of Upanishads reckoned as oldest, values altogether "pre-Buddhistic", i.e. pre-Sakyan; when on the contrary they will take just those Upanishads as the better guides to early Sakya; when they will see, not only in Commentaries but also in Piṭakas, the expressions of later strata of thought, then will they be nearer to a right conception of original Sakya. They will better understand how much and how little this was a new word following upon what was already there.

Now that which was already there in north India, and in possession of the leading religious culture of the day, itself still relatively a new word, was that immanent theism which saw in man's nature kinship, ultimate identity, with Deity.

I am not imagining that this, a religious tenet of the first importance, was a matter of popular belief. There was between the cultured and the multitude of that place and day as much difference as there is now, even anywhere. There was possibly an even greater difference. It was perhaps a tenet confined to brahmans and to men who had studied under brahmans, to wit, some kshatriyas (nobles). But the first Sakyas were mainly of these two classes. And we have no historical evidence to make us deny that these men had both been nourished on that immanent theism, and that they accepted it and brought it into their teaching.

I know that this is opposed to what is held by Buddhists and by writers on Buddhism to have been the case. But this is a result, among the former, of following a tradition, among the latter, of taking the Piṭakas at their face-value. Had there been from the first a revolt against the belief that every man was, as such and potentially, More-than-man, was as man the very Most, was Deity, we should expect to find such Suttas, as record interviews between the first Sakyas and brahmans, telling us of this very central doctrine meeting with dissentient protest and being defended. But we do not. There are quite a number of conversations with brahmans of varying degrees of worthiness in all the Nikāyas, from the eminent Soṇadaṇḍa, the rude Ambaṭṭha and others of the Dīgha Nikāya, the distinguished group named in the Brahman Vagga of the Majjhima, the Bhāradvājas and others of the Saṃyutta, to Tikaṇṇa and others of the Anguttara, but in not one of these conversations does any such protest or attack occur. Had there been such, it is inconceivable that the editors of the Sayings, and those later editors of the "Books" would have been careless in preserving them, so much would any anti-Ātman matter have accorded with the standpoint they had come to hold.

These conversations with brahmans are now all, or will shortly all be accessible to the English reader, and hence I need not swell this book with a synopsis of them. Here I will only say that where dissentience on the part of the Sakyan is shown, it is not in any way against the reality, or the overworthing of the man as man; it is in such matters as overworth, in the efficacy for salvation, of the rite without the conduct being in keeping with the prayers (Tevijja Suttanta), in the efficacy of the chanted mantra as such (Saṃyutta, Brāhmaṇa Collection), in the overworthing of the Three Vedas and of erudition in them (e.g. Anguttara, Nipāta iii, 58), and in the monopoly claimed by brahmans to such erudition and to priestly functions in virtue of birth alone (e.g. ibid., 59; and Majjhima, Brāhmaṇa-vagga).

Here then we do not find what we should have expected to find.

In another matter we find what we should have expected not to find.

One instance of this will come better at the end of this talk.[1]

Another is the three little Suttas in the Kosala Collection of the Saṃyutta, where Gotama is made to endorse certain remarks about the self (*attā*, *ātman*), without by a single word correcting the speaker, the king of Kosala, in that which he affirms about the self. The gist of the three is as follows: Evil conduct in deed, word and thought is treating the self as a foe, good conduct, as a dear

[1] Page 201, and cf. 192.

friend. The self is guarded by good conduct, not by evil conduct. No one is so dear to a man as the self.

Gotama enhances the last remark by the pregnant comment:

> Since aye so dear the self to others is,
> Let the self-lover harm no other man.

This last Sutta occurs also in another Collection, also of the second Piṭaka, known as the Udāna. The Commentary on each version is ascribed to a different editor, and the different way in which, after a similar start, they comment on the attitude towards the self is curious. The former, Buddhaghosa, evades the matter and slips past; the latter, Dhammapāla, treats the self in an un-Indian and more modern way, as just "his own". So treated, nothing can make the Suttas, especially the last, very acceptable to modern ethical standards. Using "self" as we do—as the Buddhists *came to do*—the assertion that a man is supremely dear to himself sticks in the gullet. And even the mild rejoinder that he should not harm another supremely self-loving person, falls very short of what we now require. We should want to put "Let him ward that other lover-of-self", not merely keep from hurting him. And we should turn away, saying: Ah! well, it's just old world ethics.

Yes, I would say, it is old world wording, but it's not ethics at all. It is old Indian religion. If we recollect that, when Gotama and Pasenadi conversed together, a man's "self" was used, not just as we use the term, but that it meant that More in the human self who was the Divine Kinsman,[1] the immanently Divine in every man, both in the king and in his queen Mallikā, who here speaks, as well as in the benign teacher conversing with them, then we shall read the little tale aright, and the others too. Let the reader substitute God for the self, and at once we are no longer in an atmosphere of pseudo-ethics; we are at the heart of India's religious ideal; God as our beloved friend, the Holy Thing within us warded, the Highest and Best in us, the Thing we hold most dear. It is wording the *summit of the man's standard* when our poet makes him say: I never loved thee, dear, so much, loved I not "honour" more. Honour is here the man's Dhamma, the immanent Inner Controller. And here then we find the self, as standing for this Highest in man, honoured by king and queen, and as such approved by the Man of the Sakyas.

Another unexpected thing we meet—unexpected from the usual

[1] Page 175.

standpoint imputed to "Buddhism"—is that, in certain compounds occurring in Sayings, which there is some reason for considering as "early", we find the word *attan* (self) used to describe what is evidently not the man as complex of body and mind only, but the very "man-in-man"—the "soul" or "spirit" to use Western diction. And we even find in the very much later Buddhaghosa an apology put forward for such usage, as of a term suggesting so much more than *he* would have his hearers understand in the meaning. It is possibly felt that the apology is needed, because the *attan* in the compound word is not referred to as a thing that is to be repudiated; on the contrary, it is referred to as both a very integral thing meaning the essential man, and also as a thing which is "to be made to *become* *the more*!

This is a point usually passed over and even misrepresented both by commentator and by translator. Here are such terms: *ajjhatta, paccatta, attabhāva, pahitatta, bhāvitatta.* They mean respectively, belonging to the self, only of the self, state (or encasement) of the self, having the self stabilized, having the self made-to-become. We find all of them in the Four Nikāyas, and in the (probably) early portions of the Sutta-Nipāta and Dhammapada (as well as in other books).

With the first of these I have already dealt. The next: *paccatta*, often occurs (alternatively with *svayaṃ*: this very man) in refrains describing the grasping of something learnt in the most inward way, and not superficially only; as a thing which had gone to stimulate manhood, and not the memory only . . . *paccattaṃ veditabbo viññūhi*: to be understood by the wise *each for himself* is one instance. We have the Commentator paraphrasing it as *attano attano abbhantare*: of each (man) in the inmost (man). Now it is among us maintained that, in such an idiom, merely a reflexive emphasis is intended, which does not go beyond our own idiom in self-prefixed compounds. This is assuming much. It assumes first, that the speaker of ancient India meant just what *we* have mainly come to mean, secondly, that we have always meant, and may always mean, what we have mainly *come* to mean. But it is surely incautious to assume that East and West do always mean the same in similar idioms, and have always so meant. What we find is, that it is *unlikely* there was identity of meaning here between the India of there and then and the Europe of just here and now.

The important point to note here is that, in the Nikāyan idiom, the true worth in a given matter is referred not to the mind, nor to man externally visualized, but to the inmost word for him, the valuer of the worth. There is *something more here* than goes with our prefixed "self".

The next term *attabhāva* in the Nikāyas, e.g. Dīgha, ix, is used to word the man as in one or other world of life. The word is the very direct and natural expression of what, in those different worlds, constitutes the real matter of importance: the very man (or soul, or spirit) in the "state" (*-bhāva*). The question of *how* he is, that is, in what encasement, is treated as accessory. He is he, and there was no felt need to apologize for or explain away the word *atta-*. When we meet with the word in the later Abhidhamma, in a description of each of the five senses, we find these are said to be *-pariyāpanna*, "included in the *attabhāva*." We are here a good way nearer to the growing idea of the man as being just a "complex", such as the Founder, as we shall see, warned men that he was not. And when we turn to the Commentaries, we find *attabhāva* (*a*) explained away, (*b*) apologized for as a concession to the foolish and ignorant. (*a*) In that on the Dīgha passage we are told that *attabhāva* = *dhammā* (phenomena), to wit, body and the rest, and further that the inquirer is to be shown that the word is nothing more than a term (*paññatti-mattaṃ*) and a popular idiom (*vohāra*). (*b*) In that on the Abhidhamma passage we are told, that "body and the five skandhas are so called, because of the fool-folk's opinion that 'This is for me the self'". We can see a little by this how far Buddhaghosa, when he gives us his opinion, has come away from the simple unsophisticated straightforward speech of the day, when the *attan* as word meant *attan* the thing, the very real, the thing supremely worth-while, the very man.

In the compounds *pahitatta*, *bhāvitatta*, we have words which run in very goodly company, as being of the very worthy, right through the Nikāyas, chiefly in the second and the third Nikāyas. The context is the terms "earnest or zealous, ardent, with stirred up energy, wise, well-concentrated, with the self developed, with the self made firm (or stabilized)".[1] Here there was no burking the matter by making a concession to "fool-folk's" way of speech. Here there could be no manner of doubt as to the high value placed in the older teaching in every one of these words. No teaching which belittled the *attan*, or made it anything but the very man, would have used such terms in which the making the self to grow and be firm was so commended. The one thing left for the exegesist to do was to explain away the *attan*. And this he does in two ways;

[1] *Appamatto, ātāpī, āraddhaviriyo, paññavā, susamāhito, bhāvitatto, pahitatto.*

in *pahitatta* he calls in a fanciful and impossible etymology of *pesita* for *pahita* : "sent away" instead of "made firm"; in *bhāvitatta* he replaces *-atta* by *citta*, "mind"![1] And, unfortunately, in the former expedient he has misled the translator, at least in one case, so that the many occurrences of *pahitatta* in the Majjhima are rendered as "void of", or "purged of self"!—a melancholy inversion of the true Sakyan meaning.

Of other Commentators, Dhammapāla follows Buddhaghosa in explaining the former compound by "having-sent-away-minds (*-citte*)". But that other unknown commentator on the Dhammapada, wrongly identified in mediæval tradition with Buddhaghosa, makes no such evasions. His comment on the compound is "*bhāvit' attānaṃ* : that is *vaḍḍhit'attānaṃ*"; "made-to-become-self, that is, grown-self."

The context on which he is commenting is one where the other meaning of *bhāvitatta*, namely, the abstract noun, derivative of *bhāvita* (as if we should say : self-growth) cannot possibly be meant. We should have found *bhāvitattaṃ* not *bhāvitattānaṃ*. This abstract of *bhāvita* is very rare in the Piṭakas; all such abstract forms are as rare in the Suttas as they have become plentiful in the Commentaries. Thus the phrase in Majjhima, i, 239 f. : "*bhāvitattā kāyassa . . . bhāvitattā cittassa*", nearly unique in the Nikāyas, could, in Buddhaghosa, be matched in page after page. Its presence in this context is suggestive of later rewording, when recourse was had to abstract nouns.

But, by that unknown commentator, the self (*attan*) is accepted *at the value it bears in the Dhammapada*, and this is the opposite of something unreal and depreciated. Nothing is more striking than the attitude here of this commentator compared with that of the other two commentators towards the "self", so greatly does it differ from theirs. Throughout the chapter (verses 157–66) called Atta-vagga, his word-for-word comment neither explains away, nor evades, nor apologizes for the word "self"; nor again does he try to appreciate or to analyse it when, for instance, the self is called "hard to tame", or "well tamed". He does not say with the others : here self means mind. He writes in the spirit of early Sakya :—*attan* meant the whole man, even his body too, but it also meant more, even as the word "man" means all that *and more.* That the man, the self meant more, meant more than mind plus body, needed for early Sakya no explaining.

Nothing, it were truer to say, is more striking than this

[1] For examples, cf. *Pali Dictionary* (P.T.S.), on the terms.

commentator's different attitude save one thing, the presence in the text of the Atta-vagga itself and the nature of its contents. If the men of Buddhaghosa's age had edited the Dhammapada, we should have had this Vagga included under the earlier Citta-vagga; we should have had many of the "*atta's*" altered to *citta*. Yet not all; for in this little chapter, matters are dealt with which go to the very root, the very essence of that "More" in the man, matters which no Sakyan, early or later, would hold could be expressed by just "mind". It took *a long time* to come down to the evasions and the apology of the Commentaries-as-written. Midway perhaps is a verse in the Anthology (Theragāthā), based on the Suttas, showing the placing of the "mind" in man:

> Within the little five-doored hut an ape
> Doth prowl, and round and round from door to door
> He hies, rattling with blows again, again.
>
> Halt, ape! run thou not forth. For thee
> 'Tis not herein as it was wont to be.
> Wisdom doth hold thee captive. Never more
> Shalt roam far hence (in freedom as of yore).
> (ver. 125, 126).

More than once in the Suttas the mind is compared to an ape, and the Commentary here reminds us of this. The picture is not only æsthetically effective, even haunting, it is a just valuing: we have a bodily encasement with its five sense-gates and a quasi-inner living procedure of force, i.e. ways of reacting to incoming things, and the want to react more overtly. But there is also present the man of the house ordering the mind or will with his "Halt, ape!" Without his presence as valuer, as guardian, the whole picture becomes as a dead leaf eddying in a wind-swept corner. The man-in-the-man is here, the *attan*. And the self in the Atta-vagga is similar. Here the self (the man-in-man) is the only judge of self (the whole man); here the self is judging the self as only fit to teach another if he carry out what he teaches; here the self is not the doing [1] but the doer: "by the self is evil wrought"; "by the self is the self made holy." Here not even a later Sakyan would have substituted mind for self, even where metre made it easy. In one or two places—those where the "taming" of self is spoken of—it might have been done, but not in the remainder. When the Sakyan spoke of evildoing and its retribution he no more spoke of mind,

[1] As Buddhaghosa's tradition said it *was*: *Visuddhi-Magga*, xix, pp. 602 f. (P.T.S. ed.).

he spoke of the "man", the very self, that who could alone be held to be "responsible", as no "minding" could be.

And this attitude towards the self, so different from the prevailing attitude in the Piṭakas, is strong evidence for the relatively early date of at least the first half of the Dhammapada Anthology. A (very slight) kinship in other passages in it with the Chhāndogya Upanishad have been already pointed out, e.g. by Messrs. Barua and Mitra.[1] We have to keep more in view than is usually done, that Sakya was at first consentient with the prevailing "higher" religious teaching about the Man as having in his very nature potential deity, and that this was chiefly implicit in the word *attan*, the self.

So much was already there, in India's thought, and Sakya sought to infuse a "more" into that teaching. Now that which was quickly *coming to be there* was a teaching which, in the man, distinguished from the very man not only his body but also his mind. This teaching I have already touched upon as one of the features in the environment in which Sakya took birth. I mean Sānkhya.

There is this also to be said of Sānkhya, which is usually ignored. So far was Kapila's teaching likely to worsen the belief in the uniqueness of the man (*purusha*), that it invested him rather with an added detachment from everything earthly and incarnate. Not only did that teaching distinguish from the concept "man" the mind as well as the body, but it also tended to see in the man, not the worker or user of these, but a passive detached otherness, a divinity, but will-less, disinterested, such as man has sometimes conceived elsewhere and elsewhen. The later developments in Sānkhya, by which it came to be designated as atheistic, were not of its beginnings.

We owe much to the scholars, as I have already said, Jacobi and Garbe—Pischel and Deussen follow them, and between them they practically converted Oldenberg—for drawing attention in the last generation to the way in which the Sānkhyan influence had affected Sakya. The two first-named were not right in describing Buddhism, in its "philosophy", as "derived" from Sānkhya; they had done better to have called the process an infiltration into the Sakyan mandate of a new and growing vogue, and that from its earliest days. The Sānkhyan analysis of mind as being computable, apart from the very man; of mind as revealing a very interesting, complicated procedure; of mind as resolvable into a definite number of factors, was almost certainly known to the alert thoughtful group of those new men, the first Sakya-sons.

Certain it is, that even in the least elaborated Suttas, possibly

[1] *Prakrit Dhammapada*, p. xxvii.

very early Sayings, we can see how pre-occupying, how absorbing was this idea of "mind", how it was fed, how it reacted, how it was ever changing, whether it survived death unchanged, how it might be wholly or in part suppressed. There is so much about mind and things mental in Buddhism, Rhys Davids said to me—was it forty years ago?—and no one has yet threshed it out. For a teaching aiming expressly in its early missioners at a call to Everyman to win his own salvation in his way of living, it is astonishing how much effort, time, and space is given in the Suttas, as finally compiled, to this question of the nature and ways of mind, to the man as *becoming more* in terms of mind, to the man as reckoned generally in terms of mind, to mind as to be deprecated as unworthy of the man, as "not you". Care is shown to equate the terms for mind: "*citta*, that is, *mano*, that is *viññāṇa*."[1] Questions are put (*a*) on mind-ways: "*viññāṇa* . . . *vijānāti*: what is that?" "*Paññavā*: what is that?"[2] (*b*) on values in these: "Do you declare there is in musing one highest state of mind, or are there several?"[3] (*c*) on order in mind-ways: "Does 'minding' precede 'knowing', or the converse, or are these simultaneous?"[4] (*d*) on the nature of mind: "Is mind(ing) the Self, or is it a different thing from the self?"[5] And one could lengthen the list. The question also is raised of the special senses, with distinct field and function, and who it is who "enjoys", or collectively experiences the impressions they bring? What again is it that constitutes awareness on occasion of sense? There is more detailed analysis of this kind in the later compilations termed Abhidhamma, nevertheless it is all anticipated in the earlier compilations known as the Four Nikāyas or Āgamas of the Sutta Piṭaka.

It is scarcely to be wondered at that a student, here and now, coming straight from the mill of academic psychology, should have seen with much interest in all this the dawn of an awakened curiosity —a curiosity much akin to that which, in the last three centuries of our own culture, has evolved also into a divorce of the study of mind from that of the man abstractly considered, and into the creation of an analytic study, "psychology," more or less related to the study of man's bodily organism, physiology. But herein was danger; and at present it is not so much the lure of the psychological comparisons which have proved dangerous as the results of the same, which

[1] *Saṃyutta*, ii, 94. [2] *Majjhima*, i, 292; *Saṃyutta*, iii, 87; ii, 100.
[3] *Dīgha*, i, 185.
[4] Ibid.
[5] Ibid.; cf. p. 32, 34; *Majjhima*, i, 138; 300.

have perverted our true conceptions of what this ancient interest in the mind actually amounted to in the early days of Sakya. The tendency to read our own temporary conclusions into these older gropings may blind us to the change brought about in Sakya by the influence of Sānkhya.

India was much given to thinking on the man, but she did not really get very far save in just this one point of utmost importance: that the man—and by that I do not mean his body, or his mind-ways—the man was in his nature a potential more-than-man, that he was in a word divine. Even this she did not word in a fit way. She worded it, in most of the Brahmanic teaching, as if the man were already, *here and now*, the consummate More-than-man, the Most, shall I say? could he only use wisdom enough to see it. There was no just valuing of all that the very best of men needed before that perfection could be attained. India had no conception of man as fundamentally willer, to enable her to get into the way of a juster appreciation of the nature of things human and divine. We could to-day, if we had the will to it, come at a better valuation of the long way that lies before each of us, the worst and also the best, before the perfect man is reached. But we need, I believe, to start our man-values with the Indian view that man, the very man, is by nature potentially more than our usual conception of human nature concedes.

The Sānkhyan movement, astir in north India, did nothing of purpose, I repeat, to lower that Indian view of man. But it saw the mind as a distinguishable manifold, and herein probably lay its new appeal. The cultured world began to discuss this mental manifold, and its applications. So now with us it is no longer the Academy only, in treatise and classroom, that discusses "psychology". In so seeing the mind as matter for computation, for analysis, for categorizing, Sānkhya was careful to exclude from mind, the man or self. Whatever be the age of the many Sūtras, or mantras, or curt aphorisms, as which the teaching has survived, there is in them a clear belief in the reality of the self. A typical aphorism is as follows: "Since the manifold (of sense) is for-the-sake-of what is not that manifold . . . since there must be superintendence, since there must be an enjoyer, because of the need of perfection, the man *is* (*puruṣo 'sti*).[1] And another: "The self exists, because there are no proofs of its non-existence."[2] Hereon the comment by Vijñāna, a theistic Vedântist of the sixteenth century, late in time though it

[1] *Sānkhyakārikā*, aphorism 17. Cf. Garbe, *Sānkhyaphilosophie*, p. 302.
[2] *Sānkhya-pravacana-bhāshya*, vi, 1.

be, is for the European of interest; "The existence of the self stands firm as following from the idea: 'I know' . . . we are only concerned to comprehend how he is distinguishable (from everything else)." This distinguishing was pushed to the uttermost in holding the self aloof from body and from all that Sānkhyan analysis distinguished in mind, including that mental function termed I-making (*ahaṃkāra*), by which the mind became, as it were, a pseudo-self. This may be seen in the negating phrase, which would seem to have been caught up by the men of Sakya and repeated again and again both in positive and in negative form:—"from the study of the principles there arises the conclusive, purified, because faultless, perfected knowledge: 'I am not; not of me; not I.'" This strange and probably broken down fragment of a half-lost tradition has called for explanation both from East and West. Our own Wilson explained it as "merely intended as a negation of the soul's having any active participation, any individual interest or property, in . . . possessions or feelings". Garbe amplifies it by adding to the clauses the word "active", the Sānkhyan self being conceived as a passive spectator.[1] Narâyana the commentator has also: "that is, I am not the agent; pain and the like are not of the self; there is (for him) no I-making."[2]

The Sakyan version of this is slightly less fragmentary, albeit it also is not easy to make clear. It is always given as *suggestive* of a quotation, that is, as a mantra which is adduced. And it is possible that it is an older version of the Sānkhyan "tag", older than that which has survived in the late, the mediæval Sānkhyan Sūtras, i.e. in their Commentaries. It is thus: "(It is not fit to say this, to wit) 'This (neuter) am I; this (masc.) is of me (or mine); this (masc.) of me the self.'"[3] It occurs in this form in the second recorded utterance of Gotama, and if the saying be put into the negative, the reader will better see the likeness. Thus "you should say: 'This thing am I not; this one is not mine; this one is not the self of me.'"

Let us come to the Utterance itself. Not hailed or attested by unseen hosts, as we saw was in the legend of the First Utterance, it none the less must have been valued as a mantra of the highest importance, for although I have found the opening sentences, which, as in the case of the First Utterance, are the real criterion in the mandate, in only one or two Majjhima Suttas, the expository sentences

[1] *Sānkhyakārikā*, aph., 19; cf. *Die Sānkhya-Philosophie*, 302.
[2] *Sānkhyakārikā*, aph., 64.
[3] Ibid. *Etaṃ mama, eso 'ham asmi, eso me attā.*

which follow are quoted literally scores of times in the Nikāyas, albeit in unequal distribution. Like the first Utterance, it *came* to be known by a special name: *An-atta-lakkhaṇa-sutta.* It had been possible, in Pali compound-wording, to have called it the *Attan-alakkhaṇa-sutta*, viz., the saying on the non-marks, the false marks, of the self. We should then have been at least nearer to that which was, for me, the real significance in the mandate. As it is, we get in the actual title the emphasis negating the self, which *gradually came in*, and which has so largely blotted out for the world the original Sakya. Here is very literally what the Vinaya gives us:[1]

"Body is not-the-self. On the one hand were this body the-self, this body would not be liable to oppression (illness). It might succeed in (saying) as to the body: 'Thus let body be for me.' 'Thus let body not be for me.' Mind is not-the-self. On the one hand were this mind the-self, this mind would not be liable to oppression; it might succeed in saying as to the mind: 'Thus let mind be for me.' 'Thus let mind not be for me.' Since on the other hand mind is not the-self, therefore is mind liable to oppression, nor does it succeed in saying as to the-mind: 'Thus let mind be for me.' 'Thus let mind not be for me.'"

Here for me all that can be judged as genuine in the passage ends. It goes on in a way that is different, different in this: that the man, or self is conceived in what is worse, as transient, as ill, as bent this way and that (*anicca; dukkha; vipariṇāmin*). And, as I said above, in my hypothesis of a gospel deserving to be called a world-religion, to go about bringing a "new word" of this sort to the Many, for me, cannot rightly, cannot possibly be the message in such a religion. "Not this, not this" is what follows; it is the estimate of the monastic vehicle, by which the real message was borne, and in the bearing came to be distorted. The whole passage may be read at this book's end; I give yet a portion of the remainder to show the Sānkhya-like refrain used in the negative.

"What think you of this: is body permanent or impermanent? It is impermanent. But the impermanent (thing), is it unwell or happy? It is unwell. But that which is unwell, impermanent, a changing-thing: is it now fit to consider that in this way: 'This (is) mine. This-one I am. This-one for me is the self?' It is not. Therefore here whatever body . . . whatever mind there be, whether it be past, future, present, belonging to the-self or external, gross or subtle, low or excellent, far or near: all body . . . all mind should be viewed as it really is with right *paññā* thus: in these

[1] Vol. i, p. 13.

words: 'It is not mine. This one I am not. This one is not for me the self.'"

As with the First Utterance so here we have, I repeat, a conclusion savouring strongly of the monastic traditional editing, but failing, as I hold, in the genuine brand of a world-gospel, by which life is shown to be a More, a richer, fuller thing, a thing fraught with unfolding to come, and not a shrunken thing.

The reader will there see, that after "body" as not the self, the mind is considered, not, as in some possibly very old sayings, in one term, but in four groups (*khandhā* or *skandhā*). To these I shall come presently. I believe we have here four later insertions for the one word *citra* (*citta*). The substitution itself of *rūpa* for *kāya*, as the proper term for body, is itself not without significance. The less, shall I say? academic way of alluding to body and mind was, I believe, "*kāya*, *citta*," as we may see in Sayings which give us the impression of straight talks rather than ecclesiastical discourses.[1] But the growing tendency had been to see the man, not as the unseen but very real experiencer (*paṭisaṃvedī*) by way of body and mind, but as the complex (*sasambhāra*) of these two. And hence to call the one aspect of him the thing seen, or *rūpa*, came into use in a newer, more limited meaning.

Readers of Oldenberg's German rendering of the Second Utterance should not take his *occasional* substitute of "corporeality" for "body" as accurate. In the Pali only body (*rūpa*) is used. The abstract form is in this ancient mantra out of place. It occurs once—I believe once or twice only—in the Suttas, with corresponding abstract forms for the other four skandhas: *rūpatta*, *vedanatta*, etc.[2] and very strange intruders do they appear. There will be many, many years between the date of this Sutta's compilation and that of even the editing, let alone the utterance of our mantra.

The parts of the body, usually numbered as thirty-two, form a category to which a quite surprising degree of attention is paid in the Pali books, attention which is largely of a depreciative kind, as we should expect in monastic discourses. But depreciation alone would not have entailed the meticulous attention that we find. That attention is itself a signpost pointing to the dying out of the man as real, and to the seeing the man not only in the mind, but also in the body, as a "nothing-distinct-from either". For it appears to have been the way of teaching, that when the parts were enumerated, both solid and fluid, the teacher, as we see in commentaries, made a point of insisting on the mechanical process going on in each part,

[1] E.g. *Saṃyutta*, ii, 94 f. [2] Ibid., iii, 87.

so as to oust very thoroughly any idea of personal experience from it, even as the idea of a personal experiencer was ousted from the mind, as any *plus* quantity in mind. Thus to take the liver : " the right side does not know that against it leans the liver, nor does the liver know that it leans against the right side. There is no mutual laying to heart, no reflection. Thus liver is separate, non-mental, empty (of the man) . . ." [1] " not being, not man."

As to the five khandhas, so unfortunately miscalled (=" heaps "),[2] appearing so early at the very birth of Sakya, we have here again what any reasonable reader will admit is a very actual, if lamentable " dressing ", given indefinitely later to an original record. I speak as one whose first-hand acquaintance with the native cultural methods of the India of to-day is of the most limited. Nor for that matter is modern India the India of B.C. 600–500. But I have, for better for worse, very deep convictions about the Man and his men who brought the Sakyan gospel to birth, and those convictions make it impossible for me to hear them start their mission to the Many with an academic attempt at making a most important, a most vital pronouncement about the man and his body and his mind in terms of a fivefold analysis. I am convinced that Gotama, in this old record, which I consider, apart from the glosses described, as genuine, spoke simply of body (*kāya*) and of mind (*citta*), and that he was here warning his men that neither of these two was the real indwelling Self (*ātman, purusha*), that neither of these two was to be considered as the thinker, the enjoyer, the doer. (Words for valuer, willer, chooser he had not.) That the self, the man, as these was existent, very really existent, no one as yet denied. But already there will have been growing up a tendency in students of the new ideas, such as were his few hearers, to merge the very man in his ways, physical and psychical. I say " ways ", not instruments, perhaps the fitter term. In that relatively instrumentless world, there was, I repeat, no word for instrument, nor for " using " in general.

I hold it of the utmost importance in our inquiry that the Second Utterance be estimated as I have tried to show. It is usually considered as a second Mandate or Mantra in the Sakyan gospel to stand beside the first ; a negative mandate beside the positive mandate, denying the existence in the man of the self, or (very) man, as then generally accepted. It is nothing of the sort. It was a warning,

[1] *Visuddhi Magga*, 356 (PTS. ed.). Added in the parallels in the *Khuddakapāṭha* Commy., p. 42, etc.
[2] E.g. *Atthasālinī*, p. 141.

parallel to that in the Kaushītaki Upanishad, against the tendency then beginning, to reckon as the self or man the man's instruments. The religious ideal of the day was that "the great unborn Self, undecaying, undying, immortal, fearless, even Brahman" was the self in man who "is not born, dies not, has not come from anywhere, has not become anyone, unborn, constant, eternal, primeval."[1] As the weak body or mind he was not God. But—he could, he does "become". And it was to clear the idea of the man, not only from what we call materialistic canker, but also from the inroads of Sānkhyan mind-analysis, that this new teaching of man as becoming, figured as man in wayfaring, might be the better discerned that the warning of that Second Utterance was given.

The warning ultimately failed to be heeded. Nay more: it was ultimately construed to mean the non-existence of just that reality which it was intended to safeguard. More on this later. Here this one word of late testimony.

The fourfold division of mind just mentioned may be relatively early, a result of Sānkhya stressing the manifoldness of mind, and not as such involving any ejection of the "man". But for Buddhaghosa it was made just for this latter purpose. "Why," he asks, "did the Bhagavā say there were five groups, no less and no more? Because these sum up and apportion according to their affinities all the constituents of being, because it is just these that afford a basis for the false opinion of the self and what is of the self."[2] And this deliberate ousting of the self was not yet in its infancy when Gotama first spoke.

The Utterance came to be misunderstood, because the message of man, as one whose nature and life are a Becoming, failed to grip India, and was so let wane that we have to figure it from a fragment here and there. Man as safeguarded by the Utterance was That who becomes, in a way body and mind do not. It was to leave in greater clarity the new word to men of the More in man's nature, in man's future. But the monk-dressed Utterance, as we have it in full, speaks of man not as of the More, but as the Less, the Worse, and of Stopping as held desirable. Such a gospel is no worthy world-religion. Such a gospel I cannot for the life of me imagine a Helper of the Many to have taught.

That Gotama taught here no repudiation of the very man or self is not solely hypothetical. There is a precious scrap of evidence

[1] *Bṛhad. Up.*, iv, 4, 25; *Katha Up.*, 2, 18.
[2] *Visuddhi-magga*, xiv, p. 478 (PTS. ed.).

to show that he was against looking upon the self as a figment. And I hold it is, *as far as it goes*, evidential, because it could not conceivably have been added as a gloss. It is this : a little later in the record we come upon him, a teacher yet quite unrecognized, accosted by men of his own class who ask if he has seen a woman go by ? It would appear that a woman in their employ had stolen clothes or jewellery. That the story is accurately remembered in the Vinaya seems to me doubtful. Married ladies were sensitive as to their company then as now, and there is a monkish flavour about the thief having been a demi-mondaine. I have suggested a reason [1] why Gotama was " consulted " in such a matter of purely worldly concern, but if the reader finds it simpler to believe that he was, as the narrative tells, just by the road-side, why, so be it. The one thing that matters is his reply : " What think you, gentlemen ? Is it better for you that you should seek a woman, or that you should seek the self ? " The rejoinder is : " This, sir, is better, that we should seek the self." And then : " If so, gentlemen, sit down and I will teach you *dhamma*."

What a lovely opportunity has here been lost, when we read further. The twenty-nine wives have melted away—the monk-editors would see to it that they did !—but of the thirty husbands, who are all said not only to have been " converted " but also to have been there and then " ordained ", not one appears to have been able to give a report of what it had meant to be taught *dhamma*, much less of how to " seek ", or find " the self." All that is given is a little formula we often meet with in conversion episodes, often in these of the Vinaya, twice in the Majjhima, thrice in the Anguttara Nikāyas :—Then " the Bhagavā preached to them in due course, that is to say, he talked about (alms-)giving, about morals, about heaven, about the evils, vanity and sinfulness of sense-desires, about the advantage in renunciation ".

There are few things more exasperatingly disappointing, in these precious but ragged fragments of records, than this poor little " set piece ". How can we see anything in it of the inspired Messenger of the Way, of *dhamma*, of the call to man's will, a messenger who probably never uttered his message twice in the selfsame words ? What creative genius ever made a copy ?

Yet there are who see in very reiteration of the formula—for which there may well have been some lingering tradition as at least a basis for it—something to justify the translation : seek *yourselves*. It may be said there is enough to show that the talk, as to the average

[1] See *Gotama the Man*.

man, was aimed at building up moral and religious "character", and that is what we understand by "yourself".

I will come round to this. Let us glance at the stereotyped passage in detail. We should not, as historical critics, put the patter of the later editing monk wholly on one side. There is in it one item wherein we may see at once the vista of the Way, and therewith the fact that "early Buddhism", whatever the misguided may say, is not just a system of ethics. Ethics has nothing to say about "heaven". But the Way is, in early Sakya, just the way to heaven, the Way through this world and the next and back and forth and here and there until the Goal, the "ending of ill", the utterly well be reached.

The word here rendered "heaven", *sagga*, or *svarga*, meaning approximately very lucky (world), is a very old one, used, by a people whose imagination in such matters was less atrophied than that of the modern West, to mean safe, happy rebirth, or survival at death. This included chiefly escape from the perils of hell (*niraya*), that is, from a long spell of unceasing suffering, and escape from the perils of the Petas (they who are *pra-ita*; gone on [1]), that is, from a long spell of intermittent suffering. *Sagga-kathā*, or talk about heaven, with the other word *sugati*, happy going, runs right through the Suttas in a way that nirvana does not. The survival of the former terms is fit and noteworthy. The Many needed (and need) teaching about the Next Step, and no man then or now *is fit for more*. Nirvana was a later mandate of the monk. But men as to the hereafter, as not yet enlightened, are ever vague, and even in Buddhist lands *svarga* and nirvana are much confounded.[2]

Sagga-kathā then, had the record been worded at the time of those early talks, would have come first, as being about the Way to weal (*Artha*), the importance of safety in the next step. Following it would have come *sīla-kathā*, talk about morals, or how to live so as to compass that safety. But the first and the last two items are patently a monastic framework. For in the first place, *dāna-kathā*: talk about giving, should have been included under *sīla*, as a moral admonition to be generous, liberal of hand and pocket, ready to give aid. Else it must have meant a specific sort of giving. But this is just what it did come to mean. Giving, in the Suttas, means subscribing to, supporting, not the poor and needy, but the community of monks. I am not suggesting that to support "holy men" only arose with the growing vogue of the *samana* when Sakya was still very young. It is true that when *samaṇas* became very numerous,

[1] Possibly a corrupted version of the Vedic "fathers".

[2] See (my) *Buddhism*, 1912, p. 194 f.

it was always "touch and go" in the matter of "giving" being sufficient to keep alive this or that community of world-and-work-forsakers. This we read in several Vinaya and Sutta contexts. Even in the days of Asoka, the Commentator brings forward this hazard as the reason for outsiders passing themselves off as members of the Sakyan Sangha. None the less, support of the "holy", or "worthy man" (*arahan*) was an ancient custom.

Yet it is only when we read without preconceptions, that we see how very unlikely it is, that the first "talks" to the Many by the new Sakyan men should have led off with *dāna*. Think of it! A new man uttering a new word, fraught with a pregnant shaft of meaning for the New India of his day, beginning with an injunction about a time-worn custom, a custom too manifestly in his own worldly interest, in his being dependent on alms. The idea is preposterous. It could only have been later that, in the program of the monk for the edification of the laity, *dāna* bulked large and weighty, as due, not, I repeat, to the sick and needy, but to the monk.

The two *kathās* again are just where the monk-*sīla* may be said to have superimposed itself on the lay-*sīla*. Restraint in sense-desire, of however healthy a form for lay humanity, and renunciation may well be called the *sīla* itself of the monk. He was sheltered from inducements to quarrel or covet property or woman, and hence from murder. He had no worldly projects, where lying and libel might serve his purpose, and he could not well be a frequenter of places, opportunities (*thāna* is the code-word) for drinking. It is too true, by his own records, that he actually was to a great extent a minor infringer of *sīla* in wordy strife, in foolish talk, *pace* worse offences. But he spared no pains to hedge himself about with a very multitude of little rules, and no community should be judged by its worst men. The fact remains that, for a monk, *sīla*, as vitally important, meant (*a*) the pruning away of much reckoned as of the healthy life in the world, (*b*) the attitude of turning from, or renunciation (*nekkhamma*: the word means either going out from, or not tolerating). And this makes it fairly clear that talks in such a vein would be quite out of place in a discourse to laymen.

Most of all out of place when the very motive for the talk was recorded as "teaching *dhamma* in the search for the self". What could this have really meant?

Once more we find the translator falling back on Western preconceptions. The standard translation (if one may so call it: Oldenberg's) is: "should you not rather be seeking yourselves?" The one justification (?) of this is, that the word "self" when functioning as just a reflexive pronoun is not in Pali used in the plural, as we can use it. And this also: it may be that at the back of the translator's mind, and of that of his colleague no less, there ran the traditional phrase of the relative importance of a man's gaining the whole world at the cost, the loss of his own soul.[1] This latent significance of the losing may have recognized here a complement in the seeking in order to find.

Now this sort of idiom: "his own soul", is I believe, not Indian. I have only once come upon an approach to it, namely, in the Poṭṭhapāda Suttanta of the Dīgha-Nikāya (ix), "*Saññā nu . . . purisassa attā?*" . . . This has been rendered by Rhys Davids: "Is consciousness identical with a man's soul (or a different thing)?" *Purisassa* is of, or to, *purisa*; and it was only natural, especially in early days of Pali renderings, to put it in the possessive case: man's soul. But much Pali translating has shown us that, in matters immaterial, the *meaning* is usually that of the locative: in, or as to, or by, or for, as considered by. And hence we should be more in keeping with Indian idiom if we rendered the question by "Is mind, *for the man*, the same as the Self, or is it a different thing?" The Greek, and for all I know, the Aramaic might speak of the man and "his own soul" (*psyche autoû*) as in some way distinguishable entities. For the Greek no doubt the "man" was the external visible tangible shape, in whom one inferred a working, immaterial something called mind. Added to this there was an immaterial sort of replica of him, "psyche," once pictured as just a ghostly double, till Sokrates arose and championed its very reality as that counterpart of the external man, who was not of this world only. And this is the sort of notion we have inherited in our tradition; this it is that we call "soul". This it is we are as yet content to speak of, not as "we", as "I", but as "my soul", as if there were two entities: I and my soul!

But this was not the Indian way. The emphasis in that was reversed. It was, it *is*, the psyche, the soul, who *is* the "man". The rest was appanage of him, adjunct, accessory. Hence to say "seek the self" (*attānaṃ gaveseyyātha*) would not mean in India what for the Christian it would mean, namely, "seek your own soul." For the Christian this would imply: Give heed to that in or of you which is of importance in connection with your salvation. But to say at that day to men of India: "seek the self", would

[1] *Matthew*, xv, 26.

bear a different emphasis. It would for them have meant: "Seek the Man!" It would not have meant something in, or of, or about the man; it meant the Man himself. The word *attā* meant equally *purusha*, man, or *satta*, being. It would not have meant in quite the same sense the *manussa*, the external visible man with inferable mind. It would have meant that whom we mean when saying "I", or "you". And what does not this open up as meant in that brief, but pregnant question?

I venture to reply it meant this: You should seek the self at his true value, the man as not body, not mind, the man as the most real in what is you, the man as being of the worlds, the man as able to become More in the wayfaring in the worlds, the man as able to attain in the Way to the uttermost that is there in him of his nature as man.

Now there is nothing here that a Christian, or a man of Islam, or of any other really worthy religious belief could not say in exhortation. I would only say that the Indian *would have the start of them* in that he alone worthily named the self, whose true worth and reality were to be rightly valued, as the Man; it was nothing as "the man's" that was so to be valued; it was not the "man's own", whether called soul, psyche, or spirit. It was the "very man of very man". And more: it was man as one in nature with the Divine, so that the quest of the Man involved, implied the quest of God.

We may never know now how that question was really followed up, when the men sat down and the Man showed them, no doubt in very simple words, what the quest of the Self, the very Man, would come to mean for them earnestly seeking. One explanation of the question may be raised, which I do but raise to drop it as unthinkably improbable. Yet a Buddhist, hardbitten by the dogma of the "Not-self, or *anatta*, might conceivably put it. This is, that the questioner meant: "You people are much exercized just now about the nature of the self, listening to sophists who argue, the self is this, the self is that. Well, I tell you, you may seek him, but it will prove a chimera. Will you find him? I tell you, Never." My answer to such a supposition is, that it can only be maintained at the sacrifice of the character of the Man who so taught. We are not discussing the way of a satiric disputant of the schools. We are inquiring into the first utterances of a Helper of men, eager to help the man with guidance of a gospel about the very man, a man who was yearning towards those whom he taught, calling to the more in every one of them, mothering them in his heart. Such a man would certainly not have faced those first lay listeners with a sardonic scepticism, or with a bare negation, explicit or implicit.

Reverting to the alleged emphasis in the word self, as meaning for the hearers of that day more than it as yet means for us: if we remember that "self" (*attan*) may be equated by "man" (*purusha*), the apparent abrupt transition in the teacher's question is greatly reduced, and indeed becomes highly pertinent. I mean, that if we substitute "man" for "self", we get the following sequence in the words spoken: "What have you, gentlemen, to do with 'woman' (*itthiyā*; this may be 'with "woman," "a woman," or "the woman" in question') . . . would it not be better for you, if you were to seek 'Man' (*purisam*)?" That we have here what is almost a playful, a word-playful mode of diverting the attention:—from the female through the male to the man, who is in both woman and man (*homo*, not *vir*), would be a method fully approved of in ancient Indian discourse.

There is yet an interesting piece of reconstruction to be suggested. In the records the Second Utterance is made to succeed the First at once, while the episode of the seeking noblemen follows only after the account of Yasa's conversion and that of his friends, and the sending out of the first fellow-workers. But it were to credit these fragmentary records with too much historical truth, were we to take them as safe guides in the matter of succession in time. There is no genuine interest betrayed in them as to the time-sequence in the first days and weeks of the life of the young movement. The men who compiled the collection of rules, and of episodes leading to rules, known now as the Vinaya Piṭaka, were not primarily interested to revive and draw up a historically truthful narrative of the movement *as such*. They were *Vinaya* editors, editors, that is, of the Rule, the Discipline. And what they sought to make permanent in fixed form was a highest possible sanction for the *inception* of each of these "Institutes" or Ordinances.

To take a striking instance of this: The only occasion when we see Gotama coming close to the central Jesus-mandate is when he finds a monk sick with dysentery lying neglected in bed, and proceeds himself with Ānanda's help to bathe the patient, change his clothing, and admonish the monks to tend each other's bodies, since other nurses they as monks had none. In the Jesus-mandate this would have come—so to speak—into a Sutta, a general religious talk. In the Vinaya (and it recurs nowhere else) it is relegated to the section on Rules for Monks' Wear! And it never recurs in the Suttas. In the part with which we are just now concerned, that which is mainly sought is sanctions for the rules observed in the Admission of Monks to the Order. Thus there was the original direct welcome into the Community by the Master himself, considered later a great honour : *Ehi bhikkhu !* "Come, monk !" So the nun Bhaddā, the ex-Jain :

> *. . . Come, Bhaddā, the Master said.*
> *Thereby to me was ordination given,*[1]

and the Commentator expatiates on the woman's good luck. Of this kind, it is stated, was the *upasampadā* (thing achieved, technically "ordination") of the first group of disciples. The next feature was the sanctioning the entering the community *tevāciko*, that is as a Three-worder, or in Oldenberg's rendering, by the formula of the (holy) Triad : Buddha, Dhamma, Sangha. This is recorded of Yasa's father who had come out seeking his son, a formula for the admission of lay-followers, and one that is in this context too patently premature to need further comment. The next two episodes are on the surface more historical in interest, giving a very curt account, as of "old forgotten things of long ago", of additional converts. But there is this other interest, that they are all, albeit remaining laymen, made to attain to the supreme rank of arahat, or arahant, or arahan—let us choose the last : all three are grammatically correct. Now at that time the word simply meant our own old-English holy man or friar, who, be it said incidentally, could turn on magic power an he so willed. The weight in the title came in much later, and the title was then reserved for the monk alone, albeit there were dissentients. This we see in the book called *Kathāvatthu* (iv, 1).

The two little Māra episodes which then follow have no apparent interest either historically or disciplinary. We do know from Christian ecclesiastical history that personified evil there plays a very prominent part from the very first. Nor was Māra less prominent in many monkish episodes in Sakya. But the very important episode of the entry of Sāriputta and of Moggallāna into the Community, coinciding as it is said to have done with the conversion of many others, Brahmans and Kshatriyas, is apparently only recorded to give the requisite sanction to the statute that if a man on entering the Order provoke the indignation of his circle, in that he is shirking his duties to society before he is of fit age to do so, the fuss made is to be allowed to die down as it surely will !—one of the worst monkish libels imputed to the Founder.

[1] *Pss. of the Sisters*, verse 109.

But my point is this: if we see, in the chronicled order of episodes in the Vinaya, an interest mainly in the life of the *man in the Order*, and only a secondary interest in the real history of the Sakyan Movement, we are then at liberty to effect such readjustments in the records as may seem to us *more likely* to have been the actual, rather than the recorded sequence of events. If, for instance, I were writing a history of the Sakyan movement, I should so far readjust those early episodes as to relegate both the Māra episodes, that of the sending out missioners and the Third Utterance, the Burning discourse, to a much later period of Gotama's life. I should also suggest that the Yasa conversion belongs to a later date because of that Threefold Formula in it, albeit this is probably the insertion of an editorial hand. On the other hand I should rescue the highly important episode of the conversion of the great lay patron "Anāthapiṇḍika", that is Sudatta, the millionaire merchant, from the later (?) corner where it has found insertion: the Rules about Dwellings—this, of course, because of his munificent gift of the Jeta Grove and Vihāra—and further, to come at last to our seeking gentlemen, I should place that episode *before* the account of the Second Utterance.

If this be done, we see at once the natural sequence in the quest of the Man or Self being followed up by the few weighty words against a wrong quest of the Man, namely, that neither body nor mind must be taken as being he. As the Utterance now stands, there is no apparent motive for its being uttered. But given the exhortation to seek the Self, we can well understand that it may have been in response to the interest shown by his handful of followers, or possibly by the then fast growing company of them, *when he told them of the incident*, that he then added the very far-reaching words concerning what the Man was not.

The true inference from Gotama's warning is, I here say again, not what it is usually assumed to have been. Unsupported by the Pali scriptures, the usual inference would probably have never been made, so forced, so un-Indian is it. That true inference I consider to be, that the new word of the mission was not, at least at first, an account of man's nature; as we have seen, it was more concerned with what the man had to do, to become, than with what he was. And further, that the accepted ideas about that nature needed a deeper, truer seeking than men were giving to it: "Ought you not rather to be seeking the Self?" The Founder himself did so seek; and what he found we have tried to show. It was Deity as immanent. The Highest, the Best, Whom the thoughtful had come to word in an impersonal neutral word (*Brahman*) was in and of the man as That-which-ought-to-be; That too who might be (*dhamma*). That Vedic term for code or law took for him a new inwardness, an immanence, akin to St. Paul's "law of my mind" (*ho nomos tou noos mou*)—the Indian would have said "law for me" (cf. *me attā*).

It was by no outward code or prescribed rite, of which the Brahman teaching was so overfull, by which the man was so over-guided, that he became the better; it was by heeding the Self-*dhamma*, the inner man-referee (*atta-dhamma*, *atta-saraṇa*): it was by the inward glow of the monitor within the man (*ajjhattaṃ*), that he, the wayfarer, chose aright. Here is the new word on the Self in Sakya: *dhamma* in the man will bring about the "becoming" which is more truly "he" than is "being". Man likes to be told what he is to do. Hence, it has been said, are Army and Church still our chief institutions. Here men appreciated the man who tells them what to do. Here then are mandate and mandater in one, in the very man himself.

If it is admitted that the little formula of repudiation of what is not the self represents a current saying used first by teachers of Sānkhya and then by Sakyan teachers, it is a reasonable inference that the Sakyans, especially at the start of their mission, would not have used the saying in a different sense from that used by the Sānkhyan teaching. Had they differed, at that time, in essentials from the Sānkhya, then either they would not have used the saying at all (as likely to promote error), or they would have used it to bring out the difference in their own position. Since they did use the saying both at first and afterwards, and since they never bring out any such difference, we must, I think, conclude that their object was essentially in this matter not opposed to that of Sānkhya. In other words, they were "seeking the self"; they were not denying the self. This was not all; they were going further than the Sānkhya was, in those early days, seeking to go. They were not at bottom and originally concerned with the *sānkhya*, or "computation", of mind as distinguishable from the self. Theirs was a humaner mandate; a message of life-guidance. But to begin with, it was well to define that whom they sought to guide as he who was not to be sought in certain ways; he was not—was there not a rising danger of this?—he was not to be sought in mind, any more than he was to be sought in body.

A word in conclusion on present views about the doctrine known as *anatta*—not-self, not-man—which grew up slowly out of the misrepresentation of the Second Utterance, fostered by (*a*) partial dissent from the current conception of the self, (*b*) pre-occupation with the mind, till it assumed the importance of a central, or co-central dogma.

The view is growing among modern, non-Asiatic votaries of Buddhism that *an-atta* is anti-egoism, unself-ishness. It is a case of reading our own ideals and even our language into ancient teachings. In the Pali scriptures, at any rate, there is *nothing whatever* connecting the repudiation of a certain conception of the self, nor with entire rejection of a self, with moral or ethical ideas. Nor is there any conception of a "universal self", with which the individual self, as an ultimate fiction, is held to conflict. There is perhaps no good reason why this transference of meaning and attitude should not serve to help in fostering the modern ideal of world-citizenship. But it is not a Buddhist idea; or rather it does not belong to that original teaching which India so long called, not Buddhism, but Sakya. *Anatta* may serve as a rope wherewith to choke down selfishness, but let no professing Buddhist so libel the Sakyamuni as to accuse him, as so long he has been accused, of having taught a gospel of "Not-self" as either true of the man, or as having any bearing on the good life, the *brahmachariya*.

Our own religious and ethical tradition has, in the matter of self, taken a colouring which makes it especially difficult for us to appreciate the Indian handling of the word. In the Christian wave of renaissance which surged up against the slave traffic, the prison-hell, and other social cankers, and out of which the word altruism emerged, the "self" underwent a worsening which, as word, it had not merited. Selfish, i.e. belonging to self, has long been of odious import. And over the word self has come a blight not Indian but peculiar to Europe and America. It has needed all Max-Müller's prestige of high backing at Oxford to carry through his Englishing of the Divine as the Self (capital S) in his Upanishad translations without, so far as I am aware, arousing any articulate repulsion in readers. For that matter he may have helped in some degree to rehabilitate the word, and possibly Tennyson's famous lines may be an echo unawares—or was his poem echoed by the scholar?:

> Self-reverence, self-knowledge, self-control:
> These three alone lead life to highest power.

It is only in the last that we have the self depreciated, as possibly a selfish self. The second is of course very Greek, and is ethically neutral. But the first has an Oriental flavour which is scarcely early Victorian, nor in Johnson's Dictionary.

I shall come to the Upanishadic "*nirātman*" in a later chapter.[1]

I come to the questioner—I was such myself once—who asks, why, if the Second Utterance meant no denial of the self, it included no affirmation of the same? This is again a confused perspective, this time a historically confused perspective. It is perhaps still more general than the last error, and vitiates much writing on the subject. The questioner should remember that, when this utterance with its negative emphasis (as to body and mind) was first spoken, there was no manner of doubt whatever that the self, both divine self and man-self, existed. There was no need to affirm that which went without saying. Had a teacher then said the self was not, he would have been outside the pale of decent thought. And had a teacher *affirmed* the reality of the self, very God and very man, he would have been considered a little foolish for confessing that which no one doubted.

It should not be forgotten that, at the time we are considering, the influence, power, and prestige of the Brahman cult was not unlike that of the Christian Church in the Middle Ages. These two cults taught all that was best in the religious faith of their day, as well as much that was not so good, much in which reform was needed. The earlier Upanishads might have revealed a rebuke, a warning, for instance, on the materialistic conceptions of the immanent Self, Brahman, Ātman, which are there revealed. If they do not, it is probably because the need of reform herein was not yet felt. And so we get such a warning, not in them, but only in the sayings of men who did feel the need of such a reform. Such a warning may have been uttered, and repeatedly, but in the day of compiling orthodox records, it was not suffered to survive.

Thus we may suppose a reforming Brahman teacher saying to his colleagues: "This that you are reported to be saying, that Brahman, the Ātman, is so 'big', or so 'small', and that It is 'situate just in the heart'[2]: look you, this is not fit; size is not of Brahman; locality is not of Brahman," so much he might well have said. But never would he have, by these negations, implied that either Brahman was not, or was not to be got at more correctly than in magnitudes and in locality. Yet it is just this that they do, yea, and that I did, who would see in the Second Utterance the implication that because those accompaniments of the self, body and mind, are not as such

[1] See Chapter XX.

[2] Such sayings are collected in Rhys Davids' "Soul in the Upanishads", *JRAS.*, 1899, p. 71.

the real self, *there does not exist any real self!* In so concluding, they make the historic error of placing the birth of Sakya not, as is fit, amid the earlier culture in which it actually took place, but amid the changed culture which the adolescent Sakya itself helped to bring about. Taking interval with interval, the error is as if we saw the Christian world of to-day, in which the Catholic Church is obeyed by a portion only of Europe, as the very same Christian world in which Luther came forward, lone fighter, and challenged the right of the priest to confer absolution of sins. Luther's world and our world are different. We must, we must see Sakya the new-born in its right setting; and that is much more the India of the greater Upanishads than the India reflected in the Piṭakas.

Let me now reply to those who think I am needlessly going too far; to those who would see the true position of Sakyan teaching in a *compromise*. The Piṭakas, they would say, deny only a permanent self; they have no quarrel with a changing impermanent self, to be "got at" only in the changing mind, and that this is the self in prefix or compound, worded in many teachings as true, and that as much reality attaches to it as to the self of the reflexive pronoun and as there is in any European language.

Nay, I am not going too far, or needlessly. It is for the truth of the historical evolution in Sakya that I take this stand; it is the change that came over Sakya that I see not yet taken fairly into account. At its beginning we see an admonition to seek the self, and to be heedful not to seek him wrongly. We then find a mass of sayings (suttas) of no ascertainable date on which we can rely, holding the man or self in worth as impermanent, ill, changing, and therefore not, as such, the (divine) self. Together with this, the constant iteration that neither body nor mind is the (i.e. that) self. We then get a long series of debates, the date of which is assignable, where the orthodox debater contends there can be no "getting at" the man, or self—it is now *puggala*, not *attā*—in any real, ultimate sense. We then find the Commentaries on this and other works explaining that the man is really no self, but a complex, or series of mental phenomena (*dhammā*). We finally see the man, the woman, defined to be (as entities) non-existent (*a-saṃvijjamānā*). In all this there is no compromise of the European kind, which saw, in the unseen "man", the fluttering *kêr* of the Greek, the *anima*, the *animula*, of the Roman. The one compromise long maintained, and finally abandoned, was that of the "not to be got at", as falling short of the "is not", "does not exist."

And in Ceylon to-day, as I am informed by a pious and cultured lay Buddhist, the final stage of this long descent in the debasement of the high value in the Self of India and of the Indian birth of Sakya is still taught in the Sangha. Not, for the Sangha there, is the Self That who should be sought [1]; not for it is the true nature of the Self to be safeguarded. Unheeded is the warning, for the self is held to be but a name for some group of *skandha's* or *dhamma's*.[2] And therewith is denounced as untrue the seeing in the very man that Highest towards whom he can advance in becoming by *dhamma*.

[1] In his injunction "seek the self," Gotama is but repeating the admonition of Brahman teachers before and in his day:—"this, the Self should be sought, inquired after" (*Tad anveṣṭavyaṃ*—cf. gaveseyyātha—*tad vijijñāsitavyaṃ*)—from Chhāndogya Up., 8, 1, 1, to Maitri Up., 6, 8.

[2] *Dhamma-puñja-matta*: a mere heap of appearances (*dhammā*), Comm. on Vinaya, i, 22, P.T.S. ed.

XI

THE MANDATE OF THE WARDING OF MAN

In the mandate of Causation, I was dealing with a very important fact in Sakyan origins which was there from the first, and may be said to stand second only in its teaching to the chief message of the Way. I come to a mandate which was not there from the first, but which was an adopted child of high value. Indeed were we to withdraw every reference to it from the Buddhist scriptures, one half of its credit with its Western sympathizers would wane away. That credit is based, I should judge, partly on its catholic " ethic ", partly on its claim to take its stand (as its adherents think) on the fact of the uniformity we call Causality. And the high value in which, as modern ideals demand, those adherents hold this Catholic ethic is likely to make slower the acceptance of the view I have put forward these two years, that it *is* an incomer, and not an integral part of the original Gospel.

That original gospel was not, as gospel or " God-message ", that a man should ward, care for, aid, mother his fellow-man, as it was in that later gospel after which we number our era. It was a mandate of " warding ", but it was his own " way " that the man was to ward, his own salvation he should choose, walking according to the " light " —as we should say—that was in him : the *dhamma* of the " ought to be ". That in so walking he was to think, speak and act in this way, and not in that way, inevitably involved his relations with his fellow-man. But the expression of these interrelations took a form which was negative rather than positive, and virtually amounted to this : that a man be in no way harmful to his fellow-man, his fellow-beings. He should not do aught to injure them in life, in property, in marriage, in confidence. He was not taught to call a man his brother, or even his neighbour, much less was he taught to feel that, in the great inner control of *dhamma*, there was any such potent link as bound the men of Jesus one to another in a controlling Force conceived as a common loving Father. The first men were to teach their world out of compassion—this I do not overlook —and the negatively worded code of Not-injuring occurs also, rarely, but in an important context, with a wording that is largely reclothed in *positive* terms.[1] But we have to weigh a collection

[1] E.g. *Dīgha*, No. 1 ; *Anguttara*, i, 211, etc.

of scriptures, even with regard only to one portion, i.e., the oldest, as a whole, and not by isolated passages. And the result is, that if we withdraw all reference to this other mandate, which I have called an incomer, we cannot but come to the conclusion that as an ethical system, Sakya is on the whole well expressed, in its most popular anthology, as mainly negative, as enjoining the getting the needful from one's fellow-man without injuring him, even as did the bee from the flower.[1]

Let it not be supposed that I am seeing in the morally blameless, harmless life a small thing and insignificant. On the contrary, it would, if generally carried out, insure in social conditions a very Paradise on earth, to the extent to which it would imply the absence of just those social defects, those social sores which call for a more positive mandate to man than *ahimsā*, the not-injuring his fellow-men. If we could but start our race in a Paradise of harmless bee-life, the negative code of the Buddhist sīla, or moral habit, might suffice, but man has to pull himself not only along, but upwards. And he has found after long experience that he cannot himself climb upwards, if he help not his fellow-man upwards also. And it is just here that the negative code of Not-Harm breaks down. The monk tried to climb mainly alone.

By no means should we make light of his persisting insistence on the importance of morals for both monk and layman. It is perhaps overlooked how he insisted, how large is the number of plain morality Suttas. The first third of the Dīgha Suttantas, the Sīlakkhandha, is a number of compositions setting forth a scheme of teaching, in which morals are placed first. In the Saṃyutta-Nikāya, rough reckoning shows some sixty and, in the Anguttara-Nikāya, some 150 Suttas concerned with the importance for man's present and future welfare of the moral life. The insistence on this importance was among the first things that struck me when I came, after years of pioneer work on Abhidhamma, to study the Sutta-Piṭaka. Man as having in himself the Most is not there, but there is the basis and start of man as becoming More.

As he fares further in the More, man will not rest content with basis and start. To concentrate on that is a gospel only for savage man. Yet the Buddhist, though he has a further More, though he has a worthier, a positive wording of morals, holds, as it were to a sacrament, to the reciting only of a negative five-fold code (wherein is no mention of filial or parental morals—the monk would naturally neglect these)—this I have already alluded to. For that matter the

[1] *Dhammapada*, ver. 49.

Reformed Churches, with all that Jesus taught of a more positive code, still harp on the mainly negatively worded code of the primitive Hebrew.

Not for a moment am I saying here, that Gotama had done a worthier work to have taken as his mandate, that a man should ward his neighbour as himself. *The world was not ready for that.* The world was getting ready for an earlier stage in the man's long journey homewards. This was the taking upon himself as individual the exercise of what we now call the will to compass his own salvation. The next development of his will in that was to realize, that he could not live for himself alone; that he was responsible for the salvation of his fellow-man also. But in that day this would have met with no acceptance; nor even now is it an accepted code among all men counted holy in India. It could only find partial acceptance when shouldered by that will-mandate for which the time, beginning to grow out of the swaddling clothes of Brahman prescribings in social conduct, was ready. Such a shouldering of a more positive ethical creed took place when the Sakyans adopted the mandate which is known, in Pali scriptures, as that of the Four Divine States, Moods, "Abodes," Livings (*vihārā*).

It is a strange thing that the Man of this gospel was one whose name his age and after-ages have let die, but it is a fact we have to face, when and if we find it impossible to do other than to see in it something taken over from without. We have already discussed a similar difficulty in tracing the real author of the prominent part assigned to causation, as a mandate already accepted, and men not being urged with reasons why it should be accepted, when the Piṭakas were compiled. But the difficulty as to the author of the "Four Moods" is even greater. For they do not appear, as causation is made to appear, in the records about the Founder before, during, and after the utterance of his mandate, nor is there any reference direct or indirect to them in that utterance, nor as following it.

Even when the Way came to be resolved into an eightfold code of right procedure, no place was found for any one of the Moods, not even for that *mettā* or amity which has *come to stand*, as newer ideals have demanded it should, for the leading sentiment in Buddhist ethics.

The earliest association of it with any individual is with the monk (in the Order) Subhūti, the laywoman Samāvatī, and the thera Revata, one of the leading teachers. The two former are said to have been commended for "undefiled disposition" and for "amity-disposition" respectively; the last is credited with some eloquent verses in the Theragāthā on amity. But there is nothing in the verses, nor in the Commentaries on any of the three, which is suggestive of their habitual disposition being anything more than a willing compliance with something taught, and by them thoroughly accepted. There is nothing whatever of the putting forward of a new word of their own in that compliance. The first-named is not even commended in terms of any of the Four Moods. But the "undefiled disposition" resolves itself in the Commentary to a predisposition to get so lost in "amity-musing" that, on going round for alms, he would "go off" into such a state while donors waited. He is said to have been the nephew of the great lay patron of the Sakyan movement, the merchant Sudatta, better known as Anāthapiṇḍika (Feeder of the Forlorn). Samāvatī was also of the burgess class. Revata was brahman, brother of Sāriputta. It is not impossible that one or more of them may have been first a disciple of this unknown teacher before they became associated with Sakya, but herein also all is surmise. Let us leave surmise and set down here what we find in the records, which, when all is said that can be said, brings me to the conclusion with which this chapter begins.

We find a fourfold "exercise", moulded into a formula of a quite distinctive character, a formula which emerges here and there in discourses. We also find passing allusions in the scriptures to the four heads of the formula, and we find two at least of the four expanded separately, and in a different connection.

Where there is need to refer only to the exercise, we find it called "the four divine states (or moods)", *cattāro brahmavihārā*, or later, "divine state-jhānas" (*brahmavihāra-jhānāni*), or later still, "the immeasurablenesses" (*appamaññāyo*). Under these names they are cited in the Anguttara-Nikāya, once in the Dhammasangaṇi (Abhidhamma), once in the Vibhanga. The attribute "immeasurable" is older (Sutta-Nipāta).

I have called the exercise one of states, or of moods, but this is not because either term is really adequate, Neither for that matter is the Pali term *vihāra*. The word is used, as readers will know, for abode; this was the rendering I first used for the exercises when translating the passing reference to them in the first book of Abhidhamma. The verb *viharati* is constantly used in the Suttas in its secondary intention to express a persistent, or habitual way of life or thought.

And it is not easy to get near the literal Pali in English. Nor apparently in German either: Franke has *Weltverschlingungen*, which is in no way a translation; Neumann has *Warten*, which is still less so; Oldenberg so evades a rendering when dealing with the subject that I cannot trace one. And the failure of the first two lies largely in their misunderstanding the real object of the exercise. To that we shall come. But we need the persistence, the "dwelling upon", that there is in the words "abode", "state," "mood," and hence, so far as they go—it is not far enough—these renderings are not actually wrong. It is not their fault if the Pali word, noun and verb, itself does not go far enough. That the Pali noun and verb were used by the initiator himself of the exercises we have no guarantee; indeed, I think we may believe that he did not, for his idea was not the self-concentrated static idea, such as most writers believe. Such an idea would better fit the verb of the formula of the exercise, *pharati*, suffuses, a word used in Pali for what our books call somatic resonance, a reaction in the body *of the agent*. The initiator's idea is better served by the verb used in the older Sutta-Nipāta: *bhāveti*, "make to become, make grow, create", namely, in *another*.

With regard to the first part of the compound name, *brahma-*, here I believe it is a mistake to fall in with the Commentarial definition of "best" or excellent in a purely secular sense. Not that we have better words for describing our "highest" in values; my objection is that, in the day when Sakya began, *brahma* meant Divine, and also that there is reason to think that the exercise was the work of a Brahman, or ex-Brahman, for whom especially the word would mean Divine. To use a Commentarial definition is to postdate these early Sakyan and other mandates to the day when the vehicle of monasticism was refashioning those mandates in word and emphasis to suit its altered ideals.

The other two terms are not without interest. *Jhānāni* or musings may possibly have been used from the first. The exercise involved that brooding upon, or over, with will implicit, which is the specific meaning of Jhāna. The object too, was, as in Jhāna, that of access, access to a man or men not necessarily present, as we say, in the flesh. But *appamaññāyo*, infinitudes, the later term, points to that deterioration of the exercise when the individual *as object* was lost sight of and a wide vague sweep of thought (or rather of will) was the only object of which the formula took account.

We come to the formula itself. It runs thus:

"He with amity-consorted mind abides suffusing one quarter, thus also the second (quarter), thus also the third, thus also the fourth. So above below across everyway, by everywhereness the entire world with amity-consorted mind, with abundant expanded immeasurable unhate, un-ill-will suffusing abides he. . . . And then again with pity-consorted mind he abides suffusing one quarter. . . . And then again with gladness-consorted mind he abides suffusing one-quarter. And then again with poise-consorted mind he abides suffusing one-quarter with abundant expanded immeasurable un-hate un-ill-will suffusing abides he."

I would first say that I make no apology for this curious specimen of English with its odd compounds and negatives. It is rendered literally, with the intention of giving the reader as close an access to the mind of the mantra-makers of Sakya at its second stage, the stage of the first organizing of corporate oral literature, as is now possible. If he will read with care he may come to see in it some five *aperçus*, five " things seen ", of historical interest.

Firstly, we have here a mantra, a declaration of what is, or is to be done, which is almost certainly not the way in which the teaching of these acts or disposings of benign will were originally expressed when they were being urged *upon individuals.*

Secondly, the exercise as prescribed is carried out, not by the mind " consorted " (*sahagata*) by this or that, but by a person who is using a mind and directing it. This is only one of the many ways (as we shall see later) in which the Sakyan sayings give the lie to the superimposed Sakyan dogmas.

Thirdly, the Sakyans developed and emphasized that Indian tendency to word important ideas in the negative which we see, for instance, in such expressions as " not-illness " (*ārogya*) for health, and the " not thus, not thus " for more positive attempts at expressing concepts of the highest things. It was a great gain for Sakya that the annexed gospel we are considering was worded *mainly* in positive terms, but it was not Sakyan, and when Sakya reworded it negatives may have been called in.

Fourthly, in that rewording the individual, as object of the man carrying out the exercise, is out of sight. That he was the primary object of the exercise is revealed to us in one of the only two instances in Pali literature where we have the exercise taught, not in a mantra, but in the way of the teacher expounding. This is in the *Visuddhi Magga*, a work dated by experts as of the fifth century A.D., where the teaching given is ever referring to an existing tradition about the practice, a tradition therefore of quite indefinite age. The other instance is also by Buddhaghosa, but is a later work. This is the Commentary on the *Dhamma-Sangaṇi*, first book of Abhidhamma, translated as *The Expositor.*[1] Here the learner is bidden to start

[1] *Atthasālinī*, ed. Pali Text Soc.

his amity-wish with, not an individual, but with one house, then increasing this in idea to two, and so on up to ten, then to a street, the village, a district, a kingdom, etc. (If we revert to the wordy formulas of the Piṭaka compilation, *Paṭisambhidā-magga*, we find again the four "infinitudes" as *anodhiso* exercise, modified by an *odhiso*, or delimited method, wherein seven sections of living beings are successively to be good-willed: women, men, Ariyans, Non-Ariyans, devas, humans, purgatorials.[1])

Lastly, although, in the mantra, the really essential individual is dropped out and the lowest unit is made to be one of the four quarters of the world as known to the agent, the exercise is really ethical, in a bigger worthier sense than are those "sīlas" which constitute the Buddhist ethical code, and which are, as such, to be formally taken upon himself by everyone on becoming a lay Buddhist. I say, really ethical, because the man is here mandated not merely to *abstain from harming* his fellow-man and all that is his—as in the Sīla formula—but to *help him to a "more"* in his nature and life. It is, to put it crudely, as if a man having £10 in a community, where the average had but £5, were to urge a man having less than the average to accept out of his surplus. Now this helping the fellow-man to become more, to have more is one with that higher ethic which moves the saviours, the helpers of mankind. But the more they bring is not a More in body or mind; it is a more in the growth of the very man in whom these are instruments. I shall have something to say on each of these points. Meanwhile let us resume the inquiry into what lies historically behind the formula.

This is cited from the Tevijja Suttanta of the Dīgha-Nikāya (No. xiii), it being the *first occurrence* of the formula in the Piṭakas and the Suttanta being *the last* of the section on the moral code or Sīla. The formula occurs about twenty-nine times in the Pali Canon, the wording being everywhere identical, save that the subject is sometimes simply "he", sometimes "the monk". Sometimes the formula is introduced by the exercise of "putting away" the five "hindrances" (covetousness, ill-will, sluggishness, restlessness and perplexity), which is usually made to precede Jhāna, and other work of development. Such a piece of organizing in method belongs also to the later stage of Sakya when the fourfold mandate of moods had ceased to become a direct instrument for help between man and man, and when it was more used for self-expansion.

The frequency with which the formula occurs in the Canon

[1] Note that animals are not included.

varies greatly according to main and sub-sections of the whole work. I will glance at these in order.

The Vinaya Piṭaka has apparently no use for it; it does not occur. But the first of the four Moods does occur, and in a way which shows us how the unknown man of the Moods-mandate will have found an older vehicle, current in his day, on which to base a nobler and more expanded ethic. I refer to five allusions to amity (*mettā*), and to the verb associated with it; the term "suffusing" (*pharati*), of the mandate. There are three cases in which the Founder suffuses with amity a discourteous layman, Roja,[1] and also a fierce elephant,[2] and further, prescribes such suffusing when a monk would admonish a fellow-monk.[3] Here we see what is, in my judgment, the original teaching applied to the first of the Four Moods.

Of the other two, one is but a passing reference to this first of the Moods, made about himself by the aged Revata, long after the Founder had passed away.[4] The other is of yet greater interest, in that it gives us a rival mantra wording, again, only the first Mood; wording it also with a universalizing expansion, but wording it in terms very different from those of the fourfold formula.[5]

This rival mantra occurs also in the Anguttara-Nikāya as a noteworthy group of four things, placed in the Fours Section.[6] But no mention is made of the other three Moods in this connection. It is a charm or spell against snake-bite from any of the four kinds of snakes! These four "families" (*kula*) are Virūpakkha, Erāpatha, Chavyaputta, and Kaṇhagotamaka. These "should be suffused with a friendly mind" (*mettena cittena phareyya*); then thought should proceed from apods (*apādakā*) to bipeds, quadrupeds, multipeds, culminating in

> May all beings, all breathers, all creatures everyone,
> *Sabbe sattā sabbe pāṇā sabbe bhūtā ca kevalā*
> All see lucky things! May no evil whatever come!
> *Sabbe bhadrāni passantu! mā kañci pāpaṃ āgamā ti!*

To this possibly very ancient rune the Sangha, in annexing it, has added a coda making it orthodox and linked this with the probably original affirmation of the rune: "Worked by me is the warding! Worked by me is the shielding! Let all creatures depart!"

On this and the other Buddhist "warding-runes" I have written, in introducing the most elaborate of them: the Āṭānātiya Suttanta,

[1] *Vinaya-Piṭaka*, Mahāvagga, vi, 36. [2] Ibid., *Cullavagga*, vii, 3.
[3] Ibid., ix, 5. [4] Ibid., xii, 2. [5] Ibid., v, 6.
[6] *Anguttara*, ii, 72.

Dialogues of the Buddha, iii, p. 185 ff. On the curious and interesting names for serpent-"*kulas*" Richard Morris's note on the Bower birch-bark MS., in which a version of the rune was discovered "in the ruined buried city of Mingai, Kashgaria", nearly thirty years ago, should be consulted: *JPTS.*, 1893, pp. 61 ff. My concern here is with the mental attitude in the rune. And this is not quite fitly rendered in any translation known to me. Fausböll and Rhys Davids translate "I love Virūpakkhas" and so on.[1] Messrs. Jayasundere and Woodward translate "Goodwill towards Virūpakkhas" and so on.[2] The Pali is simple and crude, such as we should expect in a "*vijjā*" or spell of popular and ancient usage. It is

Virūpakkhehi me mettaṃ, mettaṃ Erāpathehi me . . .

Literally rendered this is "with the Virūpakkhas for me the kind thing (be)", etc. And whereas the Anguttara Commentary passes it over, the Jātaka Commentary supplies the word "with" (*saddhiṃ*), and explains "me" by the (Dative or Genitive) *mayhaṃ*.[3] I have rendered *mettaṃ* as "kind thing", just as *mittaṃ* may be, but *mettaṃ* and *metti* are not unknown as variants of *mettā*.

In the Sutta Piṭaka the Four Nikāyas give the Fourfold Formula 26 times: Dīgha 7 times, Majjhima 3, Saṃyutta 4, Anguttara 12 times. Besides these there are two cases where three only of the Four are mentioned, twenty-three cases where *mettā* alone is the subject, one where "pity" alone is "practised", and one where *muditā* is to be "practised". It may be noted too, as not insignificant, that in the Etadagga Sutta of the Anguttara (the ascription of "diplomas" of excellence to individual adherents), only one person is named as best in the practice, not of the Four, but of *mettā* only, and that is a woman and a laywoman at that: Samāvatī![4]

In the Fifth, or Khuddaka-Nikāya, some of which is what may be termed apocryphal, there is, in all its fourteen books (I omit the late but included Commentary to the Jātaka) only one citation of the fourfold formula. This is in the Paṭisambhidā-magga. But that the fourfold group was known also to the recorders of the earliest book of the fourteen is seen just once. In the first part of the Sutta-nipāta we find:

Amity,[5] poise, pity, release
pursuing, and gladness betimes
without repulsion for the whole world
let him fare alone like a rhinoceros' horn.

[1] *SBE.*, x, and *Vin. Texts*, iii.
[2] *Numerical Sayings.*
[3] Fausböll's *Jātaka*, ii, 145.
[4] Eka-Nipāta.
[5] Verse 72.

And that not only the group of terms but the formula itself may have been familiar to the Sutta-Nipāta repeaters seems suggested by the phrases in verse 507 :

> He passion-rid should repress ill-will
> making to grow the friendly mind immeasurable,
> day and night ever earnestly
> he should suffuse every quarter (with) Immeasurableness.

Here in the last word is even an anticipation of the later name for all four: the immeasurablenesses, or infinitudes. In verse 987, in a passing allusion to *mettā*, we get the word *phasse*, touch, instead of *phareyya*, suffuse :

> Let him touch with amity (things) weak and strong.

In verses 143–52, or Mettasutta, repeated in another little anthology, the Khuddakapāṭha, there is a lovely combination of the first three of the four suffusion-thoughts, in which without the word "suffuse" (*bhāvāya*, "make to become," is substituted), phrases from both the fourfold formula and the warding rune are wrought together. Here, too, is the simile, known to many now, of the amity-to-be-thought being as immeasurable as a mother's warding love. It is in this poem that occurs the phrase which may well have given rise to the group-term *brahmavihāra*.

> *brahman etam vihāram idha-m-āhu.*
> divine (is) this state ! here have they said.

In the other anthologies, only *mettā* is commended : in the Dhammapada once only, in the word *mettāvihārin* ; in the Thera-therī-gāthā Revata is eloquent on *mettā* as his habitual attitude, and so is the tamed bandit Angulimāla, Sañjaya briefly echoing them ; Phussa enjoins amity and pity, and the boy Sopāka echoes the mother-simile. This is all ! [1] In the Iti-vuttaka is the very glowing eulogy of *mettā* with eloquent similes of moon, sun, and morning star. Here is no fourfold praise, nor formula, but treatment in terms of value, and that with a term of the market : *agghāyati*. This may have been at the time a novel and forced term in religious teaching. It is unlikely to have originated in a monastic atmosphere, and I can well imagine Gotama bringing it out of his own experience and his father's in intercourse with the "court-valuer" (*aggha-kāraka*).[2] There is also in this work the linking of *mettā* with the

[1] Nos. ccxliv, cclv, xlviii, xxxiii.

[2] § 27 and *Cambridge Hist. of India*, i, 216.

term mind-release (*cetovimutti*), the interpolated word, making five, which we saw in the Sutta-Nipāta verse quoted above.[1]

Expanded treatment of the first term only, *mettā*, occurs in the Paṭisambhidā-magga's "Mettakathā".[2] And a special expansion of the second term, pity, as a Buddha-attribute, is given in the chapter "The Achievement of the Great Pity", a liturgy of refrains not without æsthetic impressiveness.[3] *Muditā* is never expanded; its solitary separate use in the Anguttara I have noted. The word is just "gladness", but its meaning appears to have been always the special gladness of the German *Mit-freude*, that is, one-half of the meaning of sympathy, just as pity stands for the other half.

Nor is there any expanded treatment of the suffusing of the fourth thought *upekkhā*. Here it is the Buddhist term that is not very fit. Used to express mind-work where there is no awareness of either pleasure or pain, the word has in its background, so to speak, a positive connotation of evenness or poise[4] (*sama*). This finds expression in the verses describing the tenth and last "perfection" (*pāramī*), developed by a Bodhisat, namely, *upekkhā*.

> "They who prepare ill for me and they who give me happiness:
> to all I am even; granting and grudging exist not.
> Balanced as to pleasure and pain in honours and dishonours
> everywhere even am I; this is my 'perfection of *upekkhā*'."[5]

Now this evenness was of the very stock-in-trade of the monk, who had turned his back on world-experience. He had to face the need of it at every turn. He was especially called upon to suffuse *himself* with it. Hence probably arises the absence of any expansion of the idea of "willing" (for so of course we should say, not "thinking"), evenness in others. To this I return presently.

Lastly the Abhidhamma gives twice a place to the fourfold formula: in the first book (Dhammasangaṇi), showing it as an adjunct to "good" or Rūpa-Jhāna, and in the second book (Vibhanga), where it occupies a chapter towards the end, after that on Jhāna. There is no expansion anywhere of any separate factor.

Thus much in brief survey of the manner in, and extent to which this very remarkable subject of purposive thought is met with in the Buddhist (Pali) Canon. The reader is now in a better position to weigh the suggestion I put forward. This, I repeat,

[1] P. 275, cf. below, p. 285. [2] Vol. ii, p. 130. [3] Ibid., p. 133.
[4] Lord Chalmers's rendering. [5] *Cariyāpiṭaka*, iii, 15.

is that in the teaching, couched and half-hidden in a fixed wording, of a man so worthing and warding his fellow-man, nay, his fellow-creatures, as to practise televolition upon them in four modes for their benefit, his own included, we have the mandate of some man or woman, or both, which was not in the mission of the founder, or of the unknown co-founders of the Buddhist movement, but which was, at some unassignable time in the years of inception, introduced, accepted and annexed, together with the credit thereof.

This is not supported by reference to any other Indian scriptures which may approximately be judged to be contemporaneous with, or prior to the Buddhist Piṭakas. Worthy sayings on amity and pity and on evenness may be found in early Upanishads and the Mahābhārata, albeit not perhaps on "muditā". It is *the collocation of the four in a practice of televolition*, ranging (the formula hides this) from the individual to the very world with the idea of thereby healing and benefiting *others*, which no one seems as yet to have detected, as originating in Indian literature, save in the Piṭakas, and which throws the teaching into high relief as both original and in itself distinct from any other gospel, Buddhism included.

It is, I believe, only in the Yogasūtras (i, 33) that we find in extra-Buddhist literature, the fourfold thought and its "cultivation". But, apart from the post-Buddhistic date ascribed very generally to the compilation of the Sūtras as we have them,[1] they clearly represent, as compared with their wider scope in the Piṭakas, a shrunken practice. They are mentioned in passing as just a needed adjunct to mental stability. The chief aim is there the benefit of the yogin. Emphasis is no more on aiding the fellow-man. The only older concept in them is the word *bhāvanā*, making-to-become, and not suffusing: the verb we found in the Sutta-Nipāta version.

There is one passage, and one only, of internal evidence, pointing to its being the teaching of persons called "Wanderers (*paribbājakā*) of a different school" (*aññatitthiyā*). This is inserted without obvious reason, into the Bojjhanga-Saṃyutta (No. 46), for be it noted as significant that there is no Brāhmavihāra-Saṃyutta![2] At Haliddavasana of the Koliyas some monks, making a call in the Wanderers' Park, are asked whether the doctrine of the fourfold suffusion—the term is my own; the description is by the Buddhist formula—which the inquiring Wanderers teach, is the same as that which the Samaṇa Gotama teaches, "doctrine for doctrine, teaching for teaching," or is there a difference? The monks hastily return and consult their fountain-head.

[1] Cf. J. H. Woods, *Yoga-System of Patañjali*, xvii f.

[2] Vol. v, 115.

His reply as to wherein his own method and outlook were, not contradictory, but a taking up of the suffusing practices into something that was not merely ethical but religious, is, if it contain a true echo of the Man's words, of very great significance. He is said to have answered: "You should ask them 'How is each one of the four developed? What does it lead to? What is its perfect form? What is the result of it? What is its goal?'"

In part these are the words of a genuine religious pioneer. The rest of the reply is so different, so obviously monkish, so according to code, that I leave it there.

Not long before his death, Gotama is shown enumerating certain points which his disciples were well to learn, pursue, make to become (*bhāvetabbā*) and expand, as he had taught them, to serve for the welfare and happiness and good of mankind. These amount to seven groups, thirty-seven in all, and have been classed as the thirty-seven doctrines belonging to enlightenment (*bodhi*). Now the Fourfold Formula of suffusion is *not among them.*[1]

Again, I repeat, no disciple, let alone eminent disciple, stands out in the "official list" as best (*agga*)[2] in the fourfold suffusion. Seventy-six men and women are distinguished, two of them more than once. There are upwards of seventy ways, in life, character, and mind, for which they are distinguished, but of Brahmavihāras there is not a word save concerning the amity-habit of just one laywoman.[3] The disciple who *was* cultivator of this, Subhūti, is described, as shown above, by a different, a negative term.

There is another reason for finding that the Brahmavihāra code of practice is not of endogenic growth in what we may call the original mandate. No cult, unless it be that of the Hebrews, has more emphatically based itself as a religion on morals (*sīla*) than did Buddhism. The first Suttanta in the first book of its Sutta-Piṭaka is, in its first half, a setting forth of the good life as a threefold graded Sīla. And it is no fleshless code, but a triple grading of values, *as worthed* more or less by the judgment of its founder and *put by him into practice.* This triple Sīla is repeated, fully or in part, in nine of the twelve following Suttantas. Here then if anywhere should we have expected to find the fourfold *brahmavihāra* brought in as either the climax of *brahmacariya*, the holy or divine living, or as a special development in the carrying out of it.

We look through the first and eight more of the following connected Suttantas, each showing a different occasion for the appeal

[1] Nor, it is true, are the "Four Truths"! [2] *Anguttara*, i, 23 ff.
[3] *Manorathapūraṇī* (*A.* Comy.), i, 418 ff.

to the body of Sīla doctrine, in vain. Not till the last Suttanta, the Tevijja, does it come, and then just where we should have looked for it: as the culmination in reply to the question: "And how, Vāseṭṭha, is his conduct good?" Five stages in the purifying character and conduct are given in reply, then the ensuing joy and peace, and *then* does "he, with amity-consorted mind suffusing one quarter" and the rest, proceed to exercise the televolitional warding and helping of his fellow-beings.

But why here only? The Brahmavihāras are mentioned here, and here only, because of a tradition which had come down to the editors of the Piṭakas that Brahmavihāra practice meant attainment after death to rebirth in the Brahmā world. Thus elsewhere a monk who is an habitual practiser is called *brahmapatto*, just as a monk who is an habitual "Jhāna-practiser" is called, for reasons that I suggested in the foregoing chapter, *deva-patto.*[1] And the Tevijja Suttanta theme is how brahmans might best insure joining the community of the Brahma-devas. *That* is why we find it here.

Whence came this association of the Brahmavihāras with what was, or was believed by Buddhists at one time to be, the goal of Brahman aspiration? "I thought, sir," Sāriputta, himself an ex-brahman, is made to say to his leader, "that as these brahmans' hearts are set on the heaven of Brahmā, I would show the way to union with Brahmās."[2] But I have nowhere seen it contended by any book old or new, that the fourfold suffusion or irradiation of beings is supported by anything in Brahman literature. On the contrary, the Brahman was *not* taught to interest himself in his fellow-beings with all social and other barriers thrown down, such as the Buddhists termed *an-odhiso.* And even had the practice originated among the founders of the Buddhist movement, many of whom were ex-Brahmans, they would have taught and sanctioned it out of goodwill to their fellows, and *not* for the attainment of a particular world in rebirth. The layman was so to live as to win Sagga, happy rebirth; the monk, it came to be taught, was so to live as to win no rebirth.

I think that the founder of the social gospel of the Brahmavihāra attitude and practice may have been also an "ex-Brahman", living the homeless life as a Wanderer, and teaching the multitude the good life *in his own way*, just as Gotama taught in his. His object would be the worthy guiding of men in a *yāna*, a way leading to happy survival in Brahmā-heaven. He, too, would find that the many were just then waking to the significance for man's present and future happiness, not so much of the sacrifice, the chanted mantra,

[1] *Anguttara*, ii, 184. [2] *Majjhima*, ii, Dhānañjāni Sutta.

the priestly celebrant, as of the worthing and warding of the fellow-man. He may well have found in popular use runes for warding off danger seen and unseen by the power of what we now call the will, but for which, *with no such word to hand*, he called thought or mind (*citta*).[1] This negative idea in the runes of warding the *willer* from danger he, as a pioneer in advance of his age, converted into a willing of good to the object or *person willed*. And so much of the mother was there, as there is in all warding of creatures, in his gospel, that not only will he have had many women among his disciples,[2] but he or they will have given expression to mother-care in his teaching. There was little interest in the mother as such for the Buddhist monk. As giver and warder of life, of " becoming " (*bhava*), she would arouse in him repulsion rather than veneration. Hence I should place the credit for the mother simile of the Sutta-Nipāta to the influence of this unacknowledged source. And with that the credit also of the simile, used but not invented by Buddhaghosa, comparing the fourfold suffusion with the mother's care for her four children : tenderness for the babe ; pity for the hurt child ; joy in the success of the schoolboy ; poise for the busy young man.[3]

I would not say that there is anything in this gospel of " Ignotus ", that Gotama could not have taught, did not teach, in his own way. The facts in the evidence are, that compared with the way usually ascribed to him, the way of the Fourfold " telepathy " strikes the critical eye (and ear) as something from without, exotic, much as does the upthrust of igneous rock through stratified rock. And his own abstention from claiming it as part of his program in the Suttas of Assertion or " Lion-roars ", such as that in the Vinaya, Pārājika i, and in Majjhima, Sutta xii, or where the disciple asserts for him, as in the Sampasādaniya Suttanta, is a point not to be overlooked. Those Sayings are not, for me, Gotama's—he was too great a man to call himself a great man—but his editors'. But it remains that the Fourfold Practice is *not adduced as essentially his teaching*.

I am not saying herewith that the teaching was not of his day. I believe we can fully accept it to have been so and, I repeat, to have been taught by him and his first men. There is possibly another reason why later editors of the Sayings, why later editors still of the scriptures did not include the Moods in either the Suttas of Assertion

[1] It is significant herein that Buddhaghosa so far discerns the implicit "will" as to write: "Desire-to-do, desire (*kattu-kamyatā*, *chando*) is the beginning (*ādi*) of the Moods" (*Atthasālinī*, 194). Note that he does not use *cetanā* here where it would fit, if it did equate these two terms.

[2] Cf. above the married woman, Samāvatī. [3] *Visuddhi-Magga*, ch. ix.

or the Bodhipakkhiyā Dhammā. And that is the same reason for which they are excluded from the subjects considered under the so-called Supramundane (*lokuttara*) *Dhamma's* of the Dhammasaṅgaṇi. Admitted under the *dhammas*, analysed in the chapter on Musing associated with other worlds (Rūpa and Arūpa), they are given no distinct mention in the following Lokuttara study. That is to say, "amity," is implied in *adosa*, the negative of hate, and "poise" finds mention, but, in the words of the Commentary, "pity and joy have a being (or person) for their object, while those supramundane states have Nirvana for their object, hence those two are not mentioned here." Such was the ruling of the monk about the monk-ideals—so far are we in these from the attitude towards the Better, the More represented by Gotama and his men, by all real Helpers of men!

I do not say that any one of the points I put forward to show the Four Moods as annexed gospel is in itself convincing, but there are several points, and taken together they do constitute an obstacle to the usual assumption that the Brahmavihāras are originally Sakya teaching.

I do say, that both in tradition and by the whole purpose and work of his long mission-career, the first "state", amity or good-will, *is* a true attribute of Gotama. It was the ninth (not the first) of the ten "perfections" developed by a Bodhisat. True also of him is the attribute of pity, albeit this is not reckoned as a "perfection". Of the third state, "muditā," we do not find, either in Buddhological tradition, or in his mission-years, anything of *muditā* that we can single out as characterizing him, unless we take a sounder view of *muditā*.[1] The fourth state, poise, on the other hand is both a "perfection" (the tenth), and is testified to in the Suttas. But it tended to fall behind the others. Not without reason certain "Northern" schools maintained[2] that, if the Buddha were without passionate feeling, he could not feel the boundless pity for man and the world which the Buddhist literature constantly associates with his name. We certainly find him teaching to others *mettā*, and with it, to a very limited degree, pity and poise. But he has his own way of teaching it, according to the Sayings, and that way is *usually not* the way of the Mandate of the Moods. *This* way is for a man, willing to mend a defect he perceives in another man, to send forth into his will a stream of will, so that the other man may feel arising in him the sentiment felt in greater measure by the willer. Let us say that the man *AB* has noticed hardness in *CD* over the misfortune

[1] See below, Chapter XV. [2] *Kathāvatthu*, xviii, 3.

of *EF* and others. *AB*, himself surcharged with pity for *EF* etc., directs his will at *BC*, holds forth as it were the hands of pitiful will towards him, silently urging him to feel the pity he himself feels. This is what I would have readers of Buddhist teaching see in this mandate. This does not preclude a bringing of an ever widening sweep of altruistic will into moments when *AB* is not wrestling, so to speak, for the spiritual betterment of *CD*. No religious teacher limits his efforts to helping in the confessional or the consulting-room, or to the winged word uttered to the inquirer in the street. He can will and enjoin the willing with wider range. We read of Gotama practising the more intensive way of helping the individual. But it was a way of his own; it was not the way of this mandate; much less will it have been by way of this mandate expanded, and therewith necessarily weakened in universals. The Moods method is singular among Piṭaka methods; the terms are singular. "Suffusing, radiating" (*pharati*) is rare, and is restricted elsewhere, I believe, to the *subject*, in moments of strong emotion; here it is to affect the *object*. So little do we bear this in mind in poise that both Buddhists and we tend to see, especially in the radiating of poise, a boomerang bringing benefit not to the object but only to the subject after his orgy of altruistic emotion.

In fact Spence Hardy and to some degree Oldenberg do see in the Four Moods a sort of subjective orgy. And the treatment of the fourth mood "poise" (*upekkhā*) in the Visuddhi Magga is purely self-regarding.[1] Yet there was no need for this ignoble contraction of the will. The very simile of the mother and her four sons should have taught him better, might possibly have done so had he been a good house-father instead of a monk. The mother, he wrote, "is in no way anxious for the son who manages his own duties." No mother worthy of the name would endorse that. Once mother, always mother. There is of course a relative truth in it, but not enough to switch off one of the Four Moods from their ethical rank and make it frankly selfish. It is the son she would be urging by will that he should maintain poise in the hurly-burly of the world, in the status of lover, husband, father, in war, in travel, in pain, and sorrow. Her own feelings she would not rate as worthy of a study in poise.

That Gotama, when he came to hear of this man (or woman), and his teaching, rated it highly and adopted it, I fully accept. It was like him to appreciate the best thought and work of his day. And yet Gotama and "Ignotus" never met! But this is not stranger

[1] P. 317 (PTS. ed.).

than, not so strange as, Gotama and Vardhamāna, the Jain, never meeting. Around each was his "world". The seniors, the Jains, held their great man aloof from the younger pretender. May not the possibly senior Sakyaputtas have held Gotama aloof?

Or the welcome may have been rejected by Ignotus's world, not because he will not have thought highly of Gotama, but possibly because of tendencies among Gotama's disciples over which he shook his head. What might these be?

As brahman, Ignotus may have remained in word and in practice a worshipper of Brahman, or even and also of some personal projection of that impersonal Brahman. But I drop this as pure guessing, and suggest in the literature of the fourfold formula itself a possible guide to disagreement. Thus :—

Gotama, like other great Helpers of man, perhaps more especially than any other, addressed his message to what we may call the man-in-man, who is "neither body nor mind".[1] This it was that man should seek to find : so ran, as we have noted, his first utterances. Now his age was much pre-occupied with the analysis of mind and its action through sense on body and matter. And just as it is with us now, the man, the user of mind and body, the layer down and taker up of bodies, was being suffered to drop out of sight, was coming in fact to be reckoned as a "complex" of body and mind, and nothing more. But Ignotus's teaching was an appeal to the man, and through the man to the fellow-man, first in the individual and then to the group and the whole without class or sex or race or other distinction. In the formula, which will be the work of the formula-making Gotama-men, this *individual objective* is lost sight of. But that it was and remained the traditional way of the practice we can see by the Paṭisambhidā-magga's and Visuddhi-magga's descriptions of it. The man was to let his "thought", really his *will*, work on the thought, the will *of a man*. By this intensive telepathic willing, the *object*, the fellow-man, was, as we see in Roja, to come himself to feel amity for the willer instead of dislike, to feel the warmth of a man's compassion, to feel the cheer of sympathetic friendship, to feel the balance he needed if tossed about by praise or blame, etc. The universalized willing, besides being as the French would say *ce qui fait beau dans le paysage*, is more likely to benefit the willer than the willed. We saw this in "poise"! It is by radiating amity and the rest to society, to races, to the world, that we ourselves shall in our word and deed get on in promoting the world's peace and happiness. But it is by working on the *individual* man, woman, and

[1] The Second Discourse, and *passim* in Suttas.

child, that we can help with any certainty of effect. Buddhism has tended to lose sight of this in its ejection of the "man-in-man", and its skandha scheme of man's instruments *as* the man, in its pre-occupation with the type, the class, the process,[1] in fact, with something like a herd-psychology of its own.

There is another possible barrier between Sakyas and the disciples of Ignotus in the tendency betrayed by the word release (*vimutti*), which is often interpolated in the formula, notably where the Wanderers word their practice in the Buddhist formula *without it*, and where the reply *inserts it*. *Vimutti*, whatever else it meant to India as "mokṣa", meant in Buddhism (*a*) release from the world and (*b*) release from rebirth, both for the monk. But what if Ignotus, as a friend of man and of men, was no friend to monkdom, and disapproved of its growth among the men of Gotama?

In such tendencies I see quite enough to deter a teacher from associating in personal intercourse with the leader of a group so tending. It may have cost him much to keep aloof. He has paid heavily. To us he is as if he had never been. But not, it may well be, to beings elsewhere.

In leaving the subject of the Brahmavihāras, I commend very earnestly to my readers the recast of views both Buddhistic and European which has been here attempted.

The present view which holds the field is that the Founder, at some stage in his teaching career, thought out and put forward the exercise of the Four Moods, and that the exercise was intended as religious self-culture in layman and monk.

My view is that in the Four Moods we have an enjoining of the man to work for the welfare of his fellow-man, so as either to supplement other work of welfare in word and deed, or, where these might not be possible or advisable, to develop to a new degree of intensity and effectiveness the work, on his behalf, of mind (or as we should say, of will).

Further, that the references to this enjoining are sufficiently distinctive to lead us to the conclusion that in it we have the ethical gospel of an unknown man, a contemporary of Gotama's; that, as involving pre-occupation with the warding of one's fellow-man, it offered a very important improvement in Gotama's teaching where, as he will have come, in mixing as teacher with his fellows, to have seen, *lay its weakest side*, its ethical not its self-cultural side; and that, seeing this, he took over the Brahmavihāra cult and made

[1] Practically the whole of the Abhidhamma is a study of fixed type, group, and process.

it as his own. As acknowledged to be his very own *it never became* : this we have seen ; but the world has been growing in religious ideals to the need, in any religion still held as worthy of adoption, of a strong representation of ethical teaching. And albeit the wrong view taken with regard to the object of the Moods reduces the exercise of them to a matter not primarily of ethics properly so called, but to a mere reverberation of ethical influence in the individual only, nevertheless, as the best that Buddhism has to offer—and, indeed, in the matter of catholic sympathy it is a very good best—the exercises have come in these days to hold a very high rank in doctrines considered as early Buddhist.

I am fain after the lapse of the burying centuries to do a late justice to the work of a great and good man who is for us now not even a name. But—and I feel sure he will agree—the yet more important work in values here is the reinstating the real nature and method of the work of fellow-warding which he taught, a work which is without its equal in ancient culture, nor is adequately enjoined even to-day.

I would go further and suggest what it was, in this man's world and age, that was predisposing men to be moved by just the teaching, the new word he brought to them.

We saw, in the second chapter, that man's conception of That in whom he lived, moved and had his being had come to be taken up into the very nature of him, so that he *was* That in the way of *becoming* That. "That" was worded as not only Brahman, but as "self", thus giving to just the word self (*ātman*) a depth and sublimity of meaning it has not with us. Self included, involved, "at its highest power" that which the religious man held most precious, most valued, most "dear" (*priya*). But this Self he was also bound to infer in another. That other man was also as a mother-expectant, cherishing within her the To-Be. Each man was, as the Christian scriptures also saw, a temple of the Holy Spirit.

This is the sentiment expressed in the Sutta verse of the Piṭakas :—

> The whole wide world we traverse with our thought,
> finding to man naught dearer than the Self;
> since aye so dear the Self to others is,
> let the Self-lover harm no other man ! [1]

Writers pass over this verse—it is a close echo of Upanishad teaching—perhaps because this "love of the Self" is to us repellant.

[1] *Saṃyutta*, i, 75 ; *Udāna*, V, 1.

We have worsened the meaning of "self"; we mean, by that, body and mind with all their imperfections; we leave out the essential: the valuer, the "man". For the Indian it was, it is very different. And in the then accepted cult of the God-in-and-as-Self I see a mighty lever, exalting the anæmic, negative "not-harming" ethic of the time to a sublime ego-altruism, to a worship and a warding of the Self that is I-in-the-Becoming and You-in-the-Becoming till then unknown.

XII

ṚDDHI, OR THE MAN AS MORE

In the dark days for so many mothers, now gone I pray for ever, I once, at the suggestion of a then rising philosopher, went with him to consult incognita a professional psychometrical medium. When I told the things the medium told me to my husband, I added : " If, if only what such people so consulted can tell us is *true*, it is they who should be our seers, they who should stand in our pulpits, at our deathbeds. They know, they see more than we. Those accredited preachers only read and believe. These have more ; they are more . . . if . . ."

It is for this " more " that the man of abnormal gifts has been valued by mankind in all lands, in all ages. Hence when Sakya was born, this value in the " more " was there already. It was no longer, as in the Vedic values, a " more " to be granted by placated Great Devas ; it had become a gift extorted, as it were, by and from correctly celebrated sacrificial ritual.[1] But in India it was, to a great extent, the *man* in whom resided the gift of the abnormally, or supernormally more. Of old the Rishi could bless, or (and this especially) blast, as were he Deva. The Brahman could, and did, as being the celebrant of the rite, the chanter of the mantra, count as more in himself than the normal man. Even the *samaṇa*, the recluse was as likely as not to have developed some individual supernormal gift, rarely found in the man of the world. And in exercizing such a gift he did not judge that it was just mind putting forth power over body ; it was *he* who was " minding " body in a special way. Such at any rate appears from the various ways in which that exercise was spoken of, as we shall presently see.

Vested in the man the abnormally-more was known by the name of *ṛddhi*, a word which in Pali slipped down into *iddhi*. The root of the word has been stated to lie in *ardh*, to prosper. It may indeed be that this idea has grown from the word *ṛddhi*, and its derivatives, being used to mean prosperous, thriving, successful. But I venture to see in the root *vṛdh*, to grow, the more primary source, and herein

[1] Cf. H. Oldenberg, *Weltanschauung der Brahmaṇatexte*, 133 f. ; 149 f. ; Macdonell, *Enc. R. and E.*, art. : Magic (Vedic).

Whitney suggests a connection.[1] Those adjectives are too patently secondary, derivative, resultant, to rank as radical.

It is true that, in the Piṭakas, *iddhi* also stands for what is notable, physically and mentally, in a way of *normal* excellence or success. Rhys Davids has collected such instances concerning a lion, a king, a rich man, a hunter, etc. in *Dialogues of the Buddha* (i, 273). In such cases we are up against instances of what *we* might call "luck", which are either natural endowment, or obtained by applied industry, perseverance and so on. But we see from all such, that in *iddhi* we have the double meaning that lies in the word luck. Luck may be ours by natural endowment, by our own normal, consistently persistent effort. But in luck there is ever the "juncture", the incalculable residuum, due now and not then, here and not there, to causes over which we have no assignable control. And we may try to explain away *iddhi* in ancient India by many red herrings, but there will remain the other kind, the abnormally, the psychically more, the source of which the Sakyan after-teachers were no more able to explain truly or coherently than are the wise of our day.

A definition of *iddhi* which may best cover all the varied use of the word is to connect it with what I have elsewhere called "more-will". Many are the makeshifts in old Indian language for lack of the word will, as we have seen in these chapters. But in those two words, *saṃkalpa* and *ṛddhi*, the one meaning purpose, the other abnormal effectuating, they got near to the real thing. They blend in a way in the vision that the loving Anuruddha conjured up :

> *Mama sankappam aññāya satthā loke anuttaro*
> *manomayena kāyena iddhiyā upasankami.*[2]
> He knew my (heart's) intent the Teacher, he
> whose peer the world hath not, and came to me
> by power-to-effect, with body as 'twere by mind.

We are reminded of another lover of the Man, whose longing wrought no such effect of more-will : the aged Pingiya, of the Sutta-Nipāta :

> From Him not mine to dwell absent
> E'en for a moment, brāhmaṇa.
> I see him with the mind as with the eyes,
> unfaltering, brāhmaṇa, both night and day.
> Revering him I spend the night ;
> From him methinks absence there's none.

. . . .

[1] *Sanskrit Roots*, p. 164 f. : "√*vṛdh*, grow . . . Compare √*ṛdh*."
[2] *Theragāthā*, ver. 901.

If Gotama hither or thither goes,
't is here, 't is there that I am drawn to go.
Of me the aged strength-enfeebled man,
the body cannot run there where he is.
Ever I go faring by (heart's) intent,
for to that Man the mind of me is joined.[1]

The case, on the other hand of three nuns, disciples according to the Commentary of Gotama's foster-mother, whose couplets stand second, third and fourth in the Anthology—and that is not an unreasonable warrant of their relatively early date—we come up against experience suggesting the possession of *iddhi* similar to Anuruddha's. Muttā, Puṇṇā, Tissā all are said to have beheld, in an aura, a vision of the Founder. It is also recorded that *he* uttered the several couplets they are credited withal. But we shall see this kind of exegetical filching from women *actually in process* in the case of Vajirā,[2] and here I draw the line at what I am inclined to hold true. There is enough in this very interesting subject of *iddhi* to strain modern credulity, without needlessly exaggerating the ordeal.

Let us first discount that exegetical sanctioning, as deemed necessary in those earlier days for women's work. What there am I prepared to accept, as at once abnormal and probably true, objectively true *for some* it may be, in the visions of Anuruddha and the three nuns? The narratives do not warrant our holding that the Founder had passed away from earth. Is he held to have come near them in some supernormal way?

I think that Pingiya's verses are a sound corrective of this. We are not here concerned to make out a period of *unlimited* miracle-working for Gotama and his disciples. This might have been the alternative to our ignorance a generation or two ago. But we really have got a little further than that to-day. Pingiya in fervent devotion dwells upon his hero, and follows him, as he sits or lies alone, how? There is no "flying through the air" here. It is "by the mind as by the eyes"; it is with his "heart's intent"—the word is *saṅkappa*; *we* might have said "will"; they could not. Or we should have said: "my thoughts follow him day and night."

If we now credit our loving thinker, Anuruddha, with an abnormal visualizing power—and the three nuns perhaps with a similar power—we have here a phenomenon not unknown to abnormal psychology, and not peculiar to any one land or era: that

[1] Ver. 1140, 1142–4. Note the *me cittaṃ* "mind of me". "*I*" am not the mind.
[2] Chapter XX.

of a mental image appearing at least to the subject as a spatially external "eject". It is very possible that, in this vision, it may have seemed to Anuruddha as if his Leader had really "come to him". In that case the *iddhi* would have been *his*, not the Leader's. Or it may have been a case of *iddhi* in both. Thus it may be suggested that we have here a case of a form of telepathy now, I believe, engaging attention in psychical research, of appearances to the clairvoyant of persons known to be on earth but absent. And this, in a very different wording from that which such research would now employ, is the belief expressed by both Dhammapāla's Commentary,[1] and by that of Buddhaghosa on the same verses where recorded in the Anguttara Nikāya.[2] The latter is the inferior description; the "intent" of Anuruddha is reduced to *vitakka* (apprehending), not, be it noted (to *viriya*, or *chanda* or *cetas* or *cetanā*, or) to any terms which our translators render by "will". And the Bhagavā is said to have come to the disciple by a "mind-made body, making the body as it were mind". Dhammapāla's comment is to this extent worthier that he adduces a much more suitable term in his goodwill to explain the business. This is *adhiṭṭhāna-iddhi.*

This, or "*iddhi* by way of resolve", or determination, brings us on to dynamic ground. It is the first in a scholastic category of ten modes of "iddhi-powers" (*-balāni*), to be found in the treatise "The Way of Analysis",[3] of the miscellaneous books of the Sutta-Piṭaka. Neither Commentator persuades me that Anuruddha really had such a "visit" paid him. He was a noted psychical subject, yet he is telling of his vision in very simple, but rather poetical terms: "he came to me." But with the later growth of the Buddha-cult, it was inevitable that the gift of the disciple should be transferred to the "Buddha". So both Commentators bring the latter along to talk to Anuruddha about the eight thoughts (*vitakkā*) of a superman, and then return to the Sangha and tell it all over again in detail like any super-lecturer! How characteristic of the After-men it is! The Man of the super-values becomes the all-knower; the gifted disciple becomes the little-knower. The Man of the super-values talks in terms of fixed schedule; the venerable and eminent disciple has on the subject no words at all, fixed or otherwise.

[1] *Pss. of the Brethren*, p. 327, *n.* 5; *Anguttara*, iv (misquoted there as iii), 235; *Manoratha puraṇī*, i, 191 f.

[2] Vol. iv, p. 228 ff.

[3] *Paṭisambhidāmagga*, ii, 174; 205.

The ten items in the treatise named above, the *Paṭisambhidā-magga*, are as follows : (1) *iddhi* by resolve, (2) by transformation, (3) mind-made, (4) by suffusion with an idea, (5) by suffusion with concentration, (6) Ariyan *iddhi*,[1] (7) resulting from good deeds (in the past), (8) of the man who has merit, (9) from spells (10) *iddhi* in the sense of effecting by right application here and there. How far the later writings of Commentary and Manual agree with, or differ from this (virtually) Abhidhamma list I have gone into elsewhere.[2] With such late developments we have here little concern.

But there is in the Four Nikāyas a fixed wording which will be much older. We do not find it in process of coming to be : it is always the same, and it is the oldest thing of its kind in Sakyan records. It is called the " variously assigned modes of *iddhi* ", and it runs as follows : " Being one, he becomes many ; having become many he becomes (again) one ; here visible, there invisible, he goes without let or hindrance through wall, through rampart, through hill, as if through air ; he makes immersion-emersion in earth as if in water ; he walks on water, unbreaking it as if on earth ; he travels seated cross-legged through air as if he were bird on the wing ; he can handle and stroke with the hand this moon and sun, mighty and powerful though they be ; he has control over the body as far as Brahmā-world." [3]

My acquaintance with books about Buddhism is very deficient, but of those known to me there is but one which approaches this formula, not indeed without preconceptions of a Western sort, but without prejudice, also of a Western sort. I refer to Dr. H. Beckh's popular opuscule *Buddhismus* (Sammlung Göschen, 1919). He alone (to my knowledge) sees how integral was its import with Buddhist origins, and he alone sees it as very interesting. *How* interesting it is his preconceptions do not suffer him to see. And with his merging the whole of the central mandate of " Buddhism " into Indian Yoga I do not agree. But he does not push *iddhi* aside after the method of repellant rationalism. It stands as a ruined pillar in early Sakya, and to pass by and leave it on the other side is to evade the inconveniently obvious. Dr. Beckh's preconceptions, to my thinking, find too easily a resort to such defining terms as " super-sensuous ", " super-earthly," " ætherically mental," " higher power of mind,"

[1] " Ariyan ", in scholastic Pali, tends to be synonymous with " arahan's ", See my ed. of *Duka paṭṭhāna*, p. 366.

[2] *Compendium of Philosophy*, by S. Z. Aung, p. 60, n.

[3] *Dīgha*, i, 78 ; *Saṃyutta*, ii, 121, 212, etc.

etc. I believe that if we were to drop this—may I say—nineteenth century lumber, and come to modern psychical research, coupled with historical criticism, we might find the *iddhi*-formula not merely interesting after an antiquarian or a "mystical" sort, but one that has an appeal for the abnormal psychology of to-day. Not one of the terms I quote is even suggested by the Pali concerning *iddhi*. It is true that the word "mind" (*citta*) is used where we should and ought to use will and super-, or more-will. But that is, as we have seen, India's defect and misfortune wherever the word "will" is called for, for example, in the Four Moods, in which Dr. Beckh sees nothing whatever either super-sensuous or super-normal, or work of will miscalled in Pali "mind". And there is nothing anywhere to suggest that the Sakyan conceived he was using any but his normal mind in any but a specially strenuous way. This way is worded by two quite ordinary "exoteric" terms: *abhinīharati*, "he super-out-brings (the mind)", *abhininnāmeti*, "he super-out-bends (the mind)", namely to effect his purpose. The former term, without the "super-", is used for extracting a wedge[1]; the latter, as it stands, is used for a crab or tortoise putting forth its claw.[2] This does not exclude their implying a strenuous effort of will when associated with "*citta*".

With regard to the formula calling for historic criticism, it were well to apply this before calling out that an abnormal psychology would only see mystic dementia in a formula which includes a stroking, a touching moon and sun, or having in the body access to the world of the Rūpa, or Brahmā-devas. It does sound a little unlicensed, but it does not call, as Dr. Beckh calls, for us to help it out by reference to the very un-Buddhist Suttanta, the Pāyāsi.[3] For Sakya the unseen worlds started with that of the firmamental, or we might say, Nature devas: the Four Rajas of the four quarters, with devas of moon, sun, and stars, the rain, the clouds, and so forth. These were conceived as embodied, and as so near, relatively to the man of earth, that he could, if psychically gifted, even touch them as he could not touch the devas of the next world when seen. For this solution the reader should consult the Saṃyutta Book on Psychic Power, *Kindred Sayings*, v. in Mr. Woodward's translation.[4]

The next world is that of the Thirty Devas and of Sakka, a world also very close to earth, corresponding to our own next step. This finds no mention in the formula, possibly because it may have been

[1] *Majjhima*, No. 20; i, 119. [2] Ibid., i, 234, etc.
[3] Considered as originally Jain by Dr. Leumann. *Dīgha*, ii, No. xxiii.
[4] P.T.S. ed., 1930, pp. 225 ff.

sufficiently attended to in the original Jhāna practice. The next after that was the Brahmās' world, also very near but worthier. The conception of it as up aloft was soon to begin, but there is no "up" (*upari*) in the *Dīgha-Nikāya* to justify the use (in the translation) of that English word. It is true that Jhāna is, in the (later) Abhidhamma, associated with the Rūpa (and Arūpa) world, and here and there in the Nikāyas we find the same distinction. But we have to recollect that in the Piṭakas, in their present form, we have the editings of an age from which the object of the old Musing had waned, and which afford us no sure clue to the ideas of the day which saw the formulating of this old *iddhi*-schema.

So much then for the way in which Western preconceptions hinder our understanding the nature of *iddhi*, and entail the present neglect in discerning historical values in Buddhist records. I will now try to show how the old *iddhi*-formula is so much more interesting for me than it has apparently been for other writers, and even for the more heedful Dr. Beckh.

If we discount the last two clauses, accounting for them as I have suggested, it is not impossible that we may come to see, in the old formula, not unbridled fantasy, but a carefully limited statement of abnormal human achievement, such as has been now and then, here and there, witnessed and well attested not only in the past but also in our own times. In one and all of the clauses it is a question, not of that which would, if attempted, certainly destroy life, but of that which has been shown to be possible, where there is a faculty somewhat exceeding the normal limit. For instance, there is no question of life carried on under the earth or under water. The limit I have mentioned is that of "diving" into earth and "coming up again (*ummujja-nimujjam karoti*)". It is true that the achievement of the Indian fakirs of surviving unharmed the being buried in earth for a limited number of hours, cannot be very fitly described in the clause above, which is the reverse of passive endurance. Yet it is always possible—as was the case, I think, in Anuruddha's "he came to me"—that we have here a very ancient wording, which came to be adjusted when the value in *iddhi* had practically waned into a matter of old times. It made anyway a very convenient mnemonic quasi-alliterative cadence when taken in conjunction with the walking on water. This, indeed, is a noteworthy feature throughout the mantra. It has only just stopped short of being worded metrically. Walking on or rather over water—in Pali it would not be differently expressed—and rising in and moving through the air are phenomena not unknown to the East and West of to-day. The present generation has forgotten Daniel Home and the sensation he made in the scientific world. The passing through obstacles has likewise been attested in Houdini's wonderful feats, with his additional difficulty of the escape from a complex of knotted cord, while immured in a chest. Again, there is no claim to an *iddhi* which could endure fire. Here the limit is drawn; and similarly as to living without food. Yet had the formula been merely fanciful, there is no lack of a claim to such powers in later uncanonical standards.

There remains the first achievement, which translations sometimes misrepresent. Put into equivalent English the Pali will be: "he being one can become many, (then) being many he can (re-) become one." Now the outstanding instance of this self-multiplication—a form of abnormality which, as of to-day, in East or West, has not come to my ken—was the monk Panthaka Junior. The account of his blossoming out from shy diffidence into this height of confidence in will-work is told briefly in the verses ascribed to him in the Anthology, and in at least three Commentaries: Dhammapāla's on the poem, Buddhaghosa's on the mention of Panthaka as chief of those skilled in "transformation by intent (*ceto-vivaṭṭa*)", and that on the Fourth Jātaka about the brothers Roadling or Wayman (Panthaka), Senior and Junior. The versions are all in one or more features mutually discrepant; thus in the Anthology our Panthaka sits in Jīvaka's Mango Grove, in another version the dinner party is there, with the Order as guests, Panthaka being left at the Vihāra. In the Anthology, Gotama bids a disciple fetch him; in the Anguttara Commentary, Jīvaka the host sends a servant, and so on. I mention these misfits to show that we have a notable tradition but one of very sketchy records, which have undergone, as the Pali reader will see, a quite diligent amount of embroidery, Buddhaghosa and the unknown Jātaka Commentator being herein the chief gossips. Stripped of frills, I picture the event somewhat on this wise: Jīvaka, the Magadha court-physician, an outstanding figure among the lay patrons of the Sakyas, entertains Gotama and his earlier co-missioners in his garden. Panthaka remains alone at the mother-settlement in the Bamboo Grove. Gotama is aware that Panthaka is developing a remarkable *iddhi*-power, declines to eat till he be sent for, and sends a disciple to fetch him, who will perhaps discover him practising alone his power, and also be able to estimate rightly what he sees. *Let us say*, it is no one less than Moggallāna who is sent. He finds Panthaka so practising. He is projecting here and there a quasi-material replica of himself (the multiplication to a thousand means no more than our "a thousand thanks", just "several"). Being himself highly psychic, Moggallāna sees the forms before—Panthaka's concentrated will being disturbed—they vanish, and the two go to the party, Panthaka becoming recognized (by the testimony of the highly gifted Moggallāna) as the Ugly Duckling become a Swan.

We have here a case, fundamentally well attested, of a very abnormal gift, reckoned then also as such, but which is akin to the subjective projection of another person obsessing the thought of the subject, such as we have seen in the case of Anuruddha and the three nuns. The differences here are that the subject projects a visualized replica of himself, and—and this difference is, of course, all-important—the visions are visible to a second person who is, by his own gift, qualified to see what, for normal sight, is invisible. For that matter, we do not know that the projector himself saw what his will wrought; his metrical narrative may possibly have been only of the effect on the messenger. It is more likely that he did see. I am too ignorant of the varieties in abnormal human powers, which have been observed by the competent and competently recorded, to go further into this class of phenomena. But I incline to think that it was almost or altogether unique, and that the wonder of it led to its being set at the top of the "Various Kinds of *Iddhi*" Formula.

I am not saying that the projection of his own personal appearance by a man capable of *iddhi* was held to be unique; it was the more than one such projection that was held as so wonderful. On the other hand, I do not concede that the curiously worded achievement, in the Sāmaññaphala list of eight "Studies",[1] is a genuine reference to *iddhi*-power of projection. The willer is there said to "create a body made of mind, and from this body to create a different body having shape, made of mind, complete in all parts and faculties." What are we to make of this irrational procedure? Why is it not included under the *iddhi*-formula which follows? Franke suggests it as forming a basis[2] for the formula, but there is nothing of the nature of a Causal Succession in the eight. Why again have translators shirked using the word "create"?[3]

I believe that we have here a badly corrupted surviving memory of a time when it was a new thing in India to be distinguishing introspectively the mind, as well as the body, from the man. It is not easy for us of to-day to place ourselves within such a contemplation.

[1] *Dīgha-N.*, i, 77 (*Dialogues*, i, 87 f).
[2] Cf. his *Dīgha-N.* 78, n. 3: "Grundlage."
[3] For the Pali *abhinimminãya*, etc.

I have gone into this in the chapter on Sānkhya. We forget that it was a very enthralling novelty for the thoughtful of that day—a day, be it never forgotten, far earlier than the day of the ideas prevalent in the Piṭakas. *It was a new world of thought that was opening up.*

In the preceding, that is, the first of the eight Studies, we have the body considered both in itself and also as being valued by mind (*viññāṇa*) "now here the mind of me is resting, is here bound up." This is the older way of values. There is no attempt to consider mind analytically, as came to be done. And there is no attempt to make mind do the work of the man, as a wielder of body. Minding, or action of mind simply presented or "showed up" body as "a coloured thread passed through a gem shows up the gem's translucency", the thread here representing the ways of mind. It is the older dualism of the man and his body. The man is here ever present: "my body, my mind."

Nor should the reader bring in here the later depreciation of mind, in *viññāna*, as a reference to sensuous and emotional experience only. In this more ancient reckoning it is not mind "at a lower power"; *that* is a later refinement. The words for mind (*citta*, *mano*, *viññāṇa*) were then equivalents, as we read in a venerable Saying: *cittam, iti pi mano iti pi viññāṇaṃ* (*iti pi* is "thus too"). It was the ancient Sakyan way of speaking of that in the man, which he could contemplate and value, over against that whom he could not contemplate or value: the "man-in-man", contemplator, valuer. A similar description in another venerable Saying is to speak, not of body and mind, much less of the more pedantic five *khandhas* or aggregates, but of body as "bemindish", thus: *sasaññī, samanī, saviññāṇako.*[1]

But in the following paragraph, in the second of these eight Studies, there would seem to be a picturesque if crude effort to contemplate first body, and then evoke or educe from the body the influences which, as it were another finer body, were spread in and over the body co-operating with, and wielding, in heart, blood, sense-organs, the grosser life of the body. There was no question yet of an ejection of the real man. It was the new elaboration of the man's equipment (*parikkhāra*), the nearest word there was to "instruments". And it was a wonderful and fascinating subject—this "new psychology"—it was an expansion in man's conception of himself; it was a more in and of him, evolved from the older dualism of man and body, and it was not unnatural to picture it as a "new body" created out of,

[1] *Saṃyutta*, i, 62; ii, 252 f.; iii, 80, etc.; v, 311.

or drawn out of the material body, in idea, as like a stem, or sword from a sheath, as worded in the following similes.

This pre-occupation with this newly distinguished "mind" as along and with the body, the new values, the new terms, the new analysis that arose about it, led to a new designation for the studious disciples; they came to be called *manobhāvanīyā*, that is, developers of mind. It even appears, from the Commentaries, to have been a term of respect, parallel to the more usual "reverend" (*āyasmā*). And it is *this new pre-occupation* that I judge to be here meant in the second of the Eight Studies of the Sāmaññaphala Suttanta. It follows the contemplation of the "beminded" body as such; it is kept apart from the following study of *Iddhi*, which is, as it were, the appendix to the normal man's properties, the study of the more than the normal.

As to that "appendix", the *Iddhi*-formula, or Third of the Eight Studies, there is this further word as to its showing limitation rather than licence: a mere magical schedule, or fantasia would have been more inclusive; it makes no mention of a power to anticipate events, such as we know especially in Scotland as second sight, or of a power to conjure up unseen beings, or to exorcize the same, to heal or to curse. Once we place ourselves, with regard to those two last clauses, at the old Indian point of view, we are more likely to be struck by the restraint of the formula than by its extravagance.

For not only is it interesting in being a list differing in detail from the list that the very early Christian Fraternity would have compiled, had it been as much given to category-making as was ancient India at the time we are considering—such a Christian list would have included healing, casting out "devils", the seeing of visions (as in the case of Peter and John) and other powers recorded in the Acts—but its interest lies also largely in this, that it is a record (a partial one) of what a man can achieve, in the control of matter, in a relatively greater degree, if he happen to be born with, or has developed, a relatively greater degree of will. *Iddhi* is practically "more-will"; this is, if not explicit, implicit in its very meaning: effectuating, e.g. *sam-iddhi* is success, the having wrought or accomplished. This is best illustrated in the phenomenon, not unknown to us, of "levitation". This is to overcome the force of gravitation to a *relatively greater extent* than any leaper in the high and the long jump achieves; and by the same self-directing activity, namely, will. The leaper may look and calculate, but if he exert not will, as we usually picture will, he will accomplish no leap. In that leap he, for two or three seconds, overcomes the force of gravity to the extent of rising in the air it may be as much as five feet, or of moving through the air several feet, bringing into play a very synergy of will. Could he put forth a somewhat more sustained synergy, we should see the momentary leap become a movement of abnormal duration, and so, possibly, of elevation.

In thus associating leaping with levitation, as acts of will at a different power, I make, of course, no original suggestion. The association was made by a Buddhist monk nearly ten centuries ago. Milinda (Menandros) asks Nāgasena, how can anyone move through the air? "Do you admit, sire" asks Nāgasena, "that you have ever jumped over the earth a *vidatthi* or a *ratani*?"[1] "I do; I have jumped 8 ratanis." "How did you jump?" "I called up the thought: Here I will alight. With the calling up of the thought, my body became buoyant." "Even so, sire, a monk who has *iddhi* and has got his purpose under control, focusses the body on the thought and goes through the air."

The telling "how it's done" is here of great interest, showing how hampered (yet unaware) the Indian was, always was, for want of the idea and the word "will". We saw this hampering lack in the First Utterance of Gotama; we see it here some five centuries later. With the use here of *citta*, *cetas*, thought, or mind, or purpose, made to do service for will, the Western reader may have jumped to the conclusion that *iddhi* is explained away as merely visiting a place, earthly or otherwise by the visualizing it in mind. He would not realize, how "mind", "thought" had to serve as words for will. There was no idea, either in the Milinda Questions, or in the Piṭakas, of coming down to so cheap a rationalization as that!

And it is in the Indian wording of this abnormal will that we see so emphatically brought out, despite the poor vocabulary, the belief in the existence of the man over against body and mind. It is the man here who is the valuer and the disposer of both the one and the other. It is not only the king, Menandros, who, as not entertaining any Sakyan notion, or shall I say, Buddhist notion of the man as a fiction, naturally uses the diction current in his cultural world; it is Nāgasena, too, the monk who had challenged the king to show him how to find the man as a distinct entity, who *also acquiesces* in the same diction and uses it himself. The Buddhist will, of course, say here that the monk was only using the conventional diction in converse with a layman, and a non-Buddhist at that. But

[1] Space-measures. *Milindapañho*, p. 85. Cf. my *The Milinda Questions* p. 99 f.

if we go back from so late a work to the Canon, we find no care taken, when practice for, or performance in *iddhi* is the subject, and the performer spoken of, or to, is a monk, to merge the man in body and mind. It is "the man" who is disposer of both.

That *iddhi* in fact was a difficulty in the way of the doctrine of the "not-man" was brought forward, in the great series of debates on the subject in the Kathāvatthu. The upholder of "the man" there sees, in success in *iddhi*, or any other form of psychic abnormality, the necessity of postulating "a man". Such success is not worked from without, but is of the self (*ajjhattaṃ*). It is not insignificant that the upholder of the not-man slips past again with the question, whether the man is only real *when achieving iddhi*? [1]

So far I have been considering *iddhi* in its general recognition in early Sakya, but not as a channel for that becoming of the "man in the 'more'", or as we should say, for spiritual growth. To this we are now coming. As such, *iddhi* forms were not essential to advance in the Way, or to the forwarding the welfare of others. There was no intrinsic virtue in abnormal powers. It is not overlooked that the notorious Devadatta was so gifted. But it *is* overlooked that the fact of such gifts as being here and there inborn, or even as capable of being developed, *constituted a guarantee* that the man *was and could be more*, could grow, in intrinsic worth. A man having power of *iddhi* is already the more, even if it be a more only in the power over matter. But, in that herein he has abnormal will-force, he is capable of a worthier use of it.

We of Europe have still so much to learn before we can worthily estimate this matter of *iddhi* as abnormal will. We have to come to better conceptions of the nature of "the man", the *puruṣa*, in our religion and philosophy, of the will and the man as willer in our psychology, of the fact and significance of "becoming" in all three. The subject has been too much waved aside as either the records of childishly wonder-doting monks, or of a hankering after the unseen, the mystical, the magical, the need to impress the "sign"-loving outside world. To judge of *iddhi* with less of such pre-conceptions, we should in the first place study the subject from within, I mean within the early Sakyan movement. We may then come to see values hidden to the reader who, at the first allusion to achievements he is quite unable to do himself, treats it as horses once behaved before motor-cars.

Let us look first at those early fixed wordings, both about *iddhi*

[1] *Kathāvatthu*, i, 1, § 217 f.

and other things prescribed as highly desirable. I refer especially to the list *of* lists which came to be called *Bodhipakkhiya Things*, and to be named later as the thirty-seven such. One of the lists is known as The Four Right Efforts, another is The Four Steps to *Iddhi*. Clearly we are in the heart of a very strenuous gospel; and this comes the more as a shock when we recollect three things: that it was a religious mandate for the Many, that in the prevailing religious mandate at its birth, man and Deity were both conceived as essentially both "Being" and also "Thought", and that neither was conceived as "will", nor as fundamentally Willer, nor was either idea worthily worded.

What then were those four Steps to *Iddhi*, and what exactly was included here under the word? Here is the formula preceded by the suggestive introduction at the beginning of the section on *Iddhi* in the Saṃyutta-Nikāya: [1]

"These four steps to *iddhi*, brought about (*bhāvitā*), practised, advance to the going further and further: what are the four? (1) Here a monk brings about a step to *iddhi* consorted with a combination of concentrated effort with a 'mantra'. (2) . . . a step to *iddhi* consorted with a combination of concentrated effort with energy. (3) . . . with a combination of concentrated effort with mind (*citta*). (4) . . . with a combination of concentrated effort with intellect (*vīmamsā*)."

Hereon a word or two. I have striven to render as literally as possible the crude and inadequate Pali wording. The result in form and terms is as crude as the original. It should not be forgotten that we have on the one hand a course practised by the few, even in earliest Sakya, leading to results attainable only by yet fewer. We read in this Section of not only "monks", but also of even Ānanda asking Gotama what is "step to *iddhi*", what is bringing the step about, what is the way to do it? [2] On the other hand we have monks engaged in settling certain fixed wordings in the rudiments of Sakyan "doctrine", perhaps in the Founder's old age, probably in the growing "settlement" at Sāvatthī, who, as *corresponding to* scribes, editors, journalists, in our world of books, but as living in a world of no writing, would be very unlikely so to enter into and understand the range of the abnormal as to express it fitly. We may see similar crudities not seldom even in our writing world, in the journalism of to-day, both secular and theological.

In the next place, in rendering the word *chanda*, not in accordance with the Commentaries, nor as do other translators by "will"

[1] *Mahāvagga*, vol. v, p. 254 f. [2] Ibid., p. 286 f.

or "desire", and the like, but by its other meaning of metric speech or *mantra*, I believe my furrow as yet is quite lonely. That I am right is, of course, my conviction. To use the word in this latter sense in the formula is a far better fit. I am coming to that below. Desire (or will) is *presupposed* in the aspirant. The carrying out his desire in "energy" and the rest, such is the aim of the worded prescription. For that matter the word energy (or endeavour, *viriya*) is already provided for in the word "effort" (*padhāna*). But it is possible that we have here a tag of extra-Sakyan, of Yoga wording: *samādhi-pradhāna*, taken over (*padhāna* is a very rare word in the Piṭakas), and the term *viriya*, much valued in Sakya, had to be given distinctive place and emphasis.

As to the potency attaching to the chanted rune at that day in India, I have gone a little into the matter already.[1] And on the subject of such metric runes being held capable of producing wonderful effects, for instance, on serpents, I would refer the reader to the citations in the chapter on the Four Moods.[2] As meaning metric cadence the word *chanda* is rare in the Canon, yet we have it in both Vinaya and Sutta. Thus in the couplets on "the Bard", I have rendered the word as follows:

> Metre's (*chando*) the hidden source whence verses flow;
> Letters it is that issue from that source;
> 'Tis names of things whereon verses are hung;
> The bard is the abode wherein they dwell.[3]

We forget, in reading such lines, that we are in a world yet governed by the spell of the spoken, especially the chanted word, and not in the world of the book.

But I am not very hopeful that Buddhist or non-Buddhist will agree that I have come here to a right conclusion. The former will say: "It is clear from Suttas in the Iddhipāda-Saṃyutta, that *chanda* was understood, in the Steps, to mean desire, or volition. We see it as the first-named step, associated with the formula of the Four Right Efforts to bring about the good and repress the bad (another of the *Bodhipakkhiya* Lists). We see Ānanda associating with the Chanda Step his explanation, to the brahman Uṇṇabha, of the object of the holy life being the removing of desire." And so on. The non-Buddhist is still unwilling to accept the idea of the Suttas being a very composite result of much editing at different places and times. Let us leave it at that.

[1] *Gotama the Man*, pp. 82–5; and above, p. 53. [2] Chap. XI.

[3] *Saṃyutta*, i, p. 38; *Kindred Sayings*, i, 54.

Lastly, there is, in the fourth step, the curious word *vīmaṃsā* (Sanskrit, *mīmamsā*), literally "desiring to think", also a very rare intruder in Piṭakan Pali. Here we have probably a learned-sounding word, which would, in its association with brahman culture, have a prestige for the compilers who were only, I repeat, at the rudiments of a Sakyan thesaurus. At that date *citta* was not so much a thought or idea, as it is in the later Abhidhamma, but was equated by mind and *viññāṇa* and, as we have also seen, was used just where they, who would render *chanda* by will, would expect to find it, (*chanda*) and *do not find it*—I mean, in the exercise of the Four Moods. Nor should we forget, that in lacking a satisfactory word for will the Indian, in the words for mind, *citta*, *manas*, could and did invest these words with a certain dynamic implication. Oldenberg, as I have said, has drawn attention to this [1]; Deussen has now and then rendered *manas* by Wunsch, wollen, Wille [2]; and the association of mind with action, as one of the three forms of conduct in *manasi-karoti*, *manokamma*, is itself suggestive of this. If then we take *citta* in the third Iddhipāda as used rather for purposive mind, we can see that, where what we now call "intellectual concentration" was needed (or was it just a special idea that was needed?), a distinctive term for it was required. *Saññā* in old Pali wording was used for idea or notion. But that term had also a very wide range, and hence also would not supply the more distinctive word.

Summing up these brief comments, we get this: Much insight into the nature of *iddhi* is neither to be found in, nor expected from the fourfold formula. The first kind of "step" should be taken as meaning that potent Indian co-efficient in achievement, the metric rune. The step involving with strongest emphasis what we call will is, not the first, nor the second, but the third step or way—a meaning involved in both Vedic and Sakyan conceptions of the words *citta*, *manas*. And we may add this: the four "steps" do not mean a progressive series, any more than do the other lists in the Bodhipakkhiya Schema. We do get the idea of process, or serial thought here and there in the Suttas, e.g. in the Four Truths, and in such a mental and volitional progress as that of the Kītagiri Sutta (Majjhima, No. 70)—the learner who has faith, draws near, listens to teaching, remembers, scrutinizes the "good" (*attha*) therein, approves, thereupon desire is begotten, and zeal, and weighing, and lastly effort. "Process" in Sakyan psychology had made advance

[1] *Die Weltanschauung der Brahmana-Texte*, pp. 70 ff.

[2] *Sechzig Upanishad's der Veda*, pp. 175, 229, 460; "= *der bewusste Wille.*"

when the Milinda Questions were *written* (? soon after 100 B.C.), but a series like the above is very rare in the Piṭakas, and the rareness is attested in the Seven Lists we have in mind. The four steps are four methods, by which the few abnormally gifted, severally and according to individual idiosyncrasies, used to develop (bring about) their specific potency or *iddhi*.

I come now to the greater task of weighing the value and significance of *iddhi* in Sakyan origins. We have plainly here no infiltrating or annexed feature. Inquired about it would seem to have been, but then there will ever be such inquiry where the matter is a gift possessed only by the few, and where the source is so cryptic. And we can credit a man like Ānanda inquiring, where we should not look to find Moggallāna, Anuruddha, or Panthaka inquiring. If the Founder in turn inquire of Ānanda about it (and in the same terms), this can only have been as teacher asks pupil. That Ānanda himself came later to develop *iddhi* at his entry into the Rājagaha Congress is solely in the Commentary, and has too much the character of "frills" to call for credence. But that Gotama was himself abnormally gifted in *iddhi* lies too much in the very marrow of the records on the beginning of his career as teacher to be as lightly passed over as it usually is. With this I have dealt in *Gotama the Man*. Nor is there throughout the Suttas any inconsistent faltering about the certainty of his abnormal powers. That he strongly blamed any use of such power for display all writers have noted, and noted *with an emphasis they fail to use* in regard to the far more numerous references to his exercising it worthily.[1] We cannot it is true, point to any man similarly gifted being drawn into his company because of the leader's *iddhi*-powers. Moggallāna, himself so highly gifted, is not so credited in the account of his coming in. Yet it is quite likely that, being himself convinced of the reality of the unseen, in virtue of his psychic sensitiveness, he was drawn to join a teacher who laid no less stress *on that reality*, and on the all-importance of its being taught as real in the real meaning of the Way.

In this connection two passages about Moggallāna should not be overlooked. The one is, as we saw in discussing Jhāna, that it was his desire to use his clairvoyant, clairaudient power for "holding back the veil" of the unseen for the benefit of men by getting access to the next deva-world, and telling what he there saw of the happy

[1] Cf. esp. *Saṃyutta*, v, 282 f. Cf. also translation of vol. iv, introduction.

results of well-doing on earth. The other is that of the Lakkhaṇa-Saṃyutta, an interesting, as yet ignored passage.[1] Moggallāna and a fellow monk called Lakkhaṇa—"Mark"—are coming down Vulture's Peak to Rājagaha for the daily alms-round. At a certain point Moggallāna smiles. Mark asks why? "Ask me," is the reply, in "Gotama's presence." Eventually Mark does so. "I saw," is the reply, "a man undergoing punishment in another world. And I felt how wondrous it is that a person, that an individual will come to be like that!" Gotama thereupon remarks: "Disciples who have got vision and knowledge will know, will see, will testify that things are so. I also was seeing that man, but I did not mention it. Were I to do so, others would not believe me, and for such this would long redound to bane and ill for them. That man was a beef-butcher in this very Rājagaha; as a result of his work he has long been roasting in Niraya, and now by its residual result he is experiencing such an individuality."

There then follow nine other versions of such tragic sights, variants probably of the one episode as differently told and memorized, but all of them fairly characteristic of the monastic tendency to exaggerate the terrors of post-mortem retribution, and especially so here, where the monastic teaching grew to be ever more opposed to the value set on life as such.

Now I am glad here to take back, after seven years of study, the suggestion I made that Moggallāna's smile was to be deprecated.[2] Had he smiled out of cynical amusement we should not see him so valued, together with Sāriputta, by Gotama as to have come down in tradition as chief disciple, nor should we read here of the commendation of his vision and knowledge and testimony. It is even preposterous to associate with the man of the gospel for the "end-making of Ill" a co-worker who could be amused at suffering. No hard-hearted smiler was Moggallāna. But he was experiencing that exhilarating sense of expansion known to all who have, in this way or in that, within this limited earth-life, achieved a more than the normal. So feels the musician when to him is borne a new and divine melody; so feels the painter when to him comes vision in form and colour, and one could extend the list. Body and mind are here collaborating, but it is chiefly the very man, who in such moments of super-sight and super-hearing and super-imagining, is in very process of blossoming into the more than man, for whom the handicap of earthly encasement is for the time transcended, and who, as yet

[1] *Saṃyutta*, ii, p. 254 f.; *Kindred Sayings*, ii, 169 f.

[2] Ibid., Introduction.

man of earth, becomes deva. Many are and were the ways for accomplishing this expanding into quasi-divine Becoming ; and, in that the ways are so many fetches made by the man of earth after that Divinely-Most latent in all men, stunted in all but very few, the nature of each way is mainly unwordable. For what we clothe in words is that which we can rate, worth, value. And the outcome of the ways in abnormal achievement we can valuate and hence put into words. But the way itself is no way only of body and mind ; it is an expansion working through these of the man's very nature, in process of becoming-in-the-Divine, or, as we might say, of becoming more in That who is Most. He is possibly himself unable to find words for the experience.

He might admit that he was in a state of will, of volitional energy, and again he might not. For very likely he would not have any very sound ideas on the nature and scope of " will ", and would allow as much or as little of its working in his " way " as the very muddled psychological notions about will of his time and circumstances prompted him. He might even say, in some abnormal ways, that he did not seem to be using his own will at all ; he might therein be unaware that in his case he was in a state, not of fiercely concentrated will, but of receptive willingness. " When I have played my best," a professional violinist has told me, " I did not seem myself to be playing." " When I am acting my best," a dramatic woman-artist told me, " I am being played-through." So much is the willer, in such a state, capable of being willed " from without " by agencies unseen. In the Steps to Iddhipāda, on the other hand, we are mainly concerned with ways of fiercely concentrated will, such as are known to men of abnormal power of will over matter exceeding in degree, as I was saying, that of the athletic jumper.

But here the question arises : Is each of these four steps, or are they collectively, a preparation *merely* to attain to a man's control of matter by mind, or to a control of mind in the materializing of it ? This is a not unimportant question. For if the answer be yes, it invests the ideals of Sakya, even along this special line suited only to the few, with a pre-occupation with the disposing power of the man over material things which the main Sakyan ideals do not seem to bear out.

If we run through the book on the Iddhipāda in the Saṃyutta, we find that of the thirty-six detailed Suttas on the characteristics and advantages of these Steps, one quarter associate them with attainment of the powers listed in the *Iddhi*-formula. In the rest there is no mention of the formula. But in some, notably in the four leading

Suttas, they are said to be indispensable to what I have tried to show were the central Sakyan ideals, namely, the Going Beyond (or Further), the Way, the Becoming utterly Well (the right ending of Ill), Nirvana.

I repeat: "the Going Beyond," and that in the face of the unfortunate rendering, from text and Commentary, of the editor Léon Feer in *aparaparaṃgamanāya*. This as it stands means usually "again and again", or "to and fro": *apara-apara*. But if we look at the analogous context in the Sutta-Nipāta, the meaning I have given comes out very clearly, and to this I have already referred. The name of the poem is being explained (verses 1129–30):

Ekam-ekassa pañhassa yathā Buddhena desitaṃ
To each-several question as by the Buddha taught
tathā yo paṭipajjeyya, gacche pāram apārato,
he who thus were-to-practise would-go to-the-beyond from-not-beyond,
aparā pāraṃ gaccheyya, bhāvento maggam
from-not-beyond to-beyond he-might-go, making-become the way
uttamaṃ.
the-uttermost.
maggo so pārangamanāya, tasmā Pārāyanam iti.
this way (is) for going beyond, therefore (it-is-)thus: "Beyond-way."

And the "beyond" here is not in the books used to mean just advance in a man's religious or other progress in this life only. It means the "hereafter". This is very clear in the favourite Raṭṭhapāla Sutta, where the chief thing the thoughtful man is "up against" is not merely the futilities of just worldly aims, but death. It is true that, with the growth of monasticism and with it the growth of the theory, that the ripe man can land himself in the beyond of nirvana by a perfecting made here and now, the simpler older issue of victory over death in "the next step only" got more complicated. To each, the pro-Buddhist on the one hand, and the seeker after the original Sakya on the other, be his divergent conclusion. Here I am standing only for a sounder rendering of the term under discussion. *Pāraṃ* is the further shore of any water, as not *oraṃ*, the hither shore.[1]

This puts a very different complexion on the dignity of the Steps

[1] "All good enough for dull wit of a fool, But not for him who seeketh the Beyond", *Psalms of the Brethren*, p. 303. So Lupton: "who seeks the Shore beyond," *JRAS.*, 1894, 798. Neumann's "der die Küste sucht" sacrifices meaning to metre. Lord Chalmers's "goals beyond" is as to its plural free. *Further Dialogues*, ii, 33.

as a religious organon. It justifies us in harping on the More to achieve the Most in man's nature, as at the very centre of Gotama's mandate, pictured as progress in a Way or Road, in a world's-way-faring. So outstanding are the four, from the more or less inferior values set out in the remaining Suttas, that I give here the way in which the aim in each of them is worded. The Four are to be " made-to-become, and made much of (*bhāvitā bāhulīkatā*) ". They then " conduce to the going further and further . . . to a growing peace, to higher knowledge, enlightenment, nirvana." " To whatever things the four are opposed, the Way going to the utter weal is opposed ; whatever things the Four countenance, those things the Way countenances." " They are a worthy outfaring faring for the practiser to the utter weal." (*Saṃyutta*, v, 254 f.)

The *Iddhi*-formula can put forth no such high claims. If it is confused with, not clearly distinguished from, the religious scope of the Steps, this is but another proof that the colossal task of editing the unwritten was too much for the monk-journalist.

In one other passage the two words " made to become, made much of ", are amplified by these five others :—" made a vehicle of, made a base of, persisted in, fostered, well undertaken." This is in the Book of the Founder's Passing,[1] where Gotama is said to declare, as a possible result of all this, the greatly prolonging of one's earth-life. The amplification does not occur at all in the Saṃyutta Book in question.

In the reference to Nirvana, also in the citations given, the equivalent terms to Nirvana are those in the text of the First Utterance. But here we see them amplified and preceded by three eminently monastic views of the Goal, namely, " absolute repulsion, fading out, ending." These are but so many negations, ill-fitting with a select line of endeavour to realize the More there is in man, and not the making of him ever less and less. This becoming-the-more is more worthily brought out in the rare term " made a vehicle of ".[2] Translators are agreed as to the rendering, and I do not share the surviving editor's doubt in the *Pali Dictionary*, P.T.S. Namely, that the term does not so much connote advance, as routine. Not all of us can drive, though practically all can walk. *Iddhipāda* is essentially a practice in improved, more effective advance in the Way, attainable by the more than averagely rich in will and in means for progress.

Taken together with Jhāna (as meaning for early Sakya what I have tried to show it meant[3]) we have in these two institutes

[1] *Dīgha*, ii, xvi, p. 103. [2] *Yānikata.* [3] Chap. IX.

very notable "vehicles" for the fostering of the growth, the becoming, the development, not of body or of mind, but of the very Man. Rightly understood, they are an emphatic endorsement of the truth that world-religions, in general, start *at first* as milestones on the way leading to an expansion, an enrichment in man's life and outlook, not to a contraction, not to a lessening, not to a negating this and that. The Iddhipādas show the man willing-to-become with his own resources. Musing shows the man alert to grow from without. The latter has its analogue in what we are pleased to call inspiration; the former has its analogue in the as yet untried ways in which man by will can affect matter, ways which now and again a super-normal man proves to be do-able, ways in which the healing art has yet much to teach us, and in which the mysteries of magnetism may hold for us yet unrevealed wonders. Both are ways of progress in the Way, not within the reach of all, and probably not taught to all. But Sakya in its *Iddhi*-cult catered for the super-gifted few, as well as in other ways for the average Many. And I believe it was as a most worthy side of the Way-doctrine, that Gotama and his first and worthiest men both justified their own abnormal achievements, and encouraged a development of these in others who were fit, and "who were willing to learn" (*ye keci sikkhākāmā*).

XIII

ABHIJÑA (ABHIÑÑĀ), OR THE MAN ADVANCING

In the last chapter, under what I called the *iddhi*-formula—not the "Four Steps"—we were considering how early Sakya included in its scope those unusual, abnormal cases of power of will over *matter* which were to be found now and then among the Many, independent of learning or social status. I now come to consider certain other abnormal gifts of will, usually listed in Sakyan records immediately after the *iddhi*-formula, but having this difference: that they are more properly described as abnormal cases of power of will over what is *immaterial*. These were also to be found among the Many, independent of learning or social status.

Thus it is Sunīta, the sweeper who develops these loftier psychic propensities, as the verses ascribed to him record [1]:

> While passed the first watch of the night there rose
> Long memories of the bygone line of lives . . .

And it is C(h)andā, the destitute widow, who in her verses also claims the same powers [2]:

> The Threefold Wisdom have I gotten now . . .

This "wisdom", in Pali *te-vijjā*, represents three out of the four abnormal powers, usually made to follow the *iddhi*-formula, in a list which came to be known as the Abhiññās, or Higher Knowledges (the plural form is at least, my teacher Croom Robertson used to say, good Scottish). And it is very reasonable to find valid the record, in an early Anguttara section (Nipāta iii), that the Sakyans, in constructing a body of doctrine to set over against that which then held the field—the lore of the Three Vedas—took three of these special gifts and the sort of knowledge or conviction which they brought to the holder, and caused them to be taught as this "Threefold Lore". The three so chosen were Remembrance of former life spans, the Deva-sight, Insight into *three* of the so-called Four Truths, and also into *three* of what came to be called the Four Āsavas, or pervadings, or poisons. And they are a characteristic feature in the Anthology, especially the Nuns' Section.[3]

[1] *Theragāthā*, ver. 627. [2] *Therīgāthā*, ver. 26.
[3] *Pss. of the Sisters*, p. 26, n. 2.

This power of more-will over things immaterial is now usually called "psychic", presumably to distinguish it from "mental". Neither term is quite satisfactory, although mental processes are much involved. "Psychic" is an epithet for the minding in things which are not understood as coming within the scope of this or that natural law—as yet. "Occult" (hidden) is more or less co-incident with it. It is clear then that, in so far as psychic experience is allowed to be a kind of mental experience, and is to that extent, if abnormal, yet possibly of objective value, our psychology is no closed body of knowledge but is a charted clearing in a larger uncharted world. It is built up on a basis of sense-impressions; and these are such as our special senses and inner sensory reactions bring to us, either unaided or extended by instruments.

But there is the possibility, when our enlarging the world of matter is accomplished otherwise than by material instruments, that we shall come to enlarge that charted clearing in our psychological field. Our knowledge of the external world is, we all admit, only relative; hence there may be forms of matter, not necessarily ultra-minute, to which our senses, the senses of our visible body cannot react. This does not make those forms of matter absolutely non-existent. By our hypothesis of the relativity of knowledge they are only relatively non-existent. And if we add a further hypothesis, namely, that we have here and now not one body only, but one other, it becomes conceivable that could I but experience the reactions of that other body, as I do those of my visible body, I may at least conceive a way by which a person, having the abnormal gift of such other-experience, may have impressions not had by the more normal man, i.e. the man as normally little developed.

Now this further hypothesis has been, in many times and places, a matter of conviction, a *vera causa* as our books say, which can alone account for a whole world of experiences had by persons, whose honesty and truthfulness those who knew them did not doubt. In India it was usually called the subtle body (*sukshuma-sharīra*, in Pali *sukhuma-sarīra*). And it has been believed, albeit seldom if ever clearly expressed, that the "man" (*purusha*), or self, or soul, is invested in, and expresses himself through this other body, during sleep and other forms of unconsciousness. There is the further hypothesis, as corollary, that at death of the earth-body, this other body becomes the more permanent encasement of the "man", at least for another life-span, not on earth.

Nothing of this is recorded as *taught* in the Pali Piṭakas. That it was a current notion, held by some, when in Asoka's day the first

Kathāvatthu debate was compiled, is betrayed in the hurried-over section on Abhiññā, to which I have already referred (p. 247). It is a very unsatisfactory attempt in recording, but that is characteristic of the whole debate. And for this reason: the composition is the work of special pleading and of propaganda. Hence the stronger the point raised in defence of (the older and more Indian case of) "the man", as a very immediate and inexpugnable reality, the more is it hurried over, the defender never worded as properly setting out his case. For it cannot be said that, in bringing in *abhiññā*, the debaters were touching on a matter which had become of no importance, whatever it may have been valued at in the past. The *abhiññās* were reckoned by the compilers of the Nikāyas as both corollary and crowning features of saintship; as the Commentary has it (p. 31): *arahatta-sādhana*, "the perfecting of arahanship," a belief which is well borne out in the Anthologies.

The orthodox argument is, *contra* "the man as a *sine quâ non* in the exercise of *iddhi*": "do you maintain his reality solely on that ground? If so, is he real when *not* exercising *iddhi?* How do you support that?" The defender is merely made to say to the former question, "No, not only then." But the Commentator comes to his help (!) by giving us what the defender may well have said: "He judges, that supernormal power is wrought, not by external agency, unconnected with the man's faculties, but is of the self (*ajjhattam*), hence there must be a user of those powers. Else are *they* the fiction, yet you admit they are actual occurrences."

But the first centuries of Sakya were not days when men were intelligently inquiring into the mechanics of the abnormal. They were incurious over agency, vehicle, process, medium, just as they are, with few exceptions, even to-day. The fact and importance of the last-named, the medium (*metaxu*) between sense-organ and object was as little taken into account as it was in Aristotle's day. It is in Sānkhya records that we come upon the concept of the other, subtle body, and of them there is little we can refer with safety to the time of Gotama. That the self or man was active and abroad in another world (which was all about him), during the body's sleep, is insistently taught in the greater Upanishads, but that the self was then invested in a second body, as substantial to the experience of that world as is the body of our world to us, is nowhere stated.

We have, therefore, to consider this matter of psychic knowledge, or *abhiññā*, as rooting or not rooting in early Sakya, without presupposing any articulate teaching, or even curiosity about a "subtle body" as aiding in any of the processes.

There came in time to be a list made of these gifts, called *chaḷ-abhiññā* :[1] the six super-knowledges. We nowhere read of the number varying. (The allusion to "the five" in one work, the Saṃyutta, *may* be merely indicative of the five out of the six which are not expanded (*vitthāritā*) repeated in detail, but of this more presently.) The six are (1) Ways of *iddhi* (the formula),[2] (2) Deva-hearing, (3) Thought-reading, (4) Memory of former lives, (5) Deva-sight, (6) Insight into Āsava-destruction. I propose to consider these in reference to their status in earliest Sakya, taking them separately. But first we have to face the fact that there is *nothing "psychic" about the last.*

This, the sixth, states that the agent attains to a knowledge (*pajānāti*) of the nature, origin, ending and way to end Ill ; attains also to a knowledge of the nature, origin, ending and way to the ending of Āsavas, these being sensuous pleasure, becoming and ignorance. I have taken the list as given in what is probably the oldest statement of the Six : the second chapter of the Dīgha (the first) Nikāya. This, together with its predecessor, are the only Suttas actually named as being "chanted" in unison at the First Congress. (The other Suttas and the other Nikāyas are of course thrown in *en bloc*, but that is a gloss which is historically absurd.) The order in which the Six are recorded is not always the same, but this one is ever at the end. Are we to consider it as belonging to an original list? It is true that in the titular word we have "knowledge" and that hence, however much the achievements listed in the Six may have involved synergy of will, and however much there was of volitional coefficient included under the Indian terms for mind-work, there was, on the face of it, no misplacing of a *power of insight* under a list called Super-knowledge. On the other hand, there are not lacking reasons, to me very potent, for looking upon this so-called sixth *abhiññā* as a later addition.

Chiefly because it betrays a changed set of values. In it we have a double list of monk-values, namely, two sets of riddances. In the one the woe of life in any world has (by the adept) been gauged and its continuance ended, ended, that is, with the next dying. This list (as the "four truths") is in the edited First Utterance ; but for me it was not in the original first utterance. I have tried to deal with that. In the other list, we have a curious term "*āsava*",[3]

[1] More strictly *abhiññāyo*, but as with other fem. abstractions, it is more usually stated in the sing.

[2] As in preceding chapter, p. 239.

[3] Any oozing, spreading "flow"; a word for strong liquor, or for poison.

which we do not meet with in any of the early utterances ascribed to Gotama: the three, subsequently, the four, Āsavas. This absence does not of course rule it out decisively from the fundamental mandate. But it does point to the peculiarly monastic, or eremitic attitude of dread, depreciation, and repulsion respecting life in the world, or in any world. Thus of the three things condemned, two are "desire" and "becoming". These are not usually so rendered; the first, *kāma*, is *called* sensuality, *which it is not*; the second is *called* "rebirth"—which is but a step in becoming—or else "existence". The fact is that translators, in a laudable wish to make these doctrines rational and good for mankind, as befits a world-gospel, failed to see (as I did also) that they were not, in such doctrines, representing the world-gospel but the monkish distortion and contraction of it, which supervened after the first quarter of a century or so when the pristine, positive, glad tidings of goodwill to mankind had had its day and its purity had passed. In the Sixth Abhiññā we have come to the monk-gospel by and for the monk. *Kāma*, in the older Brahmanic teaching, older than, yet nearer in time to the birth of Sakya than the tarnished article of the Piṭakas, stood for the very nature of man. "Man is altogether *kāma*; as is his *kāma* so is his purpose; as is his purpose so is his deed . . ."[1] From *kāma*, then, arises every good and worthy thing he has ever known: his aspirations, his love, his work, his triumphs over difficulties, his coming-to-be in that which is the More in him. And that More he worded in *bhava*, becoming, not only as regarded developments in this little life-span, but in the greater becoming that lay beyond (*pāraṃ*). Something of this was in the virile teaching of India when Gotama the Man rose up and took his fellow-man by the hand, to tell him the real significance for him, for her, of its possibilities. *Kāma*, *kratu*, *karma*: the whole figure and story of the Way might be told, retold in those three words. But as in time the monk-vehicle took over complete control, *kāma* became a synonym of sense-pleasure only; the noble word *kratu* was suffered to fall into disuse; the vision of life beyond the grave became a thing of birth, disease, old age and dying over and over again, and *bhava* fell from its splendour as guarantee of perfection, to be achieved only in the long, long upward way, fell to be a synonym only for that dreaded "over and over again" (*punabbhava*). And the Wheel of the forward adventure contracted into the revolutions of a *bhava-chakka*: a Wheel of whirling, not of onward rolling.

My book is no dissertation on monastic categories; hence I

[1] *Bṛhad. Up.*, iv, 4, 5.

pass over the uncertainties, in different Piṭaka passages as to (*a*) the items in the threefold āsava-category, (*b*) the fourfold āsava-category. They find their way into the appendix to the first utterance as modes of desire and the various versions are best seen in the Sangīti Suttanta of the Dīgha.

It is not a little curious that, in his chapter on the Abhiññās, Buddhaghosa, as if abiding by some old tradition (as we saw him doing in the Four Moods), treats only of the Four I take here,[1] and *omits the Sixth*. His reasons cannot, of course, be those which make me not interested in it, as original or not original Sakya; so I do but mention this (*Visuddhi-magga*, Chap. XIII).

Now the first five Super-knowledges present a contrasted set of values to that of the Sixth. They are the worded results of exploration into the More in the man. They tell of so many ways in which it is given to some men and women to expand to a richer life even while on earth. As such they do not fit with the Sixth. So far are they from showing any odium as to *kāma* and *bhava*, so relatively in harmony are they with *kāma*, *kratu*, and *karma*, in their being expressions of man's desire to extend his sense-experience, not condemn it, in their being expressions of an instinctive fellowship with the worthy of other worlds, in their being an expression of value regarding the long upward way of the past by which the man has become so far as yet he has become, in their being an expression of desire for further-reaching communion with his fellow-men of earth, that we seem, in leaving them and coming to the Sixth, to be stepping into another world.

Such anyway are reasons which weigh with me in seeing five and not six as of the older teaching. Indeed, I would even see in the passage cited above,[2] where five are spoken of, a *very possible survival* of the earlier list with the sixth *abhiññā* added as gloss. My reason is, that nowhere else is a *peyyāla*, or elided set of repetitions so worded that the *number* of heads elided is stated. Readers of the Pali texts will follow me here, and I will pass on.

The Second Super-knowledge in the Dīgha list is called the "deva-sense-element of hearing (or of the ear)," and is described as "purified and going beyond human (hearing), whereby he hears both sounds, divine and human, whether far or near."

"Deva" and "divine" are the same word *dibba*, the Vedic *divya*, the adjective for *deva*. And *dhātu*, which I have called sense-element, is a familiar term for the organs and objects of senes.

[1] With the First he deals separately. [2] P. 260. *Saṃyutta*, ii, 216.

It is literally the thing laid down, the datum, postulate, or condition, or given set of conditions. We shall see, under the Fifth Super-knowledge, that it does not occur where we should have expected it would. The *dhātu* here, or " conditions ", differs from the ordinary hearing-*dhātu*, as being " of the devas ". And whereas the object, or thing heard, or impression may be as of something far or near, the hearing of it is a transcending the range and scope of normal earth-hearing. This may mean transcending the normal limitations of hearing, as when Gotama is asserted to have heard a talk about himself below Vulture's Peak while himself on that hill.[1] But there is plenty in the records, let alone the qualifying word *dibba*, to show that speech from another world was chiefly meant. When we once get rid of our Western tradition of worlds as being necessarily very far apart, we may understand that the Indian could mean that which was very near, yet which did not come within the range and focus of earthly sense, save of those few who were users also of another set of senses. And by the hypothesis of the dual body, room is found, in an orderly way of thinking, for such an expansion of man's sensory experience.

How little either the hypothesis, or the significance of the word *dibba* was grasped in the later Sakyan world may be seen in the work already alluded to, the Paṭisambhidā-magga, where the transcendent hearing is described in terms of the earthly quarters, to be attained by a radiating of thought (*vitakka-vipphāra*) following a thorough practice in the Iddhipādas. How much more simply and directly the deva-hearing was taken for granted in the older Suttas may be seen in that to which I have already referred,[2] where from Gotama's description of his visitor, the deceased Anāthapiṇḍika, and of the heard things he said in praise of Sāriputta, Ānanda infers that the visitor was indeed the good patron himself.

The third Super-knowledge I have called Thought-reading, using our modern term, based on our world of things written. The Pali term is *C(h)eto-pariyañāṇa*, or thorough knowing of purposive mind. The word *cheto* is here very apposite, stressing as it does what the man, whose thought is " read ", is *willing* to do, either in coming to a conclusion (work of mind), or in overt action (work of body). Hence there is a definite and limited basis laid down on which the gift should be developed. And that is how the " reader " may, in the More in himself which he is enjoying, get at the More in another

[1] *Dīgha*, iii, p. 39. [2] Above, p. 179; 183, *n*. 5.

man who is in process of choosing, deciding. It is essentially the helper's, the teacher's line, not that of the psycho-analyst's as such, but rather that of the psycho-analyst who is diagnosing for a cure.

It is necessary to bear this in mind when it is the formula that is analysed. For in this, the will to help *is entirely lost sight of.* It runs thus: "Penetrating with his own purpose the purpose of other beings, of other men, he knows the passionate mind as such and also the dispassionate mind; the angry mind as such and its opposite; the stupid mind as such and the opposite mind; and so for the collected mind, the broad mind, the inferior mind and the peerless one; the concentrated mind and the distracted; the freed mind and the not freed. Just as a woman, man, or child looking into a mirror or clear water would discern a mole on the face if there were one . . ."[1]

Here is thought-reading, without the least sign that the will thus active is spurred by a desire to help the other man. We may come to this or that conclusion why this is not mentioned: it may have been held as not needing to be said; it may have been that the insight was to serve as a warning and guide to the "reader" only as to which men he could safely approach and which not, to guard himself from contamination; or it may have been that the power to make play with such a gift was one of the assurances in himself that he had really attained to *arahatta-sādhana*: the plane of the Worthy Ones. If anyone doubts the last alternative, he should read (in the English translation if he will, just published) how Buddhaghosa treats of the gift in the *Visuddhi-Magga*.[2] There is no question of ethics here; it is a matter of a power to be used as a man would resort to his microscope.

But for me the details of the formula, and emphatically, the simile illustrating it, betray the later hand, when the monk was no longer, *by vocation*, a helper of his fellow-men. It is true, the Four Moods will have been by that time annexed. But it is surely evident that they were not admitted into these peculiarly "arahan-ish" studies aspiring to final Nirvana—we saw that they were not[3]—else had they been very much in the picture here. No one who has been a teacher but will have envied the user of such a power to get at the back of the pupil's mind, so often armed in presence of the teacher, crusted over, sluggish, distracted, baffled, so as to be able the better to draw out that which is latent within him or her. The only man I know who, himself English, developed the power in another

[1] *Dīgha*, No. 2, p. 80. [2] Chap. XIII.
[3] Above, p. 229.

country, was so embarrassed by the intrusion, the irruption on his reticent mind of the mind of others when he happened to join any gathering, that he actually bent his will to *rid* himself of the power. This man, albeit very worthy in every way, was averse from any will to help others by way of words ; the opportunity was given, and he rejected it. But that the power was used by the Sakyan founders, to give needed help in words, is repeatedly recorded in the Suttas. A monk is said to be asking himself as to how this or that can be known or the like ? And it is either Gotama, or Moggallāna, the great super-normalists, who divining his thoughts comes to his aid with an informing word.[1]

Let not the reader be cheapening the gift when he reads, that the mysterious willer known as Māra had it and used it.[2] Māra was conceived as a *deva*, if a bad one. And we are here concerned with powers, which were no monopoly of the Arahan, but belong to that original set of values of the first Sakyans, who were contemplating, not the perfection of the man in this earth-life—that was the later Arahan-theory—but with his Wayfaring towards that perfection through the worlds, and who held that the *deva* was " the man ", the self, in one of his future embodiments. Thus, to wield powers such as *devas* wielded was at once a means of communication with, as the song says, " the land I'm goin' to " and also an earnest that when gone to, such powers would become for them normal, and not merely abnormal.

The Fourth Super-knowledge is Memory of former lives. The Pali term is literally "past-dwellings-memory", the word " dwellings " being practically our "livings". As originally formulated, it was probably the brief opening words : " He remembers the variously circumstanced past life." [3] This has then been expanded, with unfortunate exaggerating garrulity, into a series of memories reaching back over one life-span to an infinite number, in which every detail of domestic and social status, weal and woe, is said to be recalled at will. With all that the Suttas record, as to many worlds of weal and woe, of rebirth as animal, of the few times relatively speaking in which rebirth as man is attained, it is not a little curious to see how, in this formula, there would seem to be none, in all the worthy one's long upward way, but *human rebirth*, or perhaps rebirth in a world so far resembling earth-life as to admit of such social institutions as " name, tribe or clan, and social class " (later, caste).[4]

[1] *Saṃyutta*, iii, 81 ; v, 294 f.
[2] Ibid., i, 119 f.
[3] *Anekavihitaṃ pubbe-nivāsaṃ anussarati.*
[4] Cf. below, 281 f.

There is in both formula and later embroidery a yet more interesting feature. The power of expanded memory is now very rarely met with, and then it is usually, I believe, met with in the very young. I have myself met with one such case in a little Roman boy, curiously adult in reminiscence, and expert in drawings of Eastern scenes of which he had seen no originals. And we hear of such cases in Asian countries here and there carefully investigated. But it is probable that the incursion of the book, largely superseding the work of memory, has made the development of a potential gift ever more and more improbable. In the days too of which I am writing, such a power will have been rare. In it we see another mode of expansion in the More in the man. And this time the main interest for my subject lies in this, that it is more explicitly the very man who is expanded down space and time. Here is life, here is changing, becoming, growing of the individual, encased now in this body, now in that, wielding body with mind, now in this way now in that. Here is no mere "bundle" of states or events, the man in the past is the man who remembers. He who is now "I" is the "I" of that remembered time. But the "I" has not remained unchanged. He was younger then, he is now more "grown", albeit not without worsenings in this life or in that. But the youth of the very man he is does not swiftly mature to be succeeded by decay, as with the youth of each body. To quote a poet of yesterday: "The thoughts of *this* youth are long, long thoughts." He, as distinct from his instruments, bodily and mental, is in a long process of becoming, of *werden.* In the framework to each Jātaka story we see how this fundamental identity is constantly kept to the fore. At the end of each story there appears what may have been, in this apocryphal folk-lore thesaurus, a surviving tradition of the way in which, exercizing his gift of the super-normal memory, the Founder would identify himself with the "me" of the recalled event: "on that occasion . . . the leader of the caravan was just I." The emphasis is strong; it is not: . . . and I was the leader . . . , it is as I give it: *satthavāha-jeṭṭhako pana ahaŋ eva ahosiŋ*: "caravan-leaders' chief (but) I just was!" Still more emphatically is the identity worded in one of these long memories not included in the Jātaka collection but told in the Majjhima-Nikāya, in the Potter's Sutta. Touring in his own country, Gotama turns aside from the road to rest in a certain spot, and smiles. Ānanda is with him, and we can discount the stereotyped "great company of monks" being along, for it is quite an intimate talk with Ānanda alone, and very charming. Explaining why he smiled, he tells what he remembers about a young brahman, who stubbornly resisted his friend's and social inferior's attempts to bring him to the then world-helper, Kassapa, and who at length yielded, and became a disciple. He then concluded thus: "Now may be, you will be thinking that Jotipāla on that occasion was someone else, but you musn't think so. On that occasion it was *I* who was Jotipāla."

The stress here is unmistakable, for it is more usual in Pali, I repeat, to use the verb without the pronoun. But the "I" (*ahaṃ*) is a frequent feature in the way of speaking ascribed to Gotama. And this is surely not a little noteworthy in scriptures which have been made the vehicle of a doctrine, imputed to just this man, that the "I", the very man, was a fiction, a mere name-label. Nay, for the Man of the Way, for the Great Caravaner, the wayfarer was, I repeat, the one chief thing in the Way. Speaking to so old, and devoted a learner as Ānanda, and not to the Many, it would have been expected that he would have said, "The complex that you now call 'me' was then the different complex I am telling you of." Here we ought to have seen a case of a "Buddha who had the two ways of talking," which Buddhaghosa, with no evidence of any pertinency trots out in his explanations.[1] I repeat this here, not only because of the mischievous effect the apologia has had throughout the Buddhist world past and present, but also because I have not yet seen the reality of the man as a postulate in this fourth of the Super-knowledges taken into account.

I am not contending that in his contracted teaching of the man as being only real in a series of momentary complexes, the Commentator had not a lofty ideal of the man as so conceived. He did believe in his man growing, becoming, as such a series in the past (when philosophically worded), and as being in some cases so ripened by a long past, that as Arahan, or utterly worthy, he was here and now rounding off the long series and closing it. But in his series so conceived, the only reality to be "got at" was the man in idea, the man as mind, the man as *dhammā*, as mental phenomena. And of these we find him saying: "in not a single *dhamma* is there the man *quâ* distinct entity." And as being a very abnormal idea-complex, the Arahan, in this abnormal memory, was to be shown as almightily abnormal. Hence it is that we get, in the elaborated formula of the Past Memories, the expansion of the more sober older opening words which show the *abhiññā* as the remembering "former life," or a former life (*-nivesam*). Your Arahan, as being second only to a Buddha, was no mere recaller of one other earthlife only but could revert mentally to past æons.

But it is in just this exaggerated idea of the man-complex as mighty rather in the mind than in, as we say, the spirit, that the monk falls

[1] *Kathāvatthu Comy.* on 1, i, last pages.

short in worthily expressing the ideal of the coming-to-be. The dry and irritating formula contains no reference whatever to a belief that in those remembered past life-spans there was growth or worsening, or at least, in the long run, positive growth. The whole essence of the Way-gospel is absent from it; it is as Dead Sea fruit.

Finally, as to the other-body hypothesis: it may be seen how it renders the older teaching of the memory of the one previous earth-life not a miracle, but an uncharted working of nature. When the man is conceived as spending many hours of the earthly body's sleep invested in the other body, and in the next world, it then becomes likely that he will remember thus and there, much of his previous life on earth. And so the Super-knowledge of remembering becomes the power of *using the other body also while he is awake.* Life in the other world in such a series of visits will bridge the gulf for the rememberer between the two lives on earth.

The Fifth Super-knowledge is that of seeing, as do the devas, the worthy of the next and other worlds. It too has its probably briefer opening and later elaborated formulas. They begin thus: "He by the deva-sight, purified, transcending human (sight), sees beings." Thereupon comes the detail, that the beings are deceasing and being reborn (lit. arising, happening), and he knows them sufficiently to recognize them as of different moral and social worth, and the way they're going, that is, according to their past conduct, being either to a lucky world or one of disaster. Then follows the parable: "as if a man who had eyes to see stood on an upper terrace over crossroads, watching men (*manussā*) entering and coming out of a house walking about the street and seated in the midst in the meeting place (the place of honour). Then would he know: 'Those men are entering and so forth.'"

Two items hitherto unnoticed may here be considered.

There is no mention in the opening formula of the word *dhātu*, i.e. *cakkhudhātu*, condition or datum of sight, as we noticed in the Abhiññā of Hearing. Yet in the Piṭakas sight, if placed always foremost, is reckoned in each category of sense-experience as in no other way distinguished from the other senses. But there is, as with us, the closer association of sight with both the mind and with the man. The terms for "seeing" flow over into those for ways of mind. We see this here in the parable. The wise man, the gifted man is the see-er (*chakkhumant*). That he was also "he who hath ears to hear" came later into the language of religion. Monastic Sakya was out to value the mind as that whereby the man could alone be in any ultimate true way " got at ". " Knowing is seeing," as runs our own adage, and hence the *abhiññā* of sight received a more honorific elaboration than is given to the *abhiññā* of hearing.

Further there is, in the elaboration, a term which so far as I know, occurs nowhere else. The see-er, beholding this and that "man" faring well or ill, calls all equally "these honourable beings" (*ime bhonto sattā*). This appellative, probably broken down from *bhagavan*, seems to betray a lingering feeling of reverence for what we should call the spirit or soul faring to and from the worlds. Anyway, after this Suttanta, we read not again of beings as betitled ; the tendency is just in the opposite direction. In that day the pupil and teacher, Brahman or Sakya, addressed each other as *bho*, plural, *bhonto* :—

> Now pay good heed, sirs (*bhonto*), to the words that he who sees, healer and hero, speaks to us,

says Sela the teacher, in the Sutta-Nipāta.

But the nun, Vajirā, replies contemptuously to the tempter :—

> Being (*satto*)—why dost thou harp upon that word ?

We are perhaps too inclined to look upon this super-normal sight, whether we believe there was " anything in it ", or whether we do not, as a sort of super-earthly panorama. This may be because it has been only considered in the formula, and not in the special cases of clairvoyance—for it is really that—occurring here and there in the Suttas. We saw a similar misconception arising from mere formula-study in the Four Moods. But in those special cases there is nothing panoramic about the experience. Gotama hesitates to start his mission. Clairvoyantly he both sees and hears a deva begging him on bended knee to begin. He both sees and hears clairvoyantly visitors from the next world : Anāthapiṇḍika, King Bimbisāra, Ajita, and many other such visitors, as the old metric portion of the Saṃyutta-Nikāya shows. And when asked if he can show a state here on earth which is of unmixed happiness, he is said to have replied : " Why yes, Udāyin, it is when one muses till devas reborn in a happy world come to be with you, and talk and discuss with you." Surely this is what anyone in the least acquainted with what we now call matters psychic would call a clairvoyant, clairaudient experience, and that of a peculiarly worthy kind.

Such are the Six ways of Abhiññā. They are not in themselves the message or gospel of Sakya. They were not in that gospel considered, as at least one writer has considered them,[1] the steps leading up to the threshold of the Goal. They were but a nobly reverent valuing of the More in the Many ways, by which it was given to a man or woman of special ability, of more will, of earnest aspirations to develop his or her nature. And that they were there at the very birth of Sakya there can be no reasonable doubt.

[1] Heiler, on Jhāna. See in that chapter above.

XIV

THE WORLDS IN EARLY SAKYA

The original Sakyan gospel, as it appears to me, and as I have here tried to show, centred in the figure of each man's life (given the datum of man's essential nature) as a Way. And a Way not of this world only, nor of one life-span only, but a Way wherein he as wayfarer journeyed, not as herded but as self-directive, through life in many worlds, in many ages. His wayfaring was, in the long run a progress, if with many set-backs. And in this chequered progress was figured the essential fact of his nature : becoming, or the bringing out the more that was in him potentially. Ahead of him was figured a Goal, an End (*pariyosāna*), figure of that Most which is potential in the More of him. I now come to consider the ways in which in that day those many worlds were conceived, and—in my subject the more important question—the extent to which they entered into his values.

That India of that day generally believed in the survival after death of the essential " man ", under no matter what name, and no matter what became of his earthly make-up, is clear enough. I pay little respect to hypotheses of his survival as " man " emerging from beliefs in his survival as tree-spirit or animal or the like. That such beliefs are still found surviving here and there in south Asia is no warrant for such an emergence. Beliefs of "primitive" folk of to-day are, as Rhys Davids was wont to say, no safe index as to origins. Such beliefs may rather represent a worsening in evolution than a secular stand-still—a thing which I hold to be an impossibility. More in keeping with religious history is it to hold, that even very early man was not left in the dark as to death and the hereafter ; that inspired helpers are not to be counted by the very few, tribute to whose mandates has survived in documents. That the majority, at the coming of new light, have never learnt, have never truly handed down, all they might have, from those helpers is no true measure of what may have been revealed. *How* the man survives has been shown distorted and debased in numberless ways. But *that* he survives has been, down the ages, an overwhelmingly preponderant conviction. That we can even now speak of this, man's birth-right and " right-of-way " in his long upward way, as doubtful, let alone untrue, is a matter over which our after-comers will marvel.

But what, if any, was the new light in the Sakyan message, concerning unseen worlds?

The changes that we encounter in cosmological concepts and names, when we leave Brahmanic literature for the Piṭakas, will have struck every reader. Together with these changes there is, in the Piṭaka-category of worlds and their governors, a definiteness which is less apparent in Vedic categories. The definiteness is more superficial than were it the result of carefully valuing thought, or attention to revelation. Its chief significance is that, in the Piṭakas, we see reflected a world over which has passed the rake of Sānkhya analytic methods, and then the enregistering grip of the written word. The list of named worlds has become more precisely hierarchical, more crystallized, but that is all. In every other respect we can see lowered values: less living faith, less serious heed given to seeing life whole. On the one hand (*a*) the cult of the Founder as "Buddha" was growing, growing too was the cult of the "more-man", the Arahan of exaggerated abnormality; on the other hand (*b*), the healthier food for the forward view, the vision of coming life, which the Founder and his men had held out, was treated with averted eyes. Imagination, constructive, and reconstructive, which is the very soil of man's growth in the More, starved itself in the latter field (*b*), because it had turned for nutriment to the former (*a*). Never materialistic, never atheistic, the later Sakya nevertheless sank, in its contracted vision of life as a whole, to the level of the materialist and the rationalist, concentrating its interest and its appreciation on this earth-life, together with much retrospective interest on the immeasurable past, but with no inspiring outlook in the forward view of progress in the Way through the worlds.

The earliest form of category of the worlds meeting us in the Nikāyas is perhaps that of eight items, occurring, for instance, as one among a number of subjects to be continually held in remembrance (*anussaraṇa*). They are first given in the talk said to have taken place between Gotama and Visākhā, in the Anguttara-Nikāya.[1] The list starts with what *we* might call Nature-gods, chiefly the governors of the four quarters of the firmament, but, as I have said above, including personifications of natural phenomena: moon, sun, etc. There follows that which we may call "the next world". This properly includes the next five divisions: Tāvatiṃsa, or world of the thirty (councillors), with a deva having the title of Sakka as governor; the world of the Yamas, or Watchers; the world of Tusita, or the Happy; the world of the Nimmānarati devas and that of the Paranimmita-vasavattī devas, or, respectively, they who delight in

[1] Vol. i, 210 (Nip. III, 70).

creating and they who delight in others' creatings. I have used the word "world" only as indicating a group within the same corporeal conditions; no new body was required in passing from one to another of these five. After these we have the Brahmā-group devas (Brahmakāyika); and lastly the Tat-uttariŋ devas, or they of the "Beyond-that". The Continuous Remembrance Sixfold Category, of which the men of these worlds or world form one head, is itself a matter of fixed wording, arranged either in the Founder's old age, or after his decease; nevertheless it may well be a wording of actual memorized sayings of his day, for the woman and the man counselled so to remember are said to have been respectively Visākhā, his eminent lay disciple and Mahānāma, his affectionate cousin, the Sakyan noble.[1]

Such a set of five or six afforded easy scope for subsequent rewording. But that the Category of the six remembrances, if indeed it was so old, was in the fixed wording we now have it is more than doubtful. The Six are Tathāgata, Dhamma, Sangha, one's own morals, generosity, devas (*devatā*). But in the talk to Visākhā we do *not* find the fifth, just as, much later, we find the six supplemented by *four more*: dying, etc.[2] And the formula of the first Remembrance abounds in Buddhological terms, which would not have been applied to the Founder till after he had ceased to be a very human memory, e.g. Tathāgata, Buddha, Sambuddha.

The way in which in the Sixth the devas are alluded to is of great interest, in view of the change in values which had come over the day of the birth of Sakya. Let the reader judge: "remembering the devas of those worlds, he thinks: the kind of faith wherein these devas, deceasing here were reborn there, that faith is mine also. And so for their morals, their education (*suta*, or things heard), their generosity, their values in Highest Things (*paññā*, *prajñā*). Thus remembering himself and the devas, his mind is not obsessed by evil, but is straightened, because of them. And thus he wins knowledge of his weal, of *dhamma*, he wins bliss belonging to *dhamma*, and from thence is born zest, tranquillity, pleasure, and the mind of him pleased is composed."[3] Do we not see here, at a time when the popular personifications of Deity were become as outgrown as were those of Olympus in Plato's day, a new conception of better-world-inmates come up: that of men who, on earth developing the more that was in them, according to their relative stage of maturity, had passed on to a world where that "More" was *habitual*, and not striven for by the minority only? It is true that, for the age, it was but a question of the More; the aspiration to a concept

[1] *Anguttara*, i, 210; iii, 284 f. [2] *Visuddhi-Magga*, chap. vii, viii.
[3] *Anguttara*, loc. cit.

of the "Most", the Highest, the Best *as externalized*, lay in ruins. But as of man's inmost nature, that concept had been pointed to as *within* (*ajjhattaṃ*), and again as a Weal, an *attha* (or *artha*) as also somehow ahead, at Way's End.

This dwelling on devas as the very worthy, as having been worthy on earth, as passing, it might be, back to earth as men, as now visiting earth with help and healing for men, or for that matter, but in very rare cases, themselves to learn of a man, is a feature which is of the earliest Sakya and which reverberates all the way down to Buddhist writers of Ceylon tradition—I am thinking of Buddhaghosa's treatment of this very Remembrance. I am also and chiefly thinking of the account in Vinaya and Nikāyas of the First Utterance, where the Mantra, heard by but a few on earth, is represented as heard and acclaimed by the worlds I have shown as listed; and with this addition, that acclamation is worded as starting with earth-devas (*bhumma-devatā*), and spreading to all worlds. Further, I have already referred to a way, ascribed at least by Dīgha-bhānakas to Gotama, of saying, when asked (evidently prior to Buddha-cult conceptions) how he had come to know something, that he had learnt it from a deva. I have also dealt with the (?) inserted clause: "knew it of myself."

One thing there is, among many, that the student of early Buddhism needs to bear in mind about this lively intercourse with good men of another world which is so salient a feature in the Sayings. This is the evident way in which, to the Sakyan of super-normal vision and hearing, the deva appears as objectively living in a world of embodied life as is the man of earth. He has visible body; he walks, he seats himself, he kneels, he is in raiment, in armour, he takes the earth man by the arm, he speaks audibly with him.[1] He may of course, even to the strongly psychic, have differed in appearance from the man of earth, as he does to-day. It is a different set of sense-apparatus which is reacting to him. But it is utterly untrue to say, as I have it asserted before me in print, that "his existence is entirely subjective", according to any Sakyan sources worth quoting, old or later.

In the enumerated list of eight deva-worlds, the items second to sixth comprise the one world of that which came to be called that of Kāma, in other words, the world of experience by way of sense-desire, as we have it on earth. The earth in fact was included in this part of the cosmology; so were the regions of unhappy experience: those of hell or purgatory (*niraya*) and the not imprisoned, yet afflicted men of the Peta world: the worsened form of the Vedic Preta,

[1] E.g. *Dīgha*, Sta. xi, xv, xviii, xix, xxi; *Saṃyutta*, i, Collections i, ii, xi, etc.

or the Fathers. The seventh or Brahmā world came to be called the world of Rūpa, that is, of the Seen, or things seen. This did not mean that the denizens were of one form of sense-experience only, or that they had a monopoly of that; their hearing appears as acute; but sight was the only sense highly ranked. It meant as we saw, as we still "see", "knowing"; it was the world of greater, wider knowledge, world-vision. It meant a higher value in mind. A sounder psychology, assigning value to the work of touch, in common with such insight in other psychological thinking, which I have considered elsewhere,[1] arose at a later stage in Sakya. And that man is more fundamentally "will" than what is chiefly meant under "mind" was not, and is not yet understood in any Indian system.

It is perhaps scarcely necessary to say here that this world of the Brahmā-kāyika devas did not, at the time of our inquiry, centre in the impersonal concept of Brahman. Here is not the place to go into a discussion on the term, when first met with in the Rig-Veda as meaning prayer, and its subsequent evolution. That evolution has been felicitously summed up in Dr. E. W. Hopkins's much-saying words: "In the Vedic hymns man fears the gods, and imagines God. In the Brāhmaṇas man subdues the gods, and fears God. In the Upanishads man ignores the gods and becomes God."[2] At the time we are considering, that is, after the few earliest Upanishads and contemporaneous with much of the thought revealed in what I am calling the Greater Upanishads, the last phase of that evolution had been for a time holding the field, with its weighty word: "That art thou". As That, the very man or self was "imperishable". But into the newer thought of the day was spreading the idea of the perishableness, the transience, the impermanence of things both of the seen and the unseen. This note of "change in everything" was affecting the concept also of man's fundamental nature. To *counteract* it here, in the man conceived as That, the Imperishable Divine, there was coming to the aid of this, the emphasis we find only in later Brahmanic writing, such as the Gītā in the Mahābhārata, to wit, of That as being the Unchangeable.

> It is not born, nor does It ever die, nor having existed does It exist no more. Unborn, everlasting, unchangeable and primeval, It is not killed when the body is killed. . . . It is said to be Unchangeable.[3]

But, in the attributes enumerated in the Sakyan books as those of the Governor of the Brahmā-world, we get no mention of such

[1] *Bud. Psych. Ethics.* [2] *Religions of India*, p. 216.
[3] *Bhagavadgītā*, ii, 27, pp. l; lxi; 117 *n*. l.

as would be ascribed in views outside the Sakyan Order. Of the eleven attributes or names of Brahmā, in the stereotyped formula compiled in the Order, the Imperishable and the Unchangeable do not occur. The eleven are rather such titles as might be bestowed upon an earthly monarch : "Overcomer, Not-overcome, Who sees whatever there be, Controller, Lord, Maker, Creator, Best, Disposer, Valuer, Father of all (things) that have come and are to come " [1]—a very fine description of a great statesman-warrior king.

Let not the freer renderings of other translators seem to put me in the wrong. I find no justification for such renderings as " Ancient of Days ", and " abiding for ever ". K. E. Neumann is closer to the Pali, and I only differ from him in taking, with Buddhaghosa, *sañjitar* (Disposer) to come from *sajati* and not from *sañjāyati*, Engenderer. The full list I find only in Dīgha and Majjhima-Nikāyas [2]; in the Anguttara-Nikāya and Iti-vuttaka the last seven epithets are absent, the remainder being applied to the "Tathāgata ".

In this description we have man imagining the Highest as a man, a super-man. He has, under monasticism, worsened the Upanishad values—" ignores the gods and becomes God "—he now rates the man as less than very man, and thereby the God, seen in man's nature by Indian seers, has in consequence become less. He can no longer conceive the Highest so worthily, because the standard held up by them *in his own nature* has been lowered. And he has reverted to the childish conceptions of the Veda values.

I come back to the five groups of the Kāma devas. The first, usually called Tāvatiṃsa, three (and) thirty, is a sort of portmanteau word, combining the frequent alternative *ti-dasa*, " thrice ten ", with *tiṃsa*, "thirty." That the council was of thirty only, governing under a chief, officially called Sakka, is curiously endorsed by the Kulāvaka Jātaka (No. 31). Sakka is almost certainly a late substitute for Indra, the great Vedic deity. The more usual way in the Suttas of alluding to Sakka is to say " Sakko devānam *indo* ", in Sanskrit, Indra. For instance, in the Sakka's Questions Sutta, dealt with above,[3] the reader will find that he is nearly always called by the triple-worded appellative, or indeed without the first name (Sakka). I believe that when Sakya began, no such name as Sakka for the governor of the Thirty-world was in use, but only 'Indra ruler of devas'. Later on with the growth of the Buddha-cult, or Tathāgata-cult, the clan whence he came will have shared in the honours poured on him—

[1] E.g. Kevaddha Suttanta (11) of the *Dīgha*; also in its Brahmajāla and Pāṭhika Suttantas.

[2] Suttanta, xi, and Sutta 49. [3] Page 156.

for that matter it was apparently a belief among the Sakyas (Pali Sakkas), that their tribe, whether of the northern Sakas, or not, was of divine origin. Hence I see in the phrase "Sakka ruler of devas" the transition from Indra to a name, for the origin of which there exists, so far as I have seen, no other explanation.

In the Yama group on the other hand we have the Vedic name, the Watchers, and the Vedic concept retained. The Vedic twins have in the Suttas become the Yāma-devas, but their chief is, in the Devadūta Sutta, repeated by both Majjhima-bhānakas and Anguttara-bhānakas, called "Yama-rājā". The composer of the Kevaddha makes here I believe his own variant, and calls him Su-Yama, the good Yama, not rājā, but a superior deva among the Yamas. As in the Vedas, so in that Sutta, he is in such a relation to the man in his passing from earth, that it is before Yama's tribunal that he must stand, to hear his fate. I alluded to this in an early chapter, but the Sutta is noteworthy enough and enough passed over to make it worth while to quote it.

It occurs among the last placed Suttas of the Majjhima-Nikāya, and among the relatively foremost in those of the Anguttara-Nikāya. That the former is a later, because it is a more edited version I shall show in a later chapter. I give a condensed version of the latter or earlier recension (Anguttara-N., i, 138f.) :—

"There are these three deva-messengers. . . . Some one acts amiss in deed in word, in thought. At the breaking up of the body after dying he rises up in the woeful way, in purgatory, warders grasping him and showing him to Yama raja as one who, unfilial, without respect for the worthy and holy things, or for his chief, deserves punishment. Him Yama raja admonishes : See here, man (*purisa*) ! Did you not see manifest among men the first messenger ? I did not see, sir. Did you not see among men any aged woman or man, feeble tottering grey ? I did see, sir. See here, man, to you, ware and mindful of the aged one, did not this occur : I, even I too shall get old ; come now, I will do good in deed, word and thought ? I will not have succeeded, sir, I will have been careless. See here, man, by carelessness you did not good in deed, word, thought. Verily, man, according to what was careless, so will they do to you. For lo ! this evil action was done not by your mother, nor by your father, nor by brother, nor by sister, nor by friends and advisers, nor by kindred, nor by devas, nor by recluses and brahmans ; it was done by you, yes, by you ; it is just you who are experiencing the result thereof."

These words are then repeated in the case of the second messenger of the devas: a sick woman or man; then again in the case of the third messenger, the dead body of a woman or man. The text actually reads: a woman or man one-day-dead . . . two-days-dead . . . three, etc. followed by adjectives expressive of decay. Monastic editors were not a little given to this repulsive embroidery; and for that matter, the custom, alternative it would seem to cremation, of exposing the dead for beast, bird, and creeping thing to devour will have rendered decaying corpses a sight less unfamiliar than in other communities. But to speak of the corpse *as woman or man* is a diction of popular materialism too prevalent yet with us, but which the Suttas usually avoid; their allusion being habitually to the breaking up of the body at death.

There follows a lurid account, a page in length, of tortures in which India's early culture found satisfaction no less than did we in our own earlier civilization. At the end of the Sutta are eight lines of verse, wherein it is said of good men, not that they do not also appear before Yama, but only that they do heed the messengers during their earth-life.

That the Majjhima version [1] is the later may be inferred, I think, from its addition of two more to the three messengers. We are first shown, not an old, but a new-born man. New birth is an opportunity, but for the monastic ideal it was as a warning messenger. Further, legal punishment on earth is inserted as a third messenger. Again the following purgatorial paragraphs are elaborated. But in the Majjhima we get that notable simile which has somehow remained, in threefold repetition, with one exception, the monopoly of this Nikāya: the worlds compared to two houses, with a going and coming into and from each, which the man who has eyes to see is mindful of.

It may be remembered, by those who have considered the Buddha-legend, that this is not the only variant of the messengers as three. Namely, that in the Suttanta Mahāpadāna (Dīgha, xiv), we find four messengers, the fourth being a *samaṇa*, as furnishing for the Bodhisat the index to a solution of the problems embodied in the other three.

It is curious perhaps, but I have never yet seen this possibly very old Saying, linking up as it does the Piṭakan cosmology with the Vedic, and very possibly with that of Zoroaster, noticed by any writer, Buddhist or non-Buddhist. Herein they are but mirrors of the lack of heedfulness, let alone of faith in the matter, which is characteristic of our age. The Christian, the Muhammadan has relegated the

[1] Sutta, No. 130.

matter to one universal judging. Their scriptures give here no certain sound. Only the Parsee has with the Buddhist a more definite mandate. But the Parsee does not hide his mandate as does the Buddhist. The latter, if of the Hīnayāna section, still needs to bring out the truth so impressively shown, that the message of Gotama was a Way not of earth only, but a Way of the worlds. The three messengers as impressing the Man of the Message are often quoted. But that he is described as saying they are world-messengers to you and to you, with serious results if you heed them not—this is pushed aside.

Whether in the parable of the other-world-, or "deva-" messengers (*deva-dūtā*, they are called), we have a teaching actually uttered by the Founder, men, so long as they are "careless" to get, as valid institutes, trustworthy well-checked communications with other worlds will never come to know. But they can at least see, in this instance of the varying nature of versions of one record, the sort of materials on which, so aided, they may in the future come to weigh evidence. Some may say: Surely he may have taught not one, but all three ways. As to that I say again: So far do I agree that an original genius, in helping not men only but the man, would maintain no stiff uniformity in either material or wording, that I imagine him as never saying the same thing twice in the same way! But as to those "inserted" messengers I would also say that two of them have a decidedly monkish emphasis very suggestive of monk-editors. Further, that the message given by earthly punishment, while it has a very plausible look, is not on a level, as the mandate of an inspired Helper, with the nucleus of those "Three". It shows man as warned to heed what earth, at one time, in one land, legally bids him not to do. That code varies with time and place. The three messengers are indexes to a code not of earth, but of the worlds, *true of man at all times in every land and world.* They stand warning not Indians only, not Buddhists only. They call to man as man. As such they belong to the mandate of a Helper.

And it is the notion each forms of the nature of that Helper, which must decide for each, whether he is likely to have spoken of the punishing in the way he is recorded to have done.

Very noteworthy is the pointed and extreme emphasis, in the Saying, on the "man" (*purisa*), personal and solely responsible, who has come over from earth. His body, and with it the minding, or mind wrought up with it, he has laid down and left. Body and intelligence he has evidently come into afresh. But he remains the "man" who was on earth. He is not judged as a mere new fivefold "group" of body and of mind. He is as he was, to the extent that he is still the same inexpugnable "thou" and "thee". He has *become*—"bhava" has taken place in him—he has *yet* to *become*, and that many times. But "he" is neither body nor mind. He is More.

More, because he knew all along that he was heedless, where he should have taken heed. More, because, as wayfarer in the Way, the *Magga* of the worlds to worlds' end, he was himself willer, he was chooser of the better way, or of the worse, a "law", as St. Paul worded it, "unto himself." "Dhamma": the "ought to be", the "may be", the immanently divine, was working on the "More" in him all the time. He does not plead *ignorance* of that which he should have heeded, only carelessness, as to there being other tribunals than that of earth. In such heedlessness verily he is a man of the twentieth century!

The Saying in its central three is evidently a talk to men and to the man, not to recluses. Nevertheless the editor has annexed it as a talk to monks. He was apt to act thus.

If I pass more quickly over the three remaining sections of the world awaiting worthy men at death, it is not because I would not say more if I could, but because Buddhist tradition has failed to keep them quick in memory. That the Tusita, or Tusita-city was considered as the peculiar home of the righteously happy appears in the pretty story of Sumanā, youngest daughter of Anāthapiṇḍika, in the Dhammapada Commentary (ver. 18). That it was held also to be the home of a helper of men before devas summon him to expect, that in dying there he will be reborn on earth with a mandate of help, appears in the same work (ver. 11-12).

The two remaining sections are of greater interest, yet about nothing perhaps is Buddhist tradition more unsettled and uninterested. They were probably later conceptions than the rest—like wisdom teeth—coming late they have petered out first. Their names, devas who joy in creating, and devas who can-at-will-possess the creations of others,[1] indicate an appreciation of the More-in-man in its finer aspects. As such, they find no fit and worthy warding of earlier tradition in the more or less degenerate Commentaries. That on the Dīgha (on Suttanta i, pt. 2) is evidently uncertain about them, associating them with the so-called Debauched-by-pleasure-devas; in another, the latter of the two groups is called the realm of the Māras! In the Mahā-Samaya Suttanta, however, where a mighty congress of the Unseen is hymned as waiting upon Gotama in the woods of his native place, they are not so associated:—

[1] Nimmāna-ratino devā, Para-nimmita-vasa-vattino devā.

. . . devas from Tusita
And Yāma heavens . . .
They who rejoice in shapes they make themselves,
And they who use creations not their own.[1]

As an appreciation of man as creator, both "worlds" would appeal to the Indian, and it may well be that they made good a want in Sakya, when the belief in a supreme personal creator-deity had waned. We have here appreciation of the artist in the widest, loftiest sense: the Player with the making-to-be, and not with the becoming better than he was; the willer making to become in sheer joy of willing and therewith the fellow-men rejoicing in such noble work of "more-will". It is significant as to this, that, in the Janavasabha Suttanta,[2] Brahmā, governor of his world, when he visits and addresses the heads of the world of the Thirty, at the rejoicing over the many Gotama-disciples who have been coming over at death, praises *first* Gotama's teaching in the worth of Iddhi, or "more-will". This was, as I said, an anticipation on earth, in the abnormal few, of a normal "more" in another world.

One word finally on the very significant but wholly neglected eighth division in devas: they who were Tat-uttariŋ, "Beyond that." The reticence in this earlier wording of the Nikāyas is so much wiser than the later attempts to build up a shadow-world of Mind-devas.[3] In Sakya the man felt he could not conceive, and therefore could not word the "Most"; he stopped at the "More". *Uttariṃ* is, like "More", a comparative word: "further than." He here showed truth and wisdom; and it is a sad thing that he went on later to try to express the perhaps ineffable, the inconceivable, but at any rate the not yet revealed. Man will only be able to word fitly a further Beyond-that, a More-than-that, when he is himself become more.

In the matter of modes of unhappy rebirth generally, under these the Suttas class Niraya (hell or purgatory, with no implication of eternity in the term), birth as Peta, or birth as animal. There was no more sense of remoteness in whereabouts of the first two, any more than of the third. The only local difference lay in the first two being of the present but unseen, as the third was or might be, at any moment, of the present and seen. It is not, I believe, till we come to the later compilation and writing of the so much longer oral Commentaries, in particular that on the Jātaka, that we find it was a considerable drive in a deva-chariot to be fetched from earth to visit first Niraya,

[1] *Dīgha*, "Mahā-Samaya" (No. xx). [2] *Dīgha*, No. xviii.
[3] Āruppa-worlds.

then the Svarga world. (Nimi-Jātaka.) That the early Sakyans believed in rebirth in those unhappy worlds as highly probable in the hereafter of the unworthy of earth is to be accepted, unless indeed the Founder drew the line at animals. That he did not so draw it is apparent in two or three Suttas, but there is no approach in such Suttas to anything in position or in teaching which is suggestive, as is the Devadūta Sutta, that we have in them something amounting to genuine memories of Founder's talk. We cannot tell. Emphasis on Peta and animal rebirth in what appear to be old sayings there is none; in these, ill doing and "carelessness" are spoken of as finding retribution in suffering referred to in very general terms: *niraya*, or going out or down, *apāya*, going off, *duggati*, bad-going or -faring, and the like. The torture business appears to be manifest appendix work, aimed doubtless at heightening the lurid picture of life anywhere as Ill, and also perhaps at catering for the lust for the terrible, to which both monk and laity would look for dramatic satisfaction, not perhaps to be enjoyed in any other way. In somewhat the same way will have been developed the custom, in the Order, of bringing in animal stories when addressing lay-congregations. In a social cleavage, such as spread wherever Buddhism gained the upper hand, of the monk as higher, the laity as lower, it would become usual to talk down to the laity in a way we do not find the Founder doing, of giving them stories and horrors as "interesting", "attractive." And thus also, the hell and beast emphasis would grow. The talks moreover being on a popular level, the fact that, however reborn, the very "man" it was who survived death, and suffering, and beasthood would not come up for debate.[1]

I return to the deva-worlds.

Modern writers are not over disposed to distinguish between the silence in the Suttas on Deity-worship and this marked feature of welcoming converse with devas and of their being held in worth as men of the "More". This is chiefly because the altered concept of the deva as no longer a Mahādeva, or what translators call "gods", has not been grasped. Rhys Davids defended the more usual depreciation of "the gods", in his own and others' writings, by saying to me that the word "gods" was very elastic in scope; the devas of the Piṭaka records, albeit no form of cult was to be paid them, were nevertheless (*a*) of the unseen things, as earth-sense went, (*b*) lived in a quasi-heaven, and (*c*) were of super-normal nature in certain respects, e.g.

[1] Cf. on these matters *Gotama the Man* and *Stories of the Buddha*, introduction, xx.

mobility, will-power, length of life; that hence they were as much within the elastic scope of the word "gods", as were many, for instance, in the Olympic group, or in those of Rome. (I should add that (*a*), (*b*), and (*c*) are rather the reasons I imputed than what he gave; I do not remember that we discussed the point.) I quite agree with the relative harmlessness in an elastic use of "gods", where there is a relative familiarity with the contents of the term. That is the case in the *dei* and the *theoi* of our own classics; the contents are in our traditions well known to us, albeit not to readers of the East and South. But when it is we who are dealing with unfamiliar traditions, it becomes right that we should not carelessly transfer our own values to these, in a more or less careless transfer of terms. We have to deal under the term *deva* with not only a different world of values, but with a difference coming up within that different world. For that matter, there is room for advance even in our historical weighing of the words *theoi, dei*; but as to historical weighing in the word *deva* we are perhaps not beyond the threshold; we have not yet duly considered how far, at any given period in the religious history of India, "gods" and devas coincide.

In a little work of suggestions like this, there is no space to include a detailed history of the changed attitude towards *devas*, but certain salient features may be indicated.

The Piṭakas passages which I have in mind as illustrations are Saṃyuttas i, ii, vi, ix, and xi; Iti-vuttaka, §§ 81, 82, Dīgha-Nikāya, Suttantas xi, xiii, xviii, and xxi.

Perhaps the most striking feature in the change is, that permanence, the Imperishable (*akshara*) of the greater Upanishads is ruled out from the attributes of the deva. This is given in the Saṃyutta as a mandate, in the Iti-vuttaka as a recurring phenomenon. The former may be consulted by the English reader in my translation, *Kindred Sayings*, i, 179, § 4, where Gotama, in communication with a deva of the Brahmā-world, is made to say: "Alas! sir, you are in ignorance, who say, that being transient, you are not transient, that being not eternal, you are eternal" . . . and so on. The latter is a little poem (following the prose version), telling of what happens when a deva, his life-span ending, and with rebirth on earth imminent, is bade an affectionate farewell by fellow devas. This changed view may not impress us who have here no "Bible" before us as we read, but it is a tremendous change, and is of itself enough to give pause to a translator using the word "gods". If only Sakya, if only Buddhism in Hīnayāna had not lost the significance of the world-truth in man's nature: "Becoming, not Being," to which this great change in deva-concept was due, translators would not have so lightly carried on with their "gods".

Another salient feature, betraying an equally tremendous change in values among the devas as fellow-men once on earth, is the moral and ethical advance in the character ascribed to devas of the next and the Brahmā world. The Vedic "gods" are unmoral when not immoral. Even Varuṇa is not hymned as commending any save the narrowest code in things moral in the sense of not harming others, while as to positive ethics, those are greatly to seek. But the devas of the Suttas named are what we should call "gentlemen"; upright, sincere, gentle, forgiving, courteous. And more: they are out, not to play with the hap of the man, but to ward him. His holding to the Way of the good life is a thing over which they are keeping watch—how should this not be, when in a brief period, he will be in and of their world, and they in and of his? His interest in them, and their world, whether this be got indirectly from "the man who sees", or through his own super-normal gifts, is ever welcomed and encouraged *by his future fellow-citizens.* The standard of conduct among Brahmā devas is such that young Brahmans, seeking the best Way of access to their company hereafter, are admonished by Gotama (according to the Tevijja Suttanta) to conform to what they believe is that standard, as greatly superior to that obtaining in the current decadent Brahmanism. And access to, converse with the devas by the very worthy of earth is hailed by the former with joy and warm welcome: "Come, sir! Welcome, sir! Long is it since you made occasion to come this way. Be seated! Here is a seat ready."

The deprecatory allusions to devas to which I have alluded tend to pass over these many pictures, in the Piṭakas, of other-world society at a distinctly higher level than the average level in the ancient Indian world. I think this passing over is mainly, though not wholly due to three things: (1) ignoring the changed meaning in the term *deva*; (2) the coming of devas of high rank to learn of and pay homage to the first Sakyan teachers, and (3) the influence of the Kevaddha, or xith Suttanta of the Dīgha-Nikāya.

Into the first reason I have gone.

As to the second, it is one I have no wish to pass over. We cannot give credit to the pleasing features recorded of what the men of super-normal gifts will have told the average Sakyans as characterizing the devas of "the better land" with whom they had converse, without also giving credit to the Suttas and poems which tell of such visits as that paid to Gotama by Sakka ruler of that land, in which teaching is sought on high subjects, or of homage and felicitations tendered to both Gotama and to several of his disciples, men and women. Picture Subhā, the goldsmith's daughter so greeted, while occupied in Jhāna-musing—seeking like other early Sakyans thereby such access—

> To her approached Sakka by iddhi-power,
> With deva-company and homage paid—
> The lord of worlds unseen!—to this Subhā,
> Daughter of workman in the art of gold.

and the yet humbler Sunīta, mentioned above, let alone the gifted Moggallāna, as testified in the Anthology, by gifted Sāriputta, and Sāriputta himself as witnessed, it is said, by Kassapa: in these cases the homage being paid by Brahmā devas:

> See how they stand, those thronging *devatās*
> Of iddhi-potency, illustrious . . .
> With hands held out in greeting reverently . . .
> Hail thou, humanity's aristocrat!
> Hail who art 'mong men incomparable!

words such as later Sakya would have reserved for the Founder alone.

But there is here no call to decry the devas as regarded by those early Sakyans, unless we persist in seeing in them real deities of the Vedic kind: mahā-devas, such as Indra, Prajāpati, Varuṇa, who have become, in the new thought of the day, *passé*,[1] and to be spoken of with a somewhat complacent patronage. If once we see in the devas of the early Sakyan days the fellow-men at a different stage in life's becoming from "the man" just now on earth, it may dawn upon us that here we have a notable anticipation of the Christian ideal worded as "the Communion of Saints"—a confraternity of the very worthy, linking world with world, and holding up it may be a light in our own darkness. Too much, may be, do we relegate that saintly communion to a vague hereafter; too little is the forward Way, for us, a wayfaring *with* the kindly warding devas of a better world.

I come now to my third reason for what we may call the cheapening of the deva in Buddhist and modern Western treatment. This is the Kevaddha, or Kevaṭṭa Suttanta, a curious irruption into the earnest and dignified tenor of the Sīlakkhandha Book of the Dīghā Nikāya. That it is not wrongly so to be described will be evident to anyone who reads this whole Book at a sitting. It is not therefore necessarily a late or quasi-accidental insertion. But its character is sufficiently

[1] In the probably very old First Sutta of the *Majjhima* Prajāpati is included, but is, in the Comy., identified with Māra!

discrepant to make it wiser for the historical critic to keep it out of the main current of the older Sayings (even as one would push aside, in the following book, the Pāyāsi Suttanta)—and to regard the exceptional features in it as somewhat of a *tour de force*, not to say a freak, in Suttantas.

In reply to a request that he would bid some monk of supernormal gift work an iddhi-miracle, Gotama, after a critical talk on the use of such gifts, is made to tell a curious story as to how a certain monk did once use his iddhi-power. Wishing to learn of the dissolution of the elements wrought up in the human body, he used the concentration of mind suitable for manifestation of the "deva-conveying way", and so visits in succession the six regions of the unseen world discussed above. I pause here to *suggest*, that the, I believe, unique idiom for access to that unseen : *devayāniyo maggo*, unlike the usual Piṭakan wording, but of the earlier Vedic diction, sets the seal of genuine early if not very worthy Sakya on this Suttanta. I have referred to the matter under the subject of Jhāna.

At every stage of the access won, first the men, then the governor of the region successfully refer the inquirer to the region where the devas are, not " higher "—I repeat that the " aloftness " is a liberty, at once late in Pali and European, taken by the translator—but " surpassing us and worthier than are we ". The monk is finally referred to the yet worthier world of the " Brahmā Group ", and then to their governor. This deva too, for all the tremendous concepts in words expressing him, enumerated above (p. 276) takes him by the arm aside, and then perpetrates an act of terrible deceit, saying that, to save his reputation of omniscience, he makes the confession privately, and that is, that even he does not know the truth in the matter, but the monk should make good his oversight, that it was in his own world, and just then, that the man was to be found who did know, to wit the Bhagavā.

As to the estimate here assigned to the world and status of devas as a whole, it were hard to find anything, for the Indian mind, more damning than this. And this being unquestionably so, it is a little curious that more " capital " has not been made out of it by Buddhists and rationalist writers on Buddhism. That this has not happened reflects credit on, rather than oversight in them. For the object of the Sutta is not, I think, so much a deliberate de-valuing of deva-worth, as an early case of apotheosizing the worth of the Founder of Sakya.

To another it may seem that the central interest is the light sought on the query. Not so, since it has no bearing on the dialogue out of which, by way of illustration, the invented story grows. That dialogue turns on the question of super-normal ability, such as we have been considering above. It is consistent that the story, illustrating, should be concerned with that ability as accredited to devas, and also as known to be possessed by the Founder and a few of his disciples. The query is chosen as it were at haphazard, to justify the quest-feature. Men were much exercized over the nature of the bodily and mental constituents and their relation to the "man", and of his identity with, or otherness from them. It was one of the problems of the "Zeitgeist", as we used to say. Meanwhile the "otherness", the "apartness" of the Great Man yet in their midst was beginning, if slowly, to grow.

I picture the author of the Kevaddha Sutta as one of the word-fluent lights in the Order, free-thinking as to the realities of the unseen, with which he himself will not have been in the least conversant at first-hand: revering the aged teacher, not as a friend and comrade, but as a sort of world-seer still keen and fiery in will, able to answer so many questions as to this and other worlds—the see-er of the Two Houses—to the many who came to ask; a compiler very ambitious to make a worthy name for himself in the busy world of Sāvatthī, in midst of the systematizing and unifying in wording of the accumulated streams of memorized sayings which were being told by repeaters of that place and from other viharas. This man I see dealing, as accredited co-editor, with a Saying of the Teachers hailing from Rājagaha when in converse with the householder, Mr. "Fisher" (Kevaṭṭa), and the luring idea occurring to him of illustrating it in his own way, by bringing in the new ideas on body, mind, and the Super-man, or Arahan.

A very "unknown warrior" has he proved in time's verdict, this *x* of the Kevaddha story, for all his ambition. Honour to the original worder, honour to the New! In them lies our hope for the earth, for the worlds. But the New is not ever the Better, though the Better is ever the New. *x*, for all his good will, fell back from the once new mandate of Sakya which was also the better. In that, the man in the Way of the worlds is shown as able to become the More, and his life is shown as the expanding in the More towards the Most. In this story, we see the man shown as less; he is, here already, becoming virtually only mind, and he is only shown as more in a super-man alone, by a shrivelling in the worth of those worlds, wherein wayfaring he can truly expand in the More. The unknown author, to bring into stronger relief the figure he was portraying, set up a dummy world of accessory figures, resembling the Indian bas-reliefs, with their central figure towering over all others. It is a childish device in hero-worship. Gotama was too great to need an apologia of that kind.

It is a little strange that Buddhist supramundane lore, and the light shed here and there on it by recent editions of the Pali books have called forth so very little competent comment. Yet again it is not strange that our generation should as yet prove so deficient therein. It is only a generation possessed of the conviction that life as a whole, in the individual, means not a lessening *for him*, let alone a becoming nothing *for him*, but a becoming more to an indefinite degree, from whom we might look for sympathetically critical interest. And it is only when those Buddhists, who, taking their stand on the Pali Theravāda, and coming to have a knowledge of the contents and history of its records, let go the doctrine of the "Not-man" as a "growth" in those records, and hold to the belief in the man as both fundamentally real and as ever becoming the More on his long upward way to the Most, that they too will take interest in this great expansion in the Way of the worlds, felt after in these neglected deva-scriptures.

XV

THE CROWN IN THE MANDATE: COMPASSION

We who are accustomed to think of one great world-helper as "moved with compassion for the multitude", who were "as sheep without a shepherd",[1] and who spent himself in exercizing that compassion—we, who read, here and there in the Piṭakas, of "compassion" as the very ground of a mandate to men, to man and deva, which would make for weal, for happiness, may hardly realize that, in coming on to that ground made wide in word, we are in what was, at the birth of Sakya, a relatively new word. Further West and much later, it was a relatively new word even in the day of Jesus. Hellenic tradition had not much mothered the sentiment; Roman culture touched lightly on it. Hellenic Greek took over, in its Christian literature, the Hebrew link between the emotion of compassion and its visceral effects, or what our psychology has come to call, its somatic resonance. And so we have it saying, of the compassionate Jesus, *esplangnisthe*: "viscerally-moved." I know not the Hebrew idiom, but for the Jew it was no new idea for Deity to be worded as moved with compassion for his people: "Thou art a God full of compassion" is a frequent refrain in the Psalms. When it is a fulness which should be shown by man to man, the Hebrew scriptures are silent, save when a woman is mothering a child[2]; and it is to deaf ears that the prophet exhorts every man "to show mercy and compassions to his 'brother'".[3] It was a world less deaf when Jesus came. In the Indian diction we do not find the visceral "resonance"; it is true that the usual term *anukampā*, in the Pali books, indicates a vibrating (*kampā*) in accord (*anu*); but the bodily effect is not emphasized. This may be because the greater emphasis on "the man", as the central fact in the matter, apart from his vehicle, needed no help from bodily reference.

The inspired prophet of the Hebrews conveys a divine mandate to his fellows. There was about the idea, in a parallel word, a similar

[1] Matthew, ix, 36; Mark, viii, 1, etc.

[2] Exodus, ii, 6; Isaiah, xlix, 15.

[3] Zechariah, vii, 9 ". . . but they refused to hearken, and pulled away the shoulder and stopped their ears, and made their hearts adamant."

if more indirect tradition surviving in India. In the Brihadārañyaka Upanishad there is, in a group of short *accretions* (v, 2), a parable telling of how the offspring of Prajāpati, world-deity, were waiting upon him for teaching: devas, men, Asuras. (Another group, the Fathers, of the Shatapatha Brāhmaṇa[1] has fallen out, as have the beasts.) In a monotony of thunder :—*da*—*da*—*da*—, the deity gives reply variously interpreted by each section as *dama* (self-control), *dāna* giving, *dayā*, compassion.[2] Now we know that in the Asuras, we have old Iranian deities lowered to demons, titans. And that in the old Persian mandate of Zarathustra we have Ahura, the Deity enjoining compassion, and hence, the idea of compassion as being at the time an ideal upon earth. *Dayā*, more usually *anuddayā* is in the Suttas an alternative term to *anukampā*. Hence we may say, that as in Palestine compassion had expanded directly as a divine precursor to its development in the life of Jesus, so in north India had it expanded indirectly as a divine idea, an Aryan, yet a foreign idea, to its development in the life of Gotama.

I say, in the life of Gotama, for I can find *no other admonition* in the Upanishads to cultivate compassion. I speak subject to correction, but I find no reference to it in any edition of the Upanishads, original or in comment. That compassion was revealed in mantra or in deed by Vedic gods is hard to find, save in the passage quoted, and that was a mantra either of Gotama's day, or earlier. But in what I believe to be early Sayings in the Piṭakas, we find a wording of *anukampā* and of *anuddayā* as interesting as it is far-reaching and long-surviving.

Long-surviving in that, both in the scenes where Sakya began, and also in the lands of its furthest penetration in later centuries, it is perhaps as the Compassionate One that the Founder left his most lasting imprint on the memories of men. The Chinese pilgrims have in their itineraries preserved this for us. Both Fa-Hien in the fourth century A.D. and Hiuen Chwang, two centuries later, wrote of Topes to be seen perpetuating the memory of some act of compassion wrought by the Bhagavā. It is true that the acts are mainly not acts of his life as Gotama, but such as Jātaka stories told about him when a "Bodhisat", when as man or beast he gave his life to save the bodily life of some beast or man. The later pilgrim has, it is true, surviving tales to tell of Gotama exercizing compassion as a Teacher in cases of tortured or condemned criminals and making no attempt to heal or rescue their bodies. The incident of Gotama's

[1] Book ii, 4, 2, 1–6.

[2] In full, *dayadhvam*.

tending the neglected sick monk [1] is also stated as the *raison d'être* for a tope. And it is perhaps noteworthy that these compassionate acts associated with his historical life are given as surviving round about Sāvatthī, where we should have expected to find just such worthy, and very possibly true memories.[2]

Characteristically different is the perpetuation of compassionate memories in the adopted Buddhism of the Far East. With a conception of the reality of the very man (or self) much less wilted and washed out than was the case in Hīnayāna, we see the ideal of compassion become the chief feature of man realizing the More in his nature in better worlds, as the Community of Bodhisattvas or Communion of Saints. Amitābha, Avalokiteśvara, Kwanyin, whether conceived as man, or as a compassionately working Madonna: all are mainly tributes in idea to the loveliness of the compassionate warding of man by them who are willing and able to help.

In all this wide-flung reverberation of the influence exercized by the life and teaching of a great son of man and his helpers, there is shown in the idea of "compassion" an inclusiveness, an indiscriminateness, which is natural enough, but which is perhaps not the real and true nature of the sentiment felt and exercized by Sakyamuni and Sakyans. That a man should feel kindness (*dayā*) toward *certain of his fellow-men*, as neighbour, father, friend, that he should put himself out to exercize it, that he should make sacrifices in exercizing it, that he should even risk, even sacrifice life itself in exercizing it: here is no new thing as first shown and taught by Sakya. Any mother could tell us that, she the Arch-compassionizer from animals upwards. Again, that a man should feel pity at the sight of suffering fellow-men—here is nothing which it can safely be claimed was a new word in the teaching of the unknown Brahman, or ex-Brahman, taken over by Sakya: the mandate of the Four Moods. That teaching was not intended to present the Four, amity, pity, etc., as dispositions not valued till then. Its teaching was how to practise them in a new and very intensive way, the way of will-suffusion.

It is true that in the prescribing of these in a universal way to include all men, all creatures, we have something that may have been in range a new word, shared in, be it remembered, by the old Upanishad quoted. So too may have been the kindness and compassion

[1] Above, p. 206.

[2] Legge: *Fa-hian*, p. 31, f.; T. Watters: *On Yuan Chwang*, i, p. 387.

characteristic, it is recorded, both of the Founder, and of the aspirant to saintship: he is "kind and compassionate to all creatures and beings",[1] not merely to "certain of his fellow-men". And so far was it a new ideal, that it is prescribed for the laity as specifically Sabbath-morals of the degree followed *daily* by the former only,[2]

> too high and good
> For human nature's daily food.

None the less is it true that, in the injunctions of the Mahābhārata, known as the Mokṣa-dharma, the wise man is bidden to check a natural tendency to pity creatures; rather should he remember that all living things must expiate the fruit of their deeds, and take no notice of them.[3] But this is no word of the time of which we are speaking; it is of a later date, being evidently saturated with the monastic spirit, which had spread over more than Sakya in northern India. We are inquiring into a time when there was no such artificial culture of repression checking men's healthier instincts; a time of expansion in the new rather than of shrinkage; a time rather of the open hand than of the averted eye.

And we ask ourselves: what was exactly the specifically New in the note of "compassion" (whether as *anuddayā* or *anukampā*), which struck so rich a chord in the taught word and the live word of Gotama and his men?

Let us consult the appearance of the word and the contexts.

We first see Gotama at home, pained and puzzled over the fate of the man as bound to a body: the ageing, the diseased, the dead man or woman so bound; the wail: "Alas! this world has fallen upon ill, and who will show a way out of that?" I have seen it asserted that here he was occupied solely with his own immediate future as bound to a body. This is as forced and unreasonable as to take the opposite extreme—that he was solely concerned with others, not himself. Verily not of such are the helpers of "the man". But I have dealt with this. We then see the implied compassion further implicit in the new departure from home and office and worldly fortune. We see, after years of seeking, the message taking form, as a mandate of hope and of expansion in outlook and possible becoming for the man, in the Figure of the Way. And at length the further exercize of compassion takes shape with the word

[1] *Dīgha*, Sta., i, p. 4.
[2] *Anguttara*, i, 211.
[3] *Adhyāya*, 215, 4. Cf. *Theragāthā* Commentary (*Pss. of the Brethren*), pp. 99 and 122 for similar sentiments.

become explicit: "Go on tour (*charatha charikaŋ*) for the good of the many folk, for the happiness of the many folk; out of compassion for the world; for the salvation (*attha*), for the good, for the happiness of devas and of men. Go not alone, but in twos . . . Teach *dhamma*, lovely for youth, lovely for middle age, lovely for latest years; declare the worth in the Highest, the utterly perfect, the very pure."[1]

This is a great gesture, yet is there here no coinciding with that which is elsewhere worded as amity, or as pity. There was not to be a declaring of either, but of *dhamma*, namely, of that inward Thing of the very man (or self, *ajjhattaṃ*), which would secure his true Becoming, whether he was man or deva. Let us look further.

We find the Founder rallied now by a Sakyan, now by some persuader to the worse, whom the age called, or came to call "Māra":—

> You a *samaṇa* who have put away all ties, are wholly free; it is not well that you teach others.

The poem makes the Founder answer thus:—

> Whatever be the cause, Sakya, from which intercourse is born, it does not fit the man of holiness. By mind to take compassion, if the mind be satisfied that he teach others, he is not thereby bound. It is from sympathy, from compassion.[2]

And this[3]:—

MĀRA: Not suitable for you is this, that you
Should teach another. Have a care lest you
In such a practice are not left to hang
Strung 'twixt supporters' zeal, opposers' ire.
GOTAMA: Compassion for his good th'awakened feels
Towards another when he teaches him.
From zeal of partisan, opposers' ire
Unloosed and freed is a tathāgata.

And this[4]:—

MĀRA: What? Lie you (here) mentally dull and vacuous?
Or are mazed over your coming discourse?
Do not affairs many and divers await you?
Biding aloof, here in a resting-place lonely
With sleepy face, why would you now be sleeping?

[1] *Vinaya*, Mahāvagga, i, 11.

[2] *Saṃyutta-Nikāya*, i, 206. The Sakyan is here called a yakkha, as the deva Sakka is called elsewhere. The Commentary would make him a "Māra". "Of holiness" = he who has *paññā*.

[3] Ibid., i, 111. [4] Ibid., 110 (trisṭubh metre).

GOTAMA: Not mentally dull lie I (here) nor vacuous,
Nor am I mazed, brooding on future discourse.
My aim is won, nor have I any troubles.
I lie at rest filled with compassion for all things.

. . . .

Nor days nor nights stir up regrets within me.
Worsening (*hāni*) see I naught in the world whatever,
Hence may I sleep filled with compassion for all things.

I quote these to me deeply interesting verses without wishing that any reader should think he has in them Gotama's actual words. I do not suppose that devas, Māras, or teachers queried and riposted in metric speech any more then than they would now. Did we but know more, we should "see" some monk of the fixed-wording-industry set to turn repeated prose *sayings*, probably of a brief fragmentary kind, into the more stable metric diction. And it may well be that, himself bitten with the new vogue as to man revealed in mind, he inserted *petits bouts* of the same in the sayings, in a way we do not elsewhere find in compassion-contexts, viz. :—"by mind to take compassion (*manasā anukampituŋ*)", if only, perhaps to give proper length to a *gāthā* or line. But in the main we have here a sentiment imputed, in the character of a world-helper like Gotama, which is very worthy of him, and which it is very likely that he both felt and uttered.

Just what is that sentiment, as distinguishable from both amity (*mettā*) and pity? For that it is distinguishable appears (*a*) from silence about it when these two sentiments are discussed, and (*b*) from silence about these two when compassion is to the fore.

In the first place the sentiment is said to be felt as in a way different from those which usually lead to human intercourse: relations domestic, social, commercial, political, æsthetic and the like. "None fits" this kind of contact felt by the *sappañño*, the man of the attribute *paññā*, which we saw belonged to him as having in himself the promise of the "Most". In the second place it is pre-eminently the sentiment of the worthy teacher towards the taught. This is, in the first place, one of warding. Buddhaghosa rightly remarks of *anuddayā*, kindness or compassion, that it "means warding (*rakkhati*)".[1] The good teacher stands *in loco parentis*, as we say, mothering his pupil in all goodwill. Thirdly, the compassionate one is shown as in no way worried, but as on the contrary quite happy. He is not cast down over the ills of the world, or of

[1] Atthasālinī on Dhammasangaṇi, § 1056.

any persons in it. He is not considering any *hāni* whatever, that is, any letting down, decline or shrinkage, as to men or the man. Hence he is on the one hand not torn with pity (*karuṇā*), on the other hand he is buoyed up, either by a conviction that the man is and will be no worse than he is believed to be, or that he can, probably will, become better.

But I am bound to add that my interpretation, as the only one possible in the case of a helper of men, filled with compassion, is opposed to that of the Commentator. He says : " When over some worry arisen for teacher or pupil, persistent exposition and question make a torment of night and day, not thus do they torment me, for there is nothing whatever left me of work uncompleted." The result of this overshadowing arahan-theory of the " all-done " man is that he leaves the lovely serenity of compassion entirely out of the picture. It is a woeful worsening in the scholastic attitude that is indicated.[1]

So far then we see, in " compassion " as here entertained, a sentiment which is not the same as, nor commensurate with, active pity. Pity, at least, in the Piṭakas and Commentarial books, is a matter of " inability (to behold) bodily ills "[2]—herein it is nearly on all fours with Cicero's " ill ease of mind growing out of the misfortune of another "[3]—and the good-will to remedy. Nor is there in compassion just what is expressed by amity (*mettā*), a word which does not appear in conjunction with *anukampā*. *Mettā* is, or may be between men, when engaged in those modes of intercourse alluded to in the poem I quoted—the causes " from which intercourse is born "—where man, with visible, mind-expressing body, meets with man.[4]

I quote a few more contexts.

A very usual one in the Suttas is that where " the favour of a visit " is worded as : " would he come to me out of compassion ? " I have not found the idiom used, save when the request is made (by a messenger) to a teacher of religion. Usually addressed to Gotama, it is also found used (after his death) for instance, to Ānanda. So used, it would appear as if compassion were held to be a prerogative of such teachers. The phrase may have been merely the suitable etiquette ; or it may have implied the conviction that such a visit

[1] *Sāratthappakāsinī*, p. 176.

[2] *Visuddhi-magga*, p. 325 : *Sattānaŋ dukkhâsahanatā*.

[3] *Enc. R. E.* : art. " Pity ".

[4] Cf. the worldly, as compared with the dhamma-compassion in *Anguttara*, i, 92.

would result in a benefit of a certain kind :—not to body nor to mind, but, as our diction would (not happily) word it, to the "soul" of the man visited. This in Sakyan diction would be (more happily) expressed as Visākhā put it: it would result in a "becoming" *in the man* visited.

Then there is this saying, made out as a frequent counsel to disciples after a teaching :—

"That, Ānanda, which should be done by a teacher for his disciples, who seeks their good, who is compassionate, and because of compassion, that have I done for you. Here are shady trees; here are empty places; muse, Ānanda, be not careless; become not one who afterwards regrets." [1]

This beautiful coda occurs in the Suttas five times. The compassionate Way-shower brings his hearer thus far; it is then for the latter himself, showing compassion to himself, to carry on in choice of the right way shown to him. And Ānanda knew and valued the compassionate Way-showing as we have seen and, as his pitiful moan shows, felt not over-wise in the matter of carrying on :—

But I am one who yet has work to do,
A learner with a mind not yet matured;
And now the Master hence has passed away
Who e'er to me such (sweet) compassion showed.[2]

Nor was homage of grateful sense of compassion paid to the best of teachers alone.

That which my teacher wished (that I should know)
Fostering in me, who for the Deathless longed,
The thing that was to do that have I done.
Yea, won and realized is *dhamma* now;
E'en for my own, not learnt as "such and such".
Worthy the speaker who instructed me;
Compassionate, 't is thou hast favoured me,

are lines from Sumana's poem to his Thera-uncle.[3] And C(h)andā, a lonely widow, tells of the mothering of Patāc(h)ārā :—

And she, out of compassion on my woes,
Patāc(h)ārā ordained me as a nun.[4]

It is in Sumana's lines that we see the kind of benefit worked by compassion. There is here no fostering of body, nor of mind *as such*. There has been the opposite of that which the resting Gotama was happy in not presaging: there has been no "hāni"; no wilting;

[1] *Majjhima-Nikāya*, iii, 157.
[2] *Theragāthā*, ver. 1045.
[3] *Theragāthā*, ver. 334.
[4] *Therīgāthā*, ver. 125.

there has been, as Buddhaghosa well says, "growth and not decline," and the growth has been in the coming to be of the More, not in body or mind, but in the very man, the self, the soul. This is the specific object of compassion, as felt indeed by every teacher worthy of the name, but chiefly by the teacher of religion, concerned not primarily with body and mind, but with the "man". And by that I have no teaching of any cult or creed in mind, any more than will have been in the will of Gotama. Here and there, very rarely, he is called the peerless physician and surgeon :—

Teacher most pitiful, healer of all the world,

but the healing given is of that stimulus to the growth of the man, even of one who, as in the last quoted speaker's case, is anticipating instant murder.[1]

There is no question here of any hard and fast limit in the meaning of compassion (*anukampā*, *anuddayā*), as a monopoly of the teacher. The word occurs as a quality of the generous donor of alms,[2] and also of the parents' care :

. . . To do me kindness (*anukampāya*) they,
My good desiring and my happiness,
Conducted me—father and mother too—
Into the presence of the Buddha (blest).[3]

And in that precious survival, the Sigālovāda Suttanta,[4] of the six kinds of social relations in which the householder stands, the one term in each of those relations is declared to be "rightly compassionate" for the other term, the latter reciprocating by "waiting upon" the former. Thus the parent, the teacher, the wife, the master, the friend, the brahman or recluse should feel compassion for child, husband, friend, servant, layman respectively. These compassionates as superseding, in the teacher's homily, the sixfold sort of nature-deity worship in which the householder was occupied, are thus made to rank as so many little devas of a cult prescribed in Sakya. So great, in Sakya, is shown the responsibility attaching to those six relations, so fine the opportunity for exercizing compassion, tender care, protection.

The warding of man as exercise of compassion cannot but *include* all fellow-feeling, whether the prevailing tinge of it be pity, or kindliness, or protection, or sympathy with joy. We see on the one hand Gotama's compassion for all things described, in a later Piṭakan

[1] *Theragāthā*, ver. 722, etc., etc. ; *Itivuttaka*, § 100, cf. § 106.
[2] Ibid., § 75. [3] *Theragāthā*, ver. 473–4.
[4] Cf. transl. *Dialogues of the Buddha*, No. xxxi, and Introduction.

book (the Paṭisambhidā-magga), as his "attainment of the great pity", in an eloquent refrain as of a "Benedicite, omnia opera":—

> On fire are the habitations of the world: so seeing great pity falls on the Buddhas the Blessed Ones; fallen into an evil way . . . without shelter . . . without refuge . . . inflated, unsoothed . . . pierced is the world with many darts, and there is none can draw them out but I; flung into a cage of corruption, wrapped in the murk of ignorance and there is none to show it light but I; . . . I have crossed over, I am able to make it cross, freed I can set free, tamed I can tame, at peace I can make peaceful, comforted I can comfort, passed to the utterly well, I can make to pass . . .[1]

and much more besides. Here is compassion conceived in terms of divine pity. Again we see Jesus as moved with compassion, now for the Many's need of guidance; but now also for their being hungry and weary in body, and here is pity in terms of compassion. We see again, in a Sutta, the Jain leader made to urge a man to challenge Gotama in debate over his commending of compassion, while yet coming none the less with his disciples to Nālandā, suffering at the time from scarcity, as if pitiless toward givers who themselves are lacking food.[2] The Sutta is so obviously a patchwork of fragments that to discuss it further were here useless. I quote it only to show the compassion, which Gotama exercized and enjoined, *confused* with the pity which is moved and exercised over bodily ills. We make the same confusion to-day ourselves.

And so much do we see, in the divine compassion of a world-helper, that pity for the earthly instruments of the man, when it is the pain and sorrow and stupidity he seeks to heal, that the word calls up in us a man of sorrows, or at brightest a grave tenderness, whether the image we have in mind be that of the Jesus who wept, or of the Gotama of serene face who smiled. In Buddhism, the monk-ideal has darkened us with the obsession of "Ill"; in the West the price of sin has overshadowed the meaning in the Helper's compassion: "the joy that was set before him."[3]

"The joy"—what did Sakya make of that third "mark (*lakshaṇa*)" of the Divine in ancient Indian conceptions of Deity: *ānanda*, bliss, happiness? Much more, probably, than the brooding on Ill of the Four Truths formula, and the Causal Chain formula and many others would let us imagine. We have here as everywhere to dig under substrata, to see the

[1] Vol. i, p. 126 f. [2] *Saṃyutta-Nikāya*, iv, 322.
[3] Hebrews, xii, 2.

glint of some much buried thing of radiant beauty. The superstructure reiterates, in piled-up stones, that the man changes ever, and is much liable to Ill, therefore, can he not possibly be Ātman, God, Divine, THAT, since, as went without saying, That was Being, not change, That was joy, not sorrow. But underneath we come on things covered over by these negations, covered over, that is, by the shadow of these rather than in fact.

Take the little heeded Third of the Four Moods approved of and taken over by Sakya : *muditā*, joy. I think that we translators and exponents have forced the note here as to *muditā* being sympathetic joy, Mitfreude. Buddhaghosa was wrong and we follow him. Both he and we misconceive the true nature of the unknown teacher's mandate. The true meaning is, for me, that the well-willer, knowing in himself the bliss that lies in the growth, the becoming of That More in the very man, radiates joy to another whom he judges to be starving for it. This is a good way above the materialistically conceived occasions for felicitation on external success, which Buddhaghosa brings to bear on the subject. To radiate Brahma-joy needs no pleasant event, present, past, or future, in another's hap, to call it forth.

I said just now not covered, only overshadowed, mindful that the refrain just cited is found in several Suttas. But we see that joy arises with growth, not in body or mind, but in the very man. It is not a question of sharpened intellectual acumen, but of spiritual growth. He who is only potentially That, is advancing in the Becoming That. And in so far as the Three Divine attributes are a true conception, it is inevitable that, with the More in becoming, should arise the More in joy. The Sutta is only to this extent "monkish", that the "becoming" is, *with one exception*, represented as riddance, the "putting off" this and that. The one exception is, that he is now the better realizing that compassion for all, which, in thus comrading joy, becomes perhaps for the first time in India verily Godlike.

But in the Vinaya, where the joy-refrain occurs, I think once only, a truer note is struck by the speaker, the good and wise Visākhā. In the episode already cited,[1] where she speaks of an opportunity for exercizing compassion as a becoming, or making to become (*bhāvanā*), she gives, not as a result of her becoming, but as the *very ground of it*, the joy that her practised compassion will engender in her. Thus it is the "more" in the divine mark of joy, which will go with the "more" in the divine becoming.

[1] Above, p. 98 f.

Here we seem to see the link between this elect woman's Wayfaring and that of the Way-shower, who could rest entirely happy while filled with that compassion for all, which made, not so much for worry over the needs of body and mind, as for the becoming more and more in that divine joyousness, which he knew in himself, and foresaw as the ultimate fate for every man.

But it is the joy in becoming that we meet with in the probably mainly authentic talk of Gotama with the king of Magadha, the Sāmaññaphala-Suttanta, and again in the saying of Visākhā, already mentioned. This divine joy, this *ānanda*, in both these episodes gleams out in its proper setting: the man in process of becoming.

Here, in the first place, we have no dropping out of the man, the self, no setting up a dummy man called mind; here is the man working his coming to be through his earth-vehicle of be-minded body. Here again is the man so working not yet realizing himself as even now That-Who-is the divinely consummate. Here is man-who-is-to-be-ultimately That, realizing himself as That in the becoming, brought to the highest that he, on earth, yea, and for long afterward, is fit to realize, ready to experience. And first, in the Sāmaññaphala Saying, we have the man of the will-to-the-better at work; he is casting out unclean spirits from his house [1]: sensuousness, malevolence, torpor, worry, covetousness, doubt; he is replacing them with "compassion with the good of all creatures" (*sabba-pāṇa-bhūta-hitânukampī*); and when all this is done "joy is born in the self, to the self joyous zest is born; the body of the zestful mind is tranquillized, the tranquillized body experiences happiness, in him, happy, the mind is stayed. . . ."

Musing he sits in Jhāna, and "with zest and happiness he anoints, drenches, fills up, suffuses the body, so that no part of it is therewith untouched."

Joy over the results of the good teacher's compassion, joy as will, I think, have been radiated to him by that happy teacher breaks out in lovely relief in the tamed disciple who had been notorious in evil-doing, Angulimāla:

> Deep in the wild beneath some forest tree,
> Or in the mountain cave, is't here, is't there,
> So have I stood and let my throbbing heart
> Transported beat. Happy I seek my rest,
> Happy I rise, happy I pass the day,
> By evil ones unhaunted—ah! behold
> The Master's sweet compassion shown to me!
>
> (*Theragāthā*, ver. 887 f.)

[1] Cf. pp. 71–3.

There is in the ex-bandit's happiness at least a silence as to that complacency which, in some of the poems of this anthology limits the true vista in joy—the joy namely in awareness of becoming—to the premature conviction that consummation has been reached. He has a long way yet to go, but he had certainly come along bravely. "Becoming" is also stressed—rather than a fancied achievement—in the happiness being sought by happiness, and not by ways of deliberate self-torment :—

> This happiness by happy ways is won—
> See the true rightness of the sense-of-right!
> (ver. 220 and 63).

an attitude which is found, in the Majjhima-Nikāya,[1] expressly opposed to the Jain leaning to austerities as being the right way to happiness : "happiness is to be won by *dukkha*."

And with the first men of Sakya, this refrain : "happiness happily won" was no mere theory. That they were happy teachers of a happy gospel may reasonably be inferred from that last touching tribute, paid by the aged king of Kosala to his contemporary and friend Gotama of the Sakyas, in the Sutta called "Shrines of Dhamma".[2] Not only, he is made to say, is it concord which he witnesses among the Sakyans, contrasting with political and domestic strife abounding elsewhere, it is that, as compared with other *samaṇas* and religious brahmans, the Sakyans he found "joyous and joyful, exultant and jubilant, buoyant and fervent, without care or worry, tranquil . . . with a mind become as a creature of the wild. Surely, thought I, this is due to you and your teaching". And if we pass from Saying to Saying of the same Nikāya, this joy-note meets the eye every now and then, amid all the stressed "ill", as a happiness evoked in and through the further becoming in the man, and in his sense of it.

Thus the Way itself is called *pītigamanīyo*, "a going to joy" (i. 117). Then we find three different versions of the following experience : "if, on reflection, a man who is "striving" toward the better, is aware of success, he may live on, in his training in good things, in joy and bliss" (i, 100 ; 419 ; iii, 294). Again, a man is as a bad cowherd, ignorant of good watering places, if, when studying, he knows neither his weal (*attha*), nor *dhamma*, nor the joy belonging to *dhamma* (i, 221). And it is with a very pæan of joy that another Cowherd Saying ends, bidding the men of such a gospel rejoice : "This world, the other world :—well declared are they by him who

[1] Sutta 14 ; cf. Sta. 85. [2] Ibid., Sutta 89.

knows, there too where evil has mastery and there where death comes not. The awakened one who knows who understands what is the world hath opened the gate of Amata for winning of Nirvana. Withered up is the stream of evil! Be joyful with much joy! Ye are they who have won to safety!" (i, 227).

So also wrote St. Paul in one letter after another, some twenty-one times: "Rejoice, and again I say unto you rejoice" and the like, and St. Peter too: "rejoice with joy unspeakable and full of glory!": men who were face to face with a near future more grim that that facing the Sakyans, and known by them to be such.

These two and the early Sakyans were close to the heart of the new mandate, and were still vibrant with the joy pulsing through it as, in each case a "More-word" in man's power to become, in man's essential nature as less a being than a becoming. But from the over-stressing which was made, in the one case, of the thing which the becoming left gradually behind, *dukkha*, and in the other case, of the price which the becoming was held to have cost, both the fact of the becoming and the joy inherent in it greatly faded. So much so in the case of Sakya, that I find no one, Buddhist or non-Buddhist, who sees, in the Way, a symbol, an earnest of *bhava*, becoming, and that I find Buddhist scriptures denouncing "becoming", or hiding it under the altered inflexion of *bhāveti*, makes to become, and rendering that by "meditation!"

This is a drab view, and to not a little degree it is the price paid for so shifting the view, that a new centre of *Buddhism* had come to take the place of the original centre. The four truths, a neatly drawn up diagnosis of "ill", with the chief emphasis laid on ill, had thrust aside the Way, and made it at best a way out from ill. But the forward view is much less concerned with ill, much more concerned with progress in the better. It is the price, too, paid for maintaining the theory of the arahan, with the yet inconceivable, ineffable consummation of "the man" crammed and stuffed into the brief, crowded hour of his little earth-day. The arahan rejoices, it is true, but he rejoices with his head over his shoulder at what he was, compared with what he has become. He has no joy in his *present becoming*; and that being so, becoming, as an ideal set before him, is no more. The religion of his day and country conceived Deity as being (*sat*) only; the arahan in turn valued himself only as become (*bhūta*).[1] Between the two, the new word in becoming, symbolized in the Way and the Wayfaring as "*going on* to joy", wilted; the very clue to it was lost.

[1] E.g. *sītibhūta*, synonym for arahan.

And so joy in becoming, as taught and shown by the first Sakyans, is not now stressed as it should be. And therewith is not felt the true significance in the word *anukampā*. *Anukampā*, I repeat, is vibrant kindliness; compassion, with pity only if there be need for it. The Greek *charis*, which our Christianized English renders by "grace", is the nearest we have to it. As a gesture of happy kindly service between shower and receiver, each of whom, as bestowing, as welcoming, is eager for some benefit to accrue, each of whom is bent on added welfare, each of whom is finding joy in the gesture—here we have *anukampā* in a sense which avails to include the "favour" of a visit (e.g. Dīgha, i, 204; Anguttara, iii, 49), the parental care of the child's good upbringing (Theragāthā, ver. 334), ministering to the sick (Majjh., iii, 258; Saṃy., v, 380), the grace bestowed on pupil by teacher, on husband by wife, on listener by priest or minister (Dīgha, No. 31), on man of earth by warding willers unseen.[1] For in every case there will be, at back of any tending of body or of mind, a joyous becoming and a joyous making to become in the very "man", to whom service of grace is shown, whether the very man be encased in vestment of woman, man, or child. There will be no "teacher's fist" in the exercise of *anukampā*[2]; there will be only good will in the hand to forward, in the "man" giving and receiving, that coming-to-be which is true wayfaring in the Way going to Joy.

And hence it is that I have called *anukampā*, not the base, but the crown in the mandate; not the *bhava*, the "becoming", as truer of man than his "being", but the joy in becoming and making to become which is man's very guarantee of final consummation. "Behold! this is the joy of his way, and out of the earth shall others grow."[3]

[1] See several Suttas in *Saṃyutta*, bk. ix, "The Forest Sayings", also in Bks. i and ii.

[2] *Dīgha*, ii 100.

[3] Book of Job, vii, 9.

XVI.

THE MAN OF THE NEW WORD

From the world of the birth of the new word, through inquiry into that word, we have been coming to the other term in our relation, the voice, the life in whom my hypothesis may be said to centre : the man of the new word. Here why should there be many words about him ? Is it not written in the book of Gotama the Man ? Yet is there one thing perhaps which may better be said about him than by him ; we who seek for true values in this great Compassionate One may best ascribe to him that which he has not fully worded about himself. We are, it is true—to refer to a great painter of my race—but as Love among the Ruins, yet even there can we perhaps get a truer perspective of this Lover of man than he himself could show.

It is good to see two such great Lovers together : their word at heart the same, yet in the accident of form so very different.

" These things have I spoken unto you, that joy, my joy might remain with you ; that your joy might be full." (Gospel of St. John, xv, 2. Note the emphasis : ἵνα ἡ χαρα ἡ ἐμὴ . . .)

" Are you indeed living happily, sir, within that leaf-hut, in winter nights ? Yes, kumāra, I am living happily ; if anyone in the world lives happily, surely I am one of such. . . . There is left in me no cause of unhappiness." " Now what say you ? Can a man who clings to ill, has gone over to ill, so cleaves to ill, that he regards ill as 'mine', 'me as ill', 'the self of me as ill'—can he either of himself thoroughly understand ill, or live casting out ill ? He could not." (*Anguttara*, i, 136 ; *Majjhima*, i, 233.)

These are, as many know, sayings attributed in two of the world's most notable scriptures, to two men of the new word. The beauty and directness of the first is an advance on the other two older sayings, but that may be a happy accident in the matter of editorship in both the Scriptures—an accident that makes us catch our breath at the vivid vital loveliness in those parting sayings of the Jesus of the Johnian tradition, and leaves us, in most of the Gotama sayings in the Nikāyan tradition, sighing over what of vivid vital loveliness may not have got lost, and which is anyway too often muffled and dimmed through the medium of a wrongly shifted emphasis.

In essence they are thus far parallel : those men are men of joy (*ānand*) bringing to any and every man a new word of joy, of joy because it was of the man as becoming, not as standing still (*sat*), or wilting to less, of joy, because the man as having mind (*cit*) could understand and word his coming-to-be. For both of those men spoke of the crown, the end of that coming to be, as not an indefinite, infinite wandering, but a quest to be consummated. The one, mid-way between east and west, spoke of it as "the Father in me" the man ; the other, of the mid-east, spoke of it in terms of (not Being, but) becoming, happiness, values, in other words of his country's conception of the man, *raised in one respect to a new power*—that of becoming. Both spoke of the Highest man can conceive as "in me", the very man, not the perishable body and the man's ways in working it, but the worker himself, the Becoming one, the Joyous one, the Valuer. "Hush, Vakkali ! What is there in seeing this vile body of me ? He who sees *dhamma*—(the divine urge in man)—sees me ; who sees me sees *dhamma*."[1]

It is inconceivable to me that such men, who knew themselves as on the one hand participants in the splendours of immanent Divinity, as yet immature, and on the other, as aware within themselves of a mandate to teach this to others less aware of it, could have been, in the day of their mission, other than men radiating the vibrant joyousness which Sakya worded as compassion. Even when in advice given, the body only came into question, the sagacious royal beneficiary stroking limbs restored to health could say : "Ah ! surely for my weal (*artha*) both in this life and in that beyond has Gotama shown compassion on me."[2] Here is health of body transcended by a giving of health when this body is discarded. And when the man ailing in body is bidden to see that the man, the self keep well[3] (no teacher at that day in India would have said "the mind" as the records have it), it was to the eternal youth in himself that his attention was turned, a youth not without the ways of wielding brain and muscle which we sum up as mind, but a youth who, when the instrument he so wielded lay useless in death, would enter upon new ways of wielding, with a new instrument.

Men of the morning : so do I conceive these sons of divine joy, far more pre-occupied with the *artha*, the "well" of men than with their ills. No one can experience some little advance in this divine hygiene in himself without increase of the joy which is inherent in it ; much

[1] *Saṃyutta*, iii, 120. [2] Ibid., i, 81.
[3] Ibid., iii, 1 f.

more will he be "abounding in joy" (*pāmojjabahulo*) to whom has come the elect destiny of forwarding others in the "happy holy plane" (*padaṃ santaṃ sukhaṃ*)[1] of a becoming in the "more".

But as long as we picture the great world-helpers concentrating on one life, and that here below only, we tend to see them as men weighed down by the burden heavy to bear, as men of the "way out", as travailing over the Many to be saved, as confronted by world, flesh, and devil, and we tend also to see the souls to be saved, the *parvulos trahendos* (in Gerson's phrase) as fugitives escaping :—

> Like forest fires behold them drawing nigh :
> Disease, decay and death, dread trinity. (450)

But once a year we, if we were born under the Christian tradition, catch a gleam of a wider, longer, truer irradiation, covering not earth only, but the worlds of the Way to the Goal ; we see, though we know it not, "life whole," if not yet "steadily" as such. We listen to faint echoes of transcendent joy : *Gloria in excelsis Deo, et in terra pax hominis bonæ voluntatis* linking up the worlds. Our own singers respond, catching the ardent glow of the altar-coal, and putting our tired concepts, our perennial deafness to shame, as they hail those other voices :—

> Sing, choirs of angels, radiant and triumphant !
> Sing, O ye citizens of heaven above !

And then we turn for another year to our muck-rakes again, and the joy-light fades. So we fail to see, in inspired helpers, men in whom that joy-light was their day's habitual wear :—

> For them is every day May-festival[2]—

their ever-burning altar-fire, making them one, as we are not yet one, with the greater life. But either the bright ardour of the memory of them has been cut short by tragic suddenness, or their glad message has been clouded over by gloomy ideas bearing on the less in man, and not on the More in him, which they came to draw out, to foster. And our Compassionate Ones become our Men of the Great Pity, with drawn features or with brooding countenance, more than our Joyous Ones, who sought to lead us "by happy ways to happiness".

Christmas comes and passes, but spring comes also, type eternal of youth. Our Great Compassionates are the men of joyous grace, because they bear, not only in themselves the joy of their own inner

[1] *Dhammapada*, ver. 381 ; *Theragāthā*, ver. 11.
[2] *Majjhima*, i, 39 ; *Suddhassa ve sadā phaggu, suddhass'uposatho sadā.*

burgeoning, but also a message—" tidings of great joy to you and all mankind "—of the capacity within each man of a similar burgeoning, earnest and guarantee of final consummation. Not theirs is it, not theirs can it be, to stress the " miserable sinner " in the man, the unreality of the very man at back of mind and body, the perils besetting him at every step, the backward view, the way of him as an escape from fire, safety from shipwreck, release from becoming, the whirling of a wheel, an eddy of rebirth. Theirs is the worth in the coming day, the forward view, the *dhamma*-wheel of the Inner Controller, the chariot that bears him onward to the home, in the glorious adolescence that the man-in-man can make-to-become, once he realizes how pre-occupation with the back and forth of the way of body and mind only has stunted it.

It is true that the man of the new word may in India have come to birth at a time when there was creeping over his world a depressed reaction from that day of an earlier new word, a time when the later followers of those men, the first " recluses ", they who had left human intercourse to taste alone the newly taught immanent Deity in man, arose : the after-men, who as *samaṇas*, as *bhikshus* profited by living near " the world ", and who flung in the face of it, that it was Ill, on fire, sick, hopeless, and that the one quest worth while was escape from it not only there and then, but for ever and everywhere.

But our Joyous Compassionate would not be the man to put himself at the head of such a movement, and teach an emphasized gospel of Getting Away. If he rated it at all, he would know, as in the words imputed to him above, that a man obsessed by ill, wrapped up in it, could not rightly judge it at its true value. Pre-occupied himself at first by the way ill loomed so large for his fellows, he set himself, not so much to lead the brooders on ill with a doctrine how to get out of it—as he is represented—but with his face set towards the neglected well-spring of joy in each man : the happy Way to happiness ; the guarantee in man, that the nature of him : becoming, minding, latent joyousness, was no matter of a mandate about ill, but was in itself a call to " fare onward unto perfection ".[1]

Great service in many ways to the study of the Indian records has been rendered by that fine scholar Hermann Oldenberg ; we all know and acknowledge it. But it was a grievous disservice that he rendered to the study of Buddhism in his insistence on " Erlösung ", release, as the " centre " of Gotama's mantra of Benares and of his teaching in general. Grievous because of his having himself arrived at such a view ; grievous because his was a pencraft to render it plausible ;

[1] Ep. Hebrews vi, 3.

grievous because of the subservient following his able presentation of it, coupled with his wide Indological erudition, has elicited in his own country and elsewhere, among both scholars and amateur votaries of Buddhism. He saw that "monkdom" was a growing vogue when Sakya was born. And virtually he made his "Buddha" place himself at the head of that vogue. He failed to discern in him, not the man of a vogue, but the man with a new word. He wrote of the changed ideal spreading over India of that day, the "wellbeing, the victory, the dominance" of Veda ideals clouded over by the calm, quiet, peace, "Erlösung" of the world-forsaker. He could write critically as to the value of such evidence as was to be looked for in the hand-to-hand transmission resulting in what are called Piṭakas; and yet he saw that later ideal, as expressed in the Piṭakas, the sufficient guide to a right estimate of the teaching of a man like Gotama! He was content to let the Piṭakas be the measure of the man who was not to be fitted into monastic formulæ and aspirations. He credited the Teacher of Will, in the Coming-to-be of the Way, with being chiefly the teacher of four texts about Ill. And thus it comes, that the whole significance of the surviving tradition of "becoming", in Buddhist scripture, and about Buddhism in Indian thought, is by him passed over; that the insistence, in those scriptures, on the "stirring up of energy and endeavour", the earnest bidding to Self-reference, to Self-guidance, in a word, all that the figure of the Way really stood for, is, in his "Buddha", left either totally or relatively out of view. Conformably with his seeing in the Founder of Buddhism one who was at once a monk of the new monkdom, and a type of the Indian mind, more contemplative and cognitive than dynamic, he sees in his teaching, a plan of salvation *by knowledge*,[1] and not, as I have tried to show it, a call to the unworded will and choice and valuing, which each man could develop for and in himself in his Becoming, *as he lived.*

Never shall we understand this Man or do him justice till we get rid of the maggot of "Erlösung" from our mind. The agitation that drove him from home as a questing student was no more the positive key-note of his inspired new word than was the Jewish call of the Baptizer to "repent" the key-note of his more inspired disciple's teaching of the fraternal warding of man by man. Not so starved and schematic are the rich and manifold natures of these elect men. They are too genuine, too vivid illustrations in themselves of "becoming" to be that. When they begin their mission they are already a taller plant in growth than those they tell of their new word; but their

[1] Wissen, Erkennen.

growth ceases not when their teaching begins. Object-lessons are they in their earth-life, be it long or short, of that very becoming more which is, if buried, yet at the very heart of their message. A poor after-concept it is which sees in the inspired teacher a man who could no more grow! a man who here and now is finished ! Poorest of after-concepts is it in Buddhism, denying, in the teacher of man's divine Becoming, the truth of that highest attribute in himself. It is only, I repeat, a most unworthy idea of what we try to say by our poor word "becoming", which prevents us from seeing in Gotama, or in any great Helper of men a very type of Godlike *Werden*, or radiant radiating becoming.

We need to learn that neither he nor That on whom mankind can cleave in faith, as to a "rock of ages", is therefore rightly conceived as a stony immobility. We need worthier symbols. The drowning sailor is lifted from his plank on to the great liner, but the ship is not immobile. The tossed shipwrecked one is borne along still, but it is now by the greater mobility, the "goer to joy". We too, and not Sakya only, need worthier symbols, worthier words. Of this I have spoken here, elsewhere, often. Before me is the title of a new book by a German : *Mein Werden und mein Wirken* : how are we to put that into equivalent English ? "My coming-to-be and my making to become ?" awkward it sounds, yet it is in itself the very essence of Gotama's mandate, having in it, as he also had, the will, in man implicit, both to become and to make become ! Are we perhaps therefore a little less blameworthy if we do not get at his meaning, when our more erudite neighbours, and not we, have these fine verbal instruments ? Yet they get at it, as lying just in those splendid terms, *werden* and *wirken*, even less than we here have done. Man, wrote Rhys Davids, is not a being, only a becoming.[1] And yet he got no farther, for he saw in the "Buddhist man" what the scholastic monk saw : only body and mind. He did not see that, whereas "impermanence", with its pseudo-becoming and its passing away, is of body and mind, *werden*, becoming, without passing away, is only of the very man, the "you and me" of whom Gotama, it is said, used to speak.[2]

But there was a blight come over the thought of this his age, similar in this respect to the blight that spread over Sakyan monasticism. We have all but lost sight of that "very man". We scarcely word him save in poetry : "The rank is but the guinea stamp ; the man's a man for a' that." Talking of "stamp", we tend to fall back on its synonym for the very man ; surely, it is

[1] *Early Buddhism*, 56. [2] E.g. *Dīgha*, ii, p. 90.

said, we value a becoming in, a growth of, "character", which is other and more than bodily or mental advance. Yes, we fall back on that, but not as meaning the man, you, me. It is in ironic drollery only, that we say of X: He *is* a character! Worthy of effort is it surely to bring here our poetry into prose, and word by "man" that which in religion we mean by soul or spirit. These are words suggestive of a disembodiment that may be wrong, and even, in case of distress, signals about the body only. We know that there has ever been in India from time immemorial the conception of a World Man from whom proceeded all things, the Puruṣa of the Rig Veda hymn and of the Upanishads. As sacrificed by Deity to Deity he may time and again have been merged in many conceptions of personal gods, of deified men. Yet he survived, and in the birth-time of Sakya had come on earth as the Mahā-purisa of the Piṭaka legends, the Super-man, born to be either world-conqueror ruling righteously, or the world-saviour. We see here India's faith, persistent through ages, in the possibility, the occasional actuality of "man in the more", of man raised to a higher power. Man so rated, in legend, in theory, led to the Founder of Sakya being held as more than man, as super-man, as "deva beyond devas," the title which had perhaps first come into use when the latter chapters of the "Questions of King Milinda" were written, let us say, about the birth time of Jesus. The title is suggestive, for us if not for Buddhists. To be super-deva on and of earth may be credible only to a Buddhist, but there is nothing inherently incredible about it if we rightly conceive our very man, and see in him Wayfarer of the Worlds.

Held in this worth, he, as bending here his will to become the More, not in just body and mind, but in himself, the very man, is seen to be exerting "Werden and Wirken" in life's supreme adventure: the becoming and the ultimate achievement of not the More only, but the Most, the very Man in the uttermost.

In this his call to man, Gotama lacked words that we have; he had words that we lack, or weaken in the using. There was with him the Indian idea of a Man-in-the-Highest associated with the word *purisa*; there was the word becoming, *bhava*, *bhavya* (*bhabba*); there was not the word will. For the last, if we may judge by reverberant Sutta-injunction, he used every available makeshift, groping after new words for new emphasis. His after-men weakened *purisa* to *puggala*, a word without the mighty associations, which in every man but the one Super-man of their cult they sought to evade. And *bhava* they had come to dread, because they saw in it, as did through them

Rhys Davids, only *bhava* of more bodies, more minds.[1] They had lost the man, who, in each new birth, " sows the To Be " in himself. So they dropped from their teaching, and then from their records, everything showing this use of the word in its true, its new value. They fell back on their " ill ", and on *bhava* as a factor in the arising of that ill, and on the stopping of *bhava* as consummation. The tragedy of it lies too deep for words.

[1] The symbol of *bhava* in Central Asian portrayal is a pregnant woman.

XVII

THE TEACHING OF THE FIRST MEN OF SAKYA

Nothing in our problems on Sakya is harder than to distinguish, in such records as we have, what will have been the teaching, in mantra or in talk, of the first few Sakyan missioners, as differing, in matter, in mode, in emphasis, from the teaching which little by little came to take its place. That this change took place is indisputable, albeit it is as yet far from being adequately recognized. There was no fixed wording of any kind to constitute a referendum. There were new views, new ideals growing apace as we have seen, where Sakya was born. And the teachers themselves were no machines, full charged and started to turn out the same theme in the same way; they were full charged it is true, with will and with a central theme: the willed growth of the self or very man evolving That who he really was (as opposed to his merely *being* That), under the figure of the Way. But they themselves grew as they taught, the Sakyamuni not excepted (was he alone to be excepted from a teaching of universal change?), and what they said as older men will have been here and there a "becoming" in that which they had said at first.

But the records as we have them were put into fixed form (yet unwritten) very long after the developments of the first decades of the Sakyan mission had come up and passed by, and all that is left is to seek here and there for a trace of them. We need not utterly despair of finding such traces half obliterated under the thicker spoor of the accumulating utterances, accumulating while growth was still active in the will to record. But we must, in seeking, imitate the man of science referred to above, and bear in mind what it is we have to look for. We have to look for the remains of a teaching, which was not for a world within a world, which was not for a little world of intelligentsia only, which was not for a world of "Protestants", of Nonconformists as such, which was not for the formation of a Set or Party or Society or Sect or Cult, which was not for the formation of a Body or Sangha of *samaṇas*, nor to place these in prestige and worth above the laity as such. Truly ours is no easy task, for our records, if read at the standpoint of their compilers, would lead us to conclude that this last-stated object was precisely the aim of Sakya, its teaching on purely religious themes being more or less incidental to that object.

We must seek under this; we must shovel on one side the teaching which reflects the standpoint of the *samaṇa* or monk: the teaching of the man who looks on life in the world as shipwreck, as walking into fire, as wading in filth, as courting disease. And more yet must be shovelled aside: the teaching which is a worsening of the nature of the man, which piles up negatives about him, as being ultimately only distinguishable as mind, which sees in the "becoming" of further life for him only a result of perverted will, which conceives the consummation of him only as a "going out". And we must see if there remain anything of salvage about this, anything which is in harmony with the gospel figured by the symbol of the Way. Does anything survive which shows man's nature as potentially the Highest, capable of evolving That Which it truly was? Anything which shows him at this or that stage of becoming That? This, I hold, is what we have "to look for", and to lift out, if indeed we find it, from the matter in which it is embedded, as being of the original Sakyan teaching. I am not saying that such fragments will be *all* that the first men taught. I indicate several matters of current interest in which they may be safely assumed to have been interested, and which will have come in varying proportions into their teaching. But these are matters which we should group around their central message, and not suffer to usurp that place.

Now we have in the preceding chapters discussed a few fragments which, for me, do tell of that central message: the words on the Way, on the associating with the Way of the word "to make become", the word on the quest of the Self, the word on the supreme value of *dhamma*, or the inner monition of the Self, the association of the Way, not with this life only, but with a goal, with the "Beyond". Were I to sift the Piṭakas from end to end for an exhaustive winnowing, I should indeed be doing a task that needs doing, but this book makes no claims to be in any respect exhaustive. But there is one feature, a very prominent one in the Suttas, to which I have in past years sought to lure students, one where our survivals may reasonably be expected. This is in the parable, the simile, the object-lesson. On the one hand this is a likely method in missioners' talk; on the other, the Eastern literature is ever prolific in it. It is even held as a valid method of reasoning, and herein is often used to make error seem plausible. A fraction of resemblance is taken as voucher for resemblance in the two wholes which are compared. Where the comparison in the simile is used with clearer vision, the usual Sutta introduction is justified[1]: "Well then, I will make a simile for you, for even by a simile some

[1] E.g. *Majjhima*, No. 21.

wise men discern the object in question." And sometimes there is added : "a simile which is original and spontaneous."

It is a little singular that, so far as I have been able to gather, so little work of cataloguing, analysis and comparison has been done in the similes of literatures. Especially in literatures which are historically obscure, such as is Buddhist literature. Especially also in literatures which are ostensibly based on a gospel message preached to the Many. For in this case we inevitably get figures and parables drawn from scenes and customs and events which strike the eye, which fill the daily life of the people taught. Hence we may get light on the place and the time where the teaching first took place. And to what extent our survey is comprehensive, to that extent are we safeguarded from over-hasty conclusions.

For instance, we open our *Iliad*, and at once we plunge into the colour and sound, the stress and bustle of agitated mass-movements, by the aid of such similes as buzzing bees, wind-waves in the corn, the refrain of roaring breakers, crests of fire running over the slopes. Had we an Index of Homeric similes we might or again we might not conclude, that, as is asserted in one popular Survey of religions, Greek professional bards were mostly as blind as Homer, the similes being mainly sound-pictures. But certainly the equal proportion of sight- and sound-pictures in our opening four does not so far support the opinion.

Be that as it may, I made an Index of Piṭaka similes,[1] and from it learnt a few fairly safe conclusions about the place and time of early Sakyan teaching. One of these centred in the river similes. These were nearly always about Ganges and her tributaries, flowing eastward. This militates against the theory, now perhaps moribund, that either "Buddhism", or the Piṭakas are a purely Sinhalese product. "See how Gangā trends down eastward, slopes eastward, is borne down eastward. If all the people came with spades, think you they could make her flow west?" There are four or five little Gangās in Ceylon —the word means simply goer—but they have compound names, and the only one of any length—a mite beside the Ganges—flows north. Nor would Gangā's feeders have occurred to a teacher of Ceylon : "Just as whatever great rivers there be, such as Gangā, Yamunā Sarabhū, Aciravatī, Mahī, all of them slide and tend to the east... even so does he who makes to become the Way flow and glide and tend towards Nirvana". The Ganges itself is now and then called "sea", and the parable of her bearing down a "great tree-trunk" as a picture

[1] In *JPTS.*, 1907; appendix in 1908. First editions published since make revision desirable, and there are other omissions and errors.

of a young man's many dangers in life is suggestive of a mighty stream, of which the Sutta-Nipāta poet spoke his verse.

> Noisily go the little rills, silent the mighty stream (ver. 720).

I think that if we saw certain early English manuscripts naming the river Forth, and not the Thames in their parables, we should, if in doubt as to their place of origin, hesitate to say this was the Abbey of Westminster. Moreover, the climate in the Piṭakas is not that of tropical Ceylon. The sun's heat and splendour comes, if rarely, into the similes, as when the Sakyan Simeon, Asita, is in a poem said to behold the baby Siddhattha "as the glowing sun after the rains freed from cloud"[1]—this is typical of the sun-figures—but cold nights and days are also mentioned :

> Dost dwell beneath bare skies? Cold are these nights
> And wintry now. See that thou perish not
> With cold foredone. Get thee within thy lodge,
> Thy door well barred.
> (*Theragāthā*, ver. 385.)

The balance is, I grant, in favour of warmth, since the bliss of coolness is a synonym for saintship : "sītibhūta." But the balance of evidence in matters topographical favours the Ganges valley rather than Ceylon. And not a region much to the north of that great watershed. The mountain majesty of the north has its fitting figure in "Himavā pabbatarājā", "the snowy king of the hills," yet is he a mythical world, and the *pabbata*, literally rugged protuberance, figuring in verse and prose, is mainly the "little hills" around Rājagaha, less high than our own highest fells, or other craggy heights.

> Like to a rock that is a monolith
> And trembles never in the wintry blast . . .
>
> E'en as a mountain-crag unshaken stands,
> Sure-based, a muser with illusions gone,
> Like very mountain stands unwavering.
> (*Dham.*, 81 ; *Therag.*, 642, 651, 1000.)

Himavā himself is far away :—

> Like to the snowy peak the good shine far,
> (*Dham.* 304)

and no truly Alpine denizen would have seen just rain as causing the spate here described :—

"Even as when in the hills above the deva rains, so that the waters according to their watershed flow down and fill the hill nullahs and

[1] *Sutta-Nipāta*, ver. 687.

these fill the becks and these fill the rivers, and these fill the ocean, so in the believing disciple, . . . do these things flow on, bearing him beyond toward the cleansing from all that poisons." Who, say, at Aosta in late June, when the placid Dora becomes a raging grey torrent, would so word the cause?

Evidence, too, might, by one who knows better than I, be drawn from the plants in the similes. Their authors are, as to place and time, between the scarcity of reference to the lotus in the older literature and the plenitude in mediæval books. So also is the fan-palm (*tāla*) about them, but not apparently the cocoa-nut palm. About them too was the sāl tree and the *karèr*,[1] but I find no trace of conifers.

Of beasts too, apart from elephant and buffalo, those of the homestead are as with us, from cow-byre and horse-stable to poultry and pigs. But the camel is all but entirely absent; bear, panther, and tiger hardly come in at all, and the lion, albeit a frequent figure :—

> As to the call of distant lions' roar
> Resounding from the hollow of the hill
> List to the psalms of them whose selves were trained
> Telling us messages anent themselves . . .
>
> (*Theragāthā*: opening verses)

is usually, like the Himâlayas, a mythical figure, as of olden memories.

"The lion, king of the beasts, at eventide comes forth from his lair . . . stretches himself . . . surveys the four quarters, utters thrice his lion-roar . . . sallies forth on his round . . . and beasts hearing fall a-quaking and hide themselves . . ."[2] It seems a graphic picture, but I mistrust the setting-out roar as unlikely to facilitate good hunting. But I may be wrong; it is the almost invariable "king of the beasts" which suggests the mythical. Anyway the "mṛiga" as hunted by kshatriya is portrayed as deer, not lion, let alone tiger. Equally mythical perhaps is the rare figure of the rhinoceros,[3] to whom as a lone wild beast the true recluse should in lone faring be like. The monkey plays a small but important part in the similes. It stands for the mind regarded from the preacher's point of view: acquisitive, inquisitive, inconstant.

> Unsteady is the mind as any jigging ape[4];

and as coming thereby to disaster by hunter's guile and snare of sticky bait, after the fashion of the well-known "Brer Rabbit" of negro story.[5]

[1] *Pss. of the Brethren*, p. 363. [2] *Saṃyutta*, iii, 84.
[3] *Sutta-Nipāta*, Vagga ii.
[4] *Theragāthā*, ver. 1111; *Sutta-Nipāta*, ver. 791; *Saṃyutta*, ii, 95.
[5] Ibid., v, 148.

But it is naturally of the human environment of the authors of the literature that the parables and so forth tell us most. We see that the life of the town, in the Suttas, does not bulk nearly so large as that of the country. These people are living mainly in villages, with their surrounding communal field (*khetta*) of rice and grain of various kinds, their cattle pastures beyond, with a communal herdsman warding the cattle from wild beast, or from trespassing on corn, or when fording streams, and with the uncleared jungle, the *kantāra* or *gahana*, stretching away in this or that direction, never, it may be, very far off: a favourite symbol of life's snares or of uncandid thinking. And as to the field culture and the cattle, we notice not only the communal use of diverting the running streams, this day for A's field-irrigation, that day for B's, as may be seen in Alpine community-culture, but also two things: the brahman at his ploughing is in no way incurring the stricture on land-tilling for brahmans of the "Laws of Manu"; and in the word "go-ghātako", cattle-butcher, the similes know of no *tabu* on beef.

If we follow our similes into the village, or the rarer city, we find a host of parables and metaphors: the gates compared, as in our Bunyan, to the avenues of sense, the bazars and workshops, where the wheelwright is planing knobs and blemishes out of his tyres, the fletcher is moulding his arrowpoints; the goldsmith is applying the ordeal of fire to his precious metal; the potter, with oven, moulds in two parts and brittle wares is here (I have not noticed his wheel in the Piṭakas); and so are ivory-workers, smiths, dyers, painters, house-builders, coopers, leather-dressers, and florists. The arts are not strongly represented in simile, but the fresco-painter's human figures symbolize a man's deeds as creating his own after-life; and the lute comes in both as typical of seductive sense-lure, and also as suggestive, in the tuning, of due measure needed in adjusted tension of what we might call will, and which the record calls effort put forth.

Along the streets, the wheel of the cart follows the beast's hoofs like dogging retribution; the well-trained elephant is symbol of self-mastery; the thorough-bred horse too, quivering at the very shadow of the whip.[1] The chariot of the Right passes along the Straight Road to the land of No-Fear, its syce of right vision running on before.[2] And the king's seven relief posting chariots, in readiness for a journey where the will to special effort is called for,[3] would have been valid for us but a little over a century ago.

[1] *Saṃyutta*, i, 7; *Dhani*, 143. [2] Above, p. 150.
[3] *Majjhima*, No. 23.

Soldiers in armour marching past suggest the armour of righteousness [1] as later to St. Paul. And the evil-doer whom they, "the king's men," hale before the king, is not man's only enemy who can "break through and steal ".[2]

Nor are the children left out, playing then as now with sand-castles, jealously guarding what "is mine ", and then knocking it down with equal zest a moment later [3] : it is a monkish simile in its application and forced the application of self-analysis killing desire. To the baby's nurse the Founder is shown likening himself, warding his new disciples even with seeming severity, as a nurse to extract a choking bit of stick will take the babe's head in her left hand and crooking her right finger will hook out the stick even if blood flow therewith.[4]

The imagery grouped about the women busied round the hearth and house reveals a patriarchal state of society, with all the standpoints implied therein. The disciple diffident in faith is compared to the newly-wed daughter-in-law's nervousness on entering her father-in-law's household. The housewife testing with finger and thumb the rice she is boiling in a sampling ladle is said to have a two-finger intelligence, in common with her sisters. And the ways of women are likened, for caprice, crookedness, wantonness, seductive power, and all the rest, to the path of a fish in the sea, the bends of the river, a public house, or highway, to fire and flood, to the cat, and other less canny beasts. As mother, it is true, she is in another category, as we might expect: she too with the father, and the teachers of old is Deity, Brahmā [5] ; she is the ideal of compassion.[6] But as wife also it would seem to be other than a monk who speaks of her as "comrade supreme ",[7] and as "the good friend dwelling in the house ",[8] "taking compassion upon her husband." [9]

The cat, the mouse, the dog are also pressed into service, and in the house, the fire, the pots, the mirrors, and the clothes-chest. The last named is of special interest in a remark ascribed to Sāriputta : that a man's mastery over the mind is as a king able to have selected, at will from his wardrobe the suit he chooses.[10] The converging rafters of the house serve to illustrate old age ; the house top terrace the retrospect won of happy survival after death ; and the here and the hereafter are likened to two houses of the life in both of which the man who has eyes to see is aware.[11]

[1] *Saṃyutta*, v, 6 ; *Therag.*, 543.
[2] *Khuddakapāṭha*, viii.
[3] *Saṃyutta*, iii, 190.
[4] *Anguttara*, iii, 6.
[5] *Anguttara*, i, 132 ; cf. Taitt. Up. 1, 11.
[6] *Sutta-Nipāta*, Mettā Sutta.
[7] *Saṃyutta*, i, 37.
[8] Ibid.
[9] *Dīgha*, No. 21.
[10] *Majjhima*, i, 215 ; *Saṃyutta*, v, 71.
[11] *Majjh.* i, 81 ; 76 ; 279.

It is very possible that in many cases, such similes, drawn from daily life, were spoken, not by way of mental images, but as what our kinder-gartens call object-lessons. The parable was itself a thing handled, shown, altered. Jesus used this method with immortal effect: "Give me a penny. Whose is the image and superscription?" And again, "he took a little child and set him in the midst: . . . except ye become as little children . . ." There is no object-parable in the Suttas so winning in truth and loveliness as this, but one, which would suggest a young hearer, was used also with immortal effect. The object-lesson, namely, given to Rāhula by his father, is still to be seen in the rock edicts of Asoka as the saying of the Laghulovada (Rāhul'ovāda), "on lying speech by the Bhagavā Buddha," in the Calcutta-Bairat inscription. In the Sutta so-called the son has brought water for foot-bathing to the father, who thereafter pours most away. "See, Rāhula, the little water (left)"; pours the rest away: "See, all is gone"; upsets the pan: "see how topsy-turvy"; shows the empty pan: "see how empty; see how little, how thrown away, how empty is the holy life of those who have no shame in consciously lying!"[1] There are also the object-lessons of pebbles or leaves taken in the hand, or dust on the finger-nail to suggest violent contrasts with greater wholes[2]; and the hand held up and waved to suggest the freely willing agent who is not the toady or otherwise mentally captive.[3] Panthaka's towel is another such, though less advertized.[4] We have considered Panthaka, snubbed as a dull boy by fellow-monks, but cherished by Gotama, who discerned his psychic gift:—

> Who laid his hand upon my head and took
> My arm and to the garden led me back
> And in compassion to me gave
> A napkin for the feet and bade me thus:
> Fix now your mind on this clean thing, the while
> Well concentrated you do sit apart.

And perhaps the best known object-lesson is that of the "mustard-seed" for which the inconsolable Kisā-Gotamī bearing about the body of her little child was to ask at any house where no man had died, to serve as medicine for a miracle-cure. We have the story solely from the Commentaries,[5] but it may be a memory that is at least partly true. The lesson drawn from her quest by the mother is not

[1] *Majjhima*, No. 61. [2] *Saṃyutta*, v, 437; 460, etc.
[3] Ibid., ii, 198. [4] *Therag.*, Cūḷa-Panthaka, see Chap. XII.
[5] *Dhammapada Comy.* on ver. 47, 287; *Therīgāthā Comy.* on No. lxiii.

that conveyed in terms of modern human sodality by Edwin Arnold's poem: "the whole wide world weeps with you." European Buddhists have gladly adopted it, and to some extent Ceylon has also. The *orthodox* solatium is, that everything, not one's own child's body only, being impermanent, the more one loves the more one will suffer. And hence, said monasticism, love not, if you would not suffer. And so, adds the commentary, "she stiffened her mind from the softness of love." So falsely rings the bigger note of to-day when struck with that of Eastern monasticism. The latter is not therefore wholly unworthy. Somehow the drug of self-pity had to be eliminated.

It is impossible in this passing reference to give more than a fragmentary survey. I included upwards of 600 parables and other forms of simile in my Index and Supplement, and still it is not exhaustive, even apart from Piṭaka books at the time inedited. The subject awaits better treatment and deserves it, for thereby may both knowledge and sympathy grow. There is no adequate sympathy in the study of any scriptures apart from their similes. These are like ancient trees round which the creepers of religious sentiment, deep, old, very moving, have twined themselves. And we cannot transplant these old trees into the love and adoration and aspiration of another creed. Or at most in some cases only, and even in these . . . The sun figures in Sakyan and Christian similes, but the tender feeling of fostering in the Jesus-word: "for he maketh the sun to shine upon the just and the unjust" finds no echo under the less pitiful sun of India. The Sakyan has recourse to the patient tolerance of earth, water, fire. It is Bunyan rather than the Gospels which have made the way of life and the river of death mighty pictures for the English Christian, pictures which for the Sakyan are so fundamentally important. But if we were to speak of the Wheel symbol (let alone the later simile of the Three Gems) to a Christian, we stir no responsive throb; as little should we do so in the Buddhist by speaking of the Lamb, or of the winged messengers. So estranging have been the separate avenues made by the growth of figurative language. So impossible is it for never so ardent a con- or pervert who has been brought up an earnest Christian to become genuinely a Buddhist, or the converse. A learned and sympathetic American spent years in travel along the Eastward path pursued in history by Buddhism[1] to try to find out "what it feels like to be a Buddhist." I venture to think this is impossible. There is not for the sympathizer the traditional background which will have told upon any Buddhist whose upbringing has been worthy of the name. It is none the less

[1] *The Pilgrimage of Buddhism*, by James B. Pratt.

well to know something about such a background, analogous to that of Islam and Christianity, and to be able to draw comparisons.[1]

I come to the special comparison pertinent to the object of this book. We have to ask, of Piṭaka parables and other similes, which, if any of them, are, I cannot alas ! say positively, but *likely* to have been actually uttered by the first men of the Sakyas ? which are more likely to have been first used by Sakyan teachers of a later date ? And I suggest the following rough guide.

If the conception put forward in these pages of the original Sakyan message be accepted, then will also those similes be accepted as early, which are in line with, and illustrations of the nature of that message. And if the hypothesis as to the essential nature of the "new word" in a world-gospel, put forward in an early chapter, be valid, then are there some similes which, as illustrating a standpoint *adverse* to that new word, will not have been uttered by the first men, who stood so close to the heart of the mandate. Here too exhaustive survey is impossible, but a few typical instances should be useful.

There is first and foremost the idea that man, as to his nature and in his life, is in a state of becoming, that is, not merely of change or of change negatively conceived as transience, but of *becoming*, if he be walking "by *dhamma*", (*dhammena*), *more* than he was before. He is, as man, not merely "being" (*sat*). To illustrate this, I see chief of all of course the way or road or course (*magga* ; *añjana*, *yāna*, *patipadā*), implying that which is its chief interest, its very cause : *the wayfarer*. With this we may associate the stream, once equated with way ("What is it we hear called 'stream'? Just this Ariyan Way . . ."[2]), and the chariot, when used, as it is in the quotation given already (p. 317), as the man or woman wayfaring to the goal (not, I need hardly say, as it is misused in false analogy by the nun Vajirā, whereof more in a later chapter). A spirited simile too of a man's stages in becoming or growth is that of the relays of chariots arranged for the king's forced rate of travel (*Majjhima*, No. xxiv). It is ascribed to Puṇṇa, when in conversation with Sāriputta, and is for me very suggestive of a genuine memory, albeit somewhat dressed up with scholastic terms, and adorned with too much mutual salaaming.

Then there is that symbol of the chariot's progress, the Wheel, nearest in importance for Buddhist tradition to the cross for that of Christianity, the wheel which stands for the Way, for wayfaring, for the wayfarer, but which in legend has got mixed up with the

[1] Dr. Burlingame has published a work on "Buddhist Parables".
[2] *Saṃyutta*, v, 347.

spread of a cult, and which by monasticism got perverted into that which revolves without progress, an idea in the air, forsooth, and not on solid ground: the wheel of rebirth severed from the faith in becoming. With these we must also associate the parable of the raft, a figure to which the Suttas themselves refer. It is so indicative of a gospel of becoming that it may be told as it stands.

"I will teach you *dhamma* by the parable of the raft. Just as if a man on a journey should come to a great water, the hither shore whereof were full of perils, the further shore whereof were the haven whence comes no fear, and he had no boat for crossing nor any ford. And he were to think: What shall I do now? What if I were to make me a raft of brushwood and rushes and boughs, and were to launch it paddling with arms and legs? And so he did and so he crossed. And coming ashore would he then think: Great service to me has been this raft. I will carry it along on my back? Nay, for he would think: Great service to me this raft has been. Now can I sink it, or leave it high and dry. And so, unencumbered, he were to go on his way. Even so do you leave behind what is *dhamma*, let alone what is not *-dhamma*."[1]

The notable "moral" is more worthily appreciated in the words of St. Paul: "Let us cease to speak of first principles and fare on unto perfection." The Pali is most unusual in form and suggests a corrupt reading, but here is not fit opportunity to discuss it.[2] The meaning is not on that account obscure. The *dhamma*-monition needed by the child, by the beginner, by the learner at an early stage becomes outgrown, and may be, *qua* specific monition, laid aside. Its message has been wrought up into the man's partially achieved becoming. He needs, he gets further monition, but the raft-stage of these he has left behind. It is a raft-stage that is explicitly referred to later on in the same book of Suttas.[3] A disciple is being reproved, that he saw the mind as the man, namely as that who "runs on, fares on"—it is the usual phrase—from life to life. This may well have been a *caveat* to the first men, of the nature of the Second Utterance.[4] And the clinging to the mind (*viññāṇa*) as the "speaker, the experiencer who faring on is here and there to feel the results of deeds good and bad" is there stated to be incompatible with the having learnt the lesson of putting aside the raft.

This Sutta has been woefully misconstrued, not to say mis-

[1] *Majjhima*, i, No. 22.

[2] i.e. in using *dhammā* for what should be *dhammo*, and in the curious term *a-dhammā*. Dictionary editors have overlooked this. Trenckner's vv. ll. note suggests uncertainty in recensions.

[3] *Majjhima*, No. 38.

[4] Above, Chap. X.

constructed by Piṭaka editors, let alone modern writers,[1] but its *application* of the raft-parable, together with the parable itself, is for me of the original stock of teachings. The man, in the first place is not a static being, but in process of becoming ; the man, in the second place, is not, in becoming, just mind ; he is he.

To me the raft-parable, as told and then as further applied in the Majjhima-Nikāya, is in my judgment of the original teaching. But if we turn to the same parable as told in the group of parables in the Sense-sphere Collection of the Saṃyutta-Nikāya, we see that the whole pith and point of the earlier symbolism has been blurred, lost. The " Snake " Sutta (xxxv, iv, 5, 197) tells of the world-wayfaring of many terrors of the average Everyman, and how finally, coming to the great water he builds him a raft, in the same wording as in the Majjhima. But the raft-journey is the one effective and final stage "the Ariyan eightfold way", which lands him, a perfected "brahman ", i.e. saint, in the great Beyond of nirvana. It is no intermediate means to be discarded for a better means of progress ; the man is now at the end, the gone-out, the finish so far as any teaching showed, of both " being " and " becoming ". Here we have no weaving of the Way into Everyman's life in the world, as the right choosing now in this, now in that crisis of will and conduct. We have first the man-in-the-life-and-work-of-the-world ; then we have the cutting himself adrift from that life, and then only, the entering upon the Way and its (relatively speedy and simple) termination.

This finality about the raft-business as achieving a final crossing is also to be seen in perhaps the purest expression of recluse-ideals : the poems of the Sutta-Nipāta (ver. 21) :—

> Bound, wellwrought, was the raft, said Bhagavā,
> Crossed, gone beyond, I could subdue the flood ;
> No further need for raft doth now arise . . .

And in that late compilation of materials early and late, the Book of the Passing Away, we find the raft no longer used to illustrate even a stage in the Way, but as contrasted with the superior method of salvation used by the wise :—

> They who to cross the mighty stream evade the swamps,
> Bind them a raft ; crossed over are the wise.

Here again is the way of the layman and the short-cut assumed as the way of the *samaṇa* held up in contrast. In other words we are, in these latter applications of the raft simile, listening not to Gotama and his men, but to the monk of the monks' world.

[1] Myself included, in *Buddhism*.

I turn to a very different picture, yet to one in which we see the same pre-occupation with the fact, the mystery, the all-importance of Becoming : the parable of the hen and her eggs. The sublimity in the mother-yearning of the Saviour of men over the stubborn city : "How often would I have gathered thee, O Jerusalem! . . ." exalts the homely metaphor of the anxious little bird to its own height. In the Sutta similes we find her at an earlier stage of her motherly cares, and concerning a matter where the emphasis is less poignant, and is more on the very fact of the coming-to-be. It was of sufficient salience to be repeated four times in three of the Four Nikāyas :—

"Let a man, if he have done his utmost in right training, not be anxious as to the result. He will surely come forth to the light in safety. Even as a hen who has brooded over duly and sat herself round her dozen eggs, may yearn : 'O that my little chicks may break open the egg-shell . . . and come forth into the light in safety!' Yet all the while those little chicks are sure to do so. Even so, etc."

The parable is given also in three of the passages in the case of a not coming to be where the man "has not done his utmost". It is for the rest much wrapped up in monastic admonition, yet in the passage I quote, the Sutta of the Fallows of the mind (Majjh. 16), the subject is introduced with the phrase : "he will surely not . . he surely will, attain to growth, development, abundance,"—words closely connected in the original with organic life—which is echoed in so many Suttas. And more : there is the significant word, *bhabbo*, the Vedic *bhavya*, here (and elsewhere) used : "the man-who-may-become." The word may well have lost its early force, nor is that force well brought out in translations. It is rendered as able to, capable of, fit for. But this for original Sakya is not enough ; the renderings are too loose, too free ; we have in *bhavya* the man who was strongly advancing in coming-to-be ; the will-full man ; the man very much awake and alive as to the very man, not just in body or mind.

Then there is the parable of the judas tree (or kiṃsuka), illustrating differing needs, differing values, differing attainments in growth at different seasons. It is analogous to the raft as a temporary need ; it is much beworded with scholastic formulas, but it may well be of the true original sayings, and is all the more to be noted, in that few parables of things so patently "becoming" as the plant have survived. It is a far cry in time and in changed views to Buddhaghosa, yet it is precisely he who reminds us of the plant tradition in teaching,[1] when trying to explain his paralogism of survival without the man to survive, and with the connection between the Way and Becoming practically lost.

[1] *Visuddhi-Magga*, xvii, p. 555 ; *Buddhism*, p. 145.

The most notable association with organic growing is the parable of the Jeta Wood[1]; Here the parable as it has come down to us has this in common with the Second Utterance: the central point in both is left unsaid. I mean that, in reminding hearers that the faggots borne away to be firewood were as body and mind, it was not necessary to say that the wood was still there, as the "man" was still there, becoming, even as the wood went on growing. Nevertheless, it may be that we have here some later editing with which I will deal later.

Another parable which has perhaps undergone similar treatment, and which has, in context and in point, much that is akin to that of the judas tree, is that of the border city. Here is a fortified six-gated city (five senses and *manas*) with a wary gatekeeper, or rather announcer: (awareness inner and outer), and swift chariots bringing a "true word" from east, from west, from north: the three avenues from without for India. All are submitted to the lord of the city sitting at the crossroads, i.e. the chief square.[1] So by this message and by that does the man grow.

Here we have, I believe, another ancient saying of the true old stock. The thing about it which is later and not true seems to me to be the interpretation. The swift messengers are called calm and insight, terms which albeit mentioned in the *mātikās* of the Anguttara are only dwelt upon in later books. And the lord of the city is mind, *viññāṇa*, the mind where we ought to have found the man, the self. Mind has already been accounted for under the "six gates". More of this too later. Clearly there has been editing, and not able editing at that. We have only to glance a little further at the jumble of application in the "poaching cow parable" and that of the lute, where the castigation of sense-desires is merged without distinction into the man as not to be found in his body or mind.

I come to a parable which has for me now a meaning transformed from that which it seemed to bear many years ago. This is the figure in one Sutta only (in the Second Book of the Saṃyutta) entitled "Nagara", the City. Gotama is represented as telling, at Sāvatthī, the story of his woe over the world's obsession by disease, age, and dying, and how light came to him in discerning that the man could be, nay, was the cause in his own becoming.

"At that thought about things not taught before there arose in me vision, knowledge, *paññā*, wisdom, light. Just as if a man faring through the forest, through the great wood should see an ancient way, an ancient road, traversed by men of former days. And he were to go along it, and going along it he should see an ancient city, an ancient

[1] *Majjhima*, i, pp. 104, 357; *Saṃyutta*, iii, 153; *Anguttara*, iv, 125.

princely domain, wherein dwelt men of old, having gardens, groves, pools, foundations of walls, a goodly spot. And that man were to bring word to the raja . . . Pardon, sir, know this : such and such have I seen . . . Lord, restore that city . . . Even so have I seen an ancient way, an ancient road traversed by the rightly enlightened ones of old. And what is that way ? . . . Just this Ariyan Way . . . "[1]

In the translation of this Book of the Saṃyutta, I, a little over mid-way between the earlier interpretation alluded to and what I now hold to be true, wrote in my *Buddhism* (p. 33) : "This beautiful Sutta which has the stamp of an *ipse dixit* stress . . . for a special purpose was held to lie on the teacher showing in it, that he was not unique, but in a series of teachers." And I likened the statement to words by Jesus and by Confucius. Six years later I saw, in the Sutta as a whole, stress laid on the antiquity of the moral instinct, the " ought ", the Way-law in human nature, shown by great teachers. I was feeling out after *dhamma* here better than before ; there was, I hope, some " becoming " shown, but at this later day I trust that where I have come-to-be is better, is truer yet.

The question here is neither of a Buddha-succession, nor of *dhamma* conceived as the dubious word instinct. *Dhamma* is for me that Alpha whereof the simile of ancient city in ruins is not fit. The Founder may, or may not have been speaking as the Sutta records. It seems quite probable that he may have. But in those musings on the mandate, urging him, travailing in him for birth, it was the nature and life of man that was occupying him. It was a renascent word concerning this that he had to utter. It was the ideas about the man and the Way of him that needed building up. These were the things that needed re-discovering. And for all the wordy glosses about cause as conceived in monkish formula and the Way in its eightfold dress, I believe we have here a true parable of the first men.

Of cardinal importance in this rediscovering of the Man and the Way of him was the new word of Sakya, emphasizing a raising the standard of conduct here, as necessary to salvation hereafter. The life must be in keeping with the prayer. The Tevijja Suttanta (Dīgha, xiii) is a talk with young brahmans, showing no dissent from their main beliefs, but making of this life a preparation for qualifying to join the company of a better moral world after death. Only in this way would there be consistency in invoking the warding of them here by that world. Now the notable simile in that talk lifts this into high relief, and is for me therefore very genuine : " As well might a man stand on the hither bank of this river Achiravatī and think to cross

[1] *Saṃyutta*, ii, 103.

over, were he either to chain himself here, or lie down and sleep, or keep calling, 'Come, O Beyond from the Beyond!'" Nay, but he must be up and doing, ridding himself of all that disqualifies him from being fit for admission yonder. Do we not see here how the Sakyan mission was no anti-brahman attack, but the building up where was a weak spot in the current teaching: the need to work for the Becoming-more in the man who potentially was the very Most?

Significantly old too for me is Sāriputta's parable of the raja and his wardrobe (*dussa-kāraṇḍaka*). In the charming Greater Gosinga Wood Sutta, where the first men are enjoying its moonlit glory, they, each of them, declare how the "man" might enhance it. (The text has "almsman", monk, but it is only one among them whose affirmation is narrow enough to fit that: Kassapa.) It is Sāriputta who has started the talk: "Fair is the wood in the clear moonlight, with the sāl-trees blossom-laden, with heaven's perfumes methinks wafted around! What think you, Ānanda?" And Sāriputta is the last to state his opinion:

"Take a man who is master of the mind, and is not under its mastery . . . It is as if an eminent man, with a wardrobe filled with clothes of divers colours, were in the morning to don the pair of robes he were to desire for early wear; at noon to don the pair he might desire then; in the evening were to don the pair he might desire then. By such a man were Gosinga made beautiful."

(The translator in *Further Dialogues* has here, I regret to see, been misleading, just where it is important, in this matter of early Sakyan ideas, to use utmost care. The telling is in Pali of the simplest description and with a slender vocabulary. The English translation is how an Englishman might now tell it. But there is *no word* in Pali for "choose" or for "select", else had they been used. "Don" is *pārupeyya*, lit. "to wrap round"; "desire" is *ākankhati*.)

Sāriputta is again associated with this parable in the Saṃyutta-Nikāya (v, 71).

Why do I think we have here an early saying? Because it is not a theme which would occur to a man of Sāriputta's culture to say, on such an occasion, *if for him* the man was merged in, was to be sought in, the mind. He might have used it in talking as teacher to the Many, the less cultured, the young, but not here to the elect few. The Sānkhyan teaching, as I have indicated, was distinguishing the man (*purusa*, *ātman*) from the mind much more clearly than ever before, and that little company would know this. But in expecting appreciation of his statement from that company, Sāriputta evidently held that the man was both very real, and also was That-who-mattered; the owner, the desirer, the don-ner; as we should now say: the chooser, the selector. The mind was for him the outward going self-expression of the man, even as were the robes.

I have referred to the many similes drawn from the many forms of human arts and crafts, such as any walk through the village, or city streets, or along the field or river, or through a wood brought to view. I am ready to admit such similes as for the most part likely to be original talk of the first men. This is mainly because I do not see them as monks vocationally, but as in the first place missioners to the Many; because I do not see them as world-forsakers, recluses, world-work-shirkers in their teaching, but as eager to help men to be better workers. They would be interested in men as workers; they would know them better as such. I quoted long ago with approval Edwin Arnold's lines in this connection:—

> Radiant in heavenly pity, lost in care
> For those he knew not save as fellow-lives.[1]

I still hold that the first men's appeal and mandate was to the very man in each man, nay, I hold it much more decidedly than I did. But I believe that the very man was in each case better "got at" by way of a knowledge of the man's life. So perhaps was Nanda the communal cowherd better revealed in his unconscientious impulsiveness to the Founder, as he halted while taking his cows home, than when not engaged with his duties:—

The parable finished, Nanda who has been listening breaks in: "Master! not one of those obstacles shall stay my log floating down-stream[2] . . . May I be ordained in your Order?" "Well, Nanda, hand over your cows to their owners." "Master, they will go home alright; they are crazy for their calves". "Do you hand over your cows to their owners . . . and then we will have a talk about these things." I was reminded of this when I heard a sagacious woman say (an officer in the "Rangers"): "I would much rather see the girl out of uniform at her work; I know much more about her then".

Especially do I see in similes of constructive activities pictures the first men will have used. Here is one out of many:—

> The conduit-makers lead the stream,
> Fletchers coerce the arrowshaft,
> The joiners mould the wooden plank,
> The self: 'tis that the pious tame.

This verse occurs twice in Dhammapada, twice in the Theragāthā. Now one of the disciples who is named as composer, is by the Commentary described as lacking in concentration, and as noticing, as he

[1] Light of Asia ("-men" had been better). [2] Above, p. 314.

walked, the concentrated industry of craftsmen and how they made things come to be. In the Dhammapada it is a little boy-monk whom Sāriputta takes for a walk and responds to the impression the seeing of effective work makes on the child's intelligence. The repetition in each book is merely the same verse and a different version of the same story respectively. The Comments have become monastically distorted, yet is the idea of the man being able to make himself become a "more" not wholly lost, even though in the former case the moral drawn is more complete ignoring the world of men, and in the other, the greater concept of "becoming" is shrivelled into a "taming".

I am not claiming for a moment that all or even any of these many similes were put into words for the first time in India, or elsewhere by the men of Sakya early or late. It is of course the application, the choice of them with which we are concerned. It is possible, that in cases where there was a borrowing, the loan was taken unawares. But it is also possible that the Sakyan teachers may have borrowed deliberately. If they did not admit the debt, that after all was the ancient way. There is, for instance, a trio of very splendid figures, occurring only in the Majjhima, which I incline to think were borrowed, and knowingly borrowed. The probably involuntary lenders will have been the man (a brahman) and his disciples who taught the little gospel of willing one's own amity pity, gladness, poise to another man who was lacking in one or the other. These efforts in telepathy I have dealt with above, and they appear as an outcrop in the Pali records, not belonging to the Sakyan gospel. The similes are as follows :—

"Men may use manifold speech to you, rough or smooth, kind or cruel. But you towards them have thus to hold your thought : we will not let our mind be disturbed, nor evil sound escape our lips ; kind and compassionate will we abide, our mind affectionate, free from secret malice. And any such man will we irradiate with mind of amity, and going beyond him, we will . . . irradiate the whole world with mind of amity, broad, deep, unbounded. As a man who with spade and basket sought to dig up and remove the whole earth and could not, for deep and immeasurable is the earth . . . or who came with paints to paint over the whole of space . . . but formless and invisible is space . . . or who came with a torch to dry up great Ganges . . . but deep and boundless is Ganges, so do you say : we will irradiate the whole world with a mind like the earth, like the sky, like Ganges."[1]

The sweep of this mind-play leaves our poet Heine, with his

[1] *Majjhima*, No. 21 ; No. 28.

Norse fir, his Vesuvius crater and his sky, writing "Agnes, ich liebe dich!" some way behind. We get near it in the elemental tolerance I have already mentioned, but it is nowhere else approached. There is a fourth figure, the perfectly dressed hide, but it is bathos after the three, and may well be a sweeping in from some other record. Once more, there is at the conclusion the simile of the Saw, which we find referred to as a known Saying: that the monk is to be non-resistant, even if men would saw him asunder. We do not read of martyrs in Sakya, and it is likely to have been a hyperbole used in the days when to become a monk brought a man some abuse, and he was eager to profess himself undaunted. Our own saying "I will see myself shot first" is such a hyperbole.

Lastly, it may well be that the rank and traditions of "Gotama the Man", as well as of his kindred who followed him, not to mention disciples such as Kappina raja, may have led to a certain predilection for similes drawn from things familiar to such men. I refer to the chariot and horse, the elephant and archery, to armour and the fight, to the raja giving orders, to sword and turban. So impressive will these have been to an Indian that at a later date we find the author of the *Milinda Questions* considering a kshatriya's insignia good evidence that, even in the absence of him, he had been [1]: *fuit Ilium*! It does not, I confess, take us far; later monks may well have been of kshatriya rank and used such parables; we will only go so far as to say that such similes are not to be ruled out from first men's talk.

Certain similes there are, however, which I should be inclined to hold *are* ruled out from that talk. Herein I suggest, knowing that many will differ; I suggest, that we first listen to a collective expression of such similes. This is from the last poem in the Nuns' Anthology—in its way a collection unique in any literature. It bears the stamp of late, i.e. the stamp of probably written work and not that of an ancient record committed when orally old to writing. Sumedhā, a fictitious princess, has, like young Catherine of Siena, herself cut off her hair, dropped the tresses before her prospective bridegroom, and is insisting that she be suffered to leave the world:—

> To him thus Sumedhā, for whom desires
> Of sensuous love were worthless, nor availed
> To lead astray, made answer: "O set not
> The heart's affections on this sensuous love.
> See all the peril, the satiety of sense.
>
> . . . .

[1] p. 207.

Nay, an the rain-god rained all seven kinds
Of gems till earth and heaven were full, still would
The senses crave and men insatiate die.
" Like the sharp blades of swords are sense-desires";
" Like the poised heads of snakes prepared to dart";
" Like blazing torches" and " like bare gnawn bones . . ."

. . . .

" As fruit that brings the climber to a fall"
Are sense-desires; evil " as lumps of flesh
That greedy birds one from the other snatch";
" As cheating dreams"; " as borrowed goods" reclaimed.
" As spears and javelins" are desires of sense,
" A pestilence, a boil, and bane and bale,"
" A furnace of live coals," the " root of bane",
Murderous and the source of harrowing dread.

. . . .

Call ye to mind how it was said that " tears"
And milk and blood flow on world without end.
And bear in mind " that tumulus of bones
By creatures piled who wander through the worlds."
Remember " the four oceans" as compared
With all the flow of tears and milk and blood.
Remember " the great cairn of one man's bones
From one æon alone equal to Vipula".
And how " great India would not suffice
To furnish little tallyballs of mould,
Wherewith to number all the ancestors
Of one's own round of life world without end."
Remember how " the little squares of straws
And boughs and twigs could ne'er suffice
As tallies for one's sires world without end."
Remember how the parable was told
Of " purblind turtle in the Eastern Seas,
Or other oceans, once as time goes by
Thrusting his head through hole of drifting yoke":
So rare as this the chance of human birth.
Remember too the " body-parable";
" The lump of froth," of " spittle without core",
Drifting . . .
Remember what was said of " crocodiles",
And what those perils meant for us.

. . . .

" Him will straw torches burn who holds them long
and lets not go": so in the parable . . .

. . . .

Cast not away, because of some vain joy
Of sense, the vaster happiness sublime,
Lest " like the finny carp thou gulp the hook,
Only to find thyself for that foredone ".
Tame thou thyself in sense-desires, nor let
Thyself be bound by them as is " a dog
Bound by a chain ", else will they do forsooth
With thee as hungry pariahs with that dog.[1]

Here we have on the one hand the world-shy recluse's ascetic shudder over any, even healthy enjoyment by way of sense, and on the other, the specifically Indian recluse's refusal to see, in life indefinitely prolonged by rebirth, the indefinitely many opportunities needed for ever further " becoming ", growth, development. It is the outlook of tired vision, which is dull of imagination and fails to grasp what it means to be reborn anew, with youth and energy as fresh as in Eden, and with who knows what more added in the will to be put forth by the man who has become the more, with as it were a brand-new battery wherewith to express himself? If it be not so with him, let him not blame the fresh opportunity.

The fault, dear Brutus, lies not in our stars,
But in ourselves, that we are underlings.

But it is just the fresh opportunity which the outlook of the monk held as an undesirable and fearsome future. The idea underlying his own Jātakas, the idea of the evolution of a Bodhisat, or Buddha-to-be ought to have taught him better—might have taught him, had he understood better, that not a Bodhisat only, but every man and woman underwent that evolution.

Now every one of the similes and parables cited in Sumedhā's verses are easily to be traced in the Suttas. She presents a relatively complete list of such baleful figures, such as suggests either assiduous note-taking or just memorizing when listening to her instructors, monk or nun, or that she had access to some Mātikā or " table " of such tropes drawn up, say, at Patna, in her day the Rome of the Sangha. In either case we must conclude that such similes were the samples mainly in use for and by monk and nun in the instruction given, as according to Vinaya and Sutta it was regularly given in the viharas. If it be said that for other poems Sumedhā may have used the similes of " becoming " sampled above, the fact remains, none the less, that the one poem which survives as hers is not such another, but just this. I do not forget that she too, in this one little masterpiece of its kind, bursts into an austere joy over the vision of the " vaster

[1] *Therīgāthā*, ver. 485 f. Cf. *Psalms of the Sisters*, p. 171 f.

happiness sublime" awaiting one whose truck is along the "never-ageing, never-dying Way". But she too shows in this that loss of the earlier symbolism which we found in the Snake Sutta. The Way has become tantamount to the End itself, not the way thither. The Way no longer "flows on into Nirvana", but is Nirvana, and can only be described, as I have said, in a very world of the Not.[1]

> This never ageing never dying Way—
> No sorrow cometh there, no enemies,
> Nor is there any crowd; none faint or fail,
> No fear cometh, nor aught that doth torment—
> The Way of a-mata, ambrosial . . .

No such Mātikā appears to have survived, yet is there in the Majjhima-Nikāya a suggestion or two that the baleful pictures Sumedhā quotes may have been listed. For instance, in No. 22: "The Bhagavā has described these sense-desires in the (ten) parables: the bare bone, the straw-torch" and so on. And most of these are expanded as schedule in No. 54.

The third[2] of the three Utterances ascribed to Gotama at the outset of his career is, as compared with the (for me) genuine portions of the first two, a very plunge from the world-messages of these into the little world-within-world of the monk. Its position is so far historical as to the Order and not to any mere rule, that the context is about the early accession of men as disciples who were already *samaṇas*. But its simile of things on fire, quaintly suggestive of the widely popular sea-chanty "Fire", has no worthy bearing on the new word of the Sakya mandate, is just the warning of one recluse to other recluses, with never a "new word" in it and, as the first, the inaugural, address of a new leader to new converts, is simply impossible. If it represents an actual opportunity, the use made of it as recorded would lower our estimate of the really great man who could so throw it away.

In speaking of the Piṭaka similes as only in part assignable to the first men, I repeat there is here no question, taking them in their totality, of a hard and fast marking off. It is for instance very possible that the similes drawn from the field and workshop have been *repeated* by worthy monks in their teaching, from the first authors of such to the present day. But that it was scarcely the genuine monk, the scrupulous recluse who would have bethought him to use them, is amusingly betrayed by the Commentary on Kula, the monk who lacked self-absorbed thought. Kula is said, in going for alms along the street, to have peeped "out of the corner of his eye" at the craftsman working

[1] *Gotama the Man*, p. 155. [2] *Vinaya*, i, 34.

as he sat tailorwise, intent on his job.[1] And this becomes clear when the Vinaya rule is read: "With downcast eye will I go amidst the houses: this is a discipline which ought to be observed," ... "that is, looking the length of a plough-and-beast" (*yuga-mattaṃ*).[2] Kula's peeping taught him a "new word", perhaps; other monks merely repeated it.

Then again, whereas the monk may well have used that other fit simile for "becoming", the tilling of the earth, namely, the field or *khetta*, he is nevertheless found diverting it to forward his own interests, *quâ* monk. Take first a parable which belongs to the treasure of a Society which, in its chief aim, and work, was a missioners' club:—

"Such a teacher may be rebuked thus: 'You are like a man who, neglecting his own field, should take thought to weed in his neighbour's field. Like that I say is this lust of yours to teach others what you have not yourself attained to.'" (Dīgha-Nikāya, i, No. xii).

Take next the charming "Ploughing" Sutta, where Gotama, watching the 500 ploughs of the Bhāradvāja brahman's estate ceasing for the noontide dinner of the workmen, is challenged by the master to show he has also earned his dinner by his ploughing. The reply has been done into verse, but may well have been in substance spoken by that First Missioner:—

"I too, brahman, plough and sow, and when all is done I eat... my seed is faith and rain my discipline, *paññā* for me is plough and yoke, the pole is conscience and the team my mind; inwyt my ploughshare and my goad . . . ; I clear the ground with truth, and my release from work is That fair Thing of innermost desire (*soraccaṃ*);

Energy is my burdenbearing team,
Drawing my plough toward the Haven sure.
Onward it goes nor ever draweth back,
And where it goeth we shall weep no more.
Such is the ploughing that is ploughed by me.
The fruit it yields is food ambrosial.
Whoso this ploughing hath accomplished, he
From suffering and from sorrow is set free.
(*Sutta-Nipāta*, ver. 76, p. 13; *Saṃyutta*, i., p. 172)

But there is another more prevailing use of *khetta* in the Suttas, and yet another, both of a very different purpose. In the latter, where the field is likened to "karma", there is a teaching parallel to Jain monasticism, wherein "action", the deed is as such deprecated,

[1] *Theragāthā*, 19, cf. 29; *Psalms of the Brethren*, p. 24.
[2] *Vinaya*, iv, 186.

(Anguttara-Nikāya, i, p. 223). In the former, the community of the monk is made the field, whereby the faithful laity ever giving may reap a plentiful crop of "merit". And here the simile is further used to show that the crop, accruing from "giving" generally, will be in direct proportion to the object of the giving being very worthy men, a view of "charity" which excludes any parallel with modern charity, since it does not countenance "rescue work" in any form.

It is a rich "field", this of the Pali similes, I have but touched on it here and there, and have in this chapter suggested a fresh guide in any attempt to treat them historically. And this is, that the earliest among them are on the whole likely to have been such as throw into greater relief the religious ideal of their birth-time : the importance of the very Man—as enhanced by the new word about him—namely, that it is truer to say of the Man he is *becoming*, than to say he *is*. It is this that we see pictured in the raft, the embryonic chick, the ploughing, the self-and-neighbour-gardens, the man and his wardrobe. Here is no man as mind only ; here is no man as monk only. Here are no wordy pundits with formulas, with stereotyped teaching, with refrains for memorizers. Here are the Sakyans with their new word.

But of course not here only. The parables and similes but served to throw the real message about the man into relief. And it is in that relief that we can divide between the early and the later with some confidence in our division as truly made. Again, it is in these figures that we get away from the standardized teaching to which I refer. Elsewhere we are for ever wandering in it. Very little is left of what we may call heart to heart talks between man and man, such as all true mission work must mainly show if truly recorded. Where they have survived we at once note the difference. The mantra was needed for the very Message itself. The fraction surviving of that, with its buttressing, I have discussed. It was needed at the start for the missioners. It will often have been repeated as mantra. But the main body of actual teaching will have been the application of the mantra, with all that it implied, in talks, rather than in finished discourses or sermons. These we find everywhere : expositions or discussions of dogma ; elaborations in a fixed wording to be "worded" on feast days ; the work of the editor, not of the first teachers. In them we are reading of a form of words as the thing of value ; there is rarely any vivid, living accosting of man by man.

This it is that we long to find, that we rarely find, that we see must have been lost save just here and there. Why "must" ? Because these first men were no staid, elderly pædagogues ; they were mainly young men, young anyway in spirit, young as to the very man, who were fired with the ardour of a new word of renascence to a world, grown a little beyond, out of, certain fixed habits of thought, and waiting to make response. "Burning with fervour" (*dahati tejasā*) is the word of an old verse, a survival probably of the metrical setting of the founder's reply, while yet young, to the king of Kosala. We may discount the, as we say, "swank" put, as in so many other passages, into the mouth of a Founder in the day of a developed Buddha-cult. But the claim here made by the new, yet young teacher from the Sakyas, that a man of his calling was not to be despised on account of his youth, may point to a certain confidence in the truth and timeliness of his message, and also in his own sincerity, and it may very likely be genuine old memory. The young noble, the yet small snake, the forest fire just started, the man strong in casting off all worldly encumbrances, were none the less things it was well to take into account without delay. We have in the Sutta the new man vindicating with ardour his new word. For that matter all the "talks" in this Kosala Collection seem relatively free from editing. Almost in them we see and hear the Man. They are, it is true, milk for babes; the king was no more than that. But his foolish little war evokes a profound word on war; he hears a New Word on woman at the birth of his daughter, at which he has pulled a long face; and the rousing parable of the imminent landslide, with the trenchant summons to be in haste to do what alone it is worth while doing, is of tremendous power (*Saṃyutta*, i, Book III).

Power, ardour, joyous energy: these and the like are what we much more need to see in those first men of the Sakyas than we do, who have too long been hypnotized by that libel on their leader, the set type of the immobile eternal cross-legged Sitter, type of a creed and a church which has come to a standstill, has cast aside its own first and central truth, that man's nature is essentially a becoming, that his salvation is thereby guaranteed, but he must look to it that he speed up that becoming.

Let us try to disentangle a few sayings which are more of meat than milk.

Tissa his cousin is depressed or bilious or both. His cousin Gotama first heartens him by a talk on the great Adventure of the Way, (before which, a pedantic section on the five skandhas has been inserted). We then see him driving in the great figure of wayfaring and the end lying beyond with words like so many magnetic shocks of will-healing:—

"*Abhirama, Tissa! Abhirama, Tissa! Ahaṃ ovādena . . . ahaŋ anuggahena . . . ahaŋ anusāsaniya . . .*" [1]

[1] *Saṃyutta*, iii, 108.

Now these words mean literally "Be of great joy, Tissa . . . I by exhorting, I by helping, I by instructing ". I know of no such sentences in Pali construction as are the last clauses. The readings differ, and the Burmese emendation does not emendate. Nor have I at hand the Commentary. With perhaps ill-advised impatience I venture to see here the very *usual* idiom for "what use is it to you that I exhort, etc. ?" Then only do we see, that here we have, from the buried years, a very shout of joyous comradeship in the new vista of the Way and the fellow-wayfarers: "Be of great joy, my lad ! (See what lies ahead ! See all the more-in-life I show you in what lies before you !). *What need for you is there that I preach, that I come to your aid, that I instruct ?*" And this with hands upon head, upon shoulders, or within handgrasp. Is not this perhaps a truer picture than the solemn cross-legged seer speaking of skandhas, of lusts, of the world and of life as only tragic ?

To that other cousin too, Mahānāma the Sakyan, a layman of worth, sincerely devoted to Gotama, we just catch (preceding the stereotyped sayings of a creed), a word or two of direct encouragement. Gotama is going on tour ; Mahānāma asks : Among men living in divers ways, how is it best I should live, while you are away ? "Keep faith," is the reply, "keep up effort (no word for 'will' here) ; watch over thought ; practise musing ; have *prajñā* (let the Self value)." [1] Here we have the early category of the five spiritual faculties,[2] and with them we may well have the founder's advice. The rest is late credal matter. Again, we have Mahānāma shrinking from death, scared apparently, in a modern way, at the danger in street traffic. What would be his fate were death sudden ? "Have no fears, cousin, have no fears," is the answer, "you have lived a good life ; not evil will be your dying, not evil will be your passing hour. Your body may become the prey of this and that, but you yourself will rise up, will go to better things (*visesa-gāmī*)." [3] The rest here too is credal.

Here again is a word, free from all credal admonition, going straight to the heart of things : The aged sick Nakulapitar comes for comfort. Gotama rejoins : "Verily, householder, your body is in poor health, and you live with pain. See to it that the man, the self, keeps well." [4] Here the credal matter is appended in an after-meeting with a disciple, highly suggestive of later editing. And further, both here and in the foregoing reply, the words self, or man are not there *now* ; what we find is "mind" (*citta*) ; mind is said

[1] *Anguttara*, v, 332 f.
[2] Ibid., i, 39, §22.
[3] *Saŋyutta*, v, 369.
[4] Ibid., iii, 1 f.

to survive death; mind is to be kept in health. The former of these two statements would be in conflict with the statement given under the raft-similes. Both are later than the day of early Sakya; both are obvious glosses.

Lastly, I see in the talk with Māgandiya, a wandering student such as the first men had been, something that is not edited out of all its first shape, albeit the editor has not been quite idle. I cannot take up space with it here, and a good translation is with us.[1] The opening is an outstanding episode, vivid, probable, with Gotama as the guest of a brahman. It is the Wanderer who is hostile. With courtesy and ardour Gotama opens up for him the vista of the Health, the Wellbeing, not of body or mind, but *of the man*. And for once the word Nirvana is worded as the consummation of man's *health*, with all that hinders that uttermost-weal extinguished.

Here then are just a few fragments surviving to show to some little extent how I hear those first Will-missioners spreading their glad tidings of good will of the Man, the Man held by the current teaching as *being* the Highest, but needing to realize that the Highest was to be a *Becoming*, a long upward Way of *making to become*.

[1] *Further Dialogues of the Buddha*, by Lord Chalmers, i, 353ff.

PART II

XVIII

SAKYA ORPHANED

I have now completed, so far as it is given me, for this work, the inquiry into what constituted the original mandate of Sakya, the gospel of Gotama, and his leading co-workers. This is not the teaching *mainly* emphasized in the Piṭakas, nor in any portion of them. Nor for that matter is it the teaching as yet discovered in any other Buddhist literature, in whatever language it survives. *But the Piṭakas betray it,* if they do not place it on the pedestal where it should be. It would be, were the Piṭakas the work of men, whose values were the values of the Founder and his contemporaries, in their prime. But they are not; they are the work of men carried out during a period lasting from, say, the last quarter of Gotama's ministry to a period *subsequent to* the time of Asoka and the Third Congress, a period not far short of five centuries. During that time, much was undergoing change; tendencies, which were in their infancy at the birth of Sakya, had grown strong and unwithstandable; values strong at that time had depreciated. And, pregnant event, north India had experienced the rapid rise, on the upheaval following Greek invasion, of a Chakravarti, a "world-monarch", an Indian emperor. Lastly, but not least, there came the transfer of that specific line in Sakyan energies which resulted in the Pali Piṭakas to a new land, to Ceylon, where "the man" was otherwise conceived, where the memorized sayings in some form of Prakrit were reworded as Pali, where the Said became in time the Written.

Of those tendencies, of those values, it is these three which we have in what follows to keep ever in view :—

(1) the depreciated value in the concept "man";
(2) the growing tendency to seek the man in the mind;
(3) the growing régime of the monk.

Nor should we lose sight of the super-monarch.

With these tendencies and values, I have already dealt to some extent. I was digging under these, the burying super-structures, and reference to the changes was, if incidental, unavoidable. I am now concerned mainly with the super-structures, in other words, *with the values emphasized in the Piṭakas*, and not merely betrayed. My book is not mainly concerned with them. But handled they must be, if only to bring the treasure buried beneath them the better to the surface. On the pregnant fact of the super-monarch I have also a word of comment.

In my book, *Gotama the Man*, I have tried to reconstruct the corporate activities as going on in, shall I say? the last decade of the founder's life. I have located these activities as mainly, or wholly at Sāvatthī, for which evidence is not wanting. Thus a quite disproportionate number of Suttas are associated with Sāvatthī, many of them with the curt heading: *Sāvatthī nidānaṃ*.[1] There are five other such curt headings, but they are all in the latter part of the Third Nikāya, and suggest a late collecting of memorized Sayings, possibly a search for and a sweeping in, made for the great revision of repeatings said to have been carried out at the Third Congress. Again, when the Founder on the tour he undertook in extreme old age fell ill, his companion Ānanda is said, in the Commentary, to have gone after the cremation to Sāvatthī, and there, steeped in grief, to have resumed his customary service on the beloved Master as if he were still there *at his home*, to be waited on; and then, rousing himself to have spread the news, causing much mourning among the townsfolk, to whom the passing of so venerable a figure must have been as was to those of Windsor and Balmoral the passing of the aged Queen at Osborne.

And as to that tour, made when walking must have been an ordeal for one whose body was, as he may indeed have said, " only kept going as was a worn-out cart," it is now a few years since I said, in the teeth of the Piṭakan refrain, that, for some reason carefully suppressed, it was *not* with " a great company ", but alone with cousin Ānanda.[2] Only one critic noted at the time, to me, that this was contradicting the books. But then very few critics or Buddhists are on speaking terms with the detailed contents of the books. I did not then give any reasons, and in my book referred to, I have again, in repeating the heresy, given no reasons which would weigh. I said only: " Reading attentively, men could see for themselves . . . " I will here try to show what, so reading, we get.

The " tour-Suttantas " of the Dīgha-Nikāya are all in the first, or Sīlakkhandha division, which comprises the first thirteen Suttantas (vol. i). They are six in number, to wit, i, iii, iv, v, xii, and xiii. In

[1] " Buddhism and the Negative," *JPTS.*, 1924–7; *Kindred Sayings*, iii, iv, Introductions.

[2] " Buddhism and the Negative."

every case the opening is with an identical formula: "Thus have I heard. The Blessed One was once wayfaring along the high road between X and Y with a great company of monks, with not more than 500 monks." The last tour of his life occurs, as readers will know, in the second Suttanta of the middle division entitled Great, = "important." It does not come at the beginning of the Suttanta, as do the earlier tours of the Dīgha. It starts with the paragraph numbered by our editors as thirteen. No start as such is worded. It begins abruptly: "Now when the Blessed One had sojourned at Rājagaha as long as he pleased, he invited Ānanda: Come, Ānanda, we shall go to Ambalaṭṭhikā. Even so, sir, assented Ānanda. Then the Blessed One with a great monk-company proceeded to Ambalaṭṭhikā." This formula is repeated for further walks eleven times, till the fateful Kusinārā is reached. Nowhere else, in any tour in any of the Nikāyas, have I come across a walk beginning with that invitation *to one man*, with its pathetic suggestion, when once we have deleted the last sentence in its oddly diminished wording, of the two aged men wearily plodding along from village to village.

Now I say not that my inference amounts to what actually took place. But there must be some reason for this departure from the previous tour-formula, repeated six times in the Dīgha. There must be some reason for the reiterated appeal or bidding to Ānanda only, and for the very evident comradeship of Ānanda throughout till he is left weeping beside the "man"-deserted body. I believe that, if this tour be read attentively and comparatively, the shadowy "great monk-sangha" will dissolve, and the two aged men will for the first time stand out in a sharp relief that is true. At the last scene too, there is no sign whatever that anyone was present save Ānanda, with whom we may imagine will have been a physician hastily fetched, and perhaps also the few women who in tears were the first to come to mourn.[1] It is incredible, that the shadowy many would have suffered him to lie there in the open, on a cloak between the two sāl-trees, with no ministering activities.

I cannot but think that this moving scene has been read with little or no reconstructive imagination on the part of writers and readers, else this matter of the tour, in its unique wording, and of the dying, little befitting the passing of a leader so entirely devoted to his followers over such a long period, would have come up for the critical discussion due to it. And if I have tried to discuss it in this book, the subject of which is not the life and passing of

[1] *Vinaya*, ii; Cullavagga, xi, 1, 10.

Gotama, but the message he lived and taught, it is to illustrate what I mean by the need, in getting at that message, to read attentively, to read between the lines, to read with a certain amount of, I think, wholesome mistrust, to read with an imagination which would get behind the records, compiled, revised, and finally written each and all at different periods of time, at different places.

And there are other features in those last days, concerning which we have been reading with sluggish reconstructive imagination. We tend to forget, to overlook, or perhaps we have not even known, that in those two aged tourers we see almost the only survivors of the original or very early Sakyaputtiyas. And that means two lonely comrades of the Old Brigade. Kaccāna was still there, but at Avanti (Majjhima, Sutta 84); and there was Kassapa, but living by choice as a recluse.

There was, it is true, still Anuruddha, also aged, but he was ever a confirmed recluse, and we have more than one account of the Leader going to visit him[1] and not, as in Kondañña's case, of him visiting the Leader.[2] Now it is true, that in the deathbed scene we have Anuruddha suddenly emerging, and correcting Ānanda's moan: "He is dead!" by saying: "Nay, he is in trance."[3] Anuruddha is also credited, both here and in a slightly different version in the Anthology, with a very lovely couple of stanzas on the passing.[4] The latter feature is of course of little or no evidential value, for he may well have uttered a response on hearing the news in his retreat, and this may have been put into metre by others whose business this work was, or by himself.

But even if we explain the verses in the Dīgha in this way, it will seem, to most, very wantonly sceptical to go further and say, that the verse-maker himself was not rightly described as present. It will be said: Surely he was, for as a noted muser, he better than Ānanda would recognize the difference between trance and death. I would be the last to discredit a line in the records, where I see no reason for doing so. It is a weary and disappointing work to be seeking the true, and to have so often to find what is not the true, even if the untrue be put in with the laudable motive of apologia or edification. Why I see no Anuruddha at that last scene is the utter silence in the record on a matter where he, of all survivors, would have been first to record what he heard and saw, but where he did neither.

If we look at the first utterance, we see in the record a glowing

[1] e.g. *Majjhima*, No. 31. [2] *Saṃyutta*, i, 193. [3] *Dīgha*, ii, 156.
[4] Ibid., 157.

account of unseen witnesses to that utterance. We do not know who testified to this, nor to what extent it was subsequently "dressed up" in the brave array of a sort of wireless message passed on from world to world. But it is there. Somehow it came there. There were, it is said, only six persons present; there may have been more; only five are named as joining the speaker at once. All were vigorous, keenly interested men. We have seen, that to testify to unseen presences was a feature in early Sakya from the very first, in both the Founder and a few others of his men. But we do not know which of those six could have then testified save only Gotama himself. But at his dying we have an event which Buddhism has celebrated as of the utmost weight, dating events from it as the beginning of an era: thus in the Dīpavaṃsa:

> Four months after Parinibbāna, the first Recital will take place; a hundred and eighteen years later the third recital will take place. . . .

Similarly, in the Mahāvaṃsa and Commentaries. Is it then likely, that an event, so very grave at the time, so very weighty in the years to come, should have been let pass in utter silence as to any such testimony to unseen witnesses, had there been a witness of known competence to testify to their presence? Granting that the monastic teaching comes in here, namely, that this man was passing, not on in the worlds, but out of all worlds, is it for all that likely, that the governors of worlds (who are recorded as making pronouncements on the passing) would have failed to testify by their presence, to so supreme a passing, and that the homage of their presence would have been suffered to pass unnoticed by a witness like Anuruddha, a "man who saw"? Anuruddha *may* have been there, summoned possibly by a messenger sent by Ānanda, as was probably the case with Kassapa; he *may* have testified to the "Musing" of the dying man, so queerly recorded; he is *said* to have ordered Ānanda to act as his messenger; he is *said* to have interpreted the wishes of unseen willers in a matter quite unimportant to them—the place, relative to the village, of the cremation—but would he not surely have witnessed to more, had he indeed been there?

Shall we say, there is here no reason to doubt Anuruddha's presence? Or shall we interpret the silence as to a tradition of unseen attendant companies in this way:—There was no such tradition, because the interest of Sakya in other worlds and in deva-intercourse was waning. When the old memorized Sayings, in different versions, underwent, at a later date, or dates, *sangaha*, or compilation into rounded-off divisions, there was a felt need to make here and there apologias for this and that shortcoming, or give some weighty sanction for this or that traditional feature. There was need to camouflage the unseemliness of the secluded passing away; there was need to explain an old saying stating that the Man, in his passing, was in Jhāna, this, as I have shown in a previous chapter, meaning "access to devas",[1] to another world; and this, according to the later theory of nirvana and parinirvana, was anomalous, and had either to be dropped out, or sanctioned by the alleged presence of a great and honoured clairvoyant like Anuruddha. There was need to give weight to the surviving tradition of a change in cremation arrangements as being somehow associated with a mandate "from without". Now in the first place, there had survived a verse ascribed to Anuruddha on the Leader's passing; secondly, of the few great First Men, Kaccāna was living afar at Avanti, Gavampati was afar and age-weakened, Kassapa came, in the tradition, after the event, when the cremation was over-due. There remained only Anuruddha. And further, Anuruddha's psychic fame would avail to sanction the keeping in of those two features: the Jhāna, ending on the Fourth Stage, which was traditionally that of entering into deva-intercourse, surviving in tradition about the Man who, *it had come to be held*, was no longer in any world of personal being; and the unexplained tradition of the changed location, explicable perhaps by the link between Brahmā and the North—the sign of his advent being "a splendid light coming from the North"[2]—but needing the endorsement by Anuruddha.

And so we have the aged recluse Anuruddha clothed for a moment in ". . . the demi-god Authority . . ." and brought to the front of the stage, bidding his cousin Ānanda, as *āvuso*, as equal or inferior, be his living letter, and obeyed by Ānanda as an inferior would answer his superior: *bhante*. To some extent, the situation is thereby saved. Let it not be thought, that the criticism is frivolous. Greater critics than I have made clear the patch-work character of this Suttanta, interweaving old sayings with much Sutta-discourse, and that for a special purpose, or purposes. They have, I think, overlooked the patchwork in the central episode, a patching which is, from the point of view of the exegesist and the apologist, even more needed, even more justifiable than the reset.

[1] *Devuppatti.* [2] *Dīgha*, ii, 150; cf. Stas., 18, 19.

I incline to think that the fact of the survivors' loneliness is dimmed by the, this time more obvious, gloss of the talk with Sāriputta inserted in the last tour, at a time when Sāriputta had passed away, perhaps many years earlier. We know from the Suttas, and also from the Jātaka "present-day" episodes, that both Sāriputta and Moggallāna died before their Leader,[1] and one of the latter episodes would lead the credulous reader to think that the former's going preceded that of the Leader by a very short interval. There is further the misleading translation somewhere, rendering Gotama's tribute to his beloved brother-in-work

> . . . that Wheel
> Doth Sāriputta after my example turn,[2]

as "will turn after me", as if he was to be the Leader's heir and successor. That the Suttanta of the Decease is to a large extent a patchwork of passages from other Sayings has been shown in detail by Rhys Davids, and this passage is such a patch, cut out from the Sampasādanīya Suttanta of the last division of the Dīgha. Its insertion here, where it is out of place (else should we have surely had the death of Sāriputta narrated as immediately following), is as I read it a word of apologia to the great man who had, for reasons I have suggested in *Gotama the Man*, left once and for all the Sāvatthī Sangha, where the framing of formulas was going on in a way he had realized to be one of which he disapproved. The old lion was, I conceive, aroused, and it may be, that sore and indignant he set out alone for the last time to tell his message.[3] If this be true, it explains the anomaly in the "Come, Ānanda". It was a very awkward situation, which the recorders had subsequently to face, and in their way they met it as best they could, with memorized sayings exalting the powers of their Founder in prophecy, in *iddhi*, in *abhiññā*, in rapt musing, in the Lokāyata or world-lore about earthquakes, and in dwelling on the three-fold institute of Buddha, Dhamma, Sangha, which the aged leader would certainly not have used as a "slogan" in his day.

I have little hope of doing more here than making suggestions which a later generation may find are not without weight. If I go on to say, that not only was the dying of the Founder an event as

[1] *Saṃyutta*, v, 163; *Jāt.*, i, 230; v, 64 f.

[2] *Sutta-Nipāta* and *Theragāthā*; Sela.

[3] The culminating pathos here is that a set lecture is put into his mouth on the subjects: morality, concentration, (divine) wisdom, which is not anywhere in the records a triple text associated with him.

lonely as it was unexpectedly sudden, that not only were the funeral arrangements of a very hurried kind, but that the first general conference, miscalled Council, was also hurriedly convened, I have little hope of carrying readers with me—at least as yet.

Agreement with the first of these three conclusions is hindered by the many, indefinitely later representations of the Dying in sculpture and other ways of graphic art, lending a sense of solemn and expected climax to a scene which actually lacked such an atmosphere. Then, too the sudden collapse of a victim to a fatal seizure of dysentery, where there may well have been a lingering for a couple of days only, is artificially softened by the Founder being represented as able, after the seizure, to arise and take a walk, as well as give more admonitions to Ānanda, and point a last convert to the Way, in words which will surely have been different from the stilted form in which they are reworded. I have been told that in our own day the empress Hsi, while suffering from dysentery before her death, was able to compose verses. Well, it is one thing to sit up and write lines, tended in luxurious surroundings, or at best to murmur metrical cadences taken down by an attendant scribe; it is another to be weathering an attack described as very violent, in the open lying on a cloak, and in the eighties.

Agreement with the second conclusion does not suffer camouflage in the record. Something of the kind there may be in Kassapa's sudden arrival being really due to a message sent by Ānanda. According to the record, Kassapa walking from Pava to Kusināra with the stereotyped retinue of a great teacher: "with a great company of the monks, with just 500 monks," meets an Ājīvaka, and says: "Sir, would you be knowing our teacher?" Apparently—I say this because the speaker of the following is not named—the ascetic replies: "Yes, I know him; the *samaṇa* Gotama passed away a week ago from to-day . . ." Thereupon follows a burst of lamentation from the monks.[1]

Is it not much more likely, that we have here the half-forgotten fact of a message sent by Ānanda, alone, uncomraded, to the influential colleague he knew to be not very far away, sent by a messenger he only secured after a few days? "Come!" his S O S will have said, "do you not know our Teacher is dead?" The question as put by Kassapa is quite meaningless. The answer, if said by Kassapa would be equally so, for the lamenting would have found utterance when Kassapa learnt the news, not when he

[1] *Dīgha*, ii, 162.

announced it to a stranger. When once we get rid of those "just 500 monks" of retinue, the situation of poor venerable Ānanda suggests such solutions.

The whole is at the best a blurred account of half-forgotten sayings, pieced together, at a much later date, with much borrowing from other portions, and with a certain amount of camouflage to cover the apparently unseemly desertion of the lonely tourer, such as the falling of sky-flowers, the suppression of Ānanda's S O S message and more ; the whole leading up to that which had come into Sakya and was new : the cult of the relics.

XIX

SAKYA IN CONFERENCE

As to the third conclusion : that the First Sangīti, commonly called Council, at Rājagaha was more or less of a hasty procedure, I am not wishing to stress this. I have come to the conclusion from the account given in the Vinaya. This is a meagre, jejune picture, about as unlike the reverent and dignified procedure, which should have followed on so great and solemn a crisis as could well be imagined. If we turn to the Commentaries, we find an attempt to make this in part good by much talk of preparations made for it at Rājagaha, and of Ānanda canvassing for attendance at it in Sāvatthī.

Let us glance at the older account. The Conference is called "that of the five hundred", as the Second was "that of the seven hundred". There may, in the former, be the result of an editorial agreement to be consistent with the number in the retinue [1] assigned to the tour-sutta formula cited above ; but it is anyway refreshingly sober in limitation, and is probably no exaggeration of the number that could be summoned in the short interval between the funeral in the Malla republic's territory and the meeting during the rainy season at Rājagaha.

That there was need for prompt action is made fairly evident. The swift outcrop, in the person of Subhadda (of course a different person from the last convert, who so soon "graduated" as arahan—the name is very common), of that tendency to divergent teaching and riven sodality, which broke out so strongly in the following centuries, shows this. Not less does that first Seceder (dating from the Passing) show it, the disciple strangely disguised under the name of Purāṇa : the Man of Old [2]—who would not wish we had his real name ! Gavampati, the senior disciple (Thera) commended in the Anthology as of mighty *iddhi*, but elsewhere coming into, I think but one brief Sutta,[3] declined to come for less worthy motives : this is according to the Chinese recensions translated for us by Professor Przyluski.[4] Namely, there seemed to be nothing worth while in trying to help the world, now that the Light of it had faded out, save in

[1] *Pañca satamattaṃ* : amounting to, or not more than 500.

[2] *Vinaya*, Cullavagga, xi.

[3] *Saṃyutta*, v, 436. In the reference *Dīgha*, Sta. 23, he is in another world.

[4] *Le Concile de Rājagriha*, pt. I, pp. 8, 30, 66, 116.

fading out also, which he proceeded to do. It may well be, that the failure lay not in Gavampati's will, but in his physical inability to travel. But that it has been allowed to come in, as a serious reason for holding aloof from a Community in whom the mission spirit was still alive, is a sinister feature in the compilers.

But if there was hurry, this rather strengthens than weakens the case for accepting the Conference as historical. And it is well that, in the face of Oldenberg's hasty assumption, that the Conference is a mere fiction, we have had, for an interval almost equally long, Rhys Davids's more sagacious rejoinder, that the assumption is ill-based and unnecessary. Mr. E. J. Thomas comments to the same effect. The reader can consult assumption and rejoinders in (*a*) *Vinaya Texts*, *S.B.E.*, I, Introd., (*b*), *Dialogues*, II, Introd. ; *The Buddha in Legend and in History*, p. 165. If, apart from assumptions and rejoinders, we consider the tradition in itself, we must surely see, that it is very likely, some Conference in Sakya should have just then taken place. The "very likely" is in itself not evidential, but it should always be suffered to have weight.

The position was more or less this : The leading men, the Centre in the Sakyan Order had been coming for some years, perhaps half unawares, to be leaning, in their attitude to the external world both lay and religious, on the support of the Word, rather than on the presence of the ageing teacher and on the teaching he had given of that inner monitor "dhamma". Hereon the way in which, in his latter admonitions, he is shown as urging attention to it, is enlightening. This is only less enlightening than it should be, *because we have modernized* the force and meaning of his words : "Be you they who have the Self, the Man, as your lamp, your referee, your *dhamma* :—your ought-to-be, your ideal !" That whom he bade his first men seek he also bade his last seek. But the modern critic holds that there lies herein no more significance than our own compounds of the word "self". Well, they are right—and so am I. But I give the weight the prefix had *for the great Teacher and his day*, and what it also has, *potentially only*, for us. It is *we* who have minimized the nature and truth of the self, and this wilted self we set up in the place of that truer (the Indian) self. But this wilted self is just what the trans-Indian Buddhism came to do also.

By speaking of the Order as leaning on the Word, I mean that, with a Leader growing old and weak, and probably much less given to "sermons" and homilies than the many Suttas of discourse, each headed by the stereotyped opening ascribed to the Bhagavā's summons, would seem to imply, the disciples' mandatory sanction was coming to be more the Mantra, the fixed form of words, than the human Source of the mandate itself. There are several Suttas in which Gotama is recorded as saying a few terse pregnant sentences, and then leaving his listeners. Now and then he pleads backache, and the need of lying down. Now and then he names a deputy to carry on: Sāriputta, Moggallāna, Ānanda. Now and then the listeners are wishful to have a clearer exposition, and appeal to a disciple like Kaccāna, noted as exponent. I am not here giving much weight to the names of the alleged supplementers. When the Suttas took their final form, the Man himself had become the overwhelmingly important feature. Any noted name would suffice to fill in and round off the full wording of the edited, then of the written sayings so long transmitted orally.

But there is on the other hand much probability that the sayings, so far as their repeaters were living at, or visiting the Central Settlement —first Rājagaha, then Sāvatthī—were being cast into some kind of fixed form, while the Founder was living his last decade or two, say, at the latter place. Hints that this was so I find in such Suttas as *make reference* to such a poem as the Pārâyana of the Sutta-Nipāta:—

> "It is said, Sāriputta, in the Way to the Beyond (Pārâyana), in Ajita's question . . . what do you make of this?"[1]

And in the Anguttara-Nikāya there are also references to Metteyya's question in the Pārâyana,[2] and to the poem itself as being recited by a woman disciple Nandamātā.[3] A further hint I see in the charge said to have been made before his decease by Gotama, that certain heads of teaching should be carefully studied and taught. And yet another hint peeps out from the *uddesas*, or "arguments" as our books used to say, summaries, with which a few Suttas begin, the *niddesa*, or exposition following. The exposition is here virtually the Commentary, the rôle of the expounding teacher, once he had uttered the mantra or, as we say, his "text". Nandamātā is recorded as "uttering the Pārâyana *with the voice* (*sārena*)", a, to me, unique phrasing, which may have had some now lost significance.

This work on the standardizing of taught Sayings will, we may be sure, have had the full consent and encouragement of the Founder. He had fought too many battles with the lions of schism and discord in his Order not to know well how swiftly that Order might split up, once the constraining bond of his presence was loosed. Had his best men been yet with him and yet vigorous, the outlook might have been more assured. In so saying, I would not make him appear an

[1] *Saṃyutta*, ii, 40. [2] Vol. iii, 399. [3] Vol. iv, 63; cf. i, 144.

anxious Church-builder. He was much greater than that. That he has come down to us as a founder of a monastic institution, when in reality, he may have been so more against than with, his own inclination, is a theory that opinion to-day will not accept. And anyway, the growing vogue of the *samaṇa* was strong enough to make any other course more or less impracticable. But the very truth rings out in his earnest words as to his one and only successor being no man, however loyal to himself, but *dhamma.* I say " the truth " here, because the other injunctions imputed to him at that very time are more or less contradictory to this saying, and are at the same time so much more what an Order, which had become a Church, would have compiled and inserted as a justification of its existence and constitution.

The word which for me rings true is this : Ānanda passes on to Gotama, when the latter had already shown symptoms of bodily collapse, in a very delicate manner, the wish he will have known existed in the Order, that Gotama would leave a testament in words to his community.[1] " Now what ", is the reply, " does the Order expect of me ? I have taught *dhamma* openly keeping nothing back. If any one thinks he will lead the Order, or that it should refer to him, it is he who should make depositions about this or that. I say not that I lead it, or that it should refer to me . . . I am old and feeble . . . I shall soon be gone. . . . Therefore do ye live as they who have the Self as lamp . . . the Self as *dhamma.*"

If with this we compare the words a little later : " Say not, Ānanda, when I am gone, the ' word ' (*pavacanaŋ*) is a past-teacher-thing. Dhamma-and-Vinaya which I have taught, set forth :—*that* for you, I being gone, (is) teacher," and still more the meticulously worded Four Allocatings (*mahā-padesā*), referred to an address given, on the tour, to the monks at a town called Bhoga, we see sentences betraying the atmosphere of ecclesiastical institutions. *Dhamma* is now no longer the Highest in the man urging the will to the higher, the Most inspiring him to the More. It is the externalized, the fixed word, nay, it is even the " Suttas ", the Rules, with which other men's teachings are to be compared. We are no longer in the world of the Many, in every woman and man of whom *dhamma* was to be assumed by the fellow-man ; we are in the chapterhouse ; we are next door to the academy.

It is true we are, in the matter of the Rājagaha Conference, not

[1] *Dīgha*, ii, p. 99. " Be ye lamps unto yourselves . . . " and " the Truth " (*dhamma*) have served, alas ! as very misleading translations ; Oldenberg's are just as bad here ; Franke's are even worse. Nor do I hold Mr. E. J. Thomas has caught the truth.

yet so far as were the editors of such glosses. But a beginning has been made. The authority of the Founder *as Teacher supreme* had waned, and was in process of being supplanted by the standardized nucleus of Sayings. I judge that to say this is probably nearer the truth than to say 'Categories', such as Bodhipakkhiyā Dhammā. It is true that those teachings are referred to in the Suttanta before us in Categories, but I shall suggest in the next chapters, that this is no sound warrant for their having been then called by such enumerations. Had this been so, we should have looked to hear of them at the First Conference. It is indeed certain that we should have found them there and then.

It does not come within the quest of this book to follow Sakya in its Conferences in detail. Let it suffice that the reader be reminded, that in the one Piṭaka record we have of that which followed the Founder's decease, two points are worthy of notice, more notice than they have, I believe, received.

In the first place, we see a more careful, more detailed attention paid to the Rule, than is paid to the Teaching. Thus: when the President Kassapa questions Upāli, the Vinaya expert, on the four Rules, infringement of which meant expulsion (*Pārājika's*), the compiler, or editor adds, after each Rule, that thus was there questioning on the matter, occasion, individual (first) concerned, the rule itself, the sub-rule, guilt and innocence. In the case of the second item of the agenda, the questioning of Ānanda about the stock of Sayings, subsequently called Suttas, or Suttantas, the compiler, or editor adds, after each of the *only two* to which reference by name is made, "Thus did Kassapa question Ānanda as to the occasion of the Brahmajāla, (and thereupon of the Sāmaññaphala), and as to the individuals." No cross-question was apparently made as to what on either occasion was taught, *pace* any first, second or third heads.

This in itself is ominous. It is not evidence, that at the Conference there was no reciting of the Sayings after Ānanda had, so to speak, given out the hymn. But it does leave us in doubt whether at that time, the one thing standardized in a "Sutta" was just what Ānanda is reported as giving out, and whether the actual episode itself was not left, as we believe the Commentaries were, to the exponent's own wording. Namely, that the telling of the episode, when once the "occasion and individual (*puggalo*)" had been stated, the teaching monk was free to tell the Sayings in his own words. If that was so, what an opening does it not leave for a gradual transformation in the emphasis, in the wording?

But this is not all that is ominous. If the reader will pursue the short account of the Conference to the end, he will find that, after all, he is yet led by the incorrigibly monastic pre-occupation about, not the history of the Order as the great work of his founders, but the occasion (*nidāna*) for telling details about Rules. The Conference, which comes at so fit a time, like the Pentecost meeting at Jerusalem, to declare both Mandate and lines of teaching, peters out in Ānanda being (most unfairly) hauled over the coals as to certain things, some of them most worthy, which he had done, and —the futility and unseemliness of it !—Ānanda being shown as giving to a local raja detailed information about the monks' worn-out wardrobes—a very rag-and-bottle talk.

I see here little blame to Ānanda and the other Sakyans in conference. They would be loudest in condemnation of such a parody of their very worthy will to meet and confer on the measures to be taken. It is the pre-occupations of the later editors over which we may feel dismay.

In the second place, the silence about the Founder is curious, or would be, if we had here any but an account of the kind I have just described : a mere matter of Rule-episode. In the Dīgha Suttanta, we see on the one hand an explosion of grief and homage at the speedy passing ; we see on the other hand, on the part of the venerable Chief, an affectionate solicitude, that his children should rightly understand what he had so long tried to teach, and should in particular question him as friend with friend (*sahāya*), comrade with comrade,[1] if there was anything which any of them was in doubt about. At the Conference *not a word of all this* ; no fitting tribute to their great father ; no word of his mandate of the Way, of his values under that and other figures of growth, of becoming, of advance as wayfarers, of the worth in which he held the things unseen in the Way to the Beyond, of the insistence on their heeding the Highest, "*dhamma*" within them. Were not these things the last solemn injunctions of him ? Surely we cannot have here the true Agenda of that Conference !

But that nothing of the kind is recorded in the proceedings may possibly point to this : that not at that day, nor for that matter, at the Second Conference, a century later, when much revision is recorded to have been carried out, can there have yet arisen that Buddha-cult, which in the Nikāyas is already an expanding blossom. In the Third Conference, we do hear that note struck. The orthodox are specified as followers with regard to one point of view attributed to the "Buddha". *Kiṃ-vādī, bhante,*

[1] *Dīgha*, ii, 154 f. Rh. D. and Franke miss the point here.

Sammasambuddho ti?": "What was the teaching of the Truly Enlightened, sir?" Asoka is made to ask, as president. Yet even there the higher worth in the Founder went no further in word.

Taken by itself, this curt reference may be no adequate guide to the stage reached at the time in Buddha-cult. Buddhaghosa's account may be brief, in that he is pre-occupied with getting past his introduction to his subject, viz. comment on Vinaya and Kathāvatthu. It may be said, that at the time of that Congress, the Piṭakas would appear to have been mostly, if not wholly compiled, and that in them the homage to the "Buddha, Sambuddha, Tathāgata" is strongly brought out, even if such titles as "Devâtideva (*deva* above *devas*) and "Sabbaññu" (omniscient), and the like appear only in yet later literature. Into this matter of completed compilation I shall go briefly presently. It does remain a curious point, that these scanty records of events, so momentous in Sakyan history as the Conferences, should have preserved (*a*) such slight reference to the Man who taught and founded, with (*b*) a patent pre-occupation about the Rule, and *dhamma* as *word*, and lastly (*c*) with the view or "school" as being orthodox, or the reverse, in the eyes of a majority in the Sangha. In the fixed wording convening the First Conference, *dhamma* is put first before Vinaya. This will have been the natural order in precedence of disciples of the Man of Dhamma; the natural order in growth. In the Conference itself, Vinaya is given the place of honour. This can scarcely be because Upāli was ranked higher than Ānanda.

But let us pass to the second meeting of Sakya in Conference.

Here we have no evidence of hurry. Here is no appearance of establishing at least the *sine quâ non* of both the constitutional basis of a sodality and the nucleus of a doctrinal tradition or Smriti. Here is recorded both the canvassing of supporters previous to the Conference, the attempt to settle points in that constitutional body of discipline in a full house, and the referring of the decisions to a "jury" of eight, to wit, four monks from the Eastern vihāras and as many from those of the West of the Ganges watershed. The fact that the points, known as the Ten Indulgences, were of a kind too trivial to have called for such a commotion has been made a ground for rejecting the historicity of the Conference. The real battleground underlying the pernickety value in the points has been too much overlooked. It is true that, at a later epoch, there would have been a serious issue in the matter of liberty to use metal currency. But scarcely then. So much traffic in goods was done in kind. Had the use of "gold and silver" been the important concession then, which it would have been, if claimed at a later date, it would have certainly been placed as Claim 1, not Claim 10.

The *real point at issue* was the *rights of the individual*, as well as of those of the provincial communities, as against the prescriptions of a centralized hierarchy. Not only as a unit, but also in the smaller groups, the man would have more weight ; he would count as a man, and not merely as the mere unit he would be, if his life, even his life in an Order of monks, were to be the carrying out of Rule this and Rule that with the monotony of herd life. He would be able as man to wayfare in the Way *atta-dhammo :* choosing, deciding according to his "conscience". So did at one time English liberties depend on a relatively insignificant matter of "ship-money", and New England liberties on a matter of tea-duties. Why is our vision so dim when it is the liberties of those long-ago monks of Vesālī we have to picture ?

Let it not be forgotten, that it was the monks of Vesālī who defended more than the right of a man to order his own wayfaring. It was they who defended his very reality. The thesis : The man is to be got at, or is an intelligible entity, in the true, ultimate sense was, we read, upheld by the Vajjian monks of Vesalī, and by others of the Order. Collectively they came to be called "of the Great Community", Mahā-sanghikas, and still later, Sammitiyas, or Sammatiyas (it may at first have been Sammutiyas).[1] These held, that the speech of conventional usage (*sammuti-kathā*) was more true than the distorting analysis used in the growing vogue called Abhidhamma. They said that, when we say "man", we do not mean, that it is truer to see reality in a complex of *dhamma's* or mental phenomena making up the man, who is but a name-label ; we mean that beneath, or behind the things seen of body, and the things inferred called mind, there is the yet more real doer and minder, experiencer and valuer. These were, I say, they who maintained more truly the teaching of their Founder, than the growing majority of Rule-men and Analysts of the men at Sāvatthī and later at Patna.[2]

What significance does not this stand, which I take as true Sakya, lend to that gesture of Gotama, turning not the head only but "the whole body like an elephant"—the old grow stiff in the neck—to give his last farewell look at the city of Vesālī ? It is a unique case : why just Vesālī only ? Was it only because it may probably have been there he first came on leaving home to inquire of Jain teaching ? Or was it also because he was leaving the men in whom lay his one hope that

[1] Later than the Patna Conference ; the term (*sammuti*) had else been used in the *Kathāvatthu*, chap. i. [2] Cf. below, p. 405.

there were yet to be found "they who will understand" (*aññātāro bhavissanti*)?

It made anyway a profound impression upon Ānanda, whether or no disciples may have escorted the two teachers up to that point. If I am right, that they were alone on the tour, it can only have been Ānanda who will have told in his last years the story of that last look. And so well did he impress it on his hearers, that Chinese pilgrims, centuries later, found a tope had been erected near Vesālī to commemorate it, the Tope of the Last Look, on the road going West from the city.

However this be, I confess to seeing a significance in the very place which was the stronghold of the Defenders of the Man being also the place where the man, in the sense in which Europe understands the word—the man-made-visible—stood up for the right to exercize private judgment in the carrying out of his life as a Sakyan. Is it possible that the Jain influence, which preceded Sakya at Vesālī, and which upheld the "man-in-man", helped in the upholding of him also in the Sakyans there?

I come, flitting across approximately two and a half centuries, to the Congress, or Conference as it should more fitly be called, not Council, of Patna. (The Pali word, as has been said, is Sangīti, the Together-Chanting. The editorial, revisional work done at the same is called Sangaha, Compiling, taking together. In saying Council, we follow presumably the traditional Christian designation of Concilium. But modern usage has come to use Council in the sense, not of *concilium*, i.e. ecumenical synod, but of *consilium*, the debating by selected authoritative debaters, in whom the Concilium centres.) The Patna gathering was much more than just a Council of experts; it was an ecumenical assembly, such as had not before been held in Sakya. And hence, although its work of elimination and of sanction was carried out by a Council, the whole event can only fitly be described as a Congress, and that of a very inclusive kind. There is no question here of the meeting of a limited number described as all of them arahans, as in the record of the First Conference, or as partly arahans, as at the Second. As to those and this, there is no fitness in calling them all "old men", with M. de la Vallée Poussin,[1] since *thera* (*sthavira*) was technically just "senior" not "aged".

To picture the "Congress of Patna" (or Pāṭaliputta), we must recall the factors in our own recent if less momentous ecclesiastical

[1] *Ency. Rel. Eth.*, art. "Councils".

crisis : a council with revisional labours of twenty years, the whole Church of England and the House of Commons. Kern was partly in error in describing it as a mere "party meeting . . . after the schism",[1] by which he seems to mean "secession", of the Mahāsanghikas. If we are to believe Buddhaghosa, this and the other schools or "sects" (*ācariyakulā*) had not seceded from the Sangha. They are expressly included in the one Sakya Sangha as distinct from teachers and teaching which were "outside this".[2] It was the very presence of such schools notably of Mahāsanghikas (or Vajjiputtiyas) in the Sangha, which contributed to bring about the "Council" and make it so momentous.

The Congress took place during the reign of King, or Emperor, Asoka, but after the middle of the third century B.C. Our Pali authorities as to the event are not contemporaneous. And Buddhist Sanskrit references to it are, Mahāyānist experts tell us, almost or wholly non-existent. The former are the Dīpavaṃsa and the Mahāvaṃsa of Ceylon, and the commentaries on the Vinaya and Kathāvatthu. These appear to have been written or to have taken written form, between six and seven centuries later. As records of a great work and a great crisis they are one and all meagre, jejune, all but childish. The Ceylon "epics" were the work of "men of letters", more anxious to interest reader and listeners than to recover the true. Buddhaghosa was earnest, but in him the historical sense is totally absent. Kern's damning the records as "full of glaring untruths" is too fierce a bark, but, albeit he too much mixes up event with "story", and Patna with Ceylon, he does bring us to this important statement : "the object of the . . . (congress) . . . was 'to prove that the Vibhajjavādins' . . . were the real and original sect, i.e. 'the Sangha'."

But who were the Vibhajjavādins, or analysts, and whence the name ? The four records deliberately affirm that the founder of the Sakya was "Analyst", and hence such were all his right followers. I pointed out long ago[3] that the Subha-Sutta of the Majjhima-Nikāya (No. 99) ascribes to Gotama the Aquinas-like saying : "I am not a generalizer, I am a *vibhajja-vādin*." Yet it is curious, that we nowhere find reference to this saying itself, nor to others like it, nor to any conscious emulating his example by disciples in teaching, nor to any naming of the orthodox debater in the Kathā-vatthu Commentary as *vibhajjavādin* ; he is termed *Sakavādi*—probably a Magadhese survival of "Sakya-speaker."

[1] *Indian Buddhism*, p. 110. [2] Kathāvatthu Commentary.
[3] *Points of Controversy* (1915), xli.

Kern sees in the term an invention of the Ceylon (Mahāvihāra) monks. To that I would suggest that at leisure far from the bustle and stress of the Patna crisis, it is highly improbable that the victorious, and hence orthodox majority in the Sangha would have invented such a name. Once victorious, any specific name, serving as a slogan, was unnecessary. At the Council of Nicæa, Athanasian fought Arian and won. Thereafter the name "Athanasian" survived only to distinguish an elaborated fixed wording of a creed; the term Arian, Arianism for a large "sect" lingered on. It was not "orthodox", not "authentic", not *the* Church. So at the Patna Congress, Vibhajjavādin fought Puggalavādin—Analyst of Man versus Defender of the (unanalysable) Man-in-man—and won. His name faded out. I find it just once in Visuddhi-Magga, p. 522—"The Maṇḍala (society) of Vibhajjavādins": so rare a reference that it was a sensation to come upon it. For me this word "the Analysts", appearing as it does only in the accounts of the Congress, not, I believe, before or after, is a party slogan invented, probably not by the party so named, but by the lay world, interested in a great and long struggle, into which monarchy itself was drawn. So our own English spoke lately of "Revisionist", "Anti-revisionist". Our history abounds in such labels, discarded in the case of the winning side.

Dr. Walleser, in his recent discussion of the term, submits a possible explanation in the idea, much exploited nowadays, that there had always been in the Sakya two ways of regarding certain terms: either the conventional, or people's meaning, and the meaning of philosophical intuition. And in considering the chief bone of contention at the time in the Sangha, namely, the reality of the "man" (over and above body and mind), he suggests, that the party who were careful to "distinguish" in which of those two meanings "the man" was taken were known as the Dividers or Vibhajjavādins.

Dr. Walleser does not stress the plausibility of this view, and I do not think it can survive historical sifting. Had the distinction been thought out and named—*sammuti-kathā*, *paramattha-kathā*—at any time preceding the Congress, we may be quite sure of one thing: it would, as a potent "silencer", have been brought forward by the orthodox debater (the "Our Speaker") in the opening and most important debate in the Kathāvatthu, ascribed, as his compilation, to the President Moggaliputta-Tissa. But "Sakavādī" never makes use of it. The first time we meet with it is in the Milindapañha, between two and three centuries later. There, anyway, such double meaning in teaching is not fathered on to the Founder. But some three centuries later we find both doctrine and libelled Father,[1] full grown, not, in the text commented upon, where it *should* have been used, *but was not*; but in the Commentary, i.e. on the Kathāvatthu. It is set forth as the peroration of the comments on that first and momentous debate. Can historical evidence, short of definite narrative, speak more plainly?

It would not, of course, help the "distinction" theory were the Kathāvatthu assigned a more recent date.[2] Such a hypothesis overlooks the old "Asokan" Pali in the first debate of the book, where *ke* stands for *ko*, and *vattabbe* for *vattabbo*, *vattabbaṃ*, archaisms in Buddhaghosa's time, and corrected by him (*Comm.*, pp. 9, 20); likewise, *se* for *so* (ibid., p. 21).

We come then to what I venture to suggest is a sounder view of the sort of "hustings" term I think Vibhajjavādin was. Let us glance at the situation.

The Founder's message was not the founding of a church of recluses over against a lay world. Hence he made no arrangements to secure church authority or church doctrine with reference to that world. He and his followers formed themselves (first as teachers) into such a dual body of religieux and laymen. But, there being no hierarchy and at first only a moral code, while the laity looked on, criticized, and supported, the monk-world began very industriously to disagree with itself, from the Founder's day onward. With the rise of the Mauryan hegemony, a new broader conception of unity must have stared the now preponderant Sakyan community in the face, at Patna and elsewhere. To this political development they presented a glaring contrast. They were in a fairly chaotic state of disunity. Their ablest divines, if Tissa be not a unique case, had retired from the city monastery in disgust to hillside viharas. But to win over the patronage of the busy sagacious king to their support was of great moment. A good shop-front, paying him the compliment of imitating the new political unity, was necessary. The Congress was summoned, and like Cincinnatus or Venizelos, Tissa was induced to come back and preside over the work of unity.

The records of the Congress make three statements, which from their obvious improbability call for criticism. A small highly efficient executive could alone cope with the gigantic task of revision, and of testing members of the Sangha by its results. We are told that the

[1] He repudiated a dual way of teaching.

[2] Cf. *Die Sekten des alten Buddhismus*, by M. Walleser, 1927.

executive numbered a thousand, that the work of "*dhamma-sangahaŋ*"[1] took nine months, and that the expulsions of the monks, not holding views then pronounced unorthodox, preceded the revision by which alone their orthodoxy could be tested.

I would suggest as a truer account that, albeit, as with the League of Nations Council, the full personnel of each general meeting was large, the actual revisers and judges may well have been, *according to precedent*, only eight.[2] The work of revision to be carefully done *must have lasted years.* With plenty of books and writing and typing materials, our own little Prayer Book Revision took twenty years. With plenty of MSS. around, the output of the gentlemen, now compiling an "authentic" version of the *Mahābhārata* at Poona, is one fasciculus per annum. But at Patna there were not even written MSS., nor any but few and awkward writing materials. There will have been repeaters (*bhāṇakas*), from different viharas eminent as living-record-viharas: I suggest the six repositories referred to, with a distinctive opening to certain Suttas, in the Saṃyutta Nikāya, to which Mr. Woodward and I have drawn attention[3]: Sāvatthi, Kapilavatthu, Benares, Sāketa, Rājagaha, and Patna itself. And these *bhāṇakas* will have come in sections before the judges, according as they were Dīghabhānakas, and so forth, and have repeated, one at a time, some *bhāṇavāra* or portion of one, something like a Welsh Eisteddfodd. Where they were all in verbal agreement, if this ever was the case, the judges may not have dared to revise, had they wished to. Where there were variant versions, *one had to be selected* as the standard version; the rest would be either ruled out, or committed to those miscellanies we find in the third and fourth Nikāyas. Thus the Magga will have been finally entered up as "eightfold"; not because there was any inherent necessity for eight, as either logical or exhaustive, or as the one and only version, but because, down the ages, teachers and so repeaters had elaborated the probably original "thought, word, and deed" of the *really* ancient tradition into variants of these, and finally, of these, eight were selected; the *ten*fold Way, for instance, being relegated to miscellaneous collections.[4]

[1] So Mhvaṃsa. Buddhaghosa uses this *and* the traditional term "reciting", *sangīti*.

[2] As at the second "Council".

[3] *Kindred Sayings*, iii, iv, v; Introduction. I wonder if the inexplicable number ejected, 60,000, may be but a multiple of these six?

[4] *Dīgha-Nikāya*, xxii, xxiii; *Majjhima-Nikāya*, ii, 29; etc. It is possible that the eight found favour, because of the judges being possibly eight in number?

And as to the inverted order in time of revision and expulsions, this may have arisen from a preliminary expulsion of those ascetics, who to get material support "without entering the Sangha . . . donned the yellow robes" and frequented the viharas. Lacking a duly attested ordination, these intruders could be summarily dealt with. To this extent I judge the order of events in the records correct ; but no further. The drastic expulsion of *ordained* monks can only have been carried through *when a unified standardized authoritative "Word" had emerged as sanction.* It was, as we saw, a traditional sanction handed down in the Sakya as accredited to the Founder's own injunction : "The disciples' Teacher was to be Dhamma and Vinaya."[1] The Founder, did he actually say so, will have meant "your inward monitor (conscience) and your outer code of rules". But Dhamma had come to mean verbalized sets of teachings. And with Dhamma and Vinaya now edited, revised, reworded in a Revised Version, it only remained to get rid of those whose views did not run on all fours with those of the revising committee.

On what did disparity in views chiefly hinge ? Let us compare the test-questions put to monks with the contents of the book Kathāvatthu. In the book, any acquaintance with it, as well as with its commentary, will *leave no doubt* as to the paramount importance of the opening debate : "Is the 'man' got at[2] ('caught', Hume would have said) in the true and supreme-meaning sense ?" Yet not nearly enough significance has been attached to this signpost of the past. It can only mean that the question of the man's real nature, either as *a being using* the body-mind khandhas, *or as only those* khandhas, was the *chief question* at issue in the fight for unity of teaching. Is our teaching to be of man as *attan*, with all that the venerable word implies in ancient Indo-Aryan tradition, or *an-attan* ? Divorced from their early mentor, the Sānkhyā, first analyser of "mind" as distinguishable from the "man", the majority in the Sangha had plumped for *anatta*, and had carried out the revision so as to make *this* appear as authoritative as repeaters' versions made possible. But they could not well put the damning test-questions save in terms sanctioned by oldest, most revered tradition, to wit, terms which were already used for wrong views in the Brahmajāla Suttanta, chanted as far back as the First Council. The views, there condemned, which were selected as tests, do refer to the nature of the "man", but not as to whether "got at" or unget-at-able. They turn on whether he survives death : that mighty test yesterday, to-day, and for ever. If the "man" survived death—not this

[1] Mahāparinibbāna Sta. [2] *Upalabbhati*. Comy. : "known."

death only, of course; the Indian mind was more logical than ours—then *he was divine*, i.e. imperishable, unchanging, not-dukkha. If he did not survive, this was the despised nihilism (*uccheda*). Now he was perishable, changing, suffering, on the one hand; on the other, he does survive.

These ancient wordings sufficed for the expelling. Either view was inadmissible, let alone the other subterfuge views of the Suttanta.[1] But there remained a *third alternative view*, by which it had come to be held, a monk's orthodoxy might be passed. This had come, *during the Congress*, to be popularly known as that of the Vibhajjavādins. Having respect to the great pre-occupation about the "man", we may conclude the nickname was because of their view about just that. If only the compiler of the "Man-talk" in the Kathāvatthu had been as clear in *positive* statement of "Saka" view, as he was in negativing the "Man"-speaker's arguments, we should not now be groping. But if we may conclude positively for him, we may say that his "Analysis" of man's nature had brought him curiously near, save in space and time, to David Hume. Namely, he does not deny that the man exists in *some* way. That came later; in the Milinda *glosses*, in the Visuddhi-magga, and in the commentaries, notably in that on the Kathāvatthu. But, analysing the concrete individual, he only finds the very "man" *in the mind*. And mind, as his Suttas entitled him to say, is "multiple, many kinded, manifold,"[2] not a unity. And there he left him. All attempts to explain survival by physical analogies in terms of result belong to later thought. The Vibhajjavādin, following his Abhidhamma as was the vogue, pulled his "man" to pieces as so many *dhammas*, mental phenomena. *Process in dhammas* belongs to post-Patna Abhidhamma: to the *Milinda Questions*, to the Visuddhi-Magga, to the Abhidhammatthasangaha.

This, then, I suggest, is how the historian of Buddhism may rightly interpret this curious name for the new orthodoxy: Vibhajjavādin. I suggest it is no invention of later records, for it is incredible that the Sangha would have called itself by a name without lofty traditional sanction. It does not occur in the (contemporary) Kathāvatthu, but then no party names of any kind do occur, so we can disregard that. It was left to the commentary to supply these. And that on the "Five Books" (Abhidhamma, iii–vii) makes no claims to derive from early sources as do those on the Five Nikāyas. Suddenly the name appears and as suddenly practically disappears.

[1] "Some only survive," and "we don't know anyway" ("Eel-wrigglers") etc.

[2] E.g. *Majjhima*, ii, 26.

I have suggested why. While the little " Council " had been pursuing its long, arduous labours with the coming and going of summoned bhānakas, companies of monks from the corresponding viharas and others will have been mustering at Patna, and, as our young people would say, no end of a hoo-ha was going on in waves of discussion, culminating in a great crescendo as it became known, that the revision was nearing completion and the day of the Congress elections drew nigh. So viewed, it is not strange that a catchword or slogan should have arisen, caught up from the monks themselves, maybe among the populace, maybe among the king's men (police, army, court), maybe among monks themselves, for the formidable party, now at last become corporate and articulate as such : the party who saw, in " the man ", one who could actually, when analysed, only be traced, beyond his bodily factor, in the manifold of the mind. Rather would it be strange, had some such name not been lit upon. If the annals of the Christian Church can show no parallel name for the matter in dispute calling for a Council, it will be because that Church had begun and grown to adolescence in Europe, not in India, the land of the Man, the Self, the Ātman in Deity and in man. I do not find in those annals a Council on so fundamental a thing as the nature of the man. The nearest is perhaps the Council at Constantinople in the seventh century, as to the will in Jesus being one with, or distinct from the will of God, where we come also on to psycho metaphysical ground. Here it was the party voted as heretical about whom the " hustings-name " centred, and which has alone survived : the Monothelites. If there was also the name : Duothelites, that has merged, as that of the victors, into " the Church ".

" Man is not to be valued save in terms of body and mind, and as such comes under the category " anatta " : this is, I hold, the decision arrived at in this Third Congress. Thereby a third milestone was set up in the way of divergence from the spirit of the Founder's message, namely, of the Man as, with *dhamma* working within him as will, most divinely Real. At the First Conference, and yet more at the Second, we see Sakya becoming ever more and more the Man of the Dhamma-as-external-Rule, of the Dhamma as becoming external precept and elaborated Word. In the Third Conference we see Sakya ejecting the very anchorage wherein *dhamma* is fixed.

XX

BUDDHA-CULT AND THE NOT-MAN

It is impossible to say, with documents where the historic sense of the compilers is practically at zero, how soon there grew up, in the still young Sakya, a loosening in the deep, the very Indian conviction of the reality, in the composite human being, of the invisible Person, whose were body and mind. It was of gradual growth, for it was not till two to three centuries later—in the time of Asoka—that we find the question of the reality of the *puggala*, that is, of the mere man, or male human being, *replacing the question* of the reality of the *attā* or *puruṣa*, that is, of the man conceived as potentially divine, and made the theme of a long and strenuous debate. It was two or more centuries after that, that we come upon further discussion in the Milinda Questions, where we find the reality of the "mere man" still evaded *in the same terms as in the Kathāvatthu*, but *traversed* by the absolute elimination of him in what will be a Ceylonese gloss.[1] It is another four centuries before we are confronted with the absolute denials of the Visuddhi-Magga, and yet another seven centuries before the assertion, that anything beyond body and mind is "non-existent," is met with in the important manual Abhidhammattha-sangaha. For us the important fact, the well-attested truth is, that this non-selfism, this *an-attā*, this disbelief in the "man", as the subject, the valuer of the object, was not of the original Sakya, but was a growth, yes, and a growth in the sense we now call malignant.

So careful have the editors of the scriptures been to invest with the highest sanction certain Suttas, which give support to the growing idea of the "man" as being "in truth and ultimately" a fiction, by putting the sayings about this into the mouth of the Founder, so readily have those sayings been accepted by modern writers, that it calls for some courage and faith to repudiate them on his behalf—repudiate them as things he would not anyway have said in his day, repudiate them as things which, as founder of a great world-message for the good of the Many, he would at no time and in no place have said. But faith in will spurs me, and I say it again. And it seems

[1] *Milindapañho*, p. 25 f; in *SBE.* trs. i, pp. 40–43. "*Na upalabbhati*" is not clearly translated.

best to discuss in this chapter those Suttas, which, at some time, *probably after* the debate was compiled for presentation at the Patna Conference, were adduced as best establishing the case, as orthodox doctrine, of the "man" as at best an "unget-at-able" entity. We can there see, where, in the records, the orthodox held, that their strongest sanctions lay for finding that the man was this and no more.

A point of possible historic significance is that these "appeals to authority", as S. Z. Aung and I have called them, are introduced, seven out of eight times, with a reference to "the Suttanta": *atth'eva suttanto ti?* "Is (this) verily Scripture?" as we should now say; or "the Elect Sayings?" *-Anto*, affixed here to Sutta, has the meaning of *-agga*, chief, worthiest. The term is used to include any Sutta quoted, yet in titles, with a very few much later exceptions, it is only the Dīgha Suttas which are so called. The significant point lies in this: that of the twenty-three Books of the Debates, appeal is made to the Suttanta in nearly every case in the first six; then up to Book XI, appeal is now to the Suttanta now to the "Bhagavā", as having said what is cited; but from XI to XXIII, *the sole appeal* is to "Was it not said by the Bhagavā?"

Is not the work trying here to tell us of the growth, during the later period when these accretions were being incorporated, of the cult of the "Buddha Bhagavā", on whom were fathered everything said as approved of in the Sayings? I blush to think, that neither of us discerned this, and as to that, that no one has since pointed it out to us.

And it is, as has been already suggested, after, and not before the Patna Congress, that the cult of Gotama the Sakyan, as super-man, and then as quasi-God, ultimately attained to such a worth as to take its place in the general reaction against immanent Theism which was going on in India, with the rise of Śiva, Vishnu and Śāktism. It is not to be expected, that the world of Sakya in India would, with such influx of recruits as may have gone on, have been immune from the spirit of the age. The more its older conception of immanent *dhamma* became externalized, as the formulated and taught and prescribed "Dhamma", the more was there left a void in "the man"—we would say, in heart and mind—for some concrete image of the Highest, the Best, the Most. Then too there was the incentive given by the actual realization of the Indian "world-monarch" ideal in the new Emperor Asoka and his empire. The way in which the early Ceylon literature wrote in adulation of Asoka, (the while it calmly admits the unspeakable fratricides of his legend), betrays the influence left by that incarnation of the old Chakkavatti, or world-monarch tradition. And with that the tradition of the Man of Dhamma-empire was, as we know, very closely linked.[1]

Now the super-normal in that Man was, and is, very much stressed as "omniscience"; he was called, and is called, *sabb'aññu*, all-knowing.[2] We find the imputation creeping up already in the Suttas and Vinaya, usually in poetic rhapsody. But, when it comes down to a direct question in prose, it is of interest to find, left in, the express repudiation by Gotama of omniscience. In Sutta 72 of the Majjhima, he is asked, at Vesālī, by the wandering (student) Vacchagotta: "I have heard, sir, that 'the samaṇa Gotama, omniscient, all-seeing, admits an absolute knowledge and vision; that whether I walk, stand, sleep or keep vigil, constantly and continually knowledge and vision is present'.[3] They who say so, do they tell what you have said, or do they misrepresent you? . . ." The reply is: "They who say so, do not tell what I have said, they misrepresent me by what is not, by what has not come to be (*asatā, abhūtena*)." Could anything be plainer? Is anything among Buddhists, in scripture, in belief, so disregarded?

Actually what was valued was, not the fancied all-knowing, but the will to teach what he knew. Gradually this distinction came to pass in the word "Buddha", "awake", or "wise": the man who knew all, and taught as he knew; the man who knew all, and taught nothing that he knew. The former became known as Sambuddha (*plus* sometimes *sammā*), or sabb'aññu-Buddha; the latter as Pacceka Buddha, or Prati-eka Buddha, awake for the one, namely himself alone. It became a thing of immense merit to give even a flower to recluses rejoicing in the latter repute; but the transcendent merit lay with the man in whose will was the helping of others. And thus it is by the teaching rather than by the knowing only, that the Awakened one reached up to Divinity. Again, in a Superman, the will to help by revealing knowledge would, though regulated by wisdom, be infinite. But it is fairly obvious, that nothing approaching a correspondingly infinite knowledge can justly be ascribed to the Sakyan who founded Sakya. He himself rejected the ascription.

In spite of him, the notion stuck and grew. And thus it is that we see, also growing, the way of referring everything in the thesaurus of monk-edited sayings, ever less to the Suttanta, ever more to the "Exalted One".

[1] See *Dīgha*, Sta. 26.

[2] Also *sabba-vidu, loka-vidu*.

[3] In the Pali Suttas the identical claim is recorded as made by the Jains for their Mahā-vīra Vardhamāna.

In examining these cited sanctions of Vibhajjavāda, I must perforce be somewhat more technical in treatment. The reader, who is satisfied with the subject, as presented in the first Part, in the chapter "Sakya, Sānkhya and the Self", can pass it over. The reader who has text and translation at hand will follow more easily.

The first quotations are declarations of the man as coming under the categories of the Conditioned [1] and of the Transient. These will have been from the Indian point of view of more weight than they may seem to us. It must never be lost to sight that, for this point of view, the man was not "*a* self", but was "of *the* Self". It was at a much later date, that the then elaborated Sānkhya philosophy came to admit the conceptions of "selves". Hence to admit that the man *was*, apart from the mind, was to value him as Divinity, namely, to give him the divine attributes of being (*a*) unconditioned, (*b*) impermanent, or, to use the Vedic word, "imperishable" (*akṣara*), (*c*) bliss.

But to value the man in this way belonged to original Sakyan, viz. Indian values, and for Sakya those values were of a day that was past. The man was not unconditioned ; he was in process of a causal coming to be. The man was not impermanent, for he was, together with all things, transient. The term "unconditioned" had become reserved for space and nirvana. The man was not bliss, but an "ill" thing.

This did not mean, I hasten to remind the reader, that anything in the world was absolutely perishable, or was unreal, an illusion. The former of these two suppositions was condemned, equally with the absolutely imperishable, as the heterodox Nihilism (literally upcutting, or upbreaking, *uccheda-diṭṭhi*). The latter view became we know, very prevalent in India, and indeed, as an attribute of deity, *māyā*, or the power of creating illusion or hallucination, much like that simulated by the juggler, is to be found even in the Vedas. But so far was it from being *applied to views* about the world of men and things in early Sakyan days, that we do not even find the word used, in the later compilations of the Piṭakas, to mean anything more than the art of the juggler, or the hallucination of mirage. There is in the Piṭakas no clear wording on the subject, but I judge, that Uccheda excludes any theory of absolute destruction, much as we now exclude absolute cessation of matter and energy.

Now this problem as to the man being, when rightly considered

[1] *Kathāvatthu*, i, 1, §§ 225 f. (*PTS*. ed.). Trs. : *Points of Controversy* (*PTS*. ed.). "Conditioned" = *sankhata*, arisen from a cause.

neither permanent, nor yet destructible, was, I believe, a very old feature in that ancient world-lore, Lokâyata, to which allusion was made in a former chapter.[1] To those vague generalizations will have belonged the antitheses: *Sassata* (eternal) and *Uccheda* (annihilation). The former term, a Pali or Prakrit corruption of the Vedic *śaśvat*, perpetually recurring, may possibly derive from the Vedic root *śaś*, "repeatedly leaping" (origin also of the name for the hare, the bounding one, *śaśa*). Both terms occur in the long Appendix to the first of all the Suttas (Dīgha, I, i), and frequently elsewhere, used as current, and demanding no explanation. (The Commentaries do explain them, but that is another thing.)

The two theories will have meant that, as to his body, the man is not permanent, either as to his earth-body, or as to any other body in any other world with which he can ever be associated. As to the man himself, on the other hand, he was *an-uccheda*, indissoluble, because he was That. As to his mind no distinction is drawn. The terms are doubtless pre-Sānkhyan, of a day when it was not yet a matter of thoughtful wording to distinguish mind from man.

So far then we elicit from that curiously muddled concoction, the Kathāvatthu debate, that "the man" (*puggalo*) does not conform to the current conception of the impermanent, in that he is "conditioned", i.e. governed by cause and effect, and that would mean that he is perpetually becoming.[2]

The next quotation is from the venerable collection of monk-verses composing the last chapter of the Sutta-Nipāta, to which we have already referred; the Pārâyana. A venerable Brahman teacher, Bāvari, it is told, sends an embassy of pupils to call on, and report to him on the famed teacher Gotama. The places on their route are described very simply, and we need not reasonably doubt, that some such visit, nay, visits will have taken place, or that the places and the names here may have been correctly recorded. But what the pupils asked and what were the several replies, or the collective reply given them is not a matter about which, at this time of day, one can feel sure we have a faithful record. In the first place, question and answer are in metric form; hence we have them only in a shape in which they will have been after-edited. Secondly, terms are used which bear the stamp of the category and the formula, notably here, in the compound *attânudiṭṭhi*:

[1] See above, p. 91.

[2] Op. cit., pp. 59–61; trs. 54 f.

Cut out the many theories as to self;
So shalt thou get past death; so an thou look,
The king of death shall no more look on thee.[1]

And lastly, the values in the verses, albeit they are not without much general religious interest, are here and there strongly monastic:

O Mogharājan, look upon the world
As void, and ever heedful bide.

"Void of a being (*satta*)" is the Commentator's chat, "contemplate the world of aggregates as void of entities,"—a view rightly representing the monastic inner-world of his day, and of that when his sources were first written down, but an unworthy view to put into the mouth of a man out to save the many in the world, with a new word of the More there was in life for the man.

The Pārâyana has probably been compiled by a monk from a number of half-forgotten Sayings telling of the many young Wandering students and pupils of Brahmans who used to come to him, to consult him with questions on life and destiny.

I return to the text of the Kathāvatthu :—The Believer in the Man quotes in his turn[2]: "Do you mean that, when the Word tells us of the Bhagavā speaking of 'the man (*puggalo*) who works for his own good', and again 'Who is the One Person who is born for the good the happiness of the many . . .', it means one who is not got at as true and as ultimately real?"

To this the Orthodox has no direct reply. The Commentator has one, but he holds it up till the end: the alleged two ways in which "Buddhas taught". With this I have dealt.[3] The Orthodox would most certainly have used it had it then been a *cliché* already invented. He only replies with an older *cliché*: The Bhagavā has said "All things are *an-atta*". He then makes the assumption—it is not explicitly stated—that this is implied in the (unusual) term, knowledge which is "not caused by another (*a-para-paccaya-ñaṇaṃ*).[4] Namely, that he who understands Ill as being transient, will of himself understand the man, liable to it, as being also transient, and therefore as not the Self.

He next quotes the famous verses of the obscure nun, Vajirā:

"Being? What dost thou fancy by that word?
'Mong false opinions, Māra, art thou strayed.
This a mere bundle of formations is;
Therefrom no 'being' mayest thou obtain.

[1] Op. cit., ver. 1119. [2] *Kathāvatthu*, p. 64 f.; trs. p. 58 f.
[3] Above, p. 358 f.
[4] In the trs. (*Points of Controversy*) "independent insight".

For e'en as, when the factors are arranged,
The product by the name 'chariot' is known,
So doth our usage covenant to say:
'A being' when the aggregates are there.
'Tis simply Ill that riseth, simply Ill
That doth persist, and then fadeth away.
Nought beside Ill there is that comes to be;
Nought else but Ill there is that fades away."

The editor of this Debate on the Man was (or ought to have been) doing a disservice to his own party, when he quoted this little poem in full, *instead of stopping half-way*, as, later on, Nāgasena did, in the discussion with King Menander (Milinda), and as, still later, Buddhadatta and Buddhaghosa did. For when we hear the whole of this little poem of utter world-woe, we see at once (or ought to), that Vajirā is sweeping aside discussion about the nature of the living being, that she may fling fuller emphasis on what for her, as a world-forsaker, is the dreadful fact about life, which will have probably whelmed her, as it did others of the nuns who have left us verses, in some tragedy of bereavement or other suffering. Here, she is saying, is the one reality worth considering: the *dukkha* that lies in our coming to be. Let be the living thing, human or other! I will show you life!

She was not right. But there are times when nothing else appears so right as this. And as she herself said: "It fades away." Or it may be, she may not have been under the waves of misery, but was keeping well to the front the world-ill, which constituted the recluse's best excuse for forsaking his and her duties to the world, to the home. At that time it was necessary to wave this banner. In the later days of those monks just named, monasticism had become too firmly instituted to need this flag-waving, and attention was more concentrated on the third of the three slogans: *anicca*, *dukkha*, *anatta*.[1]

I much wish we knew more about Vajirā. But in spite of her posthumous fame, as being the one and only woman whose words are quoted by Buddhist writings, she is not granted a place in the Nuns' Anthology; she is the last to be given room in the Nun Collection of the Saṃyutta-Nikāya, and the Commentator has practically nothing handed down to record about her.

But she had the luck, or the æsthetic *flair* to quote a figure which is a favourite to Indian as to Greek, that of the chariot, as expressing the life-way of the man. And this she applies in what was perhaps an original way.

[1] Cf. my *Milinda Questions*, London, 1930, p. 29 f.

In the instance of it, cited in a former chapter,[1] we saw it *fitly* used. The driver was *dhamma* : the will-to-the-right, or sense of what ought to be. In Brahmanic writings we get the corresponding idea of *ātman* as the driver. And this too is fit, for whereas the man is ultimately the directing master in the chariot, *dhamma* or *ātman* is That in him who suggests whither to drive. Often in Pali it is the *citta* (mind) who drives. Nor again is this wholly unfit, for the mind will then be the way, in mind, in will, of the man as self-directing ; the driver with the warrior standing by him.

But in Vajirā's simile, the man and the driver are left out, forgotten ; all that made the simile apt is not there. In chariot similes the fitness lies in movement, in direction, in advance, in compassing the aim. But in this very limited figure we have only the passive, the stationary, the man-used, the man-made thing, a mere sort of extra-body, enlarging man's efficiency in bodily work directed by way of his mind.

I do not think that Vajirā is here chiefly to blame. She was compiling a poem, giving ideal, that is, artificial emphasis to the tragic side of life ; and we make allowance for poets. She was saying : " Are you speculating over the fact of the individual being ? See him rather, human or animal or other-world being, as swept along in the greater world-fact of misery." They who are chiefly to blame are the learned Doctors of the Sangha, who attached such importance to her metric wailing, citing her ; then citing her as " saying it in presence of the Founder ",[2] then citing the Founder as having said it himself.[3] And not the Doctors only, but modern Buddhists and writers on Buddhism, who have failed (with one exception)[4] to see how vapid the simile is. On such inept similes I have said more in *The Milinda Questions*, and shall return to them in the next chapter.

The last scriptural (but still unwritten) sanction cited in the

[1] Above, p. 150. [2] *Milindapañho*, p. 28.

[3] Buddhadatta, *Abhidhammâvatāra*, (*Manuals*, i), p. 87 f.

[4] L. de la Vallée Poussin, *The Way to Nirvāṇa*, chap. ii. I regret that I overlooked his *mot juste* on the chariot, and Milinda's reply, in my *Milinda Questions*. This distinguished scholar rightly deprecates the *emphasis* laid on the imputation of " not-self " to early Buddhism. But for me he does not discern sufficiently the historical perspective. This is, not to see in monastic efforts to reconcile not-self with survival, a *camouflaging* of an *earlier* anomaly. The anomaly was *not there at first* ; it grew out of values changing in time. Anomaly, in fact, only appears, if we juxtapose values belonging to different stages of time.

Kathāvatthu is a group of three passages, which are apparently intended to clinch the matter finally with a denial, that in the world there is an ultimately real Self. These are so important, as claiming in the first place to be utterances of the Founder, and in the second as apparently going in denial beyond the qualified, Humian scepticism of the orthodox debater himself, that it is worth while examining them carefully.

The last group (text p. 68[1]) I take first. I do this because, though I have done my utmost, I can not find that the passage and the terms quoted, *as quoted*, are in the Pali Canon. If I am right in failing to find them, there will have been, at least of the passage, a later excision. It is in brief as follows :—" There are, Seniya, three sorts of teachers. One declares, that the self is real, persistent in this life and in the next. One declares that the self is real, persistent in this life, not in the next. One declares that the self is real, persistent neither in this life, nor in the next. Now the first teaches Sassata ; the second teaches Uccheda ; the third is the Rightly Enlightened Teacher."

If the passage be indeed non-canonical, we may dismiss it without breaking our heads over it. I would only say, in passing, that (1) the Pali way of stating the negative clauses, " does not declare that . . . is," does not soften the denial but is as positive in negation as I have rendered it ; (2) the title at the end, " Satthā Sammā-sambuddho " is so far as I know a unique grouping ; I imagine the latter title to be much later than the former *Satthā* (teacher) ; (3), the only Seniya mentioned in the Canon is an ascetic Cynic, or Dog-cult man, who, I presume, to make his world-forsaking the more marked, affected—God help him !—doggish ways.[2] His fate in the next life is asked about, and the Man, who was *said* to deny the self in any world, says that " he " will be reborn into the company (world or kingdom) of dogs. There is no hint at any complex which will break up at death save that of the body (*kayassa bhedā*)

Following this we have : " The Bhagavā spoke about ' oil-jar, honey-jar, butter-jar, and the like ; perpetual meal, constant soup (-charity) ". The argument is then abruptly concluded, but we are to understand, that the different sense in which words are used, e.g. " jar " to contain butter, not made of it, " perpetual " signifying a period by no means eternal, is to apply to the words : man, permanent, and so on.

[1] Trs., p. 62.

[2] *Majjhima*, i, 387 f. The dog-and-ox cult of the Suttas were merely forms of the worsened values in the " man ".

The debate here terminates in the way usually observed in the work: with a denial of the thesis. But Buddhaghosa makes it give him the opportunity to perorate in the way we saw in our last chapter, on a Buddha's popular and learned ways of teaching. I shall have another word on this later. Its historical significance is great, but is as yet passed over.

Let us come finally to the remaining pair of quotations in the Kathāvatthu debate.[1] The one first cited is in the Saṃyutta-Nikāya (iv, 54: "Suñña"). The second is from the Alagaddûpama Sutta of the Majjhima (No. 22). Both state in different ways, that the world is empty of the self, or of the "selfic" (*attaniya*). The first merely asserts; the second gives this much of explanation: "because it is impossible to get at what these, as such, truly are." This being so, to affirm, that world, that Self, that "I" am imperishable is "wholly and completely a fool-thing".

In these passages we dig in a stratum of very great interest. I will not stay over the pregnant word "empty". Negative, vacuous, it became none the less a very potent vehicle in the Buddhist development known as Mahāyāna, and is still in Eastern philosophy a word to conjure withal. But I seek here for the roots, and first developments of, not a philosophy, but a religion for the Many. And I have to look for terms of positive value, such as would be a new word in the *more in man*, and not in the *less*. Now the "man" in such a new word is the most central, most important idea. And to teach something new about him in terms of a sweeping out, as void, i.e. as not real, as foolish, as making him out to be Less, is, in a new gospel, inconceivable. Inconceivable unless there had been placed beside such a negation something of positive value, equally central and important. There was time, in the Founder's long mission, for the idea "suñña", void, to have come into the compiling of these doubtless early Majjhima Suttas, at the hands of the early Sāvatthī compilers. I know of nothing to account for the emergence of the term, save the wilting of the More in man conceived, as he was in India, as having in his nature the Most. It is the monk's answer to the First Bidding: "Seek the self!"—He replies: *The world is empty of the self.*

There is interest, also not of a kind belonging to the original Sakya, in the curious, made-term "selfic". There was coming into use, when Sakya was born—so we have seen—the term *adhy-ātma*, an adjective conveying in its form just what *attaniya* (selfic) amounted

[1] p. 67; trs., p. 61.

to, and which we have in the Suttas both as *ajjhatta* and as *ajjhattika.* Why should it have seemed necessary to make up a second term?

As to that, we ourselves have had to find a second adjective for self. "Selfish" damns the "self" to whom it is applied.[1] Hence our schoolmen in the eighteenth century or earlier coined the term "subjective". We wanted to get an undepreciated term. The Sakyan schoolmen wanted to get just the opposite: a term conveying depreciation. Hence they devised the word selfic, *attaniya.* It was because the rather older word *ajjhat(tik)a* (or its Prakrit namesake) commended, instead of damning the self, that a word, when the self was coming to be depreciated, was felt to be needed, as conveying only depreciation.

Perhaps not just only depreciation; perhaps also as belonging to another "universe of discourse". For the gist of the passage lies in this, a very often repeated deduction, that in the man as "got at", we see change and "ill". Now this is neither God, nor god-like (Self, selfic). But the depreciation is there, else had there not been used so forcible a word as *bāladhammo*, "fool-thing, child-thing."

The passage cited is in full as follows: "Given a Self, would there be attributes of the Self (*attaniyaṃ*)? Yes, sir. Given attributes of the Self, would there be for me the Self? Yes, sir. But given that both Self and attributes of Self are not to be got at as true, as persisting, then the opinion as to these things:—that the world, that the Self, that I hereafter shall be permanent, everlasting, eternal, unchanging, (that) I shall persist even as the eternal—is not this, monks, wholly completely a fool-thing?"

I do not think I am imagining anything impossible in seeing, in this apparently unneeded word "selfic", a special device to score a point in ecclesiastical special pleading, because to have used the adjective *ajjhatta* was a term of appreciation. For it certainly was so. We have but to consider such passages as that of the altar quoted above:—

> I lay no wood, brahman, for fires on altars.
> Only within (*ajjhattam eva*) burneth the fire I kindle.

On this line the Commentary has: "*niyakajjhatte, attano santānasmiṃ*," that is, "in one's own very-self, in the self's continuity."[2] There is here no sign of depreciation. And why? Buddhaghosa has lost sight, after the centuries, of the original meaning

[1] Above, p. 210.

[2] *Sāratthappakāsinī*, p. 236.

of *ajjhatta* when Sakya began. The term has become for him just what "subjective" now means for us; a term of mind-import, not *of the man who is minding*. And a quaint point about that is, that he unaware uses, in the word *niyaka* (one's own), a word which was first used for self-reference as meaning the "permanent". For *niya-ka* is a lingual slide from *nija*, and that from *nicca* (*nitya*). But the Sakyan argument was based on the man being *a-nicca*! Such are the ironies of language.

And in our own tongue we have other such dual terms nearer in form than selfish and subjective. Have we not lusty and lustful, the latter coming in, I believe, with Milton's Puritan prose, and surviving with the "lusty" of happy, healthy import of Chaucer's day and of earlier Anglo-Saxon. We have again "willing", and also "wilful", or full of perverted will, a sadly worsened word we much need in appreciative import now.

Just, then, as we in our present day have by the word "selfish" largely banned the very self or man from our ethics, and in the word "subjective" have banned the very self or man from our psychology, so did the Sakyans, even with the very words for the very man: *ajjhatta*, *ajjhattika*, *attaniya*, *attabhāva*, banish the self, who in India had stood at the birth of their movement for not the man only, but also for That who was "in" and of the man, and to realize Whom was the man's noblest aim.

We shall be wrong, I think, if we do not keep in view, that in this ejection of the self, there were at least three distinguishable stages. In the first stage, man was reckoned no longer as that "inwardly More who would become the Most", the "That Who he is". In the second stage, he 'is', but is not to be got at save somehow as, or in mind. In the third, he is reckoned as only mind, that is, as *dhammā*, or mental phenomena. In the end—as we see in classic manuals—he is not; there are but body, mind and "mentals" (*cetasikā*); a nihilism which is already anticipated in the concluding chapters of the Visuddhi-Magga.

Now in the cited passage we have last discussed, we are in the first stage of this decline. When the Alagaddûpama Sutta was first compiled—let us say, in the last decade of the Founder's life on earth, when the pressing need of fixed forms of "doctrine" was beginning to be felt—I believe that the compiling Thera, by *attā* and *attaniya*, meant God and the God-like in man. On the face of it, it is *more likely* that this is what he meant. But more: it is the only way by which the following deduction about the man being changing and "ill" becomes intelligible. Man as changing is not Being (*sat*); as liable to ill, he is not Bliss (*ānanda*). The one attribute of Deity left: Mind (*cit*): this alone could be maintained as befitting the man. And so we merge into the second stage of decline.

But it is the second stage of decline which, with the foregoing exceptions, is chiefly represented in the Piṭakas. The man is still there, using, controlling body and mind, especially in autobiographical sayings ascribed to Gotama. For example: "Then I bethought me forcibly to restrain thought by mind,"[1] and in the parable ascribed to Sāriputta, of the man as agent to, owner of his mental processes, namely the king and his wardrobe.[2] It is here not just conventional usage dictating the form of their talk; it is *their attitude* in the matter, which leaves no doubt as to the reality of the Man for them. But he has become, for the compilers, no longer the Self of the earlier teaching. We may even see Elders in the Order debating the difficulty of fit ideas about the man, in a way that is at times very Humian. Thus, in the Aggregate (*khandha*) Saṃyutta, there is this remark in such a debate: "I see that, with respect to body and mind, 'I am' comes to me, yet I do not discern this I 'am'."[3]

Later than this will be the inter-canonical Commentary on the Sutta-Nipāta, called the Niddesa, of the Sutta-Piṭaka. Here we find, concerning the Sutta quoted above from the Pārâyana, the reply to Mogharājan commented on thus: "Look upon the world as void"—it is void in twelve ways: 'body' is not being (*satto*), not soul (*jīvo*), not *poso*, *naro*, *māṇavo*, *puriso*—these are all terms for man—not woman, not self, not selfic, not I, not mine, not anyone whatever. And the list is repeated for each of the four mind-aggregates; "feeling," etc.[4] It was orthodox to see the "world" (*loko*) in these five, viz. body and mind. And it is to be noted, that we are still, in wording, not exceeding the teaching of the Second Utterance. It was only in the *inference drawn from that wording*, namely, that to be Not in body, Not in mind means to be Not at all, that we see the way opening up for the ejection of the man. It had at last come to be necessary to say that Utterance as: "The man is, but is not either body or mind," for the divergence in Sakya from the preponderant Brahman teaching of its infancy had grown great. But there was no one to say it. The Sānkhyan interest in mind and the mental had also grown great, and it was here that the man had been made to take refuge.

The one thing I do not understand in the foregoing Niddesa

[1] *Majjhima*, i, 242 f. (No. 36).
[2] Above, p. 327.
[3] Vol. iii, 130, "Khemo."
[4] *Culla-Niddesa*, p. 278–80.

comment is the absence of the word for man, *puggalo*. This curious ugly word is, in the Abhidhamma, made to replace the older word *puriso* (*puruṣa*). Here and there it has got inserted in a Sutta. And that, in the records, the Bhagavā, so the repeaters said, used it in a division of men ethically considered, as working each for his own good, for another's, for both, for neither, served as a sheet-anchor to the Upholder of the man's reality in the great Kathāvatthu debate. If the truth-speaking Teacher, it was urged, could speak of this and that *puggalo* as real, as actual agent in the world, why try to be reducing this being to an unget-at-able idea?

But I doubt that, in the Founder's day, the word *puggalo* was used for more than just the male. And I think it is likely, that it was brought to have a more general meaning as "homo" precisely because the words, till then current in religious utterance for the "man", involved and implied immanent Deity; I mean *attā* and *purisa*. Fortunately the excision of *purisa* (as a religious term) was not carried out wholesale. In the duplicated Sutta of the after-death judgment, it is not the *puggala* but the *purisa* who is there arraigned as such: "ambho purisa!" before the judge.[1]

It is true that *purisa* is also used as just male over against female in the Suttas. There is further the duplication *purisa-puggala*, possibly emphasizing *homo*, occurring in the Nikāyas, albeit rarely.

Well, it is in usage a question of the more or less, but I strongly incline to the conclusion that *puggala* was (more or less) deliberately taken into use, by Sakyan teachers and wording-fixers, as a mark and label of the shrunken meaning of the man, which appeared to them to be the more true. That it was also a new word in the day of the movement's adolescence is fairly certain, for Vedic literature knows it not, and that is to include all the earlier Upanishads. Meaning a "male", it has in later Sanskrit the derived meaning of "handsome". But the religious emphasis which it had for its Sakyan adopters is betrayed by the odd meaning in Commentaries, where it is parcelled out exegetically as "hell-crier", or "-gobbler".[2] To such a depth had the man akin to Deity sunk in Buddhist monasticism! And that, once the word had become the orthodox term for the disdeified man, it would be a natural and pious work, when the spoken sayings were under revision, and the prose sayings especially were editable, to make repeaters say *puggala* for *purisa*, I have little doubt.

The last descent we see definitely operating in the writings of

[1] See above, p. 227. [2] E.g. *Visuddhi-Magga*, p. 310.

Buddhaghosa and Buddhadatta, less obtrusively perhaps in Dhammapāla's Commentaries. It is true, that the first-named defines the word "not got at", in the Kathāvatthu, as "is not known, not approached by understanding". But he, in the same work, and elsewhere, makes it plain enough that for him the man is nothing more than a complex and a series of *dhammas*, or mental phenomena. A few centuries before him, Nāgasena, the Buddhist exponent in the *Questions of King Milinda*, still halts at the "not got at" of the Kathā-vatthu stage. He cannot discern an "experiencer" (*vedagu, vedako*), but he nowhere says: "He is not," albeit the translation suggests it somewhat freely. Still for him it is, not exactly that there is no man, but that nothing can be definitely stated about him save as I have said.

But in the later day, when the Commentaries were finally written in Pali, the man, save as a word-label, is dead. "The puggala," we read, "is divisible into fifty-seven kinds of *dhammas*, beginning with *rūpa* (material shape)." Again: "*anatta* means deserted by (*rahita*) self, soul, man (*puggala*). The man is not in even a single *dhamma*." Again: "Given body and the mind, it is customary to say 'of such a name, such a family'. It is by this customary convention and speech that we say the man is."[1] Once more, in the Vinaya Commentary (I, p. 22): "Those persons who have the notion 'I', 'mine' in what is a mere mass of *dhammas* (*dhamma-puñja-matte*)."

But in still later manuals, to say e.g. "woman", is to name *dhammas* which really exist by a *something that does not really exist!*[2]

The three-staged descent is betrayed in the wide-spread Buddhist symbol for mental complexes or *sankhārā*. In an Ajanta fresco these are illustrated as potter at his wheel making pots; in later Tibetan pictures, the potter is dropped out; in a later Japanese picture we have the pots alone.[3] How significant is not this of the history of "the man" in Buddhism!

Verily we seem here to be worlds away from that realm of Indian religious values, which was also so largely in essence that of the new-born Sakya teaching. Yet are we not so far as it might seem. For when that teaching began, it may well be, that the word *nirātman*, "selfless," was creeping into Upanishadic teaching. The Maitri Upanishad is the first to use it, and use it repeatedly, but with this meaning, so different from the term *an-attan*, of implying such

[1] *Kathāvatthu Comy.*, pp. 8, 33.

[2] Abhidhammattha-Sangaha (Compendium of Philosophy), pt. viii, § 14.

[3] Rhys Davids, *Buddhism* (*American Lectures*), p. 156.

'vision' of the highest Self that 'the man' merges his own worth in Divine values, and "abides in his own greatness." The term soon petered out again, and whereas I believe it is to be found in Mahāyānist writings, there too it tended, in the world of Amida Buddhism, where more positive ideals prevailed, to 'lapse into obsolescence'.[1] But in the Maitri it is indicative of a temporary sickening in the sublime quest of the earlier Upanishads. Emphasis is thrown on to the Less in the man, which spread over Sakya as a very canker. It was a more in becoming toward the Most that those earlier men of the new word, Brahman and Sakyan, taught, and not a Less. And herein they are nearer in spirit than the later men to that Paul who wrote: "till we all come into a perfect man, unto the measure of the stature of the fulness of Christ . . . no more children, but growing up into him in all things."

[1] J. B. Pratt, *The Pilgrimage of Buddhism*, p. 659.

XXI

SAKYA AND THE RECORDS

Men as seeking to know and to forward the very nature of the man in mind-values are specially likely to be testifying to such efforts by the machinery and legacy of the Word. This is what we find in the testament of words bequeathed to the world by Sakya, and associated in the ecclesiastical way called Canonical. In bulk it far exceeds the Vedic works which might be strictly called Canonical or "sacred", or the Avestan scriptures, or the Christian Bible, or the Kuran. It exceeds any of these, even when the much repetition in it is deducted. And not a little of this bulk is due to the speakers going about, in their laudable intent at Sāsana, or instruction and edification, to get at the *mind* of man.

A little reading in the Suttas (let alone Abhidhamma) will make this evident. We are ever being fetched up at passages dealing, not with the man *tout court*, but with the alleged factors of him. Now they are many, and it takes more telling. The force and truth of many sayings are frittered away in his being trotted out as groups, faculties, elements and the like. We have only to recall the passages referring in reiterated detail, not to "mind", but to four ways of minding, or phases of mind, to have before us the wrecking of many a forceful saying by this mistaken editing. And not in prose, only. Even in poems treating of conversion, of salvation assured, the poet will say things like this:

> Dhamma she taught to me, wherein I learnt
> The factors, organs, bases (of this self)[1];

that is, *khandhâyatana-dhātuyo*; and this:

> Herein myself I'll exercise:—the startingpoints of mindfulness,
> The powers five, the forces too, the factors of enlightenment . . .[2]

lines which in slightly varying words reverberate through the Anthology.

It is true, that in one of these the poet adds:

> One who wardeth parts and powers,
> He may do to self his duty (*attano kiccakāri 'ssa*),
> Nor work harm on any other.[3]

Here we have the man kept in view, and not merely the states and ways of him. And the Commentator, Dhammapāla, in keeping

[1] *Therīgāthā*, ver. 43; 69.

[2] *Theragāthā*, ver. 352; cf. 437; 595; 672; 1114 etc. [3] Ibid., 749.

herewith, reports the Teacher as having said: "I have taught the Ariyan who has his faculties developed (made-to-become)"; not merely "the faculties and their development".

But this is only one of the inconsistencies which attend the teaching about the man who is, and yet is not, inconsistencies which are delightful, yet ever warning, and which we find throughout the Pali literature from Canon to Milindapañha and to the Commentaries, inconsistencies which Hume himself could not write one sceptical sentence about the self without falling into. We have the very man in the language, even when we have the rejecting of his reality in the mandate. For no amount of analysis, of valuing, of judging can ever expunge the analyser, the valuer, the judge. Nor does man in what we call literature ever expunge him or try to do so. But in the Piṭakas, the "literature", man's expression of himself, is traversed by the grown and growing tendency to value, not the man as such, but the parts and ways of him. Hence the inconsistencies and the jolts that they are bestrewn withal.

Thus there is first the Founder, whose reality as man is never doubted. There are the first leading disciples, of whom the same is true. There is the Wayfarer who alone gives meaning to the Way, be he *tathāgata*, thus gone, *sugata*, well gone, *duggata*, ill gone. All are discussed as very real. There is the man who, in the Suttas, "fares from this world to that," unquestioned, however emphatically in the Milindapañha and in Commentary he is said not to fare. Identical, unchanged, he in his faring is not; he is in process of becoming; but he is said to fare thither from hence. It is the "becoming" which as "ill", has been left unsaid; the "man" is inexpugnable. Even when the mind is said to be warding, judging, resolving, as e.g. the city-guardian in the parable, it is a pseudo-man functioning, and the Commentator, as if falling into a trap, comments in terms of the man, not the mind. The arahan theory itself is a vindication of the reality of the individual, the person, the man in process of "werden", or becoming more in worth. And that there is a goal (*attha, pariyosāna*), an utter ending of ill, i.e. an utter joy, or health, implies, not that there is ending of the man (*which renders the goal meaningless*), but man's entry on perfection, on consummation as That, as the Most, after graduating in the More.

The reason is, that in literature, that is, in all utterance where man is addressing himself to man, it is not to body or to mind that he is speaking, nor even to the complex, or product of these; he is speaking from very man to very man. He is not even thinking of just body or mind only; he is speaking to, because he is thinking of, the user of these, the valuer through them of what he experiences; and through them he is calling to another user, experiencer, valuer. Of the world, mondial, is he when thus calling to the world; of the worlds, mondial again is he when thus calling past earth to the worlds; of the More faring to the Most is he when calling on, when wording the Will of the Highest. But he is a wilted world, a contracted expression of man, when he sees in himself, in others, in the highest, a not-self, a being of no reality.

Then it is that his literature, born it may be of utmost good will to help and to guide, to uplift and to inspire, falters in carrying its high mission into effect, and lets us down, now here now there, where it should have led us upward. It lies not within the scope of these few suggestions to illustrate this fully. To do so would involve a twentieth century Commentary of the Piṭakas. Such comments partial in range will come to be made when greater accessibility to text and translation, now being carried out, makes the Pali Canon more of an open book than it has been, and when translators are more capable of checking their renderings of terms and phrases by other contexts.

The suggestions I have yet to make would point the reader to (*a*) the special liabilities to, the special openings for changes in wording in such compilations as the Piṭakas, (*b*) the changes in wording as due to changes in values. To take the latter first: When the mind came to be appraised and analysed in a way it was not at the birth of Sakya, when, again, the 'self', conceived not as becoming but as being, came to be depreciated in a way it was not at the birth of Sakya, it was likely, that the man would come to be worded in terms of mind, not of the self or the man. I am not saying, that the change in wording was deliberately done by a revising, either in writing, or before that, orally. It was the teachers, the expounders who will little by little have used, for the man, *viññāṇa* here, *mano* there, *citta* in another context. I have given instances of this above. This would result in a number of what, in written records are called various readings. When the time came for a standardization of wordings ("readings" belongs to a later culture), it would be found, that the live books, the repeaters, were repeating varying versions. Some would say "man", "self," where others said "mind" in one of its terms. The Revisers would have to choose. They, because of their changed values, would tend to keep in the mind-words, and drop the others. And the "authentic" version would be worded in this way.

This is but to say in other words what I pictured as happening at such notable revisions as the Patna Conference. I say it again, if only I may clear away the supposition that I am taxing old-world revisers with any wanton dislocations of their records. They did not so much *substitute* a word which was not there for a word which was there. *Both* words, possibly more than two words, were there already. They had to choose. They chose as they deemed best. They chose according to the values of their day. Those values were not of the earliest days; they had been gradually coming in.

And they have remained "in". A reformation might have caused them to be changed again, either to the older, or to yet other "readings". I may remind readers of a somewhat similar rewording in Christian documents. In St. Bonaventura's Psalter to the Virgin, of the 13th century, the titles "Mary", "Lady," "Mother of God," are substituted for "the Lord", "Jehovah," "God," in verses of the Psalms and the Te Deum :—Let Mary arise and let her enemies be scattered . . . In thee, O Lady, have I trusted. . . . We praise thee, Mother of God. . . .[1] Here was a change in values from the dates when those verses were compiled. It was a change which was later rejected for a resumption of the older version, but rejected by only a portion of the Christian churches, who came to look upon the substituted terms as a worsening in values. It is true we have here a case of deliberate altering on the part of Bonaventura. I am not claiming as much for the preferred versions in the Piṭakas.

I now come to the other matter to which my suggestions point: special openings for such changes.

I would first remind the reader of what we can gather to have been the history of the Piṭakas, both in the making and after it. It was one in which the likelihood of change was greater perhaps than in any other literature of the kind we call Scripture. He knows doubtless, that we have in them, so far as we can see, nothing that was at any time the thing we now call "a new book". He knows that, in the palm-leaf manuscripts, or writings on other substances, containing this and that whole Nikāya, or portion of a Nikāya, this and that portion of Vinaya or Abhidhamma, he is not looking at the work or copy of a work, which was written down as I am now writing this—just as the thoughts, as we say, came into his head. He will know on the contrary, that the written lines before him, in whatever script they are, were handed down, as folksongs and

[1] I owe the knowledge to Dr. Cutts's *Turning Points of Church History*, p. 152 f.

tunes still are largely done to-day, from generation to generation, at certain centres of the cult in question, where lived repeaters, who in turn taught other younger repeaters. But one thing he is less likely to know, and another thing he may not have visualized.

Namely, that there is no mention in the Piṭakas of these repeaters, called in the Commentaries *bhāṇakas*. There is nothing ever said, beyond the one frequent opening phrase: "Thus have I heard", that when Gotama is said, in the Suttas, or in pronouncing a Vinaya ruling, to be uttering anything of mantra-like importance, one or more repeaters were sitting near like modern reporters. The nearest to it is the coda now and then, that what has been said is to be borne in mind (*dhareyyātha*): "Learn what has been said; master it, bear it in mind."[1] But even this it is very unusual to find at the end of any discourse. Sometimes it is thus: "Go and ask him, and remember what he may tell you." And so little is there any suggestion of any literal memorizing, when it is Gotama who speaks, that he is found as exhorting listeners to remember, as the subject of the talk, terms not once used by the speaker. Thus after King Pasenadi's touching testimonial to him in the last days of both, the listeners are bade to learn, master and bear in mind the "dhamma-shrines" of which the king had spoken, and by which, judging by the context, he will have meant men who foster, as "shrines", the inner monitor *dhamma* (the translation "Doctrine" is here unfit). Even when he comes nearer to memorizing of words, as when he is made to endorse Kacchāna's exposition,[2] it is only the matter, or meaning, not the words which are to be remembered.

From all this I infer, that the first memorizings, those which were carried out as we say *in situ*, and at the time of speaking, were not of any *form of wording*, but were rather of the ideas, matter, substance, of what had been uttered. The repeating was more of the spirit less of the letter, and we think of the woman of Samaria: "Come, see a man who has told me all things that ever I did. Is not this he who should come?" and of how freely she would reproduce the talk she had had with Jesus.

It is of course inevitable that many of the words in which such

[1] Let the reader of translations not be misled by the ending in another *Majjhima Sutta* rendered thus: "And word for word the Lord repeated it himself again right through." There is a Western thoroughness here scarcely borne out by the eliding *pe* . . . in the text. All that is said to have been repeated is a little verse, not the homily. Gotama acting as a repeater is to me out of the picture altogether.

[2] *Majjhima* iii, 199.

things, such home-truths were said, would be abiding. Such a word-memory would alter greatly according to the listener, as we may see to-day; listeners who are verbal phonographs, and listeners who *naturally reword* anything heard. I believe that had it been otherwise, we should almost certainly have come upon the *bhāṇaka*, in the narrative part of the Suttas. The usual opening to a discourse or *kathā* is: "Monks, I will teach you the so-and-so. Ay, ay, sir, is the response," and there is often then the injunction: "Attend well" or similar words, "and I will speak." We never read of *bhāṇakas* being seated "on one side".

Neither, for that matter, do we now say: press reporters were present; but we should look for their verbatim report in this or that paper next morning, or for the "paper" in some journal or review, after a longer interval. The address if new would not be lost. Here on the other hand it would have had to be repeated, either verbally or in substance, by the speaker, or else reproduced by listeners. And herein would lie various openings for a different wording.

When these various versions began to grow in number with the years; when too the Chief was growing old and, while never weary in interviewing this man and that, seldom addressed a congregation, or only in a few words, and left all preaching to his men, and seeing finally that the "new men" were drifting apart, both from the original mandate and from each other, it would become a very urgent business to secure the teachings, on which all or a majority could agree, in some fixed form of words. And for reasons given in the last chapter, I incline to think, that this standardizing of Rules, of heads of teaching (*bodhipakkhiyā dhammā*) and of Sayings in outline (*uddesa*) kept many earnest and sincere monks very busy at Sāvatthī.

I do not go so far as to think, that the outlined sayings were so early expanded into the finished Sutta discourses we have in the Nikāyas. If they had been, we should be nearer to the original mandate in them than is the case. With the Uddesa, or "text", alone prescribing the subject, it would be still open to the individual teacher to develop his theme as he thought best. And in so doing, he might be very near his Chief and the first men in spirit, or again, he might be far from them. I believe it was not till the Patna Congress, that the more extensive and ambitious standardizing in exposition, and not in outline only, took place; I believe, it was then, that the Saying was expanded into the Sutta, the "text" or *uddesa* into the threaded (*suttam*), or connected talk, with its frequent feature of "refrains" of repetition. The *bhāṇaka* of the many Sayings may then have become the repeater of one of the new divisions of the Sayings, made either according to length, as the Dīgha (long) Suttas, or according to grouping, such as the Saṃyutta Suttas, and have been called accordingly the Dīgha-bhāṇaka, etc., as we find in the Commentaries, and not till these. Yet so persisting was the tradition of alluding to the talk (or Sutta), and not the newer grouping or "nikāyas" of talks, that even when the talks had, after the Patna revision, come to be written, maybe first in Ceylon, maybe *before that* in India, as the *lanchakas* we read of in the Milinda Questions, even Buddhaghosa does not quote a group or complete collection by name; he usually quotes as from a certain Sutta, that is, if he is kind enough to help us so far.

But further, it would not be only the listener, and later the *bhāṇaka* who, not being an automaton, would be capable, the *bhāṇaka* little, the listener far more, of altering a wording here and there. The teacher was much more likely to do so. As teacher he was, if worth his salt, giving a mandate through the prism of his own individuality, giving in a way himself to his hearers; and the more original he himself was, the less would he be capable of reproducing the mandate of another. He may not necessarily have snppressed his mandate, or brought in others, yet could he, by varying emphasis and values, end in teaching with a tendency much changed from that of a fellow-teacher. In such a case his listeners, his pupils in the Order would come to hold in worth a somewhat changed teaching.

And meanwhile, on both teacher and listeners there would be falling influences from which they could not wholly escape, not even in the monastery: the influences we sum up in such a word as *Zeitgeist*. All either had lived, or were living in "the world"; all would, as more or less in earnest about the things that really mattered, be concerned with the Better, with the New and with the "morewill" to further the need therein of their world. And we have considered to some extent what those influences were, under which they would come. That the influences were there is as yet curiously ignored by writers of to-day. "The unchanging East" it is perhaps, which still disinclines us to look for causes at work, which were sapping, even in ancient India, the views of any one age. We are ready to admit, that the Upanishads reveal, even in the older ones, a change from the earlier Arya which produced the Rig-Veda, that the Piṭakas reveal a world differing in many respects from that of the earlier Upanishads, that Sānkhya, that Yoga are in their origins earlier than the elaborated systems surviving in Sūtras and Commentaries, and earlier than the birthday of Sakya, just as these, their Scriptures, are later than the Pali Piṭakas. All this is now admitted.

But in the case of the Piṭakas we have yet to admit more. Confining ourselves for present purposes to the four chief books: the first four Nikāyas of the Sutta-Piṭaka, we have to get rid of the notion, if we have it, that in them we are reading records faithfully wording what the first Sakyans said, or would have said. We need to see in them the work of men who, with changed values, worked upon the records with altered emphases, and hence with altered wording. We need to see in every portion of those records something which has undergone more or less of change. I am convinced, that if those first men were with us to-day, they would tell us, that they hardly recognize in the Suttas the sayings of the mandate they gave their world.

And beside this general transformation thus undergone, there is the further feature to be kept in mind, namely, that, to mention no other book, each of the Nikāyas has been the result of accretions.

In other words, to take only the Four Nikāyas of the Sutta-Piṭaka, we have to consider, in each Nikāya, the earlier portions as (for the most part of them) the oldest portion, and that accretions were being made in course of time. The changing values are here less evident than they are if we compare, say, one of these Nikāyas with the Apadāna, the Paṭisambhidā-magga, or with the Abhidhamma-Piṭaka, yet can they be traced. I have gone into one such instance of accretion, as well as of emergence of new words, in the case of Sutta 111 of the Majjhima-Nikāya, in the Preface to the Second edition of the translation of the Dhamma-sangaṇi, first book in the Abhidhamma-Piṭaka. We are, in that Sutta, well beyond the earlier world of the early Majjhima Suttas, and are not far, it may be, before the compilation of that first book.

There is, it is true, one respect in which we shall err, if we see, in the end of each Nikāya, the latest expression in values. I refer to the Sayings, which may have been collected at a later date, and brought to an editorial centre, long after they may have been treasured in some perhaps outlying district by way of oral transmission. I referred to this feature in speaking of the Patna revision, and shall return to it presently. Here, I would only refer to the last Suttantas but two of the Dīgha-Nikāya: the advice given, as by a fatherly man of the world, to a younger such, known as the Sigālovāda Suttanta, and the old Warding Rune called the Āṭānāṭiya Suttanta. Here is nothing late; here are no monastic values, no teaching of the world as ill, or of man as unreal, or of "escape" as the only way.

Nor would I see in the last two Suttantas, of scheduled items in arithmetical or other succession, late accretions. Such schedules would be, in oral teaching, a special and early desideratum in memorizing, or at best as stencilled on metal plates. Moreover, the terms in them are old in emergence and in simplicity, e.g. we find only three, not four "āsavas". But it is conceivable that, when writing had at last come in, the discussion, the mantra, the narrative would take front rank, following the traditional position of the Suttas elaborated from the Sayings, and that the listed aids to memory would be just appended, as still valuable, as still held in reverence, as by no means to be dropped.

But save for such exceptions, I judge it probably true, that the later position in the total compilation means an accretion made later in time. On this I have another word presently (p. 397).

Now I seem to see, in modern dealings with the Pali scriptures, that we are yet far from admitting, in them, between date and date, the changing world which I maintain had come about. That, till to-day, the East was in many respects relatively "unchanging", is far from untrue. Had it been absolutely unchanging, we should not now be comparing the religious thought, in it, of one epoch, with the changed religious thought of another. For in such thought, whereas we have a new word mainly in the hands of this or that section of the social structure, Brahman, Kshatriya or other, no section is water-tight; the object of mantra and then of written scripture has not been solely the benefiting, the instructing of the given section. And further, we are in them not concerned mainly with the relatively unchanging features of a civilization, such as belong to man's bodily needs on the one hand, and on the other to the accidents of his place at the time on the earth, to his geographical environment. We are mainly in populated centres, where man is quickly accessible to man, where in exchanging speech he, "as iron unto iron, sharpeneth the face of his friend." Here it is, other things not hindering, more likely that he will change, change, that is, as man, rather than in material ways. As very man, he may change in any place, remote or urban. But in the town it is probable that the becoming in his nature will proceed more quickly, because of the very man having intercourse with very man in other men. And this he will express through his mind-ways.

The influences of time and place which were active between those dates of source of Sakyan mandate and final redaction of the yet unwritten Four Nikāyas I have in my earlier chapters tried to show. They may be summed up as:

(1) A shrinkage in the prevailing concept of the man, namely as being less inherently divine, and as only existent in a different way, and with altered emphasis.

(2) A new and ever growing tendency to distinguish mind from the man, with this dual result :—that either, as in Sãnkhya, the man as ultimate reality was made impracticably remote, or else the man was hidden in the mind, as only to be got at in mind (or in mindings, *dhammas*).

(3) A tendency to turn away in religion from the plane of things unseen, and therewith from "musing" as an avenue to them.

(4) The new importance assigned to earth-life as being possibly the stage of the consummation in man's becoming. Hence the arahan theory.

(5) A broadening out of the conception of a man's duties, as denizen of a world grown wider, in consequence of first Persian, then Greek infiltration and the growth of commerce. India was no longer virtually his "world".

(6) A reactionary tendency to estimate life in the world as an absolute barrier to spiritual betterment ; to see in coming forth from it as *samaṇa* the only way thereto, and therewith a wording of life in the world, and in any other world as "ill".

(7) Lastly, dating only from the fourth century B.C., the renascence of the legend of the Super-man of the external world, as a result of the inrush of world-rule in Alexander, followed by the actual hegemony over India in the persons of the Mauryan kings, especially of course of Asoka.

Now in any one of these seven, let alone all seven, there are openings for the gradual incoming of modifications in a religion as originally conceived and taught. More especially when the religion will have been taught in ways of utterance as unchecked as they were at first and for years afterwards. We have far too tidy a notion of the growth in wording of such a religion. And we tend therewith to impute to the new men of Sakya that high pitch of efficiency in verbal memory, which was quite possibly the, almost I had said, monopoly of the Brahman world, and *only* of a limited set in that world. For that matter textual purging (*sodhăna*) was not unknown among Brahmans. In the Sakyan history, meagre as it is, such work of *sodhăna* stands out as an admitted fact, admitted as urgently necessary in all the three Conferences dealt with in this book. It is only our meagre data about the Fourth, or Kanishka Conference, not to mention two or three later ones, which hinder us from being probably able to say as much of them. Why else all the pother of them ?

We saw that the end to be attained at each of them was authenticity of mandate, so that certain movements in teaching, or in rule of life might be shown to be "correct" and according to that authenticity, or not.

As to what made this or that "wording", in things unwritten, "authentic", when the wordings submitted for revision differed as pronounced by this vihara's repeaters and by that, this could only be, I repeat,[1] the decision of a majority in the Revisionist Council, or of some one in it of an influence submitted to by the majority. And he, or the majority, or both would decide, in their choice, by that view which had come to be theirs at the time of revision. Their choice would not in every case be in agreement with the wording of such repeaters as had a genuinely or approximately original wording. The influences to which they and their viharas had been subject would tend to make them cast their vote otherwise. Hence there would get established, in the bodies of oral sayings, certain changes embodying one or other of those changed views due to those influences.

Of what nature would be these verbal changes? Are there any about which we can make plausible surmise? I can see four occasions at least where we may see changes: changes brought about not by carelessness, not by repeaters' and later by scribes' blunders, but by what will at the time have seemed good and weighty reasons. They are :—

First, as a result of the influence numbered as (1), I see room for both new meaning and new values in terms. The emphasis will have altered with the values. If we compare such a sentence as "Empty is the world of the self and of what is of the self (*attan*, *attaniya*), which we considered in the last chapter, we see the word *attaniya* replacing the older *ajjhatta*; we see, not a bidding to seek the Self, but the assertion that there is none to seek. Yet is this not the human self as yet; it is the Divinity and divine attributes in the man's self. That the man's self was also a fiction came later, but it came. Before that, the man's self, used much as we use the term, was commended when the self was resolute (*pahitatta*),[2] made-to-become or grow (*bhāvitatto vaḍḍhitatto*).

Parallel with this we may place the growth in value placed on utterances which, little valued at first, came to be a very slogan when it was the very man's dis-deified self who was voted a fiction. I

[1] Above, p. 360.

[2] The Commentator, with a not-self emphasis, gives here the inadmissible explanation of *pesit-atto*: "having the self sent (away)." Unfortunately misleading the English translator.

refer here to Vajirā's wording of the man and her parable, discussed above (p. 369 f.).

I come to probable changes in wording, by which I mean, preference given, at the time of revision, to one wording over others —a wording which will have come-in in the way I have suggested. Under the influence numbered (2), in brief, the Sānkhyan influence, co-operating with the lowered prestige of the (especially East Indian) brahman world, we probably have terms for the mind functioning not as *way* of the agent, but *as* the agent. Such instances, as I have said elsewhere, I see, not only in figurative talk, as where the mind (*viññāṇa*) is seated at the city's centre, as recipient of news from without, but in more literal teaching. When, namely, the mind (*mano*), and not the man, is called the "centre of resort" and enjoyer of the senses' tributes—"like a king enjoying the revenues of five villages," is the Comment, rightly falling back on "the man" in our natural language—and again where the sick man is bid to keep *citta* well amid his ailments of body, when, with the apparent exception where the bodily ailment is brain lesion, it is the spirit's, the very man's health, which he has in his power, and of which the mind is merely the vehicle and "loud speaker". But the vogue had arisen to use one or other of these three terms for the man, the *attan*. It was not any one of them which Gotama bade those men seek, but it was the self. And it was in all of them, as also in body that he is shown warning his men, that the self was not to be sought: "body is not the Self; nor is mind."

Under this influence No. (2) will also have come the accepting of repeaters' versions, where here and there a teacher, or line of teachers, at one vihara, will have *suppressed* some clause in a Saying which inconveniently threw emphasis on to that, in the older wording, which had come to be less valued, less believed in. Here once more—for here I am incorrigible—I refer to the parable of the wood and the faggots.[1] I still think, that to careful critical reading, *where are no preconceptions*, the suppression of the application of the wood as signifying the "man" is likely to have been made. Faggots are being collected for kindling :—"If folk take such away, would you say they were taking away the Jeta Wood? You would not. So are neither body nor mind You, of You. Put away from (your idea of) You that these are You, who are as the Wood is to the trees." Told in these words there is sense in the story. As told in the Suttas (twice at least), I used, when I read it, *even in days* when I accepted the "not-man" as genuine Sakya, to come up against the defective

[1] *Gotama the Man*, p. 61.

ending with a jolt. It may be said: There is here no greater lacuna than when, in the Second Utterance, the Teacher may have omitted assertion of the Self, when rejecting either body or mind as the self. It may have been held, in the parable also, as unnecessary. Well, be it so. Yet is a parable different from a mantra. It is to help explain something. I leave it at that.

Under the man-as-mind influence, as also under other influences, will come *inserted glosses.* Such as the resolution of the agent not only into "mind" in one of its three terms, but also into (*a*) the fourfold mind-groups of a crude psychological analysis, which had eventually, in this changing East, to give way; and (*b*) much redundant sense-categorizing of "dhātu, indriya, āyatana", mentioned above.[1] All were machinery in the rise of "ill", and to be grimly noted down as such: ways of *upādāna*, a word in which we have a *double-entendre* of *grasping* at things of the worlds, and *fuel* nourishing the fires that maintained rebirth.

And at the same time it all pointed to the increased interest in the extended and quasi-scientific study in the features of the human personality, whose earth-career, as just earth-denizen, held such wonderful possibilities.

To the complementary waning of interest in denizens of the unseen is perhaps due in part the curious Nikāya gloss already alluded to,[2] when Gotama is said to have replied to the questions put him: "How came you to know this?" with: "A devatā told me," and —here comes the gloss, held to be a worthier sanction than that: "I knew it of myself." I said "in part" only, because it will have been the growing magnification of his nature which will have called for the gloss. The first clause rings very true, for only he is likely to have said it. Had he known it of himself, that clause was less necessary, and certainly the after-men would not have put it in.

Another of these few samples—to which a later generation, when once more Pali studies worthy of the name come to be taken up, will add many more—is the universalizing of that mandate of the four Moods or ways of will-suffusion which I see as annexed, not created by Sakya. I have suggested, that the unknown messenger of this warding-gospel taught mainly a will-suffusion of individual by individual. Diluted into a will-suffusion of "quarters" and of the "whole world", it is admirable only for the suffuser, and, through his own expanded attitude, contributes a unit to the weal of the world, no more. Hence it did actually become a mode of self-benefit and, as such alone, unworthy as a world-gospel. But the

[1] Above, p. 380. [2] Above, p. 274.

very dilution into universal terms betrays a mondial expansion which may be due to the influences I have named.

It is true, that when we consider those four universals, and lay them beside that mandate of "compassion" which is of the original Sakya, they are seen rather as shrinkage than as expansion. The four universals are concerned with *loka*, the world of earth. The compassion, which is the crown of Sakya, embraces the worlds: "*devas* and men." We, in our earthly catholic ideals, commend the dilution in the Brahmavihāras, while we "graze" unheeding over the oft reiterated greater ideal of "the weal, the happiness of *devas* and men".

I come lastly to that which is by far the most intrusive gloss of all: the so often repeated reference to "Buddha, Dhamma, Sangha", with the occasional addition of the "virtues dear to Ariyans", (the calling of the three constants the "Threefold Jewel" is commentarial only). The influences tending to change, such as I have named, have here been all of them more or less at work, but more especially, I think, those numbered (1), (2), and (7):—shrinkage in "the Man", pre-occupation with mind, namely, with *ideas* of things, and the ideal of ordered world-dominance.

In a new world-word, or "gospel", the original centre of attention is man, the very man, his nature, life, destiny. In course of time it will be *less* he, the Thing, and *more* the mandate itself about him, as worded idea, as orderly attestation about him, as vehicle for conveying to men that attestation. The *ideas* about the thing and the wording of them have taken first place in importance. And so we have the *idea* of the Founder raised to ideal majesty; we have the *idea* of *dhamma*, the successor named in the tradition by himself, but changed in worth from the inner experience to the worded teaching of it; we have the *idea* of the company of the teachers out to help, now become uppermost in a social hierarchy of inferior laity and superior monk. The laity is now to be loyal to, believer in, the Idea of the Origin incarnate, the Word, the Worders. It is not easy to check the growth of the Idea, loosened from contact with the original Thing. The first idea will expand to a concept of Super-man (*dev'âtideva*), the second will stiffen into a Super-Word; the third will exalt the position of the Monk as a being on a higher plane than the layman.

Hence the many glosses of titles and of formulas, notably those which came to be worded in the Dīgha-Nikāya, announcing the arrival of the Founder and his retinue, and were later called the *kitti-sadda*, the Word of Fame. This sort of gloss begins early in the pages of the scriptures. In the Vinaya, when the kumāras inquire whether Gotama knows of their thieving woman, the question has been thus reworded: "Has *the lord the adorable one* seen a woman?" Now Gotama had then no claims, as a distinguished teacher, to be addressed in terms of reverence; he was unknown as such; he had just begun. They who will not admit glosses to the same extent as myself, will hardly refuse to see a gloss here. But if here, of all places, why not much more elsewhere? There is no idea, in saying this, of begrudging much merit, much effort of goodwill, much natural eagerness to the editorial workers, who sought to commend the world-within-world of the monk to the world of the monk-in-posterity. Nor, as to that, need there be dispraise for their "catering", as we say, for that posterity only. It is asking too much to see, in those editors, men labouring to benefit a posterity of lay-readers. They arranged, selected, dropped out, inserted for the monk, explicitly for the monk.

When we come to the main groupings of the Sayings in their embroidery as Suttas, and of those Suttas which have no original Sayings (of the Co-founders) in them at all, we are, as all will admit, in the field of later editorial work. Not that there are not, here also, many problems to solve, many problems as yet insoluble. There is for instance the question, why a limited number of Suttas should have been set relatively apart and grouped in two Nikāyas according, so it is alleged, merely to their length. And of these so grouped why, for instance, the Dīgha Suttanta "On Causes" (No. XV) should have been put there, and not with the special Group on that subject in the Saṃyutta-Nikāya. The reason is probably simple enough, had we the clue. Possibly Ānanda was the repeater of the few brief Sayings on cause, out of which the "great dialogue" was framed. And we have it, that he figured at the First Conference as vouching for certain facts about Suttas, which came to form at least *the beginnings* of the Dīgha Nikāya. Moreover, in the Commentary, these Suttas were, by name at least, handed over to Ānanda to take charge of, but that may be a very posthumous piety on the part of a Ceylon Sangha.

But on this subject, too, I must confine these last considerations to sampling how the mere pondering over the contents and their Order of the canonical books may yield at least some results by intensive study. I have found, namely,[1] that, in the canonical book

[1] Introduction to Mr. F. L. Woodward's translation, *Kindred Sayings*, v, 1930.

of Groupings of Groups, called Saṃyutta-Nikāya (third of the four Nikāyas), there are, in the very order of grouping itself, one or two interesting derangements. And I think that from these we can gather what may have been the earlier arrangement, order of importance, or of growth, in formulated doctrines. This may prove suggestively instructive as to the evolution in values which had been going on.

The last or "Great" Group in the Saṃyutta-Nikāya, is, for the most part, a grouping of Suttas under seven heads, the heads known and referred to in former chapters here, as the Things belonging to Enlightenment. Now the order of the seven, where they are given as teachings specially commended, i.e., in the Book of the Decease, is different from the order in which they are grouped in the Great Group. In the former the order is merely numerical. Thus, three heads of four items, two heads of five items, one of seven, one of eight. In the latter group the order is other, thus, the last in the former is here the first: the Magga or Way. The seventh is here the second (factors of enlightenment). But this will be clearer in tables:

Dīgha, II, Suttanta XVI.	Saṃyutta, V, Mahā-vagga.
(4) stations of mindfulness.	(8) the Way.
(4) right efforts.	(7) factors of enlightenment.
(4) stages to psychic power.	(4) stations of mindfulness.
(5) powers.	(5) faculties.
(5) faculties.	(4) best efforts.
(7) factors of enlightenment.	(5) powers.
(8) eightfold Way.	(4) bases of psychic power.

The first thing here suggested is, that the numerical order in the Sutta will be later than the order in the other. Numerical ordering is a tidy work of after-editing. It is difficult to conceive that, once introduced, it would be departed from. This points to the Decease Book being the relatively late composition it is already held to be. This does not mean that all its factors are of late composition. It is mainly, if not wholly, the editing that is late, as late perhaps as the Patna revisions. Relic-worship had grown up, and the old Sayings of the last injunctions and of the last tour, together with many teachings already in Suttas perhaps, of matters mainly magnifying the growing Buddha-concept will have been threaded together, leading up to a relic-sutta at the end. Some sort of Vinaya account there will have already been of the two Conferences. These were the concern of Vinaya repeaters and experts. The Relic-apologists were not interested in that subject, hence the silence so puzzling to exponents, about the Conference in the Decease (i.e. Relic-) Book.

Even to satisfy a lust for numerical ordering, it is difficult to imagine the main teaching, the Magga, put at the end in any list fixed, in wording and in value, at a relatively early date in Sakya. We have only to recall Ānanda's estimate of his lost Leader, in terms wholly and solely of the Way,[1] to see how this just could not be. And here, in the Grouping of Groups, we see the Way put at the forefront, the true place, especially in Buddhist estimates, of highest value.

It may be said: is this true in general of Buddhist estimates? What of the order, begun already in early Sayings (e.g. in Anguttara-Nikāya, vol. i) of *sīla*, *samādhi* (or *citta*), *paññā*: morals, mind-culture, wisdom (to give it no higher name); adopted in the stereotyped form of address put into the mouth of the Leader on his last tour, and elsewhere, and culminating, as to embroidery, in the three sections of Buddhaghosa's Visuddhi-Magga?

This is a fit rejoinder, for it throws into relief that which was, not the Buddhist, but the Sakyan estimate. That order refers us, as did Sakya, to the Man; to the way of his nature, the way of his becoming, his wayfaring, to the More in him growing towards the Most. His feet, as it was said in Sayings, were to be, *had* to be, on the solid earth of *sīla*, but that was basis only, albeit it came first. Worthily warding the mind, the ways of his self-expression, he grows in that holy thing in him, *paññā*, the reaching forth to know (the will) conceived as the Highest in him, who he is. The order of the highest value placed first has its merits, but it is derived, secondary, external. It is the order of things as valued, contemplated; it is not the order of things in the valuing, of things experienced from within, of life itself. And as with the reverberating of the word Magga down a teaching which had, in value, depreciated the Way, so is this reverberating of values in the Man, in a cult which had shrunk these values to a smaller, a more limited thing.

Something of these lost values we see in the latter, or Saṃyutta-order of the Seven Heads. The First Call, the Central Symbol, it is true, stands foremost, but studied, as I have said, from within, the Way is the Means whereby the Man may grow. He must himself be willer in way. We then get ways of growth (*Bojjhangā*); then ways of estimating growth introspectively (*Satipaṭṭhānā*); then ways of growth considered as modes of the growing will (*Indriya*, etc.). Lastly, and for the few—a sort of Appendix—

[1] Above, p. 146; *Majjhima*, iii, No. 108.

modes of revealing the "More" in man (*Iddhipādā*), as if holding out guarantees of what only the few here, but hereafter each one may become.

We now turn to the latter third of the Great Grouping. We are now at the end of the Things belonging to Enlightenment, and we might have expected to find the Group itself ending therewith. That there are five sub-divisions or vaggas, added on to this very distinctive theme of the "Things" aforesaid, is somewhat evidential. Evidential, namely, that the Book of the Groups (Saṃyutta-Nikāya) was already completed as to form, that is, as to its fifty-one Groups before, let us say, the great revision of materials at Patna brought in from distant viharas, through special summons, much fresh material. Or if not then only, then from time to time till the Patna Conference. Such winnowings of sources gave rise to a special Rule in the Vinaya, permitting travel during the rainy season to collect Sayings, which through death of a repeater, or closing down of a vihara settlement, or other reason, would be lost.[1] And maybe it was not thought wise, or for that matter necessary, to increase the established number of the Groups on those four central bodies of Sayings. So we have much other matter dumped on to the "Bodhipakkhiyadhamma-Saṃyutta", the fifty-second, and the total dubbed as the Great Group.

What are the five appended Groups about? Suttas about Anuruddha, Musing, Breathing as a culture, Entry on the Stream (another figure for the Way), and the Truths. What is it that the Great Vagga is here trying to tell us if we have ears to hear?

Why, for instance, is the teaching, now almost everywhere dinned into us as the centre of (Hīnayāna) Buddhism, put here at the very end? Why is it not included in the Things the Leader is said to have bequeathed as he was dying? Anyone who is conversant with the ousting, in the Truths, of Way from its central position to the fourth of the truths, anyone who knows how this monastic diagnosis of life as "ill", as only to be cured by suppression of the will, i.e. of desire, submerged in the "dog-with-a-bad-name" of "craving"— a suppression which leaves no other spring from which betterment can come—how this is still harped upon as the true centre of Buddhism, cannot but be amazed when he comes to find, that in those so-called final injunctions, the four truths are not mentioned at all. There will certainly have been a cause for this omission. And I suggest that the Great Vagga is dumbly trying to tell it.

[1] *Vinaya* i, p. 141.

Thus: when the "Great Group", the fifty-first Saṃyutta, was first compiled, the "Way" was still nominally central, chief. Hence it was taken first, and not last as in the more mechanical numerical list in the Dīgha. In the day of the Patna revision, on the other hand, the teaching of the Truths, the monks' Diploma, the sanction of their life as monks, had come to loom very large, and it was felt incumbent to remedy the omission by an inclusive treatment in the Nikāya, where it was least inconvenient to insert it. There is no leading up here to a climax, as in the triad of the Man: *sīla*, *samādhi*, *paññā*. The titles given above preclude that. Evidence can scarcely shout louder to us than this, that the Four Truths should, historically considered, be, *as formula*, ejected from the First Utterance.

As to the other four Appendixes: a special group on Anuruddha becomes a thing looked for, when we remember him as closely associated in kinship and origin with Gotama, as surviving his chief, and as a mysterious figure of wizard powers. Kassapa we should have expected to find thus singled out, had he not got given distinctive group-treatment earlier in the Groups (Vol. ii, 194), a priority which may have been due to his eminence as a teacher, a man of a "school" of his own, a man of organizing energy, a man typical of the ever prevailing *samaṇa*-vogue, a man not easily to be passed over. To Ānanda a special section had, it may be already, been consecrated in the early part of the Anguttara-Nikāya. We find no special section on Upāli, so notably eminent at the First Conference. But if we drop the mere legend, which sees in this Canon Law expert the former valet or batman of the young Sakyans who joined their kinsman Gotama, when he had established his mission work, if we see in him the cultured Jain of the Upāli-Sutta and noted debater,[1] we have a man who would not, in duration of adherence, have counted as one of the very veterans, deserving a special section.

As to the other three Appendixes, whereas that on Jhāna adds nothing of value historical or otherwise, that on "Breathing", as a line of exercise by which more than bodily health might be improved: this, which finds repeated and also early attention in the Majjhima-Nikāya, seems nevertheless to be in no way of the original Sakya. There is nothing vital in the wording of the Suttas dealing with it; nothing which has the zest of the new. It will have been a vogue which had come in, or come on in India, and so new men coming into the Order may have introduced the practice, and the teaching will have in some measure exploited it. But on

[1] *Majjhima*, No. 56.

the whole the editors of the Suttas passed it by, with a relatively faint interest. The (late) Paṭisambhidā-magga is voluble on it.

In the last of the three, the Sotâpatti Group, on the other hand, there is interesting material, to some extent repeated from the earlier fifth section of the Nidāna-Saṃyutta[1]: the Housefathers' chapter, with additions over which I stay for a moment.

We have here not only repeated the conversation with his friend the benevolent Sudatta, called Feeder of the Forlorn,[2] when Gotama is shown giving him that glad assurance of a happy hereafter, which is for me much more his original teaching than the blank and negative assurance of the arahan formulas; we have *two* versions of that friend's illness and of the visiting him, at his request, of Sāriputta and Ānanda. The record of this visit occurs once in one of the concluding Suttas of the Majjhima-Nikāya. There, the illness is mortal; Sāriputta exhorts him in much detail to be utterly detached from clinging to, depending on, anything in this or any other world, Sudatta weeps because this is a talk he has never heard. He is told it is not for laymen, but only for the monk. He entreats, that laymen may also be taught it, and dies. The teaching was apparently premature, even for so exceptional a layman, for he *is* reborn in the next world only, and as *deva* makes himself seen and heard by the Founder. In the Saṃyutta versions, the illness does not prove mortal, but yields to the Couéism of Sāriputta's cheering words. He is bidden, namely, to fix his thoughts on the way in which he has steadfastly followed the better, and has no need to worry. Now were there two illnesses, or but one, which was so visited? If so, which is the true version? Did "Anāthapiṇḍika" really predecease Sāriputta?

I am inclined to think, that we have here oral materials which were, as I have suggested, gathered in, say, for the Patna Conference from other, more outlying viharas. The earlier collections were left in the order to which repeaters had grown used, and these were made "accretions" at the end of the many groups of "Kindred Sayings".

But it is not the end only of each Nikāya which offers historical problems of interest. The whole table of contents of the Saṃyutta-Nikāya is trying to tell us something of the changing values under which its accretions took place. Take, for instance, the first main division of it, called the Sa-gāthā-Vagga; the poetical section. It has not a monopoly of verses; there are only relatively more. But the whole section, prose and verse, bears the stamp of the relatively old and early, and is hence very precious material. We have the

[1] Vol. ii, p. 68 f. [2] Anāthapiṇḍika.

very short oral saying, with the gist of it metrically fixed in stanzas less easy to alter than prose. And we have, out of eleven chapters, *six* which are concerned, not with this world only, but with other worlds. Men of the next world come to the Founder, or to some other psychically gifted man to advise or be advised; the men too, of the worthier Brahmā-world come or are visited; they ward and watch the progress of the earth-helper. We meet with *devas* here and there throughout the Nikāyas, but the interest in them is more diluted, less concentrated and living, than it is here.

Then there are the talks with his friend the king of Kosala, all bearing the stamp of actual if hoary memories. But with the beginning of the second main section, the section on Cause, we move on into the growing value in *ideas about things*, rather than in things; forward into Suttas about Elements, mind-and-body Groups, Suttas about varieties of sense-experience, Suttas about ideas belonging to enlightenment—all testifying to the busy path of monastic pre-occupations, which at length debouched in the scholastic work of Abhidhamma: the work of the cloister far from the mission-work of men among men, of the first Sakyans.

Such are but a few examples, and those very sketchily treated, of the problems in Sakyan and in Piṭakan history, which we older workers in Pali literature hand, as we pass on, to younger men and women, who may see the day of a revival of interest in that literature, coupled with the comparing of it with a widened field of Buddhist utterance in other literatures.

XXII

SAKYA AND ABHIDHAMMA

I have just spoken about the growing tendency in Sakya to a pre-occupation with, not things, but ideas about things. This finds fullest expression in the Third, or Abhidhamma Piṭaka, and on this I would add here, by permission, a few considerations published elsewhere.[1] To the Book of monastic rules, the First or Vinaya Piṭaka, I do not propose to return. It is patently a code, and a very elaborate one, not intended as a new, a saving Word for the Many, but as a guide in many minutiæ for life, in the world within the world, of the man who had turned his back (if not his stomach) on the world. For a man here and there, seeking nothing so much as the support of a Way of the Rule, and lacking the will to "make become" in himself the New Word: Let the Self be your lamp, your way (*gati*), the Vinaya may have been an apparently sufficing substitute for Dhamma. And the more so, the more elaborate it grew as the years went on. But it is not monastic development with which this book is concerned.

Nothing more than that monastic régime is now associated with the First Piṭaka. Incidentally much, as we have seen in the foregoing, has been of suggestive usefulness, and indeed now and then of utmost value in our sifting grain of Sakya from chaff. In this way the survival of the Vinaya is infinitely more valuable in the search for Sakya than is the Third Piṭaka. But in the days before this became accessible in printed text and to some extent in translation, as now it is, there existed a certain hope that, in Abhidhamma, in its most archaic form, we might come upon something worth calling "early Buddhist philosophy". There was, in the first place, the name "abhi-dhamma"; in its meaning, the term metaphysic, *ta meta ta phusika*, suggested a corresponding content. And then there was the notion, gathered from commentarial Buddhism, of an exalted value attaching to that content, namely, that "it exceeded and was distinct from dhamma", much as a deva might be eminent among his peers (*ati-* or *abhi-deva*). Thanks to Maung Tin's translation of this context, the Commentary on the first book of the Abhidhamma-Piṭaka, Dhammasangaṇi,[2] the reader can now swiftly

[1] *JRAS.*, April, 1923.

[2] The Expositor (*Atthasālinī*), P.T.S. ed. 1920–21, pp. 3–19.

gauge the curious hyperbole of diction in which the Piṭaka, and notably the latest accretion, is belauded. On these two grounds then, we were half hoping to find in it a plank here and there of positive exposition, esoteric rather than exoteric, bridging over the lacunæ and the reserves and the silences in many of the Suttas.

Anyway, the workers set forth, one now, another then, to explore our seven hills of Abhidhamma, and after forty years of labour[1] intermittent—workers were few, and printing even then costly—we brought back our quarry. The cynical may say, nor are they wholly wrong, that this—is it not the mountain's way?—amounted to a bag of mice. The Piṭaka had revealed much meticulous catechizing, some inconclusive dialectic, and quite a little world of word-permutations. Had our knowledge grown by it? Had labour and time been utterly wasted?

Speaking, if I may, for my spade-mates as well as for myself, we think not. We think we have, in these seven books of Pali texts, contributed a chapter to the history of the growth, within limits of time and place, of the human spirit. Considered in its due context, this chapter reveals how a certain kind of intensive culture may on the one hand stimulate, and on the other stultify that growth. And by all such considerations we ourselves grow.

Among these Abhidhamma compilers of the cloistered lives, and among the commentary compilers, a certain growth may be discerned. It was of the kind that intensive culture in close-barred conditions naturally brings about. About the great world of earth they knew nothing. The teacher whom they had come to call "omniscient" had told their forefathers in the Order nothing about it. They were secluded in their work, even from the little world of their fellow-men without the vihāra walls. They inherited as members of the Order an ample oral tradition of Vinaya and Sutta and Mātikā. And the Mātikā or tables of classification they expanded into a so-called Abhidhamma, with certain patches of commentary in parts. The Vinaya was largely framed to meet special cases. The Suttas were largely records of how other special cases were met. Mostly, that is, they were precepts *ad hominem*. Thus the precept was served up in a way called *pariyāya* (a tiresome work to translate; etymologically a going round about). The Ābhidhammikas sought how to serve up the precept *ni-ppariyāyena*; in the abstract, stripped of its accessories and no longer an *œuvre d'occasion*.

[1] For a table of years and of editions see *JRAS.*, loc. cit., *J.P.T.S.* 1920–23, p. 54.

Engaged on such work, they would inevitably clarify their concepts, adjudge definite meaning to terms, co-ordinate and subordinate among terms and, where necessary, evolve new terms. In brief, it was, as I have said above and elsewhere,[1] a discipline in consistency of thought and language. And this, at that stage of Indian thought, was not a little needed.

We may illustrate this kind of intensive and introspective growth —for it was mainly psychological—by detecting how the dual division of mind into *citta* and *cetasika's* (i.e. the bare cognitive reaction to stimulus, and all the phases, factors, or co-efficients of the same, when analysed) is beginning to intrude itself in the first book. Ultimately, that is, in the course of perhaps a few centuries, this division swept away, for all academical purposes, the clumsy old quincunx of the five skandhas. Again, we note the useful term *bhavanga* appearing in the seventh book, a word as much needed for "continuum" or "flux" of organic, including sub-conscious life, as these were by our modern psychology. Again, there is the very thoroughgoing expansion of the term *paccaya* (*pratyaya*) in a theory of relations. Twenty-four of these are distinguished, yet all are, at least by the Commentary, presented as species of the one genus, the relation of causality. This theory is quite one of the finest mice in our game-bag. It would be a noteworthy contribution by any philosophic school, ancient or modern. It does not appear to be anticipated in the Suttas even in a crude inchoate way, as are, in the Anupada Sutta,[2] the psychological introspective analyses expanded in the Dhamma Sangaṇi. But it is, in a way, a natural outcome of the central significance imposed by the Sāsana on the doctrine of the cause and extirpation of suffering. *Paccaya*—"cause," "reason for"—is in the Suttas undifferentiated from *hetu*. By intensive culture, *hetu* and twenty-three other relations are distinguished as aspects of natural causal agency.

These few instances must here suffice to show, that the cloistered Ābhidhammikas were doing their best to let shine such light of thought about body and mind as the earlier tradition of their church had been able to kindle. There was probably not very much of the real original teaching of the founder in that tradition. The Eightfold Path is no longer central, is chopped about in all manner of ways, and the idea of carrying on his beneficent work seems undreamt of. Indeed, he has himself become a very shadowy figure,

[1] *Buddhist Psychological Ethics*, Introd., pt. iv; *Vibhanga*, xx; *Buddhist Psychology*, pp. 139, 177, etc.
[2] *Majjhima Nikāya*, iii, 125.

a person only alluded to in formulas, and in the fifth book Docetic and other heresies about him are discussed in a very cut-and-dried manner.

Herein, however, these early scholastics were not different from Christian teachers in the secular education of to-day The academic teaching of the Theravāda was becoming practically no less secular. In the twelfth century manual,[1] generally used ever since, the name, let alone the teaching of the founder, has faded out utterly, save for a grace-before-meat allusion. They might claim, in this, to be carrying out his injunctions to be (not *Sattha-saraṇā*, but) *attasaraṇā*, *dhammasaraṇā*—to be dependent not on him, but on the self, on the inner monitor.

And had those monks been living in closer, saner touch with their fellows, had that doctrine not become a closed tradition bound up in iron formulas, they might, in this *atta-dhamma*-dependence have let the lessons of earth-life play over them, they might have discerned that life to be in the throes of new moral growth, they might have let the light of this moral awakening shine on their church-built Dhamma; they might have seen in rebirth and the karma-force a wonderful field for the growth of that self on which, for salvation, they were to depend; they might have grasped the truth—O! the triumph of it over tradition!—that, whereas body after body was used and laid down, whereas the force, the *śakti*, which they called mind, in this term and that, informed, innervated body after body, it was just that *attā* on which they were bidden to depend, it was that self which was really "theirs",[2] "they", as neither body nor mind could be, it was that "self", which at the very outset of his career, the master bade men go and seek,[3]—*this* it was which, down the ages of rebirth, was to grow and grow till it blossomed into the very nature of the final goal.

But the artificial life decreed by ancient India, with its cleavage between lay and religious, shut them up in a paddock And the formulas of a church which taught that all had been told, so that expansion of import and exposition was alone lawful, shut them up in a cellar. What their missionary brethren could learn, serving their fellows more directly, they could not Hence in their psychology, all and every kind of reaction is pre-determined. The essential creativeness of life and mind is undreamed of. Confronted with this creativeness, complex and unpredictable, any theory of relations

[1] *Abhidhammatthasangaha.*

[2] "Yours": *tumhākaṃ*. *S.* iii, 33 f.; iv, 81 f.

[3] *Vin.*, i, 1, 14.

has always, even in our own day, proved a quite sterile subject. Buddhaghosa makes play with the twenty-four in his Visuddhi Magga expositions, but they led him to no new vista of truth Truth, in his day, as the result of centuries of this cloistered culture, had very largely become a knowledge of "marks" (*lakkhaṇāni*), or salient features in just those concepts (and no others) which made up the little world of thought occupying the mind of the wise man in orders. So far he was at least positive, if circumscribed. Beyond this, truth consisted, according to that tradition with which he associated the name "men of old" (*porāṇā*), largely in negations. Where, ages before, the founder had been silent, where the founder had rejected alternatives without making any sweeping denials, there Buddhaghosa has been taught to say: there is not, there is nothing, there is no one. He does not seek to convince. He dogmatically denies.

And as we leave this house of cloistered lives, of a closed tradition, of a past dominating present and future, we have a sense of rooms swept and garnished, clean and tidy, of sealed windows, of drawn blinds, of no outlook towards the dawn.

Yet are there in these seven books two sayings, the finding of which was worth all the long work of delving in them. The one, revealing the Sakyan aim in jhāna: access to other-world converse—with this I have dealt (pp. 168ff.). The other is the stand taken, at Patna, by the Defender of the man, from Vesālī, when asked: "How does the man survive?" "It is in dependence on becoming that the man survives." (Kathāvatthu, 61, § 228) The baser materialistic view of becoming is hurled at him, the becoming of body and of mind, not of the man, spirit, soul. He protests, but the special pleading does not suffer more than his protest to survive. And we shut the book and remember that last look of farewell to the faithful city! (p. 355). And the shrine built there in memory thereof! (*Travels of Fa-Hien*, ch. xxv.) *Annātāro bhavissanti*. . . .

How near once or twice was Hermann Oldenberg to being a Knower (*aññātar*) of that Becoming! He hovers over it only to flit off to his Change and *Erlösung*. Yet the two passages:—"the Upanishads saw in Being all Becoming," and "the recording monks could not depict or discern inner Becoming, nor could they, if they had, impute it to a perfect leader" (*Buddha*, 6th. ed., pp. 143, 289)—call for a recast, on sounder historic lines, of his whole book.

XXIII

SAKYA REVIVED IN ASOKA

So much has recently been written about this remarkable emperor-king of India, that it has become easy to be wise about him, easy to say what I am moved to say about him briefly. And the knowledge that he said what he did is a comparatively simple problem. We have not to dig among a host of Suttas, and bring out here and there a saying at best "ascribed" to him. We have but to read the fine reproductions of inscriptions on rock and pillar scattered about India, recording what the "king dear to devas" will without reasonable doubt have caused to be made. We have but to note on one of the last discovered of these the written identification of that king with Asoka. We have but to consult recent scholars' work on the date of his reign. This done, we can place this man in space and time and sayings in a way it is much harder to do in the case of the founders of Sakya.

What then remains for me, in such a work as is here attempted, to say about Asoka is but a very few points which I have so far not seen made.[1]

The first is, that in his edicts, Asoka revives for me, in a way in which the greater part of the Suttas, let alone Vinaya and Abhidhamma do not, that which is very near to the sort of teaching given, as I believe, by the First Men of Sakya to the Many. It resembles the talks, scattered very thinly about the Four Nikāyas, to such men as Anāthapiṇḍika, Citta, Sigāla, the "householders", and to Visākhā. It does not resemble the discourses "ascribed" to the Founder as addressing monks, nor even most of the talks to individual monks. Those householder-talks and the edicts have led a scholar here and there to credit the Founder with a double gospel—one for popular teaching, one for the religious world—somewhat coinciding with Buddhaghosa's ill-founded notion of reading the conventional, as distinct from the ultimate meaning, into certain terms: somewhat coinciding with the exoteric and esoteric doctrine much fancied by some Mahāyānists. In the popular gospel, fit for

[1] I have consulted, besides Senart's classic work *Inscriptions de Piyadassī*, Hultzsch's *Inscr. of Asoka*, Corpus Inscrip. Indic, 1925. My apologies, if I repeat as mine points which have been made, unread by me, elsewhere.

the relatively immature layman, we have the good life as insuring salvation from ill rebirth, and the assurance of happy rebirth, with no monastic upheaval breaking off the man's or woman's development in life and work and play in the world. In the other teaching we have such an upheaval, to be followed by a development of certain powers and possibilities, such as would culminate in insuring salvation from any kind of rebirth, with final transformation into the unknowable because ineffable *amata* or nirvana.

This idea for me errs in placing the two teachings side by side in time. I have here been trying to show, that the monk-teaching grew up *after*, *and out and away from* the teaching for the layman. It will take many antecedent conditions to make a "church", but it does not *start* with many mandates. It starts with a new word on "man", about something "man" is then ready to come to know, something new in the long way of his coming to be. "And God said: 'Let there be light'" is the way of the new message. It is a More, never a less; a coming to be, never a "going out". But a secondary, evolved system may well merge in time out of, or more rightly around the mother-logos, such as may eventually largely drive-under that logos, and assume the place of honour. Such was the case with Sakya.

But in Asoka's case, so far was the original teaching in his day from being driven under, that it makes a lively appearance in his edicts, the while the secondary teaching *makes no show at all.* It will here be said: "But of course Asoka composed those edicts for 'the man in the street'; it is just the lay-gospel he was himself able to absorb, and knew that his lay-world would understand." Well, I hold no brief for Asoka's culture; but whereas he appears, in his edicts, as what we should here and now call a sincerely religious, and a growingly religious man, we have to quicken our imagination a little as to the men he had in view, who would be the *readers* of his public inscriptions. When, in the Middle Ages, notices were pinned on the doors of Christian churches, religious notices by order of the superior clergy, civil notices by order of sheriff, maybe, or mayor, readers of these will have been very few. These will have been mainly men of the order called "clerus": clerici, clercs, or clerks, who could both read and write. The many would come to them in most cases, to learn what the writing was about. So do I picture the many of Asoka's day, the more, in that writing of any but a few words was a new art in India in that day.; books were unknown; written letters were unknown. Hence the rock and pillar messages would have to *pass through the mind* of a relatively "educated" reader before they were read out, or expounded to our "man in the street", much as in our time new theories published about science, religion, philosophy, history, have to filtrate through popular addresses and the like before they reach him. And my conclusion is, that so far from talking down to the many, or so far from talking as "low-brow" to "low-brows", Asoka's communications were, for his time, on the level of the best general culture of his day.

And, I repeat, so little have his values been overshadowed by monastic slogans, such as *anicca*, *dukkha*, *anatta*, being given place of honour, that it is the former teaching which appears in his edicts, and nothing else. There is in these not a word about any one of the three, or about the arahan, about nirvana, about *dhamma's*, about the man as just body and mind, or only knowable as such, about rebirth as a misfortune, about the advisability of men yet young entering into orders, or indeed of any man doing so. He prescribes respect to *samaṇa* as to brahman, but the only attitude he takes toward the Sakya Sangha, beyond, once, a respectful greeting, is that of a fatherly adviser.

On the other hand, whereas he does not mention the symbol of the Way, he is repeatedly insistent on that, in the nature and life of the man, of which the Way was, as I have said, but a figure, namely, on the nature of man *as a becoming*; on the importance of furthering that becoming; on the guiding principle, *dhamma*, by which it might be furthered; on the goal towards which that becoming tended; on the happiness in life in this and other worlds attending that becoming; on the implied reality of "the man" as thus progressing in growth from one world to another. In all these essentials Asoka stands out as a genuine disciple of the "Saka", the "Budha-Saka" in its original worth, to which in the Rupnath and Maski edicts he attests open profession.

In so far as these ideals, set out in the inscriptions, were distinctively Sakyan, and not just those of a well-educated Indian gentleman of the third century B.C., it is clear that Asoka had been very lucky in the teacher from whom he had learnt. The tradition in the Ceylon epics[1] is that this was a young monk, whose holy expression, seen by the king from his palace window, had attracted him: the monk Nigrodha. (The legend of kinship with the king is less credible than the attractiveness.) It may well be, that it was in some such way, and not so much by the seven days' coaching from the dignitary Moggaliputta-Tissa, as alleged in Buddhaghosa's Commentaries,[2] that he will have learnt the real heart of Sakya.

[1] *Dīpavaṃsa*, vi, *Mahāvaṃsa*, v. [2] *Points of Controversy*, p. 6.

This, and the spirit of his edicts are in striking contrast to the dogmatic pose he is made to assume as President of the Patna Conference, in adopting the point of view of his tutor as to the man being "analysable" (into *dhamma's*).[1] And as to that, we are, in the years of promulgating by Edict, prior to the date of that much-debated Conference. Asoka, in the edicts, had not yet been coached.

I will now point out how the genuine Sakyan emphasis comes out in the Edicts. As to (*a*) the remarkable crisis in the very man (or soul), to which he confesses, after the war in which he conquered the Kalingas, in the eighth year after his coronation, and as to his growing abhorrence, before or after that, at the slaughter, for food or sacrifice, of animal life, these are not expressions we should look for from just an educated Indian kshatriya. They point to the influence either of Jain teaching or Sakya teaching, or both. All true education evokes growth in the man, but this will at any given time be checked by current prejudice and "vested interests". To get over any of these the stimulus of a New Word is needed, and this a man might *then* get in contact with either of those New Words, but not as one educated by brahman chaplains.

That Asoka reacted in that religious crisis as he did, by his notable confession of remorseful pangs, and yet more by the progress in becoming, shown in his zeal to wage solely henceforth victories of *dhamma*, brings out well his pre-occupation with "growth", "vaḍḍha", which is ever emerging in what he utters. There is here no emphasis on growth in body or mind; it is the growth of the very man. "Growth" is his usual term, but occasionally his use of *bhavati* has more in it than the mere meaning of "happening". Thus in the Girnar and Mansehra edicts occurs the unusual compound *bhava-sudhi*, "salvation in," or "by becoming"—a wonderful word, but quite obscured by the translators in "*pureté de l'âme*" and "*purity of mind*"![2] Here is no general Indian culture, that I know of; here is pure Sakya of the Way.

But his use of "growth" is also striking; thus, in the Kalsi and other edicts: "In these ways (not killing, courtesy, filial obedience) and many others, living (*calana*)[3] by *dhamma* is made to grow; the king and his descendants will forward that growth (*pavaḍhayisanti*) . . . for this has been written, that they should devote themselves to this growth. . . ." And as to insistence on it, in Hultzsch's excellent Index-vocabulary to the Edicts, there are no fewer than *eighty occurrences of some form of the word* "grow".

[1] See above, pp. 375–8. [2] Senart and Hultzsch respectively.
[3] Pali: *caraṇa*.

As to the "filial obedience" on which Asoka is often insistent, he here goes beyond the *sīla*-limitations, and more worthily reflects the older Sayings. Thus: "With God (Brahma) are those families, where the parents are revered by the children. . . . Parents are (as) God, so are teachers of the past. . . . Children who are thus wise are praised here, and rejoice hereafter in *svarga*." There is nothing of this in the Sīlas, even though they are considered layman's religion down to the present day. But home duties came not into the monk ideal; and hence even the rudiments of morality have been annexed and tampered with by the cloister. I return to the term "growth".

I do not say, that were Asoka giving his world here the secondary, derived monk-ideals, we should have heard nothing of growth. We do meet with the word here and there in the Suttas; and the Way, worded as fourfold, or, with the "fruit"-stages included, as eightfold, is only intelligible as a scheme of growth not in this world only. But in the first place, the emphasis, judging by repetition of the word in the Suttas, would be much diminished, and secondly, the fourfold Way is worded as a *getting away* from life. Asoka admits, that to become better "is a hard thing". But he is often recurring to the happiness of the growth in betterment, and his forward view towards the better things awaiting such efforts hereafter, as a man in a happier world, is very positive. "What," runs Girnar ix, "is more desirable than this: the attainment of Svarga?" Now, says the viiith, "that the king tours not for hunting or other amusements, but to visit and support the religious world, the aged and his people generally, this "becomes a greater pleasure to him". "Let pleasure be in effort, for this is both of this world and of the next," he writes in Kalsi xiii, "firm becomes this joy, the joy of victory by *dhamma*"—a glad cry which is dulled by *pīti* being Englished by the unfit, drab word "satisfaction".[1] Forty-four are the references to things of happiness in terms of happiness; to terms of unhappiness (*dukkha*) there are but three. And if we render, as does Hultzsch, *hita* (welfare) by happiness, we get twenty-six more allusions, by this untiring planner of the "hita-sukhe" of his people.

From becoming or growth, and the joy of it, I come to the other true Sakya trait in Asoka's religion. This is the right, the original, the Indian use of *dhamma*. There is a striking difference here in his use of the term *after* he has, in later life, come to profess himself a zealous Sakyan. This later usage we see in the Bairat edict, where he at length makes allusion to "all the sayings of Bhagavatā Budhena as well said," greets the Sangha, professes faith in "Budhasi dhammasi

[1] Hultzsch: Corpus Inscrip. Indicum, New Ed., 1925.

sanghasi", and, that the "sadhamme" (the good [?] *dhamma*) may persist long, advises monks and nuns, and the laity to listen to, and reflect upon certain passages in the sayings which he refers to as "these reverend *dhamma-paliyāyāni*" (pariyāyāni, or ways of exposition). These interesting citations have been competently dealt with by Rhys Davids,[1] Dr. Walleser[2] and other writers,[3] and are a very precious asset in our all-too scanty historical materials. But that Asoka here toes the line as a devout follower of Sangha terms has somewhat obscured his different way of using *dhamma* in the edicts carved in the years of his prime, round about the twelfth year of his reign. In these, *dhamma* is for him no collection of Sayings, however well said; nor does *dhamma* stand midmost in a Trinity. *Then* we have the man, becoming, in his efforts, in the better; we have the bright prospect further on of happy rebirth; we have that by, or according to which he can grow, or advance, namely *dhamma*:—these three. "Dhamma", runs one pillar-edict, "is excellent (*sādhu*), what (or how much) is *dhamma?*" Little of āsava, much good, kindness, giving, truth, purity."

This is not a code of morals; it is expressly distinguished from such a code, which was termed *sīla*; it is attached to the word behaviour, literally "walking", *caraṇa*, and it was in "walking by *dhamma*" that a man became moral (*sīlasa*). Thus: (The king and his descendants) "persisting in *dhamma*, in morals, will teach *dhamma*". (Girnar iv; Dhauli, iv.) "Moreover walking by *dhamma* (*dhamma*-walking) is not in one (who is) immoral." (Kalsi iv.) But the distinction has been lamentably obscured in Hultzsch's sumptuous work on the Edicts by his translating *dhamma* as "morality"! Senart's rendering: "religion" clears "sīla", and is so far better, yet is "religion" too weighted in meanings to fit *dhamma*. As I have maintained, we have no word coinciding with *dharma*, *dhamma*, and it is really wiser to retain it, as we have retained karma and nirvana. It is tempting, when we get, in many compounds, *dhamma* in adjectival force, *dhamma-niyama*, *dhamma-mahāmātā*, etc., to use the word "moral", but the temptation should be resisted.

It is true, that so far as we can judge, Asoka's ideal was merely that of Man in the More (as we might say, the spiritual man); it reveals no Man in the Most (as we might say, Deity). But we shall not on that account interpret his ideal more truly by rendering his

[1] *Buddhist India*, "Asoka".
[2] *Materialien zur Kunde des Buddhismus*, 1, and 9.
[3] E.g. V. Smith: *Early History of India*.

words in terms of Western rationalism. That rationalism takes no account of man as a creature of the worlds, but as of earth only. But Asoka did so very emphatically. That rationalism has not understood the phase of immanent Godhead, through which India had been passing and was passing in Asoka's day. In that phase "Man in the More" was always potentially "Man as the Most": "thou art That." If the Most, the Highest, finds no mention in the Edicts this may well be because the need of *the More in man's conduct* had been so brought to the front in the reformed teachings of Jain and Sakya. Now the new spiritualized meaning imparted to the notion "dhamma" by that reformed teaching in its earliest form was of *dhamma* as the very motor-principle, the main-spring, the inner urge of the More in conduct, such as now we word by conscience. *Dhamma* had for Sakya ceased to be the gentleman's external norm of behaviour. It had gone within, as a divine Goer (*antarayāmin*), to be worshipped by very Buddhas.[1] Through Its monitions, the un-, or im-moral man became in conduct moral: so far the edicts do go. To go farther and explain "dharma" was unnecessary, both for an Indian reader, and in particular for an Indian reader of that day of moral awakening.

So far was Asoka from feeling any need to explain "*dhamma*-growth", that we overlook how elliptical is the compound. We read it as growth of *dhamma*, instead of growth of the more in man *by dhamma*. Much as when we speak of a person having a sensitive, or a robust conscience. We mean a person who is sensitive, or less sensitive, to the urge of conscience. Asoka's sentence runs: "The king says thus: *Dhamma*-growing is growth (or it may mean grower, -*vadhitar*) by two ways: by *dhamma*-law and by approval; of these *dhamma*-law is a light (matter), by approval is much-more."

Here "law", lit. restraining, *niyama*, was already allied with *dhamma*, in the sense of "law of conscience" in such impressive sayings as that of the Paccaya-Sutta (Saṃyutta-Nikāya, Nidāna-vagga, 20): "Whether or no a Man of the Way (Tathāgata) arise,[2] and call Behold! there is *dhamma*-law, there is *dhamma*-persistence." It was of no man's invention; when he came to be, it was there. Then, "approval" is the ambiguous word *nijjhati*; it may mean "thinking upon"; it is akin to *jhāna*, musing. But I think the collective meaning of the sentence is clear, namely, that conscience may drive us, but we can also thoughtfully approve of its monition, and this is of the higher worth or "growth". It is true, that in view of Asoka's vigilance-officials, or regional supervisors, whom

[1] *Saṃyutta*, ii, 138 (vi, 2). [2] See p. 416, *n*.

he refers to as Dhamma-mahā-mātras, he may, by *dhamma-niyama*, mean moral coercion exerted by them, as by so many externalized consciences; outer, not inner "law". I do not stress the inner law to that extent. But here again, it is regrettable, that Hultzsch uses for approval (or reflection) the impossible word "conversion".

In his growth by *dhamma*, his walking by *dhamma*, Asoka went far. He may not seem in this very far to us. His time is not ours. His new rescripts to his people are, for our self-exhortations in church, on the platform, in prospectuses of public welfare, so many commonplaces. But we find no other public statements, by monarchs or anyone, of welfare-warding remotely approaching his in high motive and fatherly zeal. His day was one of moral awakening, and he put himself at the head of it. He made Sakya great, not because it was not at the time growing in moral warding of life, but because it had become a great movement needing his patronage and leadership. It was a case of mutual service between king and people—the majority of his people.

That he went worthily as far as he saw, or thought his people would see, does not lift him to the level of the Founder of Sakya. But he was a good disciple in that he placed the "very man" foremost in his mandate, in that his pre-occupation was with the man as in process of becoming, in that his vision was not limited to earth only. Further than this he did not go. He did not see *dharma* as a really cosmic fact, true of and for man in all the worlds. The thing not restricted to this world was less *dharma* than *dharma-mangala*, "luck-by-*dhamma*" (here again Hultzsch obscures the edict[1] by using, for *mangala*, the word used for walking, or behaviour, *caraṇa*; *mangala* is of entirely different meaning). "Luck-acts bring fruit in this world. But *dhamma*-luck is not of earth-time only." (*kālika*, lit. time-ish, means time as measured on earth, into days, etc. So the Commentaries. It was a superstition, that deva-time was only to be reckoned in kalpas, or great time-periods.) It brings, he continues, one's welfare to pass here, and endless merit in other worlds, or at least the latter. So in the Suttas,[2] *dhamma* is described as both concerned with things seen (*sandiṭṭhika*) and also as not-of-(earth-) time (only): *akālika*. The term is, I think, obscure to Buddhaghosa, who either passes it over, or gives optional interpretations, which have misled me and others. We owe it to Asoka, non-scholastic though he be, to have given us an unmistakable meaning to the word!

We owe more to him than that. The day was even then at hand,

[1] E.g. Kalsi, ix. [2] E.g. *Majjhima*, i, 37, etc.

when the newly strengthened and consolidated Sakya, as the great emperor-king's church, was about set to at its great work of editing its treasure of Sayings, and then armed with these, to turn and rend the very "man" in the edicts, as a valuing only to be known in mind, in *dhammā*, or ways of mind. But in the Asoka-words we have yet the main things of original Sakya: we have the man of the worlds; we have him in *bhava*, becoming, we have him in becoming by *dhamma*. Herein is for him the very guarantee of his ultimate consummation, the crown of that *bhava-suddhi*, the crown on which Asoka is silent.

There is yet one other way in which Asoka may be said to be of the genuine Sakya breed, a way indeed in which, unless he was borrowing credit due to others, he was also more truly Sakyan than the Sakyan Sangha. I refer to what we call his "missions". Much scholarly attention, again, has been expended on the edicts referring to his will for inclusive instruction in the advantages of "*dhamma*-walking" and "*dhamma*-luck" over his whole empire. And further, his naming certain contemporary rulers, as reigning beyond the districts where lived his borderfolk, rulers who have in nearly [1] every case been identified, has helped to place him yet more firmly in time as a very live historical character, in so far as such one-sided references can do so.[2] In this book then I need only to bring out one or two points about them, which seem to me to have been passed over.

The edicts in question are Kalsi, xiii, and Shahbazgarhi, xiii, and Mansehra, xiii. In them is first the announcement of his past victory over the Kalingas, and his turning with regret at the woe it entailed, to the strenuous cultivation of more worthy victories. "These," he goes on, or rather, "this has been won again both here and among all the borders, even as far as 600 yojanas, where is the Yona king named Antiyoka, and beyond this Antiyoka four kings named Turamaya, named Antikini, named Maka, named Alikasudara, down to Chodas and Pandiyas as far as Tamraparni (Ceylon) likewise, likewise here in the king's territories, Yonas-Kambojas, Nabhakas-Nabhapantis, Bhojas-Pitinikyas, Andhras-Paladas, everywhere (folk) are conforming to the king's (Asoka's) instruction in *dhamma*, moreover they to whom the messengers of Him-dear-to-devas do not go, they too having heard of *dhamma*-duties, ordinances, *dhamma*-instruction of Him-dear-to-devas, are conforming to *dhamma* and

[1] It is only not certain which Antiochos is meant, first or second.

[2] We have no records by them referring to Asoka.

will conform. This that has thus far everywhere been won has the taste of joy, firm becomes that joy, the joy of *dhamma*-victory."

We have here Asoka testifying to a benevolent interest in the welfare both of every corner of his empire, at the hands of those he calls *dūtā*, and even, in some way not specified, in the welfare of certain other living rulers. No Asiatic monarchs are named, none, that is, of the Middle and Far East. Apart from Persia, it was natural, that the result of Alexander's invasion should have turned the thoughts of Indian rulers Westward, opening up to them quite new worlds beyond Jambudvīpa, lands where, somewhat as in Europe over a century ago, the satrap-generals of a mighty conqueror reigned over divided spoil—Antiochus of Syria and its wide eastern appanages, Ptolemy of Egypt, Magas of Cyrene, Antigonos of Macedonia and Alexander of Epirus. And it is generally assumed, I think too lightly, that the *dūtā*, or messengers sent, by Asoka's own admission, to some of the peoples he names, not to all, were "missionaries". A missionary is of course a man on a mission, but our own word for such a man is a very specialized one, such as *dūta* is not. A *dūta* is just envoy, and it is very possible, and indeed I think likely, that if envoys were sent to the kings named, they were charged with gifts and amicable and peaceful political greetings (in which are also features of *dhamma*-victory), rather than with religious and moral advice.

Of the embassies confined to his own realms, we get, it may be, an endorsement in the Ceylon Chronicles: in Dīpavaṃsa viii, and Mahāvaṃsa, xii. Here, not Asoka, but the head of the Sangha, during the Patna Revisions, Moggaliputtatissa is said, in chronicles postdated by six to seven centuries, to have sent nine, not *dūta's*, but *thera's* (elder, i.e. senior monks), each with four associates, to the northernmost districts, and one, the monk-prince Mahinda, to Ceylon. Two of the nine names on tope-relics excavated near Sānchi, may possibly be a most interesting confirmation of these missionary labours.[1] But neither of the Chronicles has a word on "missions" sent to the courts or countries of the five kings named in the edicts. Nor do any positive traces appear of any mark left by any Sakyan teaching in the history of ideas and customs in those five countries. The nearest approach to such traces is claimed for the philosophy of the Egyptian Basilīdes, in Kennedy's "Buddhist Gnosticism".[2] Kennedy makes some good points, and I see nothing impossible in Basilīdes having had access, in his day, the much later second century (A.D. 117–138), to Indian ideas.

[1] Cf. Rhys Davids, *Buddhist India*, "Asoka." [2] *JRAS.*, 1902.

But I see more likelihood of Buddhist influence in Egypt resulting in the Christian monk-recluses of Egypt, and as having been effected through missions, but much later than those of Asoka's time. And I do not see why Christian historians should in any way resent this particular channel of influence, as at least possibly true.[1] Monasticism, whether cenobitic, or monachistic, is an important feature in Christian history. But in aim it has been more preponderantly social than Buddhist monasticism. It has mainly devoted its energies to the culture of letters and to healing—the warding of the sick, the poor, the otherwise ailing, the unwarded young. The true recluse, the man of the alone, is, for it, rather an offshoot than the man who is most at its centre. We do not look upon St. Jerome and St. Anthony, let alone Simon Stylites, as the typical, the ideal monk. We give the palm by preference to the little Brother at Assisi. But, for the monasticism of the Piṭakas, whereas the Vinaya Rules keep us mainly in the world of the cenobite (where rules were mainly needed), the typical monk, the monk heading directly for the aim of the "going forth", is described in the formula, so often repeated, of the lone sitter, a formula *devoid of any reference whatever*, save by wide compassionate feeling, *to the welfare of anyone save the sitter alone.*[2] This, at a time of some spiritual crisis, such as I have touched upon above, as possibly at the root of the *samaṇa*-movement, may have been natural, perhaps even wise; but from the Sakyan point of view it can be less excused. In both of the great creeds, it had in it the seeds of unwholesome excess, and the Western writer, recognizing this, need have no qualms in discerning, in the desert-monks of the Thebaid, an exotic growth of probably Indian origin.

But that we should have to wait for so many centuries till we find any sign of wider missionary zeal attempted by the Sangha in India, referred to in ecclesiastical commentary and epic, is a little strange. I do not forget, that the eminent disciple Puṇṇa appears in a late Majjhima Sutta—late in position only (No. 145)—as a devoted missionary, self-sent to the border folk of the Sunas, but I can place nothing beside it. And in those later works, we have the curious contrast, that the Sangha is made to appropriate the inter-Indian mission work, without a word of admission of the claim made to them as his by Asoka, and further, that there is no claim made by the Sangha to any extra-Indian mission work, such as is claimed here for Asoka,

[1] Cf. *Ency. Rel. Eth.* art.: "Monasticism," Christian.

[2] *Dīgha*, Sta. ii (p. 63), etc.; *Majjhima*, Sta. 27 (i, 179), and a dozen more passages; *Saṃyutta*, ii, 219; *Anguttara*, ii, 210, etc.

with the sole exception of Ceylon, the country in which both commentator and chronicles were solely interested. Were the Sangha, in the years between the Patna Conference and these later men, carrying on any zealous work in the mission field, we should almost certainly have found some testimony to it in Nāgasena's Milinda discourses, some touch of pride in the mondial religious spirit being shown by his "church", some echo of gratitude, of complacency in the patronage of a mightier ruler than Menandros. But I have found no word on missions, and only a Canute-like reference to Asoka, which is in all probability not in the sayings of Nāgasena, but is the writer's own.[1]

We fall away, in the Piṭakas, from the active, the positive missionary spirit with which Sakya, in the dispatch of the first men on short tours in pairs, appears to have started. We do not find anything like the close following up of the dispatch of thirty-five pairs of his first men by Jesus in work of healing, or the dispatch of missionary pairs recorded in the Acts of the Apostles as taking place a few weeks only after they had lost their leader. Nor do we find any of that joy with which the seventy returned to tell him of results, and with which he received them. In the first return of Gotama's men, their only word as recorded is the inquiry who is to make monks of men at a distance. Yet here, had the Vinaya anxiety about Rules not been the real object in perpetuating the oral record, we should surely have found something about the gracious joy of the compassion, which is worthily worded at the outset, and which had found, in bearing "*dhamma*-victory", "*dhamma*-walking" to others, so goodly an outlet.

There is something wrong here. And I turn again to look if haply there be no way of at least assuming a propagating of (1) culture in general from India, (2) Sakyan religious culture in particular, from and after the day of the Mauryan empire?

(1) If we can once more try to think in terms of a bookless, manuscriptless India, we see at once that, for India to make her culture in ideas known, the one way was by the man telling about it, or any branch of it. If, further, we recollect, that there had recently been opened up to India centres of culture other than her own, and that this would stimulate her commerce on all sides, to east as well as to west, and further, that on both sides of her there lay certain centres of culture older even than her own: Egypt, China, for instance, we may see something more. Men want various things; the more cultured they are, the more diversified will be

[1] *Milindapañho*, p. 121.

their needs. And the merchant will cater for all of these according to his professional intelligence. If customers who are heirs of older culture wish him to procure documents on the "wisdom", the "lore" he has perhaps heard of and "advertized", as revered in other cultural centres, such documents will eventually by the purveyor, eager for such wares, be procured. But if, as non-existent, they cannot be got, the merchant will find a way; he will purvey a human "wireless broadcaster", he will at a price engage an expert to come aboard, spend many months at sea—or it may be no fewer on the road—and on landing hand him over to the man who pays to have him supplied with native teachers, till he can worthily tell his "wisdom" in the language of his employer. The same thing—"only in words a little different"—is going on to-day, when experts from Europe and America go to India and China to give courses of lectures, or otherwise instruct, in their own speciality. They take much less time; they get along with English. And we can the more admire the courage of the old world effecting the same under difficulties so much greater.

It is just this, that survives in one sentence by a Greek historian—a well-known line, yet I think, too lightly passed over. Vincent Smith's *Early History of India*[1] gives it in full. In a fragment of the Greek writer Hegesandros, surviving in a quotation by Athenaios, Bindusāra, father of Asoka, asks Antiochos Sotēr, the Antikinos of the edicts, to procure for him, presumably from his more western "Syria" (it extended into N.W. India) some figs, some wine and grapes, and an expert (*sophistēs*). The reply is stated to have been: "Figs and glycus (the wine) we send thee, but a sophist among Greeks it is not lawful to trade in."

Greece had at that time her stores of written literature, and copies could be made for the market of readers, both Greek, Hellenic, and foreign. Her experts, or, as our writers are pleased to call the sophists, her "professors" did not then accept handsome fees to venture on distant voyages and enlighten "the barbarian", after first learning his tongue, where Hellenic Greek could not help them out. It was rather by her art, than by her wisdom, or her religious ideas, that we are now learning from explorers, how Greece penetrated as far as the centre of Asia and into Kashmir. But the letter of Bindusāra reveals, as by one slender ray of light, that for India "to trade in" the living book, the man of the mantra, *was* a feature in her commerce with other peoples. The will to purchase the knowledge of her ideas, her wisdom, her ideals is likely to have been

[1] 2nd ed., 138, n. 2.

a demand only from clients of cultures as old as, or even older than that of India herself. And I judge it likely, that it is in this way, even more than by deliberate missionary effort and organization, that China derived her first acquaintance with Buddhism, and that Egypt also quite possibly learnt of it.

How otherwise are we to account for the transmission of early "Buddhist" wisdom into China, traceable as yet from the first century A.D., but which may well be older than that? The Ceylon sources, including the Vinaya Commentary, which is Singhalese by adoption at least, claim no part in extra-Indian missions for the Sangha's activities, save only the legend of a conversion of Ceylon, as effected directly from Asoka's capital, and the very much later mission to Burma, five to six centuries later. What were the heads of the Sakyan church doing in missionary work during, say, the last two centuries of the era preceding ours, and the first three in that era, that we should find as yet no mention of it, not even any worthy pride over it in the works ascribed to Buddhaghosa and Buddhadatta? When men hold anything in high worth, they will surely give voice to it. Are we not then driven back on the assumption that, where no trade in books from India was possible, a trade in paid "tellers" was going on, and that a demand in such a supply, as was put forward by Bindusāra, was no more out of the usual than a request for figs or wine?

Yet does this not answer the question: why are such Buddhists documents as we have, hailing from Theravāda (or Hīnayāna) sources, so silent on the subject of missions? This being so, how is it that they have come to be credited with activity in these? Credited indeed so unquestionably, that one eminent Indologist sees, in Buddhist addiction to categories and schedules, a machinery deliberately fashioned for purposes of aiding in propaganda![1] Where is the evidence, that such work of synopsis, précis, and formula, among the treasures of memorized Sayings, was carried out, less to aid confessors and teachers of the faith to hearers close by, and more to assist the bringing in of confessors afar?

I incline to think we must seek the answer in a cause, which had a twofold result. In these pages I have sought to show, that Sakya, at its birth, was a new word of a certain "More" to be recognized in man's nature and life: he was very real, not as a "being", but as one who becomes; that, as becoming, he is capable at length, of consummation as That (Most)—the form which Deity as immanent had assumed in Indian religious teaching *of that day*.

[1] M. Walleser, *Die Sekten des alten Buddhismus*, Introd.

And his becoming had to show itself, not in a work of thought (or mental realization), as Brahmans taught, but in conduct. Only in that was advance in rebirth of the becoming toward the Most made certain. I have also shown that, as time went on, certain influences of the time militated against this concept of becoming as process, or Way, lasting through life in many rebirths. That there thereby came (1) a falling off from this high concept of the man (2) a pre-occupation with man as in mind, and then as mind, (3) a preference for seeking reality, not in the man, but in ideas about him: ideas of him as impermanent, as ill, as not real—ideas which included the world, and all worlds. In brief, the "man" himself, as in himself real, nay, as highest reality, *underwent shrinkage*. And his world, his birthright of all the worlds was turned from, as ill, as not to be "saved", not to be "redeemed", as we should say.

It leaps to the eye, if once this is conceded as a true presentation, that both faith and zest in the effort to bring men in, to share the creed of a shrunken man and a wilted outlook on the earth, would not be of vigorous growth. Here we come to the results. On the one hand, the decision made at Patna, in Asoka's day, pronouncing only orthodox that section of the Sangha who analysed the man into aggregates, into *dhammas*, who virtually (and later actually) denied the fundamental, the outstanding reality of the very man, the valuer in body and mind: this decision would turn by degrees the energies of the Sangha ever more and more into its own self-contained inner world of the monk-kingdom. And the book in which this intro-version is realized in a manner most startling, were it not a foregone result of the cause I have named, I mean the Visuddhi-magga, should be carefully considered before my conclusion is waved aside. Here the Way of Purity, that is, in Indian idiom, of Salvation, is conceived as entirely in the world and interests of the monk, *samaṇa*, almsman. Of its three sections, the moral habit, or *sīla*, is worthy conduct *in the monk*; the study in *samādhi*, or ways and postures of thought, is prescribed *for the monk*; the *prājnā* (*paññā*), which has utterly lost its lofty meaning (as spiritual movement within the man of the Most Who he potentially was), is a number of ways by which *the monk* can realize the mainly negative concepts under which he views life and mind. There is an all but total absence of any outward look or aspiration, mothering the world or worlds of men *as men*. The one exception is the chapter on the Four Moods, a solitary ray of mondial sunshine. And the book slopes down in its latter chapters into a very swamp of the Not Man, the Not Deity. It is dumbly telling us, while we read, why, for nearly seven centuries since Asoka, no missionary effort can be associated with Theravāda. It needs great faith, not only in your gospel, but also in the capacity and the destiny of the man you take it to, to make a missionary. Failing this, you will go, in blind loyalty to faith in That Who controls your action. Failing that, you will not go.

And yet there remains the association of Buddhism with missions. But why not? It certainly could be upheld by Sakyans, that to bring in men as converts to "the God-life"[1] was a mandate in their religion. Is the association then all a mistake? We can see that, however embroidered are the mediæval chronicles about the missions to Burma and elsewhere with what has been called "a worsening by an insatiable national vanity",[2] the legends exist and the work of missions is by *some section* of Sakya, held in worth. This argues past energies born of great good will. I do not overlook the fact, that Buddhist missions of to-day have infused into their upholders the influence of modern ideals not hailing from Buddhist traditions. The West has had such ideals in its own tradition; the East has had them for some generations in the example set, no matter if imperfectly set, by Christian missions. But, to go back again, there remains the fact of Buddhism reaching the Far East long before them. Do we need to fall back entirely on the supply of speakers of religion as an article of commerce?

Not entirely and merely as such. If we assume, that we have in the Pali Piṭakas an inclusive record of the world of Sakya, we should be compelled so to fall back. But in Pali literature we are now fairly aware, that we have the scriptures of only a corner of the Sakyan world. It is true, alas! that such scriptures as there may have been of other corners of it have mostly perished. But we read that, when Fa-Hien came a-pilgrimaging to India in the fourth century A.D., he was wanting a written Vinaya-Piṭaka, and that when after long seeking he got one, it was a *Mahā-Sanghika recension.*

How does this not give us to think! I know that, after my day on earth, Europe will come to be able to compare completed translations of Chinese and Manchurian translations of Sakyan scriptures with such Pali and Sanskrit recensions as we have—a work of translation now only begun. Pending that time we must help ourselves out with a little reconstructive imagination. Thus:—

Whether we accept the wretched little account of the procedure at the Patna Congress as it is stated, or not, there can be little doubt that, during the centuries following the spread of Sakya, something

[1] *Brahmacariyaŋ.* See above, p. 70; *Vin.* i, 21.

[2] L. Finot, *La Légende de Buddhaghosa,* Paris, 1921.

or some things supervened, causing divisions in the original Indian Sakya Community. Those divisions may have been fissions after a growing divergence in teaching at certain centres, or they may have been given separate existence through some such great congress, with revision of the oral records, and sentence of expulsion by a central Council, such as I went into in a previous chapter. Now the fact of segregation from the mother community, which called itself Theravāda, and at least for a time Vibhajjavāda, would in no way signify, that the separated, or self-separating branches of Sakya *petered out in religious energy*. On the contrary, it may have resulted in an increase of liberated teaching and propaganda. We have, through the testimony of the Kathāvatthu and its Commentary, good reason to think, that the most influential opponents to the "orthodox" majority of the central group were the Mahāsanghikas of Vesālī. And we read that it was their Vinaya recension which was procured for use in China by Fa-Hien.

Now the Sakyan wing which believed in the reality of "the man", the *puruṣa*, *attan*, self, soul, spirit, would also, it seems likely to me, keep alive a faith in the man as becoming, in the man so becoming as waiting, wherever on earth he was, to be helped in that becoming by his fellow-men. In other words the "world" was not hopelessly sunk in "ill", but was calling for man to teach it the "supreme God-life" of the first Sakyans. I think it is very possible, that much missionary work may have been effected by those dismissed, or self-dismissing Mahāsanghikas, of which no records remain. And not by Mahāsanghikas only. It is at least equally likely, that the great group of the "Everything-is" School, the Sarvâstivādins, who are also closed with in debate early in the Kathāvatthu, albeit not given the first place, were no less active in propaganda to the North and East. It is they who largely find mention in Chinese pilgrims' records. And if we have as yet access only to their Abhidhamma scriptures, wherein is no context calling for reference to missions, we may come to know more about their other surviving documents.

But I confess, that I do not see how, in those old days of little save commercial access to other lands, and of ignorance of other peoples and other languages, any genuinely missionary work was possible, save by way of commerce, in response to a demand from the cultured of some other old civilization, wanting to learn something about the "wisdom" of another land, rumours of which will have come, it may be, through merchants' talk Given the demand, and the questing merchant purveying, *then* arose the opportunity of the teller, who combined with a curiosity to learn, and a love of adventure, the will to impart what will have counted for him as the wisdom most worth while. Whether he will, if monk, have gone as monk, who can now say? Probably not. The difficulties before him were immense enough, without his presenting himself as a "shaveling" and in a garb, which might possibly make him appear to his patron and tutors as irrational.

NOTE.—With Dr. Walleser's learned article on the origin of "Tathāgata" (Jl. Taisho University, 1930), received too late to find earlier mention, I so far agree, that I see in it a general term monopolized later in ascription to one Man. But so too is Sugata, Wellfarer. I deem the words were in use later than the day of the founders, as designations of the Men of the Way-teaching:—the Thus-goners, Well-goners = Sakkaputtiyā. Still later they were reserved, practically, for the Buddha. Yet mediaeval India still equated Saugatas with Bauddhas (*sarva-saṃgraha-darśana*).

EPILOGUE

In the book *Gotama the Man*, he is made to say: "The man is my theme." By the man was meant he who is there and here sometimes termed the man-in-man. That is, the man considered as having body and mind as adjuncts, instruments, which are not he. It is we here who have not the good word, or rather, have not the good usage of the good word. It is we who cheapen our treasures. And the man, in that sense, was the theme in that the book was concerned with that which we call religion. This book is also concerned with the man-in-man, and hence with religion. And it has been an effort to disentangle, in the oldest documents yet available of a religion with a long, but most defective history, the things in them which are truly values belonging to the " man " from the things which do not come rightly into those values.

Now there are some five of these latter things which belong not to those values :—

(1) A teaching of the man-in-man as not real.

(2) A teaching which sees in man made perfect one who can no more become.

(3) A teaching holding of little value the world and man as in the world.

(4) A teaching which places at a low value the man as such.

(5) A teaching which sees the man as becoming in the worlds, that is, Man in his life-in-its-entirety as evil.

The man-in-man (who is the Best in each of us) will value the things which are the opposites of these five. For him the " man " (not mind and body only) is very real, is the most real thing in life. For him, becoming is eternal, both after as well as before he wins perfection. For him, the man in the life of the world is the man becoming in the way meant as " in the Whole ". For him, every man has in him the promise of the More, even of the Most, no matter at what stage he be. For him, the worlds are the Way in the More towards the Most, no matter how long be the Way. End, Goal, Highest, Best, Most; the man has ever and everywhere This, a more-than-excelsior, ahead in his visions. He may often be more bent over the riddance of the undesirable; he may often confine his view to the Excelsior only. But he is never long without the acme, unseen, yet postulated, in his thoughts. We see it in his

Utopias, his Golden Ages, his Heavens, his perfect worlds, his perfect man. The being well for him is not always recovery from illness, not always maintenance of normal health ; in the depths, *au fond*, he conceives a "well" which is supreme, utter, perfect, or, as in Pali, having no beyond, an uttermost-well, no matter whether he call it less felicitously a *summum bonum*, or happiness. In this ideal the man and his world properly fuse into one. Conceived as a Utopia, the world can never be a more than physical universe ; in all other respects it is the man who makes his world. The man at his highest *is* his world at its best. Man as perfect will need no world save the man. World at its worthiest is in the worthiest man.

There is here no will to belittle man in the more. At our best we are that ; we can here, and for a long, long time, be no more than that. But without the conception, beyond that, of an ungrasped, yet believed in "Most", the More itself has the less value. It is reduced to meaning not so much the more, as the less bad. It has become a scale in terms of ill, not a scale in terms of "well". It ceases to become a stage onward in the way towards the "most" ; the emphasis is then on ill, less ill.

In Sakya there arose a theory of man at his worthiest. It was not the mandate of Gotama. This had pointed to the man as wayfarer faring, that is growing, becoming, towards an uttermost end, positively worded as *artha*, *paramartha*, a consummation not to be won on earth, but referred to as *Pāraṃ*, beyond. In the theory of man become "worthy", arahan, the man is conceived as finished, in becoming, here, now, or at most in one more onward stage only elsewhere.[1] Here we have no fit picture of man as the "most". It is the man in the "more" only. As such he is estimated according to plan, not according to his very nature. It is at best a contracting of the man-consummated to the man-only-as-more. Later, in Commentarial language, he is, as such, termed *sādhako*, the accomplisher, but the *sādhana*, the accomplishing, is in the "More" only. For the vision of a Most to come has vanished in the unbelief in any positive values as to that. He has no more a mandate in a positive *artha* ; it has become for the theorist merely "an end of ill (*dukkhass'anta*)". How indeed could there be a valuing of the positive when there was to be no man to value ? Both *artha* and *attan* have been lost to sight. Values in the perfect were in a man who was, as man, a no-thing, a fiction.

But in the true Sakya, the message of Gotama, we have the word

[1] Often asserted in the *Anguttara-Nikāya*, i, 232, 245, 290 ; ii, 5, 89, 238 ; iv, 399, 423 f.

positive : the Way is there, Wayfarer is there, without whom Way were meaningless, and the End is to come as *paramartha*, ineffable because inconceivable, yet with a word which, if as yet not describing, points ahead to a meaning which is for to come.

To this end has my very provisional, inexhaustive attempt to disentangle original "Buddhism" from Buddhism brought me. And once more I am reminded of the parable of the swift messengers [1] —a saying worthy of the Sakyamuni—who came from east, north, west (India only looked for the new, then, from land, not from the sea), each bearing tidings of the true to the governor of the city, tidings of things as become (*yathabhūtaŋ vacanaŋ*). Still is the study of Sakya, as I thus hinted twenty years ago,[2] awaiting other swift messengers, this time from east, north and south, bringing other such messages of how Sakya came to be, and maybe in versions less monastically sophisticated than are the tidings we yet have had from the "south" and have here been weighing. And it is in order that they who will in turn weigh what is indeed in the Piṭakas more worthily, more truly, over against what may yet be brought to that city, where the man, and not merely mind, sits in judgment, that I have set down the things in this book.

[1] *Saṃyutta*, iv, 194.
[2] *Compendium of Philosophy*, 1910, p. vi.

APPENDIX I

PALI

The student who takes this book as more or less of a guide in Buddhist, here called Sakya, origins, may justly ask : What is this Pali language, in which the sayings and other mandates herein discussed, came to be transferred from oral to written transmission ?

The subject is one which has much engaged the scrutiny of philologists, among whom I have no claim to be ranked. Rightly to master the extent and variety of this scrutiny he would need to study the opinions about Pali expressed by Rhys Davids, R. O. Franke, W. Geiger, G. A. Grierson, Berriedale Keith, Sten Konow, Kuhn, S. Lévi, E. Lüders, E. Müller, Oldenberg, Pischel, R. L. Turner, M. Walleser, Westergaard and Windisch, to mention no others. If his interest and field be not mainly philological, he can, fortunately for him, read all their opinions grouped and discussed with concise critical acumen in Professor Berriedale Keith's article "Pali, the Language of the Southern Buddhists", *Indian Historical Quarterly*, 1925, i, 3. Let him also consult the later contribution by my senior colleague, Professor R. L. Turner, *Ency. Brit.* xivth ed., art. : Pali Language. In these he will see, among much else, how difficult it is to locate the source of Pali when we look upon it as a dialect among dialects of India. And he must free himself from the orthodox tradition of Buddhists, that Pali is only another name for Magadhese, that is, the Prakrit spoken in Asoka's day at Patna. Much is now known about Magadhese and the allied Ardha-Magadhese to which Asoka's pillar inscriptions approximate, and it is truer to say, that in Pali, here and there, we see forms of these two dialects peeping out, than that Pali has its base in them, and them only. He will take the path of least obscuration if he will see, in Pali, not any dialect, but a literary diction, evolved, by the labours of standardizing editors, from sayings repeated in many shades of Prakrit dialect. As such it is as hard to explain as is the emergence of literary English from varying Anglo-Saxon dialects, blended with a current official use of late Latin and Norman French. But perhaps no harder. And this holds analogously for other European tongues.

Pali in fact is not the name of any localizable tongue. The meaning of the word is "Row" (cf. our "paling"). There are a dozen meanings of the word *pāli* distinguishable in Sanskrit, of which "row" is one, but in no case does it mean "language". We have it in the name of the famous courtesan convert, Ambapālī, "mango-orchard-er", lit. mango-row-er, whose birth-tradition suggested her name. Again, the teeth are said, in the Visuddhi-Magga, to be in a "pāli", *dantapāli*. And it is almost in juxtaposition to this term that we read "gave him the Pali of the thirty-two bodily parts to learn", in other words gave him either a *written leaf* of that list of parts, or merely the *repeated* "row" of terms.

We must, I say once more, put ourselves back to the new use of the word there and then. When India was bookless, and and laboriously punching letters on little metal plates, she was cutting shapes in stone, she was carving. For these two operations she appears to have had but the one word *likh-*, *lekh-*, to scratch or incise. We began our writing relatively earlier; we had the two words: *ceorfan* (carve), and *writan*, which may have (if I may venture to suggest it against Skeat's derivation) the same Aryan root as *likh*, *l* and *r* being, as we know, so widely interchangeable. With the growing need, and the new material for setting down not mere lists, donations, contracts in writing, but also the expanded masses of her mantras, there came to pass the new and impressive phenomenon of seeing that which had been a time-series in air, become a "row" of things in space. And for a long time it remained customary to allude to the two series in juxtaposition: the "Row" as not the "Talk on the Meaning" (*atthakathā*). Still later, when more were learning to read the Row, the word "reading" (*pāṭha*) was substituted for "row", e.g. "The reading is also thus", alluding to variant readings: "*Ayam pi pāṭho*." But not at first; and so in "Pali", in default of an alternative term for graphic presentation, we have emphasis thrown, not on to the handicraft, as in *lekhana*, *likhi*, but on to the thing produced by handicraft, the visible, finished act. Pali is just "Text", and I have seen no reason to believe it was ever more than that.

And it is not unreasonable to see the term Piṭaka, as applied to three closed sets of "rows" of writing, emerging at the same time as the use of the word Pali. Sayings and Rules were earlier alluded to as Dhamma-vinaya, never as the two Piṭakas. Besides these, there appears, especially in Vinaya contexts, the word Mātikā, literally, watercourse or channel. This referred to a summary of heads of teaching, surviving at the beginning of the first book of the third Piṭaka,[1] into which it seems to have been expanded. (Other

[1] *Dhammasangaṇi*; cf. *Buddh. Psychol. Ethics*, 2nd ed. preface.

Mātikās occur early in the Anguttara-Nikāya.) Piṭaka, in its literal meaning, is "basket", in its secondary meaning is "traditional handing on". The Majjhima-Nikāya gives both uses: "As a man taking spade and basket might try to dig away the earth . . ." (i, 127); "A certain teacher teaches *dhamma* by . . . piṭaka-tradition, which is both true and false, both so and otherwise" (i, 520), etc. In this secondary meaning it was no far cry to accept the word for that which, by the time the third or Abhidhamma Piṭaka was finished, considerably later than the date of the Patna Congress, was an accomplished fact.

II

BUDDHIST PHILOSOPHY

My book deals with a time and place, in which men made no distinction, such as has since been made, between philosophy and religion. Religion, or the relation of man to life as a whole, including life in other worlds, in respect to his weal, is and has ever been the *matrix* only of philosophy. The philosophy, derived from, associated with, a religious mandate, namely, the attempt, out of that mandate, to rationalize it, that is, present it as an intellectual appeal in a carefully studied form of words, must necessarily be a later "becoming". This is the case with anything that can justly be called philosophy in Buddhism. The (true) teacher works to show man a "More" in his life and nature. The philosopher as such is as much concerned with the Less as with the More, and works analytically and synthetically to build a temple of the worded idea out of what he finds, irrespective of man's weal as such.

In the birth-time of Sakya we, by the Pali records, note memories of an elementary set of worded ideas on being and causal effect and the like, called Lokâyata, to which I have alluded, and which was of course Indian and not Sakyan. There was also growing up the "secular" point of view which came to be known as Sānkhya, and was, much later, elaborated into a "philosophy". We read further of several teachers, *aññatitthiya's*, each of whom is quoted as holding some theory in their teaching opposed to what was held by early Sakya. Some six of these are mentioned by name,[1] and one is the founder of the so-called Nirgranthas, whom we now call Jains. We know that the theory, by which he is in this context

[1] E.g. *Dīgha*, 2nd Suttanta; *Saṃyutta*, i, iii, 1, etc.

referred to, is not the whole, nor the centre of his teaching. We know very little about each of the others, but it is equally reasonable to infer, that neither did anti-causation, or the other sayings, imputed to them in the Suttas, imply that they were in the first place philosophers.[1] Had this been the case we should find a distinctive term for them as such. But we find none, not even a word equivalent to the Greek "sophist". They will almost certainly have been Brahman teachers, who within their own cults were known as putting forward some view concerning what I may call "man in the Less", and were as such antipathetic to the true teaching of original Sakya, and *only in so far* as they did so. They were in the first place "Vedic" teachers, not philosophers. The Greeks, having a distinctive term for the latter, but none for the professional religious teacher of India, called brahmans "philosophers", when, after Alexander, they wrote about India.

Philosophy, as applied to Buddhism, means inevitably later Buddhism, not Sakya. And this is why there is no reference in these pages to Buddhist or European works on philosophy in Buddhism properly so called. An eminent Indologist has recently written of "The Central Conception of Buddhism" in terms of a metaphysic of conceptual units called *dhamma's*, of which Sakya had not even dreamed! He is concerned with the ideas of men who lived a thousand years after the birth of Sakya! I too found, when I sought to set down the basic notions, such as might be now called philosophic, in Buddhism in any articulated form,[2] that I was after all compelled to call in Buddhaghosa, of almost as late a date. In Sakya there are sayings which may be elaborated into "a philosophy", but there is not yet anything that can rightly be so called.

In fact I would here say finally and with all possible emphasis concerning early Buddhism or Sakya that which I judge it is not:

Sakya is not atheistic;

Sakya is not just ethics;

Sakya is not a philosophy, does not contain what can be rightly called a system of philosophy.

We hear these three things said about "Buddhism", no historic distinction being made, in the far East by scholarly writers, in the middle East by Buddhists and their representatives in Europe, and in the West by writers not without thoughtful emphasis. The

[1] Cf. B. M. Barua's *Pre-Buddhistic Indian Philosophy* (Calcutta), pp. 277 ff.

[2] *Buddhism*, Home University Library, 1912. (I was not permitted to call the book, as I had much wished, by a more restricted title.)

effort to weigh and to grasp is ever commendable, but less so is the short cut to the all-inclusive word. Never is that a safe way to the True. For the Man is manifold, the Man is individual, the Man is wayfarer in many worlds. Not so easily is the truth about him and his life and his destiny, or his mandates about these to be set down in one term, in one phrase. And never shall we state the truth about these in a word of the Not.

III

CONCLUDING PORTIONS OF THE FIRST AND SECOND UTTERANCE

(Vinaya-Piṭaka, i, 6, §§ 23-9)

" 'This Ill-Ariyan truth :'—in me, monks, as to things unheard before vision arose, knowledge arose, *prajñā* arose, *vidyā* (Veda-lore) arose, light arose. 'But now this Ill-Ariyan truth is to be understood :—this, monks, have I understood : (hence) in me, as to things unheard before vision . . . knowledge . . . light arose.

" 'This Genesis-of-Ill-Ariyan truth' :—in me, monks, as to things . . . vision . . . light arose. 'But now this Genesis-of-Ill-Ariyan truth is to be got rid of :—this, monks, has in me been got rid of ; (hence) in me, as to things . . . vision . . . light arose.

" 'This Ending-of-Ill-Ariyan truth' :—in me, monks, as to things . . . vision . . . light arose. 'But now this Ending-of-Ill-Ariyan truth is to be realized' :—this, monks, has in me been realized ; (hence) in me, as to things . . . vision . . . light arose.

" 'This Course-going-to-the-Ending-of-Ill-Ariyan truth :'—in me, monks, as to things . . . vision . . . light arose. 'But now this Course-going-to-the-Ending-of-Ill-Ariyan truth is to be made to become ; (hence) in me, as to things . . . vision . . . light arose.

"And as long as in me, monks, as to these four Ariyan truths knowledge and insight as-become, thus thrice modified, of twelve modes, was not very purified, so long, monks, did I not recognize : 'thoroughly awake (am I) to the supremely right awakening as to the world where are devas, Māras, Brahmās, as to mankind, where are *samaṇas* and brahmans, devas and men.' But from the time when in me . . . (this) knowledge and insight . . . was very purified, then did I recognize: 'thoroughly awake (am I) to the supremely right awakening . . . devas and men.'

"And now insight arose in me thus: 'Unshakeable is in me release of purpose (*cetas*)! This: the last birth! There is not now re-becoming!'"

CONCLUSION OF THE SECOND UTTERANCE
(Vinaya-Piṭaka, i, § 46)

Seeing this, monks, the Ariyan disciple who has learning (lit. hearing) holds in no worth either body, or feeling, or perception, or activities, or mind, holding in no worth he wanes; through waning he is set free; knowledge comes:—'As freed I am free!' He understands: Destroyed (is) birth! Lived (is) the holy life! Done the what should be done![1] No hereafter in thusness."

IV

THE DATE OF THE BIRTH OF SAKYA

Since there is a consensus drawn from several sources, that Gotama Sakyamuni began to teach when about 35 years of age, this date must be referred to those of his birth and his so-called Parinirvana. He is made to admit more than once that he was "asītiko", that is eightyish, in the eighties, or it may be, just eighty. And the date of his passing soon after has been discussed round about other events, especially the accession of Asoka, an event which, it is held, Greek historians (not to omit the edicts referring to contemporaries) have made approximately clear. The problem remains however. Western discussion has settled, that the Parinirvana was in 483 B.C. Eastern tradition dates it sixty years earlier: 544 B.C. And recent discoveries of cave-inscriptions, giving an approximately greater antiquity to two kings of Magadha, contemporary with Sakyamuni—Bimbisāra and Ajātasattu—suggest, that the tradition may after all be at least less incorrect than had been made out. The question is succinctly stated in Mr. E. J. Thomas's *The Life of Buddha*, p. 27, and also in Dr. G. P. Malalasekera's *Pali Literature in Ceylon*, p. 15 (London, 1928).

[1] Or, may be done.

V

THE PALI PIṬAKAS

	Text	English Translation
	VINAYA-PIṬAKA	
I.	Khandhakas (Mahāvagga, Cullavagga)[1]	Vinaya Texts (*Sacred Books of the East*, xiii, xvii, xx).
II.	Sutta-vibhanga (Pātimokkha and Commentary)	
III.	Parivāra (Summaries).	
	SUTTA-PIṬAKA	
I.	Dīgha-Nikāya	Dialogues[2] of the Buddha (*Sacred Books of the Buddhists*, ii, iii, iv).
II.	Majjhima-Nikāya	Further Dialogues of the Buddha (Ibid., v, vi).
III.	Saŋyutta-Nikāya	Kindred Sayings (*Pali Text Society*, 7, 10, 13, 16, 19).
IV	Anguttara-Nikāya	Gradual Sayings (Ibid., *in the press*).

[1] The canonical order of the Vinaya-Piṭaka is thus :—II, I, III. I find no reason alleged in his *Editio princeps*, given by Oldenberg, for changing this order. In the translation, by himself and Rhys Davids there is this much of revision, that the Pātimokkha only, without Commentary, is replaced. There was at the time perhaps good reason to hurry in producing the valuable historical material in II. That the monk-régime put I in the first place has a significance to which justice has hitherto not been done.

[2] The Pali titles of I and II mean simply Long and Medium, viz. as to length. The adjectives are misfits if the whole of each collection be taken into account. Some of I are short, e.g. Nos. x and xi are, respectively, less than a quarter and one-third the length of No. I in the Dīgha ; and are also less than one-half *plus* a few pages less than the length of No. 20 in the Majjhima. But *all* of the Majjhima Nikāya are severally shorter than the *two first Suttantas* of the Dīgha Nikāya. And of the first ten Suttas of the Majjhima only one is even one-quarter the length of the second of those two. We seem here to be at the birth of these compilations, when the first two batches of systematized oral discourses were fitly dubbed Long and Medium. There is, it is true, the fact that the opening tenth of Dīgha I—the "Lesser Morals" talk—is pretty clearly older than the following nine-tenths. But if the final redaction be much later, the original wording (however it ran) may be no older than the early Suttas of the Majjhima.

V. Khuddaka-Nikāya

Work	Translation
1. Khuddaka-Pāṭha	By R. C. Childers (*JRAS.*, 1869).
2. Dhammapada .	By Max-Müller (*Sacred Books of the East*, x).[1]
3. Udāna . .	By D. M. Strong (Luzac).
4. Iti-Vuttaka .	By A. J. Edmunds (*in preparation*).[2]
5. Sutta-Nipāta .	By Lord Chalmers (*Harvard Oriental Series*).[3]
6. Vimāna-Vatthu	
7. Peta-Vatthu .	
8. Thera-therī-gāthā	Psalms of the Early Buddhists (*Pali Text Society*, i, 4).
9. Jātaka with Commentary	The Jātaka, by R. Chalmers, W. H. D. Rouse and others (*Cambridge University Press*).
10. Niddesa, i, ii .	
11. Paṭisambhidā-Magga . .	
12. Apadāna .	
13. Buddhavaŋsa .	
14. C(h)ariyā-Piṭaka	

ABHIDHAMMA-PIṬAKA

Work	Translation
1. Dhamma-Sangaṇi .	Buddhist Psychological Ethics (*Royal Asiatic Society*).
2. Vibhanga . .	
3. Dhātukathā . .	
4. Puggala-Paññatti .	Designation of Human Types, by B. C. Law (*Pali Text Society*, 12).
5. Kathā-Vatthu . .	Points of Controversy (*Pali Text Society*, 5).
6. Yamaka . . .	
7. Paṭṭhāna . . .	

[1] There are other translations made since, by A. J. Edmunds (Chicago), by Wagiswara and Saunders (London), by F. L. Woodward (Madras) and a re-translation (from German) by "Sīlachara" (London). Yet another by myself, bringing out the historical strata in the anthology will probably appear in Sacr. Books of the Buddhists Series. I may include the Khuddaka-pāṭha.

[2] There is another translation by J. H. Moore (New York).

[3] There is the earliest English translation by Fausböll, in *SBE.*, x.

INDEX